Teaching Students
with
Learning Problems

THIRD EDITION

Teaching Students
with
Learning Problems

Cecil D. Mercer • Ann R. Mercer

Merrill, an imprint of
Macmillan Publishing Company
New York
Collier Macmillan Canada, Inc.
Toronto
Maxwell Macmillan International Publishing Group
New York   Oxford   Singapore   Sydney

Cover Art: Cathy Johnson
All photos were supplied by the authors.

This book was set in Italia

Administrative Editor: Vicki Knight
Production Coordinator: Carol S. Sykes
Art Coordinator: Ruth A. Kimpel
Cover Design Coordinator: Cathy Watterson

Library of Congress Catalog Card Number:
   88-80957
International Standard Book Number:
   0-675-21027-5
Printed in the United States of America
      4 5 6 7 8 9—93 92 91

To our sons, Kevin, Greg, and Ken, who constantly remind us of the value and joy of good instruction and the frustrations of inadequate instruction. As they grow from adolescence to adulthood, we hope their lives continue to be touched by good teachers and they learn the joys of teaching themselves and others.

PREFACE

Most educators can recall key events that made lasting impressions on their thinking or feelings. One such event occurred in 1968 during a PTA meeting at a small elementary school next to the Blue Ridge Mountains in Virginia. The officers of the PTA were very concerned about the uninterested, unmotivated, and misbehaving children in their school, and they asked me to discuss the topic. More than 70 people—parents, teachers, and central office staff—entered the small cafeteria for the PTA meeting.

Within a few minutes I was introduced. I told them I was delighted to be there and wanted to begin by giving them a short test. The test consisted of a problem involving the transporting of a chicken, a fox, and a bag of chicken feed across a lake. However, the problem was designed so that it was impossible to answer correctly. I gave these instructions: "This is a short test which most people with average ability finish in 1 minute. When I say 'Begin,' please start. Ready?" Toward the end of the minute, mumbling, fidgeting, and attempts to look at others' papers were widespread. I told them time was up and asked how many had solved the problem. Nobody raised a hand. With a puzzled expression I said, "You must be tired. I'll give you another minute. Slow learners can usually solve it in two minutes."

Although I had anticipated some frustration, the behavior of this group of adults during the next minute was somewhat surprising to me. Many cheated, some cursed, others broke my pencils, and still others crumpled the test up and tossed it. At the end of this minute I informed them that time was up. I asked several people how they felt. Responses included: "I feel like punching you in the mouth"; "I want to leave and never come back"; "I'd like to give you a piece of my mind"; "What's the answer to this _____ thing?"

Within 2 minutes this situation had prompted adults to cheat, swear, want to leave, destroy property, threaten physical violence, and talk rudely. I pointed out that what had happened to them was the same thing that often happens to students with learning problems: Tasks are assigned that are too difficult or practically impossible for them to do correctly. Moreover, failure to do these tasks generally is viewed as a reflection of one's ability. The point was clear: Both children and adults are inclined to act aggressively or avoid situations in which they are given inappropriate tasks.

With adults reacting so quickly and intensely to this type of failure, I was reminded of what happens to youngsters who customarily face failure within the schools. Ann and I enthusiastically share the conviction of many educators that students with learning problems have a right to educational programs tailored to their unique needs. To us, individualized programming involves *the student working on appropriate tasks over time under effective motivational conditions.* The primary purpose of this book is to prepare special education professors and teachers, resource room teachers, remedial education teachers, and regular classroom teachers for the challenges of individualized programming for students with learning or behavioral problems.

Individualized programming requires an understanding of subject matter, assessment, teaching approaches for each content area, instructional activities, seatwork activities, and commercial programs. As teachers of children and university students, we have had difficulty finding a text that covers all of these areas. Resource and classroom teachers as well as special education professors often refer to one text for instructional activities, another for teacher-made materials, another for scope and sequence skills lists, another for assessment, and yet another for descriptions of commercial materials. This text provides a comprehensive, practical *text* for special education and remedial education methods courses; a *resource* for special education and remedial education in-service programs; and a *handbook* for individual teachers.

As a result of feedback from reviewers and users of the second edition, this third edition features some noteworthy changes, including additional coverage of research-based teaching principles with expanded coverage of learning strategies, generalization training, self-monitoring techniques, and techniques for increasing the time students spend on academic tasks. More in-depth discussions of peer tutoring, motivational techniques, teacher coaching, and computer-assisted instruction are presented. Descriptions of tests, software, and materials have been updated throughout this edition. Other significant changes include an expanded coverage of study skills and a discussion of the stages of learning. We hope this edition will help other teacher educators and teachers to accomplish instructional goals more easily.

Many individuals deserve special attention for their contributions to this book. Appreciation and thanks go to Martha Bock for her initial help in writing Chapters 8 and 9. Sincere thanks go to the reviewers who exceeded expectations in providing insightful suggestions: John Beattie, University of South Carolina; Joyce Gerard, Santa Clara University; Anita Herman, University of Wisconsin at Milwaukee; Selma Hughes, East Texas State University; Sam Minner, Murray State University; Robert D. Morrow, University of the Pacific; Lydia Smiley, Florida Atlantic University; Paula J. Smith, Illinois State University; Ada Vallecorsa, University of North Carolina at Greensboro; and Melinda Fassett Welles, University of Southern California.

We also express our gratitude to the many students who read the second edition and provided valuable suggestions for improving it. Continued thanks go to Vicki Knight, Merrill editor. Her encouragement, support, patience, and gentle reminders of deadlines made this edition a reality. After conversations with Vicki, Ann and I always felt positive and encouraged. Finally, we will always be indebted to children, parents, and teachers who have shared their successes and frustrations with us through the years.

CONTENTS

PART ONE

Foundations of Teaching

CHAPTER 1

Educational
Programming

All students are unique, differing from one another intellectually, emotionally, socially, and physically. Most students are taught in regular classes, without the need for special services, and the classroom teacher feels capable of meeting their instructional needs. Some students, however, deviate so greatly from "normal" limits that the regular classroom teacher must seek special help in dealing with their learning and behavioral problems.

Students with learning difficulties may have problems in one or several of the academic areas (such as reading, arithmetic, language, and spelling). These individuals may lack social adjustment, motivation, or self-management skills and often are described with such terms as *hyperactive, poor attention span, explosive, underachiever, clumsy,* and *poor memory.* Their estimated intellectual ability may differ markedly from their actual achievement. Some of these students exhibit wide spans between the skills they excel in and those that are problem areas. Others are merely slow in acquiring school-related skills and behaviors. Some of these youngsters may have only one problem area, such as reading comprehension, whereas others may have a combination of learning and behavior problems—for example, reading and arithmetic difficulties, and disruptive behavior.

Students with learning problems are identified with a variety of labels, such as *learning disabled, mildly retarded, emotionally disturbed, economically disadvantaged,* and *educationally handicapped.* Most of these students need special education services to enable them to develop to their potential. To secure special education services, the student must be diagnosed and assigned a label that identifies the student as handicapped.

When a label is applied appropriately, it may have some general implications for instruction. For example, the mildly retarded youngster may need basic academic training as well as a functional curriculum that stresses consumer education, family management, and job training. A disturbed student may need special affective interventions that stress self-awareness and managing stress. The learning disabled student may need adapted instructional materials and extensive practice to acquire specific academic skills. Although the labels may have general implications for instruction, Hammill and Bartel (1986) note that "an educational program must be prepared by a teacher in response to an individual student's educational needs and behaviors, not in response to a diagnostic label or definition the student may or may not satisfy" (p. 2). No matter what the label is, the individual student's characteristics—age, type of handicap, severity of problem—determine (a) when specific content is taught and (b) the intensity of the intervention.

In the past, many students with learning problems were placed in special education classes. Recent legislation and court decisions direct that the special needs of these students must be met, as much as possible, in classes with nonhandicapped peers. The placement of handicapped learners in regular classes necessitates that regular and special education teachers cooperate in planning and delivering instruction. Currently, regular teachers are providing more direct instruction to handicapped learners than before and are working closely with special education teachers.

Meeting the needs of these students continues to be a formidable task for both regular and special education teachers. Primary and elementary teachers are faced with helping youngsters acquire basic tool skills, explore careers, and develop independent work skills and numerous other skills. While teaching more than 100 students daily, secondary teachers are faced with helping adolescents to acquire academic content, vocational skills, and life-management skills.

To meet the educational needs of students with learning problems, teachers must develop strategies and techniques that enable them to alter the *type* and *amount* of instruction. Altering the type of instruction might involve putting reading passages on tape or using a contract; altering the amount of instruction means increasing demonstration and practice activities.

To succeed in school, students with learning problems need a systematic instructional program that is planned according to their individual needs. This individualized approach does not imply that each student must be taught in a one-to-one or small-group instructional format. It *does* mean, though, that the student receives daily instruction tailored to his educational needs.

INDIVIDUALIZED PROGRAMMING

Individualized programming refers to an instructional program in which the student works on appropriate tasks over time under conditions that are motivating. It may occur within various instructional arrangements, including seatwork, small-group, peer teaching, and large-group. Individualized programming attempts to match the learner, the task, and instructional interventions to ensure optimal student growth. As presented in Table 1.1, Talmage's (1975) comparison of traditional and individualized instruction highlights some of the prominent features of the two systems.

Individualized Programming Process

The process of individualized programming may be subdivided in numerous ways; however, the four steps presented in Table 1.2 cover the essential components. These steps are necessary for maintaining individualized instruction on a daily basis.

Step I: Identify target skill via assessment. The purpose of Step I is to determine *what* to teach the student. Successful instruction begins with the selection of an appropriate learning task. Siegel and Gold (1982) note that a teacher's thorough understanding of the instructional task is germane to effective teaching. To identify the target skill the teacher first conducts an assessment. The tests for the assessment may be based on a variety of

TABLE 1.1
Comparison of traditional and individualized instruction.

Traditional Instruction	Individualized Instruction
Fixed instructional objectives for all learners	Varied instructional objectives as a function of direct skill assessment
Fixed entry points into curriculum	Variable entry points into curriculum
Fixed time and pacing	Variable pacing
Limited participation of learner in decision making	Active participation of learner in decision making
Large-group intervention	A variety of instructional arrangements as a function of task
Norm-referenced evaluation of learner	Criterion-referenced evaluation of learner

→ Q- compare traditional v individualized

TABLE 1.2
Four steps of individualized programming.

	Theory	Example
Step I	Identify target skill via assessment	Subtract two-digit number from three-digit number with double regrouping
Step II	Determine factors likely to facilitate learning	Student is easily discouraged, especially when given a lot of work. Student continuously wants to know how he is doing. Student has some difficulty with oral directions.
Step III	Plan instruction	Provide oral directions slowly and have student repeat them. Give practice worksheets that feature a few items. Provide immediate feedback verbally when teaching and via self-correcting materials during seatwork. Use contingency contract.

Step IV	Begin daily data-managed instruction through three phases:
	1. Presentation
	   a. Advance organizer
	   b. Demonstration and modeling
	2. Controlled practice
	3. Independent practice
		1. Provide rationale for task. Present task via explanation, prompts, cues, and modeling. Require student to use imitation and/or verbal rehearsal. Provide feedback (via assessment) and reinforcement.
		2. Begin controlled practice activities on worksheet. Provide feedback and reinforcement.
		3. Begin independent practice activities in various materials and settings. Provide feedback and reinforcement.

sources such as a scope and sequence skills list (see Appendix A) and may include criterion-referenced tests or teacher-made tests. The teacher analyzes the student's test performances to discover which specific skills have been mastered. Then instructional objectives are selected. These target skills must be described as precisely as possible. Mager (1975) advocates the use of instructional objectives that (a) specify the target behavior in observable terms, (b) delineate the conditions under which the behavior occurs, and (c) describe the criterion for successful performance. For example, an instructional objective in geography might be as follows: Given an unlabelled map of the world, the student will label the seven continents with 100% accuracy within two minutes. Once the initial instructional objectives are selected, subsequent objectives are derived from day-to-day assessment procedures.

During instruction, the teacher decides if the difficulty level of the task is appropriate; that is, the pupil should perform the task without prolonged failure or frustration. Earned success is a key concept in monitoring task difficulty. The student must view the task as demanding enough to realize some sense of accomplishment when the task is completed. An optimum success-to-error ratio varies from child to child.

Informal reading inventories have suggested a 95% success to 5% failure ratio for instructional tasks. Lovitt and Hansen (1976) suggest the following guidelines for placement in a basal text: a correct reading rate of 45 to 65 words per minute with eight or fewer errors and 50 to 75% comprehension. This area needs research, however; therefore, teachers must rely on observation to establish a good ratio for each learner.

Step II: Determine the factors and conditions that are likely to facilitate learning. This step focuses on determining *how* to teach the individual student. Knowing how to teach the student greatly increases the *efficiency* of instruction. For example, Tony's teacher noticed that Tony completed his seatwork much faster when responses did not require the writing of small-sized letters or numbers. The teacher then gave him worksheets that provided large spaces for writing responses, and Tony's performance on seatwork tasks greatly improved. The key to obtaining this type of information is using sources and opportunities for direct observation (for example, interviewing the parents, chatting with the student, reading cumulative files, using behavioral checklists). Thus, this type of information is obtainable without administering standardized tests. Chapter 2 presents a detailed discussion of assessment for determining how to teach.

Step III. Plan instruction. This step is guided by the tenet of data-based instruction; that is, any humane teaching procedure that produces appropriate progress toward instructional objectives is good teaching. As Blankenship and Lilly (1981) state, "Good teaching is good outcomes" (p. 44). This orientation reduces the time spent planning elaborate teaching methods because it stresses that good teaching is a function of student progress. Thus, a teacher uses fundamental teaching principles (discussed later in this chapter) and monitors student progress to determine if instructional changes are needed. However, the efficiency of instruction improves if the teacher is sensitive to learner behaviors that cue the teacher concerning how to instruct the student. Thus, this step entails the development of a teaching plan that combines the *what to teach* information gathered in Step I with the *how to teach* information gathered in Step II. Chapter 2 presents a detailed discussion of instructional planning.

Step IV: Begin daily data-managed instruction. Teachers of students with learning problems encounter variable performances from many of their students. Teachers must know, however, if a student is making adequate progress toward specified instructional objectives so that they can modify instructional procedures. Evaluation must be frequent, even daily. Evaluation results provide the information for making instructional decisions. If the student masters a task, the teacher initiates a new task and repeats the teach-test-teach cycle. If a student does not master the task, four options are available for the teacher: repeating the same instructions, modifying the instructional procedures, introducing a new teaching strategy, or changing to an easier task. Again, when the teacher selects one of the options, the teach-test-teach cycle is repeated.

Typically the learning of a new skill is viewed as occurring through progressive stages. The instructional sequence of presentation, controlled practice, and independent practice includes the tactics that foster acquisition and generalization. Moreover, the data-managed instructional cycle is used throughout the instructional sequence to guide the aforementioned decision-making process. The following activities illustrate the teaching sequence.

Presentation

1. Advance organizer. Teacher discusses the need for learning the target skill and obtains student commitment to learn it.
2. Demonstration and modeling. Teacher breaks down the target skill into component parts and models or demonstrates a skill or subskill to the student. He carefully explains each step to the student.

Controlled practice or *Guided practice*

3. Student practices the selected task (skill or subskill) with guidance (instructions, cues, prompts) from the teacher. Teacher provides corrective feedback and reinforcement.
4. Student practices the selected task (skill or subskill) in controlled materials to a specified criterion. Teacher provides corrective feedback and reinforcement.

Independent practice

5. Student practices the total task to a specified criterion. Teacher provides corrective feedback and reinforcement.
6. Student practices the task presented in various materials (probes and regular curriculum workbooks) and settings (resource room, regular class, and home) to a specified criterion. Teacher provides corrective feedback and reinforcement.

A detailed example of a similar teaching sequence that has been successfully used to teach low-achieving adolescents is presented in Chapter 14.

Although many teachers share common orientations, no two teachers teach exactly alike. They select from numerous theories, strategies, and techniques to create individual styles. In creating an individualized programming approach, the teacher strives to achieve optimum growth in his students. As noted, to accomplish optimum growth it is essential for instruction to be planned according to student progress—instructional decisions must be based on student performance data. Evidence exists that teachers' perceptions of student progress without learner data are frequently incorrect (Miramontes, Cheng, & Trueba, 1984; Utley, Zigmond, & Strain, 1987). It is not sufficient for a teacher to "feel" that an approach is effective. Evaluation results need to document the effectiveness of specific interventions. Various ways of monitoring student progress are presented throughout the book. In Chapter 2 the procedures used in data-based instruction, which includes precision teaching, are discussed. These procedures are among the most precise and effective techniques currently being applied in the classroom setting.

STAGES OF LEARNING

Numerous authorities present stages of student learning that are fundamental to designing and implementing effective instruction (Haring, Lovitt, Eaton, & Hansen, 1978; Idol-Maestas, 1983; D. D. Smith, 1981). Nelson and Polsgrove (1984) report that a data base is emerging for the practice of matching teaching procedures to the student's stage of learning for a specific skill. Thus, teaching practices for each stage in the learning sequence are being recommended and evaluated.

Many educators feel that the entry-level learning stage is a critical factor in planning teaching activities. Although reinforcement is a viable technique, other strategies (e.g., antecedent changes and stimuli modifications) are needed to promote optimal learning at various learning stages. D. D. Smith (1981) presents the stages of learning that are commonly recognized. As featured in Figure 1.1, the stages include initial and advanced acquisition, proficiency, maintenance, generalization, and adaption. This section briefly describes the stages of learning and suggested teaching strategies for each stage.

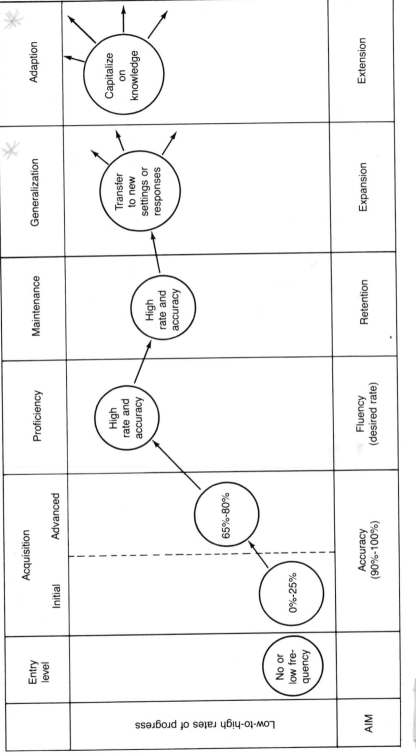

FIGURE 1.1

Stages of learning.

Source: Adapted from *Teaching the Learning Disabled* (p. 68) by D. D. Smith, 1981, Englewood Cliffs, NJ: Prentice-Hall. Copyright 1981 by Prentice-Hall. Reprinted by permission.

Acquisition Stage

During the acquisition stage, the learner performance ranges from 0% accuracy (i.e., no knowledge of how to perform the task) to a 90–100% range of accuracy. During this stage the instructional goal focuses on helping the student perform the skill accurately.

D. D. Smith (1981) recommends some major strategies for teaching a student at the acquisition stage. During initial acquisition, priming tactics are suggested, including physical guidance, shaping, demonstration, modeling, match-to-sample tasks, and cueing and prompting. Also, during initial acquisition, programming tactics are used and feature backward and forward chaining and errorless learning. For the advanced acquisition stage, refinement tactics are used and feature feedback, specific directions, error drill (practice items missed), reward for accuracy, and response cost.

Proficiency Stage

In the proficiency stage the learner attempts to learn the skill at a rather automatic level. The aim is for the student to perform the task both accurately and quickly. The tactics differ from those used at the acquisition stage. Tactics at this level focus on increasing speed of performance.

Learning at the proficiency stage is enhanced by the use of modeling, teacher expectations, drills, positive reinforcement, and manipulation of reinforcement schedules. Moreover, for social skill development, management is suggested.

Maintenance Stage

After high levels of learning have occurred at the proficiency stage, the student enters the maintenance stage. The goal of instruction here is to maintain the high level of performance. Idol-Maestas (1983) notes that students at this stage demonstrate the ability to perform the skill at a high level once direct instruction or reinforcement has been withdrawn. Students with learning problems frequently encounter much difficulty at this stage because it requires retention (memory) of the skill. Tactics at this stage concentrate on maintaining high levels of learning.

Learning during the maintenance stage involves periodic practice; however, for the mildly handicapped student, practice is not always sufficient and other tactics are necessary. Maintenance and retention are also fostered by overlearning, intermittent schedules of reinforcement, social reinforcement, and intrinsic reinforcement (self-management).

Generalization Stage

During the generalization stage, the learner performs the skill in different times and situations. For example, generalization to new situations occurs when a student demonstrates proficiency in math facts and continues to respond quickly and accurately when these facts are embedded in calculation problems. D. D. Smith (1981) reports that generalization is an area of great difficulty for the mildly handicapped, and unfortunately, it remains an area of limited research. Investigators have discovered that one cannot expect that generalization will just happen with mildly handicapped students. It must by systematically taught. Several groups of behaviorists (Gardner, 1978; Stokes & Baer, 1977; Wildman & Wildman, 1975) provide guidelines for teaching generalization. For example, Stokes and Baer (1977) recommend the following tactics for promoting generalization:

1. Teach responses likely to be maintained in the student's natural environment.
2. Vary the training models (e.g., use different teachers and stimuli).
3. Gradually loosen control of environmental

factors while teaching the student (e.g., vary instructions, stimuli, and reinforcers).

4. Conceal reinforcement contingencies when possible (e.g., delay reinforcement when possible).
5. Use stimuli in training that are found in the natural environment (e.g., use peers as tutors).
6. Teach the learner to self-monitor behavior (e.g., self-record and self-reinforce).
7. Reinforce correct responding in a variety of settings (e.g., regular class and home).

In their analysis of research on generalization, Deshler, Schumaker, and Lenz (1984) found that specific tactics employed throughout the instructional stages promote generalization. Therefore, Deshler et al. (1984) report that generalization might be conceptualized better as a framework for the entire instructional sequence than as a stage that the learner passes through after acquisition.

Similarly, Ellis, Lenz, and Sabornie (1987) report that various types of generalization are stressed throughout the instructional process. Specifically, they identify four levels of generalization.

1. *Antecedent generalization*. This level involves changing negative student attitudes that might eventually affect generalization behaviors.
2. *Concurrent generalization*. This level involves learning the skill well enough for generalization to occur.
3. *Subsequent generalization*. This level involves applying the skill to various situations, contexts, and settings.
4. *Independent generalization*. This level involves the student using self-instruction (e.g., cognitive behavior modification) to mediate generalization.

Wehman, Abramson, and Norman (1977) note that generalization is more likely to occur if people (e.g., parents, siblings, peers) in the student's environment carry out training procedures used at school. Moreover, D. D. Smith (1981) reports that the people in a youngster's environment can be taught to deal systematically with the social and academic skills of the student.

Adaption Stage

In the adaption stage the learner applies a previously learned skill in a new area of application without benefit of direct instruction or guidance. Simply, this skill may be referred to as problem solving. To illustrate, problem solving occurs when a student who has mastered multiplication facts "discovers" that division is the reverse of multiplication and proceeds to answer division facts accurately and independently (Idol-Maestas, 1983). D. D. Smith (1981) maintains that although it is important to teach mildly handicapped students adaption-level skills, this area is basically neglected. Strike (1975) notes that a discovery method of learning may be useful in helping students learn selected problem-solving skills.

Conclusion on Learning Stages

Unfortunately, research documenting successful approaches for developing generalization and problem-solving skills is sparse. Most behavioral studies only document effectiveness for short-term effects; however, some recent research in the area of skill generalization appears promising. For example, Idol-Maestas (1983) reports on eight projects in which generalization occurred through the use of behavioral tactics. Other investigators (Lloyd, Saltzman, & Kauffman, 1981; Schumaker, Deshler, Alley, & Warner, 1983) are using behavioral tactics in teaching rule or strategy learning with positive results regarding generalization.

Several behaviorists recognize shortcomings regarding teaching generalization to mildly handicapped students (D. D. Smith, 1981; Treiber & Lahey, 1983). Moreover, the combination of behavioral with other approaches (e.g., cognitive) is being suggested to teach higher-order skills (Schumaker et al., 1983; D. D. Smith, 1981; Tarver, 1986). Several sources (Blankenship & Lilly, 1981; Haring et al., 1978; Idol-Maestas, 1983; D. D. Smith, 1981) provide detailed coverage of strategies to use at the various stages of learning. The learning strategies approach is also presented in Chapter 14 of this text.

TEACHING PRINCIPLES

Teaching styles are developed individually, but they should not be based on whims, biases, or personal opinions. Teachers have the responsibility of examining the research and applying the findings as they develop teacher practices. Historically, the research on desirable teacher attributes has been inconclusive (Rosenshine & Furst, 1973); however, Stevens and Rosenshine (1981) report that recent research on teaching has been more informative.

The teaching guidelines that follow highlight the major findings of selected research in regular and special education. When a teacher incorporates these practices into daily instruction, the likelihood of improving the achievement of students increases.

Use Direct Instruction

Instructing students on appropriate tasks under conditions that motivate the students requires careful planning and monitoring of progress. To deliver this type of individualized programming, the teacher must be highly organized. This highly organized approach to instruction is often called *direct* or *systematic instruction*. Many studies support or encourage the use of direct or systematic instruction for students with learning problems (Carnine & Silbert, 1979; Stephens, 1977; Tarver, 1986; Treiber & Lahey, 1983).

> Direct instruction refers to high levels of student engagement within academically focused, teacher-directed classrooms using sequenced, structured materials. . . . [D]irect instruction refers to teaching activities focused on academic matters where goals are clear to students; time allocated for instruction is sufficient and continuous; content coverage is extensive; student performance is monitored; questions are at a low cognitive level and produce many correct responses; and feedback to students is immediate and academically oriented. In direct instruction, the teacher *controls* instructional goals, *chooses* material appropriate for the student's ability level, and *paces* the instructional episode. Interaction is characterized as structured, but not authoritarian; rather, learning takes place in a convivial academic atmosphere. (Rosenshine, 1978, p. 17)

Numerous investigators (Blankenship & Lilly, 1981; Deshler et al., 1984; Stevens & Rosenshine, 1981) offer support for the use of systematic instructional procedures. The most efficient teaching process involves five steps: advance organizer, demonstration, modeling, guided or controlled practice with prompts and feedback, and independent practice with feedback. These steps are inherent in the validated teaching sequence developed by Deshler and his colleagues at the University of Kansas Institute for Research in Learning Disabilities. Moreover, these procedures (demonstration, practice) are consistent with the emphasis on teaching mastery of the skill at a generalization level. Some research suggests that demonstration, modeling, and feedback enhance the acquisition and generalization of academic skills (Blankenship & Lilly, 1981; Deshler et al., 1984). Blankenship and Lilly (1981) provide some systematic instructional strategies that have been used successfully to promote academic performance. Selected strategies include the following:

1. Use instructions to explain how to perform a task.
2. Demonstrate the skill and have the student model it.
3. Provide drill activities and have the student practice the task to a specified criterion.
4. Give prompts and cues during student performances. Schloss and Sedlak (1986) provide the following hierarchy of prompts:
   a. Cue prompt—teacher simply cues the student to perform the task by a prompt such as "Read the second sentence."
   b. Oral prompt—teacher orally describes the aspects of the task prior to student performance.
   c. Modeling prompt—teacher performs the task immediately prior to the student's response.
   d. Manual prompt—teacher physically guides the student through the appropriate response.
5. Provide feedback during instruction of new skills.
6. Provide reinforcement for correct responses.

The teaching sequence presented earlier in the individualized programming section of this chapter incorporates many of the systematic instructional procedures supported in the research. Similarly, the teaching sequence presented in Chapter 14 provides an elaborated model of direct instruction.

Focus on Academic Instruction

Students with learning problems exhibit deficits in academic performance. The direct approach concentrates on improving specific academic skills without dealing with inferred process deficits. In a review of the literature

dealing with learning disabled students, Treiber and Lahey (1983) report success with this orientation. Specifically, they state, "This is not to say that learning disabled children do not have process deficits; rather that direct treatment of these inferred deficits is neither possible nor necessary for academic improvements to occur. This assertion is not a statement of faith, but rather a conclusion based on empirical evidence" (p. 79). Treiber and Lahey discuss literature that indicates the success of direct instruction (DI) across such academic areas as reading comprehension, handwriting, letter identification, sight-word vocabulary, arithmetic, and oral reading. Moreover, in a review of instructional approaches, Tarver (1986) concludes that strong support exists for direct instruction. Specifically, she states that "current knowledge suggests that DI theory, principles, and programs provide a strong base on which to build effective instructional programs" (p. 374).

In their review of teaching research, Stevens and Rosenshine (1981) reported that successful teachers maintained a strong academic focus. Effective teachers instructed students to spend more time working directly on academic tasks in texts, workbooks, and instructional materials. They assigned and held students responsible for more homework and tested students more frequently. In another review, Rosenshine and Furst (1973) found that being task-oriented or businesslike correlated positively with student achievement. These findings support the practice of establishing specific instructional objectives and maintaining activities that relate to those objectives.

The importance of an academic focus also receives support from research on engaged time. *Engaged time* is the time a student actually spends performing an academic task (e.g., writing, reading, computing). An extensive study of teaching activities that make a difference in student achievement was conducted

incl. in plans

as part of a six-year Beginning Teacher Evaluation Study funded by the National Institute of Education through the California Commission for Teacher Preparation and Licensing. Denham and Lieberman (1980) report that one of the major contributions of the study is its emphasis on academic learning time—that is, the time a student spends engaged in academic tasks of appropriate difficulty. As expected, the study found that academic learning time is related to student achievement. Specifically, Fisher et al. (1980) report that (a) the time allocated to a content area is positively associated with learning in that area, and (b) the engaged time that students spend performing reading or mathematics tasks with high success is positively associated with learning. Thus, a cornerstone of good teaching is establishing appropriate academic instructional objectives and designing intervention programs that maximize opportunities for the student to work successfully on tasks related to the objectives. Unfortunately, several researchers (Borg, 1980; Will, 1986; Ysseldyke & Algozzine, 1984) report that the engaged time of students in many classroom settings is relatively low.

Wilson and Wesson (1986) report that instructional time, time on task, and student success are the essential variables of academic learning time. For increasing actual instructional time, they recommend

1. Scheduling more instructional time.
2. Reducing transition time.
3. Shortening free time.
4. Improving the efficiency of organizational activities (e.g., teaching students self-management skills).
5. Being prepared.

For increasing teacher-directed instructional time, they recommend

1. Creating more teacher-led instructional groups.

2. Increasing the use of the direct-instruction teaching sequence.
3. Seeking a balance between teacher-led and seatwork time.
4. Making seatwork tasks relevant.

For increasing time on task during teacher-directed instruction, they recommend

1. Increasing teacher questioning.
2. Involving all students.
3. Using signals effectively (e.g., "Look at me").
4. Increasing teacher enthusiasm.

For increasing on-task rates during practice sessions, they recommend

1. Rewarding correct responses.
2. Using a reinforcing error-correction procedure (e.g., instead of putting Xs on incorrect responses, putting check marks on correct responses). *circles rather than X's*
3. Giving concise instructions.
4. Organizing seatwork practice (e.g., planning for students to finish at different times).
5. Using novel, motivating seatwork activities (e.g., self-correcting materials, instructional games).

The organization, management, and content chapters in this book provide guidelines, procedures, and activities to help the teacher design instruction that maximizes engaged time.

Provide Success

One of the primary findings of the Beginning Teacher Evaluation Study (Fisher et al., 1980) is that learning improves the most when students have a high percentage of correct responses during teacher questioning and seatwork. Furthermore, Stevens and Rosenshine

(1981) report that a high percentage of correct responses given rapidly correlates with academic achievement. They suggest that a reasonable success rate appears to be at least 80% during instruction and 90% at the end of a unit. Ideally, the task should maintain an appropriate level of challenge (i.e., require effort to succeed). Fisher et al. (1980) highlight this point in the following statements:

> Common sense suggests that too high a rate of high success work might be boring and repetitive and could inhibit the development of persistence. Probably, some balance between high success and more challenging work is appropriate. Also, we found that older students and/or students who were generally skilled at school learning did not require as high a percentage of time at the high success level. Apparently these students had learned problem solving—how to take a task they did not completely understand and work it out. Such students are able to undertake the challenge of more difficult material, as long as they eventually experience success. . . . When students worked with materials or activities that yielded a low success rate, achievement was lower. (pp. 17–18)

Moreover, Stevens and Rosenshine (1981) note that individualization is considered a characteristic of effective instruction if it refers to helping each student achieve a high percentage of correct responding in a confident manner. In summarizing the work of Denny (1966), Mercer and Snell (1977) note that one of his basic tenets in creating an optimal learning environment is to prevent incorrect responses and elicit as many correct responses as possible.

It is apparent that in good teaching the importance of providing the student with success cannot be overemphasized. Lack of success can lead to anxiety, frustration, inappropriate behavior, and poor motivation; in contrast, success can improve motivation, attitudes,

academic progress, and classroom behavior. Techniques that enable mildly handicapped learners to be successful are as follows: Use continuous assessment to mark the student's daily progress (Blankenship & Lilly, 1981). Base instructional objectives on assessment data. Use simple vocabulary in directions and in teacher–student interactions (Archer & Edgar, 1976). For seatwork, use one type of response for each assignment, and use standard formats (Archer & Edgar, 1976). Provide visual, auditory, and physical prompts to help the student perform correctly (Archer & Edgar, 1976; Polloway, Payne, Patton, & Payne, 1985). Use demonstration and modeling to insure correct performances (Archer & Edgar, 1976; Polloway et al., 1985). Use task analysis to break down difficult tasks into simpler tasks. Use self-correcting instructional materials (Mercer, Mercer, & Bott, 1984). The Analysis of Student Learning Form presented in Table 2.1 *on p. 47* provides a list of factors a teacher may manipulate to enhance success in the classroom.

Provide Feedback

Another significant finding of the Beginning Teacher Evaluation Study (Fisher et al., 1980) is that academic feedback is positively associated with student learning. In a study with learning disabled adolescents, Deshler, Ferrell, and Kass (1978) found that teachers should provide specific feedback on what is both correct and incorrect in order to improve performance. Denny (1966), who studied optimal learning conditions, stresses that immediate feedback is germane to effective learning. Blankenship and Lilly (1981) note that feedback serves two important functions. First, it assists students in distinguishing between correct and incorrect responses. Second, it informs students of their progress. The use of self-correcting materials provides the teacher with an effective tool for providing feedback to students during independent work. Self-correcting materials are presented in each academic area throughout the book.

Be Positive

A teacher's moods and attitudes greatly affect the classroom environment. When the teacher is cheerful, supportive, and enthusiastic, students tend to model his actions and attitudes. This can result in a very pleasant, productive learning environment. It is easy for teachers to notice when things go wrong in the classroom; however, *effective* teachers comment on positive classroom happenings, in addition to addressing misbehavior (Eaton & Hansen, 1978).

R. M. Smith, Neisworth, and Greer (1978) convey the importance of the positive approach:

> Liberal amounts of praise, support, and encouragement are found in every good classroom. By emphasizing children's good points, the teacher can build their confidence and desire to tackle more difficult activities. Failure to use such encouragement is a mistake teachers cannot afford to make. The development of a healthy social interaction in the classroom has never been accomplished through criticism and ridicule. (p. 85)

Students' descriptions of good teachers (Lovitt, 1977) reflect the importance of being positive. The children in Lovitt's study noted that a good teacher compliments children, lets children come to him for help, helps each child, uses good manners, shows trust for children, joins in class humor, explains more than once, and asks children for help. The children were concerned with fair play, inclusion in the action, and getting work done in a quiet and orderly room. They wanted the teacher to be a real person with a sense of humor. When the teachers engaged in these behaviors more, the academic performance of the children improved: "As the teacher did more things that pleased the students, they did more to please the teacher" (Lovitt, 1977, p. 94).

A positive approach is enhanced by the appropriate use of reinforcement for desirable academic, on-task, and social behaviors. The positive effect of reinforcement on academic achievement and work behaviors is well established (Blankenship & Lilly, 1981; Lovitt, 1984). Although the use of reinforcement to improve student behavior and learning has substantial support, some researchers caution against the indiscriminant use of rewards. For example, Kleinhammer-Tramill, Tramill, Schrepel, and Davis (1983) found that indiscriminant rewards on correct performance resulted in poorer performances by low-achieving adolescents than contingent rewards on correct performance. Finally, the use of intimidation, threat, and criticism are highly questionable as learning techniques to foster.

Strive to Motivate

Many mildly handicapped learners need support and encouragement from others to sustain interest in schoolwork. In many cases, they are not motivated by the reward of knowledge for its own sake. Positive reinforcement is one of the primary techniques used to motivate students. A number of teaching activities help to motivate students. Lovitt (1977) recommends active involvement of students in instructional activities. Schumaker, Deshler, Alley, and Warner (1983) also stress the need to involve the adolescent in understanding the purpose and need for the instructional activities. In addition, instructional games and self-correcting materials may be useful for maintaining interest. In a review of research on strategies for motivating students to learn, Brophy (1987) highlights 33 strategies (see Table 1.3).

TABLE 1.3
Highlights of research on strategies for motivating students to learn.

Research on student motivation to learn indicates promising principles suitable for application in classrooms, summarized here for quick reference.

Essential Preconditions
1. Supportive environment
2. Appropriate level of challenge/difficulty
3. Meaningful learning objectives
4. Moderation/optimal use

Motivating by Maintaining Success Expectations
5. Program for success
6. Teach goal setting, performance appraisal, and self-reinforcement
7. Help students to recognize linkages between effort and outcome
8. Provide remedial socialization

Motivating by Supplying Extrinsic Incentives
9. Offer rewards for good (or improved) performance
10. Structure appropriate competition
11. Call attention to the instrumental value of academic activities

Motivating by Capitalizing on Students' Intrinsic Motivation
12. Adapt tasks to students' interests
13. Include novelty/variety elements
14. Allow opportunities to make choices or autonomous decisions
15. Provide opportunities for students to respond actively
16. Provide immediate feedback to student responses

17. Allow students to create finished products
18. Include fantasy or simulation elements
19. Incorporate game-like features
20. Include higher-level objectives and divergent questions
21. Provide opportunities to interact with peers

Stimulating Student Motivation to Learn
22. Model interest in learning and motivation to learn
23. Communicate desirable expectations and attributions about students' motivation to learn
24. Minimize students' performance anxiety during learning activities
25. Project intensity
26. Project enthusiasm
27. Induce task interest or appreciation
28. Induce curiosity or suspense
29. Induce dissonance or cognitive conflict
30. Make abstract content more personal, concrete, or familiar
31. Induce students to generate their own motivation to learn
32. State learning objectives and provide advance organizers
33. Model task-related thinking and problem solving

Source: From "Synthesis of Research on Strategies for Motivating Students to Learn" by J. Brophy, 1987, *Educational Leadership, 45*(2), p. 45. Copyright 1987 by the Association for Supervision and Curriculum Development. Reprinted by permission.

Insure Attention

During direct instruction, the teacher should continuously observe the students to make sure they are paying attention. Attention is an essential factor in the learning process (Ross, 1976), and teachers should try to strengthen students' attention behavior. Among mildly handicapped learners, the inability to master a task has been related to attention problems (Broadbent, 1977; Fisher & Zeaman, 1973; Ross, 1976). To learn a new task, the student must select and pay attention to only the relevant stimuli. How stimuli are presented can greatly affect attention. For example, novelty, change, and uncertainty have been used to increase attention.

Archer and Edgar (1976) offer several suggestions for maintaining attention:

1. Make sure all learners can see the teacher during instruction. Arrangement of chairs in a semicircle maintains visual contact with students during instruction.
2. Use physical proximity. This enables the student to see and hear the teacher easily. Moreover, when the teacher notices a student daydreaming or looking away, touch may be used to gain the student's attention.
3. Use cue words. "Get your ears [eyes] ready," "listen," "look," and "ready" are words that alert the student.

During instruction, the teacher should scan the students for attention behavior and should make adjustments to improve attention when necessary.

Enjoy Teaching

Good teaching is a difficult job, requiring a lot of physical and mental energy. When examining all the aspects of good teaching, remember that students can bring enjoyment to teaching. As Lovitt (1977) points out, "Youngsters are, by definition, fresh. . . . They see life differently. . . . They often develop their own approaches and language systems for dealing with and talking about their lives. . . . Children entertain teachers; they keep them sane, pure in spirit, and incorruptible" (p. 201). The teacher should develop an attitude of appreciation and should expect to enjoy his students— enjoy their freshness, their humor, their questions, and their ideas.

INDIVIDUALIZED EDUCATIONAL PROGRAMS

Public Law 94–142, the Education for All Handicapped Children Act, was enacted by Congress in November 1975. The major purpose of the law is to insure that all handicapped children receive a free, *appropriate* public education. The four basic educational rights that the law provides for handicapped children are as follows:

1. A thorough assessment of the nature and degree of specific disability, in a nondiscriminatory manner, and with no single measurement being the sole criterion for evaluation,
2. The overall right to a free education appropriately tailored to the needs of each child,
3. Placement in the "least restrictive environment" with maximum emphasis on placement of the disabled child with nondisabled children whenever possible (mainstreaming),
4. The provision of supplementary aid and services to help insure the success of the program. (Arena, 1978, pp. 7–8)

An *individualized education program* (IEP) must be developed and implemented for each handicapped student who receives special education. According to the law, the IEP must state (a) the child's present performance levels; (b) annual and short-term instructional objectives; (c) the specific education services to be provided and the extent to which the child will be able to participate in regular education; (d) the projected date for initiation and anticipated duration of such services; and (e) criteria, evaluation procedures, and schedules for determining whether objectives are being achieved.

Table 1.4 illustrates an IEP format that incorporates the essentials of a plan. Part B-I enables the teacher to outline the short-term objectives for the academic year. Part B-II provides more space for short-term objectives but does not segment the objectives into grad-

TABLE 1.4
Individualized educational program.

Part A: IEP

Identification Information

Name __John Doe__

School __Beecher Sixth Grade Center__

Birthdate __5-15-76__ Grade __6__

Parents' Name __Mr. & Mrs. William Doe__

Address __1300 Johnson Street__

__Raleigh, N.C.__

Phone: Home __none__ Office __932-816__

Continuum of Services

	Hours Per Week
Regular class	20 hrs.
Resource teacher in regular classroom	
Resource room	6 hrs.
Reading specialist	4 hrs.
Speech/language therapist	
Counselor	
Special class	
Transition class	
Others:	

Yearly Class Schedule

	Time	Subject	Teacher
1st semester	8:30 - 9:20	math	Franks
	9:30 - 10:20	language arts	Bambara (Resource)
	10:30 - 11:20	Social Studies	Bambara
	11:20 - 12:20	science	Franks
		lunch	
	1:10 - 2:00	art	Shaw
	2:10 - 3:00	P.E.	King
2nd semester	8:30 - 9:20	math	Franks
	9:30 - 10:20	language arts	Bambara (Resource)
	10:30 - 11:20	social studies	Bambara
	11:30 - 12:20	science	Franks
		lunch	
	1:10 - 2:00	art	Shaw
	2:10 - 3:00	P.E.	King

Testing Information

Test Name	Date Admin.	Interpretation
P I A T	9-10-88	spell -1.7 Read.comp -NA; math -5.7 Gen.Inf.-6.3; Read.recog 1.2 Total -2.0
tests of initial consonants (CRT)	9-11-88	Knows 8 out of 21 initial consonant sounds
CRT		oral comprehension - 6th grade
Reading Checklist	9-12-88	reading skills - primary level
Oregon Diagnostic Reading Inventory	9-2-88	low ratio on areas of vowel & consonant sounds, irregular words, and oral reading

Checklist

9-5-88 Referral by __Louise Borden__

9-6-88 Parents informed of rights; permission obtained for evaluation

9-14-88 Evaluation compiled

9-20-88 Parents contacted

9-21-88 Total committee meets and subcommittee assigned

9-26-88 IEP developed by subcommittee

9-27-88 IEP approved by total committee

Committee Members

__Mrs. Louise Borden__

Teacher __Mrs. John Thomas__

Other LEA representative __Mrs. William Doe__

Parents __Mrs. Mary Franks__

__Mrs. Joan Bambara__

__Mrs. Alice King__

Date IEP initially approved __9-27-88__

Health Information

Vision: __good__

Hearing: __excellent__

Physical: __good__

Other:

(continued)

TABLE 1.4, continued

Part B. I.: IEP (Complete for each subject area)

Student's Name __John Doe__

Subject Area __Reading__

Level of Performance __can identify 8 of 21 initial consonants & 1 of 5 short vowels; can identify few words at pri primer level; can orally comprehend stories from 6th grade books.__

Teacher __Mrs. Bambara – Resource Teacher__

Annual Goals:
1. John will successfully complete the primer level of the Bank Street Reading Series.
2. John will recognize and correctly say 180 new sight words.
3. John will master 14 initial consonants and 4 short vowels.

	First Grading Period Sept.—Oct.	Second Grading Period Oct.—Nov.	Third Grading Period Nov.—Dec.	Fourth Grading Period Jan.—Feb.	Fifth Grading Period Feb.—Apr.	Sixth Grading Period Apr.—June
Objectives	Referred 3. 2. 1.	1. Recognize and correctly state the sounds of the initial consonant phonemes "b," "f," "s," and "m" 100% of the time. 2. Recognize and correctly say 40 new sight words 100% of the time. 3. Complete the first six stories in the primer, reading at a rate of 90 words per minute correct.	1. Correctly recognize and state the sound of the initial consonant phonemes "h," and "g" 100% of the time. 2. Recognize and correctly say 10 new sight words 100% of the time. 3. Complete the next story in the primer, reading at a rate of 90 words per minute correct.	1. Review and correctly state the phonemes "l," "s," "m," "g," "h," and short e 100% of the time. 2. Review and correctly say 50 previously learned sight words 100% of the time. 3. Recognize and correctly say 10 new sight words 100% of the time. 4. Review the previously read stories in the primer, reading at a rate of 90 words per minute correct.	1. Recognize and correctly state the phonemes "l," "d," "r," "w," short e, short i, and short u 100% of the time. 2. Recognize and correctly say 60 new sight words 100% of the time. 3. Complete the next 6 stories in the primer, reading at a rate of 90 words per minute correct.	1. Recognize and correctly state the phonemes "c," "t," "n," and "y" 100% of the time. 2. Recognize and correctly say 60 new sight words 100% of the time. 3. Complete the next 6 stories in the primer, reading at a rate of 90 words per minute correct. Evaluation
Agent		Resource teacher – 1,2 Regular classroom teacher – 2,3	Resource teacher – 1,2 Regular classroom teacher – 2,3	Resource teacher – 1,2,3 Regular classroom teacher – 3,4	Resource teacher – 1,2 Regular classroom teacher – 2,3	Resource teacher – 1,2 Regular classroom teacher – 2,3
Evaluation		1. informal assessment, including probes 2. Criterion Referenced Test (CRT)	1. informal assessment, including probes 2. CRT	1. informal assessment, including probes 2. CRT	1. informal assessment, including probes 2. CRT	1. informal assessment, including probes 2. CRT

Part B. II.: IEP (Complete for each subject area)

Student's Name _____ Subject Area _____

Level of Performance _____ Teacher _____

Annual Goals: 1. _____

2. _____

3. _____

Date Initiated	Objectives	Materials	Evaluation	Date Achieved	Person Responsible

Source: Adapted from *Developing and Implementing Individualized Education Programs* (pp. 18, 23–25) by A.P. Turnbull, B.B. Strickland, and J.C. Brantley, 1978, Columbus, OH: Merrill. Copyright 1978 by Bell & Howell Company. Reprinted by permission.

ing periods. The teacher may select either form of Part B, depending on needs and preferences. For an example of an IEP that stresses behavior management the reader is referred to Kerr and Nelson (1983, pp. 142–143).

It is a good practice for the special education teacher to work with a student for several sessions prior to the IEP conference. During this time, he can determine realistic objectives and specific teaching techniques. According to Turnbull, Strickland, and Hammer (1978a),

> The IEP has the potential of being the catalyst for a more individualized and specified approach to education, increased accountability of educators, and shared decision-making between teachers and parents. It can be viewed as a burden of more paperwork or as an opportunity to improve the quality of education for handicapped students and the diagnostic-prescriptive skills of teachers. (p. 46)

Participants in IEP Meetings

The law specifies who must participate in IEP meetings: (a) a representative of the schools, other than the child's teacher, who is qualified to provide or supervise special education; (b) the student's teacher (the special education teacher if the student is receiving special education; otherwise, the regular teacher); (c) one or both parents; (d) the student, when appropriate; and (e) others at the discretion of the parent or school personnel. For handicapped students evaluated for the first time, a member of the evaluation team or an individual knowledgeable about the evaluation procedures must attend the IEP meeting.

Schools must follow certain procedures regarding parent participation to insure the presence of parents at the meeting. Specific steps include the following:

1. Notify them early enough. The purpose, time, and location of the meeting and the persons who will be in attendance should be included in the notice.

2. Schedule the meeting at a mutually agreed upon time and place.
3. If neither parent can attend, the school should use other methods to insure parent participation, such as telephone calls or home visits.
4. If a meeting is held without a parent in attendance, the school must document attempts to involve the parents. These attempts include telephone calls, copies of correspondence, and records of home visits.
5. Provide a copy of the student's IEP to the parent upon request.

Finally, the law states that, when appropriate, the student is to participate in the planning of his IEP. Although the participation of the student in the meeting would often be minimal, it may be especially effective to include the secondary level student in the planning of his program.

Components of an IEP

Levels of performance. The student's present level of performance may be obtained from placement information (for example, evaluations of academic, language, and cognitive skills). However, additional assessment usually is necessary for creating specific objectives in various subject areas. On the IEP, level-of-performance data must be precise enough to aid the teacher in formulating initial objectives. *Norm-referenced* or *criterion-referenced* evaluation instruments are designed to provide such data. In norm-referenced evaluation a student's performance is compared to others' scores; in criterion-referenced evaluation a student's performance is described in terms of fixed criteria. Criterion-referenced instruments and informal measures seem to be more suitable than tests that primarily yield comparative scores. These instruments typically include systematic skill sequences and provide information that directly leads to objectives (for example, instruct student in sums to 9 facts). Levels of performance may be assessed in the following areas: social adaptation, emotional maturity, prevocational-vocational skills, psychomotor skills, and academic achievement. Formal and informal assessment devices are discussed in Chapter 2, and specific tests are presented in each of the respective curriculum area chapters. In addition, scope and sequence skills lists are included in Appendix A.

Annual goals. Annual goals must be tailored to individual needs—academic and otherwise—and must encompass the entire spectrum of short-term objectives in each specified area. They must describe what the child should be able to do at the end of the school year. Turnbull et al. (1978b) note that "although teachers are not legally responsible for achieving the annual goals, they are responsible for setting realistic expectations and for providing relevant, systematic instruction toward these goals" (p. 71). Annual goals that are likely for a mildly handicapped learner include the following:

1. Student will successfully complete Level 9 of the Ginn 720 Basal Reading Series.
2. Student will learn the multiplication facts through times 9.
3. Student will work steadily and independently and complete his task before moving to next task.

For the teacher who uses a scope and sequence skills list to identify instructional objectives and to monitor progress, the process of writing annual goals may be less time-consuming. By coding the scope and sequence skills list, the teacher can simply write the annual goals by using the code. For example, a student's present level of performance may be reading skill No. 3.14, and the annual goal may be to reach reading skill No. 4.26. In this

approach, the short-term objectives become the skills listed between 3.14 and 4.26. When using coding, the teacher must ensure that parents understand the organization of the instructional objectives.

Short-term objectives. Short-term objectives must be listed and described in specific, measurable terms. These objectives help boost present levels of performance toward annual goals. As noted earlier, this task is much simpler if criterion-referenced evaluation measures are used, because the mastery of specific skills is readily pinpointed on a continuum of listed competencies. Short-term objectives that are likely to be used with some mildly handicapped learners are as follows:

1. Student will recognize and say the sounds of the initial consonants *r* and *w* 100% of the time.
2. Student will correctly write his name within 30 seconds.
3. Student will read the next story (section) in his basal reader at 150 correct words per minute with two or less errors and 90% comprehension.

Description of services. A statement of the specific services and materials provided for the child includes (a) who teaches the child, (b) what content is included in the instructional program, and (c) what materials are used. Also, since Public Law 94–142 requires that the child be educated in the least restrictive environment (that is, placed with nonhandicapped peers as much as possible), the extent of the child's participation in the regular program must be established. For example, the plan may state that the child functions in the regular classroom all but one hour a day. The role of the regular teacher then is noted. (For example, the child will sit in the front of the regular classroom and will use individualized spelling tapes developed jointly by the regular teacher and the special education teacher.)

Dates of service. The plan outlines the projected dates for initiation and anticipated duration of services.

Evaluation. The use of objective criteria and frequent assessment are encouraged. However, the law requires only an annual evaluation to determine if the annual goals are being achieved. Evaluation procedures are presented in Chapter 2 and in each of the respective curriculum area chapters.

Although the IEP is a substantial improvement over planning procedures used by many educators in the past, it is not sufficient for delivering an individualized program. Bateman (1977) compared the components of *diagnostic prescriptive teaching* (an individualized programming approach) and the IEP. Prescriptive teaching and the IEP both require assessment of the child's present level and specification of goals and objectives. However, only prescriptive teaching specifies the teaching tasks inherent in the objectives (such as antecedent events, child responses, consequent events, and daily evaluation for each task). Thus, the IEP requirements are not sufficient for providing individualized programming instruction on a daily basis.

Requirements of an IEP insure a certain amount of common ground in planning instruction for handicapped students. However, the teacher retains much flexibility in selecting assessment, instructional, and evaluation procedures. It is hoped that the requirements and the flexibility of the IEP jointly will foster individualized, resourceful instructional programs.

Providing Educational Services

In developing the IEP, educators are faced with the task of placing the student in an educational setting tailored to the student's learning and social-emotional needs. The setting in which services are provided has a strong influence on the student, the teacher, and the family.

For years, educational programs for students with learning problems were operated by special education teachers in special classes or resource rooms outside the regular class. Under Public Law 94–142 the regular classroom teacher assumes more of the responsibility for educating students with learning problems.

Least Restrictive Environment and Mainstreaming

According to Public Law 94–142, the term *least restrictive environment* (LRE) means that, to the extent appropriate, handicapped students should be educated with nonhandicapped students. Idol-Maestas (1983) states, "LRE roughly means selecting the most normal educational setting in which a special education student can profit from learning opportunities that afford the maximum amount of progress in the least amount of time" (p. 8). Historically, handicapped pupils were pulled out of regular classrooms and placed in self-contained classes. LRE is based on the premise that placement of handicapped with nonhandicapped youngsters results in improved academic and social development for handicapped pupils and reduces the stigma associated with being educated in segregated settings. The least restrictive principle stresses the need for using a continuum of services sensitive to diverse needs.

A perspective on this idea is enhanced by examining Deno's (1970) "cascade" system that describes services in terms of seven levels. As a student moves from Level 1 to Level 7, the degree of segregation from regular class peers increases.

1. Regular class assignment with or without supportive services.

2. Regular class assignment plus supplementary instructional services.
3. Part-time special class.
4. Full-time special class.
5. Special school assignment within public school system.
6. Homebound instruction.
7. Placement in facilities operated by health or welfare agencies.

Mainstreaming. Public Law 94–142 does not mention the term *mainstreaming*; however, its use is widespread. Mainstreaming springs from the least restrictive environment concept and is used extensively to refer to the practice of integrating handicapped pupils socially and instructionally into regular education as much as possible. Some authorities debate about the similarities and differences between mainstreaming and LRE; however, when both are *responsibly* practiced, they appear very similar. When mainstreaming involves simply placing handicapped learners with the nonhandicapped and disregarding their social and academic needs, it is not being responsibly practiced.

The research on the efficacy of mainstreaming has been inconclusive (Carlberg & Kavale, 1980). Several investigators (Gottlieb, 1981; Gresham, 1982) report that mainstreaming has not resulted in significant social and educational growth for handicapped learners. Others (Haring & Krug, 1975; Macy & Carter, 1978) report that regular class placements have had positive effects on handicapped students. Mixed results are probably in part the result of a lack of precise guidelines for implementing mainstreaming.

Guidelines for successful mainstreaming. Salend (1984) identified the following factors that, according to the literature, appear to contribute to successful mainstreaming.

1. Development of criteria for mainstreaming. Not all handicapped students can be success-

fully mainstreamed. Educators need criteria to determine whether a student possesses the necessary skills to benefit from and perform successfully in the mainstream. Salend and Lutz (1984) have begun by identifying 15 critical social skill competencies relating to three general areas: interacting positively with others, obeying class rules, and exhibiting proper work habits.

2. Preparation of handicapped students. For mainstreaming to be successful, the handicapped student should be prepared for the behavioral and academic demands of the regular class (Gresham, 1982). The regular environment demands (e.g., notetaking, independent work) should be duplicated in the special education setting, and the learning environment within the regular class should be examined to develop specific preparation of the student to function in it. Salend and Viglianti (1982) provide a format to assist educators in analyzing the critical factors of a regular class. Finally, Gresham (1982) notes that many handicapped students need social skills training to help them function successfully in mainstream settings.

3. Preparation of nonhandicapped students. Nonhandicapped students can be a major factor in the success of a handicapped student, and they can help the educational process by interacting positively with handicapped peers. To do so, they need positive attitudes toward students with learning and/or behavioral difficulties. Positive attitudes can be fostered through the use of films, disability simulations, children's books about the handicapped, and group discussions. With positive attitudes, the regular students can help handicapped pupils by being role models, tutors, and friends.

4. Promotion of communication among educators. The education of handicapped students is now the shared responsibility of special and regular educators. Several investigators (Ammer, 1984; Miller & Sabatino, 1978) report that the success of mainstreaming greatly depends on how well these two groups interact. To help the communication process, Salend and Hankee (1981) recommend that special educators need to provide regular teachers with such information as handicapped students' academic achievement, social development, and preparedness for entering the mainstream. Moreover, behavioral consultation programs, in which the special educator guides the regular teacher in modifying a student's behavior in the regular setting, have been effective (Idol-Maestas, 1983).

5. *Evaluation of student progress.* When handicapped students enter the mainstream, their progress needs to be monitored systematically to determine whether interventions are working or need modifying. Information about a student's progress can be obtained from parents, regular educators, and the mainstreamed student. Data-based instruction (see Chapter 2) is one approach that provides an ongoing record of student progress and enables the teacher to make instructional adjustments as soon as the student experiences difficulty.

6. *Provision of in-service training.* Powers (1983) notes that in-service training is consistently identified as a major factor in successful mainstreaming. He presents an extensive literature-based set of in-service guidelines to help educators plan effective inservice for those involved with mainstreaming. To date, most inservice efforts have focused on developing positive attitudes toward mainstreaming and teaching needed competencies to implement it successfully (Salend, 1984).

Mainstream programs. In an examination of highly successful mainstreaming programs (G. Smith & Smith, 1985; Wang, Peverly, & Randolph, 1984), the six factors highlighted by Salend (1984) are apparent. Encouraging results from their program led Wang et al. (1984) to recommend trying full-time mainstreaming for educable mentally retarded, learning dis-

abled, and emotionally disturbed students before more restrictive placements are used.

Placement Selection

Large numbers of students have academic and behavioral problems, and learning disabilities teachers are being asked to serve more and more students. The concern over the growing number of students with problems has stimulated special and regular educators to join efforts and create some innovative and productive activities. These approaches focus on meeting the needs of handicapped learners within the regular class before considering formal special education services and more segregated placements. Through an approach called regular education initiative, Will (1986) *REI* recommends that the pull-out model of educating handicapped students be decreased and that regular educators assume more responsibility for teaching mildly handicapped learners. Many issues exist concerning the regular education initiative (McCarthy, 1987), and its impact remains uncertain. Much of the promise of these activities rests on the assumption that, in a supportive and trusting environment, teachers can support and teach each other in individualizing instruction for a diversity of learners. Consequently, as teachers become more competent, the regular and/or mainstream setting improves, and referrals to special education decrease.

Teachers helping teachers. Kirk and Chalfant (1984) discuss a Teacher Assistance Team model that has proven effective in helping teachers reduce the number of inappropriate referrals and in resolving many students' problems. Each team consists of three elected teachers, the teacher seeking help, and parents or others as needed. The referring teacher provides information concerning the student's strengths and weaknesses and interventions that have been tried. The team conducts a problem-solving meeting on the following pattern: (a) delineate specific objectives with the teacher; (b) brainstorm intervention alternatives; (c) select and/or refine intervention(s); and (d) plan follow-up activities. The teacher leaves the meeting with a copy of the interventions. A follow-up meeting is planned in 2 to 6 weeks to determine if the suggestions are working.

The Teacher Assistance Team model was evaluated in three states for a 2-year period. Of the 200 students served in the study, the teams helped the classroom teacher resolve the difficulties of 133 students, or 66.5%. Of the 116 students who were underachieving, the teams could meet the needs of 103 (88.7%) without referring them to special education. Moreover, schools with Teacher Assistance Teams cut their diagnostic costs by approximately 50% (Kirk & Chalfant, 1984).

Moreover, Graden, Casey, and Christenson (1985) report success with a prereferral intervention system that uses teacher-to-teacher consultation and group problem-solving sessions. Ammer (1984) surveyed 70 regular educators concerning their views of mainstreaming. In the survey, regular teachers reported that the lack of communication among teachers is a serious hindrance to successful mainstreaming. One of Ammer's major conclusions highlighted the need for peer teaching among teachers.

Another team approach generating enthusiasm among educators is *coaching* (Garmston, 1987; McREL Staff, 1984–1985; Showers, 1985). Peer coaching involves the formation of a small group of teachers and peer observation. Teachers observe each other's classrooms, get feedback about their teaching, experiment with improved techniques, and receive support (McREL Staff, 1984–1985). Coaching teams of three people engage in a three-phase process involving discussion and planning, observation, and feedback.

In the discussion and planning phase, the teachers focus on the improved technique or strategy they want to learn and outline the specific essential behaviors or actions for implementing the new technique. In the observation phase, teacher 1 observes teacher 2, who observes teacher 3, who observes teacher 1. A format (e.g., checklist, log, tape recorder) to guide data collection helps observation. In the feedback phase, the observer and the teacher meet to discuss the observations. To help maintain the professional nature of coaching, the teachers must never talk to a third person about observations or let a team member draw others into personal problems. Periodically, the coaching teams meet in a support group of 6 to 12 with other coaching teams to plan and offer support for each other. Showers (1985) reports that one purpose of coaching is to build a community of teachers who continuously engage in the study of improved teaching. The coaching process becomes a continuous cycle in which common necessary understandings emerge for improved teaching through collegial study of new knowledge and skills.

The effects of coaching are impressive. Showers (1985) reports that coaching provides the essential follow-up for training new skills and strategies. Also, it is more effective than lecture and demonstration in providing classroom applications (McREL Staff, 1984–1985). Coaching appears to hold much promise as a technique to help educators develop a broader repertoire of skills for meeting the diverse needs of students in mainstream settings.

EDUCATIONAL SERVICE PROVISIONS AND RELATED PRACTICES

Students with learning problems have a wide range of needs, and schools vary concerning the types of resources available. Needs and resources must be examined *student by stu-*

dent and must not be guided by trends or philosophies insensitive to uniqueness. Regular class service or placement options include (a) special materials, equipment, and consultation, (b) itinerant services, and (c) a resource room with a special education teacher. Table 1.5 presents some advantages and disadvantages of each respective service alternative.

Special Materials, Equipment, and Consultation

The educational needs of some students with learning problems are met by using additional materials and equipment. The materials may consist of a high-interest/low-vocabulary reading series, a programmed reader, a Language Master, manipulative materials for math, a pencil holder, or any material or hardware that makes individualized instruction possible. Also, if needed, the teacher may be provided with consultation.

Numerous professionals (Freeman & Becker, 1979; Idol-Maestas, 1983) maintain that the counseling and consulting role is becoming increasingly important for the special education teacher. Idol-Maestas (1983) defines consultation as *support* provided to regular classroom teachers to help them with academic and social behavior problems of handicapped learners. Graden et al. (1985) note that consultation facilitates the identification of areas of concern, the exploration of alternative interventions, and the implementation and evaluation of interventions. Houck (1984) reports that the consultant's task is to guide the referring teacher through the problem-solving process while simultaneously creating a sense of joint responsibility for instruction. A modification of Bergan's (1977) consultation model includes the following steps:

1. A positive and collaborative relationship is developed between the consultant and teacher.

2. The consultant assists the teacher in identifying the behavior of concern in specific, measurable, and objective terms.
3. The discrepancy between the student's actual performance level and the desired or expected level is assessed. Problem areas are prioritized, and classroom factors that influence the student's performance are analyzed.
4. The referring teacher and the consultant collaborate to design an intervention program. Factors identified as affecting the student's learning are taken into consideration.
5. The interventions are implemented and evaluated. If successful, consultation may terminate; if not successful, follow-up consultation is provided.

Safran and Barcikowski (1984) examined the impact of information offered by consultants on teacher expectations for mainstreamed learning disabled students. Generally, they found that regular teachers are highly influenced by information received from consultation. To enhance the effectiveness of consultation, they recommend that learning disabilities consultants clarify *individual* student problems and relate services to the specific needs of each child. Idol-Maestas (1983) provides a wealth of support for the consultation process and offers many techniques for consultants.

Itinerant Services

Regular class teachers sometimes need to instruct students whose difficulties are not severe enough to warrant resource room instruction or special class placement. To aid these teachers, an itinerant teacher usually visits the schools periodically. He focuses on the skills of the teacher. Miller and Sabatino (1978) describe him as a facilitator who conveys best-practice skills to regular teachers. Since these consultation services range from daily to bi-

TABLE 1.5

Advantages and disadvantages of service models for students with learning problems.

Model	Advantages	Disadvantages
Regular Classroom (Student remains in regular class all day)	Provides for interaction of handicapped and nonhandicapped peers in least restrictive setting. Prevents needless labeling.	May compound learning disabilities with instructional factors. Includes large number in class population. Uses a teacher not specifically trained. May not provide small group or individual instruction.
Consultant (Consultant teacher works with regular teacher)	Can reach more teachers. Can supply specific instructional methods, programs, and materials. Can serve more children. Influences environmental learning variables. Coordinates comprehensive services for the children.	May not foster inclusion in teaching staff. Does not provide firsthand knowledge of students that comes from teaching them. Can separate assessment and instruction.
Itinerant (Itinerant teacher travels to various schools consulting with regular teachers)	Aids in screening and diagnosis. Provides some help in area of consulting. Offers part-time services. Covers needs of children in different schools or areas. Is an economical way to address mild problems.	Does not provide consistent support for more involved students. Does not promote identification with staff. Presents difficulty in transporting materials. Lacks continuity of program. Lacks regular follow-up.
Resource Room (Child spends portion of school day—45–60 minutes—with resource room teacher; most widely used model)	Reduces stigmatization. Emphasizes instructional remediation. Supplements regular classroom instruction. Separates handicapped learner from nonhandicapped peers for limited periods of the school day. Provides individualized instruction in problem areas through specially trained teacher. May provide consulting services to regular teachers. Prevents needless labeling. Focuses on mainstreaming students.	Is not well suited to serve severely learning disabled students. Presents scheduling problems. Tends toward over-enrollment. Can create misunderstanding of teacher role. May inspire conflicts in teacher role. Provides no time to observe or consult. Provides little time to assess and plan.

weekly visits, the classroom teacher still has the basic responsibility for the child. Obviously, the itinerant teacher must be careful in scheduling his visits. Occasionally, itinerant services are bolstered through the use of volunteers or teacher aides.

Miller and Sabatino (1978) examined this program's effectiveness, noting impressive academic gains. Thus, tentative support is available for the consultation model.

Resource Room

Many students with learning problems spend the majority of the day in a regular class and go to the resource room for a specified period of time (e.g., 45 to 60 minutes) each day. The resource room teacher, located in the school, works closely with numerous teachers to coordinate the instructional programs of the pupils. Figure 1.2 indicates how this commonly used plan accommodates the different needs of both students and teachers.

Friend and McNutt (1984) conducted a survey in the 50 states and District of Columbia regarding the use of the resource room model. Results indicated that in all states and the District of Columbia the resource room is the most frequently used alternative to the regular classroom for serving the mildly to moderately handicapped. Friend and McNutt report much variation in the types of services offered within this approach. Given the alternatives (see Figure 1.2), this variation is not surprising.

Sargent (1981) examined the time use of 30 resource room teachers from five states. Using a time-sampling procedure, Sargent found that the teachers used their time in these activities: direct instruction, 51.48%; preparation for instruction, 16.38%; general school duties, 9.22%; assessment and evaluation, 8.82%; consulting with staff, 8.51%; record keeping,

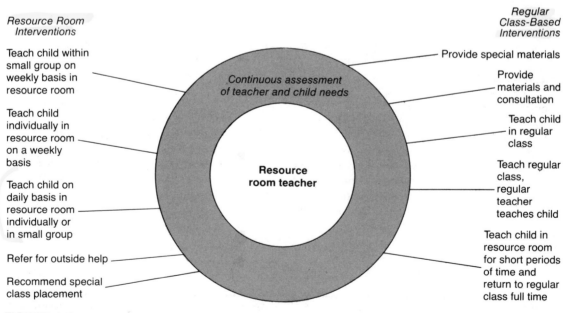

FIGURE 1.2
Service alternatives for the resource room teacher.

3.77%; consulting with parents, 3.6%; staff-ings, 2.8%; working with IEPs, 1.38%; and conducting in-service, 0%. In addition, he found that the resource teachers' estimates of their time and actual time spent were consider-ably different.

Since the resource room teacher provides daily services to approximately 20 students with learning problems and their respective teachers, obviously the role demands a highly competent, personable individual. Specifically, Wiederholt (1974) feels the following qualities are essential: (a) the ability to work effectively and harmoniously with teachers and ancillary staff; (b) the ability to assess the educational needs of pupils; and (c) the ability to design and implement prescriptive teaching.

Speece and Mandell (1980) surveyed 228 regular educators about resource room ser-vices. These regular classroom teachers thought the following nine services of resource room teachers were critical:

1. Attending parent conferences (74.2%).
2. Meeting informally to discuss student prog-ress (74.2%).
3. Providing remedial instruction in the re-source room (67.0%).
4. Providing information on behavioral char-acteristics (54.5%).
5. Providing academic assessment data (53.9%).
6. Scheduling meetings to evaluate student progress (52.7%).
7. Providing materials for classroom (52.1%).
8. Suggesting materials for classroom (52.1%).
9. Providing written reports of students' activi-ties and progress (51.5%).

Since many of these services require consulta-tion from resource room teachers, Speece and Mandell encourage more in-service and pre-service programs that emphasize the develop-ment of consultation skills.

Wiederholt, Hammill, and Brown (1983) specify numerous advantages of the resource room:

1. Students can benefit from specific resource support while remaining integrated with their friends and age-mates in the school.
2. The resource teacher has an opportunity to help more students than does a full-time special class teacher. This is especially true when the resource teacher, by consulting extensively with teachers, provides indirect services to students with mild or moderate problems.
3. Resource teachers can serve as informa-tional resources to other school personnel, to parents, and to the students themselves.
4. Because young children with mild, though developing, problems can be accommo-dated, later severe disorders may be pre-vented.
5. Flexible scheduling means that remediation can be applied entirely in the classrooms by the regular teacher with some resource support or in another room by the resource program personnel when necessary; also, the schedule can be quickly altered to meet the students' changing situations and needs.
6. Since the resource program will absorb most of the handicapped students in the schools, the self-contained special education classes will increasingly become instruc-tional settings for truly and relatively se-verely handicapped students, those for whom the classes were originally developed.
7. Because resource teachers have broad ex-perience with many students exhibiting dif-ferent educational and behavioral problems, they may in time become in-house consult-ants to the school.
8. Resource teachers can serve as ombuds-men for the students they serve.
9. Most handicapped students can receive help in their neighborhood schools; thus, the necessity of busing them across the town or county to a school that houses an appropriately labeled class is eliminated or at least reduced. (pp. 12–13)

Although the resource room is gaining popularity as an instructional plan for serving mildly handicapped youngsters, its effectiveness has not been extensively measured. Until further research suggests otherwise, however, the resource room will continue to be used as a model to serve mildly handicapped learners.

In planning an educational program for the handicapped learner, it is important to make a tentative commitment to a program level and not consider placement as permanent. Educators must provide youngsters with programs that will continuously respond to their unique needs. Moving pupils from the more segregated programs to the more integrated programs needs to be regularly considered and undertaken whenever feasible. In addition, placement in a particular program alternative needs to be considered when it appears that such a change would be beneficial. For example, a change from one regular classroom to another may be advisable because a teacher has certain qualities or an instructional program is specifically suited to the student.

Reintegration of Students

When students in special programs are functioning consistently well, consideration of reintegrating them into their regular programs is warranted. Sabornie (1985) stresses the need for educators to consider the social consequences of integrating handicapped learners with regular students. He notes that, according to research, young learning disabled students are not popular in regular classes, and he concludes that educators must both teach essential social skills to handicapped learners and help nonhandicapped students overcome any negative biases toward those with learning and/or behavior problems. Salend and Lutz (1984) surveyed regular and special educators in elementary schools to ascertain which social skills are considered critical to successful functioning in the mainstream setting. The 15 identified competencies are organized into three categories: (a) interacting positively with others, (b) obeying class rules, and (c) displaying proper work habits. They report that social skill criteria provide placement teams with critical information for determining whether or not the student is ready for reintegration into the mainstream setting. Moreover, the criteria for successful mainstreaming (Salend, 1984) discussed earlier in this chapter apply to the reintegration of mildly handicapped youngsters. Some specific guidelines for reintegration include the following:

1. Make placement changes on the basis of the youngster's performance. For example, determine if the student's academic performance is commensurate with his ability.
2. Help students and parents adjust to modifications of or a reduction in special education services. Moreover, due process procedures should be used (Stephens, 1977).
3. Include the respective teachers and solicit their observations of the youngster in relation to placement decisions.
4. Use fading techniques when changing placements (Stephens, 1977).
5. Be sure the new classroom teacher can make the necessary minor adjustments (Chalfant, 1985).
6. Make certain the exiting criteria include the same variables used in identifying and placing the student (Chalfant, 1985).

Demers (1981) examined the success of a point system for completed work and on-task behavior to facilitate a smooth transition. All teachers who worked with the student used the same point system; thus, the program was consistent throughout the day. The method works when used in its entirety.

Epstein and Cullinan (1979) suggest that a social comparison method may help determine when reintegration is feasible. First, data are collected on the performance of regular classroom peers. When the pupil performs similarly to regular peers on several critical skills, reintegration is appropriate. They note that such peer data may be better criteria than teacher intuition or norms on standardized tests.

Obviously, dismissal from a special education program originates from a reevaluation of the student's needs and progress. The IEP format offers the teacher an excellent opportunity to examine the possibility of reintegration. If observations show a change is warranted, he can initiate a meeting or reevaluate the existing IEP.

REFERENCES

Ammer, J.J. (1984). The mechanics of mainstreaming: Considering the regular educators' perspective. *Remedial and Special Education, 5*(6), 15–20.

Archer, A., & Edgar, E. (1976). Teaching academic skills to mildly handicapped children. In S. Lowenbraun & J.Q. Affleck (Eds.), *Teaching mildly handicapped children in regular classes* (pp. 15–112). Columbus, OH: Merrill.

Arena, J. (1978). *How to write an I.E.P.* Novato, CA: Academic Therapy.

Bateman, B.D. (1977). Prescriptive teaching and individualized education programs. In R. Heinrich & S.C. Ashcroft (Eds.), *Instructional technology and the education of all handicapped children.* Columbus, OH: National Center on Media and Materials for the Handicapped.

Bergan, J. (1977). *Behavioral consultation.* Columbus, OH: Merrill.

Blankenship, C., & Lilly, M.S. (1981). *Mainstreaming students with learning and behavior problems: Techniques for the classroom teacher.* New York: Holt, Rinehart, & Winston.

Borg, W.R. (1980). Time and school learning. In C. Denham & A. Lieberman (Eds.), *Time to learn.* Washington, DC: National Institute of Education.

Broadbent, D.E. (1977). The hidden preattentive process. *American Psychologist, 32,* 109–118.

Brophy, J. (1987). Synthesis of research on strategies for motivating students to learn. *Educational Leadership, 45*(2), 40–48.

Carlberg, C., & Kavale, K. (1980). The efficacy of special versus regular class placement for exceptional children: A meta-analysis. *Journal of Special Education, 14,* 295–309.

Carnine, D., & Silbert, J. (1979). *Direct instruction reading.* Columbus, OH: Merrill.

Chalfant, J.C. (1985). Identifying learning disabled students: A summary of the National Task Force report. *Learning Disabilities Focus, 1*(1), 9–20.

Demers, L.A. (1981). Effective mainstreaming for the learning disabled student with behavior problems. *Journal of Learning Disabilities, 14,* 179–188, 203.

Denham, C., & Lieberman, A. (Eds.). (1980). *Time to learn.* Washington, DC: National Institute of Education.

Denny, M.R. (1966). A theoretical analysis and its application to training the mentally retarded. In N.R. Ellis (Ed.), *International review of research in mental retardation* (Vol. 2). New York: Academic Press.

Deno, E. (1970). Special education as developmental capital. *Exceptional Children, 37,* 229–237.

Deshler, D.D., Ferrell, W.R., & Kass, C.E. (1978). Monitoring of schoolwork errors by LD adolescents. *Journal of Learning Disabilities, 11,* 401–414.

Deshler, D.D., Schumaker, J.B., & Lenz, B.K. (1984). Academic and cognitive interventions for LD adolescents: Part I. *Journal of Learning Disabilities, 17,* 108–117.

Eaton, M.D., & Hansen, C.L. (1978). Classroom organization and management. In N.G. Haring, T.C. Lovitt, M.D. Eaton, & C.L. Hansen, *The fourth R: Research in the classroom* (pp. 191–217). Columbus, OH: Merrill.

Ellis, E.S., Lenz, B.K., & Sabornie, E.J. (1987). Generalization and adaptation of learning strategies to natural environments: Part I: Critical agents. *Remedial and Special Education, 8*(1), 6–20.

Epstein, M.H., & Cullinan, D. (1979). Social validation: Use of normative peer data to evaluate LD interventions. *Learning Disability Quarterly, 2*(4), 93–98.

Fisher, C.S., Berliner, C.D., Filby, N.N., Marliave, R.,

Cahen, L.S., & Dishaw, M.M. (1980). Teaching behaviors, academic learning time, and student achievement: An overview. In C. Denham & A. Lieberman (Eds.), *Time to learn.* Washington, DC: National Institute of Education.

Fisher, M.A., & Zeaman, D. (1973). An attention-retention theory of retardate discrimination learning. In N.R. Ellis (Ed.), *The international review of research in mental retardation* (Vol. 6). New York: Academic Press.

Freeman, M.A., & Becker, R.L. (1979). Competencies for professionals in LD: An analysis of teacher perceptions. *Learning Disability Quarterly, 2*(1), 70–79.

Friend, M., & McNutt, G. (1984). Resource room programs: Where are we now? *Exceptional Children, 51,* 150–155.

Gardner, W.I. (1978). *Children with learning and behavior problems: A behavior management approach* (2nd ed.). Boston: Allyn & Bacon.

Garmston, R.J. (1987). How administrators support peer coaching. *Educational Leadership, 44*(5), 18–26.

Gottlieb, J. (1981). Mainstreaming: Fulfilling the promise? *American Journal of Mental Deficiency, 86,* 115–126.

Graden, J.L., Casey, A., & Christenson, S.L. (1985). Implementing a prereferral intervention system: Part I. The model. *Exceptional Children, 51,* 377–384.

Gresham, F.M. (1982). Misguided mainstreaming: The case for social skills training with handicapped children. *Exceptional Children, 48,* 422–433.

Hammill, D.D., & Bartel, N.R. (1986). Meeting the special needs of children. In D.D. Hammill & N.R. Bartel, *Teaching students with learning and behavior problems* (4th ed., pp. 1–21). Boston: Allyn & Bacon.

Haring, N.G., & Krug, D.A. (1975). Placement in regular programs: Procedures and results. *Exceptional Children, 41,* 413–417.

Haring, N.G., Lovitt, T.C., Eaton, M.D., & Hansen, C.L. (1978). *The fourth R: Research in the classroom.* Columbus, OH: Merrill.

Houck, C.K. (1984). *Learning disabilities: Understanding concepts, characteristics, and issues.* Englewood Cliffs, NJ: Prentice-Hall.

Idol-Maestas, L. (1983). *Special educator's consultation handbook.* Rockville, MD: Aspen Systems.

Kerr, M.M., & Nelson, C.M. (1983). *Strategies for managing behavior problems in the classroom.* Columbus, OH: Merrill.

Kirk, S.A., & Chalfant, J.C. (1984). *Academic and developmental learning disabilities.* Denver: Love.

Kleinhammer-Tramill, J.P., Tramill, J.L., Schrepel, S.N., & Davis, S.F. (1983). Learned helplessness in learning disabled adolescents as a function of noncontingent rewards. *Learning Disability Quarterly, 6*(1), 61–66.

Lloyd, J., Saltzman, N.J., & Kauffman, J.M. (1981). Predictable generalization in academic learning as a result of preskills and strategy training. *Learning Disability Quarterly, 4,* 203–216.

Lovitt, T.C. (1977). *In spite of my resistance: I've learned from children.* Columbus, OH: Merrill.

Lovitt, T.C. (1984). *Tactics for teaching.* Columbus, OH: Merrill.

Lovitt, T.C., & Hansen, C.L. (1976). Round one—Placing the child in the right reader. *Journal of Learning Disabilities, 9,* 347–353.

Macy, D.J., & Carter, J.L. (1978). Comparison of a mainstream and self-contained special education program. *Journal of Special Education, 12,* 303–313.

Mager, R.F. (1975). *Preparing instructional objectives* (2nd ed.). Belmont, CA: Fearon.

McCarthy, J.M. (1987). A response to the regular education/special education initiative. *Learning Disabilities Focus, 2*(2), 75–77.

McREL Staff. (1984–1985, Winter). Coaching: A powerful strategy for improving staff development and inservice education. *Noteworthy,* pp. 40–46.

Mercer, C.D., Mercer, A.R., & Bott, D.A. (1984). *Self-correcting learning materials for the classroom.* Columbus, OH: Merrill.

Mercer, C.D., & Snell, M.E. (1977). *Learning theory research in mental retardation: Implications for teaching.* Columbus, OH: Merrill.

Miller, T.L., & Sabatino, D.A. (1978). An evaluation of the teacher consultant model as an approach to mainstreaming. *Exceptional Children, 45,* 86–91.

Miramontes, O., Cheng, L., & Trueba, H.T. (1984).

Teacher perceptions and observed outcomes: An ethnographic study of classroom interactions. *Learning Disability Quarterly, 7,* 349–357.

Nelson, C.M., & Polsgrove, L. (1984). Behavior analysis in special education: White rabbit or white elephant? *Remedial and Special Education, 5*(4), 6–17.

Polloway, E.A., Payne, J.S., Patton, J.R., & Payne, R.A. (1985). *Strategies for teaching retarded and special needs children* (3rd ed.). Columbus, OH: Merrill.

Powers, D.A. (1983). Mainstreaming and the inservice education of teachers. *Exceptional Children, 49,* 432–439.

Rosenshine, B. (1978). The third cycle of research on teacher effects: Content covered, academic engaged time, and quality of instruction. In *78th yearbook of the National Society for the Study of Education.* Chicago: University of Chicago Press.

Rosenshine, B., & Furst, N. (1973). The use of direct observation to study teaching. In R.M.W. Travers (Ed.), *Second handbook of research on teaching* (pp. 122–183). Chicago: Rand McNally.

Ross, A.O. (1976). *Psychological aspects of learning disabilities and reading disorders.* New York: McGraw-Hill.

Sabornie, E.J. (1985). Social mainstreaming of handicapped students: Facing an unpleasant reality. *Remedial and Special Education, 6*(2), 12–16.

Safran, S.P., & Barcikowski, R.S. (1984). LD consultant information in mainstreaming: Help or hindrance? *Learning Disability Quarterly, 7,* 102–107.

Salend, S.J. (1984). Factors contributing to the development of successful mainstreaming programs. *Exceptional Children, 50,* 409–416.

Salend, S.J., & Hankee, C. (1981). Successful mainstreaming: A form of communication. *Education Unlimited, 3,* 47–48.

Salend, S.J., & Lutz, J.G. (1984). Mainstreaming or mainlining: A competency based approach to mainstreaming. *Journal of Learning Disabilities, 17,* 27–29.

Salend, S.J., & Viglianti, D. (1982). Preparing secondary level handicapped students for entry into the mainstream. *Teaching Exceptional Children, 14,* 137–140.

Sargent, L.R. (1981). Resource teacher time utilization: An observational study. *Exceptional Children, 47,* 420–425.

Schloss, P.J., & Sedlak, R.A. (1986). *Instructional methods for students with learning and behavior problems.* Boston: Allyn & Bacon.

Schumaker, J.B., Deshler, D.D., Alley, G.R., & Warner, M.M. (1983). Toward the development of an intervention model for learning disabled adolescents: The University of Kansas Institute. *Exceptional Education Quarterly, 4,* 45–74.

Showers, B. (1985). Teachers coaching teachers. *Educational Leadership, 42*(7), 43–48.

Siegel, E., & Gold, R.F. (1982). *Educating the learning disabled.* New York: Macmillan.

Smith, D.D. (1981). *Teaching the learning disabled.* Englewood Cliffs, NJ: Prentice-Hall.

Smith, G., & Smith, D. (1985). A mainstreaming program that really works. *Journal of Learning Disabilities, 18,* 369–372.

Smith, R.M., Neisworth, J.T., & Greer, J.G. (1978). *Evaluating educational environments.* Columbus, OH: Merrill.

Speece, D.L., & Mandell, C.J. (1980). Resource room support services for regular teachers. *Learning Disability Quarterly, 3*(1), 49–53.

Stephens, T.M. (1977). *Teaching skills to children with learning and behavior disorders.* Columbus, OH: Merrill.

Stevens, R., & Rosenshine, B. (1981). Advances in research on teaching. *Exceptional Education Quarterly, 2*(1), 1–9.

Stokes, T.F., & Baer, D.M. (1977). An implicit technology of generalization. *Journal of Applied Behavior Analysis, 10,* 349–367.

Strike, K.A. (1975). The logic of learning by discovery. *Review of Educational Research, 45,* 461–483.

Talmage, H. (1975). Instructional design for individualization. In H. Talmage (Ed.), *Systems of individualized education.* Berkeley, CA: McCutchan.

Tarver, S.G. (1986). Cognitive behavior modification, direct instruction and holistic approaches to the education of students with learning disabilities. *Journal of Learning Disabilities, 19,* 368–375.

Treiber, F.A., & Lahey, B.B. (1983). Toward a behavioral model of academic remediation with learning disabled children. *Journal of Learning Disabilities, 16,* 111–116.

Turnbull, A.P., Strickland, B., & Hammer, S.E. (1978a). The individualized education program—Part 1: Procedural guidelines. *Journal of Learning Disabilities, 11,* 40–46.

Turnbull, A.P., Strickland, B., & Hammer, S.E. (1978b). The individualized education program—Part 2: Translating law into practice. *Journal of Learning Disabilities, 11,* 67–72.

Utley, B.L., Zigmond, N., & Strain, P.S. (1987). How various forms of data affect teacher analysis of student performance. *Exceptional Children, 53,* 411–422.

Wang, M.C., Peverly, S., & Randolph, R. (1984). An investigation of the implementation and effects of a full-time mainstreaming program. *Remedial and Special Education, 5*(6), 21–32.

Wehman, P., Abramson, M., & Norman, C. (1977). Transfer of training in behavior modification programs: An evaluation review. *Journal of Special Education, 11,* 217–231.

Wiederholt, J.L. (1974). Planning resource rooms for the mildly handicapped. *Focus on Exceptional Children, 5,* 1–10.

Wiederholt, J.L., Hammill, D.D., & Brown, V. (1983). *The resource teacher: A guide to effective practices* (2nd ed.). Austin, TX: Pro-Ed.

Wildman, R.W., II, & Wildman, R.W. (1975). The generalization of behavior modification procedures: A review—With special emphasis on classroom applications. *Psychology in the Schools, 12,* 432–448.

Will, M.C. (1986). Educating students with learning problems: A shared responsibility. *Exceptional Children, 52,* 411–415.

Wilson, R., & Wesson, C. (1986). Making every minute count: Academic learning time in LD classrooms. *Learning Disabilities Focus, 2*(1), 13–19.

Ysseldyke, J.E., & Algozzine, B. (1984). *Introduction to special education.* Boston: Houghton Mifflin.

CHAPTER 2

Assessment for
Teaching

Ysseldyke and Algozzine (1984) aptly state the basic goal of assessment practices:

> The ultimate goal of assessment is improvement of instruction for the learner. The only valid special education process is one in which assessment leads to treatments that have known outcomes. Frankly, a good share of assessment activities today consist of meddling. . . . To the extent that collection of assessment data leads to improvements in instruction, collection of those data is a reasonable activity. (p. 288)

To aid in instructional programming, the assessment must provide information in two areas. First, it must help the teacher select *what* to teach the individual student. Second, it must help the teacher determine *how* to teach the student for maximum progress. When the teacher has determined how the student learns best, she can arrange variables such as physical setup of the class, social interaction patterns, and reinforcement strategies to make the instructional program most effective.

Information for determining what and how to teach an individual is gathered by both formal and informal evaluation procedures. Formal evaluation consists of administering standardized tests, whereas informal evaluation involves nonstandardized assessment devices and procedures. Formal testing is primarily used to document the existence of a problem and identify the appropriate label (e.g., learning disabled) for a student. Informal testing is primarily used in planning instruction and evaluating student progress on a continuous basis. Many educators prefer informal over formal assessment, and in recent years informal assessment has gained in popularity (Salvia & Ysseldyke, 1988; Stiggins, 1985). For example, the curriculum-based assessment section in this chapter presents an informal assessment approach that is receiving extensive attention. Each of the content chapters in this book discusses formal and informal assessment procedures.

ASSESSMENT FOR DETERMINING WHAT TO TEACH

Assessment areas for determining what to teach may include academic skills (such as reading and arithmetic), content subjects (such as science and social studies), motor skills, personal-social skills, and vocationally related skills (such as career knowledge and specific vocational training). This type of assessment is required at all grade and age levels.

Assessment Model

The model shown in Figure 2.1 provides guidelines for assessment of what to teach.

1. Determine Scope and Sequence of Skills to be Taught

↓

2. Decide What Behavior to Assess

↓

3. Select an Evaluation Activity

↓

4. Administer the Evaluation Device

↓

5. Record the Student's Performance

↓

6. Determine Specific Short- and Long-Range Instructional Objectives

FIGURE 2.1
Assessment model for determining what to teach.

Determine scope and sequence of skills to be taught. Teachers frequently have the responsibility of determining short- and long-range instructional objectives in numerous curriculum areas (such as reading, math, science, and vocational education). To do this effectively, the teacher must have an understanding of the scope and sequence of skills in the curriculum areas. For example, a sixth-grade teacher may have students whose arithmetic skills span several grade levels; some students need help with regrouping in two-digit subtraction problems, whereas others are working with decimals and percentages. A knowledge of scope and sequence skills provides the teacher with a clear understanding of the skills a student has mastered and those that need to be mastered.

Task analysis is very useful in helping teachers adopt, adapt, or make a material. It is essential for determining the sequence of skills included in a material or program. Task analysis consists of dividing learning tasks into parts in order to identify the skills used in performing the task. The notion that learning is cumulative—that skills build upon one another—is basic in task analysis.

Precise instructional objectives are used in task analysis because they allow the teacher to sequence instruction. A well-formulated objective for a task includes a condition (parameters of the task), a criterion, and a terminal behavior. *Enabling behaviors* are the skills prerequisite for performing the specified behavior. Enabling behaviors are determined by working backwards from the terminal behavior. Through this process, a hierarchy of skills is built. The implication of task analysis for instructional sequencing is clear: Teach the student the easiest skill that she is unable to perform.

The following example illustrates task analysis with the terminal behavior of reading a simple sentence:

Terminal behavior: Read a simple sentence.

Prerequisite skills:

Uses left-to-right eye mo
Associates sounds of lett
Blends sounds into words
Reads words in isolation
Reads words in context

Frank (1973) outlines four steps in task analysis: (a) clearly state the terminal behavior, (b) identify the subskills of the terminal behavior and sequence them from simple to complex, (c) informally assess to see which subskills the student already can perform, and (d) start teaching in sequential order, beginning with the easiest subskill the student has not learned.

Commercial programs and criterion-referenced tests are good sources of scope and sequence skills lists. Scope and sequence skills lists vary in organization, detail, complexity, and comprehensiveness. A list in reading may include 1,000 skills within the K–12 period. Lists of this size are often too complex for teachers to recognize the basic sequence of skills in a curriculum area. To be useful, a scope and sequence skills list should organize the sequence into component areas and present the major skills in each area. This type of list helps the teacher to grasp the total sequence and to see it in a hierarchical, logical nature.

For each skill listed in a sequence, the teacher can develop a device or procedure for assessing it. For example:

Skill:
Given the two base words on contractions, the student writes contractions.

Sample assessment item:
Write a contraction for:

1. can not _____
2. you are _____
3. they are _____
4. we will _____

5. I am   _____
6. he is   _____
7. do not   _____

Criterion 7/7

Scope and sequence skills lists that are useful in designing assessment programs are in Appendix A. Lists are provided in the following areas: arithmetic, reading, spelling, handwriting, and written expression. Although scope and sequence skills lists have content validity and logic, their content and ordering have not been confirmed through research. Therefore, teachers should use their own judgment in selecting and adapting them.

Decide what behavior to assess. Deciding what behavior to assess begins at a global level and becomes very specific. At the global level the area of assessment is selected (e.g., spelling or reading), usually based on referral information, teacher observation, or results from standardized testing. Assessment at the global level involves sampling the student's behavior within a wide *span of skills* in the area. In the area of reading, skills in word attack, word recognition, word comprehension, and passage comprehension might be sampled. *Skill-span* tests are also referred to as *sequence-related* tests (Archer & Edgar, 1976) or *survey* tests. Resources for constructing tests that assess across a span of skills include graded curriculum materials, scope and sequence skills lists, and standardized tests. Problem areas are then identified, and these problem areas help the teacher to select the specific skill areas for further assessment. For example, in reading, the student might demonstrate a problem with word recognition. Word recognition becomes an area for *specific skill testing*. The specific skill assessment provides information that leads directly to determining instructional objectives (e.g., student needs to work on short-vowel sounds). In summary, determining

what behavior to assess follows four stages: (a) select the global area, (b) conduct assessment across a wide span of skills, (c) note problem areas, and (d) conduct specific skill assessment.

Select an evaluation activity. The teacher has many choices in selecting evaluation activities: commercial tests, curriculum tests, criterion-referenced skill inventories and checklists, and teacher-made instruments (e.g., curriculum-based assessment device or informal reading inventory). In making the decision several factors are considered, including purpose, cost, time, and relevance of the activity or test for classroom instruction.

The teacher must consider whether the activity is for surveying a span of skills or for assessing a specific skill. If skill-span assessment is needed, the activity is usually noncontinuous (for example, twice a year), whereas with specific skill assessment it is continuous (perhaps daily or weekly).

Specific skill assessment is used during the initial evaluation to determine instructional objectives. Also, it is used in *daily* instruction to evaluate a student's progress in specific skills. Because of its frequent use, the teacher must select activities that are easy to use and not time-consuming. Additional information on frequent assessment is provided in the section on daily assessment for data-based instruction presented at the end of this chapter.

Administer the evaluation device. The teacher usually administers the evaluation device for the initial assessment. As noted earlier, the initial assessment involves evaluating both a wide span of skills and specific skills. Since this procedure involves much decision making—identifying problem areas, noting error patterns, selecting specific skills for assessment—it is usually done by the teacher or a diagnostician. After the initial assessment is completed and instructional objectives are determined, procedures for monitoring progress are established. These procedures are usually easy to administer, score, and interpret. The teacher may assign this evaluation to the student, teacher aide, classroom volunteer, or a classmate. Many students enjoy monitoring their own progress.

It is important for the evaluator to establish rapport and to note the student's attitude. Since the teacher is trying to determine if a student has *mastered* a skill, the evaluation can be administered in a flexible manner. For example, if a student does not appear to be trying, the teacher may wish to stop the activity, talk with the student, and then start the activity from the beginning. During self-evaluation activities, the teacher periodically must check on the student to insure that the student is making serious efforts and following the correct procedures. When standardized tests are primarily used to obtain a quantitative score, the administration and scoring procedures must be closely followed. Only when tests are given to determine skill mastery can administration procedures be flexible.

Record the student's performance. A teacher needs to record two types of student performance: performance on daily work and mastery of skills. Daily progress usually is recorded by means of teacher-made activities (such as spelling tests, learning charts, and performance on worksheets). Overall skill mastery usually is recorded on individual progress charts. Scope and sequence lists provide a good format for recording skill mastery. In addition, some commercial materials provide individual progress sheets for recording student performance. A detailed discussion of record-keeping procedures is presented in Chapter 3.

Determine specific short- and long-range instructional objectives. After administering the assessment, the teacher must analyze the data and create instructional objectives. As noted in Chapter 1, good objectives specify the target behavior in observable terms, delineate the conditions under which the behavior occurs, and describe the criterion for successful performance (Mager, 1975). Short-term objectives should directly contribute to the mastery of long-term objectives. For example, the following short- and long-term objectives are related:

Long-term objective: Given the graphemes of 44 phonemes, the student will say the correct phoneme with 90% accuracy.

Short-term objective: Given the graphemes for consonant blends, the student will say the phoneme with 90% accuracy.

When the instructional objectives are established, the first step in individualized programming is achieved.

Curriculum-Based Assessment

Under the rubric of curriculum-based assessment (CBA) many informal assessment procedures are being applied within the context of a local school's curriculum. CBA refers to "any procedure that directly assesses student performance within the course content for the purpose of determining that student's instructional needs" (Tucker, 1985, p. 200). Some authorities define CBA more specifically. For example, Blankenship and Lilly (1981) define CBA as "the practice of obtaining direct and frequent measures of a student's performance on a series of sequentially arranged objectives derived from the curriculum used in the classroom" (p. 81). In essence, the essential feature of CBA is that the student's progress is assessed in terms of the classroom curriculum, so that instruction can be better tailored to the student's needs.

Blankenship and Lilly (1981) provide the following steps for developing a CBA:

1. Select a curriculum material (e.g., math or reading basal) and examine the skills covered.
2. Evaluate the skill sequence and select the skill areas to be assessed.
3. Sequence the skills to be assessed.
4. Write an objective for each skill.
5. Make the assessment measures and plan how to administer the CBA (e.g., directions, number of testing sessions, scoring).
6. Administer the CBA and record the student's performance.
7. Determine the criterion for placing the student in the curriculum.

Applications of curriculum-based assessment. Although the essential feature of CBA is as old as education itself (e.g., prescriptive teaching), its systematic application is generating some practical tools, novel ideas, and impressive results. Teachers using this approach report dramatic increases in the percentage of students mastering unit objectives.

Marston and Magnusson (1985) report that CBA procedures have proven efficient and effective across a variety of assessment goals: screening, identification, program planning, and monitoring the progress of mildly handicapped students. Moreover, they note that CBA data indicate that special education students are learning in their special settings.

Blankenship (1985) describes the successful use of CBA to monitor progress in a math curriculum. She reports that CBA offers useful information at three points in the teaching process: before instruction, immediately after instruction, and periodically during the year to measure long-term retention. Germann and Tindal (1985) report good results from using CBA to monitor academic and social behaviors. They note that CBA provides a continuous data base to help with numerous educational decisions, including problem identification,

program planning, program implementation and evaluation, and program certification.

In a study of CBA, Deno (1985) concludes that achievement in basic skills can be measured reliably and validly by using the school's curriculum to generate test items. He notes that CBA holds much promise for the following reasons:

1. It is *curriculum referenced,* so that a student's competence is measured in terms of the local school curriculum.
2. It is *individual referenced,* so that judgments can be made about an individual student's progress.
3. It is *peer referenced,* so that the "normality" of a student's performance can be reliably determined using locally developed peer sampling.

In discussing the legal parameters of using CBA, Galagan (1985) notes that CBA, with its focus on individual needs, is capable of meeting the specific individual needs of children and therefore the legal requirements of the Education for All Handicapped Children Act. Gickling and Thompson (1985) capture the essence of the CBA movement:

> This focus has led to an equally important concern, that of providing low-achieving and mainstreamed children with similar types of learning conditions . . . enjoyed by their more successful peers. This statement is not to imply that they will be able to function at the same ability levels as their average and above-average peers, but that they will have similar opportunities for task success in relationship to their own entry skills and that they will begin to make more systematic progress in school. (p. 217)

Blankenship and Lilly (1981) and Howell and Morehead (1987) provide detailed descriptions of how to develop and use curriculum-based assessment.

ASSESSMENT FOR DETERMINING HOW TO TEACH

Once the teacher determines the instructional needs of the student by assessing what to teach, the very important process of determining how to teach begins. The second process focuses on environmental variables that influence the student's achievement. Traditionally, too much emphasis has been placed on "diagnosing" the student with learning problems. Learning deficits often are attributed to problems within the student, and so the student is viewed as responsible for the learning problems. Many educators now recognize that environmental factors (e.g., poor teaching) may trigger and sustain low achievement and inappropriate behaviors. Ysseldyke and Algozzine (1984) recommend the use of instructional diagnosis as a procedure for determining the extent to which poor instruction is contributing to the student's learning or behavioral difficulties.

> Instructional diagnosis . . . is designed to identify the extent to which the student's poor performance is caused by poor instruction and what the teacher might do to remedy the problem. Information on the predispositional state, history, or current characteristics of the learner is seen as of limited value. Teachers do not have an opportunity to manipulate neurons or learner histories, but they can change instruction. A factor to consider before instructional diagnosis is the extent to which an individual is actually being taught. (p. 297)

Thus, in planning for the student with learning problems, it is essential to consider both student and environmental factors.

The ability to assess how best to teach a student is a very critical skill. Unfortunately, too little emphasis has been placed on it in teacher training and material development. The efficiency of the instructional process depends on how well a teacher determines and manipulates factors that best facilitate a student's learning. For example, Ms. Allen, a classroom teacher, observed that because Ronnie is constantly asking classmates if his responses are correct, he is not using his time wisely during spelling seatwork. To improve the situation, Ms. Allen made a spelling tape with the week's word list spelled correctly on it. Ronnie uses the tape in studying the words. If the result of this adjustment is that Ronnie learns an average of one word more a day without increasing the time spent on spelling, the instructional program has become more efficient. Ronnie will learn many more spelling words during the school year without increasing the amount of time he spends on spelling seatwork. This ability to analyze how a student learns best influences the selection of materials, methods, and procedures used in the intervention program. It is perhaps the foremost skill that distinguishes the professionally trained teacher from other supportive instructional personnel.

Formats for Determining How to Teach

Systematic observation. Systematic observation of the student is one of the teacher's most valuable ways of obtaining information about a student's optimal learning conditions. In systematic observation, it is often important to record more than a specific behavior. Information for determining how to teach often comes from observing *antecedent* and *consequent* events as well: (a) what precedes behavior (teacher asked Johnny to read in a large group), (b) behavior (Johnny cried), and (c) what follows behavior (teacher coaxed Johnny). Systematic observation is simple to use and can be done in a variety of settings. Stephens (1977) recommends several guidelines for successful observation:

1. Select the behavior to be observed. Make sure the target behavior is identifiable to the extent that it is measurable.

2. Select a method of recording the behavior and record the frequency of the target behavior.
3. Describe the conditions under which the observations are made. These include time, place, activity, antecedent event, and consequent event.

Observation is improved when the observer has a specific reason or question formulated to guide the observation (Archer & Edgar, 1976). Furthermore, observational data collected over time can strengthen the teacher's confidence in the data. Technology for measurement of systematic observation focuses on two key factors: (a) select the target behavior and (b) record the frequency of the behavior. For a presentation of observational recording techniques, see Table 2.7 in the section on data-based instruction.

Formal assessment. Only a few formal tests focus on assessing factors relating to how to teach. These tests have not proven promising with regard to aiding in instructional programming. Factors that can be manipulated to improve learning are not readily assessed by formal testing. Most formal tests are administered only once, and repeated observations are needed to analyze the effects of various factors on behavior.

Criterion tests. The primary use of criterion tests is to assess for what to teach. However, since they can be used to evaluate the effects of instruction, they also are useful in determining how to teach. For example, a teacher may divide a list of spelling words into two lists to determine whether a multisensory spelling activity or a flash card drill is more effective. By administering a criterion test on each set of words, the teacher can compare the student's performances and make a decision about the effectiveness of the two treatments.

Rating scales. A rating scale is a series of statements or questions that require some judgment about the degree or frequency of the behavior or characteristics described in each statement. Sample formats of rating scales include:

Numerical Scale

Select the number that best describes the individual.

_____ Frequency of adult supervision required

1. Always
2. Often
3. Occasionally
4. Rarely
5. Almost never

Graphic Scale

Select a place on the line that best describes the individual.

Frequency of adult supervision required:

Always	Often	Occasionally	Rarely	Almost never

Some formal rating scales that may be useful in assessing students with emotional and behavior problems are presented in Chapter 5. Occasionally, teachers make or use rating scales for parents to complete. These are helpful to use with parents who do not have the time to observe and record their child's behavior systematically. A teacher also may wish to give a rating scale to students to obtain information about areas such as the student's reinforcement preferences, interests, and attitudes about school.

Interviews. Information obtained from interviews with parents, teachers, and students can be useful in determining how to teach a student. Through interviews the teacher can obtain information about specific techniques to use with the student. Also, much information can be obtained about the student's interests, favorite activities, problem areas, and attitudes, as well as how the student is perceived at home.

An interview should be conducted with definite ideas about the types of information desired. Also, it is important to remember that persons interviewed may report highly idiosyncratic and subjective perceptions.

Charting. Charting holds much promise for determining how to teach. In charting, a student's daily performance on a probe sheet is recorded on a graph. The graph provides a measure over time of the student's progress. The teacher analyzes the graph pattern and makes instructional decisions regarding which antecedent and consequent events to maintain or change. The teacher can manipulate an antecedent event (such as seating arrangement) or consequent event (for example, award points for work) and analyze the chart to see if performance improves, declines, or remains the same. Charts mainly have been used to determine what to teach, but educators now are beginning to use probe assessment and charts to evaluate learning style (Koenig & Kunzelmann, 1980). Charting itself is reinforcing to some students and may help to improve student performance.

Checklists. Checklists can be very helpful in determining how to teach. To help the teacher recognize factors that may influence a student's learning, checklist-rating scales are presented in this chapter. Together these scales form the Analysis of Student Learning Form, which presents key variables for each of the major areas.

DETERMINING HOW TO TEACH

The first step in determining how to teach is to identify the major areas of assessment. Figure 2.2 presents the major areas that are basic in assessment for determining how to teach. The areas include expectancy factors, stimulus events, response factors, and subsequent events. Once these areas are selected, it is necessary to identify the important factors included under each of them. Some of the important factors of each major area are outlined in the Analysis of Student Learning Form (Tables 2.1, 2.2, 2.4, and 2.5). The form is divided into four parts, one for each assessment area. A complete analysis of this type is usually conducted to help design instructional programs for students who are extremely difficult to manage or teach. Also, a complete analysis usually involves observations by various diagnostic team members. The primary function of this section is to *alert* the teacher to areas that contribute to how students learn. A general awareness of relevant instructional factors can be useful in teaching all students. For example, if a teacher is "sensitive" to expectancy, stimulus, response, and subsequent factors in daily observations, subtle changes can lead to improved student learning.

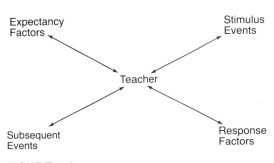

FIGURE 2.2
Important factors in assessing how to teach.

Expectancy Factors

Expectancy refers to an individual's orientation to the learning situation. Two types of generalized expectancies are recognized. One involves the expectancy for a particular type of consequence, such as social approval, achievement, tangible reward, failure, or punishment. In this type of generalized expectancy, the consequences govern whether a person perceives a situation as similar to past situations. The second type of generalized expectancy is the kind that generalizes from other situations involving a similar problem-solving activity, but differing in consequence. Thus, problem-solving activities encountered in a variety of situations may generalize to another situation, no matter the consequence. *Motivation* is often equated with expectancy, since expectancy may serve as an incentive (or deterrent) for approaching, continuing, or avoiding the learning task. If a student receives verbal praise for writing her spelling words, she comes to expect that if the words are written, some desirable event will follow. Conversely, if a student receives a low grade or criticism for writing her spelling words, expectancy can serve as a deterrent, and the student avoids the learning task. Thus, expectancy of success or failure can greatly influence the student's motivation toward the learning task.

Numerous expectancies significantly influence learning outcomes and student behavior. Four expectancies are identified for discussion: learner expectancies, teacher expectancies, peer expectancies, and parental expectancies (see Table 2.1).

Learner expectancies. Section I of the Analysis of Student Learning Form, Part I, presents several factors to be considered in analyzing learner expectancies. By using a checklist-rating scale similar to the Analysis of Student Learning Form, the teacher can answer three important questions:

1. Does the student frequently exhibit negative expectancy reactions?
2. To whom or to what are the negative reactions directed?
3. What are the stated reasons for the negative reactions?

By answering these questions, the teacher obtains information that is helpful in planning instruction. For example, if the student dislikes reading because she is embarrassed to read orally around others, the teacher may allow her to record her reading on a tape recorder or read in a one-to-one situation with the teacher or a friend. Minor instructional adjustments can often result in increased student motivation, more efficient learning, and better student expectancies.

Self-report activities are excellent ways to obtain information about a student's negative and positive expectancies. Sentence completion is a popular self-report activity. For example:

1. I learn best when _____.
2. I'm really happy when _____.
3. When I work hard my teacher _____.
4. My least favorite thing at school is _____.
5. When I don't try, my teacher _____.

Rating scales are another type of self-report that is commonly used. For example:

(a) I learn math quickly	1 2 3 4 5	I don't seem to understand math
(b) Classmates really like me	1 2 3 4 5	Classmates don't like me much
(c) I have a lot of friends	1 2 3 4 5	I don't have many friends

TABLE 2.1
Analysis of student learning form.
Part I: Expectancy factors.

	Key
	Key
	3 always happens
	2 frequently happens
	1 sometimes happens
	0 never happens

I. Learner Expectancies

A. Negative Expectancy Reactions
   Note reactions that are characterized by negative comments regarding one's own abilities, avoidance remarks, and comments which reflect the anticipation of failure or problems.
   1. Student comments about being dumb.   3 2 1 0
   2. Student comments about hating certain subjects or activities.   3 2 1 0
   3. Student comments about not being liked by peers.   3 2 1 0
   4. Student comments about not being liked by teacher(s).   3 2 1 0
   5. Student comments about anticipating failure on tests, seatwork, etc. 3 2 1 0

B. Target of Avoidance Reactions
   By listening, interviewing, and/or observing the student the teacher is able to ascertain the situations about which the student has negative expectancies. The avoidance situation may be a person, place, or activity.
   1. Student complains about attending school in general.   3 2 1 0
   2. Student complains about attending a certain class (_____).   3 2 1 0
   3. Student complains about a specific teacher or other school
      person (_____).   3 2 1 0
   4. Student complains about a specific academic subject (_____).   3 2 1 0
   5. Student complains about physical education classes.   3 2 1 0
   6. Student complains about extracurricular activities.   3 2 1 0
   7. Student complains about certain peers (_____).   3 2 1 0
   8. Student complains about riding the bus.   3 2 1 0
   9. Student complains about a certain day (_____).   3 2 1 0

C. Stated Reasons for Negative Reactions
   1. Student hates _____ because he has to: read, speak in class,
      wear gym clothes, turn in homework, sit next to the teacher, take
      notes, learn unimportant information, etc.   3 2 1 0
   2. Student claims the teacher always criticizes him.   3 2 1 0
   3. The class or teacher is so boring.   3 2 1 0
   4. The class or teacher is too hard.   3 2 1 0
   5. Student is always failing tests in _____.   3 2 1 0

(continued)

TABLE 2.1, *continued*

	Key 3 always happens 2 frequently happens 1 sometimes happens 0 never happens

II. Teacher Expectancies

    A. Assignments

        1. Teacher frequently assigns work that is too difficult or too easy.   3 2 1 0

        2. Teacher frequently assigns work just to keep the student busy.   3 2 1 0

        3. Teacher makes negative or sarcastic remarks about the student's work (e.g., "John, do you think you'll ever do your work on time?").   3 2 1 0

        4. Teacher grades the student's work hard (i.e., teacher never gives the student a break).   3 2 1 0

        5. Teacher expects the student to misbehave.   3 2 1 0

        6. Teacher expects the student to do poorly on his work.   3 2 1 0

    B. Interactions

        1. Teacher is quick to tell the student about a wrong response.   3 2 1 0

        2. Teacher criticizes the student.   3 2 1 0

        3. Teacher ridicules the student (e.g., "Are you sure you were listening, Sarah?").   3 2 1 0

        4. Teacher makes accusations (e.g., "Who took the game dice, John?").   3 2 1 0

        5. Teacher openly exhibits dislike for the student (e.g., in the teachers' lounge, in the classroom, etc.).   3 2 1 0

        6. Teacher makes negative predictions about the student's future (e.g., "He'll drop out of school").   3 2 1 0

        7. Teacher does not encourage self-expression by the student.   3 2 1 0

        8. Teacher has trouble listening to the student.   3 2 1 0

III. Peer Expectancies

    A. Social Patterns

        1. The student is an isolate.   3 2 1 0

        2. The student is a leader.   3 2 1 0

        3. Many peers criticize the student.   3 2 1 0

        4. Peers tease the student.   3 2 1 0

        5. Peers really like the student.   3 2 1 0

        6. A certain group likes or dislikes the student.   3 2 1 0

        7. Nobody appears to like the student.   3 2 1 0

        8. One student especially dislikes the student (_____).   3 2 1 0

        9. Peers view the student as dumb.   3 2 1 0

      10. Peers view the student as smart.   3 2 1 0

TABLE 2.1, *continued*

	Key
	3 always happens
	2 frequently happens
	1 sometimes happens
	0 never happens

B. Peer Values
    1. Aggressive inappropriate behavior is reinforced by peers.   3   2   1   0
    2. The student has a skill the students value.   3   2   1   0
    3. The student has knowledge the students value.   3   2   1   0
    4. The student displays no quality the peers value.   3   2   1   0

IV. Parental Expectancies

A. Negative Expectancies in Relation to School
    1. Parents tell student not to worry about getting good grades.   3   2   1   0
    2. Parents do not support the teacher in front of the student.   3   2   1   0
    3. Parents openly complain about school in front of the student.   3   2   1   0
    4. Parents reinforce (laugh, tell others) for misbehavior at school.   3   2   1   0
    5. Parents do not encourage student to do homework.   3   2   1   0
    6. Parents allow student to stay home from school when he is not sick.   3   2   1   0

B. Unrealistic Expectancies
    1. Parents select a vocational goal for the student which is not
       compatible with the student's interest or ability.   3   2   1   0
    2. Parents always take away privileges for low grades.   3   2   1   0
    3. Parents frequently insist that the student be placed in a higher
       reading or math group.   3   2   1   0
    4. Parents insist that the student take courses not suited to his
       abilities or interests.   3   2   1   0

C. Too Low Expectancies
    1. Parents talk about how the child will never achieve.   3   2   1   0
    2. Parents constantly make unfavorable statements about the child's
       future.   3   2   1   0
    3. Parents constantly ask that the child be excused from activities.   3   2   1   0
    4. Parents foster child dependency.   3   2   1   0
    5. Parents do not encourage self-expression from the child.   3   2   1   0
    6. Parents do not give the child responsibilities.   3   2   1   0
    7. Parents do not challenge the child to participate in activities.   3   2   1   0

V. Summary of Expectancy

_____

_____

_____

Teacher expectancies. Teachers develop perceptions of a student which, in turn, create certain expectancies of the student. When the teacher expects and accepts less from the student than the student is capable of giving, the expectancies may impede both learning progress and social development. Rosenthal and Jacobson's (1966) work generated much interest in this phenomenon, and it is frequently referred to as the self-fulfilling prophecy. Brophy and Good (1974) report that "the idea that teacher expectations can function as self-fulfilling prophecies appears to be an established fact rather than a mere hypothesis" (p. 77).

Characteristics such as race, special education label, sex, appearance, and achievement level of older siblings have been shown to influence teacher expectancies (Algozzine & Mercer, 1980). If a teacher expects inappropriate behavior or poor academic progress, she may likely get it. Fortunately, the reverse of this phenomenon holds much promise. Smith, Neisworth, and Greer (1978) affirm the importance of the teacher's influence.

> The teacher's attitude toward children and education determines to a very real degree how children perceive school, themselves, and each other—and how much progress they actually make. Teachers can make learning pleasant or punishing; they can create motivation or fear; they can produce excited anticipation or dread. A teacher's personal style and approach, more than anything else, create the climate and mood which will characterize the classroom. (p. 84)

Because of the influence of teacher expectancies on the success of students, an assessment of how to teach must include examination of teacher expectancies. Section II of Table 2.1 presents several factors that deserve consideration in analyzing teacher expectancies.

Peer expectancies. Through daily interactions with classmates, students learn to view themselves as leaders, followers, fringers, or isolates (Archer & Edgar, 1976). Acceptance by peers helps children gain confidence and self-assurance which, in turn, foster better performance on academic tasks; peer rejection can produce anxiety and self-doubt. Peer influence is a function of numerous factors including age, home stability, and socioeconomic level. Since elementary-aged and younger children tend to value home and adult praise more than adolescents do, there is less peer influence with them than with adolescents (Mercer, 1987). Children from lower classes appear to be highly susceptible to peer influence (Tasseigne, 1975), and children from stable family situations are less likely to conform than children from inadequate family situations (Rice, 1975). Above all, the teacher must avoid contributing to one student's negative perception of another student. Archer and Edgar (1976) report that teachers must recognize student leaders and understand classroom alliances if they wish to promote a healthy social climate. Archer and Edgar also note that the teacher must be aware of peer values, especially those relating to academic achievement and social behavior. Once the social climate is ascertained, the teacher can use peer tutoring, modeling, role playing, seat assignments, and the control of peer attention to promote peer expectancies that foster the growth of an individual student or students.

Questionnaires on class norms and personal values as well as observations of student behavior provide very useful information about peer values and class social patterns. Section III of Table 2.1 presents several factors of importance in analyzing peer expectancies.

Parental expectancies. Parental expectancies can greatly influence a student's academic and social growth. If a parent highly values and reinforces academic work, the student is likely to receive encouragement and praise from parents for doing homework and performing well in school. Parental support is often a key factor in maintaining a child's motivation and achievement. Positive parental expectancies can be very helpful in the development of the child; however, parental expectancies that are negative, too high, or too low can be harmful to the child's academic and social development. The student who must constantly face living up to her parents' unrealistic expectations may begin to hate school and eventually may rebel against both the school and the parents. Also, the student may start getting in trouble to receive parental attention. If parents do not value academic achievement, the child does not receive much encouragement or praise from parents for doing schoolwork. In home situations in which fighting or goofing off in school is valued, the student receives encouragement for behavior that is directly opposed by the school.

Given the trend toward more parental involvement in the identification, placement, and educational programming of mildly handicapped learners, school personnel must prepare themselves to work more closely and effectively with parents. The teacher must be sensitive to both helpful and harmful parental expectancies. Helpful expectancies should be encouraged, and harmful ones should be approached in a problem-solving manner. The common goal of optimal growth for the child frequently enables the teacher and parents to overcome obstacles and work cooperatively. Section IV of Table 2.1 presents several factors that deserve attention in assessing parental expectancies.

Stimulus Events

Stimulus (or antecedent) events include an array of materials, instructional methods, and classroom settings that "set the stage" for the student to respond. Since teachers control or determine many of the stimulus events in the classroom, it is important to examine them in order to understand how students learn best.

The teacher can observe the student, directly ask the student, or use questionnaires to gather information about individual preferences. Stimulus events can be sorted into the categories of (a) physical setting; (b) instructional arrangements, techniques, and materials; and (c) learning style preferences.

Physical setting. Section I of the Analysis of Student Learning Form, Part II (Table 2.2), presents variables of interest in analyzing the environmental conditions that affect a student's performance, both positively and negatively. Physical properties—noise, temperature, lighting, and spatial factors—can be manipulated to suit the student's learning preferences. When choices are available, the student or the teacher can choose a setting suitable to the activity and individual preferences. For example, Smith et al. (1978) recommend that teachers provide special places for students to go for (a) isolation, (b) rest and quiet, (c) letting off steam, (d) rewarding themselves, (e) private instruction, (f) talking with the teacher, and (g) working alone or in a group.

Instructional arrangements, techniques, and materials. This area covers a wide range of stimulus events that dramatically affect learning (see Sections II, III, and IV of Table 2.2).

Once the teacher identifies preferred instructional factors, the task of determining what to do is usually simple. For the student who readily models peers, seat him near peers who are models of desirable behavior. For the student who is easily frustrated during seatwork or always wants feedback, give the student self-correcting activities. For the student who lacks interest, constantly remind the student of the importance of the skill or use instructional games. For the student who writes slowly, provide larger spaces on worksheets to write answers or allow the student to work on a chalkboard.

TABLE 2.2
Analysis of student learning form.
Part II: Stimulus events.

	Key 3 always happens 2 frequently happens 1 sometimes happens 0 never happens

I. Physical Properties

  A. Noise

1. The student likes to work in a quiet area.	3 2 1 0
2. The student likes to work with a little background noise.	3 2 1 0
3. Others talking distracts the student.	3 2 1 0
4. The student frequently asks the teacher to repeat directions or questions.	3 2 1 0

  B. Temperature

1. The student prefers cooler areas of the room (e.g., near a window).	3 2 1 0
2. The student prefers warmer areas of the room.	3 2 1 0
3. The student has difficulty adjusting to outside temperature changes (e.g., develops colds, allergies).	3 2 1 0
4. The student has allergies which are sensitive to air quality (e.g., when furnace is first turned on).	3 2 1 0

  C. Lighting

1. The student prefers well-lighted areas of the room (e.g., reads near a window).	3 2 1 0
2. The student prefers darker areas of the room.	3 2 1 0
3. The student has trouble seeing the chalkboard or other areas of the room because of light reflections.	3 2 1 0

  D. General Physical Factors

1. The student likes to work in a lot of space (e.g., on a table top).	3 2 1 0
2. The student likes to work in close proximity to other students.	3 2 1 0
3. The student is distracted near windows, pencil sharpener, sink, etc.	3 2 1 0
4. The student likes to work in close proximity to the teacher.	3 2 1 0
5. The student likes to work in a carrel, corner, next to the wall, or beside a room divider.	3 2 1 0
6. The student is distracted by messy or cluttered areas.	3 2 1 0
7. The student prefers to work at: desk, library, table, learning center.	3 2 1 0

II. Instructional Arrangements

1. The student works well in a large group.	3 2 1 0
2. The student works well in a small group.	3 2 1 0
3. The student works well in a one-to-one situation with the teacher.	3 2 1 0
4. The student works well in peer tutoring situations as the tutor.	3 2 1 0
5. The student works well in peer tutoring situations as the tutee.	3 2 1 0

TABLE 2.2, *continued*

	Key 3 always happens 2 frequently happens 1 sometimes happens 0 never happens

6. The student works well alone with seatwork.	3 2 1 0
7. The student works well with small group on a project.	3 2 1 0
8. The student works well with a teacher aide or volunteer.	3 2 1 0

III. Instructional Techniques

1. The student needs much demonstration of expected behavior.	3 2 1 0
2. The student needs to be reminded of the value or importance of specific schoolwork.	3 2 1 0
3. The student likes input regarding instruction (e.g., game, material, time).	3 2 1 0
4. The student needs simple written instructions.	3 2 1 0
5. The student needs verbal directions to be simple and repeated.	3 2 1 0
6. The student readily models the behavior of peers.	3 2 1 0
7. The student readily models the behavior of the teacher.	3 2 1 0
8. The student needs prompts and cues to maintain expected behaviors.	3 2 1 0
9. The student needs much attention in learning new behaviors.	3 2 1 0
10. The student likes working with equipment (e.g., tape recorder, Language Master, overhead projector).	3 2 1 0
11. The student has low frustration tolerance for difficult seatwork.	3 2 1 0
12. The student responds well when the teacher asks questions.	3 2 1 0
13. The student needs his interest stimulated for drill or practice work.	3 2 1 0
14. The student works better with knowledge that work will be checked.	3 2 1 0
15. The student needs a lot of time to complete his work.	3 2 1 0
16. The student works best in: morning, afternoon.	3 2 1 0
17. The student works slowly and inaccurately.	3 2 1 0
18. The student does not perform well under timed conditions.	3 2 1 0
19. The student enjoys working against a timer.	3 2 1 0
20. The student enjoys charting correct and incorrect responses in one-minute segments.	3 2 1 0
21. In approaching a new task the student gives up easily.	3 2 1 0
22. In approaching a new task the student becomes easily frustrated.	3 2 1 0
23. In approaching a new task the student eagerly tries it.	3 2 1 0
24. In approaching a new task the student tries to distract the teacher.	3 2 1 0
25. In approaching a new task the student refuses to attempt it.	3 2 1 0
26. The student responds well to different academic materials or activities (specify _____).	3 2 1 0

IV. Materials

1. The student likes or needs self-correcting materials.	3 2 1 0

TABLE 2.2, *continued*

	Key 3 always happens 2 frequently happens 1 sometimes happens 0 never happens

2. The student likes or needs instructional games using game boards.	3 2 1 0
3. The student likes or needs instructional games using cards.	3 2 1 0
4. The student dislikes worksheets.	3 2 1 0
5. The student needs worksheets with only a few items.	3 2 1 0
6. The student needs lots of writing space on worksheets.	3 2 1 0
7. The student needs visual cues on seatwork (e.g., arrows, green dots to note starting place, lines to show place for responses).	3 2 1 0
8. The student prefers commercial materials.	3 2 1 0
9. The student prefers teacher-made materials.	3 2 1 0
10. The student enjoys chalkboard activities.	3 2 1 0
11. The student responds well to manipulative materials (e.g., puppets in language, cubes and abacus in math, calculator in math or spelling).	3 2 1 0
12. The student enjoys doing work with flash cards.	3 2 1 0
13. The student enjoys making his own materials (e.g., flash cards, game boards, card decks).	3 2 1 0
14. The student dislikes cluttered or "busy" materials.	3 2 1 0

V. Learning Style Preferences

  A. Visual Preference Indicators

1. The student enjoys reading a book.	3 2 1 0
2. The student enjoys seeing a filmstrip.	3 2 1 0
3. The student enjoys looking at pictures.	3 2 1 0
4. The student enjoys looking at a movie.	3 2 1 0
5. The student enjoys playing a concentration game.	3 2 1 0
6. The student needs someone to demonstrate behavior.	3 2 1 0
7. The student remembers material from an overhead.	3 2 1 0
8. The student remembers what someone shows him.	3 2 1 0
9. The student remembers what is seen in a film.	3 2 1 0
10. The student remembers what he has written.	3 2 1 0

  B. Auditory Preference Indicators

1. The student enjoys hearing a record.	3 2 1 0
2. The student enjoys hearing a tape.	3 2 1 0
3. The student enjoys hearing a story.	3 2 1 0
4. The student follows auditory directions.	3 2 1 0
5. The student remembers what the teacher says.	3 2 1 0
6. The student remembers what is heard on the radio.	3 2 1 0
7. The student likes talking to people.	3 2 1 0
8. The student listens to people well.	3 2 1 0
9. The student likes to study with friends.	3 2 1 0

TABLE 2.2, *continued*

	Key 3 always happens 2 frequently happens 1 sometimes happens 0 never happens

C. Tactile Preference Indicators	
1. The student likes to draw.	3 2 1 0
2. The student likes to manipulate objects.	3 2 1 0
3. The student likes to trace things.	3 2 1 0
4. The student likes to work with clay or finger paints.	3 2 1 0
D. Kinesthetic Preference Indicators	
1. The student remembers material from motor activities.	3 2 1 0
2. The student remembers what he writes.	3 2 1 0
3. The student likes to play motor games.	3 2 1 0
4. The student likes to do experiments.	3 2 1 0
5. The student likes to take pictures.	3 2 1 0
6. The student likes to operate a tape recorder, typewriter, calculator, or other machines.	3 2 1 0

VI. Summary of Stimulus Events

_____

_____

_____

Learning style preferences. Determining learning styles has received much attention, and assessing modality (form of sensation) preferences has been a key concern in this area. Diagnosticians and teachers usually administer various tests (such as *Mills Methods Learning Test, ITPA, Detroit Tests of Learning Aptitudes*) to determine a student's modality preferences and make instructional recommendations. If the student performs better in the visual modality, for example, instruction that stresses visually oriented materials and techniques is recommended. Although this strategy is commonly practiced, much research (Arter & Jenkins, 1977; Kavale & Forness, 1987) asserts that it is ineffective. Salvia and Ysseldyke (1988) provide reliability data on many of the modality preference tests

(*ITPA, Developmental Test of Visual Perception, Bender Gestalt*) and point out that the reliability coefficients are too low for use in applied settings. Logan (1977) states that such low reliability coefficients should make educators extremely cautious.

Although it seems premature to disregard the modality preference factor, educators should not rely heavily on tests for determining modality strengths and weaknesses. Using informal measures, the teacher may discover both a student's modality preference and the conditions under which the preference exists—that is, it may depend upon the particular task.

Stephens (1977) uses a criterion-referenced approach to modality assessment. Table 2.3 shows how Stephens used classroom tasks to assess modality strengths and weaknesses.

TABLE 2.3
Summary of modality assessment.

Sense / Skill		Stimulus	Criterion Score	Performance Score	Analysis Code
A U D I T O R Y	Discrimination	20 pairs of similar words read aloud	18/20	20	+
	Immediate Recall	Read primer story and answered 4 questions	4	4	0
	Delayed Recall	Referred to—five days later previous story	4	4	0
V I S U A L	Discrimination	10 pairs of words	9/10	9	0
		10 picture words identifications	9/10	9	0
	Immediate Recall	5 tests of removing different letters	4/5	4	0
		Study 4 words and then identify correct spelling	4	3	—
	Delayed Recall	4 words repeated in 45 minutes	4	3	—
H A P T I C	Discrimination	Recognize 10 upper-case letters by touch only	9/10	4	—
		Recognize 8 lower-case letters	7/8	5	—
	Immediate Recall	Identify 8 lower-case letters	7/8	6	—
	Delayed Recall	45 minutes later	7/8	5	—

Note. 0 = at criterion; — = below; + = above.

Source: From *Teaching Skills to Children with Learning and Behavior Disorders* (p. 193) by T. M. Stephens, 1977, Columbus, OH: Merrill. Copyright 1977 by Bell & Howell Company. Reprinted by permission.

Using a probe format, Koenig and Kunzelmann (1980) developed an instrument titled *Classroom Learning Screening*. This instrument is designed for preschool through grade 6 and includes readiness, math, and reading skill probes. At each grade level, three learning channel combinations are assessed: see–write, hear–write, and see–say. The see–write channel includes only math skills (for example, see multiplication facts through times 9–write answers), and the hear–write and see–say channels include only reading

skills (for example, hear word–write word; see word–say word). Koenig and Kunzelmann state that most reading and math learning occurs in these three channel combinations.

Once the examiner determines an appropriate difficulty level—a probe on which the student initially performs between 10 and 80 correct per minute—each of the three learning channel probes is administered for several days. The results are then analyzed for channel strengths and weaknesses.

As illustrated by Stephens (1977) and

Koenig and Kunzelmann (1980), the practice of examining modality preferences by using classroom tasks can render useful information in determining how a student learns. Section V of Table 2.2 presents some factors that may point to a student's modality preferences. If a modality strength or weakness is suspected, classroom observations can validate or refute the suspicion. However, if a pupil has a visual learning problem, for example, it does not necessarily mean that an auditory strength exists.

Response Types

Tasks usually require students to make a motor or verbal response, or both. Selecting the type of response for an instructional activity can be crucial in designing instruction for a student. Some students function better if the response requires extensive motor involvement (e.g., write numerals, connect dots, push button, operate tape recorder, color items, arrange items on feltboard); others function better with simple verbal responses (yes, no). Also, speed of responding deserves attention. If a student writes numerals slowly or talks rapidly without thinking, these response tendencies need to be considered in planning instruction. The Analysis of Student Learning Form, Part III (Table 2.4), presents several factors of importance in analyzing response preferences.

Subsequent Events

Consequences greatly influence behavior. Polloway, Payne, Patton, and Payne (1985) report that consequences motivate students and manage their behavior. Social praise, special activities and privileges, evaluation marks, positive physical expression, awards, tokens, and tangible objects are some positive consequences frequently used to reinforce—and therefore influence—student behavior. The teacher has many ways of finding out what reinforces a student. The teacher can simply ask

the student, or note free-time preferences for activities or objects. Some teachers use a reinforcement "menu," featuring a variety of consequences from which a student chooses her favorite.

To use consequent events most effectively, the teacher must consider timing, amount, and ratio of reinforcement. Some students need immediate reinforcement to maintain a behavior; others can tolerate a delay in reinforcement without decreasing the occurrence of the behavior. Some students require a great deal of reinforcement only for certain changes. For instance, when the teacher is attempting to establish a new behavior, much reinforcement may be needed. As the learning proceeds, reinforcement may be reduced. The Analysis of Student Learning Form, Part IV (Table 2.5), features numerous variables that are important in assessing subsequent events.

The Analysis of Student Learning Profile

Expectancy factors, stimulus events, response types, and subsequent events must be weighed in relation to one another in planning instruction. It is necessary to consider all four factors together to form instructional strategies that best facilitate learning. After each section of the Analysis of Student Learning Form has been completed, a profile may be written. The profile can display numerous patterns and supply a simple list of do's and don'ts for designing an individual program. Table 2.6 presents a learning profile and treatment plan.

The Analysis of Student Learning Form is useful primarily for guiding teacher observations in the different assessment areas. An instructional plan based on an assessment for determining how to teach should be viewed as a "guesstimate." When the right variables are manipulated appropriately, the plan is effective; but when the assessment is wrong, adjustments are needed in the plan. All treatment plans should be monitored closely to insure their efficacy and the student's progress. As-

TABLE 2.4
Analysis of student learning form.
Part III: Response types.

	Key
	3 always happens
	2 frequently happens
	1 sometimes happens
	0 never happens

I. Verbal

1. The student likes simple one-word responses (e.g., yes, no).	3 2 1 0
2. The student likes simple sentences.	3 2 1 0
3. The student likes brief discussions.	3 2 1 0
4. The student likes extensive dialogue.	3 2 1 0
5. The student likes fast responding.	3 2 1 0

II. Verbal-Motor

1. The student likes to verbalize his response while touching the item.	3 2 1 0
2. The student likes to operate hardware while verbalizing.	3 2 1 0
3. The student likes to write and say his response.	3 2 1 0
4. The student likes to sing and clap.	3 2 1 0
5. The student likes to operate hand puppets.	3 2 1 0

III. Motor

1. The student likes to respond by pointing.	3 2 1 0
2. The student uses manuscript writing.	3 2 1 0
3. The student uses cursive writing.	3 2 1 0
4. The student writes numbers.	3 2 1 0
5. The student can trace.	3 2 1 0
6. The student copies work from a near position.	3 2 1 0
7. The student copies work from a far position.	3 2 1 0
8. The student likes to use gross motor skills.	3 2 1 0
9. The student likes to use fine motor skills.	3 2 1 0
10. The student uses a pencil holder.	3 2 1 0
11. The student writes slowly and sloppily.	3 2 1 0
12. The student writes slowly and neatly.	3 2 1 0
13. The student writes quickly and sloppily.	3 2 1 0
14. The student writes quickly and neatly.	3 2 1 0
15. The student writes too big for the space allowed.	3 2 1 0
16. The student exhibits speech problems.	3 2 1 0
17. The student perseverates with a motor response.	3 2 1 0
18. The student perseverates with a verbal response.	3 2 1 0
19. The student has physical abnormalities that interfere with writing or speaking.	3 2 1 0

IV. Summary of Response Types

TABLE 2.5
Analysis of student learning form.
Part IV: Subsequent events.

	Key 3 always happens 2 frequently happens 1 sometimes happens 0 never happens

I. Verbal Praise

1. The student likes one-word praises.	3 2 1 0
2. The student likes phrase praises.	3 2 1 0
3. The student likes extensive "talk" praises.	3 2 1 0
4. The student likes humor.	3 2 1 0

II. Physical Approval

1. The student likes a smile or gesture (e.g., thumbs up, wink).	3 2 1 0
2. The student likes a touch.	3 2 1 0
3. The student likes a hug.	3 2 1 0
4. The student likes a handshake.	3 2 1 0

III. Evaluation Events

1. The student likes immediate feedback.	3 2 1 0
2. The student has difficulty with feedback on incorrect responses from the teacher.	3 2 1 0
3. The student has difficulty with feedback on incorrect responses from his peers.	3 2 1 0
4. The student has difficulty with feedback on incorrect responses from the material.	3 2 1 0
5. The student likes feedback on correct responses from his peers.	3 2 1 0
6. The student likes feedback on correct responses from the material.	3 2 1 0
7. The student needs "sensitive" feedback when incorrect (e.g., "You're almost right. Let's do it together.").	3 2 1 0
8. The student likes evaluation marks: A 1, happy face, stars, checks, number correct, letter grade, rubber stamp.	3 2 1 0
9. The student likes awards: happy grams, report cards, citations.	3 2 1 0
10. The student likes tangible items: trinket, candy, cookie, sugar pop, toy.	3 2 1 0
11. The student likes token rewards: points, chips, check marks, tickets.	3 2 1 0

IV. Summary of Subsequent Events

_____

_____

_____

TABLE 2.6
Learning profile and treatment plan.

Assessment Area	Ineffective	Effective	Treatment
Learner expectancy	Feels like teacher dislikes him		Ask for a favor once a day. Ask child a personal interest question each day (e.g., "Did you like that football game?").
	Feels defeated in reading		Pair reinforcement with effort in reading. Focus on positive reinforcement.
Teacher expectancy	Assigns work that is too difficult in reading		Provide realistic successes in reading.
	Tends to pick on student		Use sensitive responses to incorrect responses.
Peer expectancy	Selected peers do not value reading	Peers really like and respect the student	Seat student near peers who value reading. Use peer teaching with student and involve him as tutor or tutee.
Parent expectancy	Parents push student too much to work hard	Parents are concerned and interested in cooperating	Encourage parents to praise effort as well as correct product. Tell parents not to tutor child unless it is a pleasant event.
Physical properties	Allergic to dust	Prefers cooler areas of room Prefers well-lighted areas of room	Seat student away from chalk trays. Allow student to work away from furnace ducts. Seat student near a window.
		Likes to work close to other students	Assign work at table with students who work hard.
Instructional arrangements	Dislikes one-to-one with teacher	Enjoys small-group activities	Make one-to-one pleasant. Use small-group instruction.

TABLE 2.6, *continued*

Assessment Area	Ineffective	Effective	Treatment
Instructional techniques	Gets bored with same task	Needs prompts and cues to maintain behavior	Consider using contingency contracting with a variety of activities in it.
	Has low frustration tolerance in reading	Needs a variety of activities	Allow student to practice reading on tape recorder before reading orally to teacher.
	Works very slowly		Let student work against a timer.
Materials	Dislikes reading worksheets	Needs worksheets with only a few items	Consider using Language Experience Approach in reading. Use games.
	Dislikes cluttered worksheets or materials	Likes instructional games	Use worksheets that are partially completed. Use Language Master. Use tape recorder.
Learning style		Responds well in all input modalities	
Response types	Writes slowly and sloppily	Prefers short verbal responses coupled with simple motor responses	Use point-and-say responses.
	Writes too big for space allowed		Try a plastic pencil holder. Give lots of room for writing. Use chalkboard for writing.
Subsequent events	Doesn't respond to one-word praises	Enjoys smiles and handshakes	Follow good effort with a smile, touch, and encouraging phrase.
		Requests immediate feedback	Use answer keys, peer feedback, and self-correcting materials.
		Likes high letter grades	Write big letter grades on good work.
	Has difficulty with feedback on incorrect items		Use a variety of sensitive responses for incorrect work.

sessment for determining *how* to teach is similar to assessment for determining *what* to teach, in that both are ongoing processes.

Ysseldyke and Christenson (1987a) report that the systematic assessment of learning environments has been ignored. They have developed *The Instructional Environment Scale (TIES)* (Ysseldyke & Christenson, 1987b) to help professionals obtain a comprehensive description of a student's instructional environments. According to Ysseldyke and Christenson (1987a), there are two major purposes for using *TIES:* "(1) to systematically *describe* the extent to which a student's academic or behavior problems are a function of factors in the instructional environment, and (2) to identify starting points in *designing appropriate instructional interventions* for individual students" (p. 21). Instruments of this type provide professionals with a systematic procedure for examining stimulus factors that facilitate the assessment of how to teach.

DATA-BASED INSTRUCTION

Data-based instruction is a widely used approach to teaching which has roots in the areas of applied behavior analysis, directive instruction, and criterion-referenced instruction. It is a direct skill model of instruction which focuses on the direct and continuous measurement of student progress toward specific instructional objectives (Blankenship & Lilly, 1981). Many educators (Alberto & Troutman, 1986; Blankenship & Lilly, 1981; Evans, Evans, & Mercer, 1986; Kerr & Nelson, 1983; Lovitt, 1984; Stephens, 1977) concur that it holds much promise for both current and future teaching practices.

In a national survey of 136 learning disabilities teachers, Wesson, King, and Deno (1984) found that the majority (53.6%) of learning disabilities teachers ($N = 110$) who knew of direct and frequent measurement used it; how-

ever, those not using it felt it was too time-consuming. The position that data-based instruction is very time-consuming is prominent among users and nonusers of direct and frequent measurement. Wesson et al. report that time involved in direct and frequent measurement does not have to be extensive. Fuchs, Wesson, Tindal, Mirkin, and Deno (1981) report the results of a study in which teachers were trained to reduce by 80% the time they spent in direct measurement (e.g., preparing, directing, scoring, and graphing). According to Wesson et al., "Trained and experienced teachers require only 2 minutes to prepare for, administer, score, and graph student performance" (p. 48). They also report that direct and frequent measurement is no more time-consuming than other evaluation activities. Wesson et al. sum up the time-consumption issue involving direct and frequent measurement as follows:

> [S]ince related research reveals that frequent measurement improves achievement (Bohannon, 1975; Mirkin et al., 1979), the proposition that direct and frequent measurement is a waste of critical instructional time is without a factual basis. . . . Given its benefits, direct and frequent measurement must be used on a more widespread basis in special education. One implication of the present study is that teachers may need more training and experience in procedures for conducting direct and frequent measurement. (p. 48)

The major features of data-based instruction include (a) selecting a target skill, (b) selecting a measurement system, (c) collecting and graphing data, and (d) setting instructional aims and analyzing data.

Selecting a Target Skill

As noted in the section on assessment for determining what to teach, a functional assessment within the instructional setting is germane to the development of appropriate

plans should be monitored closely to insure their efficacy and the student's progress. As-instructional objectives. This assessment usu-ally entails the use of scope and sequence skills lists, classroom curriculum materials, and task analysis. The student is assessed in terms of skill mastery, and instruction begins at the lowest skill not mastered.

Selecting a Measurement System

One of the most important features of data-based instruction is its emphasis on direct, continuous, and precise measurement of be-havior. Direct measurement entails focusing on behaviors that can be observed and counted directly. Haring (1978) lists three basic criteria of target behavior:

1. Movement must occur, so that it is clear that behavior is present.
2. The behavior must be repeatable to assure an adequate opportunity to work with and change the movement.
3. It must have a definite cycle (beginning and end) so that each occurrence is fully defined by its beginning and termination.

Seeing words—saying words, writing sums to 9 facts, and taking turns in a game are examples of instructional behaviors that can be mea-sured directly.

Continuous measurement requires that a behavior be counted and recorded over a pe-riod of time, usually daily. Howell, Kaplan, and O'Connell (1979) note that performance is a single measure of behavior on one occasion, whereas learning is a change in performance over time. When more than one performance is recorded, it is possible to tell if the student is staying the same, getting better, or regressing. As more data are gathered, a teacher's percep-tion of learning becomes more accurate. Such

continuous data help the teacher make daily instructional decisions.

Kerr and Nelson (1983) provide some prac-tical guidelines for adjusting the frequency of monitoring:

1. Use session-by-session (one or more daily) recording when student progress is rapid through small-step sequences.
2. Use daily recording when student behavior fluctuates and daily program adjustments are needed.
3. Use daily recording when the daily progress of the student is needed for intervention modifications.
4. Use biweekly or weekly probes when stu-dent progress is slow.
5. Use biweekly or weekly probes when gen-eral monitoring of behavior is needed and frequent program adjustments are not needed.
6. Use biweekly, weekly, or monthly probes when evaluating maintenance or generali-zation of previously mastered skills.

Precise measurement requires that obser-vation and recording systems be reliable. Reli-ability is often determined by comparing the findings of two or more observers of the same behavior during the same time period. The greater their agreement, the more reliable the data.

In addition to the most common practice of recording permanent products, a variety of observational recording techniques are avail-able. Recording techniques are presented in Table 2.7 and include event recording, interval recording, time sampling, duration recording, latency recording, anecdotal recording, and permanent product recording. For more de-tailed descriptions of recording techniques the reader is referred to Kerr and Nelson (1983), Alberto and Troutman (1986), or Blankenship and Lilly (1981).

TABLE 2.7
Observational recording techniques.

Technique	Data Collection Method	Example	Illustration	Summary Data
Event Recording Focus: Frequency of behavior Aim: Increase or decrease frequency of behavior Advantages: Provides exact count of behavior occurrences Ease of data collection (e.g., tallies on card) Suitable to recording academic responses (e.g., tallies of reading errors)	Record each observed occurrence of behavior.	Count the number of times a student completed his assignments for five school days.	Assignments Day Due Completed 1 5 // 2 4 // 3 5 /// 4 6 //// 5 7 //// 27 16	Total number (frequency): 16 Number of assignments completed out of total assignments: 16/27
Interval Recording Focus: Frequency of behavior Aim: Increase or decrease frequency of behavior Advantages: Can observe several behaviors or students simultaneously Good for very high frequency behaviors	Divide a specified observation period into equal intervals that are typically 30 seconds or less. Within each interval record whether the behavior occurred (+) or did not occur (−) at any time during the interval.	Record whether or not a student was "attending" to the seatwork materials at some time during the interval.	1 minute 1 minute 1 minute 1 minute | + | − | + | + | − | − | + | | − | + | − | + | − | + | + |	Percentage of time in which the student exhibited the behavior: $\dfrac{\text{number intervals attending}}{\text{total number of intervals}} = 5/8 = 62.5\%$

Time Sampling

Focus: Frequency of behavior

Aim: Increase or decrease frequency of behavior

Advantages:
Can observe several behaviors or students simultaneously
Can record behavior without continuously observing

Divide specified observation period into equal intervals of several minutes or more duration. Observe at the end of each interval and record whether the behavior occurred (+) or did not occur (−).

Record whether a student was or was not "on task" at the end of every 5 minutes during a 40-minute period.

40 minutes

+	−	+	−	−	−	+	+

Percentage of time the student exhibited the behavior:

$$\frac{\text{number of intervals on task}}{\text{total number of intervals}} = 4/8 = 50\%$$

Duration Recording

Focus: Duration of behavior

Aim: Increase or decrease duration of behavior

Advantages:
Provides the amount or percentage of time the student engages in behavior

best type

Record the amount of time the student is engaged in the activity during the observation period. Turn a stopwatch on when the activity starts, and turn it off when the activity is over. Repeat this process throughout the observation period.

Record the amount of engaged time the student spent on the math assignment.

Observation time:
10:00–10:30

Start	Stop	Duration (minutes)
10:04	10:08	4
10:11	10:16	5
10:21	10:23	2
10:26	10:30	4
		15

Percentage of time the student engaged in the activity:

$$\frac{\text{number of minutes engaged}}{\text{total number of minutes}} = 15/30 = 50\%$$

(continued)

65

TABLE 2.7, continued

Technique	Data Collection Method	Example	Illustration	Summary Data
Latency Recording Focus: Duration of latency behavior Aim: Increase or decrease latency duration Advantages: Easily collected Provides data on how long it takes student to begin appropriate activity Provides data on how long student can delay response (e.g., going to bathroom)	Record the time it takes for a student to begin an activity once the antecedent stimulus (signal) has been provided. Turn a stopwatch on after the signal to begin an activity has been provided, and turn it off when the student begins the activity.	Record the amount of time it took a student to get his reading book and join the reading group after being instructed to do so.	Signal Begin Latency (minutes) 11:02 11:05 3 11:03 11:06 3 11:01 11:02 1 11:04 11:07 3 10:59 11:01 $\underline{2}$ 12	Daily average of time lapse between being told to begin and actually beginning: $\dfrac{\text{latency time}}{\text{number of days}} = 12 \div 5 = 2.4 \text{ minutes}$
Anecdotal Recording Focus: Complete description of student's behaviors Aim: Determine which behaviors are important for designing intervention and determine tactics to enhance intervention Advantages: Provides data which facilitate the development of instructional objectives and interventions	Record all behaviors of the student during a specified time period.	Record behaviors displayed during science laboratory period.	Time: 1:05 Antecedent: Teacher passes out lab materials and explains experiment. Behavior: Sally stares out the window. She talks to students around her. Consequence: Teacher talks to Sally about the experiment.	Narrative report.

Permanent Product Recording

Focus: Student outcomes which result in a permanent product (e.g., written work or tape)—most common recording procedure used by teachers (e.g., math papers, book reports, projects)

Aim: Monitor student progress and provide feedback on correct-incorrect responses

Advantages:
Easy to collect
Teacher does not have to observe student directly
Provides data on student progress
Extremely versatile (e.g., useful in all content areas)
Sample of behavior is a durable product
May be recorded at teacher's convenience

Collect assignments and provide feedback regarding correct and incorrect responses.

Collect spelling papers and return with percentage correct on top of paper.

60% correct
Spelling Test
1. ~~~~~
2. ~~~~~
3. ~~~~~

Number correct (frequency)
Percentage correct:
$$\frac{\text{number correct}}{\text{total number}} \times 100$$
Rate correct/incorrect per minute

Collecting and Graphing Data

For data to be useful the information must be displayed in an easy-to-read format. This process involves creating a visual display so the raw data can be analyzed. In data-based instruction, graphing is the most common method of presenting data. Kerr and Nelson (1983) report that graphs serve three important purposes: (a) they summarize data in a manner that leads to daily decision-making, (b) they communicate intervention effects, and (c) they provide feedback and reinforcement to the learner and teacher.

Data conversion. Data must be converted into a form that allows for consistent graphing. Ba-

sically, this involves reporting three types of data: number correct, percentage (the number of correct responses divided by the total number of responses and then multiplied by 100), or rate (the number correct divided by the time). Table 2.8 provides guidelines for converting various types of data for graphing.

Types of graphs. The basic format for graphing is a *line graph* that includes two axes. The horizontal axis is the abscissa, or x-axis. The vertical axis is the ordinate, or y-axis. As presented in Figure 2.3, the x-axis is used to record the time factor (i.e., the observation period). The y-axis is used to record performance on the target behavior. An example of a line

TABLE 2.8
Data conversion procedures.

Type of Recording	Data Conversion	
Permanent product recording Event recording	Report number of occurrences . . . *(# words read per min.)*	if both time and opportunities to respond are constant.
	Report percentage . . . *(⊖math probs, spelling wds)*	if time is constant (or not of concern) and opportunities vary.
	Report rate . . . *(# of worksheets completed to criterion/wk)*	if both time (which is of concern) and opportunities vary, *or* if time varies and opportunities are constant.
Interval recording Time sampling	Report number . . .	if constant.
	Report percentage of intervals . . . *(on task)*	during or at the end of which behavior occurred.
Duration	Report number of seconds/ minutes/hours . . . *(reading rate, sight rec. drill)*	for which the behavior occurred.
Latency	Report number of seconds/ minutes/hours . . .	between antecedent stimulus and onset of behavior.

(handwritten annotation: How long it takes to count out change, on task, self-stim, seizures)

Source: From *Applied Behavior Analysis for Teachers* (p. 132) by P. A. Alberto and A. C. Troutman, 1986. Columbus, OH: Merrill. Copyright 1986 by Merrill Publishing Company. Reprinted by permission.

graph on equal-interval graph paper is presented in Figure 2.4.

A *bar graph* uses vertical bars to display data (i.e., vertical bars represent levels of performance). A bar graph is easy to interpret and provides the teacher and student with a clear picture of performance. Some sample bar graphs are presented in Figure 2.5.

Another type of graph, the *ratio graph,* is particularly suited to charting rate data. Data for ratio graphing are converted into rate per minute and are charted on a semilogarithmic chart. Number of correct and incorrect responses on an instructional pinpoint (for example, see word–say word) for a specified time period (frequently one minute) provides the data for the graph. Such graphs are a major tool of applied behavior analysis or, more specifically, precision teaching.

Precision teaching. Specifically, in precision teaching, the teacher does the following:

1. Selects a target behavior (pinpoint).
2. Develops a task sheet or probe for evaluation of pupil progress in daily timings.
3. Graphs the data daily and sets instructional aims.
4. Designs the instructional program.
5. Analyzes data and makes instructional decisions.

Target behaviors are usually determined by administering probe sheets. These sheets include academic tasks and are used to sample the student's behavior. Typically, the student works on the probe sheet for one minute; the teacher records the rate of correct and incorrect responses and notes any error patterns. Figure

FIGURE 2.3
Sample *x*- and *y*-axes.

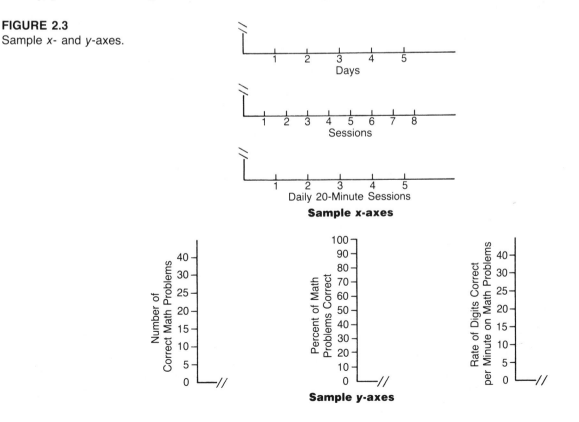

FIGURE 2.4
Sample line graph.

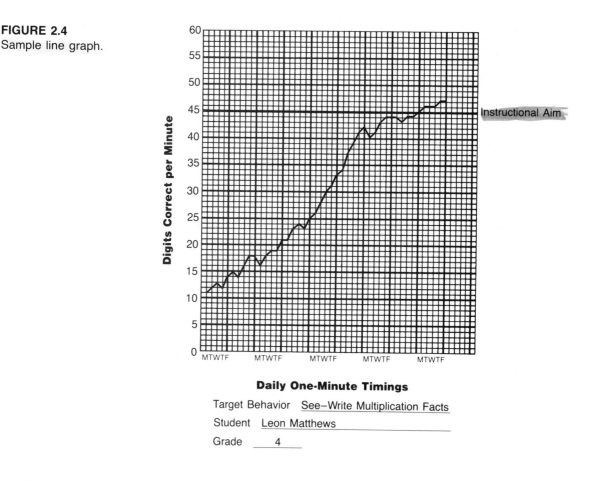

Target Behavior   See–Write Multiplication Facts
Student   Leon Matthews
Grade   4

2.6 displays a probe sheet of a task for assessing addition facts with sums to 9. The instructional objective is not usually established until the student has performed the task on the probe sheet several times, providing a more reliable index of the student's performance than one test would provide. The original assessment probe may be used, or a new probe sheet can be designed to stress specific facts—for example, addition involving zero.

With the expanded use of precision teaching, several materials are now available for implementing a precision teaching system. All of these materials contain an extensive list of academic skill probes which can be used to determine instructional objectives and to monitor student progress. Some of these materials are the following:

Classroom Learning Screening Manual (Koenig & Kunzelmann, 1980)
Psychological Corporation
555 Academic Court
San Antonio, TX 78204

Precision Teaching Project
Skyline Center
3300 Third Street, Northeast
Great Falls, MT 59404

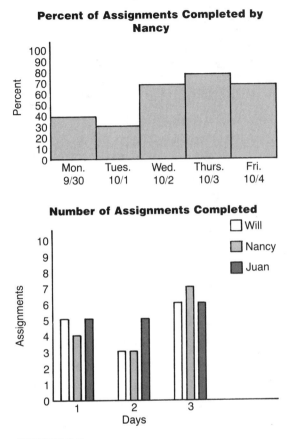

FIGURE 2.5
Sample bar graphs.

Regional Resource Center Diagnostic Inventories
Clinical Services Building
University of Oregon
Eugene, OR 97403

Sequential Precision Assessment Resource Kit (SPARK II) (Trifiletti, Rainey, & Trifiletti, 1979)
Precision People
P.O. Box 17402
Jacksonville, FL 32216

SIMS Reading and Spelling Program; SIMS Written Language Program

Minneapolis Public Schools
807 N.E. Broadway
Minneapolis, MN 55413

Precision teachers record the daily performances and graph the results.

The Standard Behavior Chart (six-cycle chart) is widely used for charting (see Figure 2.7). The chart is semilogarithmic; that is, the vertical axis is scaled so that the distances are proportional. (The distance between 5 and 10 is the same as the distance between 50 and 100.) The horizontal axis is an equidistant scale for recording days of observation. On the horizontal axis, each heavy line represents a Sunday.

Following are some advantages of the Standard Behavior Chart:

1. Rates of movement ranging from 1,000 per minute to 1 to 24 hours (.000695 per minute) may be recorded. This enables the teacher to record a wide range of behaviors on the chart.
2. Changes in performance are displayed proportionally. In this procedure, the *relative* rate of learning is more apparent than the *absolute* amount of learning (Haring, 1978). For example, if a student increases her rate of writing multiplication facts from 10 per minute to 20 per minute in a week, her rate of change ($\times$ 2) is as great as that of a student who goes from 20 to 40 in the same time period.
3. A standardized chart facilitates communication among teachers. In addition, it reduces the possibility of misinterpreting the data across various treatment strategies. (All learning is plotted on the same proportional scale.)

Berquam (1979) developed a chart (see Figure 2.8) that is especially designed for classroom use. Like the Standard Behavior Chart, it

Name _____ Correct _____ Error _____

Date _____ Comments _____

_____

6	5	4	9	8	2	5
+ 2	+ 3	+ 4	+ 0	+ 1	+ 7	+ 0

8	4	1	3	5	3	5
+ 0	+ 3	+ 1	+ 2	+ 2	+ 6	+ 4

7	4	3	8	7	2	4
+ 1	+ 2	+ 3	+ 1	+ 0	+ 5	+ 0

1	3	2	6	5	1	0
+ 0	+ 1	+ 2	+ 1	+ 4	+ 6	+ 0

3	2	2	3	3	4	5
+ 4	+ 4	+ 1	+ 1	+ 0	+ 5	+ 1

6	7	1	1	1	1	1
+ 3	+ 2	+ 2	+ 3	+ 4	+ 5	+ 8

FIGURE 2.6
Probe sheet used to present addition facts—sums to 9.

features a proportional scale; however, the range of rates is reduced to the rate span needed for charting academic skills. Also, the chart provides space for recording raw data. This helps in checking the chart and enables the student to note progress by examining the slope of the raw data.

Teachers who prefer a simpler graph may use an equal-interval chart as illustrated in Figure 2.4. This kind of chart can be drawn on square-ruled graph paper. The teacher records the frequency of the behavior along the vertical axis and the number of sessions or timings on the horizontal axis. An example of an equal-interval chart on unlined paper is presented in

Figure 2.9. Two advantages of equal-interval charts are that they are easy to understand and use and that students like the growth patterns because they accelerate so quickly.

Setting Instructional Aims and Analyzing Data

An instructional aim provides the student and teacher with an instructional goal. It offers a framework from which to analyze data and evaluate student progress. Stephens (1977) provides a detailed description of data-based instruction when instructional aims are expressed in terms of percent correct. He sug-

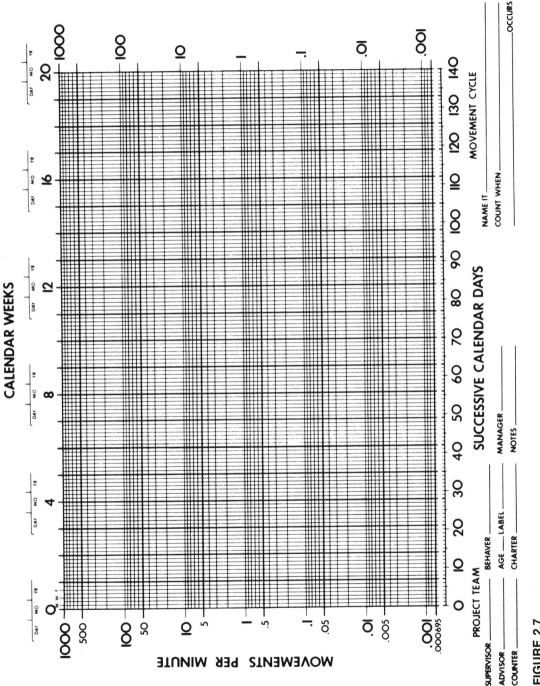

FIGURE 2.7
Standard behavior chart.

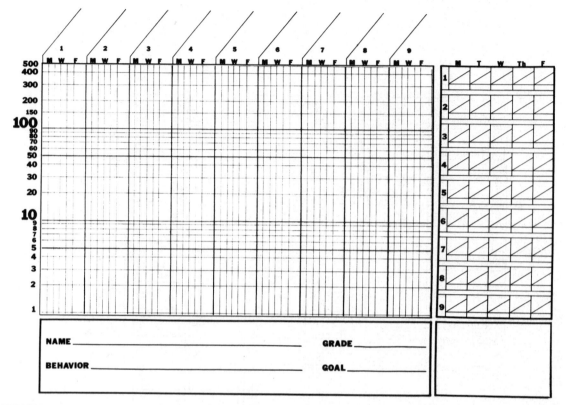

FIGURE 2.8
Proportional chart for classroom use.
Source: From *Academic Behavior Chart* by E. M. Berquam, 1979, Gainesville, FL: Behavior Development Systems. Copyright 1979 by E.M. Berquam. Reprinted by permission.

gests the following guidelines for determining level of learning:

1. *Mastery*—100% correct responses
2. *Learned*—90–99% correct responses
3. *Instructional*—70–89% correct responses
4. *Frustration*—69% or less correct responses

The instructional aim may also be expressed in terms of rate. In precision teaching, the aim is usually defined in terms of rate of correct and incorrect responses per minute. Rate is a very sensitive ratio measure that readily reflects the effects of instructional interventions. (Rate is equal to the number of movements divided by the number of minutes observed.)

Ideally, the aim should represent a mastery level of the skill. Data concerning rates that reflect mastery (proficiency) in academic tasks have long been lacking. Although there is still disagreement concerning proficiency level rates, enough data (Mercer, Mercer, & Evans, 1982) are now available to indicate proficiency level trends on selected academic tasks. Rates collected by various investigators either suggest proficiency levels or indicate the performance levels of high-achieving peers. Rates for

Name _____

Setting _____

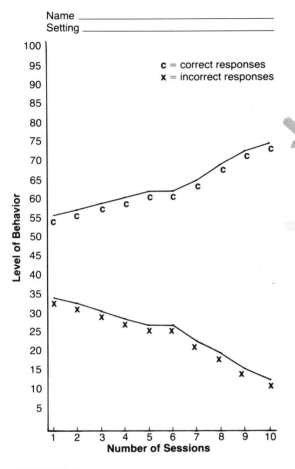

FIGURE 2.9
Equal-interval chart.

that derive from empirical support or from considerable experience (Haring & Gentry, 1976). One way of facilitating aim selection is to collect rate data from children who are achieving satisfactorily and use their performances as aims. Another way involves the teacher performing the task and using a proportion of this performance as an aim.

Rate of correct and incorrect responses has primarily been used to determine proficiency levels. Although this approach has yielded very helpful information, it may be beneficial to examine learning patterns to determine proficiency. For example, suppose that a student *celerates* at a desirable rate on a task for a two-week period and then levels off. (*Celeration* refers to charted slope without regard to direction and includes *acceleration* and *deceleration.*) Once the learning levels off, it may be extremely difficult to produce celeration that is worthy of the intense instructional effort. If a reader achieves 100 to 150 words per minute correct, it may not be worthwhile to spend a lot more time trying to obtain 200 words per minute; it *would* be appropriate to introduce more difficult reading material and strive for 100 to 150 words per minute correct again. Thus, the leveling-off rates of some students may indicate that the instructional aim has been achieved and a new skill needs to be introduced.

Charted data enable the teacher to determine if the pupil is making acceptable progress. The analysis of data is enhanced when it is charted to display both baseline data (present levels of performance) and intervention data (gathered during intervention). Each time an intervention change is made, a vertical line is drawn on the chart to indicate the change. Haring (1978) notes that the purpose of charting data is to help the teacher make accurate decisions about teaching strategies—for example, when to continue or change a procedure. Significant learning patterns often

academic readiness skills, reading skills, spelling skills, and arithmetic skills are reported throughout this book.

Certain learner characteristics, such as age, grade level, and achievement level, influence the establishment of appropriate aims. Since research has not conclusively determined specific aims for academic tasks, the teacher must use her own judgment in setting aims with individual pupils. The teacher should select aims

emerge, enabling the teacher to find possible reasons for success or failure and make decisions based on data. The most desirable pattern is clear-cut: an increase in the rate of appropriate or correct responses and a decrease in the rate of inappropriate or incorrect responses.

In a detailed discussion of patterns, Koorland and Rose (1978) present numerous common patterns. Table 2.9 shows several of them. Students with learning problems are often identified because they have difficulty keeping up with instruction. These students fall further and further behind. Analyzing a student's learning pattern or celeration can help the teacher identify learning problems in order to make appropriate decisions about instruction.

TABLE 2.9
Common learning patterns.

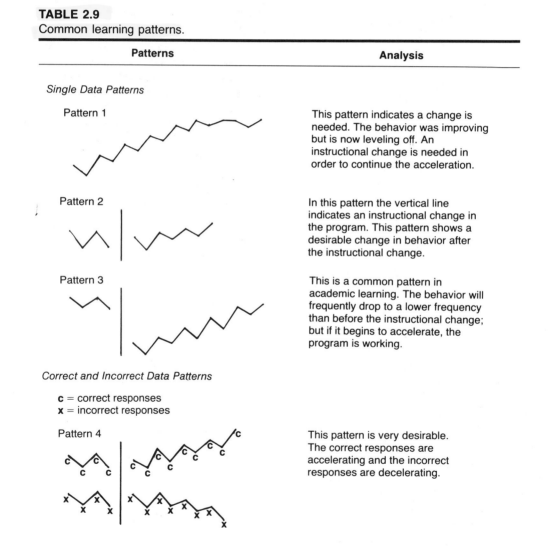

Patterns	Analysis
Single Data Patterns	
Pattern 1	This pattern indicates a change is needed. The behavior was improving but is now leveling off. An instructional change is needed in order to continue the acceleration.
Pattern 2	In this pattern the vertical line indicates an instructional change in the program. This pattern shows a desirable change in behavior after the instructional change.
Pattern 3	This is a common pattern in academic learning. The behavior will frequently drop to a lower frequency than before the instructional change; but if it begins to accelerate, the program is working.
Correct and Incorrect Data Patterns **c** = correct responses **x** = incorrect responses	
Pattern 4	This pattern is very desirable. The correct responses are accelerating and the incorrect responses are decelerating.

TABLE 2.9, *continued*

Patterns	Analysis
Pattern 5 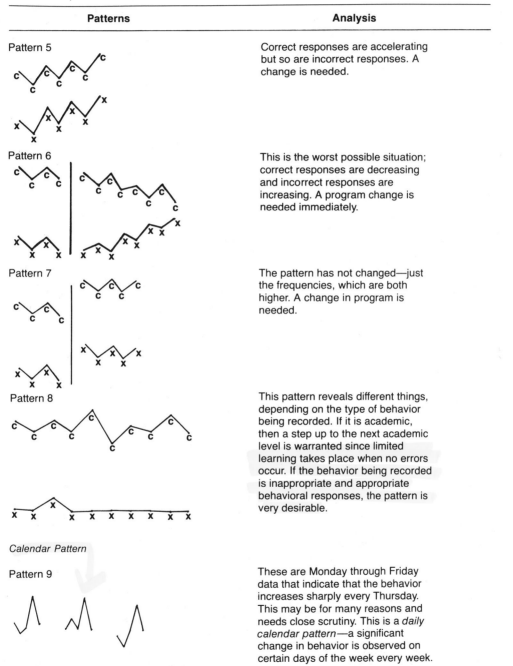	Correct responses are accelerating but so are incorrect responses. A change is needed.
Pattern 6	This is the worst possible situation; correct responses are decreasing and incorrect responses are increasing. A program change is needed immediately.
Pattern 7	The pattern has not changed—just the frequencies, which are both higher. A change in program is needed.
Pattern 8	This pattern reveals different things, depending on the type of behavior being recorded. If it is academic, then a step up to the next academic level is warranted since limited learning takes place when no errors occur. If the behavior being recorded is inappropriate and appropriate behavioral responses, the pattern is very desirable.
Calendar Pattern **Pattern 9**	These are Monday through Friday data that indicate that the behavior increases sharply every Thursday. This may be for many reasons and needs close scrutiny. This is a *daily calendar pattern*—a significant change in behavior is observed on certain days of the week every week.

Basic Guidelines of Data-Based Instruction

Data-based instruction emphasizes (a) using direct and frequent measurement, (b) making instructional decisions on the basis of student performance, (c) establishing instructional aims, (d) using task analysis, (e) maintaining records of student performance, and (f) applying the principles of behavior modification (e.g., reinforcement). Howell et al. (1979) offer numerous guidelines for implementing data-based instruction by means of precision teaching.

Precision teaching will be most successful when:

1. The teacher initially counts only priority behaviors.
2. The teacher identifies strategies to make timing and recording behavior easier.
3. The teacher evaluates the recorded data frequently (preferably daily).
4. Probing or criterion-referenced testing is used.
5. The system remains a tool for teaching rather than a "cause." Precision teaching should only be used as long as it helps the student.

Strategies to facilitate timing and recording behaviors include:

1. Take group timings. This works best with written activities. Some teachers, for example, time one-minute handwriting samples, one-minute math fact sheets, one-minute spelling problems.
2. Students can record time stopped and started. This can easily be done with a rubber stamp of a clock on the students' worksheets.
3. A kitchen timer or prerecorded tape can be used to time sessions.
4. Students can work together and time and record data for each other. This has worked well with flashcard drills.
5. Students can read into a tape recorder. Teachers can later record correct and error rates for either samples of behavior or the total session.

6. Use mechanical counters. Single and dual tally counters are available as well as beads and golf score counters.
7. Count for a fixed period of time each day. Counting for different intervals confuses the data pattern since such factors as endurance, boredom, and latency of response may enter into the data analysis.
8. One-minute timings are easy to chart (no rate plotter is necessary).
9. Aides, peers, student teachers, and volunteers can be trained to help develop materials and to count and record behaviors. (p. 185)

REFERENCES

Alberto, P.A., & Troutman, A.C. (1986). *Applied behavior analysis for teachers.* Columbus, OH: Merrill.

Algozzine, B., & Mercer, C.D. (1980). Labels and expectancies for handicapped children and youth. In L. Mann & D.A. Sabatino (Eds.), *The fourth review of special education* (pp. 287–313). New York: Grune & Stratton.

Archer, A., & Edgar, E. (1976). Teaching academic skills to mildly handicapped children. In S. Lowenbraun & J.Q. Affleck (Eds.), *Teaching mildly handicapped children in regular classes* (pp. 15–112). Columbus, OH: Merrill.

Arter, J.A., & Jenkins, J.R. (1977). Examining the benefits and prevalence of modality considerations in special education. *Journal of Special Education, 11*(3), 281–297.

Berquam, E.M. (1979). *Academic behavior chart.* Gainesville, FL: Behavior Development Systems.

Blankenship, C.S. (1985). Using curriculum-based assessment data to make instructional decisions. *Exceptional Children, 52,* 232–238.

Blankenship, C., & Lilly, M.S. (1981). *Mainstreaming students with learning and behavior problems.* New York: Holt, Rinehart, & Winston.

Bohannon, R. (1975). *Direct and daily measurement procedures in the identification and treatment of reading behaviors of children in special education.* Unpublished doctoral dissertation, University of Washington, Seattle.

Brophy, J.E., & Good, T.L. (1974). *Teacher-student relationships.* New York: Holt, Rinehart, & Winston.

Deno, S.L. (1985). Curriculum-based measurement: The emerging alternative. *Exceptional Children, 52,* 219–232.

Evans, S.S., Evans, W.H., & Mercer, C.D. (1986). *Assessment for instruction.* Boston: Allyn & Bacon.

Frank, A.R. (1973). Breaking down learning tasks: A sequence approach. *Teaching Exceptional Children, 6,* 16–29.

Fuchs, L.S., Wesson, C., Tindal, G., Mirkin, P., & Deno, S. (1981). *Teacher efficiency in continuous evaluation of IEP goals* (Research Report No. 53). Minneapolis: University of Minnesota Institute for Research in Learning Disabilities.

Galagan, J.E. (1985). Psychoeducational testing: Turn out the lights, the party's over. *Exceptional Children, 52,* 266–276.

Germann, G., & Tindal, G. (1985). An application of curriculum-based assessment: The use of direct and repeated measurement. *Exceptional Children, 52,* 244–265.

Gickling, E.E., & Thompson, V.P. (1985). A personal view of curriculum-based assessment. *Exceptional Children, 52,* 205–218.

Haring, N.G. (1978). Research in the classroom: Problems and procedures. In N.G. Haring, T.C. Lovitt, M.D. Eaton, & C.L. Hansen, *The fourth R: Research in the classroom* (pp. 1–22). Columbus, OH: Merrill.

Haring, N.G., & Gentry, N.D. (1976). Direct and individualized instructional procedures. In N.G. Haring & R.L. Schiefelbusch (Eds.), *Teaching special children* (pp. 72–111). New York: McGraw-Hill.

Howell, K.W., Kaplan, J.S., & O'Connell, C.Y. (1979). *Evaluating exceptional children: A task analysis approach.* Columbus, OH: Merrill.

Howell, K.W., & Morehead, M.K. (1987). *Curriculum-based evaluation for special and remedial education.* Columbus, OH: Merrill.

Kavale, K.A., & Forness, S.R. (1987). Substance over style: Assessing the efficacy of modality testing and teaching. *Exceptional Children, 54,* 228–239.

Kerr, M.M., & Nelson, C.M. (1983). *Strategies for managing behavior problems in the classroom.* Columbus, OH: Merrill.

Koenig, C.H., & Kunzelmann, H.P. (1980). *Classroom learning screening manual.* San Antonio, TX: Psychological Corporation.

Koorland, M.A., & Rose, T.L. (1978). *Consulting with classroom teachers: A behavioral approach for special educators.* Unpublished manuscript, University of Florida, Gainesville.

Logan, D.R. (1977). Diagnosis: Current and changing considerations. In R.D. Kneedler & S.G. Tarver (Eds.), *Changing perspectives in special education* (pp. 105–121). Columbus, OH: Merrill.

Lovitt, T.C. (1984). *Tactics for teaching.* Columbus, OH: Merrill.

Mager, R.F. (1975). *Preparing instructional objectives* (2nd ed.). Belmont, CA: Fearon.

Marston, D., & Magnusson, D. (1985). Implementing curriculum-based measurement in special and regular education settings. *Exceptional Children, 52,* 226–276.

Mercer, C.D., (1987). *Students with learning disabilities* (3rd ed.). Columbus, OH: Merrill.

Mercer, C.D., Mercer, A.R., & Evans, S. (1982). The use of frequency in establishing instructional aims. *Journal of Precision Teaching, 3*(3), 57–63.

Mirkin, P., Deno, S., Tindal, G., & Kuehnle, K. (1979). *Formative evaluation: Continued development of data utilization systems* (Research Report No. 23). Minneapolis: University of Minnesota Institute for Research in Learning Disabilities.

Polloway, E.A., Payne, J.S., Patton, J.R., & Payne, R.A. (1985). *Strategies for teaching retarded and special needs learners* (3rd ed.). Columbus, OH: Merrill.

Rice, F.P. (1975). *The adolescent.* Boston: Allyn & Bacon.

Rosenthal, R., & Jacobson, L. (1966). Teachers' expectancies: Determinants of pupils' IQ gains. *Psychological Reports, 19*(1), 115–118.

Salvia, J., & Ysseldyke, J.E. (1988). *Assessment in special and remedial education* (4th ed.). Boston: Houghton Mifflin.

Smith, R.M., Neisworth, J.T., & Greer, J.G. (1978). *Evaluating educational environments.* Columbus, OH: Merrill.

Stephens, T.M. (1977). *Teaching skills to children*

with learning and behavior disorders. Columbus, OH: Merrill.

Stiggins, R.J. (1985). Improving assessment where it means the most: In the classroom. *Educational Leadership, 43*(2), 69–74.

Tasseigne, M.W. (1975). A study of peer and adult influence on moral beliefs of adolescents. *Adolescence, 10,* 227–230.

Trifiletti, J.J., Rainey, N.S., & Trifiletti, D.T. (1979). *Sequential precision assessment resource kit (SPARK II).* Jacksonville, FL: Precision People.

Tucker, J.A. (1985). Curriculum-based assessment: An introduction. *Exceptional Children, 52,* 199–204.

Wesson, C.L., King, R.P., & Deno, S.L. (1984). Direct and frequent measurement of student performance: If it's good for us, why don't we do it? *Learning Disability Quarterly, 7,* 45–48.

Ysseldyke, J.E., & Algozzine, B. (1984). *Introduction to special education.* Boston: Houghton Mifflin.

Ysseldyke, J.E., & Christenson, S.L. (1987a). Evaluating students' instructional environments. *Remedial and Special Education, 8*(3), 17–24.

Ysseldyke, J.E., & Christenson, S.L. (1987b). *The Instructional Environment Scale.* Austin, TX: Pro-Ed.

CHAPTER 3

Planning and
Monitoring Instruction

The emphasis on direct instruction continues to gain support in special and regular education (Stevens & Rosenshine, 1981; Ysseldyke & Algozzine, 1984) (see Chapter 1). Educators are requesting that more time be allocated to academic instruction and that academic instructional time be used efficiently; that is, student response time to academic tasks should be maximized. In essence, efforts are being made to help teachers increase the intensity of academic instruction. The following specific suggestions are offered to increase the intensity or amount of time students are engaged in academic learning:

1. Increase the "opportunity to learn" for students by allocating as much time as feasible for student instruction.
2. Use time scheduled for academic instruction efficiently.
3. Promote student attention and involvement by presenting academic activities that require the student to respond.
4. Plan academic tasks that generate a high percentage of correct responses.
5. Monitor student progress on academic skills and provide daily feedback.
6. Establish an expectancy of work and success in the classroom.
7. Use contingencies to reinforce task completion and student responding.
8. Consider summer or tutoring programs for students who need intense instruction to accomplish important immediate goals (e.g., prevention of learning problems, grade promotion, and graduation).

With the increased interest in systematic instruction, some authorities fear that it is being overemphasized. Stephens (1977) responds to this concern:

Certainly, systematic instruction has the inherent danger of being overly mechanical as in an assembly line activity. Objectifying and routinizing instruction may obliterate those interpersonal values that are so helpful to the human experience, but such an omission need not occur. And, nonsystematic teaching does not guarantee sensitive teachers. Those who like children, enjoy helping them and interacting with them can maintain those feelings while using instructional technology purposefully. (p. 182)

The teacher must be able to adjust or modify plans during the day. Interesting, spontaneous events provide excellent on-the-spot instructional activities, and these situations should not be overlooked for the sake of carrying out a preplanned lesson.

This chapter discusses several important areas in planning and monitoring instruction. They include classroom rules, physical arrangements, instructional arrangements, scheduling, consulting with teachers and parents, material organization system, and record keeping.

CLASSROOM RULES

Classroom rules are essential for establishing the expected behaviors of students and teacher. Rules help structure the learning environment. They provide students with guidelines to follow and offer the teacher a framework for reinforcing behaviors. At the beginning of the year the rules should be presented to the students, and the rationale for each rule should be explained and discussed. Positive consequences for following the rules and negative consequences for breaking the rules should be clearly established and enforced in a consistent and equitable manner. The rules should be posted in a prominent place in the classroom. Worell and Nelson (1974) provide guidelines for establishing effective classroom rules:

1. Select the smallest possible number of rules. It is difficult to remember and enforce

a large number of rules. Also, in stating a rule it is better to say, "Remain in your seat unless you have the teacher's permission to be up," than, "No going to the pencil sharpener," "No visiting," or "No going to the game area without permission."

2. Use different rules for different situations. For example, rules for the playground and cafeteria may be different from those for classroom academic activities.

3. State rules that are observable and enforceable. For example, the rule, "Show respect toward others," is not easily enforced, whereas the rule, "Speak and act in a courteous manner toward classmates," is enforceable because action and words can be observed.

4. Make sure rules are reasonable. The rule, "All homework must be turned in before first period," is reasonable only if students have the opportunity to meet it (i.e., no one is absent or has been ill).

5. Determine consistent consequences for rule fulfillment or infraction. The consequences for keeping and breaking rules should be understood by all classmates. (For example, students who keep rules earn free time, and students who break rules lose recess time.) Rules without consequences have little effect on behavior; thus, consistent teacher follow-through is critical. Also, rules and their consequences should be applied in an equitable manner; bending the rules for specific students or situations should be avoided.

PHYSICAL ARRANGEMENTS

The physical arrangement of a classroom greatly influences both the instructional program and the attitudes of the students. One of the most important considerations in planning the arrangement of a classroom is to designate selected areas for specific activities (for example, math area, language area, study area). In addition, space must be provided for small-group instruction, individual student storage, individual work areas, interest centers, and material display and storage.

Academic Areas

In organizing the classroom, it is necessary to divide instructional spaces in the academic areas. In the elementary grades, these areas typically include reading, math, language, handwriting, spelling, and subjects such as science, social studies, and health. Each area should provide room for several students and a space for storing materials. In the intermediate and secondary grades, fewer academic areas are specified in a classroom; however, instructional areas may be set up for various branches of a particular subject. For example, an English teacher may have areas for literature, grammar, listening, and free reading; a math teacher may have geometry, computation, consumer math, and self-checking areas.

Teacher Area

The teacher needs areas for small-group and large-group instruction. In addition, the teacher needs some space for storing materials. The teacher's space should provide a good vantage point for monitoring the ongoing activities in the room. In the proper location, the teacher can quickly scan the room without moving. Being able to scan the room is very important when students are working on independent assignments.

Individual Student Area

Each student needs a place to store his materials, sit during whole-class activities, and go to for independent seatwork. Typically, students are assigned a desk. It is often helpful to provide students who are highly distractible or who are having a bad day with a quiet work area, such as carrels or desks located away from the flow of activity. However, it is important that such carrels be viewed as a positive place to learn and never be used as punishment.

Recreation Area

Many teachers designate an area for fun activities. Such an area is often used to reinforce students and provide those who have finished an assignment with a rewarding place to go. Some common materials that are placed in this area include a carpet, bean-bag chairs, magazines, a record player with headphones, electronic games, and recreational games.

Audiovisual Area

It is helpful to designate areas for using movie, filmstrip, or overhead projectors. Also, listening centers are needed for using a tape recorder, Language Master, phonograph, or computer. Many rooms do not provide a separate audiovisual area. In these situations, some space may serve dual functions—for example, a reading area/listening station.

General Environmental Considerations

In planning a classroom arrangement, the total effect should be pleasant and inviting. Teachers must take the resources and space available and arrange the class to suit their style and the content being taught. A sample regular classroom floor plan is presented in Figure 3.1, and two resource room plans are featured in Figures 3.2 and 3.3. Teachers may modify these to fit their needs. The sample arrangement of a regular classroom (Figure 3.1) provides for approximately 24 students, with good vantage positions for the teacher, four academic material areas, an interest and recreation area, a listening center, a quiet study area, small-group instructional areas, and an

audiovisual storage area. In addition, a screen for movies, filmstrips, and the overhead projector may be placed in front of the audiovisual materials. Since resource room programs are housed in all types of settings (such as part of a library, furnace room, or auditorium stage), two plans are presented. The plan in Figure 3.2 is for a small area, and the plan in Figure 3.3 is for a larger space.

INSTRUCTIONAL ARRANGEMENTS

Five basic instructional arrangements are available to teachers. These are presented in Figure 3.4 and include (a) large group with teacher, (b) small group with teacher, (c) one student with teacher, (d) peer teaching, and (e) material with student.

Large-Group Instruction

The large group is appropriate for numerous classroom activities, including having show and tell, discussing interesting events, discussing social studies or science content, taking a field trip, watching a play or movie, brainstorming, and playing a game. Large-group instruction is inappropriate for teaching the acquisition of specific skills. In a large group the instructional needs of the students vary considerably, and the teacher is usually unable to respond effectively to these differences.

Small-Group Instruction

Student participation is related to both group size and proximity to the teacher (Adams & Biddle, 1970). Students tend to participate more in smaller groups and when they are physically closer to the teacher. The small-group arrangement usually consists of three to five students, and it is the major vehicle for teaching academic skills. The teacher divides students into groups according to common skill needs. Groups may be based on place-

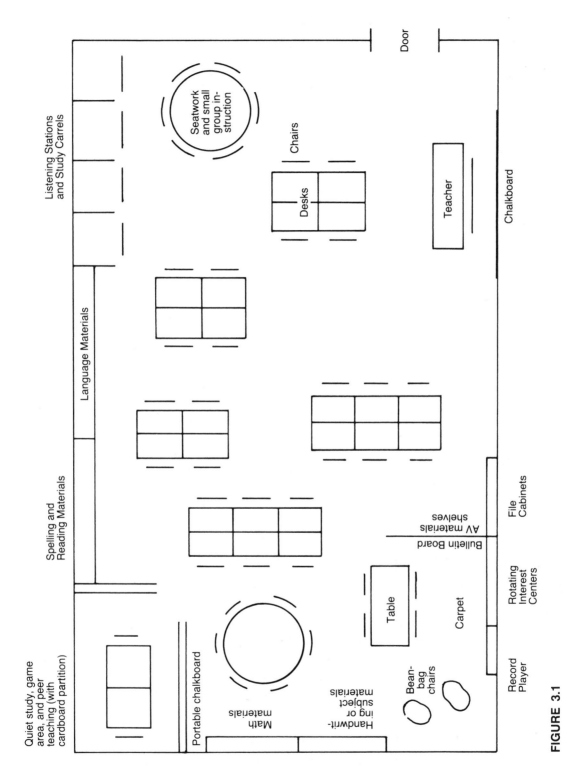

FIGURE 3.1
Sample floor plan for a regular classroom.

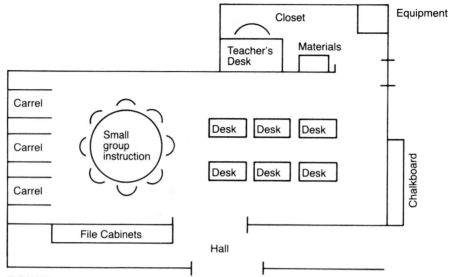

FIGURE 3.2

Sample floor plan for a small resource room.

Source: From *The Resource Teacher: A Guide to Effective Practices* (p. 57), 2nd ed., by J. L. Wiederholt, D. D. Hammill, and V. Brown, 1983, Austin, TX: Pro-Ed. Copyright 1983 by Allyn & Bacon. Reprinted by permission.

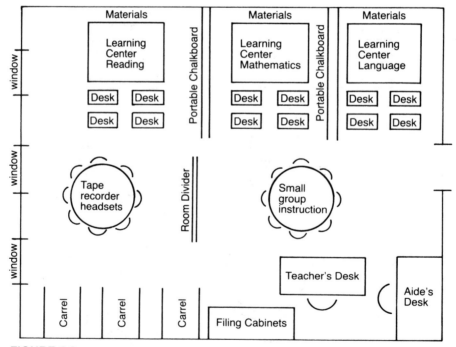

FIGURE 3.3

Sample floor plan for a large resource room.

Source: Adapted from *The Resource Teacher: A Guide to Effective Practices* (p. 56), 2nd ed., by J. L. Wiederholt, D. D. Hammill, and V. Brown, 1983, Austin TX: Pro-Ed. Copyright 1983 by Allyn & Bacon. Reprinted by permission.

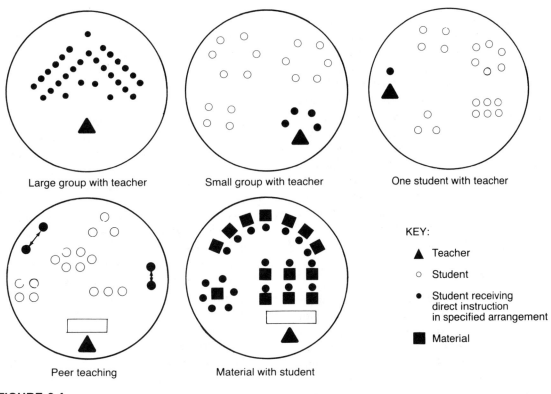

Large group with teacher   Small group with teacher   One student with teacher

Peer teaching   Material with student

KEY:

▲ Teacher

○ Student

● Student receiving direct instruction in specified arrangement

■ Material

FIGURE 3.4
Instructional arrangements.

ment in a basal reader or on need for instruction in selected phonemes, sight words, or specific math facts. These skill-specific groupings are terminated when the students master the skill (Archer & Edgar, 1976). Furthermore, the groupings must be flexible to accommodate different rates of learning. If a student makes rapid or very little progress, it may be advisable to place the student in a different group for instruction (Gearheart, Weishahn, & Gearheart, 1988).

Research on small-group instruction generally indicates positive benefits (Carnine & Silbert, 1979). To improve the effectiveness of small-group instruction, Carnine and Silbert recommend placing the students in a semicircle facing the teacher. They note that distractible students tend to perform better in the middle of the group, and that spacing the students about two feet from the teacher is helpful.

One Student with Teacher

One student with the teacher (tutorial teaching) allows for intensive instruction. It is frequently used to help students with learning problems to learn a new skill. In addition, one-to-one teaching can be used spontaneously to prevent or relieve frustration. When the teacher observes that a student is having difficulty during group instruction or seatwork, it is often helpful to give him one-to-one attention at the first opportunity.

One-to-one instruction does not have to

occur in long time segments. Three to five minutes are often very effective in helping a student understand a concept, receive corrective feedback, understand directions, and feel motivated to continue working. Archer and Edgar (1976) recommend that one-to-one instruction be scheduled daily for students with learning problems. The student then knows he will have some time with the teacher to ask questions and receive help. Elementary teachers and resource room teachers are with fewer students or with students for a longer time; thus, it is easier for them to offer one-to-one instruction than it is for intermediate and secondary level teachers to do so.

Peer Teaching

In this strategy, one student who has proficiency in a skill teaches another student with the teacher's supervision. When using peer tutors, the teacher must assume the responsibility for the instructional plan. The teacher determines the skills to be taught, the materials to be used, and the instructional activity. Also, it is helpful for the teacher to demonstrate the procedures for the pair. Initially, the planning and demonstration require some teacher time; however, the result is usually better instructional support from tutors and reduced demands on the teacher. Tutors may perform a variety of tasks that require little preparation or teacher time. For example, they may check and score student assignments, use an answer key to provide feedback to students playing an instructional game, or use an answer key to help students check their seatwork.

Peer tutoring is commonly practiced in regular education (Cloward, 1967). Allen (1976) reports that the results of research on peer tutoring indicate a positive effect for the tutor. (That is, it can help a tutor who has academic or behavior difficulties or both.) Allen notes that the effects on the tutee are generally positive, but the results are not conclusive. He re-

ports that the critical factor in establishing a mutually beneficial tutor-tutee arrangement is the competence of the tutor regarding content. As a result of his review of the research in peer teaching, Allen suggests the following:

1. Young children prefer a tutor of the same sex, but the sex of the tutor has not produced differential effects on the tutee. However, youngsters of the same sex tend to have more mutual interests.
2. Tutoring sessions that last too long may produce negative effects. Recommended are 20- to 30-minute sessions held two to three times a week.
3. Tutoring should occur in a location with minimal disturbance. Hallways and playgrounds are generally too distracting.
4. It should be explained to parents that tutoring supplements teacher instruction but does not replace it.
5. All types of students (low achieving, high achieving, etc.) may be used as tutors. However, the teacher should make sure the tutor has mastered the instructional content before tutoring occurs.
6. The goals and the activities of the tutoring sessions should be specified.

Scruggs and Richter (1985) reviewed 24 investigations in which learning disabled students were involved in tutoring interventions. They note that all authors favored the use of peer tutoring, and most studies support the continued use of tutoring with learning disabled pupils. Nevertheless, Scruggs and Richter caution against widespread endorsements. Because the tutoring studies have methodological flaws, they note that solid empirical support is lacking. Specifically, they state, "It is difficult to imagine another instructional intervention in the field of learning disabilities which meets with such unqualified enthusiasm and, yet, is so lacking in empirical evidence. [We] have also encountered the methodological challenges . . . and agree with the conviction that peer tutoring has great power and utility in special education" (p. 297).

Peer tutoring seems to hold much promise. It can improve academic skills, foster self-esteem, develop appropriate behaviors, and promote positive relationships and cooperation among peers. Tailor-made for the mainstreamed youngster, peer tutoring benefits both tutor and tutee and requires little of the teacher's time.

Eaton and Hansen (1978) note that students are a valuable source as peer teachers. They report that "chain teaching" can save energy and time: the teacher shows one student how to perform a skill, and the student in turn trains a second and so on. Additional information on peer teaching is presented in the section on peer tutoring in Chapter 5.

Material with Student

This instructional arrangement does not require the teacher's presence. It is widely used because it provides students with independent seatwork activities while the teacher engages in small-group and one-to-one instruction with other students. These independent student activities provide practice on skills in which the student has received previous instruction and has acquired some mastery (Archer & Edgar, 1976; Stephens, 1977; White & Haring, 1980). The teacher selects from numerous materials such as worksheets, self-correcting materials, instructional games, tape recorder, Language Master, microcomputer, and commercial materials. Teachers need to be very careful with this arrangement: Students frequently spend much time in this setting, and inappropriate materials can lead to frustration, failure, and the practicing of errors. Some suggestions that may be helpful in using the material-with-student arrangement on a daily basis follow.

Be consistent with learning activities. Consistency is needed in daily learning activities so the teacher can evaluate the effectiveness of activities and the students can become familiar and comfortable with the tasks. Consistency is especially important when a student is learning a new skill (Eaton & Hansen, 1978).

Use work folders for daily assignments. A work folder is a flexible system of communication between the teacher and the individual student. Work folders can be used to communicate the day's assignments. They provide a place for keeping charts and completed work and for giving feedback. After the students have used the work folders for a while, they can enter the room, pick up their folders, and begin work without teacher intervention. A check-off sheet may be placed in the folder to help the student determine which tasks are completed and which need to be studied.

Provide for self-checking feedback. Self-checking sheets and self-correcting materials enable students to verify their own work and offer immediate feedback. Several safeguards that help remove the temptation to change answers when self-checking is used include: (a) use a colored pen for correcting work, (b) correct work in a special supervised area, and (c) periodically conduct a random check of student corrections and give reinforcement for careful and accurate corrections.

Teach students self-regulation. Eaton and Hansen (1978) assert the importance of self-management skills:

> Students who can successfully manage their own social and academic behaviors learn critical life skills. They learn to accept responsibility for their own actions and for their own learning. Students who can manage their own learning experience the thrill of knowing they can succeed at some very difficult tasks. They

can replace their image of failure with one of self-confidence. In actuality, self-management is the *real* goal of schooling. It teaches a person "how" to learn. (p. 215)

Students with learning problems typically have difficulty with self-regulation (Rooney & Hallahan, 1985). Consequently, many lack self-control strategies that are fundamental to achieving success at school and home. Self-regulation is an essential component of the independent behavior that is needed to succeed as a student and as an adult. When students work independently, the teacher can more freely perform essential teaching activities. In essence, it allows students to do independent practice while the teacher instructs students who need demonstration, modeling, or guided practice. Fortunately, recent research suggests self-regulation can be successfully taught (Gelfand & Hartmann, 1984; Grimes, 1981; Workman, 1982).

Numerous approaches exist for teaching self-regulation. These approaches are often combined with aspects of learning strategy training (see Chapter 14) and/or cognitive training (see Chapter 5). This section focuses on three specific techniques for teaching self-regulation: self-recording, self-evaluation, and self-reinforcement. The steps for teaching each of these three techniques are (a) provide the rationale, (b) demonstrate and model, and (c) practice with feedback (Hughes, Ruhl, & Peterson, 1988). Each technique can be used alone or in combination with related techniques.

Self-recording involves counting and recording one's own behavior, on the assumption that such actions will influence one's behavior. For example, the daily recording of one's weight is likely to influence one's intake of calories. Event and interval recording are appropriate for most self-recording situations. The steps for teaching self-recording include the following:

1. Provide the rationale. This step involves selecting a behavior that needs changing (e.g., the need to complete more seatwork) and discussing how self-recording can be used to change it.
2. Demonstrate and model. In this step a recording form and a method of observation are selected. The teacher demonstrates self-recording by using the observation method and recording the results on the form. Next, the student performs self-recording and receives feedback until understanding is assured.
3. Practice with feedback. This step involves the student practicing self-recording with prompts and corrective feedback. As the student becomes proficient in self-recording, the teacher reduces prompts, praise, and feedback.

Self-evaluation is the component of self-regulation that focuses on teaching students to judge how well they are doing. The following steps for teaching self-evaluation are used:

1. Provide the rationale. The importance of evaluating one's work is discussed. The notion that evaluation enables the student to determine if his performance is satisfactory is stressed. Also, the point is made that it helps the student to know whether more effort is needed.
2. Demonstrate and model. In this step a self-evaluation form is selected. It usually requires the student to mark digits (e.g., 0, 1, 2) that correspond to a grading scale of poor progress (0), some progress (1), and good progress (2). The teacher demonstrates use of the form and has the student model the behavior to insure that the student understands the process.
3. Practice with feedback. The student practices self-evaluation with teacher feedback until proficiency is achieved.

Self-reinforcement is a technique of self-regulation that involves the student reviewing his progress to determine if reinforcement has been earned. The steps for teaching self-reinforcement include the following:

1. Provide the rationale. This step focuses on teaching students the importance of earning reinforcement by helping them identify appropriate reinforcers. The rationale establishes standards of performance for earning of reinforcements, and it specifies when and how the student is to be rewarded.
2. Demonstrate and model. The teacher uses mock data, recording sheets, and a reinforcement menu to demonstrate self-reinforcement (Hughes et al., 1988). The teacher tells the student if the reinforcement criteria are met and selects the reward. The student performs the same behavior with teacher feedback until understanding is apparent.
3. Practice with feedback. The student practices self-reinforcement by using self-recording and self-evaluation. Students are encouraged to praise themselves subvocally when they select the reinforcer (e.g., "I worked hard and now I get a reward"). The teacher provides corrective and positive feedback until the student becomes proficient at self-reinforcement.

Hughes et al. (1988) used a combination of self-recording, self-evaluation, and self-reinforcement to help mildly handicapped learners improve their independent work behavior during seatwork. They note that some generalization to other times occurred among their students.

Individualized instruction is easier to organize and carry out if students are involved in managing their own programs. Students may participate in the following activities involving self-management:

1. Select activities from a list designed to help them achieve objectives.
2. Manage their own work schedules using check-off sheets.
3. Use audiovisual equipment independently.
4. Select instructional materials and return them to the proper place.
5. Tutor each other when feasible.
6. Ask for adult help when necessary.
7. Self-correct work.
8. Administer timings on probes for targeted behaviors.
9. Model appropriate learning and social behavior for each other.
10. Develop techniques for modifying their own behavior.
11. Find solutions to social conflicts without teacher intervention.

Schloss and Sedlak (1986) provide the following procedures for increasing useful practice:

1. Precede independent practice with demonstration, modeling, and guided practice.
2. Match the guided practice directly to the tasks involved in independent practice.
3. Move among the students and provide praise, corrective feedback, and periodic demonstrations of correct procedures.
4. Intersperse short seatwork sessions with additional presentations and guided practice.
5. If needed, provide external reinforcement for arduous seatwork and repetitive drill activities.

SCHEDULING

Schedules are vital for accomplishing instructional goals in an organized manner. They indicate *what* activities will occur and *when* they

will occur. Most students with learning problems need the organization and routine typical
of systematic scheduling. Furthermore, scheduling greatly affects the pace of instruction. It
ensures that enough classroom time is spent in
high-priority curriculum areas and that enjoyable activities are interspersed with less appealing activities.

A well-planned daily schedule greatly aids
the teacher in providing effective instruction.
However, it takes much work to develop an
appropriate schedule. A teacher needs knowledge and skills in individualized programming
(Chapter 1), instructional approaches and techniques (Chapter 1), assessment for teaching
(Chapter 2), curriculum materials (Chapter 4),
and classroom management (Chapter 5).
Scheduling techniques presented include general scheduling techniques, scheduling in the
elementary school, scheduling at the intermediate and secondary levels, and scheduling in
the resource room.

General Scheduling Techniques

The suggestions and techniques in this section
apply to improving scheduling practices in various program settings (resource room and regular classroom) and at all grade levels.

Schedule for maximum instructional time.
Schloss and Sedlak (1986) provide guidelines
for allocating academic time. They include:

1. Plan time to practice new skills within a
   demonstration-practice-feedback-mastery
   paradigm.
2. Examine the weekly schedule and compute
   time (minutes) allocated to each student
   per week, and adjust the schedule for effectiveness.
3. Build planning time in the schedule and
   adhere to it.
4. Consider time needed for transition and set-
   ups when developing the schedule.

5. Pace the instruction quickly during sessions
   allocated to academics to obtain maximum
   use of time.

Move from definite to flexible schedules. At
first, every minute of the student's day is
planned. Times are specified for activities such
as taking off coat, washing hands for lunch,
getting ready to go home, and participating in
instructional activities. With this type of scheduling the student always knows what behaviors are expected (Gallagher, 1979). After students have become familiar with the routines
and know what is expected of them, they usually are ready to assume more independence.
Now some flexible scheduling can be used.
Students may begin to choose the seatwork
assignment they wish to do first or the interest
center they prefer to work in after completing
their math. Lovitt (1973) found that students
were able to manage their own schedules effectively. Moreover, when students were allowed to sequence the order of their own
tasks, their performances improved.

Extend daily planning gradually. In the beginning, schedules are often revised significantly on the basis of each student's daily performance (Gallagher, 1979). Events that may
cause schedule revisions include (a) work pace
of individual students, (b) incompatible groupings, and (c) change in type or schedule of reinforcers. If scheduling is planned on a weekly
basis, many time-consuming revisions might
be necessary. Once the teacher is able to anticipate students' behavior in various activities,
longer-range scheduling can be accomplished
efficiently.

*Proceed from short work assignments to
longer ones.* At first, some students are unable to work on a seatwork assignment for a
long period (such as 30 to 45 minutes). The
teacher can break the task into short lessons

that can be managed independently by the student. Gallagher (1979) points out that task complexity, rather than time, is a problem for some students. In this case, breaking the task into steps may be helpful. Eventually, time and task complexity can be increased as the student develops academic and self-management skills.

Alternate highly preferred with less preferred tasks. In scheduling, it often helps if a less preferred activity is followed by a highly preferred activity. For example, if reading is preferred over math, math is scheduled first and followed by reading. If none of the academic subjects is preferred, it may be necessary to use nonacademic activities (art, recess, music, physical education, interest center) as preferred activities.

Plan for leeway time. Gallagher (1979) notes that it is very important for the schedule to include leeway time. This time is for events such as providing feedback, explaining new directions, taking off or putting on jackets, collecting materials, and preparing to go home. Without leeway time, students may rush to finish work and make careless mistakes. They might become very anxious about catching the bus, not finishing an assignment, or missing a homework assignment.

Provide a daily schedule for each student. A daily schedule provides students with learning problems with needed structure. It also presents them with expectations and a sequence of events in advance. Developing a daily schedule is made simpler by training the student to understand the routine of events that occur at the same time each day. This is accomplished by giving the student a schedule form, perhaps on a ditto or chalkboard, that specifies the time of events for the day. On assignments that are progressive—such as as-

signments in a text or workbook, or projects that are long-term, such as a story, an art project, or a science project—the student may record his starting point for the next day on the schedule. In this manner, the subject area and specific activity are included on the schedule without involving much teacher time. When scheduling changes are needed, the teacher explains the new events or assignments.

Schedule assignments that can be completed in one school day. Gallagher (1979) very aptly points out that students need the opportunity to begin each day with a "clean slate." Students then do not have to worry about yesterday's incomplete or incorrect work. To make sure students are able to complete work, several techniques may be used:

1. Be certain assignments are at the student's instructional level.
2. Make initial assignments short and increase them gradually.
3. Provide leeway time for completing work.
4. Reinforce on-task behavior.
5. Provide answer keys and self-correcting materials.
6. Make some assignments continuous (weekly), with daily aims and a completion date specified.
7. Do not assign more work to students who complete assignments ahead of schedule.

Provide time cues. The schedule designates the time allotted for each assignment. Many students with learning problems have difficulty managing their time and need reminders or cues. The following techniques may be useful as time reminders:

1. Cut sections out of circular pieces of cardboard that are the same size as the face of the classroom clock. When these circular pieces are placed on the clock face, they

display blocks of time on the clock. For example, a circle with ¼ section cut out displays a 15-minute block of time. The student receives time cues by observing (a) the proportion of time exposed on the clock and (b) the location of the minute hand in that exposed section.

2. Set a kitchen timer for the amount of time allotted to an activity. On occasion a kitchen timer may be used with an individual student on a given activity. The sound of the timer ticking and the movement of the dial both remind the student to continue working.

3. From time to time, write the time remaining for an activity on the chalkboard, or tell the class or individual student. Some students may be selected to perform this activity.

4. Stamp cardboard clocks or clock faces on a student's paper as a time reminder.

5. Highlight certain assignments on a student's schedule—for example, underline or write with colored ink pens.

Include feedback in a student's daily schedule. Students should receive written and verbal feedback throughout the day. Feedback is essential in effective teaching. Not only should the teacher use feedback while instructing a student, but time also should be allotted for monitoring the room during seatwork activities and giving feedback (happy faces, check marks, verbal encouragement) to individual students.

Schedule activities in a complementary manner. In an individualized program teachers must organize student activities and plan time to provide individual assistance. Since some subjects require more teacher assistance than others, it often helps if the entire class is not working on the same subject at the same time (Eaton & Hansen, 1978). Arithmetic, spelling, and handwriting usually require less teacher

assistance than reading. Thus, a teacher may be able to provide more individual assistance if part of the class is scheduled to work on arithmetic while others are working on reading.

Plan a variety of activities. Sometimes academic instruction is more effective if one activity is not too long and if a variety of activities are planned. Many teachers organize a 60-minute instructional period into four 15-minute segments. A sample math lesson may include the following activities: (a) direct teacher instruction, (b) listening station (for taped instruction), (c) seatwork at desk or peer teaching activity, and (d) self-correcting material activity. In this plan, students may be divided into four groups and rotated through the activities. For students who complete their work early the option of working in an interest center may be added. Stephens (1977) notes that interest centers often are reinforcing and may help in managing students.

Scheduling in the Elementary School

Elementary regular and special class teachers often teach the same students for a large portion of the school day. This requires scheduling a variety of activities: opening exercises, reading, math, recess, art, and so on. The following techniques and suggestions are helpful in scheduling entire school days.

Analyzing the day's events. The first step in developing a daily schedule is to analyze the daily events and determine how much time the teacher is responsible for planning. This time is affected by nonacademic school activities and supportive instructional services. After the teacher has determined the amount of time students are at lunch, resource room instruction, physical education, art, and so on, the teacher knows how much time must be scheduled. In a 6-hour school day, the classroom teacher probably needs to schedule 4½ to 5 hours. Planning 4½ to 5 hours of daily instruction for 180 days a year certainly is a sizable project.

Planning opening exercises. Opening exercises usually require 15 to 20 minutes. They serve mainly to develop rapport and prepare the students for the day's activities. Also, the teacher uses this time to observe the attitudes, moods, and physical appearance of the students. Common activities for opening exercises include collecting lunch money; taking attendance; saluting the flag; recognizing special days (such as birthdays and holidays); discussing the schedule of activities for the day; and discussing current events, weather, or the date.

Introducing the schedule of activities for the day may be simple or complex, depending upon the needs of the student. Some of the options available for explaining the schedule are as follows: (a) write schedule on the chalkboard, (b) pass out dittos of schedule, (c) use picture cues to display sequence of activities, (d) review individual work contracts, and (e) use peers to help one another with scheduling. For the young child who cannot read, Polloway, Payne, Patton, and Payne (1985) suggest using pictures to designate activities:

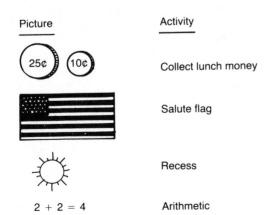

Picture	Activity
25¢ 10¢	Collect lunch money
(flag)	Salute flag
(sun)	Recess
2 + 2 = 4	Arithmetic

Planning closing exercises. Closing exercises usually require 10 to 15 minutes. They are designed to tie together the school day in a pleasant, orderly manner. Some closing activities include cleaning up, returning materials, determining what to take home, reviewing the day's activities, discussing the next day's major events, and putting on jackets. Also, the teacher should make a concentrated effort to finish the day in a *positive* manner with each student. With students who have had a frustrating day, the teacher may make a special effort to offer encouragement.

Scheduling academic instruction. Most students are more alert and easier to motivate in the morning than in the afternoon. Therefore, many teachers plan intensive learning activities in the morning. Also, since students function at different academic levels, students should be divided into small groups for academic instruction. To do so, the teacher plans activities for those students with whom he is not working directly—independent seatwork, learning center activities, peer teaching, instructional drill games, measuring and recording progress, taking a test, and working with an aide or volunteer.

Sample schedule. The sample schedule presented in Table 3.1 stresses systematic and intensive academic work in reading and math in the morning hours and more group-oriented activities in the afternoon. The schedule provides time to complete unfinished work. This extra time permits slower students to finish their work and other students to work ahead or select interesting activities. Also, the teacher may use this time to provide more individual attention or conduct assessments. These flexible time periods reduce pressure and enable the teacher to individualize instruction.

It is often easier to assign math or spelling seatwork than reading seatwork. In this case,

TABLE 3.1
Sample schedule.

Time	Activity			
8:30	Opening exercises			
8:50	Setting up and beginning work			
9:00	Reading period (small groups)			
	Group A	Group B	Group C	Group D
9:00	Group with teacher	Listening center	Paper-pencil task	Instructional game
9:15	Listening center	Paper-pencil task	Instructional game	Group with teacher
9:30	Paper-pencil task	Instructional game	Group with teacher	Listening center
9:45	Instructional game	Group with teacher	Listening center	Paper-pencil task
10:00	Recess			
10:20	Math period (small groups)			
	Group 1	Group 2	Group 3	Group 4
10:20	Paper-pencil task	Self-correcting material	Group with teacher	Criterion test, timing, or math game
10:35	Self-correcting material	Group with teacher	Criterion test, timing, or math game	Paper-pencil task
10:50	Group with teacher	Criterion test, timing, or math game	Paper-pencil task	Self-correcting material
11:05	Criterion test, timing, or math game	Paper-pencil task	Self-correcting material	Group with teacher
11:20	Prescribed and selected activities including: choosing a free activity, going to the library, using an interest center, working on unfinished tasks, performing timings, taking a test, or playing an instructional or recreational game. The teacher may use this time to work with children who have been absent or out of the room, provide feedback, and give individual attention.			
11:45	Story time, handwriting, or curriculum area (science, social studies)			
12:00	Lunch			
12:30	Spelling, language arts			
1:00	Physical education, music, art, and/or motor development			
1:30	Recess			
1:45	Curriculum area (science, social studies, geography, career education, or citizenship)			
2:05	Prescribed and selected activities			
2:20	Closing activities			
2:30	Dismissal			

	Reading period (small groups)			
	Group A	*Group B*	*Group C*	*Group D*
9:00	Group with teacher	Listening center	Paper-pencil task	Math self-correcting material
9:15	Listening center	Paper-pencil task	Math self-correcting material	Group with teacher
9:30	Paper-pencil task	Math self-correcting material	Group with teacher	Listening center
9:45	Math self-correcting material	Group with teacher	Listening center	Paper-pencil task

the teacher may wish to give math or spelling seatwork to students during the reading period (for example, see the schedule above).

Scheduling at the Intermediate and Secondary Levels

A typical high school schedule includes a homeroom period, five or six class periods, and a lunch period. Class periods are approximately 50 minutes, and the teacher usually has one period for planning. Since a fixed schedule of periods exists at the high school level, it might seem that teachers do not need to do much daily scheduling. However, since lessons must fit into 50-minute segments, planning is essential to insure efficient use of instructional time.

Regular class and resource teachers develop a minischedule for each class period. Each minischedule may include a brief opening exercise, the instructional activities, and a brief closing exercise. An opening exercise may be limited to an explanation of the activities for the period; a closing exercise may simply consist of allowing time to put away materials. Some high school classes are structured so that students enter the room, get their work

folder, and begin working. The teacher moves from group to group, or individual to individual, to offer assistance and reinforcement to the students. In this arrangement opening activities are omitted, but time is scheduled for returning folders.

In planning for a period, it may be a good idea to divide the students into groups and schedule appropriate activities for each group. With this format a teacher may rotate through the groups. Some content is adequately taught to the whole group; however, when this arrangement is used, the teacher must insure that all students understand the lecture material (for example, by taking questions from the students). The teacher should expect students with learning problems to need additional help during seatwork. This help may be provided by a classmate, special material, an aide, or the teacher.

General scheduling considerations that may be useful with adolescents with learning problems include the following:

1. If there is flexibility in scheduling electives, students can select courses in which they have a good opportunity to succeed

(Marsh, Gearheart, & Gearheart, 1978). Scheduling that results in a heavy load or an unsympathetic teacher can cause serious problems for a mildly handicapped learner.

2. A course load must reflect the needs of the student. There should be a balance between courses that are demanding and those that are less demanding. Course substitution may also be used. If the school offers courses that are less demanding but satisfy required credits, the student with learning problems can avoid those courses in which he is likely to be unsuccessful.

3. Expanded course offerings are used in some settings to accommodate the student with learning problems. In these situations the special education staff teaches some content areas in a different setting (Marsh et al., 1978).

Scheduling in the Resource Room

The resource room teacher is faced with a very tedious and time-consuming scheduling task. Most of the difficulty stems from the fact that the student is participating in more than one instructional setting with two or more teachers. The following issues complicate resource room scheduling:

1. The student's academic, emotional, and social needs must be considered when determining the best time to schedule resource room instruction. If the student leaves the regular class for the resource room during an academic lesson, will he miss needed academic instruction? If he goes during a nonacademic activity (such as art, physical education, or music), will the student resent missing a desirable activity?

2. Classroom teachers usually have preferred times for sending students to the resource room.

3. Students who come to the resource room

at a specified time may have very different instructional needs. For example, one student may need help with a specific math skill, whereas another student may need to work on reading comprehension.

4. In some situations it is helpful if the resource room teacher teaches in the regular class setting.

5. Since students are participating in parallel and complementary instructional programs, with different teachers working on the same instructional objectives, the resource room teacher must schedule some time for conferring with classroom teachers.

Despite numerous scheduling difficulties, the resource program remains an important instructional model for serving students with learning problems. For example, Wood (1984) reports that the resource program exposes mainstreamed students to more teachers, a broader knowledge base, and a wide range of role models, and it also affords them the opportunity to build and maintain relationships with nonhandicapped peers. The following techniques and suggestions are helpful in resource room scheduling:

1. Students may come to the resource room at different times depending on the day. For example, they may come at a certain time three days a week and at another time on two days of the week. With this schedule the students do not consistently miss a given subject or activity in the regular class.

2. A resource teacher may choose to provide instruction in the various academic areas at fixed times during the day. With this type of schedule, reading, math, handwriting, and spelling are taught at a specified time, and students may come to the sessions they need. Thus, a student may come to the resource room for a half-hour of instruction

one or more times daily to receive help in problem areas. Wiederholt, Hammill, and Brown (1983) refer to this as a *staggered* schedule.

3. Hawisher and Calhoun (1978) provide two resource room schedules that have been successfully used in South Carolina.

Schedule A

8:00–9:00	Planning/Conferences
9:05–9:50	Group A
10:00–10:45	Group B
10:55–11:40	Group C
11:45–12:15	Lunch
12:15–1:00	Group D (or Conferences)
1:00–1:55	Group E
2:00–2:45	Group F
2:45–3:30	Planning/Conferences

Groups A, B, and C are filled with students needing a heavy concentration of remedial assistance. . . . Groups D, E, and F lend themselves to alternate scheduling. For example, Group D could be split into D^1 and D^2. The students in D^1 would attend on Monday, Tuesday, and Wednesday; D^2 students would attend on Thursday and Friday, or D^2 could be a time period reserved for observations and conferences. Group F would be meeting at a time of day which is suitable for rewarding those students who had controlled specific target behaviors in their planned behavior management programs.

Schedule B

8:00–9:00	Preschool Planning
9:00–9:45	Group A
9:30–10:15	Group B
10:00–10:45	Group C
10:30–11:15	Group D
11:15–11:45	Planning Time
11:45–12:30	Lunch
12:30–1:15	Group E
1:00–1:45	Group F
1:30–2:15	Group G
2:15–3:10	Postschool Planning

Schedule B is more demanding and offers some distinct advantages. The teacher meets with two or three students for 30 minutes of active individualized instruction. When the second group arrives for its period, the first group works independently for 15 minutes. This schedule allows individualized tutoring and demands independent desk work. . . . Both schedules call for 45-minute periods of tutorial instruction. The 45-minute period is strongly encouraged as it provides enough time for the pupil to be taught, to learn, and to assimilate (or drill). A period of less than 45 minutes tends to provide only 15 minutes of instruction time because of the arrival-departure confusion. (pp. 84–85)

4. To maximize the efficient use of time, the resource room teacher must encourage and reinforce (a) being on time and (b) making a quick transition from task to task within the resource room.

5. Several techniques are used to decrease the likelihood that students will disrupt the regular classroom when they return from the resource room. The resource teacher may give the student an assignment to work on until the regular teacher can involve the student in the ongoing activities. Also, the classroom teacher may assign a student the responsibility of helping the returning student to begin work.

CONSULTING WITH TEACHERS AND PARENTS

The role of the special educator as a consultant to regular teachers is widely accepted. Effective consultation results in better services for students with learning problems. Some important goals of teacher consultation include the following: (a) increase the skills of the regular class teacher in serving students with special needs, (b) promote a positive attitude toward special education students and services, (c) assist the regular teacher's confidence in serving students with problems, and (d) coordinate services to students involved in regular and special education programs.

The special educator must function in the delicate role of peer and expert. For meaningful consultation to exist it is helpful if the regular teacher perceives special education as an extension of the regular program with both parties sharing the instructional responsibility. A productive partnership between the regular classroom teacher and the special education teacher is facilitated when it becomes a continuing relationship. This type of relationship is enhanced by a special educator who is genuinely interested in consultation and pursues such activities with regular classroom teachers as having occasional after-school coffee together, arranging brief regular meetings, and making frequent room-exchange visits.

Marsh, Price, and Smith (1983) provide some suggestions for the teacher-consultant:

1. Clarify the role of special education.
2. Identify specific strengths that can be shared in a competent manner. Competence facilitates respect and support.
3. Expect some resistance and criticism but try to avoid defensiveness.
4. Maintain a professional yet personable attitude.
5. Make known the types of services available in the special education program. Describe the program in detail in the faculty handbook, complete with sample forms used. Present the program at a faculty meeting at the beginning of the school year.
6. When a request for service is made, respond as quickly as possible.
7. Schedule services with input from the teacher.

Parent-Teacher Conferences

Parent-teacher conferences develop and maintain a cooperative partnership. Many school districts encourage the special education teacher to meet with the parents before the child begins receiving special education services. Duncan and Fitzgerald (1969) have supported this practice. They found that early meetings with parents served to prevent or reduce attendance problems, the number of dropouts, and discipline problems. Moreover, early meetings were associated with higher grades and good future communication.

The initial conference is extremely important. To prepare, teachers should examine the child's records and follow an initial interview guide (Kroth, 1975). Other professions (e.g., medicine, social work, counseling) consistently use guides to help conduct the session in a systematic rather than haphazard fashion. Kroth recommends these emphases:

1. Present status (chronological age, grade, class, prior teacher)
2. Physical appearance and history
3. Educational status
4. Personal traits
5. Home and family
6. Work experience (usually for older children)
7. Additional information

Rigid adherence to the guide is not necessary. Some flexibility may be needed regarding the topics covered, sequence of events, and length of session.

After the initial session, conferences typically consist of four parts: (a) establishing rapport, (b) obtaining pertinent information from the parents, (c) providing information, and (d) summarizing the conference (Stephens, 1977). Stephens suggests that starting with neutral topics and providing a comfortable seat help establish rapport. To obtain information, the teacher should state the purpose of the conference, ask specific questions, recognize parents' feelings as reflected in their statements, and avoid irrelevances (e.g., marital problems). To provide information, the teacher should start with positive statements regarding the child's behavior and provide samples of work when possible, avoid educational jargon, and share anticipated plans. To summarize the conference, the teacher should briefly review the conference, answer questions, and thank the parents for coming. Heward, Dardig, and Rossett (1979) provide a parent–teacher conference outline that is helpful in conducting effective conferences (see Table 3.2). In addition, Kroth and Simpson (1977) discuss various strategies, ideas, and activities to maximize the benefits of parent conferences.

Stephens (1977) offers several suggestions for evaluating a conference. For example, written outcomes can be compared with the actual outcomes. The areas in which planned outcomes and actual outcomes are discrepant represent areas that need improvement. Finally, he notes that three objectives are usually a maximum goal for a 45-minute conference.

Both parties must listen. A good listener gains much information that oftentimes can help solve problems. Schlesinger and Meadow (1976) identify listening as an important professional tool. Parents like to talk to a teacher who listens in a sympathetic, calm, and nonjudgmental manner. Several authors (Dinkmeyer & Carlson, 1973; Gordon, 1970) stress the importance of active listening (being involved in helping another define problems and clarify beliefs and values). Kroth (1975) equates such a listener to an excellent dancing partner "who seems to feel the rhythm of the conversation and moves accordingly" (p. 30). Fatigue, strong feelings, word usage, too much talking, and environmental distractions deter active listening.

Reporting Pupil Progress

In most school districts, teachers send home progress report cards six times a year, each covering a 6-week period. Parents receiving such reports cannot reinforce and encourage specific skill development on a daily basis. Several studies (Edlund, 1969; Kroth, Whelan, & Stables, 1970; Simonson, 1972) have explored the use of daily report card systems.

When daily report systems are used, the child's report card usually remains on his desk all day. The teacher records the progress or instructs the child to record it during the instructional activities. At the end of the day, the teacher signs each card.

Teachers who use precision teaching or who chart the child's progress can send the child's charts home each day. The charts record progress on specific skills (pinpoints). The teacher usually measures the progress by the number of correct items and incorrect items performed in a 1-minute sample (see Chapter 2). For parents who want to reinforce specific skills, the chart has the advantage of listing the pinpoint. A teacher may choose to report the child's progress using any metric system (percent, rate, number correct, checklist) that the teacher-parent-child triad understands.

Not all children can benefit from the daily system. Some teachers and parents prefer weekly progress reports giving the child the opportunity to recover from a "bad day." Such reports take less of the teacher's time.

Teachers should also consider sending home notes, happy grams, or achievement certificates when the child masters a specific skill. Kroth (1975) describes numerous methods that have been used successfully with parents of handicapped learners.

TABLE 3.2
Parent-teacher conference outline.

Conference Outline

Date _____ Time _____

Student _____

Parent(s) _____

Teacher _____

Other staff present _____

Objectives for conference:

Student's strengths:

Area(s) where improvement is needed:

Questions to ask parents:

Parent's responses/comments:

Examples of student's work/interactions:

Current programs and strategies used by teacher:

Suggestions for parents:

Suggestions from parents:

Follow-up activities:

   Parent(s):

   Teacher:

Date called for follow-up and outcome:

Source: From *Working with Parents of Handicapped Children* (p. 233) by W. L. Heward, J. C. Dardig, and A. Rossett, 1979, Columbus, OH: Merrill. Copyright 1979 by Bell & Howell Company. Reprinted by permission.

MATERIAL ORGANIZATION SYSTEM

To plan and deliver individualized instruction in a systematic and continuous manner, a great deal of organization is needed. For the beginning teacher the development of a system is a large undertaking; however, without it much frustration and anxiety can result. For example, without a system of filing instructional materials that accounts for storage and retrieval, the beginning teacher can spend hours trying to locate needed materials. Thus, one of the initial jobs for a teacher is to develop a filing and storage system and refine it with use.

Before the first day of teaching, the teacher begins to make bulletin boards, dittos, instructional games, worksheets, interest centers, overheads, and special project activities. A filing system helps the teacher organize and add to these materials. In addition, the system can be refined as the teacher develops priorities.

Table 3.3 presents a very general filing system. The categories would change depending on the subjects being taught. As it develops, the system would become much more specific. For example, numerous subcategories would be listed under phonics as materials and activities are collected and developed (for example, individual consonant sounds, blends, vowel sounds, digraphs). In the academic areas a highly specific filing system may be developed from scope and sequence skills lists, commercial programs, or curriculum guides. By making the system open-ended, the teacher can add categories as needed. New ideas or materials collected from teachers, books, in-service meetings, university classes, or commercial programs can be filed into the system readily and used when needed.

RECORD KEEPING

Record keeping for instructional purposes refers to the process of collecting and organizing data on student progress. Keeping a record of

TABLE 3.3
Sample categorical outline for filing system.

I. Academic Areas

  R. Reading
    R-1 Readiness materials and activities
    R-2 Phonics materials and activities
    R-3 Comprehension materials and activities
    R-4 Whole-word materials and activities
    R-5 Language experience materials and activities
    R-6 Basal related materials and activities

  A. Arithmetic
    A-1   Readiness materials and activities
    A-2   Quantity materials and activities
    A-3   Place value materials and activities
    A-4   Addition materials and activities
    A-5   Subtraction materials and activities
    A-6   Multiplication materials and activities
    A-7   Division materials and activities
    A-8   Fractions materials and activities
    A-9   Percentages materials and activities
    A-10 Word problems materials and activities
    A-11 Money materials and activities

Other academic areas (language, spelling, social studies) would be developed according to subareas and specific skills.

II. Management and Motivation Areas

    B.B. Bulletin boards
    I.C.   Interest centers
    L.C.   Learning centers
    C.R. Classroom rules
    S.   Scheduling materials (e.g., forms)
    E.C. Evaluation center materials (e.g., charts, forms, stopwatches, logs)
    G.   Games
    A.V. Audiovisual materials
    S.C. Self-correcting materials
    B.M. Behavior modification materials
    C.A. Classroom arrangement materials

student progress enables the teacher to make timely instructional decisions. Also, record keeping is necessary for planning and implementing IEPs and for reporting student progress to parents.

Because students receive instruction in a wide range of skills that vary greatly in complexity, the task of recording student progress is not simple. Data collection can become quite cumbersome and awkward; thus, teachers might find it a negative part of the instructional process (Cohen & Plaskon, 1980). However, record keeping provides the teacher with essential information and therefore is a positive component of the instructional program. When record keeping is correctly developed and managed, many benefits are realized:

1. Students often enjoy participating in recording their progress.
2. Teachers can gain satisfaction from having documented student progress.
3. Teachers can pinpoint learning difficulties and make timely interventions.
4. Teachers can share the progress of students with parents, principal, and other school personnel.
5. The data can be used to help make program and placement decisions.

A record-keeping system must serve two primary functions. First, a composite or master form is needed to record the progress of students on major objectives across all curriculum areas. For the elementary teacher this form includes several curriculum areas, whereas for a high school teacher it may include only one area. Progress recorded on the composite form serves as a basis for evaluating students and reporting information to others. Second, a system is needed to record and evaluate the progress of students on daily instructional objectives. This daily system is a major part of individualized instruction, and it provides data for making instructional decisions.

When several short-range objectives have been accomplished, the progress is recorded on the composite form. In reading a ten-page story, short-range objectives might include:

1. See—say vocabulary words with 100% accuracy.
2. Match vocabulary words to meanings with 100% accuracy.
3. Read pages 1–3 with 90% accuracy.
4. Read pages 4–6 with 90% accuracy.
5. Read pages 7–10 with 90% accuracy.
6. Answer comprehension questions with 90% accuracy.

After these short-range objectives have been accomplished, pages 1–10 under reading would be checked off as completed on the composite progress form.

Many options are available to the teacher for establishing a record-keeping system, including commercial materials, curriculum guides, scope and sequence skills lists, and school district curriculum guidelines. A teacher must select or develop a system that reflects his individual preferences.

Composite Record Keeping

The first step in developing a composite record-keeping system is to organize instructional objectives. These objectives must be specific, measurable, and organized in steps small enough to reveal short-term progress (days to weeks). Instructional objectives that are in a sequence must be listed in a hierarchical manner. Nonsequential objectives—for example, social skill objectives such as taking turns in a game or raising a hand to talk—should be clustered in a meaningful way. The sequential objectives on the composite form should be in larger steps than the daily instructional objectives.

The composite record of student progress provides the teacher with information for *grouping* the students for instruction. Students who are working on the same or similar objectives in a specific subject area may be organized into a small group for instruction. Once the initial instructional groups are established, the daily recording of student progress enables the teacher to change grouping patterns throughout the year. The student thus can move to and from groups on the basis of progress. The composite record also helps the teacher with the difficult problem of grading students.

Some commercial materials organize the objectives and provide the teacher with record-keeping forms. Curriculum guides developed by school curriculum committees often outline the instructional objectives by subject area across grade levels. In addition, scope and sequence skills lists (such as those provided in Appendix A) provide a framework for organizing objectives.

A composite record-keeping form should be kept simple. Also, since it is used for a long period by numerous people, it helps to use sturdy material. The sample form presented in Table 3.4 is organized by subject area for simplicity; for sturdiness, it may be constructed on a manila folder. When a folder is used, material (such as criterion test results) may be put in it for recording.

Daily Record Keeping

To establish a daily record-keeping system, short-term instructional objectives must be identified and arranged in a sequential order whenever possible. Criteria for mastery of the objectives must be established. Students should learn to evaluate and record their daily performances as much as possible.

Charting, described in Chapter 2, is an excellent system for recording the progress of students on selected daily instructional objectives. Figure 3.5 shows a chart used to record the progress of a student on reading objectives for which the criterion is 140 words correct per minute with three or fewer errors. Many students learn to time and score their own performances and record them on the chart. An adult occasionally can conduct the timing to insure that the student is evaluating and recording his performances accurately. When the

TABLE 3.4
Class progress record.
Curriculum area: Reading.

Students' Names	Instructional Objective: Pages in Textbook											
	1–5	6–11	12–20	21–26	27–31	32–40	41–43	44–47	48–51	52–58	59–64	65–68
1. Archer, B.	9/3	9/10	9/19	9/26	9/30	10/6	10/11	10/19	10/24	10/31		
2. Dillard, W.	9/3	9/16	9/30	10/11	10/24	10/31						
3. Gruggs, G.	9/7	9/18	10/4	10/23								
4. Hiller, D.	9/8	9/20	10/7	10/20	10/27							
5. Hunt, T.	9/7	9/19	10/4	10/22								
25. West, R.	9/4	9/15	9/19	9/30	10/6	10/12	10/27					

Note: Each objective is based on pages completed in a commercial material (for example, workbook or reader).

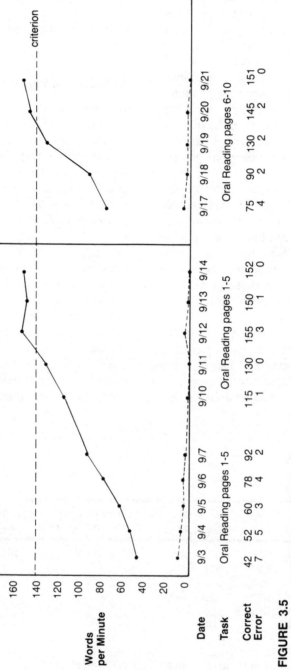

FIGURE 3.5

Chart of progress on a series of reading objectives.

student feels he has reached the criterion on an instructional objective, it is a good time for the teacher or an adult to conduct the assessment.

A student progress book is frequently used. This is especially suited for the secondary teacher who teaches many students the same subject. Table 3.5 presents a progress book of daily or short-term objectives in social studies.

For some instructional objectives that relate to social skills, observations may be recorded on tally sheets. For example, the teacher may wish to reduce out-of-seat behavior during math seatwork. Also, a tally sheet may be used to record academic responses. The teacher could make a tally of each time the student capitalizes the first word in a sentence or responds correctly to a specific question.

Archer and Edgar (1976) suggest a format for recording performances on spelling words. In this format, presented in Table 3.6, the number of correct and incorrect responses is recorded.

The record-keeping formats presented in this section provide the teacher with a variety of options for establishing a daily recording system. No matter which format is selected, the following steps must be followed in plan-

TABLE 3.6
Format for recording performances on spelling words.

Name: Bobby Richards			
Date	Spelling List Number	Correct Responses	Error Responses
10/2	1	14	6
10/3	1	16	4
10/4	1	17	3
10/5	1	20	0
10/6	2	15	5
10/9	2	16	4
10/10	2	19	1
10/11	3	11	9
10/12	3	16	4
10/13	3	17	3
10/16	3	19	1
10/17	4	17	3
10/18	4	20	0

TABLE 3.5
Progress book of short-term objectives in social studies.

Students' Names	Social Studies Objectives							
Boyer, R.	79 9/20	80 9/21	81 9/22	82 9/24	87 9/25	88	89	90
Chestnut, W.	91 9/14	92 9/17	93 9/18	101 9/19	102 9/20	103 9/22	104	105
Martin, A.	49 9/20	52 9/22	53 9/24	54 9/25	55	80	81	82
Parker, D.	79 9/8	80 9/10	81 9/11	82 9/12	87 9/13	88 9/14	89 9/19	90
Rice, S.	91 9/17	92 9/19	93 9/20	101 9/22	102	103	104	105

Note: Since social studies objectives may not always be sequential, the numbers may not always be consecutive.

ning a data-recording system (Archer & Edgar, 1976):

Step 1: Write a measurable short-term objective.

Step 2: Determine the measurement dimension to be used (for example, accuracy, rate correct and incorrect, or frequency).

Step 3: Decide how often to assess the behavior (1-minute sample daily, 10-minute criterion test, weekly unit test, all out-of-seat behavior during math seatwork).

Step 4: Establish a consistent schedule for measuring the behavior.

Step 5: Select a recording format.

REFERENCES

Adams, R.S., & Biddle, B.J. (1970). *Realities of teaching.* New York: Holt, Rinehart, & Winston.

Allen, V.L. (Ed.). (1976). *Children as teachers: Theory and research on tutoring.* New York: Academic Press.

Archer, A., & Edgar, E. (1976). Teaching academic skills to mildly handicapped children. In S. Lowenbraun & J.Q. Affleck (Eds.), *Teaching mildly handicapped children in regular classes* (pp. 15–112). Columbus, OH: Merrill.

Carnine, D., & Silbert, J. (1979). *Direct instruction reading.* Columbus, OH: Merrill.

Cloward, R. (1967). Studies in tutoring. *Journal of Experimental Education, 36,* 14–25.

Cohen, S., & Plaskon, S. (1980). *Language arts for the mildly handicapped.* Columbus, OH: Merrill.

Dinkmeyer, D., & Carlson, J. (Eds.). (1973). *Consulting: Facilitating human potential and change processes.* Columbus, OH: Merrill.

Duncan, L.W., & Fitzgerald, P.W. (1969). Increasing the parent-child communication through counselor-parent conferences. *Personnel and Guidance Journal, 47,* 514–517.

Eaton, M.D., & Hansen, C.L. (1978). Classroom organization and management. In N.G. Haring, T.C. Lovitt, M.D. Eaton, & C.L. Hansen, *The fourth R: Research in the classroom* (pp. 191–217). Columbus, OH: Merrill.

Edlund, C.V. (1969). Rewards at home to promote desirable school behavior. *Teaching Exceptional Children, 1,* 121–127.

Gallagher, P.A. (1979). *Teaching students with behavior disorders: Techniques for classroom instruction.* Denver: Love.

Gearheart, B.R., Weishahn, M.W., & Gearheart, C.J. (1988). *The exceptional student in the regular classroom* (4th ed.). Columbus, OH: Merrill.

Gelfand, D.M., & Hartmann, D.P. (1984). *Child behavior analysis and therapy* (2nd ed.). New York: Pergamon Press.

Gordon, T. (1970). *Parent effectiveness training.* New York: Peter H. Wyden.

Grimes, L. (1981). Learned helplessness and attribution theory: Redefining children's learning problems. *Learning Disability Quarterly, 4,* 91–100.

Hawisher, M.F., & Calhoun, M.L. (1978). *The resource room: An educational asset for children with special needs.* Columbus, OH: Merrill.

Heward, W.L., Dardig, J.C., & Rossett, A. (1979). *Working with parents of handicapped children.* Columbus, OH: Merrill.

Hughes, C.A., Ruhl, K.L., & Peterson, S.K. (1988). Teaching self-management skills. *Teaching Exceptional Children, 20*(2), 70–72.

Kroth, R.L. (1975). *Communicating with parents of exceptional children: Improving parent-teacher relationships.* Denver: Love.

Kroth, R.L., & Simpson, R.L. (1977). *Parent conferences as a teaching strategy.* Denver: Love.

Kroth, R.L., Whelan, R.J., & Stables, J.M. (1970). Teacher application of behavioral principles in home and classroom environments. *Focus on Exceptional Children, 3,* 1–10.

Lovitt, T. (1973). Self-management projects with children with behavioral disabilities. *Journal of Learning Disabilities, 6,* 138–150.

Marsh, G.E., II, Gearheart, C.K., & Gearheart, B.R. (1978). *The learning disabled adolescent: Program alternatives in the secondary school.* St. Louis: Mosby.

Marsh, G.E., II, Price, B.J., & Smith, T.E.C. (1983). *Teaching mildly handicapped children: Methods and materials.* St. Louis: Mosby.

Polloway, E.A., Payne, J.S., Patton, J.R., & Payne, R.A. (1985). *Strategies for teaching retarded and special needs learners* (3rd ed.). Columbus, OH: Merrill.

Rooney, K.J., & Hallahan, D.P. (1985). Future directions for cognitive behavior modification research: The quest for cognitive change. *Remedial and Special Education, 6*(2), 46–51.

Schlesinger, H.S., & Meadow, K.P. (1976). Emotional support for parents. In D.L. Lillie & P.L. Trohanis (Eds.), *Teaching parents to teach: A guide for working with the special child* (pp. 35–47). New York: Walker.

Schloss, P.J., & Sedlak, R.A. (1986). *Instructional methods for students with learning and behavior problems*. Boston: Allyn & Bacon.

Scruggs, T.E., & Richter, L. (1985). Tutoring learning disabled students: A critical review. *Learning Disability Quarterly, 8*, 286–298.

Simonson, G. (1972). *Modification of reading comprehension scores using a home contract with parental control of reinforcers*. Unpublished master's thesis, University of Kansas, Lawrence.

Stephens, T.M. (1977). *Teaching skills to children with learning and behavior disorders*. Columbus, OH: Merrill.

Stevens, R., & Rosenshine, B. (1981). Advances in research on teaching. *Exceptional Education Quarterly, 2*(1), 1–9.

White, O.R., & Haring, N.G. (1980). *Exceptional teaching* (2nd ed.). Columbus, OH: Merrill.

Wiederholt, J.L., Hammill, D.D., & Brown, V. (1983). *The resource teacher: A guide to effective practices* (2nd ed.). Austin, TX: Pro-Ed.

Wood, J.W. (1984). *Adapting instruction for the mainstream: A sequential approach to teaching*. Columbus, OH: Merrill.

Worell, J., & Nelson, C.M. (1974). *Managing instructional problems: A case study workbook*. New York: McGraw-Hill.

Workman, E.A. (1982). *Teaching behavioral self-control to students*. Austin, TX: Pro-Ed.

Ysseldyke, J.E., & Algozzine, B. (1984). *Introduction to special education*. Boston: Houghton Mifflin.

CHAPTER 4

Choosing and Developing Materials

Choice of instructional materials greatly influences any educational program. As much as 75 to 99% of each student's instructional time is planned around classroom materials (Bartel & Hammill, 1986). In most classrooms a student spends much of the school day working alone with a material while the teacher instructs other students. Since materials affect the content, quality, and general efficiency of the instructional program, teachers should take care in choosing, developing, and changing materials.

CHOOSING MATERIALS

Archer and Edgar (1976) note that the teacher has three options in choosing materials: (a) adopt a commercial material and use it as designed, (b) adapt a commercial material to fit the instructional needs of a specific student, or (c) make materials. Given the great number of commercial materials, selection often is very difficult. Production of instructional materials for handicapped students has increased tremendously since the passage of Public Law 94–142 (Hickman & Anderson, 1979). Unfortunately, most of these new materials are not accompanied by field test data or research data supporting their effectiveness.

Most teachers are faced with the difficult, tedious task of selecting materials on a limited budget. A good plan in making this selection includes the following steps:

1. Identify the curriculum areas in which materials are needed.
2. Rank the areas from highest to lowest priority.
3. List affordable materials that are designed to teach in the selected skill area or areas.
4. Obtain the materials and evaluate them so that a decision can be made regarding a purchase. On request, many publishers will provide a sample of materials or a manual for the teacher to examine. Also, many school districts have resource or curriculum centers which contain materials for teachers to inspect. The following sources offer questionnaires or models for evaluating materials: Bleil (1975), V.A. Brown (1975), VanEtten and VanEtten (1978), Watson and VanEtten (1976), and Wiederholt and McNutt (1977).

The major factors involved in material evaluation are presented in Table 4.1.

TABLE 4.1
Factors in material evaluation.

General Information
1. Name and publisher
2. Major skill concentration
3. Cost and durability
4. Target age
5. Research and field test data

Characteristics Relating to Teaching
1. Sequence of skills
2. Organization of material, including considerations for individualization
3. Clarity of directions
4. Task levels
5. Stimulus-response modality combinations
6. Pace of content presentation

Characteristics Relating to Classroom Management
1. Evaluation and data recording
2. Space requirements
3. Time requirements
4. Extent of teacher involvement
5. Interest level
6. Reinforcement

General Information

The area of *general information* includes descriptive information that usually is included in advertisements. This information helps the teacher decide which materials to consider further and which to eliminate.

Name and publisher. This is basic identification material.

Major skill concentration. For what instructional area is the material designed? What are the major goals of the program? For example, if it is a reading program, does it stress word-attack skills, comprehension skills, or both?

Cost and durability. Are the costs of the materials within the teacher's budget? Once the material is purchased, do additional materials have to be purchased to maintain the program? Are the materials sturdy enough to last in the classroom? How does the cost compare to costs of other materials designed to teach similar skills? Can other materials that concentrate on similar instructional objectives be developed that are cheaper and easier to use?

Target age. The teacher needs to know if the material is appropriate for the age span of his students. Some materials may focus on the same skills but may differ in format and content to appeal to different ages. For example, the *Reading Mastery: DISTAR Reading Program* (Science Research Associates) focuses on word-attack skills for elementary students, and the *Corrective Reading Program* (SRA) concentrates on the same skill for adolescents.

Research and field test data. Many instructional materials do not provide such data. However, when the data are available and reported in a usable manner, the teacher can find answers to important questions: For what group is the material suitable? Was it effective in teaching stated goals or objectives? Was its use compared to other materials? Is the pro-

gram effective as a total program, or does it need to be supplemented? Is it a supplement to any other program? Are prerequisite skills for using the material outlined?

Characteristics Relating to Teaching

Sequence of skills. *Sequence* refers to the order in which the skills are presented. Some materials are sequenced so that the student must succeed at each level in order to advance to the next level. Other materials (for example, social studies, reading comprehension) do not directly link success at one level with success at the next level. The teacher can ask several questions regarding sequence: Is the sequence evident in the material, and is it logical? Does the sequence proceed from simple to complex? Are the objectives stated in behavioral terms? Are the steps in the sequence small?

Organization of material. *Organization* refers to how the content is arranged. Specifically, units, lessons, or chapters are examined. Is the material organized so that lessons or activities can be used separately in an interesting, meaningful way? Are there any suggestions for modifying the materials for individual students? Does the material provide for determining entry skill level and for monitoring student progress? Is the material coordinated with any other material?

Clarity of directions. Are the directions written in concise, simple language? Are the directions for seatwork activities easy to follow? Are the directions to the teacher easy to understand, and do they apply to group instruction, assessment, and follow-up activities? If written responses are required, is the format understandable? In a popular reading series, some adolescents were confused by the use of single worksheets that required four different responses: fill in blanks with words, draw a line to the correct answer, circle the correct answer, and fill in blanks with a letter (Gallagher, 1979).

Task levels. VanEtten and VanEtten (1978) discuss four levels of task difficulty. From simple to complex, the levels are as follows:

1. Imitation (reproduce stimuli).
2. Match to sample (for example, circle the letter *r* in the following: a c r b m t n).
3. Restructure stimulus and then respond (for example, classify objects into categories—concept formation).
4. Creative responses—constructing entirely novel responses (as in creative writing or essay writing).

For most students with learning problems, corrective instruction occurs at the first three levels.

Some important questions about task level include: Does the material present information at a concrete level (three-dimensional manipulatives), a semiconcrete level (two-dimensional materials—picture), or an abstract level (symbolic), or does it use combinations of these? Does the material primarily use (a) imitation tasks, (b) match-to-sample tasks, (c) concept formation tasks, or (d) creative response tasks? Is the readability level of the material appropriate for students? Sometimes the readability level set by the publisher and the reading level obtained by the teacher are quite different.

Stimulus-response modality combinations. For some students, the modality emphasized is important. Is one stimulus modality primarily used? If so, which one? Is one response modality primarily used? If so, which one? What stimulus-response combinations are primarily used (such as visual stimuli—motor response)? Can the responses be performed

by an individual student without disturbing others?

Pace of content presentation. How fast are new concepts presented? Are adequate practice activities included? Are previously learned skills reviewed periodically? Can students move at different speeds through the material?

Characteristics Relating to Classroom Management

Evaluation and data recording. Are evaluation forms and tests included for individual students? Is a composite evaluation form and assessment system included? Can the evaluations be administered by the student or a peer? Do the evaluations occur often enough to be useful in making instructional decisions? What type of evaluation tests are used: placement tests, mastery tests, chapter tests, unit tests, daily probes, or teacher-made criterion tests?

Space requirements. Can the material be readily stored in a learning center? Is the material packaged well for storage? Does the material distract other students when it is being used? Is the material easy to move from place to place?

Time requirements. How long does it take to set up the material for use? Can the material be used in flexible time limits? Is the time lapse between instructions and activities appropriate? Does it take long to clean up and return the material to its place?

Extent of teacher involvement. Does the material require continuous involvement during (a) initial instruction, (b) review, or (c) practice activities? Does the teacher have to intervene as the child moves from one activity to another? Are independent seatwork activities provided? If so, are they organized concisely enough for the student to manage the tasks independently? Does the material provide feedback to the student (self-correcting or answer keys), or does the teacher have to provide most of the feedback? How many students can use the material at the same time?

Interest level. Is the material packaged attractively, and is it of good quality? Do the illustrations enhance the material? Do the pages have more than one concept or task per page? Are illustrations appropriate for the students? Is the material free of sexism, and does it represent ethnic populations appropriately?

Reinforcement. Does the material include special reinforcement events such as take-home reinforcements, happy messages, symbols of achievement, and so forth? Is reinforcement spaced appropriately for maintaining a desired rate of responding? Does the material include suggestions for reinforcement schedules and reinforcement activities?

Depending on their own needs and teaching styles, teachers stress different aspects of materials. Table 4.2 highlights the major areas of interest in material evaluation.

Procedures that are helpful in choosing and evaluating materials include:

1. Compare materials with the same major skill concentration.

TABLE 4.2
Sample material evaluation.

I. General Information
  A. *Name:* Reading for Concepts
     Publisher: Webster Division, McGraw-Hill Book Company
  B. *Major Skill Concentration:* The materials are designed for young, reluctant readers to grow in reading experience while exploring a wide variety of areas within the sciences, the social sciences, and the humanities. The main purpose includes not only the general improvement of study reading, but also the improvement of those areas of comprehension in which the student is weak. Vocabulary work and questions dealing with critical thinking skills are constant throughout the series.
  C. *Cost:* Current prices are unavailable; however, the teacher could not design similar materials easily.
  D. *Target Age:* The materials seem most appropriate for students between the ages of 7 and 15 years.
  E. *Research Data:* Unavailable

II. Characteristics Relating to Teaching
  A. *Sequential Development of Tasks:* The comprehension skills in this series are carefully structured to develop a broad comprehension background. Not only facts are elicited, but also meanings of words in context, use of antecedents, substantiation from content, and meaning of the whole, inference, and implication. The series progresses from recall—one of the more simple thought processes—to synthesis—an abstract level of thinking.

(continued)

TABLE 4.2, *continued*

The specific skills developed include:

1. Recall of factual detail
2. Recognition of the meaning of a word in context
3. Competency with structural skills—finding the antecedent
4. Recognition of implications and inferences
5. Ability to make substantiation from content
6. Recognition of the meaning of the whole (the main idea)
7. Recognition of the meaning of antonyms
8. Recognition of and ability to interpret cause and effect
9. Recognition of the concept (the theme of the entire book)
10. Recognition of correct form and use of adjectives, predicates, and so on

B. *Organization:* The material is highly organized and suitable for use with an individual as well as with a group. Individual lessons may be used separately, and it is easy to monitor progress. The material is not specifically used in conjunction with another material.

C. *Clarity of Directions:* Specific directions are outlined at the front of each book for both the teacher and the student. The directions appear simple enough for most students to follow.

D. *Task or Grade Level:*

Book	Grades	Average Readability Level
A	2–4	1.9
B	2–4	2.5
C	3–5	3.2
D	3–5	3.9
E	5–7	4.6
F	5–8	5.2
G	6–9	5.8
H	7–10	6.4

Although the tasks primarily involve concept formation, tasks that require creative responding are also included.

E. *Modalities Emphasized:* Auditory, visual, verbal, motor

F. *Pace:* The pacing of the content appears to provide the student with adequate instruction at each level before new content is introduced. Practice exercises are included.

III. Characteristics Relating to Classroom Management

A. *Evaluation and Record Keeping:* There is one page of reading with one page of questions opposite it. These questions are designed to improve specific skills in reading. There are also charts at the end of each book in which the student may record scores of each skill tested. Thus evaluation is frequent and related to specific skills.

TABLE 4.2, *continued*

B. *Space Requirements:* The materials are nicely packaged and do not require much space. They can be readily stored in a learning center or moved from one area to another.

C. *Time Requirements:* The materials are easy to set up and may be used for short or long periods because there are many short lessons (such as one-page stories).

D. *Teacher Involvement:* The material is primarily teacher directed. But the student is also expected to participate actively in order to see reading in relation to thinking, both in written exercises and the group discussions. Teacher-directed discussion of the responses and determination of the correct answer is an important part of the instructional procedure. It would be possible, however, to provide the student with access to the answer keys found in the back of the teacher's guide. In this way, and by having the student record his own scores on his progress charts, the material becomes more self-instructional as the student comes to recognize his own strengths, weaknesses, and improvements.

E. *Interest Level:* The content is written to include a sequence of reading levels that maintain the interest of students whose chronological age has outstripped their reading skills. The variety and relevance of the range of content, as well as the fictional narratives based on worldwide folktales, make the material highly appealing to the imagination of students throughout a wide age span.

F. *Reinforcement:* Many students will find the progress charts and short stories reinforcing. No specific recommendations are offered for consequent events.

2. Work with colleagues and compare perceptions.
3. Ask experts in the content area to comment on the material.
4. Talk with teachers who use the material.
5. Obtain materials for trial usage whenever possible.

Teachers can obtain descriptions of available materials from commercial catalogs and material resource centers in local schools, state agencies, and universities.

A federally funded, computerized retrieval system is available to help educators examine instructional materials. Since 1975 the *National Instructional Materials Information System* has provided a retrieval service. The system clearinghouse is located in the National Center for Educational Media/Materials for the Handicapped in Columbus, Ohio. It features telecommunications hookups with all regional Area Learning Resource Centers and Specialized Offices. Requests for information can be directed to the Columbus center of the Area Learning Resource Center serving a particular geographic area. The system includes abstracts of more than 45,000 items appropriate for the needs of handicapped learners.

ARRANGING AND MANAGING MATERIALS

When the teacher has selected instructional materials, the next task is to organize and use them efficiently. Teacher-made materials must be developed to supplement the commercial materials; both kinds of material must be organized in the classroom so that students can easily locate, use, and return them. Many teachers use learning centers or work stations for organizing instructional materials in the curriculum areas (such as reading and math), while interest centers are used for organizing materials that focus primarily on reinforcement and enrichment activities.

Learning Centers

For many teachers, learning centers are a major way of managing the classroom and providing individualized instruction. Learning centers have materials of many levels and activities that accommodate a variety of individual needs. Learning centers offer follow-up to the teacher's instruction and provide an opportunity to practice specific skills; thus, these centers may be very helpful to students with learning problems. Also, since the centers are individualized, students with learning problems can work at their own pace and develop responsibility and self-discipline through accomplishment and success (Gearheart, Weishahn, & Gearheart, 1988). Learning centers may be gradually added to the classroom. Over time the teacher can refine and improve them by eliminating ineffective materials and introducing new materials.

In this book, a *learning center* is a designated area where instructional materials in one major curriculum area are located and organized. Intermediate and secondary teachers may divide learning centers according to sub-areas within a major curriculum area. For example, in math, learning centers may be in the areas of geometry, algebra, consumer math, and basic computation.

Some authorities refer to a learning center as a single instructional activity or material, such as a learning packet or instructional game. However, when the learning center is viewed as a designated *space* for organizing materials in a major curriculum area, the center includes all instructional games, packets, and activities that provide instruction in the particular skill area. Also, the type of learning center depends on the area of skill concentration. Learning centers could be developed in the following skill areas: phonics, consumer math, written expression, handwriting, reading comprehension, and career education.

For a learning center to be successful for the teacher and the student, it should include the following components.

Subject area and related skills. The teacher selects an area of instruction in which to develop a center. Once the area is identified, the skills and concepts that are to be taught, reinforced, or enriched must be determined. These skills and concepts aid the teacher in organizing the center activities.

Directions for use. Since students normally work independently in a center, the directions must be simple and clear. Because students perform different tasks at the center, individual student folders frequently are used to provide instructions to each student. In addition, the folder provides the teacher with a means of communicating with the student (feedback, assignments, reinforcement), and it gives the student a place to store work.

System of material organization. For the student to retrieve and return materials efficiently, the materials must be carefully organized. *Codes* involving colors, letters, or numbers often are used. Colors may symbolize a specific skill area (such as word attack). Letters may indicate a more specific skill (for example, *Dig* for digraphs). A number is used to pinpoint an activity under a specific skill—for example, *Dig #4* is an activity for *oa* words.

Work space. The work space in a center depends on the space available and how the teacher uses the center. Some teachers instruct students to do the work at their desks, whereas other teachers have students work at the center. In all centers, work space should be available for at least two students. Not only can two students use the center simultaneously (for getting instruction or working), but also space for peer teaching is provided. Teachers who have small groups working in the center need a work space for four to six students.

Format for recording progress. Once the student has completed her daily work in the center, a record of her progress needs to be made. This record may be in the form of (a) a teacher's checklist in a folder with student names and center activities, (b) a large wall chart for checking off activities in the various centers, (c) a checklist in the student's own folder, or (d) assessment devices including criterion tests, mastery tests, graphs, and charts.

All of the components mentioned are necessary for the successful management of a learning center. However, the materials within the center must meet certain criteria for the center to be successful. In addition to including single worksheets or single activities that the teacher instructs the student to do, the center should include *learning guides*. A learning guide is any instructional format (learning unit, learning packet, contract) that includes an objective and a list of materials and activities designed to help the student achieve the objective (Dell, 1972). Dell suggests the following items for developing more effective learning guides:

1. *An objective.* It is usually given a number to facilitate the record-keeping system.
2. *A pretest.* Sometimes the pretest consists of one item or example. More frequently it consists of several items.
3. *A list of materials and activities* that a student may use to help him achieve an objective. They could be divided into several lists based on different types of activities to be assigned according to student learning characteristics.
4. Several *self-checks* interspersed within the list of activities to help a student monitor his own progress.
5. *A posttest,* which may be a paper and pencil test or a list of behaviors to observe for evaluation. (pp. 61–62)

In developing a learning guide, Schulz and Turnbull (1983) suggest including corrective teaching procedures for students who do not pass the mastery test. These procedures might include additional practice activities, for example.

Selected materials for centers. The materials included in a learning center will vary as a function of available resources, teacher preferences, and space. Each curriculum chapter of this book includes a description of numerous activities, instructional games, self-correcting materials, commercial materials, and computer software programs that are suitable for inclusion in learning centers.

Developing and using centers. The following suggestions may be helpful in creating effective learning centers:

1. Make them neat and attractive.
2. Make them a pleasant and comfortable place to work.
3. Appeal to student interests and curiosities.
4. Give simple and clear directions.
5. Make the evaluation activity important. (For example, the teacher should follow up student work as much as possible.)

6. At first, organize the center according to specific instructional objectives and gradually add materials and activities as resources and time permit.
7. Include activities that involve more than one student.
8. Explain and demonstrate how to use the center, particularly when a new material or activity is added to the center.
9. Coordinate movement to and from the center with other activities (usually via scheduling).
10. Do not limit the use of center activities to the physical area designated as the learning center. In many instances, students may be directed to other areas in or outside of the classroom for completion of activities.
11. Make changes to maintain enthusiasm for a given center. Some centers will change every day, and others will change once a week. Still others may remain constant for a longer period.
12. When several centers are in use in one classroom, give careful attention to the balance of design in the centers. Some provide for active involvement, and others are for more quiet activity. Some require only short attention; others demand time for long-term development. Some offer experiences in reading and writing; others require extensive motor activity. Some are designed for individual work; others, for the cooperative efforts of pairs or small groups. Some are open-minded and experimental in nature; others are more structured in presentation of content. Some are completely pupil structured; others are totally prepared by the teacher.

Sample learning center. Stephens (1977) provides some excellent examples of centers that organize activities and materials according to instructional objectives. These centers may be expanded by increasing the number of objectives or the types of materials and activities. The following center is from Stephens (1977).

Math Center

Purpose: To discriminate cups, pints, quarts, gallons, ounces.

Activity A

Materials: Milk, juice cartons, filmstrips or tapes, water, recipes.

Directions: 1. Present containers, water, basin. List of things to discover by experimenting. *Ex:* How many cups can fit into the pint, etc.? Evaluation—Make a record sheet of "What I Discovered." Compare with correct answer sheet.
2. Make up—Collage, magazine pictures of containers and labels from home.

Purpose: To discriminate inches/feet.

Activity A

Directions: Have different items at center to measure—measure a book by width and length—measure top of desk width and length—measure height of board (or similar area).

Activity B

Directions: Measure area of specified part of room, i.e., blackboard, bulletin board in square feet, square inches.

Activity C

Directions: Given a number problem pertaining to measuring—student draws picture, makes equation and answer and self-checks equation and answer.

Activity D

Directions: Draw classroom according to scale, drawing in furniture in classroom.

Activity E

Directions: Design a floor plan according to scale—placing pieces of furniture specified.

Purpose: To write and say correct answers when given multiplication facts.

Activity A

Materials: 8″ × 8″ cardboard square, 18 snap-type clothespins, magic marker, pencil and paper.

Directions: Divide a cardboard square into 8 diagonals. Write a multiplication fact in each space. Write answers in snap clothespins. Give cardboard and clothespin to the student, together with a worksheet for writing problems. Student is to snap appropriate clothespin to each problem. Provide an answer key. After student checks answers, he is to write the problems.

Activity B

Materials: Game board, game card 3″ × 6″, party favor helmets.

Directions: Place cards face down in pile. Each child places a marker at opposite goal posts. Player draws a card and checks if he has the answer to any of the next three equations. Advances 10, 20, 30 yards depending on the position of match. Card is returned to bottom of pile. If not a match, no yardage gain is made. First to make touchdown wins game.

Activity C

Materials: Game board, cards with facts 3″ × 6″.

Directions: "The Road Runner" game. Place markers at start of race. Place cards face down in a pile. Player draws a card and moves his marker to the correct answer. Special citations and awards are offered during play. Winner finished game first.

Activity D

Materials: A grid, using cross number puzzles.

Directions: Fill in grid with multiplication facts, leaving blank spaces for the answer. Also have addition along with the multiplication problems. Provide answer sheets.

Activity E

Materials: 4 egg cartons, numbered 1 to 12; 2 bottle caps for each egg carton.

Directions: The child places the bottle caps inside the egg carton and closes the lid. He shakes the carton for a few seconds. Then he opens the lid. He looks at the 2 places the caps landed and these are his numbers to multiply. He then writes these two numbers on his paper and computes the fact.

For working in pairs—one child may shake and then ask the resulting combination of another—if he answers correctly the second child then shakes for the first. When a child misses, the partner can then shake another fact for him. (pp. 294–295)

Adapting Materials

Many of the materials available to the teacher need to be adapted for use with students who have learning problems. Complex directions, fast pace, reading level, boring content, confusing formats, lengthy assignments, and other factors may contribute to the problems of mildly handicapped learners. To individualize instruction, the teacher needs to adapt these materials to fit the individual needs of students. Teachers have successfully used the following adaptation techniques.

Use a tape recorder. Many problems with materials are related to reading disabilities. The tape recorder is often an excellent aid in overcoming this problem. Directions, stories, and specific lessons can be recorded on tape. The student can replay the tape to improve understanding of directions or concepts. Also, to improve reading skills, the student may read the printed words silently as they are presented on tape.

Clarify or simplify written directions. Some directions are written in paragraph form and contain many units of information. These can be overwhelming to some students. The teacher can help by underlining or highlighting the significant parts of the directions. Rewriting the directions is often a good idea. For example:

Original directions:

This exercise will show how well you can locate conjunctions. Read each sentence. Look for the conjunctions. When you locate a conjunction find it in the list of conjunctions under each sentence. Then circle the number of your answer in the answer column.

Directions rewritten and simplified:

Read each sentence and *circle all conjunctions.*

Present small amounts of work. Gallagher (1979) recommends tearing pages from workbooks and materials to present small assignments to students who are anxious about the amount of work to be done. This technique prevents students from examining an entire workbook, text, or material and becoming discouraged by the amount of work. Finally, the teacher may wish to reduce the amount of work when it appears redundant. This is easily accomplished by requesting the student to complete only odd-numbered problems or items with stars by them. Or the teacher could provide responses to several items and ask the student to complete the rest.

Block out extraneous stimuli. If a student is easily distracted by visual stimuli on a full worksheet or page, the student can cover sections of the page not being worked on with various sizes of oaktag. Also, line markers can be used to aid reading, and windows can be used to display individual math problems.

Repeat directions. For students who have difficulty following oral directions, it is often helpful to ask them to repeat the directions. The student can repeat the directions to a peer when the teacher is unavailable. Lewis and Doorlag (1983) provide the following suggestions for helping students understand directions:

1. Give both written and oral directions.
2. Give oral directions in simple language.
3. Give only a few (one or two) oral directions at a time.
4. Define or explain new terms.
5. Keep written directions at the reading level of the students.

Change response mode. For students who have difficulty with fine-motor responses (such as handwriting), the response mode may be changed to underlining, selecting from multiple choice, sorting, or marking. Provide extra space for writing answers on worksheets, and allow responding on individual chalkboards for students with fine-motor problems.

Highlight essential information. If an adolescent can read a regular textbook but has difficulty finding the essential information, the teacher may use a highlight pen on this information.

Locate place in consumable material. For consumable materials in which students progress sequentially, such as workbooks, the student may diagonally cut the lower-right-hand corner of the pages as they are completed. With all the completed pages cut, the student and teacher can readily locate the next page that needs to be corrected or completed.

Provide additional practice activities. Some materials do not provide enough practice activities for students with learning problems to acquire mastery on selected skills. Teachers must then supplement the material with practice activities. Recommended practice exercises include instructional games, peer teaching activities, self-correcting materials, computer software programs, and additional worksheets.

Provide a glossary in content areas. At the secondary level, the specific language of the content areas requires careful reading. Students might benefit from a glossary of content-related terms.

Cut and paste textbook content. The teacher can cut the main ideas or specific content from the text or material and paste the information on separate sheets of paper. Advantages of this procedure include the following:

1. The material can be arranged sequentially.
2. Headings can be inserted to facilitate organization and retention of ideas.
3. Small segments can be presented to allow for closure.

4. Distracting illustrations, colors, and nonessential information can be removed.
5. The material can be used without rewriting and can be photocopied for use with two or three students.

Additional information on adapting materials (i.e., advance organizers, guided practice, rewriting texts, and textbook usage) for older students is presented in Chapter 14.

Classroom Equipment

Instructional equipment can be used to individualize programs and meet the specific needs of students with learning problems. For example, audiovisual equipment can be used to instruct students with specific modality preferences, and manipulative devices often help in holding the attention of a distractible learner.

Computer and software programs. The computer can be used as a tool for classroom management as well as classroom instruction. Hofmeister (1984) suggests that the most appropriate use of the computer is as a supplementary tool to allow teachers more time to teach. Teachers can be partially released from time-consuming tasks through computer-assisted management, particularly in developing individualized educational programs (IEPs) and in computer-managed record keeping (N.P. Brown, 1982; Hayden, Vance, & Irvin, 1982). Computers can store sequences of instructional objectives and student performance information as well as track student progress, complete proper forms, and provide required record-keeping data (Hooper, 1981; Koehler, Ossler, & Raucher, 1981).

The computer offers some unique advantages in instructing students with learning problems (Kolich, 1985; Schiffman, Tobin, & Buchanan, 1982):

1. The computer can be made "user friendly" by programming it to use the student's

name when giving lessons. A computer also allows the student to make mistakes in a nonthreatening environment and is non-judgmental.

2. The computer gives the student its undivided attention and is not concerned about other students in the room.

3. The computer waits patiently while a student with learning problems slowly works out a problem.

4. Reinforcement of individual student responses is immediate. The computer can provide continuous and positive feedback and praise, thus giving the student a higher sense of self-esteem.

5. The use of animation, sound effects, and game-playing situations makes drill and practice exciting.

6. The computer is suited to the discovery method of learning. Programs that simulate real-life experiences allow the student to make decisions and see the consequences.

7. Strategies related to problem solving can be adapted for the computer. For example, adventure game programs, as well as learning to program, present exercises in problem solving.

Educational software differs in method or mode of delivery as well as in quality. Watkins and Webb (1981) delineate six modes of delivery:

1. Drill and practice: This common use of computers in education serves as a supplement to other forms of instruction. It is designed to integrate and consolidate previously learned material through practice on the computer.

2. Tutorial: In the tutorial program the role of teacher is assumed and material is presented in a programmed learning format. The student moves from one step to the next by answering questions and may be branched to remedial or review segments as well as to more advanced levels of the program.

3. Educational games: Games are designed to develop general problem-solving methods and strategies while maintaining interest and motivation.

4. Simulations: Simulations attempt to model the underlying characteristics of a real phenomenon so that its properties can be studied. They may incorporate many game features but are intended to model some reality.

5. Problem solving: The computer can be used to solve real-world problems. For example, students may write computer programs to test possible solutions to a variety of real problems.

6. Computer-managed instruction: The teacher may use the computer in diagnostic, prescriptive, and evaluative tasks. For example, student test scores might be utilized by the computer to generate tests, new prescriptions, and grades.

Research on computers and instruction is promising but inconclusive, and little information is available on how microcomputers can best be applied in the classroom (Stowitschek & Stowitschek, 1984; Torgesen & Young, 1983). However, through the use of appropriate software, the student with learning problems can be provided with individualized instruction and needed academic practice in a motivating manner. Hannaford and Taber (1982) note that for software programs to be effective they must be compatible with the teacher's instructional style, instructional goals, organization of the classroom, and curriculum, as well as with the learner's needs and characteristics. Other factors that should be considered are the adequacy of instructional design (e.g., presentation of material such as appropriate reading level, use of multisensory channels, ability to branch to different levels of instruction based on performance evaluation, and provision of reinforcement and feedback) and technical adequacy (e.g., extent to which the software can be controlled by the teacher or the student).

In addition to the many general uses of the computer, several investigators report on specific applications that are especially suited to students with learning problems. Grimes (1981) notes that for students who have difficulty maintaining on-task attention, computer programs can promote attention with color cueing, animation, underlining, and varying print sizes. For students who respond impulsively, the computer can provide cues or hints to inhibit impulsive responding. For those who take a lot of time to respond (i.e., reflective responders), computer programs can be tailored to allow extra response time.

Torgesen and Young (1983) report that the computer is especially useful for assisting instruction in word recognition. Specifically, they note that microcomputers offer varied word recognition practice activities that help maintain interest and attention. Moreover, they can monitor, measure, and influence response rates. For example, response rate is influenced by such motivational tactics as games, immediate feedback, and progress reports. LOGO, a computer language that provides a context for "learning by doing," has been found effective in teaching problem-solving skills to students with learning problems (Chiang, Thorpe, & Lubke, 1984; Papert, 1979).

Kolich (1985) reports that the future key to successful computer-assisted instructional application depends on a closer working relationship between educators and software manufacturers. Various software programs in arithmetic, reading, spelling, and written expression are presented in their respective chapters; and programs pertaining to learning strategies, science, social studies, functional living skills, and career-related instruction are included in Chapter 14. In addition, Appendix C lists addresses of producers and distributors of educational software.

Tape recorder. Cassette recorders have several advantages. They are simple to operate, the recorder and tapes are small and easy to store, and tapes are relatively inexpensive. Headphones enable individual students to operate a recorder without distracting classmates. Instructional applications of the tape recorder include the following:

1. A tape can be made of reading material (for example, basal reader, stories, and magazines). The student can read along with the tape to practice reading. Thus, the tape can provide feedback, increase speed, and help the student identify and practice difficult words.
2. In a language experience activity, the student can use the recorder to make a tape of a story. Later, the student can write out the story from the tape with a peer, aide, or teacher.
3. Oral directions may be put on tape to accompany seatwork activities. The student who has difficulty with oral directions can play the tape until she understands the directions.
4. Spelling tapes are useful for practice and taking tests. One commonly used format includes (a) the spelling word; (b) the word used in a sentence; and (c) a pause, a beep, and the word spelled correctly. The pause can be eliminated by having the student stop the recorder while she writes the word and then start it to check the spelling.
5. Stories, facts, or a report of an event may be recorded. News programs, commercials, telephone messages, weather re-

ports, and teacher-made content may be used. The student listens and then responds to comprehension questions. For example, a weather report is taped, and the student is required to answer such questions as these: High temperature? Low temperature? Any rain? Forecast for tomorrow? What season is it?

6. One-minute samples of instrumental music may be taped for students to use in conducting timings. These tapes usually begin with the word "start" and end with the word "stop." The teacher may prefer to use only the words and omit the music. In place of a kitchen timer, tapes of different time spans can be used to mark the end of any timed activity.

7. Correction tapes can be used to provide feedback to students who have completed math seatwork.

8. Polloway, Payne, Patton, and Payne (1985) suggest using a tape recorder for self-evaluation in telephone etiquette and for instruction in proper ways to introduce friends and relatives.

9. Music may be recorded on tapes for students to listen to when they have completed an assignment. Also, pleasant background music may be played while students are engaged in activities such as cleaning up, settling down after recess, free-choice, seatwork, or art.

10. At the secondary level, class lectures and discussions may be taped. These tapes can be used to help the students review or understand the material.

Overhead projector. The overhead projector is readily available to classroom teachers and can be useful in the individualized classroom. The overhead projector is used to display an image on a screen from a transparency. Transparencies may be teacher-made or purchased. They allow the user to write on, color in, and point at specific details while discussing them. Overhead projectors can be used to project images on light-colored surfaces without darkening the room. Since the overhead projector greatly accents the visual image, it is helpful with students who are easily distracted by extraneous visual stimuli. The teacher can block out all stimuli that do not relate to the item being studied or completed.

Some guidelines for effective use of transparencies on the overhead projector are as follows:

1. Prepare transparencies ahead of time.
2. Type or write in clear, bold lines on plain paper. Use a pencil or marker containing a carbon base, or put the original through a copy machine. Then make the transparency quickly by putting the original through a Thermofax copier or transparency maker.
3. Make letters at least ¼" high. Orator or bulletin type from a primary typewriter projects adequately.
4. Simplify and be concise. Use a maximum of six or seven lines of copy and six or seven words per line.
5. Use simple graphic drawing. Have diagrams ready ahead of time rather than using teaching time to put complicated illustrations on the transparency.
6. Emphasize key points by capitalizing, underlining, circling, and boxing.
7. Use color for clarity, emphasis, and variety. The acetate background itself may be a color instead of clear. Also, colored pieces of acetate may be attached in key spots or colored markers may be used on the acetate.
8. Turn the projector off and on to shift students' attention.
9. Use the revelation technique (covering the visual with a sheet of paper and revealing items one at a time) to avoid distractions

and keep the class interested. Students who are taking notes would probably appreciate being shown the complete visual first as an overview before the masks are applied.

10. Use the techniques of overlays and masking (revelation) to break down a whole into its component parts.

11. Locate the screen so that everyone in the room can see it clearly. Position it as high as possible, and tilt it forward to project an appropriate image.

12. When writing while talking, check the screen periodically to be sure the students are seeing what you want them to see. Write clearly.

13. Keep extra markers or pencils on hand in case of breakage or loss during presentation.

14. Make color lifts of artwork on magazine paper.

15. Use transparencies in place of the chalkboard to focus attention, thereby saving time and space, since the lesson may be used again. Also, class control and eye contact can be maintained better than at the chalkboard.

Uses of the overhead projector include the following:

1. Class schedules and homework assignments may be put on the overhead to save chalkboard space for student and teacher use throughout the day. If the student needs to check on the schedule or finish copying her homework assignment, she can turn on the overhead projector and complete the task.

2. The overhead projector can be used for administering many kinds of tests: computation facts, word problems, cloze spelling tests, fill-in-the-blank items, multiple-choice items.

3. The overhead projector can be used to display the category being discussed. Words, phrases, sentences, poems, drawings, and pictures are useful stimuli in facilitating relevant interactions.

4. The overhead projector is useful for playing reading comprehension and spelling games. The teacher gradually exposes the letters of a word, the definition of a word, a sentence, or a paragraph. The students attempt to respond correctly with the fewest cues possible. With the letters of a word, the students attempt to finish spelling the word; with the definition, they identify the word that matches the definition. In the sentence task, students try to complete the sentence correctly. The paragraph task involves providing a title for the paragraph. It often helps to divide the students into teams and allow each group to give a response as another cue is presented.

5. Spinners may be made on a transparency, placed on an overhead, and used for a variety of instructional activities and games. The teacher or student spins it, and it points to letters, numbers, words, or math facts. The spinner can be used to (a) determine the number of points a specific task item is worth, (b) select a math problem (by pointing to it), (c) select one word at a time until the student can make a sentence, and (d) select a letter for the student to sound out or add to previous letters to spell a word. These games are suitable for the student-teacher pair, two or more students, or a large group divided into teams.

6. The overhead projector may be used in developing experience stories with small groups of students. In this activity, the group contributes to the telling of a story or a description of an event while the teacher writes it on the transparency.

7. The overhead projector is an excellent

means for students to display stories developed in language experience activities. The stories may be read to the class or copied by selected students. In addition, the class may help the student title the story.

8. Polloway et al. (1985) point out that it is often easier to lecture by using an overhead projector than by using a chalkboard. It is easier to point to material on an overhead than to underline material on a chalkboard. Also, it is easier to uncover additional material on the overhead than to write on the chalkboard. With the overhead the teacher does not have to write and talk simultaneously or have students wait while the teacher writes.

9. Many students enjoy writing on a transparency and seeing it presented on a screen. This activity is especially useful in practicing handwriting.

10. The overhead projector can be used to project figures, pictures, letters, or numbers on a blank chalkboard. The student can trace over the projected images to practice handwriting or develop fine-motor skills, or this activity may be used as reinforcement.

Language Master. The Language Master is a very useful instructional tool. It is an adaptation of a tape recorder which plays and records cards that have tape attached along the bottom. Most cards are 4" × 14", but other sizes are available. When the stimulus card is inserted in the machine, a recorded voice is heard as the card moves from left to right. Blank cards are available and may be recorded on as they move through the machine. The audiotape, like a tape recorder, can be erased and cleared. Also, the Language Master enables both the student and the teacher to record on the same tape without erasing each other's response. For example, a teacher may record a word which is played when the student pushes the instructor button and inserts the card. Once the card is heard the student can set the machine for recording, push a student button, and record the word. Then the student can set the machine for play and listen to both words by inserting the card once with the instructor button down and once with the student button down. Visual cues also can be displayed on the cards. By writing the visual cue on a small card and attaching it to the stimulus card with a paper clip, it is easy to use the stimulus cards for a variety of activities without permanently attaching a visual stimulus. Laminating or putting acetate on the top portion of the card makes it possible to use felt pens and grease pencils to provide removable visual stimuli. (If lamination is used, the teacher should be careful to avoid putting the taped portion of the card in the lamination machine.)

Many different commercial Language Master programs are available in speech therapy, language arts, math, and science. Blank cards are available for developing one's own programs and may be ordered in several sizes: regular, extra long, or extra tall. A brochure is available from Audio-Visual Products Division, 7100 McCormick Road, Chicago, IL 60645.

The Language Master may be used in the classroom in the following ways:

1. Spelling words may be presented on the Language Master. Only the audio portion is used to present each word, and the correct spelling of the word is written on the back of the card. The student inserts the card, hears the word, writes the word on a worksheet, and then turns the card over to check her answer.

2. Sounds of phonemes may be recorded on the cards, with each corresponding grapheme written on the back. The student lis-

tens to the phoneme, writes the corresponding grapheme on a worksheet, and then turns the card over to check her response.

3. The visual portion (V) of the card may be used to present a task or problem, and the audio portion (A) can provide the correct response. Sample activities for this format include the following:

   Unravel scrambled letters: V = tac; A = "cat"

   Solve math problem: V = 6 × 7; A = "forty-two"

   Answer social studies question: V = What is the capital of Florida? A = "Tallahassee"

4. With the tall-sized cards, the visual task–auditory answer format can be used to include the following types of activities:

   Reading comprehension: V = reading passage with question; A = answer to question

   Math word problems: V = the word problem; A = the answer

   Categorize words: V = list of related words (such as food words); A = common category

   Correct grammar: V = paragraph with several incorrect verb tenses; A = incorrect verbs with corresponding corrections

   Word meaning: V = definition of a word; A = correct word

5. Only a portion of the card will play if a notch is cut in it—for example,

With the auditory and visual stimuli placed on the right side of the notch, a task can be presented and the card will stop. Then the student can respond to the task and push the card to the right until the machine finishes playing the remainder of the card with the correct answer on it.

6. The instructor portion of the tape can be used to record feedback and praise.

Small-item materials. Some useful, inexpensive materials that are very handy in running a classroom include the following:

1. *Miniature chalkboard.* One side of a piece of three-ply cardboard, approximately 15″ × 18″, can be painted with several coats of chalkboard paint (available at school supply and paint stores). Also, the smooth side of a Masonite board can be painted and the rough side can be used as a flannelboard (Gallagher, 1979). These boards can be made for individual students to use at their desks or in a learning center.

2. *Flannelboard.* A heavy piece of cardboard can be covered with flannel. Also, the rougher side of a piece of Masonite can be used for a flannelboard. Figures for the board can be made from foam-backed material or felt. Flannelboards are available commercially in various sizes, and some have easel backs. Uses include presenting vocabulary or spelling words, listing important rules, displaying parts of an outline, displaying graphs and fractions, presenting pictures representing difficult concepts, and displaying map outlines.

3. *Game materials.* Materials commonly used with game boards can be collected and stored in an accessible location. Golf tees, people from Playskool, and items from old games are good markers; dice and spinners are good number indicators. Manila folders are excellent for drawing start-to-finish game-board formats and are easy to store.

4. *Construction materials.* Various materials should be collected, such as pictures (for

example, of specific sounds, story starters, and so on); school supply or cigar boxes; oatmeal boxes; egg cartons; shoe boxes; water-base marking pens; plastic term-paper holders; tobacco or coffee cans; tongue depressors; library card holders; poster board; oaktag paper; wooden cubes; pizza discs; envelopes; and clothespins. These and other materials are useful for constructing instructional materials. The instructional games and self-correcting materials presented later in this chapter use many of these items. Also, the instructional activities discussed throughout the book require many of these materials.

5. *Typewriter.* A manual typewriter can stimulate learning and can be fun to use (for example, in practicing spelling and typing stories). Also, the typewriter is helpful for students with handwriting problems.

6. *Durable coverings.* Materials used frequently can be covered with a transparent, adhesive material or with plastic spray. The student can mark on the material and wipe off the markings with a damp cloth. Also, a consumable workbook can be protected for repeated use. Trim two pieces of acetate to the size of the workbook, lay the acetate on the inside of each cover, and tape it to the cover along the outer edge. To do the work on a page, the student simply flips the acetate over the page and uses a crayon or grease pencil. This can be erased, leaving the workbook blank so that it can be used by the next student. Another method is to cut cardboard into 8″ × 11″ pieces and tape acetate to it, either along the left side only or along both the sides and the bottom. A pocket can be formed to hold worksheets.

7. *Magnetic board.* The magnetic board can be used for students to respond on, to present tasks, or to display work. Work or tasks are displayed easily by taping a paper clip to the back of the stimulus card or worksheet. The paper clip clings to the magnetic board and holds up the material.

8. *Tracing screen.* A wire screen with a cardboard edge makes an excellent tracing screen. When paper is placed over the screen and written on with a crayon, the letters become raised and are good for tracing.

9. *Mirror.* A door-mounted or full-length mirror is excellent for teaching grooming and self-concept-related activities. It provides direct feedback to a student about her appearance.

DEVELOPING MATERIALS

In teaching students with learning problems, it is often helpful—and sometimes necessary—to supplement or replace commercial materials with teacher-made materials. These materials can provide additional practice, highlight relevant stimuli, provide feedback on progress, and increase motivation. Teacher-made materials include worksheets, games, flash cards, drill sheets, self-correcting activities, and probe sheets. Students spend much classroom time working with instructional materials on their own; thus, it is important that the materials used not lead to frustration, failure, and the practicing of errors.

To some degree a material serves as a teacher. The more teacher functions it can serve, the more useful the material. Inexpensive materials can perform these teaching functions: (a) providing instructions, (b) presenting a stimulus or task, and (c) providing feedback about correctness of student responses (Mercer & Mercer, 1978).

Self-Correcting Materials

Self-correcting materials provide the student with immediate feedback without the teacher being present. Self-correcting materials are especially useful with students with learning problems, who often have a history of academic failure. It is important to reduce their failure experiences, particularly those that take place in public. When the student makes a mistake with a self-correcting material, it is a private event—it happens without anyone else knowing it. Only the student sees the error, and she can correct it immediately. Furthermore, if immediate feedback is not provided, the student will practice mistakes until the teacher corrects her at a later time. With self-correcting materials, the student is corrected immediately and practices only the correct response.

Self-correcting materials help some students maintain attention to academic tasks. The student may approach each response with a game-playing attitude: "I bet I get this one right!" However, when a self-correcting material is used, some cheating should be expected at first. Many students initially enjoy beating the system, but eventually it becomes more fun to select an answer and see if it is correct. If cheating persists, a checkup test or posttest on the content featured may be administered. It does not take long for the student to realize that cheating on the material will not help her on the checkup test.

The importance of immediate feedback is well documented as a valid teaching procedure. Self-correcting materials provide the student with immediate feedback, yet the teacher is free to work with other students. In a study reported by Mercer, Mercer, and Bott (1984), students who used self-correcting materials and traditional worksheets learned considerably more with the self-correcting materials.

Self-correcting materials should be simple in design so that a demonstration enables students to operate them. The best use of these materials may be to practice or drill on subject matter that the teacher already has introduced.

Finally, do not require students to use the same self-correcting material for a long time. Vary the content periodically, exchange materials with another teacher, give students a choice of which material they wish to use, have students make their own content for the self-correcting device, or put away selected materials for a while. By changing self-correcting material from time to time, a teacher can maintain student interest and involvement.

The next section provides examples of feedback devices that can be used to make self-correcting materials. The self-correcting materials are presented in two categories: those with construction guidelines and those that are very simple to make. The same device or material can often be used with different content. Throughout this book self-correcting materials are presented in the different content areas.

Self-Correcting Materials with Construction Guidelines

Flap. A flap may be made of any flexible material such as cloth, vinyl wallpaper, construction paper, or thin cardboard. When using the learning material, the student can bend the flap up or to the side to reveal the answer to the question or problem. Figure 4.1 illustrates an Answer Box with a flap to provide feedback.

Selected instructional pinpoints:

1. See math fact or problem—say answer.
2. See math fact or problem—write answer.
3. See contraction words—write contraction.
4. See percentage problem—write answer.

Feedback response:

A flap is placed over the mouth. When the flap is raised, the answer is revealed. Vinyl wallpaper is flexible and serves as a good flap.

Materials:

1. A cardboard box (for example, cigar or school supply box)

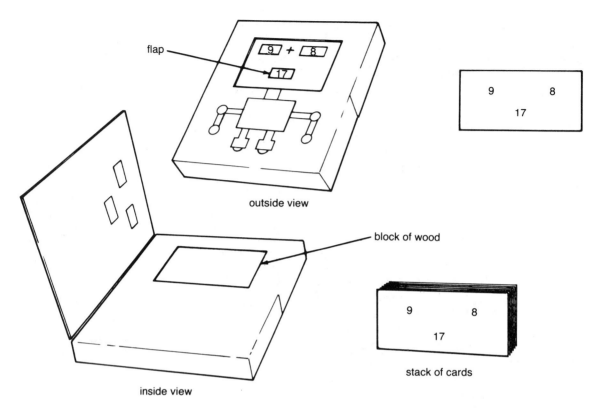

FIGURE 4.1
Answer Box.

2. 3″ × 5″ index cards
3. Contact paper or lamination
4. A small wooden block, approximately 3″ × 3½″

 Construction:

1. Cut out three squares in the lid of the box so they form two eyes and a mouth.
2. Cut a section out of the right side of the box so the index cards can be fed into the box from the side.
3. Paint the box inside and out.
4. Laminate a picture of a face on the box and place the eyes and the mouth over the squares.
5. Place a flexible flap over the mouth.
6. Prepare index cards with problems and answers so that the problem appears in the "eyes" and so that the flap over the mouth can be lifted to re-

veal the answer. For math problems, a grease (overhead projector) pencil can be used to write the math operation (+, −, ×, ÷) in the space between the "eyes."

Directions:

The student inserts a stack of selected cards into the Answer Box. Then the student responds (orally or by writing) to the problem presented in the two windows. He lifts the flap over the mouth to reveal the answer and check his response.

Modifications:

Vary the card formats so that a variety of math problems and numerous reading tasks are available. Some possible card formats include the following:

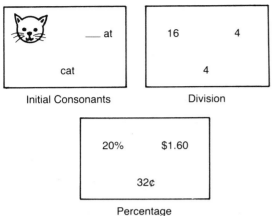

Initial Consonants   Division

Percentage

Windows. Small windows may be cut in materials to provide feedback. The correct answer may be in the window, or, when two or more windows are used, the items in the windows can match to show a correct response. Figure 4.2, Spinning Wheels, illustrates the use of windows.

Selected instructional pinpoints:

Any pinpoint can be selected in which a matched pair can be devised (problems on one wheel and the correct answers on another wheel). For example:

1. See math problem—select answer.
2. See picture—select word.
3. See picture—select initial sound.

Feedback response:

Windows provide feedback. When a correct match is obtained in the front windows, the objects, symbols, or numbers match in the back windows. Thus, to check an answer the student looks at the back windows.

Materials:

1. Poster board
2. Brass fasteners
3. Small pictures or symbols

Construction:

1. Cut two horizontal pieces of poster board with matching dimensions.
2. Cut two windows on the same horizontal line in each piece. The windows should line up with each other when the pieces are placed together (back to back).
3. Decorate and laminate each piece, and make the center holes for the fasteners.
4. Cut circles with dimensions that enable the outer 1″ ridge to pass through the windows when the center of the wheel is lined up with the poster board hole.
5. Write, draw, or paste problems in one wheel and put answers on a corresponding wheel. Write, draw, or glue symbols, objects, or numbers on the back of each wheel set.

Directions:

The student selects a wheel set that presents the task that the teacher wants her to work on. She places the wheels between the two rectangular pieces, lines up the holes, and inserts the brass fasteners. The student then rotates the task wheel until a problem is presented in the window. Next the student rotates the other wheel and selects one of the answers that passes through the window. Once an answer is selected, the student flips the material over and checks to see if her answer is correct. A correct answer yields matching objects in the two windows on the back.

Modifications:

Teachers can make many wheel sets and code them according to skill area. Wheels that are to be used together (a wheel set) should have matching codes on them. The tasks that can be placed on the wheels are almost limitless. The size of the material can be varied to accommodate different sized windows.

Stylus. Feedback may be provided by using a stylus with certain types of stimulus cards. The Poke Box (p. 135) illustrates the use of the stylus.

FIGURE 4.2
Spinning wheels.

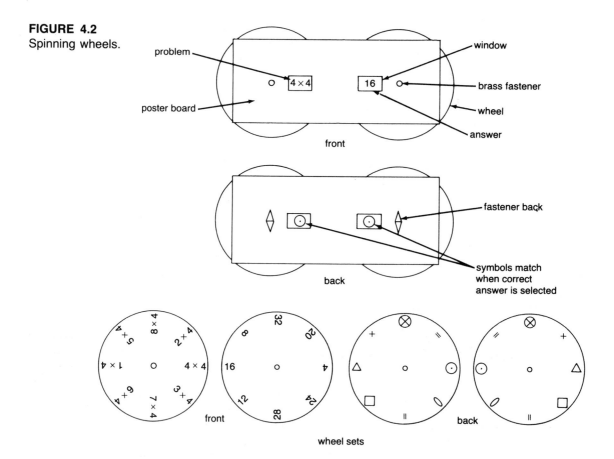

wheel sets

Selected instructional pinpoints:

1. See math problem–choose answer.
2. See math problem–write answer.
3. See sentence–choose missing word.
4. See paragraph–choose title.
5. Any instructional pinpoint that features a multiple-choice answer format may be used with the Poke Box.

Feedback response:

The student inserts a stylus in one of the holes below the answers and pulls the card to see if it comes out of the box. If the right hole is selected, the card is easily removed from the box (the area below the correct answer is cut and offers no resistance to the stylus).

Materials:

1. A cardboard or wooden box big enough to hold 3″ × 5″ or 5″ × 8″ index cards
2. A large rubber band
3. A thin stick or poker
4. Index cards

Construction:

1. Cut the front end of the box so most of the index card is visible, but leave a horizontal strip at the bottom of the box about 1″ high.
2. Using a hole punch or drill, make three evenly spaced holes across the front of the box about ½″ from the bottom.
3. At each end of the front of the box, drill or punch a hole that extends beyond the dimensions of

Poke Box

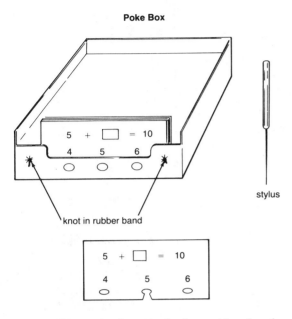

5 + □ = 10
4   5   6

knot in rubber band

stylus

5 + □ = 10
4   5   6

the index cards. Insert a broken rubber band from the inside of the box on both sides, and tie the ends in knots on the outside of the box. The rubber band holds the cards and pushes them to the front of the box.

4. Paint the box inside and out.
5. Make holes in the index cards so they line up with the holes in the box.
6. Cut out one answer slot on each card.
7. Attach the stylus to the box.
8. Prepare index cards with problems or questions on top and possible answers beneath. Line up the answers with the appropriate holes.
9. To prevent a student from tearing the card by pulling too hard on a wrong choice, strengthen the holes with gummed reinforcers.

Directions:

The student says, writes, or chooses his answers. Then he pokes the stylus in the hole representing his answer. If the choice is correct, the problem card can be pulled up and out of the box and the next problem card is presented.

Modifications:

The size of the box may vary so that large cards can be used. Some Poke Boxes feature 8″ × 11½″

cardboard cards. The large space provides room for short stories and multiple-choice comprehension questions. The teacher may put the problem or story on a separate worksheet and put the answer selections on the cards.

Light. A light may come on to provide feedback for correct responses. The Electric Learning Board shown in Figure 4.3 is used by many teachers, and it illustrates the use of this feedback device.

Selected instructional pinpoints:

1. See picture—select word.
2. See math fact—select answer.
3. See paragraph—select fact.
4. See word—select plural.

Feedback response:

The student inserts the stylus in one of the holes to indicate her response. The light turns on to indicate a correct response.

Materials:

1. Cigar box (wooden or cardboard)
2. #12 bare copper wire (single-strand)
3. #16 insulated wire (stranded)
4. Light bulb and socket
5. Battery
6. Plastic tape
7. ¼″ quarter-round wooden sticks
8. Epoxy glue
9. 5″ × 8″ index cards (unlined)
10. Hole puncher

Construction:

1. Drill holes in the top of the box to cover the area of a 5″ × 8″ index card. Six holes across and seven rows down are enough.
2. On the inside top of the box, place copper wire so that it passes under two holes on each row. Glue the wire. Connect this wire to one terminal of the battery. These are the correct answer holes which will cause the light to turn on.

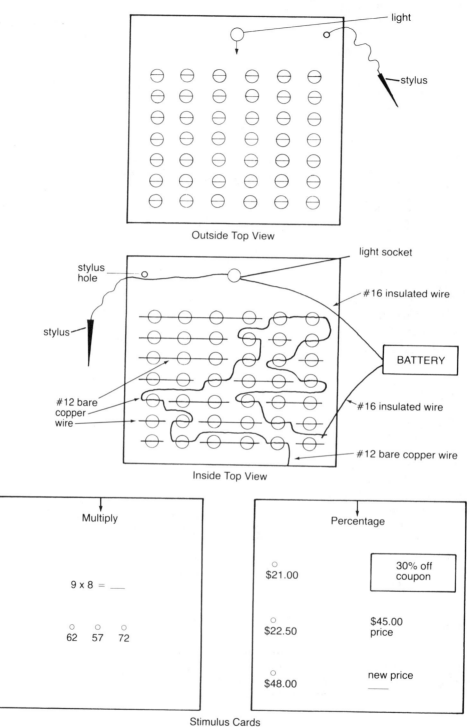

Outside Top View

Inside Top View

Stimulus Cards

FIGURE 4.3
Electric Learning Board.

3. Glue copper wires over the other holes. Be sure that none of the copper wires touches the live wire, so that the correct-answer holes cannot be figured out. All the holes have copper wire passing under them, but only underneath *two* holes per row is copper wire that is hooked up to the battery.

4. Connect the second terminal of the battery to one terminal of the light socket.

5. Drill a hole in the top of the box to the right of the light socket. Make a stylus using #16 insulated wire with #12 bare copper wire at the point. Wire the second terminal of the light socket to the stylus.

6. On the outside top of the box, make a border for the 5″ × 8″ index cards so that they can be fitted over the holes properly. This may be done by gluing the ¼″ quarter-round sticks around the three sides of a 5″ × 8″ area. The bottom side is left open to slide the card into the space. Make an arrow on the box to indicate where the top center of the stimulus card should be when properly inserted on the Learning Board.

7. Make a key card with the correct-answer holes marked so that other cards may be made easily by fitting them over the key card.

8. Make stimulus cards that present a task and a multiple-choice answer format using holes in the cards. Place the hole for the correct response so that when the stylus is placed in it the light turns on.

Directions:

The student places a stimulus card on the Learning Board and inserts the stylus in the hole for her answer. If the choice is correct, the light turns on.

Simple Self-Correcting Materials

Puzzle. In this type of feedback, pieces of material fit together to indicate a match or correct choice. The top or side section of each puzzle shows an object or problem, and the bottom section or other side provides the name of the object or the answer to the problem. The sections will interlock only if they belong together.

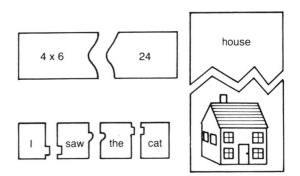

Matching cards. Sets of cards are prepared with the problem or question on one card and the answer on another card. The back of the set of cards contains a match of some sort or a picture completion. When the student selects an answer to a problem, she turns over the cards. If the appropriate answer is chosen, the objects, numbers, colors, or pictures on the back will either match or fit together to complete a picture.

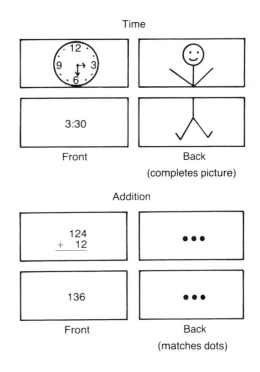

Answer on back. A problem is presented on one side of a stimulus card, and the answer is placed on the other side.

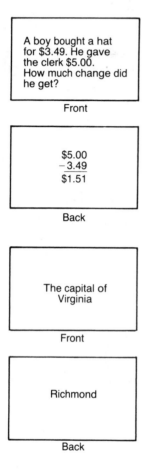

Tab. A tab is pulled from a pocket in the learning material to reveal an answer or answers.

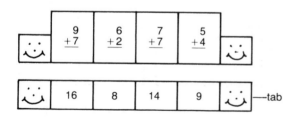

Pocket. Pockets may be made easily of envelopes stapled to the back of the learning material. Pockets usually hold some type of answer key. In addition, pockets may be coded to provide feedback. For example, library card pockets may be used for sorting stimulus cards. A code is on the back of the stimulus card and the library pocket. If a card is placed in the correct pocket, the codes match. Many instructional pinpoints can be taught with this format. For example, if the stimulus cards show words from the categories of noun, pronoun, verb, and adjective, there would be a pocket corresponding with each category.

Holes. Problems are written on one side of a card or sheet, and a hole is punched beside or underneath each item. The answer to each problem is written on the back of the card next to or under the hole. (See the figure below.) The student sees the problem, writes or says the answer, puts a pipe cleaner or pencil in the hole, and turns the card over to check her response. This format is good for teaching opposites, plurals, synonyms, word problems, and

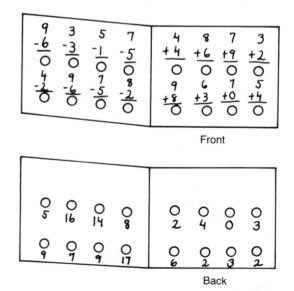

so on. Manila folders may be used to make this material.

Clips. Clips such as clothespins or paper clips may be used to provide feedback. For example, a cardboard pizza wheel can be divided into segments with a task stimulus presented in each segment. Responses are made by clipping clothespins to the edge of the segments. To check answers the board is turned over to see if the code on the pizza board matches the code on the clothespin.

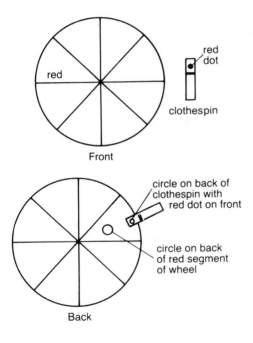

Front

Back

Strips in a folder. Strips are cut in one side of a manila folder and then the folder is laminated. Worksheets containing problems and answers are inserted into the folder so that only the problem is presented. The student uses a grease pencil or a felt-tip pen to write her responses under each problem. Then the worksheet is pulled upward, and the answers appear in the strip.

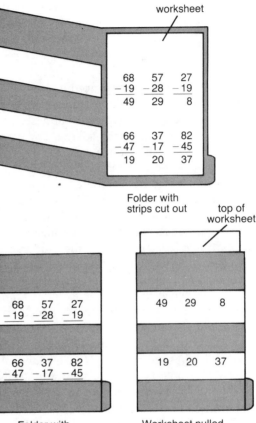

Folder with strips cut out

Folder with strips closed

Worksheet pulled up to reveal answers

Instructional Games

Students with learning problems frequently need a lot of drill and practice in academic skills. Because drill can be tedious, creative teaching must motivate students. Positive reinforcement, charting, self-correction, and high-interest formats frequently are used to enrich drill. Instructional games are a popular way of maintaining interest during practice.

First, the purpose of the game needs to be examined. The game must include the intended outcome, and the student must have the skills necessary to play the game. Usually the game is used to practice or reinforce a skill that has already been taught. Of course, the game must not be mere busy work. By monitoring student progress, the teacher can evaluate the effects of an instructional game on a specific skill.

Next, the basic game procedures must be selected. Familiar game materials such as checkers, cards, dice, spinners, and start-to-finish boards should be considered. The game should involve both chance and skill.

The games should be individualized for student needs. If a game has many uses, it saves the gamemaker's time and helps the student learn new skills in a familiar format. Games may be made self-correcting, or an answer key can be provided. This allows the students to play the game without direct teacher supervision. Surprise factors boost interest in the game—*go to jail, skip a space, fix a flat*. Moreover, they add to the element of chance.

MacWilliam (1978) recommends making a rough draft of the game and testing it before making the finished product. Manila folders are good game boards because they are sturdy, are a handy size, have tabs for easy reference, and are easy to store in a file cabinet. Rules are readily available if written on the back of each folder. Lamination makes the game board more durable and attractive.

The teacher can purchase kits with blank laminated boards which have established routes for markers to travel, unmarked spinners, and blank playing cards. Several publishers market these materials.

Figures 4.4 and 4.5 show teacher-made instructional games. In addition, games involving cards, dominoes, chips, dice, and so on are presented in the curriculum area chapters.

Simple Game Board

Instructional objective:

Any instructional task that can be presented on a card and performed in a few seconds is suitable.

Feedback device:

Answer key and peer correction provide feedback.

Materials:

1. Poster board
2. Index cards
3. Golf tees
4. Dice
5. Tasks for the cards

FIGURE 4.4
Simple game-board format.

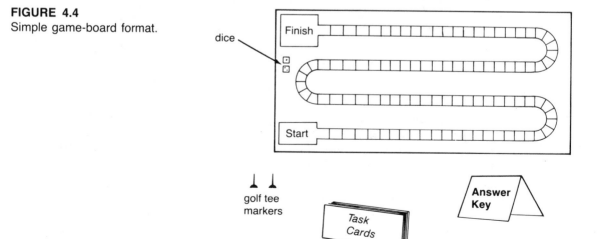

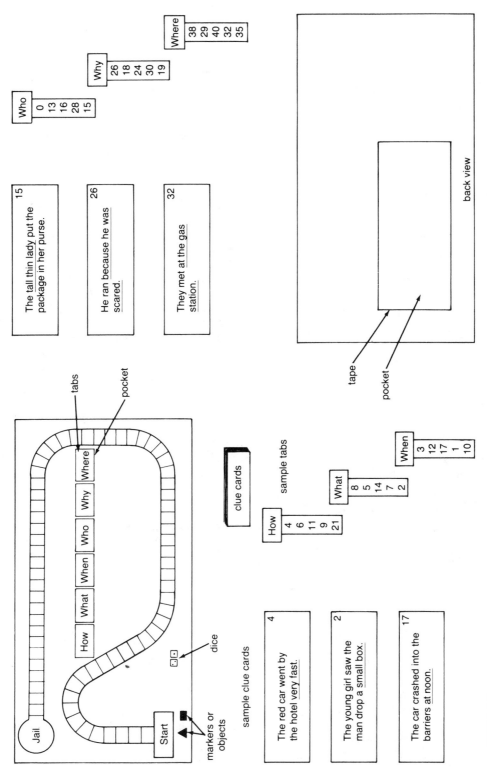

FIGURE 4.5
Mystery detective.

Construction:

1. Draw on a poster board a segmented road, race track, rocket path, football field, mountain path, or any other start–finish sequence.
2. Decorate the board to accent the game theme (racing cars, football, joggers, mountain climbers).
3. Make a stack of task cards with an accompanying answer key. For example, if the task card says

$$4 \times 4 = \underline{}$$

the answer key would read

$$4 \times 4 = \underline{16}.$$

Directions:

1. A player rolls the dice, picks up a task card, and says an answer.
2. If no player challenges this answer, she moves her marker the number on the dice.
3. If a player challenges her answer, it is looked up on the answer key. If it is correct, the player gets another turn. If it is incorrect, the marker is not moved and the challenger takes a turn.

Modifications:

1. The challenge factor may be omitted.
2. Spaces may be marked so that when a player lands on them a chance card is picked up.

Mystery Detective

Instructional objective:

Reading comprehension. See sentence clue card and select the meaning of underlined portion in terms of how, what, when, who, why, or where.

Feedback device:

Tabs with numbers that match those on the clue cards are used to provide feedback. For example, a number on a *What* card will be on the tab labelled *What*. Thus, a correct response results in a number match between the card and the tab.

Materials:

1. Poster board for game board, tabs, and clue cards
2. Dice
3. Pictures or drawings for decoration
4. Objects to move from start to jail

Construction:

1. Cut a slot in the poster board and tape an additional piece of cardboard to the poster board so that a pocket is formed with the slot at the top of it.
2. Cut six tabs of a length that exposes the name of the tab, but not the numbers, when inserted fully in the pocket.
3. On the game side of the board draw a "start-to-jail" winding, segmented road.
4. Make a stack of sentence clue cards. Underline a portion of each sentence that corresponds to one of the how, what, when, who, why, or where questions. Place a number in the right top corner of each clue card. Do not repeat the numbers.
5. Make six tabs, one for each of the questions. On each tab list the numbers that match the clue cards.
6. Laminate the material to increase its durability.

Directions:

1. A player rolls the dice and picks up a clue card.
2. The player determines if it is a how, what, when, who, why, or where clue and selects one of the tabs.
3. If the number on the sentence clue card is on the tab chosen, the player gets to move her marker the number of spaces indicated on the dice.
4. If the number on the sentence clue card is *not* on the tab, the player does not move her marker.
5. The next player does the same thing, and the first player to put the marker in jail wins.

Modifications:

1. Use this game format to practice syllabication. Label each tab with a number to indicate the number of syllables on corresponding word cards.

2. Instead of using the pocket on the game board, put each tab in an envelope or in a separately constructed pocket.
3. To make the game more exciting, mark "Trouble" or "Good News" on certain squares. When a player lands on a marked square, she picks up a card and does the activity on the card—for example, *go ahead three spaces.*

Toss A Disc

Instructional objective:

Any instructional task that can be presented on a card and performed in a few seconds is suitable.

Feedback device:

Answer key and peer correction provide feedback.

Materials:

1. Poster board
2. Index cards
3. Discs (checkers, laminated circles of poster board or oaktag)
4. Tasks for the cards

Toss A Disc

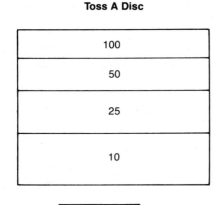

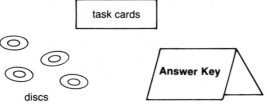

discs

Construction:

1. Divide a piece of large poster board into zones, with the zones getting larger as the points decrease.
2. Put points for each zone in the center of the zone.
3. Use checkers as discs or make discs out of oaktag or poster board.
4. Decorate the poster board with a theme.
5. Laminate the poster board.

Directions:

1. Place the game board on the floor, with the highest point zone flush against the wall.
2. Approximately 8–12 feet away, mark a space for the player to stand behind while he is tossing the disc toward the game board.
3. After the disc is tossed, the player picks up a task card and answers the question on it.
4. The player checks his answer on the answer key. If he is correct, he gets the points indicated for the zone his disc landed in. If he is incorrect, no points are awarded.
5. The first player to earn 500 (700; 1,000) points wins.

REFERENCES

Archer, A., & Edgar, E. (1976). Teaching academic skills to mildly handicapped children. In S. Lowenbraun & J.Q. Affleck (Eds.), *Teaching mildly handicapped children in regular classes* (pp. 15–112). Columbus, OH: Merrill.

Bartel, N.R., & Hammill, D.D. (1986). Important generic practices in teaching students with learning and behavior problems. In D.D. Hammill & N.R. Bartel, *Teaching students with learning and behavior problems* (4th ed., pp. 347–377). Boston: Allyn & Bacon.

Bleil, G. (1975). Evaluating educational materials. *Journal of Learning Disabilities, 8,* 12–19.

Brown, N.P. (1982). CAMEO: Computer-assisted management of educational objectives. *Exceptional Children, 49,* 151–153.

Brown, V.A. (1975). A basic Q-sheet for analyzing and comparing curriculum materials and proposals. *Journal of Learning Disabilities, 8,* 409–416.

Chiang, B., Thorpe, H.W., & Lubke, M. (1984). LD students tackle the LOGO language: Strategies and implications. *Journal of Learning Disabilities, 17*, 303–304.

Dell, H.D. (1972). *Individualizing instruction: Materials and classroom procedures.* Chicago: Science Research Associates.

Gallagher, P.A. (1979). *Teaching students with behavior disorders: Techniques for classroom instruction.* Denver: Love.

Gearheart, B.R., Weishahn, M.W., & Gearheart, C.J. (1988). *The exceptional student in the regular classroom* (4th ed.). Columbus, OH: Merrill.

Grimes, L. (1981). Computers are for kids: Designing software programs. *Teaching Exceptional Children, 14*, 48–53.

Hannaford, A.E., & Taber, F.M. (1982). Microcomputer software for the handicapped: Development and evaluation. *Exceptional Children, 49*, 137–142.

Hayden, D., Vance, B., & Irvin, M.S. (1982). A special education management system. *Journal of Learning Disabilities, 15*, 374–375.

Hickman, M.R., & Anderson, C.R. (1979). Evaluating instructional materials for learning disabled children. *Journal of Learning Disabilities, 12*, 355–359.

Hofmeister, A.M. (1984). *Microcomputers applications in the classroom.* New York: Holt, Rinehart, & Winston.

Hooper, G.A. (1981, November/December). Computerize your IEPs. *Classroom Computer News,* pp. 34–36.

Koehler, T., Ossler, A., & Raucher, S. (1981, April/May/June). Computerized support systems for individual educational plans. *Monitor,* pp. 14–15, 28.

Kolich, E.M. (1985). Microcomputer technology with the learning disabled: A review of the literature. *Journal of Learning Disabilities, 18*, 428–431.

Lewis, R.B., & Doorlag, D.H. (1983). *Teaching special students in the mainstream.* Columbus, OH: Merrill.

MacWilliam, L.J. (1978). Mobility board games: Not only for rainy days. *Teaching Exceptional Children, 11*(1), 22–25.

Mercer, C.D., & Mercer, A.R. (1978). The development and use of self-correcting materials with exceptional children. *Teaching Exceptional Children, 11*(1), 6–11.

Mercer, C.D., Mercer, A.R., & Bott, D.A. (1984). *Self-correcting learning materials for the classroom.* Columbus, OH: Merrill.

Papert, S. (1979). *Final report of the Brookline LOGO Project, Part II: Project summary and data analysis.* (ERIC Document Reproduction Service No. ED 207 801).

Polloway, E.A., Payne, J.S., Patton, J.R., & Payne, R.A. (1985). *Strategies for teaching retarded and special needs learners* (3rd ed.). Columbus, OH: Merrill.

Schiffman, G., Tobin, D., & Buchanan, B. (1982). Microcomputer instruction for the learning disabled. *Journal of Learning Disabilities, 15*, 557–559.

Schulz, J.B., & Turnbull, A.P. (1983). *Mainstreaming handicapped students: A guide for classroom teachers* (2nd ed.). Boston: Allyn & Bacon.

Stephens, T.M. (1977). *Teaching skills to children with learning and behavior disorders.* Columbus, OH: Merrill.

Stowitschek, J.J., & Stowitschek, C.E. (1984). Once more with feeling: The absence of research on teacher use of microcomputers. *Exceptional Education Quarterly, 4*(4), 23–39.

Torgesen, J.K., & Young, K.A. (1983). Priorities for the use of microcomputers with learning disabled children. *Journal of Learning Disabilities, 16*, 234–237.

VanEtten, C., & VanEtten, G. (1978). A working model for developing instructional materials for the learning disabled. *Learning Disability Quarterly, 1*(2), 33–42.

Watkins, M.W., & Webb, C. (1981, September/October). Computer assisted instruction with learning disabled students. *Educational Computer Magazine,* pp. 24–27.

Watson B., & VanEtten, C. (1976). Materials analysis. *Journal of Learning Disabilities, 9*(7), 408–416.

Wiederholt, J.L., & McNutt, G. (1977). Evaluating materials for handicapped adolescents. *Journal of Learning Disabilities, 10*(3), 132–140.

CHAPTER 5

Developing Social-Emotional Skills

hildren with learning difficulties often have social and emotional behavior problems. The child with social problems may be unable to behave appropriately with peers and in social situations (teasing, withdrawing, interrupting conversations). Emotional problems are generally considered to be within the person (poor self-concept, anxiety). Problems in these areas overlap; for example, a child with a poor self-concept may withdraw from social interaction with peers and adults. Although it is not always apparent whether social and emotional problems are contributing to a student's academic difficulties, it appears that these aspects of a student's behavior are usually counterproductive to learning and thus limit academic success. On the other hand, learning difficulties may contribute to social and emotional problems by causing the student to face excessive academic failure and frustration.

The teacher can help foster the student's emotional development as well as the acquisition of social skills. Direct instruction may be the best means of reducing problems related to social-emotional development.

ASSESSING SOCIAL-EMOTIONAL BEHAVIOR PROBLEMS

The problem behavior may be disturbing either to the student himself or to peers or adults who interact with him. During assessment, consideration should be given to the type of behavior and its frequency, intensity, and duration. Assessment procedures aid the teacher in identifying social-emotional behavior problems that require immediate attention. Assessment of social-emotional problems is presented according to five categories: (a) direct observation, (b) commercial instruments, (c) Q-sort technique, (d) sociometric techniques, and (e) informal self-report techniques.

Direct Observation

Direct observation of social-emotional skills includes observing the behavior, the teacher-student interaction, and the environment.

Observation of behavior. Direct, systematic observation of student behavior can provide information and insights about the child's social-emotional skills. Many teachers have training in personality development of children and work with students for several hours each day in different situations; therefore, many teachers are highly qualified to observe and assess behavior. If behaviors are *described* and reported as responses seen or produced (such as *gets out of seat, butts in the cafeteria line, calls Bill a sissy during math seatwork*) instead of as interpretations (such as *hyperactive, disruptive, impulsive*), the validity of teacher observations increases (Stephens, Hartman, & Lucas, 1983). The teacher thus should observe the conditions under which the behavior occurs and record the frequency of occurrence. Careful observation may reveal, for example, that out-of-seat behavior occurs only during arithmetic seatwork, or that singing in class occurs when the child is sitting near Maria. The target behavior may also be measured by duration—how long the child exhibits the behavior—or by a time sampling, in which the child is observed during certain periods for specified lengths of time. Techniques for recording observations (discussed in Chapter 2) include event recording, duration recording, interval recording, time sampling, latency recording, anecdotal recording, and permanent product recording.

In addition to the behavior itself, the teacher should also note the events that occur immediately prior to the behavior and the events that immediately follow and reinforce the behavior. Information about the conditions surrounding the behavior may enable the teacher to choose management strategies. For example, a child's swearing might receive the reinforcement of attention from peers (laughter). The teacher could concentrate on eliminating peer reinforcement of undesirable behavior and encouraging peer attention to desirable responses.

Finally, observation and daily measurement of behavior can provide feedback on the success of strategies used to resolve the behavior.

Observation of teacher–student interaction. Flanders (1970) presents the *interaction analysis system* for measuring the interactions between the teacher and the students in the entire class. Flanders specifies ten behavior categories: seven involve teacher's verbal behavior (for example, praising, asking questions, criticizing); two involve students' verbal behavior; and one is for silence or confusion. Teacher–child interactions are observed and behaviors are recorded every 4 seconds. Data are collected for several days during short observation periods. Smith, Neisworth, and Greer (1978) suggest a simplified version of the Flanders technique in which a tape recorder is used instead of a trained observer. The teacher can interpret the recordings made during the day and can categorize the verbal interactions according to Flanders's 10 categories. By using this assessment device the teacher can identify verbal patterns of student–teacher interaction in the classroom.

Brophy and Good (1969) developed a system called *dyadic interaction analysis* that measures interactions between the teacher and a student. The system includes five types of interaction: (a) response opportunities, (b) recitation, (c) procedural contacts, (d) work-related contacts, and (e) behavioral contacts. Daily observations are made over a period of time. A coding system is used to record the type and duration of each interaction and whether the teacher or student was the initiator.

In teacher–child interactions, a teacher occasionally may overreact to a certain behavior. Teachers must show understanding and awareness in order to control inappropriate reactions.

Observation of environment. In assessing social-emotional behavior problems, the teacher should observe different environments in which the child operates. The teacher then considers the environment's influence in starting or maintaining the problem behavior. Some observation may be made outside the school setting; however, the teacher mainly should observe in-school environments (such as art class, physical education class, lunchroom, playground). Perhaps the target behavior surfaces only in certain settings or instructional conditions. The student may become disruptive when he is required to remain seated for long periods of time during a lecture. But when he is allowed to move about or participate in class discussions, his behavior may be acceptable. Or a child may exhibit anxiety and may withdraw when required to read orally in front of his class, or when required to compute timed math problems, but may be quite comfortable when working alone in untimed situations or in small-group activities. Thus, teacher observation of various environments may result in making adjustments in the child or in the environment in which he experiences difficulty. Additional information on observation techniques is provided by Cartwright and Cartwright (1984).

Commercial Instruments

Checklists, rating scales, and self-report tests have been published that focus on assessing social-emotional problems. These devices provide methods for obtaining and recording judgments of teachers, students, peers, and parents concerning undesirable social-emotional behavior. Checklists generally are used to record the presence or absence of specific characteristics or behaviors. Rating scales are designed to indicate the frequency of a particular behavior or the degree to which certain characteristics are present (Wallace & Larsen, 1978). Self-report tests usually assess attitude or self-concept.

Generally, the instruments assist the teacher in identifying areas for further assessment and intervention. The teacher may choose to supplement a published instrument by developing teacher-made assessment procedures (checklists, direct-observation techniques) that help in identifying specific problem areas or that locate strengths and weaknesses.

Interview instruments. The instruments in this category feature the interview technique for obtaining information about social-emotional factors. The interviewer (school psychologist, social worker, guidance counselor, or specially trained teacher) follows systematic procedures as he interviews one or several persons (such as family members, peers, other teachers) who know the student.

The *AAMD Adaptive Behavior Scale— School Edition* (Nihira, Foster, Shellhaas, & Leland, 1981) covers social and daily living skills and behaviors of students aged 3 to 16 years. Part I evaluates personal independence in daily living (e.g., independent functioning, self-direction, responsibility). Part II measures personality and behavior disorders (e.g., aggressiveness, rebelliousness, trustworthiness). The scale domains are grouped into five factors: personal self-sufficiency, community self-sufficiency, personal-social responsibility, personal adjustment, and social adjustment. The responder (any person familiar with the student) must check statements that apply to the

subject or rate the statements in each item as occurring occasionally or frequently.

The *Behavior Rating Profile* (Brown & Hammill, 1983) is designed to study the behavior of children and adolescents (grades 1 through 12) at school, at home, and with their peers. Information is collected not only from the student but also from teachers, parents, and peers. Six independent measures are included: teacher rating scale, student rating scale (school), parent rating scale, student rating scale (home), sociogram, and student rating scale (peer). The results of the profile may be used to identify students with behavior problems and to distinguish between learning disabled, emotionally disturbed, and normal students. Also, the profile may be useful in identifying settings in which behavior problems occur and those that are free of problem behaviors.

The *Scales of Independent Behavior* (Bruininks, Woodcock, Weatherman, & Hill, 1985) provide a noncognitive measure of adjustment in the social, behavioral, and adaptive areas. The instrument is designed for infant through adult ages and assesses functional independence and adaptive behavior in motor skills, social and communication skills, personal living skills, and community living skills. Also, a problem-behavior scale focuses on general, externalized, internalized, and asocial maladaptive behaviors. Because the instrument is conceptually and statistically linked to the *Woodcock-Johnson Psycho-Educational Battery,* adaptive behavior can be measured based on cognitive ability.

The *Vineland Adaptive Behavior Scales* (Sparrow, Balla, & Cicchetti, 1984) assess personal and social sufficiency for individuals from birth to adulthood. Three versions are available: (a) interview edition, survey form— aids in screening or classification decisions, (b) interview edition, expanded form—provides specific prescriptive information that can be used for educational programming, and (c) classroom edition—allows for direct observation of adaptive behavior of students aged 3 to 13 and uses a checklist format. Thus, information about an individual can be interpreted from the points of view of a parent or primary caregiver and a teacher. The scales assess adaptive behavior in four areas: communication, daily living skills, socialization, and motor skills. The survey and expanded forms also measure maladaptive behavior. Standard scores and percentiles are available for each area and subarea as well as total adaptive behavior, and norms are provided in the interview editions for students in various categories (e.g., nonhandicapped students, mentally retarded, emotionally disturbed).

Observer-rater instruments. With these instruments an observer (teacher, guidance counselor, social worker, school psychologist, or family member) either completes a checklist on the presence of selected behaviors or attitudes or uses a scale to rate the degree to which the selected attitude or behavior is present.

The *Behavior Problem Checklist* (Quay & Peterson, 1983) uses a rating system that distinguishes among behavior not observed, observed but mild, and observed and severe. The checklist is used for children and adolescents and can be completed by parents, teachers, or anyone familiar with the student. Problem behaviors are classified as (a) conduct disorders, (b) personality disorders, (c) inadequacy and/or immaturity, and (d) subcultural (socialized) delinquency.

Burks' Behavior Rating Scales (Burks, 1977) are designed for children in first through ninth grade and may be administered in approximately 10 minutes. There are 18 categories of behavior, including (among others) (a) self-blame, (b) anxiety, (c) withdrawal, (d) dependency, (e) poor attention, (f) poor impulse con-

trol, (g) poor sense of identity, (h) poor anger control, (i) aggressiveness, (j) resistance, and (k) poor social conformity. The manual provides suggested intervention techniques for each category.

The three Devereux scales are the *Devereux Child Behavior Rating Scale* (Spivack & Spotts, 1966), the *Devereux Elementary School Behavior Rating Scale* (Swift, 1982), and the *Devereux Adolescent Behavior Rating Scale* (Spivack, Spotts, & Haimes, 1967). The *Devereux Child Behavior Rating Scale* is designed to describe and evaluate behavior disorders of emotionally disturbed and mentally retarded children aged 8 to 12. It can be completed in 10 to 20 minutes by a rater who is familiar with the child's behavior in a home-type situation. There are 17 behavioral factors, such as emotional detachment, need for adult contact, social aggression, and unethical behavior. The *Devereux Elementary School Behavior Rating Scale* focuses on behavior problems in children in kindergarten through sixth grade. Scores are obtained for 11 behaviors (such as classroom disturbance, impatience, inattention and withdrawal) and three additional items— inability to change, slowness, and quitting before completing a task. The *Devereux Adolescent Behavior Rating Scale* is appropriate for children aged 13 to 18. It provides 12 factor scores (such as poor emotional control) and 11 item scores (such as peer dominance, plotting).

The *Hahnemann High School Behavior Rating Scale* (Swift & Spivack, 1972) is administered by the teacher to measure observable classroom behavior of students in grades 7 through 12. Eight general factors are measured: (a) general anxiety, (b) quietness and withdrawal, (c) poor work habits, (d) lack of intellectual independence, (e) dogmatic and inflexible behavior, (f) verbal negativism, (g) disturbance and restlessness, and (h) expressed inability. In addition, five factors related to academic success are rated: (a) reasoning ability, (b) verbal interaction, (c) originality, (d) rapport with the teacher, and (e) anxious production (anxiety related to learning or mastery of classroom tasks).

The *Pupil Rating Scale* (Myklebust, 1981) is used with students in kindergarten through sixth grade. The teacher evaluates specific behaviors and rates each child on a 5-point scale. The items evaluated include auditory comprehension, spoken language, orientation, motor coordination, and personal-social behavior.

The *Social-Emotional Dimension Scale* (Hutton & Roberts, 1986) is a 32-item norm-referenced rating scale used to assess students aged 5 through 18 who are at risk for conduct disorders, behavior problems, or emotional disturbance. Student performance is assessed in six areas: physical/fear reaction, depressive reaction, avoidance of peer interaction, avoidance of teacher interaction, aggressive interaction, and inappropriate behavior.

The *Walker Problem Behavior Identification Checklist* (Walker, 1983) is designed for use with students in kindergarten through grade 6. It consists of 50 statements describing behaviors that may interfere or compete with successful academic performance. The checklist takes about 15 minutes to administer. The items are designed to measure five behavioral factors: (a) acting out, (b) withdrawal, (c) distractibility, (d) disturbed peer relations, and (e) immaturity.

The *Weller-Strawser Scales of Adaptive Behavior* (Weller & Strawser, 1981) consist of two scales: elementary scale for students who are 6 to 12 years old and secondary scale for students who are 13 to 18 years old. The adaptive behavior of students with learning problems is assessed in four areas: social coping, relationships, pragmatic language, and production. Each scale consists of 35 items that present pairs of descriptions of an adaptive behavior characteristic, and the examiner marks the alternative that best describes the student's behavior. A profile is obtained of either mild to moderate or moderate to severe adaptive behavior problems in each of the areas. Recommendations for programming and environmental modifications are included for each possible profile.

Self-report instruments. With self-report instruments the student responds directly to test items. These instruments usually focus on measuring self-concept or personality variables.

The *Coopersmith Self-Esteem Inventories* (Coopersmith, 1981) are self-report questionnaires that consist of short statements ("I'm a failure"; "I can usually take care of myself") to be answered "like me" or "unlike me." The inventories are designed to measure attitudes toward the self in social, academic, and personal contexts. The school form contains 58 items that can produce a total score, a lie score, and attitude scores toward self/peers, home/parents, and school.

The *Piers-Harris Children's Self-Concept Scale* (Piers & Harris, 1969) is a self-report instrument for children in grades 3 through 12. The child responds with yes or no to 80 declarative statements (such as "I am good looking," "My classmates make fun of me"). The items are written on a third-grade reading level, and both positive and negative statements are included. The scale covers many areas of self-concept, among which are physical appearance, popularity, and happiness-satisfaction. The suggested administration time is 15 to 20 minutes.

The *SRA Junior Inventory* (Remmers & Bauernfeind, 1957) is a checklist of problems and needs designed for use with students in grades 4 through 8. The problem areas included in the inventory are (a) about me and my school, (b) about me and my home, (c) about myself, (d) getting along with other people, and (e) things in general. It can be administered in approximately 45 minutes. Response boxes of different sizes enable the student to indicate the size of each problem—big box, middle-sized box, little box, and circle (to indicate no problem). The *SRA Youth Inventory* (Remmers & Shimberg, 1957) uses a similar procedure but has a slightly different set of problem areas for students in grades 7 to 12.

The *Tennessee Self-Concept Scale* (Fitts, 1965) requires approximately 20 minutes to complete. It is a self-report scale designed to measure self-concept of students 12 years of age and older. The scale includes five general categories: (a) physical self, (b) moral-ethical self, (c) personal self, (d) family self, and (e) social self. There are 90 statements (such as "I have a healthy body"; "I have a lot of self-control"), and each item is answered on a 5-point scale from *completely false* to *completely true*.

Q-Sort Technique

The Q-sort technique, developed by Stephenson (1953), is a procedure for investigating self-concept that may be used to identify areas for behavior modification (Kroth, 1973). According to Wallace and Larsen (1978), "This technique is based upon the theory that individuals have a 'real' and 'ideal' self and that it is profitable to determine the degree of discrepancy between these two evaluations of self" (p. 117). The technique offers a way to select specific social-emotional behaviors for intervention.

The student is given a set of cards containing statements which he must sort onto a pyramid formboard. A sample list of 25 statements suitable for elementary school students is presented in Table 5.1. Figure 5.1 shows the behavior formboard. The formboard contains nine categories which form a continuum from

TABLE 5.1
Elementary-level school items on the behavioral Q-sort.

1. Gets work done on time
2. Pokes or hits classmates
3. Out of seat without permission
4. Scores high in spelling
5. Plays with objects while working
6. Scores high in reading
7. Disturbs neighbors by making noise
8. Is quiet during class time
9. Tips chair often
10. Follows directions
11. Smiles frequently
12. Often taps foot, fingers, or pencil
13. Pays attention to work
14. Works slowly
15. Throws objects in class
16. Reads well orally
17. Talks to classmates often
18. Scores high in English
19. Talks out without permission
20. Rocks in chair
21. Scores high in arithmetic
22. Asks teacher questions
23. Uses free time to read or study
24. Works until the job is finished
25. Walks around room during study time

Source: From *Communicating with Parents of Exceptional Children: Improving Parent–Teacher Relationships* (p. 46) by R. L. Kroth, 1975, Denver: Love. Copyright 1975 by Love Publishing Company. Reprinted by permission.

"most like me" to "most unlike me." The student is given the same number of descriptor cards as there are squares in the pyramid. In sorting the items, he must arrange the cards so each square is used and none is left blank or used twice. First the student is asked to complete a *real sort*, in which he is instructed to sort the items onto the formboard in a manner that best reflects how the student believes his own everyday classroom behavior really is. After the responses of the real sort are recorded, the student is asked to complete an *ideal sort*, in which the same items are ar-

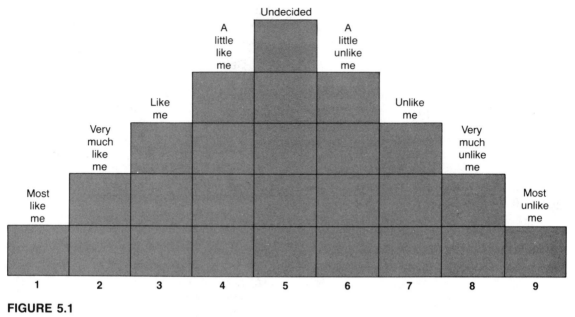

FIGURE 5.1

Behavior formboard.

Source: From *Communicating with Parents of Exceptional Children: Improving Parent–Teacher Relationships* (p. 44) by R. L. Kroth, 1975, Denver: Love. Copyright 1975 by Love Publishing Company. Reprinted by permission.

ranged on the formboard to indicate how the student would *like* to be in daily classroom activities. During sorting, the student may rearrange the cards until he is satisfied with his responses. The teacher compares the student's responses on the real sort with the responses on the ideal sort and notes items which differ greatly—that is, by 4 points or more. These items may become target behaviors for intervention. For example, if the student rates "Is quiet during class time" as "very much unlike me" (value: 8) on the real sort, but "like me" (value: 3) on the ideal sort, this may be an area for the child and teacher to work on together for improvement.

The behavioral Q-sort also may be administered to parents or teachers. Thus, comparisons can be made between others' perceptions of the child's school behavior (both real and ideal) and the child's own perceptions of his behavior. For example, the teacher can rate

the student on the same behavior that the student rated himself on, and the two ratings can be compared. When the comparisons on a specific behavior (such as "Pays attention to work") are very different, that behavior may be selected for examination and intervention.

Sociometric Techniques

Sociometric techniques, developed by Moreno (1953), record a child's standing and the various peer relationships within a classroom. Each student is asked to choose one, two, or three classmates with whom he would like to study, work, eat lunch, play, or perform any classroom or social activity. It helps if a printed list of the names of all class members is provided. Responses should be kept secret. Although students sometimes may be asked to make negative choices, it is better for the questions to be worded positively:

With whom would you most like to study?
Whom would you most like to sit with at lunch?
Whom would you most enjoy working with on an art project?
Whom would you most enjoy being with during break?

Sociometric ratings are considered to be one of the most dependable rating techniques (Fiske & Cox, 1960; Lindzey & Borgatta, 1954). The number of raters is large—sometimes an entire classroom—and a student's peers are most likely to observe behavior that is typical of the person.

Responses from a sociometric questionnaire indicating the number of times each child is chosen may be recorded on a tally sheet, or a *sociogram* may be constructed to provide a visual record of the social structure within the class. Figure 5.2 shows a sociogram of 10 fourth-grade students who were asked to write the names of two classmates with whom they would most like to play.

In this example, for the most part the girls preferred to play with girls, and boys with boys. Among the girls there seems to be a close relationship among Alice, Debby, and Judy. Within this group there were no choices of other classmates. Joan did not receive any choices, and Kim was selected as first choice only by Joan. Kim was the only girl to choose a boy. Among the boys, Bob and Steve were mutual choices, as were Ken and John. Adam received no choices, and John was the only boy to choose a girl.

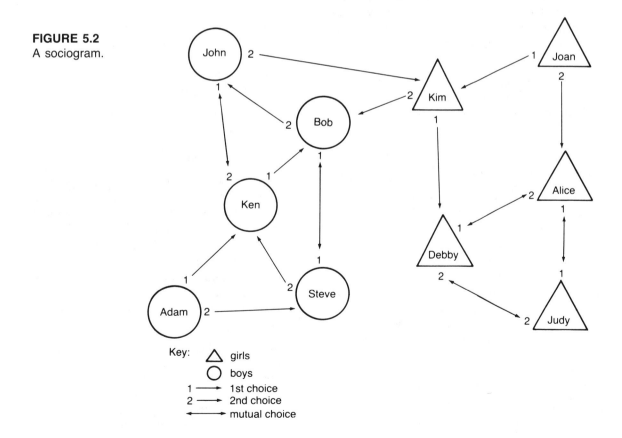

FIGURE 5.2
A sociogram.

Key: △ girls
      ○ boys
1 ——→ 1st choice
2 ——→ 2nd choice
◄——→ mutual choice

The information obtained from the socio-gram can help to identify isolates as well as leaders and can give the teacher a basis for congenial, effective group activities. In addition, the social preferences discovered provide insight about which social patterns should be changed and which should be encouraged. In this example, activities involving Adam and either Ken or Steve may be a positive for Adam, who in general is an isolate. Among the girls, situations should be planned to foster relationships outside of the clique. Different patterns probably will be revealed for different activities or settings. A student may be selected by several classmates as their choice for a study partner but may receive no choices for social activities.

Information also may be provided through *peer nomination* techniques, in which each student responds to statements about attitudes or behavior by naming classmates. For example:

Which students are very popular?
Which student does the teacher like the most?
Which students cause a lot of trouble?
Which students are selfish?

Informal Self-Report Techniques

Self-report techniques provide the student with an opportunity to report on his own specific behaviors. Self-report procedures obtain information directly from the subject, so the information is totally subjective. Its validity depends on the student's willingness to report the information and his ability to understand and perform the task. Self-report techniques provide a general idea of the student's problems. The student should be assured that the information provided is confidential and that only honest answers are helpful to the teacher. Four frequently used informal self-report techniques are checklists, questionnaires, interviews, and autobiographies.

Checklists. In a teacher-made checklist, the student is asked to indicate which behaviors or descriptions he feels apply to himself (such as "Has a lot of friends"; "Finishes classwork"; "Gets mad quickly"). Checklists are easy to administer and may give the teacher some insights concerning how the child views himself. For example, the student is presented with a list of adjectives and is instructed to check all words he considers to be descriptive of himself. Sample items may include the following:

____ absent-minded	____ happy
____ athletic	____ popular
____ likable	____ cooperative
____ friendly	____ intelligent
____ lonely	____ quiet
____ nice looking	____ neat
____ careless	____ noisy

Questionnaires. There are several kinds of questionnaires designed to obtain information about a student's personal, social, and emotional behaviors. The yes–no or true–false format is useful and is easy to administer:

Do you get mad often?	Y N
Are you usually very friendly?	Y N
I usually like to be by myself.	T F
Nothing gets me too mad.	T F

Questionnaires using open-ended questions or sentence completion require the student to complete the statements. Thus, the student expresses himself in his own words. Such a format requires more time and ability on the part of the student, but it often yields more meaningful information than the yes–no or true–false format. Sample items from a sentence-completion questionnaire might include the following:

1. I get angry when_____
_____.

2. I wish I could_____
_____.

3. When I feel lonely I_____
_____.

4. I work best when_____
_____.

5. I don't know how to_____
_____.

Interviews. Specific information also can be obtained from the student through interviews. They provide an opportunity for the child to express opinions and feelings about himself and others. Interview techniques may even be extended into daily conversations with the child, thus providing a flexible and ongoing source of assessment information.

Lister (1969) offers several guidelines for interviewing as an informal assessment technique. First, the teacher should relate the discussion questions to the student's particular area of difficulty. The interview is often most effective when conducted in private, and rapport should be established to communicate an honest interest in the child. Interview questions should be kept to a minimum and should be broad instead of specific; in this way, the child is required to develop a topic or express an opinion. If the teacher receives proper consent to do so, the interview may be recorded so that it is available for later study. If recording is not possible, notetaking during the interview should be minimal, with most notes made as soon as possible.

Autobiographies. In autobiographies the student gives a written account of his life or reveals his feelings about himself and others. Personal experiences, ambitions, or interests may be described. Students who have difficulty in expressive writing could record oral presentations of the autobiography. The type of autobiography depends upon the age and maturity of the student. The child may be asked to respond to specific questions or may be given a topic, such as "Things That Upset Me." Autobiographical material may then be analyzed for present or potential problem areas.

MANAGING BEHAVIOR AND DEVELOPING SOCIAL-EMOTIONAL SKILLS

Depending upon the situation and individuals involved, teachers may use a variety of strategies to improve social-emotional skills. In this section, the following methods for managing behavior problems and developing social-emotional skills are discussed: (a) behavior modification, (b) applied behavior analysis, (c) cognitive behavior modification, (d) modeling, (e) peer tutoring, (f) structured classroom, (g) providing support and success, (h) attribution retraining, (i) interview techniques, (j) managing surface behaviors and assertive discipline, (k) social skills training, (l) bibliotherapy, and (m) projective techniques.

Behavior Modification

Behavior modification derives from the concept of *operant conditioning* (Skinner, 1953). The basic premise is that behavior is learned and is a function of behavior's consequences. According to Wallace and Kauffman (1986), "Behavior modification refers to any systematic arrangement of environmental events to produce specific changes in observable behavior" (p. 21). Thus, it is a highly structured and systematic approach that results in strengthening, weakening, or maintaining behaviors.

After identifying and collecting baseline data on a target behavior, the teacher must observe events that happen just before the child's behavior (antecedent events) and just after the behavior (subsequent events). (A form for recording antecedent and subsequent events is presented in Chapter 2.) These events are then manipulated, and various reinforcers or rewards are used to elicit a change in the behavior. A *reinforcer* is any event that follows a behavior and results in maintaining or increasing the behavior. *Positive reinforcement* means adding something pleasurable or positive to the environment, whereas *negative reinforcement* means withdrawing something unpleasant or negative from the environment. Reinforcement results in strengthening or increasing the target behavior. Various social or tangible reinforcers may be used—praise, hugs, treats, free time. Praise is one of the most effective and convenient positive reinforcers for teachers to use in managing student behavior. Paine, Radicchi, Rosellini, Deutchman, and Darch (1983) report that effective praise has several important features:

1. Good praise adheres to the "if–then" rule. The "if–then" rule states that *if* the student is behaving in the desired manner, *then* (and *only* then) the teacher praises the student.
2. Good praise frequently includes students' names.
3. Good praise is descriptive.
4. Good praise conveys that the teacher really means what he is saying. (That is, it is convincing.)
5. Good praise is varied.
6. Good praise does not disrupt the flow of individual or class activities.

In using reinforcement techniques, it should be kept in mind that reinforcement immediately following the behavior is most effective. In addition, attention may act as a reinforcer for inappropriate behavior. For example, when the teacher frowns or speaks sharply, the child may interpret this as reinforcing attention. Thus, the teacher should be careful not to reinforce inappropriate behavior with attention.

The *schedule of reinforcement* (that is, the plan of conditions under which reinforcement occurs) may be either continuous or intermittent. On a *continuous schedule,* the desired behavior is reinforced every time it occurs. On an *intermittent schedule,* reinforcement is given according to either an *interval* (reinforc-

ers given at certain times) or a *ratio* (reinforcers given after a specific number of responses).

Shaping refers to reinforcing steps toward the target behavior. The goal is broken down into an ordered sequence of steps or tasks, and reinforcement is given to those behaviors that come close to the desired behavior. The desired behavior thus is shaped by gradually increasing the requirement for reinforcement until the target behavior is obtained.

Punishment, as opposed to reinforcement, refers to presenting something negative or withdrawing something positive following the behavior. This results in decreasing the undesirable response. One procedure frequently used to decrease undesirable behavior is *time out.* Time out is a short period of time during which no reinforcement is available. Thus, the child is removed from a positively reinforcing situation. Time out may be used while the child is at his desk simply by removing the opportunity for reinforcement (for example, avoiding any contact with the child for 30 to 60 seconds), or by not allowing him to participate in a reinforcing activity for a certain amount of time. Also, time out may be used by actually placing the child in a specific time-out area for a brief amount of time (3 to 5 minutes), during which he is isolated from the teacher and peers. Time out is based on the idea that behaviors followed by no reinforcement tend to decrease in frequency.

Response cost is another punishment technique that involves the loss of a reinforcer contingent on inappropriate behavior. The consequent loss may be an activity, points, a privilege, or a token. Kazdin (1972) reports that response cost has been used successfully without the undesirable side effects (escape, avoidance, aggression) sometimes observed with other forms of punishment. Although punishment and negative reinforcement are sometimes necessary to manage behavior, the teacher should strive to maintain a positive reinforcement system. Also, when it is necessary to use aversive techniques, it is most effective if they are combined with positive techniques (Walker, 1979). Blankenship and Lilly (1981) and Kerr and Nelson (1983) provide detailed discussions of the appropriate uses of aversive techniques and their drawbacks. Moreover, they strongly recommend the use of a positive reinforcement system as much as possible to manage behavior.

Paine et al. (1983) provide a step-by-step management system which combines positive reinforcement, a warning technique, and response cost. It includes the following steps:

1. When a student is misbehaving, give praise to nearby students who are exhibiting correct behavior. Once praise is given to several students, wait a brief time (30 seconds) to see if the misbehaving student responds. If the student responds by giving the correct behavior, praise that student. *DRO*

2. If the student fails to respond positively, talk to the student in an unemotional manner. Tell the student that he is receiving a warning and instruct him to begin work. The warning is more effective if it is delivered near the student and eye contact is established. The teacher should avoid getting into a conversation while giving the warning. After a short time, praise the student if the student begins correct behavior.

3. If the student does not respond to the warning, calmly remind the student about the warning, then write his name on the board, and put a mark next to it.

4. If the student fails to comply, place another mark by his name. This should be done without comment. Moreover, continue to praise other students for appropriate behavior.

5. At this point, if the student fails to comply, repeat step 4.

6. For behaviors that are unacceptable, use predetermined consequences. Unacceptable behaviors and resulting consequences should be explained at the beginning of the school year.

7. Have each mark after a student's name represent a loss of privileges. One mark could stand for 5 minutes taken from recess, two marks mean 10 minutes are lost, and so on. The consequence may be similar for everyone or varied for different students. The marking system is only effective if students lose privileges that they value.

8. Finally, be sure not to give the student extra attention when he is missing time from recess or staying after school. Consequences of the marking system should not be reinforcing in any way.

Knowledge and application of reinforcement principles are very helpful in managing a classroom. Many teachers apply these principles in a "natural" way, without taking the time to write a behavior modification plan specifying the target behavior, consequent events, schedule of reinforcement, and so forth. However, the behavior of some students does not change unless a highly systematic behavior modification plan is developed and applied.

Figure 5.3 presents a record of an individual behavior modification plan to increase staying-in-seat behavior. The teacher used a time-sampling technique to record whether the student stayed in his seat during seatwork activities. Observation sessions were 30 minutes in length, and the teacher used a recording sheet marked off with a row of 10 squares. The teacher looked at the student every 3 minutes and recorded a "+" if he was in his seat and a " − " if he was not. As Figure 5.3 shows, the student's percentage of staying-in-seat behavior was low during baseline. However, when the teacher began giving the student praise and attention for appropriate in-seat behavior (in sessions 11 through 20), the level of the de-

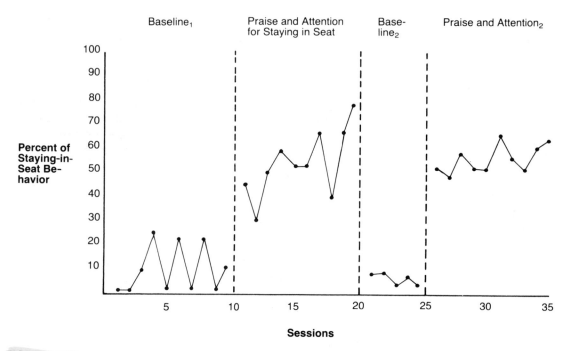

FIGURE 5.3
Record of a behavior modification plan to increase staying-in-seat behavior.

sired behavior increased greatly. When praise and attention were withdrawn in baseline₂ (sessions 21 through 25), the student's staying-in-seat behavior sharply diminished. But when praise and attention were provided again (in sessions 26 through 35), the level of the appropriate behavior quickly increased. Thus, the teacher was able to note the effects of teacher attention on modifying the student's out-of-seat behavior.

Contingency contracting. Contracts between a student and the classroom teacher may help to motivate the student toward desirable behavior changes. A *contract* is an agreement—verbal or written—between two parties. The term *contingent* means that there is a relationship between what one does and the consequences. In behavior modification, contin-

gency contracting is based on the Premack Principle (Premack, 1959). This principle states that the frequency of a less preferred activity increases when it is followed by the opportunity to engage in a more preferred activity. For example, if the student would rather play outside than sit quietly at his desk, the contingency contract might state that sitting quietly for a certain amount of time will be followed by outside play.

The following steps are involved in writing a contingency contract (Stephens, 1977):

1. The teacher outlines the specific behavior required of the student.
2. The teacher identifies the reinforcement for which the student will work. This reinforcement should be available to the student *only* for performing the specified behavior.

The required behavior or the consequent reinforcement may be determined through student–teacher discussions.

3. The teacher specifies the terms of the contract, which should include the amount or type of behavior required and the amount or type of reward.
4. The teacher watches for the specified behavior to occur and then rewards the student according to the terms of the contract.

A sample contingency contract is presented in Figure 5.4.

In developing a contingency contract there should be mutual agreement between the student and the teacher. The terms should be clearly stated in a positive manner, and the terms should be fair for both student and teacher. After both parties have signed the con-

tract, the conditions should be monitored frequently to assess progress. In addition, all parts of the contract should be followed systematically, and the student should receive reinforcement as soon as the contract is completed.

Various types of contracts may be used. The agreement may or may not specify a time limit within which the required behavior must be performed. Intermittent reinforcers can be used in long-term contracts, and steps toward the desired behavior can be rewarded. Contracts may include agreements between the child and other school personnel or parents. Group contracts may also be used: The entire class agrees to behave in a certain manner or perform a specified task by a designated date, and the teacher agrees to reward the students who fulfill the agreement. Contingency con-

---

CONTRACT

Beginning date: *10/21/88*

Ending date: *10/25/88*

STUDENT: I agree to *finish my math seatwork during math period on Monday, Tuesday, Wednesday, and Thursday.*

Signed *Timmy*

TEACHER: I agree to *give Timmy free time during math period on Friday.*

Signed *Mrs. Jackson*

FIGURE 5.4
A sample contingency contract.

tracting thus can promote desirable actions (social or academic) by involving the student in managing his own behavior.

Token systems. Token reinforcement systems are widely used in behavior modification. O'Leary and Drabman (1971) note that these systems have three basic characteristics: (a) behaviors to be reinforced are clearly stated, (b) procedures are devised for giving out a reinforcing stimulus (token) when the target behavior occurs, and (c) a set of rules is explained to govern the exchange of tokens for reinforcing objects or events.

A *token* is an item given to a student immediately following the occurrence of a target behavior. Usually the tokens have little intrinsic value; they acquire value when they can be exchanged for a desired object or activity. Tokens may consist of play money, trading stamps, poker chips, stars, or any other object that is easy to dispense and store. These tokens may be accumulated and then exchanged for a desired object or activity. A classroom store may be established where, at designated times, each child may "purchase" reinforcers by trading in earned tokens. Objects (balloons, comics, jewelry, sports trading cards, pennies, coloring books, magazines) and activities (playing a game, listening to records, coloring, watching a filmstrip) may be available in the store. A reward menu is posted which lists the store items and their costs—for example, listening to records for 10 minutes—20 tokens; purchasing a baseball trading card—15 tokens.

Vernon (1972) discusses several advantages of token systems. First, boredom is avoided because tokens may be traded for a variety of reinforcing objects or events. Second, a token system is useful with students who generally do not respond to social reinforcement. Third, tokens are easily administered, and the number can be adjusted to reflect the time and energy required to perform the target behavior. Fourth, token systems help students appreciate the relationship between desirable behavior and reinforcement. Students learn that behavior has consequences, and this is likely to enhance self-control.

Blackham and Silberman (1980) stress that a token system must be developed and applied thoughtfully. They also report that problems should be expected at first, and the teacher will have to refine the system. Blackham and Silberman suggest guidelines for planning and using a token system:

1. The target behaviors that earn tokens should be clearly specified. For example, individual behaviors may be posted on a student's desk. Rules governing group behavior contingencies should be reviewed frequently.

2. The reinforcers that the tokens are exchanged for must be appealing and available *only* within the token system.

3. The number of tokens earned must match the effort required for performing the target behavior. If a student has a lot of trouble staying on task during math seatwork, the reward for staying on task must be sufficient to encourage on-task behavior.

4. If possible, the teacher should keep a record of the number of tokens earned by each child and the group. This type of record often provides an additional incentive to students.

5. If *response cost*—token fines—is used, the conditions under which tokens are earned and lost must be clearly specified. Awarding and taking away of tokens must always be related to student *behavior*. Arguments about token loss should be avoided.

6. It is usually best if token exchange is scheduled for the end of the day.

7. The system should be devised so the stu-

dent competes with himself rather than with others.

8. A well-planned token system should gradually withdraw material reinforcers and stress reinforcing activities and events. Also, praise should be combined with the tokens so that social reinforcement alone eventually can be used to maintain desirable behaviors.

9. The token system should be simple, functional, and not distracting to the learning process. In school, checkmark tokens are often the easiest to use. Each student is given a card with his name on it, and the teacher puts checks on it as they are earned. A special pen may be used to distinguish these checks. Other students cannot use a student's card, whereas tangible tokens may be traded or stolen.

Additional information on token systems is provided by Ayllon and McKittrick (1982) and Stainback, Payne, Stainback, and Payne (1973).

Applying consequences with adolescents. In managing secondary students Kerr and Nelson (1983) report that structure and consistency are essential. The likelihood of power struggles and defiance of authority is greater with adolescents. Thus, it is very important for both the teacher and student to function in a structured environment; that is, expectations (rules), consequences, and routines should be clearly established. Techniques that have been effective with secondary students include token economies, contingency contracting, verbal feedback, mutual goal setting, and self-control training (Deshler, Schumaker, & Lenz, 1984; Polsgrove, 1979). Moreover, the importance of involving adolescents in curriculum and management decisions is stressed throughout the literature.

Some suggestions for managing consequences with adolescents include the following:

1. Stress the natural consequences of behavior. For example, the natural consequence for stealing is arrest, for being tardy is detention, and so on. Thus, if a rule is broken, the stated consequence is applied. This helps reduce power struggles between the student and teacher because the student is likely to view the teacher as a person who follows rules rather than as an authority figure who maliciously applies punishment (Kerr & Nelson, 1983).

2. Use conditioned reinforcers (e.g., points) with adolescents. They are easily administered or withheld with a minimum of teacher verbalization (Kerr & Nelson, 1983).

3. Consider using peer interactions as reinforcers for adolescents.

4. Develop a continuum of consequences for managing inappropriate behaviors. Public reprimands should be avoided because they increase the probability of further conflict. Use little verbal interaction and eye contact when administering a negative consequence. Response cost is a good beginning step in dealing with inappropriate behavior. Time out is another effective consequence with adolescents. The management system by Paine et al. (1983) presented previously provides an excellent framework for managing adolescents. It stresses a positive approach but incorporates a warning system and response cost.

Applied Behavior Analysis

Applied behavior analysis emphasizes direct, continuous, and precise measurement of behavior. Direct measurement entails focusing on behaviors that can be observed and counted directly. Continuous measurement requires that a behavior be counted and recorded over a period of time, usually daily. Precise measurement requires reliable observation and recording.

Lindsley (1964) developed specific techniques (known as *precision teaching*) for the measurement and analysis of behavior. Charting is its main feature. The steps include the following:

1. The teacher selects a target behavior or a pinpoint.
2. An aim is determined that provides the student and teacher with an instructional goal. The teacher must decide the rate (i.e., frequency of observation) at which the target behavior should occur.
3. The teacher counts the number of times the behavior occurs and graphs or charts the data daily. (Graphs and charts for recording behavior are presented in Chapter 2.)
4. The teacher analyzes the data and makes instructional decisions. If the student's performance is improving, the current instructional technique should be continued.

Blankenship and Lilly (1981) discuss the use of data-based observation as a systematic method to observe, measure, and record student behavior. They present various procedures for identifying, defining, observing, and charting behavior, as well as methods for making instructional decisions based on data. (See Chapter 2 for a discussion of data-based instruction.)

Cognitive Behavior Modification

Cognitive behavior modification analyzes the thinking processes involved in performing a task. Meichenbaum (1977) discusses *self-instructional training* as a method to encourage appropriate responses and discourage inappropriate responses. The following sequence may be used:

1. Instruction by another person—for example, an adult model (teacher) performs a task while talking out loud to himself.
2. Overt self-instruction—for example, while performing a task, the child verbally instructs himself or whispers instructions to himself.
3. Covert self-instruction—for example, the child performs the task by guiding his performance through private speech.

Thus, inner speech is considered an aspect of the thinking process, and the student is encouraged to verbalize prior to acting. Language is thought to enhance thinking and, in turn, affect behavior. In the classroom the student might be taught to use the following self-verbalizations: (a) questions about the task ("What does the teacher want me to do?"), (b) answers to the question ("I'm not supposed to talk out in class"), (c) self-instruction to guide the student through the task ("First I raise my hand and wait for the teacher to call on me"), and (d) self-reinforcement ("I really did well that time!").

In cognitive modeling, the teacher should not only model strategies for performing a task but should also model actions and language appropriate for dealing with frustrations and failures. In addition to talking to himself, the student may be taught to use *images* (for example, thinking of sitting in the classroom during recess as an image to reduce out-of-seat behavior).

Modeling

In modeling, the student learns appropriate behaviors by observing and imitating others. When the student observes one of his peers being rewarded for desirable behavior, he tends to follow the example of the model. Thus he learns those behaviors which have positive consequences. Likewise, unacceptable behavior may be discouraged when the student watches another receive punishment for such behavior. In addition, the teacher may call attention to behavior that he would like to see modeled: "I like the way Jimmy raised his hand instead of talking out, so I will answer his question first."

In using modeling to influence a specific behavior, the following steps are helpful:

1. Select the behavior.
2. Select the model.
3. Give the model and the observer directions concerning their roles.
4. Reinforce the model for exhibiting the behavior.
5. Reinforce the observer for imitating the behavior.

The modeling process can have three effects on the student: (a) new behaviors may be learned from the model, (b) previously acquired behaviors may be strengthened as the child observes similar desirable behaviors of the model being reinforced, or (c) previously acquired behaviors may be weakened as the child observes the model receiving punishment for similar unacceptable behaviors.

Peer Tutoring

Peer tutoring typically involves pairing a competent student with a student who has difficulty in a particular academic area. Peer tutoring also may be used to improve social skills. If assessment procedures reveal that a student has no friends or is not accepted by his peers, peer tutoring can be a strategy for enhancing the child's social growth. Using information from a sociometric device, such as a sociogram, the teacher may pair a student with a

preferred tutor. The child thus will be likely to model the appropriate behavior. The teacher should train the student tutor in teaching and reinforcement techniques. Tutoring sessions should have easy-to-use materials and a set routine. Self-correcting materials and instructional games provide excellent materials for peer teaching arrangements.

Paine et al. (1983) provide guidelines for establishing and maintaining a peer tutoring program:

1. *Determine the roles of tutors.* Decide what role tutors can serve in the classroom. Peer roles may be ascertained from a list of useful activities including instruction in academic and social skills, record keeping, timings, observations, modeling, and feedback.
2. *Select the tutors.* Select tutors who are capable of demonstrating the task to be performed. Also, match tutor and tutee for compatibility.
3. *Train the tutors.* Train the tutors to model the instructional task and provide appropriate feedback.
4. *Supervise and reinforce peer teaching arrangements.* Reinforce tutors for presenting stimuli, providing feedback, and maintaining pleasant interactions. Reinforce tutees for following directions and responding to task materials.

Allen (1976) reports that peer tutoring has a positive effect on the tutor. (That is, it helps the tutor with academic or behavior difficulties, or both.) As noted in Chapter 3, peer tutoring can be successfully used to improve academic skills, foster self-esteem, help the shy youngster, help students who have difficulty with authority figures, improve race relations, and promote positive relationships and cooperation among peers. Additional information on peer tutoring is provided by Ehly and Larsen (1980) and Pierce, Stalhbrand, and Armstrong (1984).

Structured Classroom

The structured approach to teaching students with social-emotional behavior problems may help to control disruptive behavior. Structure should be used in the following areas: environment, program, relationship between the child and adult, teaching materials, and success (Cruickshank, 1976). Distracting visual and auditory stimuli should be reduced to a minimum, and the student should be provided with a reasonably quiet place to work. A small cubicle or a carrel with cardboard partitions helps to eliminate all nonessential and distracting stimuli from the learning environment.

Structure is also provided by careful planning of days that feature schedules, routines, or contracts. The student should have assignments throughout the day, with specified activities at certain times. Each assignment should be checked by the teacher. After completing a task, the student should have a choice of activities to engage in—for example, games or interest centers—until the teacher returns to him. A classroom routine should be established, with the teacher providing consequences for behavior on a consistent schedule.

Carefully organized and stimulating teaching materials draw the student's attention to the learning task. Use uncluttered worksheets and widely spaced written materials. In addition, reading materials may be covered to expose only a small area of the reading selection at a given time. Structure in the classroom may thus aid both learning and the management of behavior problems.

Providing Support and Success

A teacher who establishes rapport and appreciates each student as a person may effectively help the student with learning problems to realize his potential. Good teachers practice feedback techniques and know how to correct a wrong response without hurting the student's feelings (e.g., "You're almost right. Let's do it together"). They make positive statements and praise appropriate actions rather than attending to misbehavior.

Success in learning can enhance feelings of self-worth. When a student is continuously given tasks that are too difficult, frustration develops, which may be followed by behavior problems, aggression, or withdrawal. All assignments should be within the student's learning capacity, frustration level, and attention span. The teacher may display charts and graphs showing progress and may provide extrinsic rewards for increasing accuracy and mastering progressively more difficult tasks.

Success is also accomplished by having the student work with self-correcting materials. Because the student can immediately check the answer and not practice mistakes, failure is reduced, and it becomes a private event, since only the student sees the error and he can correct it immediately.

In addition, the teacher can create a classroom atmosphere conducive to positive social interaction among students. The teacher may pair students having learning difficulties with popular students for social group activities or on teams in instructional games so that the paired students can share positive and pleasant experiences. Also, using the student with learning problems as a tutor in peer teaching activities may boost the pupil's self-esteem and indicate that the teacher has confidence in the individual's ability to handle the task. The use of support and success techniques may not only build students' self-concepts but may also motivate those who have experienced much failure because of learning problems.

Attribution Retraining

Attributions refer to a person's beliefs concerning the causes of events. Students differ in their ideas concerning the causes of their successes and failures. Those who believe in an internal locus of control explain the outcomes of their actions on the basis of their abilities or efforts. In contrast, persons with an external locus of control believe that factors outside their control, such as luck or task difficulty, determine their fates.

Some students with learning problems may believe that their successes are a function of external factors. Bryan (1986) notes that it would seem advantageous to induce such students to have more positive and self-serving expectations of their academic successes. As students experience many academic failures, they may doubt their intellectual abilities and doubt that anything they do will help them overcome their difficulties. Thus, these students may lessen their achievement efforts, especially when presented with difficult material. In other words, repeated failure can lead students to believe that they are not capable of overcoming their difficulties, and their beliefs about their abilities can affect achievement efforts and accomplishments.

Attribution retraining studies have found that teaching students to attribute their failures to insufficient effort may result in increased persistence and improved performance when confronted with difficulty. In these studies, students are engaged in academic tasks and are given feedback that emphasizes the importance of their effort. Fowler and Peterson (1981) note that prompting and reinforcing students for verbalizing the appropriate effort attributions may be more effective than simply telling them when they fail that they need to try harder. In addition to stressing effort as a determinant of a student's difficulties, it may also be helpful to teach students to attribute their failures to ineffective task strategies (Licht, 1984). Bryan (1986) notes that teachers should convey to students that they are learning new skills and that effortful application of the new skills may help them overcome their difficulties.

Interview Techniques

Life-space interviewing. Life-space interviewing can be used in the classroom to manage a crisis or an everyday problem. This technique attempts to structure a situation so that the child works out his own problem. The interview is designed to be free of judgment; the teacher is simply a listener and helper for the student as he makes decisions about how to handle the problem.

Morse (1971) outlines the steps in life-space interviewing:

1. Each student involved in the specific incident is allowed to give his own impression of the occurrence without interruption.
2. The teacher listens and, without casting judgment, asks questions to determine how accurate each child's perception is.
3. If the students cannot agreeably resolve the problem, the teacher may have to suggest an acceptable plan to deal with the problem.
4. The students and the teacher work together to develop a plan for solving similar problems in the future.

The classroom teacher may best use life-space interviewing to provide emotional first aid on the spot at times of unusual stress. Thus, the technique is used to (a) reduce the child's frustration while supporting him during an emotional situation, (b) reinforce behavioral and social rules, and (c) assist the child to solve his own everyday problems. For example, after a fight on the playground, the teacher may engage in life-space interviewing to allow the child to release frustration and anger. The teacher provides support and aids the child in viewing all sides of the situation and the rights of others.

The attitudes and behavior of the teacher as interviewer influence the effectiveness of life-space interviewing. The teacher should be polite to the child and should maintain eye contact with him. Asking "why" questions should be avoided, and the interviewer should try to reduce any apparent guilt feelings. In addition, the teacher should encourage the child to communicate and ask questions as they work together to develop a plan of action for present or future use. The life-space interview technique is time-consuming and requires sensitivity and emotional control from the teacher. However, it can be effective in helping a child see the consequences of his behavior and finding ways to deal with a problem.

Reality therapy. Reality therapy, developed by Glasser (1965), is used to manage behaviors by teaching the child to behave responsibly and to face reality. An interview technique similar to life-space interviewing attempts to help the student make sound decisions when confronted with a problem. In reality therapy each person is assumed to be responsible for his own behavior. Inappropriate behaviors are not excused on the basis of unconscious motivations. During interviews the child is provided with emotional support, and no judgments are made of the present behavior. The teacher and the student jointly develop a plan to increase the student's responsible behavior, and the student is encouraged to make a commitment to carry out the plan. No excuses are accepted for irresponsible behavior; the student is expected to realize the consequences of such behavior. Thus, the morality of behavior is emphasized, and the student is taught socially accepted ways to handle problems.

Glasser (1965) presents a three-step format for applying reality therapy. The first step is to help the student identify the problem. This is accomplished by asking questions such as "What happened?" and "Where are you going?" The second step is to help the student develop a value judgment, asking questions such as "Is the behavior helping you?" or "Is the behavior against the rules?" The third step is to involve the student in carrying out a plan to correct the inappropriate behavior. An application of reality therapy is featured in the following scenario:

Teacher: "Michael, what just happened?"

Michael: "Nothing."

Teacher: "I thought I saw you push Susan."

Michael: "Yeah, maybe I did."

Teacher: "Tell me about it."

Michael: "I was running to get in line and she got in my way."

Teacher: "Well, I'm sure you didn't push her on purpose, but is pushing students against the rules?"

Michael: "Yeah."

Teacher: "What do you think should be done?"

Michael: "I don't know."

Teacher: "Why don't you sit over there at the reading table a couple of minutes and think about what you can do to solve the problem."

Michael: "O.K."

(Five minutes later.)

Teacher: "Got an idea?"

Michael: "Yeah, I think I should line up after the others for the rest of the week."

Teacher: "Does that help Susan?"

Michael: "No."

Teacher: "What can you do to help Susan?"

Michael: "I can tell her I'm sorry and let her line up in front of me tomorrow."

Teacher: "Can you do that?"

Michael: "Yeah."

Teacher: "Fine, I think that's an excellent plan."

Managing Surface Behaviors and Assertive Discipline

Long and Newman (1971) discuss 12 techniques for managing surface (observable) behaviors and helping to prevent the buildup of behavior problems:

1. Planned ignoring: Many behaviors will stop if they are ignored rather than given teacher attention.
2. Signal interference: The use of a cue (such as finger snapping) may alert the student to stop a particular behavior.
3. Proximity control: Some disruptive behavior may be prevented by the teacher's presence in the area of potential trouble.
4. Interest boosting: Behaviors may be managed when the teacher shows a genuine interest in the child as an individual.
5. Tension decontamination through humor: A humorous remark by the teacher may release tension in an emotional situation.
6. Hurdle lessons: The teacher may lessen frustration by providing individual academic assistance.
7. Restructuring the classroom program: A change in the classroom program may reduce behavior problems.
8. Support from routine: A familiar routine may provide support to the child.
9. Direct appeal to value areas: The teacher needs to be aware of the student's personal values in order to appeal to them.
10. Removing seductive objects: Items that distract the student may be removed from the classroom to avoid provoking disruptive behavior.
11. Antiseptic bouncing: The child may be removed from the classroom without

punishment; for example, ask him to run an errand.
12. Physical restraint: The teacher may restrain the child when he has lost self-control and may injure himself.

Assertive discipline, as advocated by Canter and Canter (1976), is an approach to classroom control that allows teachers to deal constructively with misbehaving students while maintaining a supportive environment for student growth. Charles (1985) presents a series of five steps to implement assertive discipline:

1. Recognize and remove roadblocks to assertive discipline. First, negative expectations about students must be replaced with positive expectations. Teachers must realize that all students need limits and that teachers have a right to set limits as well as ask for and receive backup help from principals, parents, and other school personnel.
2. Practice the use of assertive response styles. With the assertive response style, teachers clearly define their expectations and continually insist that students comply with those expectations by backing their words with actions.
3. Learn to set limits. Teachers must establish specific behavioral needs and expectations of their students and then decide how to respond to students when established expectations are either complied with or broken.
4. Learn to follow through on limits. Teachers must take appropriate actions for students' compliance with or refusal to meet demands. Thus, the students choose their behavior but have advance knowledge of the good or bad consequences that will result from their choice.
5. Implement a system of positive assertions. When teachers follow through with positive consequences when students behave in

appropriate ways, the influence of teachers with their students increases, the amount of problem behavior decreases, and the classroom environment becomes much more positive.

Thus, Canter and Canter's (1976) model of assertive discipline integrates such ideas as behavior as choice, logical consequences rather than threats or punishment, positive reinforcements for desired behavior, and addressing the situation rather than the student's character. The approach maintains that teachers must care enough about students not to allow them to behave in ways that are damaging to themselves and that teachers must firmly guide students and apply natural consequences of student behavior while receiving full support from administration and parents. Individual or group training in assertive discipline is available through teacher or media kits published by American Guidance Service.

Social Skills Training

A variety of procedures have been used to improve the social skills performance of students with learning problems (Schumaker & Hazel, 1984). One technique involves the manipulation of antecedent and consequent events associated with the target social behavior. For example, environmental events can be changed in an effort to increase the probability of future occurrence of appropriate social behaviors while decreasing the probability of occurrence of inappropriate behaviors. Approaches of this technique include the use of cooperative goal structures, the delivery or the withholding of particular consequences contingent upon the occurrence of social responses, the application of group contingencies, and the use of home-based contingency management systems. Another technique that has been used to reduce the rate of inappropriate social

behaviors is cognitive training aimed at teaching self-control of personal behaviors (e.g., self-recording and self-evaluation of behaviors).

Also, interpersonal social skills can be increased through direct instruction. Schumaker and Hazel (1984) discuss four types of instructional interventions that have been used to facilitate the acquisition of social skills:

1. Description—primarily oral techniques in which the teacher describes how to perform a skill appropriately.
2. Modeling—demonstrations of the social skill either by live models or by film, audiotape, or pictorial models.
3. Rehearsal—verbal rehearsal of required skill steps to ensure that the individual has memorized the steps in sequence and can instruct himself in what to do next, and structured practice (e.g., role-play activities) whereby the learner attempts to perform the skill.
4. Feedback—verbal feedback following rehearsal to inform the individual on what steps he performed well and which behaviors need improvement. Frequently, combinations of these procedures are included in social skills training interventions.

In addition to procedures that are frequently used to teach social skills, a social skills curriculum can be used. For example, the following social skills curriculum consists of four main areas:

1. Conversation skills—using body basics, greeting, introducing yourself, applying active listening, answering questions, interrupting correctly, asking questions, using goodbye skills, and conversing.
2. Friendship skills—making friends, saying thanks, giving compliments, accepting thanks, accepting compliments, joining

group activities, starting activities with others, and giving help.

3. Skills for difficult situations—giving criticism, accepting "no," accepting criticism, following instructions, responding to teasing, resisting peer pressure, and apologizing.

4. Problem-solving skills—negotiating, giving rationales, persuading, problem solving, getting help, and asking for feedback.

Bibliotherapy

Bibliotherapy is a teaching technique in which reading materials are used to help the student better understand himself and his problems. Characters in the books used learn to cope with problems and situations similar to those faced by the student. Through identifying with the character, the student releases emotional tensions and achieves a better understanding of himself and the problem. Also, characters, attitudes, values, and situations in reading selections may serve as models for the student.

Hoagland (1972) notes that for bibliotherapy to be effective, the student must move through three phases during or immediately after reading a book: (a) *identification*—The student must become personally involved and must identify himself or see a situation similar to some of his own situations; (b) *catharsis*—The student must release emotional tensions regarding the problem; and (c) *insight*—Through empathizing with the character or plot, the student must reach a better understanding that tempers his emotional drives.

Cianciolo (1965) suggests the following steps for discussing a book:

1. Retell the story and emphasize incidents, feelings, relationships, and behaviors.
2. Discuss changes of feelings, relationships, and behaviors.

3. Identify similar events from the student's life or other reading selections.
4. Explore the consequences that occurred.
5. Make a conclusion or generalization about the consequences or helpfulness of alternative behaviors.

The student should come to realize that he is not the first person to encounter a particular problem and that there is more than one way to solve a problem.

Books chosen for a bibliotherapeutic program should focus on a particular need and should be written on the student's level. The selections also should depict realistic approaches and have lifelike characters (Cianciolo, 1965). Suitable books can be selected from various sources (such as Kircher, 1966; Moody & Limper, 1971; Reid, 1972) that have bibliographies cross-indexed by theme and age level. Russell and Russell (1979) provide various activities to be used in conjunction with bibliotherapy.

Projective Techniques

Various projective techniques may be used by the teacher to encourage students to project or express their feelings and emotions. Creative activities, such as role playing and puppetry, provide an opportunity for the student to express feelings and reduce frustrations with few constraints.

Role playing. In role playing, students assume the role of a character and act out a brief episode that involves a problem. The role-playing process includes four steps:

1. A specific problem is identified—classroom problems or conflicts or other relevant situations.
2. After the problem is described, the roles must be established and assigned to vari-

ous students. Volunteers should be sought; students should not be forced to play a role.

3. The actual role playing takes place and should be brief. The same situation may be repeated several times with different children to present many solutions to a single problem.
4. A discussion follows, focusing on the role or behavior rather than the child portraying it.

Thus, through role playing the student faces reactions of other people and learns ways to cope with similar situations.

Puppetry. Puppets can help children experience different events and express feelings and emotions. Fairy-tale characters (such as king, witch, giant, animal) are used to represent human emotional experiences. Students can make hand puppets and a stage. The puppet theater provides a nonthreatening atmosphere in which children can express their feelings freely as they engage in problem solving. Following each puppet show, other solutions to the problems presented can be discussed.

ACTIVITIES AND MATERIALS

Problem Areas and Management Activities

The following selected problem areas cover a wide range of social and emotional behaviors. Within each area, several management activities are suggested.

Academic behavior problems. Some social-emotional behavior problems result in lowered academic performance. A child whose tolerance for frustration is low may become frustrated easily when attempting to complete academic tasks that require great effort. The problem behaviors of task avoidance and task interference also hamper the completion of academic work. The student who seldom completes timed assignments within his capabilities may have a problem in slowness in work.

Activities:

1. Allow the student who avoids academic tasks to choose from a variety of activities within a skill area. This will allow him to think he selected his own work rather than having it forced on him. Also, consider letting the student complete academic tasks in various ways, such as using a red pen or working in a different area of the classroom. A variety of stimuli (tape recorder, Language Master, computer, manipulative materials) may be used to maintain the student's attention to the task.
2. Shortly after assigning an academic task, provide a reward for those students who have started the work and completed several problems. This will encourage the student who avoids tasks to become more involved. Rewards may also be given upon task completion to encourage the student to work steadily to finish an assignment.
3. To increase the student's speed in performing academic tasks, have him work against a timer and chart his progress. For example, the number of addition problems completed correctly during a specific period of time may be recorded on a graph each day. As progress is made in the student's rate of work, the difficulty of the tasks may be increased.
4. To discourage slowness in work, draw up a contingency contract. The student and teacher can agree that if the student finishes a specific part of an academic task within a certain amount of time, he will not have to complete the remainder of the assignment. The contract should also specify an accuracy criterion (such as 85% or more correct responses) to discourage the student from rushing incorrectly through the task. Thus, accurate work performed in a reasonable amount of time is rewarded.
5. When a student shows a task interference behavior, such as looking out the window, move

physically closer to him so he is aware of your presence. Also, the student may be paired with a productive worker, and modeling may be used to elicit appropriate behavior.

6. Prepare a series of tasks at different levels of difficulty. Allow the student with low frustration tolerance to complete the first task at his own pace. Gradually introduce time limits. Record the student's progress and reward steps of progress. After the student has mastered the first task at various time intervals, repeat the procedure with a more difficult task.

7. Provide the student who avoids tasks with an incentive to start working. Give him a worksheet with the first few problems already completed.

8. Present academic tasks in game formats, such as start-to-finish races or card playing.

9. Use self-correcting materials, which provide immediate feedback and reduce the practicing of errors. The student may avoid academic tasks in order to avoid failure; however, with self-correcting materials, failure is not publicly known, and the student can immediately correct his responses.

10. Use assistance cards to help manage requests for assistance. Paine et al. (1983) suggest folding a 9″ × 12″ piece of construction paper into a triangular shape with two 4″ sides and a 2″ base. Tape the triangle together and write "Please Keep Working" on one side and "Please Help Me" on the other side. When the student wants help, he places the side stating "Please Help Me" toward the front of the room, thus leaving the side stating "Please Keep Working" facing the student. The teacher provides each student with a work folder which occupies the student until the teacher is available to help. Frustration is reduced and success is increased if the work folder includes a self-correcting material. The work folder should include tasks that relate to the student's instructional needs (e.g., practice in a specific skill). The assistance card enables the student to request help without raising his hand or disrupting engaged academic time. The supplementary work folder enables the student to continue to work productively on another academic task in which

immediate teacher assistance is not required. Also, the assistance card reminds the student to keep working.

11. Use feedback charts for managing student behavior. Paine et al. (1983) note that feedback *show Behav. rating scale* charts provide the student with a visible display of progress and also generate valuable data to help make educational decisions. The chart is displayed where all students can see it and is divided into four areas. For example:

Begins assigned activities promptly	Follows directions
Completes work or works entire time	Receives less than two warnings

Each student receives a blank card divided into four squares. Throughout the day the teacher marks each square with plus marks (+) when the student performs the desired behavior. At the end of a specified time period, the student may be allowed to trade the marks for free time, playing a game, and so on. The teacher may use separate cards for different academic periods. Also, a group chart may be made and laminated so it can be used repeatedly.

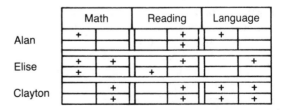

	Math		Reading		Language	
Alan	+		+		+	
			+			
Elise	+	+	+			+
	+		+			
Clayton		+		+	+	+
		+		+	+	+

12. For the student who does not complete homework, have him earn the privilege of being al-

lowed to do homework at home (Lieberman, 1983). Place the student on a 5-day probation during which he must stay after school and complete his homework assignments within an agreed upon period of time. Then have him alternate doing his homework at home and at school every other day for 5 days. Finally, he can be allowed to do full-time homework at home. However, if any assignments are not completed at home, the student is placed on probation for another 5 days. Thus, for the student the positive consequence is earning the ability to do homework at home, as opposed to the negative consequence of staying after school for not completing the homework.

Disruptive classroom behavior. Disruptive behavior in the classroom includes actions that interfere with instruction or activities of an individual or a group. Inappropriate talking out and out-of-seat behaviors are frequently disruptive to the classroom. Moreover, the use of sarcasm, swear words, and temper tantrums are disturbing behaviors that need to be modified.

Activities

1. As much as possible, ignore disruptions and reward the student's complying behaviors. For example, when a child talks out during class, completely ignore him and do not respond to what he has said; however, when he raises his hand during class, immediately recognize him and praise his behavior. This is effective only if teacher attention is reinforcing. It may be necessary to also control peer attention to the inappropriate behavior.
2. Ignore out-of-seat behaviors and give verbal praise to students who remain in their seats. Students who remain seated during work periods may be rewarded by being allowed to participate in a game involving movement (musical chairs, kick ball).
3. Use a timer to see how long an active child can stay in his seat. Time him at various intervals during the day and reward him when he remains in his seat during the interval. Record his progress on a graph so that the student com-

petes with himself to improve his behavior. As he progresses, gradually increase the time interval for staying in the seat.
4. Give the active child periodic breaks that allow him to get out of his seat. He may be given errands to run, during which he can move around or leave the room.
5. Contingency contracts may be devised. The student agrees to stay in his seat for a period of time, and if he does so, the teacher agrees to reward him with some free time out of his seat, such as extra recess. Likewise, a student may agree in a contract not to talk out during class for a specific amount of time in return for the reward of free talking time.
6. Cut out a figure of the student which includes a large pocket and tape it to the wall. Whenever the student behaves appropriately, place a chip or token in the figure's pocket. When the student engages in an inappropriate behavior (out of seat, talking out, use of swear words), remove a chip from the pocket. At the end of each day the chips may be traded for a reinforcing activity—free time, playing a game, watching a filmstrip.
7. To reduce swearing, suggest to the student other words that may be used (for example, *darn, heck, shoot*). Reinforce the student every time he refrains from swearing and uses another word.
8. Use a graph to record the number of swear words or sarcastic remarks made by the student during a specific time period. This will call his attention to his inappropriate remarks. Have him compete with himself, and reinforce him for improved behavior.
9. When a child starts a temper tantrum, immediately remove him to a time-out area in which he is isolated from the teacher and his peers. When he is able to remain quiet, allow him to return to the classroom. In this way the child receives little attention for inappropriate behavior. Also, be aware of the chain of behavior that leads the student to an outburst or tantrum. Apply time out or another management technique before the chain has gone too far.
10. At the beginning of the day, make 15 numbered marks on the chalkboard. Explain to the class that they have an opportunity to have a 15-

minute recess at the end of the day. However, for each disruptive behavior one mark will be erased from the board. At the end of the day, give the class the number of minutes of extra recess remaining on the board. Instead of recess, the minutes could be used in a special game, story time, or field trips.

Problems with authority figures. Some students have inappropriate reactions to school personnel or authority figures. The student may resist coming to school and may frequently challenge the authority of his teacher and principal by constantly arguing and disobeying school rules. This negative reaction needs to be changed to promote a healthy attitude toward school and authority figures.

Activities

1. Provide the student with positive reinforcement for attending school. For example, give the student a special treat or plan a rewarding activity each day he arrives on time. Special privileges, snacks, and activities may be made contingent on regular school attendance.
2. Pair the student who is absent frequently with a well-liked peer who has regular attendance. (Use a sociogram to determine a good match for modeling purposes.) With the teacher's guidance, the model may plan to meet the student at school for various activities and thus encourage attendance.
3. Allow class members to establish some of their own rules of behavior and consequences for disobeying a rule. Discuss the need and reasons for the rules. When some rules are made by peers, students may be less inclined to challenge the teacher's authority.
4. When the student repeatedly disobeys rules and instructions from his teacher, give him several courses of action to choose from. When possible, avoid conflict and "showdowns" in which he is forced to obey. Sometimes a peer can explain an assignment or rule to a student who resists adult authority and the student will comply.
5. Ignore the student whenever he argues with the teacher or disobeys instructions. Walk away from

him when he argues. Isolation also may be effective in dealing with the student who argues. Reinforce obedient behavior and positive language through praise and attention.
6. Invite various authority figures in the community to speak to the class and share some of their problems and experiences during their school years. This sharing of experiences may make a positive impression on the student who shows a negative attitude.
7. Use an "emotion box" in the classroom. Give the class members several forms that ask for name, date, emotion, and reasons. Ask the students to complete a form and place it in the emotion box whenever they react strongly to an event in the classroom. Through this method the teacher may gain understanding about each student's reasons for undesirable and negative behaviors. To foster a positive attitude toward authority figures, ask the student "planned interest" questions every day. For example, ask what he did last night, if his team won its ball game, and so on. Also, remember the student on special days, such as his birthday. A teacher's genuine interest in individual students encourages a positive feeling toward school attendance and authority figures.

Poor self-concept. *Self-concept* refers to a person's perception of his abilities and of how others important to him feel about him. A person with a poor self-concept has feelings of inferiority and inadequacy and may express these feelings—"I can't do that," "I'm not very smart." Such a student may lack self-confidence and be reluctant to interact with others. He may resist academic work because he fears failure.

Activities

1. To make the student feel special and important, select him to be "Student of the Week." Seat him in a special chair and give him a badge to wear. Each day ask the other classmates to write something special about the student being honored. They may write positive statements about his abilities or his personal attributes.

Also, the students can decide on other special activities they can do for the child—perhaps write a story about him or play his favorite game at recess.

2. To develop self-awareness, have students collect items that tell something about themselves (for example, magazine pictures, small objects, photographs). Encourage each child to make a collage of these items on tagboard. The center of the collage may contain a picture of the student, with the items arranged around the photograph. The students can share with others what the items represent and why they were chosen.

3. Write short, personal notes to the student to provide him with encouragement and to let him know you have an interest in him. Also, have brief conversations with him. He may need extra encouragement when trying a new task or suffering from a disappointment.

4. Use the student as a tutor in peer tutoring situations. This may boost his self-esteem. It also shows that the teacher has confidence in the student's ability to handle the task.

5. Make some academic tasks look more difficult than they really are. The student will gain self-confidence when he successfully completes a task he thought was very difficult. For example, a simple math worksheet to practice subtraction facts may be replaced by a worksheet that *appears* to contain very difficult problems but really requires the same basic skills. The problem

$$394876$$
$$-173472$$

requires the same basic skills as

$$\begin{array}{cccccc} 3 & 9 & 4 & 8 & 7 & 6 \\ -1 & -7 & -3 & -4 & -7 & -2 \end{array}$$

6. Provide success activities and limit failure as much as possible. Before requiring the student to participate in oral reading, have him review difficult words or go over the story on a tape recorder. Also, using self-correcting materials keeps incorrect responses a private event and gives the student a chance to correct his re-

sponse immediately. Provide verbal praise and correct wrong responses without hurting the child's feelings: "You're almost right"; "Let's do it together"; "Nice try."

7. Help the student compile a scrapbook about himself. Include pictures or drawings of family, friends, and pets. If possible, take photographs in the class. The scrapbook can include written accounts of trips, interests, and favorite activities.

8. Set realistic goals with the student on selected tasks. Record the child's daily progress toward the goal. When the goal is achieved, the child should be rewarded. In addition, point out the student's progress to make him feel proud of his accomplishments.

9. Emphasize the importance of student effort on academic tasks, and teach the student to attribute his successes and failures to amount of effort. This may result in increased persistence on difficult material and reduce doubts of intellectual ability.

Social immaturity. The socially immature student lacks the ability to get along with his peers and lacks other social skills common to his age group. He may engage in antisocial behavior, failing to recognize his responsibilities and the rights of others. Social withdrawal may result from lack of academic success.

Activities

1. Pair a withdrawn student with a competent, socially mature peer for various activities. They must cooperate in completing an academic task together or being a team during a game. Thus, in these situations success or failure is shared by both students.

2. If a child frequently teases another student, ask the teased child to ignore the child who is teasing him. Reward the teased child each time he makes no response to teasing. Thus, the child who is teasing does not receive attention from either the teacher or the peer for his inappropriate behavior. Also, self-recording may be used to reduce teasing. Give the student a slip of

paper with lines for his name and date and spaces in which he is to mark each time he teases. The marking should be monitored. Having to mark down his own inappropriate behavior may help the student decrease his teasing.

3. Use the socially withdrawn or rejected child in peer teaching situations as either the tutor or student being tutored. A sociogram may indicate an appropriate match. Peer tutoring encourages appropriate peer contacts in a secure and structured activity.

4. Use modeling techniques to teach various social skills. Praise the model for appropriate social behavior in the presence of the socially immature student.

5. Encourage the withdrawn student to use a tape recorder when he feels like talking. The teacher tells the student that if the student would like to share it, he (the teacher) will be glad to listen. The teacher may respond on tape if the student prefers. This is a first step in encouraging a withdrawn student to talk out loud and discuss his feelings.

6. Use role playing to present a variety of possible social situations. Discuss several different mature reactions to specific problems. Thus the student is presented with a choice of solutions to use when coping with similar social occurrences.

7. When a student frequently is aggressive toward a peer, ignore him and pay attention to the child who was his victim. Reinforce cooperative and peaceful behavior in the presence of the aggressive student, and reward him when he behaves appropriately.

8. Encourage the student to develop a vocabulary that expresses feelings. Pockets may be glued on a large piece of tagboard, and on each pocket a face may show a different expression (smiling, frowning, serious). Words expressing feelings (sad, cheerful, troubled, anxious, pleased, miserable, nervous) may be written on index cards. The child is instructed to match each word to a picture expressing that emotion. The correct face can be drawn on the back of each card so the child can check his response. Another activity with feeling words is to give the

child a list of words and ask him to write each word in a way that shows the emotion:

Afraid	
Shy	
Excited	
Jumpy	

Secondary students may increase their vocabulary to include feeling words which may be divided into unpleasant and pleasant:

Unpleasant	*Pleasant*
Ambivalent	Accomplished
Betrayed	Confident
Condemned	Ecstatic
Distraught	Fascinated
Dubious	Gratified
Exasperated	Infatuated

9. Have each student express his mood or feeling at different happenings. Write events on index cards (such as, "It's time to go to school"; "I don't know what to do"; "I don't have any money"; "My teacher smiles at me"; "It's my birthday.") Use a piece of tagboard with pockets labelled with various moods. Each student selects a card, reads it aloud, tells how the described event makes him feel and why, and places the card in the pocket that corresponds to his feeling. Also, during classroom situations take pictures of students showing various emotions. These photographs may be displayed with captions telling the emotion shown and the situation in which it occurred: "Kevin is very proud. He is wearing his badge for captain of the safety patrol." By observing the pictures, students may become more sensitive to facial expressions.

10. Conduct class meetings during which the students discuss any question that seems relevant to them at the time. This opportunity for personal involvement is especially appropriate for secondary students. The teacher should keep the discussion moving and see that everyone is given an opportunity to participate as much as possible.

Games

Many activities may be presented in a game format to stimulate interest and involvement. Games also promote positive peer relations and enable the teacher to work on specific social-emotional skills—for example, cooperating, staying on task, taking turns, or expressing feelings. The following games are designed to foster appropriate social-emotional skills.

Picture Puzzle Game

Materials:

A large picture of something the child is interested in or wants, cut into pieces.

Directions:

Encourage the student to show appropriate behavior over a period of time by rewarding him with something he wants. The student and teacher agree on the desired behavior to be reinforced and the type of reward. Each time the student shows the desired behavior, the teacher gives him a piece of the picture puzzle. Each time *inappropriate* behavior is observed, the teacher takes away a puzzle piece. When the student has received all the puzzle pieces to the picture, he is reinforced by receiving the reward.

Work Around the Circle

Materials:

Classroom chairs arranged in a circle; a timer.

Directions:

Set a timer to go off at various times during intervals of from 1 to 4 minutes. When the timer buzzes, each student who is working may move to the next chair. Students who are caught not working must remain in their seats for that turn. Thus students who are working appropriately rotate around the circle. When a student has completed the circle, the teacher should check his work and give him free time until all students have worked their way back to their own seats.

The Principal's Game
(Paine et al., 1983)

Materials:

Timer; chalkboard area for recording points.

Directions:

Use this game to improve the behavior of a disruptive class of students. Begin by telling the students they need to work harder, and there is a game that can help them. In the game, teams are formed according to seating clusters or rows (i.e., one team for each row or cluster). A timer is set to ring six times during the class or day. Each time it rings the teacher determines which teams are following classroom rules and working. If all team members are working the whole team receives a point; however, if one or more members are not working no points are awarded. To win, a team must receive a minimum of five points, and it is possible for all teams to win. At the end of the day or class, invite the principal to come into the room and recognize the winning teams and praise their fine work. In addition to the principal, other significant people (e.g., counselor, another teacher, local sports figure, parent, etc.) can be asked to visit and recognize winning teams.

Behavior Monopoly

Materials:

A game board similar to a Monopoly board which has a variety of reinforcers (including some booby prizes) written in the squares; a die; student markers.

Directions:

Use the game board to provide the student with some type of reinforcement. Randomly identify a student displaying an appropriate behavior. Allow him to roll the die and move his marker on the board. The student receives the reinforcer indicated on the space he lands on. He then leaves his marker on that space so it can be moved next time he gets a chance.

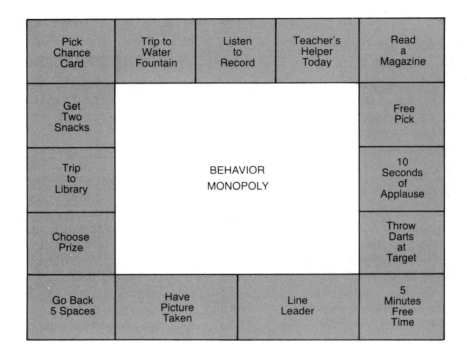

Pick Chance Card	Trip to Water Fountain	Listen to Record	Teacher's Helper Today	Read a Magazine
Get Two Snacks		BEHAVIOR MONOPOLY		Free Pick
Trip to Library				10 Seconds of Applause
Choose Prize				Throw Darts at Target
Go Back 5 Spaces	Have Picture Taken	Line Leader		5 Minutes Free Time

Chance Cards may include: "Arm wrestle with teacher," "Hop on one foot for 5 seconds," "Send note to a friend," "Hug the teacher," "Pick up trash," and so on.

Speed Chase

Materials:

Poster board with large speedometer dial drawn on it; cardboard arrows, each of which has a student's name on it; various small prizes.

Directions:

Allow groups of children to compete to see who can accurately complete the most classwork during the day. After the teacher has checked an assignment, each student attaches his arrow to the speedometer to indicate the number of items he performed correctly on the task. His speed on the speedometer increases according to the number of correct items on each assignment. At the end of the day the student with the highest speed wins and picks a prize.

Modifications:

Rather than competing in all subject areas for an entire day, students may record their speed in one subject area for several days. Also, the speedometer may be used to record specific behaviors during the day, such as staying in seat or raising hand instead of talking out. Two students who need to change the same behavior could compete. Each time the student displays the appropriate behavior the teacher moves his arrow on the speedometer; the arrow is moved *back* for inappropriate behavior. The student with the highest speed at the end of the day wins the speed chase.

The Lottery
(Paine et al., 1983)

Materials:

Prerecorded tape with randomly spaced "beeps"; tape recorder; space on chalkboard for recording checks by student's names.

Directions:

Hold a daily lottery in which students work for the opportunity of having their names drawn at random. During the day play a tape with six randomly distributed "beeps." Students who are following classroom rules (e.g., on task, in seat, not talking) when the beep sounds receive a check by their names on the chalkboard. Students who receive five or six checks in a day are eligible for the daily drawing. At the end of the day, two names are selected from the qualifying students. The principal or teacher phones the respective parents and tells them about their child's good behavior.

Good Behavior Game
(Barrish, Saunders, & Wolf, 1969)

Materials:

Tally chart.

Directions:

Divide the class into two teams and explain that talking out and out-of-seat behaviors are going to be recorded. Whenever a student engages in either behavior, place a mark on the tally sheet for his team. At the end of the day the team with the fewest marks wins. If both teams have fewer than six marks, the whole class wins. The members of the winning team receive a previously agreed upon reward. If both teams win, reward the entire class with a 30-minute special project period.

Timer Game
(Wolf, Hanley, King, Lachowicz, & Giles, 1970)

Materials:

Timer; point chart; prizes.

Directions:

Set the timer to ring on the average of once every 20 minutes during a range of from 1 to 40 minutes. Each student who is in his seat when the timer rings is awarded five points. Each student's points earned are recorded on a point chart. At the end of a specified period of time, the points may be traded in for prizes such as snacks or privileges.

Best and Worst Game

Materials:

Paper and pencil.

Directions:

Describe a social situation and have each student write down what would be the *best* and the *worst* thing to do in response to that event. Each child reads his response, and the choices presented are discussed. The student with the best response (decided by the presenter of the problem) gets to describe the next social incident and lead the discussion.

Personality Game
(Bailey, 1975)

Materials:

Start-to-finish game board; cards with personality traits written on them; markers.

Directions:

Place the cards face down on the playing board. The first player takes the top card and reads it aloud. If he feels the card describes him, he may move forward five spaces. However, if he feels the statement on the card does not apply to him, but the majority of the group feels it does (or vice versa), the player must move his marker three spaces back. If neither the player nor the others feel the card applies, the player stays where he is. The players may tell why or why not they think a trait is or is not descriptive of their personality. After each turn the card is placed face down in the discard pile. If a blank card is picked, the player may make up a trait. Players may choose the top card from either the original card pile or the discard pile. The purpose of the game is to help each student better understand himself. The first player to move around the board and reach the finish space is the winner.

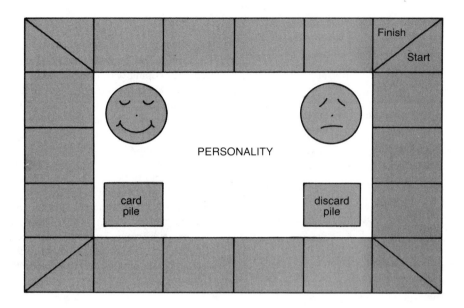

Sample cards may include: "I am impatient," "I joke around a lot," "I am kind to animals," "I don't ever like school," and so on.

Socialization Game

Materials:

Start-to-finish board; dice; set of cards containing personal questions; markers.

Directions:

Use the game board to improve social skills by providing the players with an opportunity to talk freely about feelings, relationships, or activities. Each player rolls the dice and moves that number of spaces on the board. He then must take a card and respond to the question by explaining his answer to the other players. The first player to reach the finish space wins.

Sample questions may include: "Do you like to be alone? When?" "If you could be anyone in the world, who would you be? Why?" "What happened on the happiest day of your life?" "What would you do if you didn't go to school?"

Decision Game

Materials:

Five parallel lines marked on the floor with masking tape.

Directions:

Explain to the students that the five lines represent (from right to left) absolutely right, somewhat right, undecided or neutral, somewhat wrong, and absolutely wrong. Tell a story or describe a situation; then ask the students to move to the line that indicates their decision about the story or situation. Each student should explain why he moved where he did.

Stories or situations such as the following may be used:

John saw William take two quarters from the teacher's desk and put them in his pocket. He told William to put the money back but William refused to do so. John then went to the teacher and told her William had taken the money. Was the decision to tell the teacher right or wrong?

Ms. Adams asked her class to be very quiet before recess. Three boys continued to whisper and giggle. Because of this, Ms. Adams kept the whole class in from recess. Was the teacher right or wrong?

Commercial Programs and Materials

Various programs and materials are designed to help students better understand themselves and get along with others. The following selected programs and materials may be used to enhance self-concept and general social and emotional growth. (The publishers' addresses are included in Appendix B.)

Asset: A Social Skills Program for Adolescents
(Hazel, Schumaker, Sherman, & Sheldon-Wildgen, 1982)

Publisher: Research Press

Description:

This video program is specifically designed for teaching social skills to a wide range of adolescents in grades 6 through 12. The program features modeling scenes that show teenagers interacting with peers, parents, teachers, and other adults. Scenes of teenagers modeling both appropriate and inappropriate social interaction skills lead to stimulating discussions, and students have the opportunity to get actively involved by relating the video presentations to their own personal experiences and feelings. An individual videocassette is available for each of the following social skill areas: (a) giving positive feedback, (b) giving negative feedback, (c) accepting negative feedback, (d) resisting peer pressure, (e) problem solving, (f) negotiation, (g) following instructions, and (h) conversation. The Asset manual provides the leader with training procedures, lesson plans, skill sheets outlining the steps for each skill, home notes, checklists, consent forms, and various questionnaires.

Coping With Series
(Schwarzrock & Wrenn, 1984)

Publisher: American Guidance Service

Description:

Four sets of five paperback books are included in this series. The books present information in four areas: (a) coping with personal identity (focuses on self and self-improvement, such as making better decisions, living with loneliness), (b) coping with human relationships (focuses on getting along with others—social skills, communication, thoughtfulness, acceptance), (c) coping with facts and fantasies (provides factual information about drugs, alcohol, smoking, unhealthy eating habits, and roles of men and women), and (d) coping with teenage problems (addresses a variety of teenage problems such as cliques, parents, and common crutches). The books are appropriate for adolescents and may be helpful in discussion groups and counseling sessions. A leader's manual is included with each set of books.

Developing Understanding of Self and Others
(Dinkmeyer & Dinkmeyer, 1982)

Publisher: American Guidance Service

Description:

These instructional kits are designed to encourage the social and emotional growth of children in kindergarten through fourth grade. *DUSO I,* for children in kindergarten through second grade, is used to develop appreciation of individual strengths and acceptance of limitations, beginning of social skills, and awareness of feelings, priorities, and choices. *DUSO II,* for third and fourth graders, helps develop a greater understanding of the purposive nature of behavior, more effective communication skills, a greater understanding of feelings and empathetic behavior, and skill in recognizing and making choices. The central character of both programs is a puppet, Duso the Dolphin. A problem situation and a story are presented and are followed by role-playing and puppet activities. The kit provides hand puppets, posters, activity cards, and audiocassettes of stories and songs.

Human Development Program

Publisher: Human Development Training Institute

Description:

This program, also known as Magic Circle, includes a teacher's manual and activity guides for students aged 4 through 11 (preschool through sixth grade). The program includes daily 20- to 30-minute teacher-led discussions that take place in a circle. A topic is suggested in the form of an unfinished sentence (for example, "Others make me angry by _____"; "One time I didn't give up was _____"). Students in the group take turns completing the sentence. The teacher acts as a catalyst, and the participants are encouraged to share their feelings as well as listen and observe others. Through working as a group, the students learn to communicate and develop more meaningful relationships with one another. The program, as described by Bessell and Palomares (1971), focuses on feelings and individual recognition and seeks to improve self-control and the ability to listen and express.

Self-Control Curriculum
(Fagen, Long, & Stevens, 1975)

Publisher: Merrill

Description:

The self-control curriculum is designed to help elementary-aged children overcome problems in self-control. Eight curriculum areas are included: selection (focusing and concentration, figure–ground discrimination); storage (visual and auditory memory); sequencing and ordering; anticipating consequences; appreciating feelings; managing frustration; inhibition and delay; and relaxation. Each curriculum area contains an introduction, a statement of rationale, a description of units and goals, and suggested learning tasks or activities. The teacher has the option of teaching any curriculum area according to her own schedule. Objectives of the curriculum include reducing disruptiveness, strengthening emotional and cognitive capacities, building control skills, and promoting balance between cognitive and affective development.

Toward Affective Development (TAD)
(Dupont, Gardner, & Brody, 1974)

Publisher: American Guidance Service

Description:

The *TAD* program consists of activities, lessons, and materials designed to stimulate psychological and affective development in students aged 8 to 12 (grades 3 through 6). The kit is organized into five general sections containing 21 units (191 sequential lessons). Activities (such as self-awareness, working with others) may be added into the classroom schedule. The kit includes a manual, picture cards, posters, duplicating masters, a cassette, shapes and object cards, color chips, feeling wheels, a filmstrip, and career folders. The lessons, designed to involve students actively with one another, take 20 to 25 minutes.

Transition
(Dupont & Dupont, 1979)

Publisher: American Guidance Service

Description:

This program is designed to help students aged 12 to 15 (grades 6 through 9) understand and cope with various social and emotional situations. The five units included in the program are communication and problem-solving skills; openness and trust; verbal and nonverbal communication of feelings; needs, goals, and expectations; and increasing awareness of values. Each unit has its own teacher's manual. A scope and sequence outline of the entire program is included. There are instructions for 91 sequential activities such as scenarios of conflicts and dilemmas, debates, games, discussions, and questionnaires. The program also includes 88 cartoon posters; six cassettes; eight script booklets; duplicating masters; discussion cards; 48 "feeling word" cards; and 28 illustrations of facial expressions, postures, and gestures. Through the program, students are confronted with real-life issues and problems. They are encouraged to communicate successfully, solve problems alone and with others, and get along with peers and adults.

Walker Social Skills Curriculum

Publisher: Pro-Ed

Description:

The ACCEPTS program (Walker et al., 1983) teaches

classroom and peer-to-peer social skills to students in kindergarten through sixth grade. The 28 classroom competencies and social skills are presented in five areas: (a) classroom skills (e.g., listening to the teacher, following classroom rules), (b) basic interaction skills (e.g., eye contact, listening, taking turns talking), (c) getting along skills (e.g., using polite words, sharing, assisting others), (d) making friends skills (e.g., good grooming, smiling, complimenting), and (e) coping skills (e.g., when you express anger, when someone teases you, when things don't go right). The ACCESS program (Walker, Todis, Holmes, & Horton, 1987) teaches peer-to-peer skills, skills for relating to adults, and self-management skills to students at the middle and high school levels. A total of 30 social skills are presented in three areas: (a) relating to peers (e.g., interacting with the opposite sex, being left out, handling group pressures), (b) relating to adults (e.g., disagreeing with adults, working independently, developing good study habits), and (c) relating to yourself (e.g., being organized, using self-control, feeling good about yourself). The curriculum is designed for use by both regular and special education teachers and can be taught in one-to-one, small-group, or large-group instructional formats.

REFERENCES

Allen, V.L. (Ed.). (1976). *Children as teachers: Theory and research on tutoring.* New York: Academic Press.

Ayllon, T., & McKittrick, S.M. (1982). *How to set up a token economy.* Austin, TX: Pro-Ed.

Bailey, E.J. (1975). *Academic activities for adolescents with learning disabilities.* Evergreen, CO: Learning Pathways.

Barrish, H.H., Saunders, M., & Wolf, M.M. (1969). Good behavior game: Effects of individual contingencies for group consequences on disruptive behavior in a classroom. *Journal of Applied Behavior Analysis, 2,* 119–124.

Bessell, H., & Palomares, U. (1971). *Methods in human development: Theory manual.* San Diego: Human Development Training Institute.

Blackham, G.J., & Silberman, A. (1980). *Modification of child and adolescent behavior* (3rd ed.). Belmont, CA: Wadsworth.

Blankenship, C., & Lilly, M.S. (1981). *Mainstreaming students with learning and behavior problems: Techniques for the classroom teacher.* New York: Holt, Rinehart, & Winston.

Brophy, J., & Good, T. (1969). *Teacher-child dyadic interaction: A manual for coding classroom behavior.* Austin, TX: Research and Development Center, University of Texas.

Brown, L.L., & Hammill, D.D. (1983). *Behavior Rating Profile.* Austin, TX: Pro-Ed.

Bruininks, R.H., Woodcock, R.W., Weatherman, R.F., & Hill, B.K. (1985). *Scales of Independent Behavior: Woodcock-Johnson Psycho-Educational Battery* (Part 4). Allen, TX: DLM Teaching Resources.

Bryan, T.H. (1986). Self-concept and attributions of the learning disabled. *Learning Disabilities Focus, 1,* 82–89.

Burks, H.F. (1977). *Burks' Behavior Rating Scales* (Rev. ed.). Los Angeles: Western Psychological Services.

Canter, L., & Canter, M. (1976). *Assertive discipline: A take-charge approach for today's educator.* Seal Beach, CA: Canter and Associates.

Cartwright, C.A., & Cartwright, G.P. (1984). *Developing observation skills* (2nd ed.). New York: McGraw-Hill.

Charles, C.M. (1985). *Building classroom discipline: From models to practice* (2nd ed.). New York: Longman.

Cianciolo, P.J. (1965). Children's literature can affect coping behavior. *Personnel and Guidance Journal, 43*(9), 897–903.

Coopersmith, S. (1981). *Coopersmith Self-Esteem Inventories.* Monterey, CA: Publishers Test Service.

Cruickshank, W.M. (1976). William M. Cruickshank. In J.M. Kauffman & D.P. Hallahan (Eds.), *Teaching children with learning disabilities: Personal perspectives* (pp. 94–125). Columbus, OH: Merrill.

Deshler, D.D., Schumaker, J.B., & Lenz, B.K. (1984). Academic and cognitive interventions for LD adolescents: Part I. *Journal of Learning Disabilities, 17,* 108–117.

Dinkmeyer, D., & Dinkmeyer, D., Jr. (1982). *Developing understanding of self and others* (Rev. ed.). Circle Pines, MN: American Guidance Service.

Dupont, H., & Dupont, C. (1979). *Transition.* Circle Pines, MN: American Guidance Service.

Dupont, H., Gardner, O.S., & Brody, D.S. (1974). *Toward affective development: A program to stimulate psychological and affective development.* Circle Pines, MN: American Guidance Service.

Ehly, S.W., & Larsen, S.C. (1980). *Peer tutoring for individualized instruction.* Austin, TX: Pro-Ed.

Fagen, S.A., Long, N.J., & Stevens, D.J. (1975). *Teaching children self-control: Preventing emotional and learning problems in the elementary school.* Columbus, OH: Merrill.

Fiske, D.W., & Cox, J.A., Jr. (1960). The consistency of ratings by peers. *Journal of Applied Psychology, 44,* 11–17.

Fitts, W. (1965). *Manual: Tennessee Self-Concept Scale.* Nashville: Counselor Recordings and Tests.

Flanders, N. (1970). *Analyzing teacher behavior.* Menlo Park, CA: Addison-Wesley.

Fowler, J.W., & Peterson, P.L. (1981). Increasing reading persistence and altering attributional style of learned helpless children. *Journal of Educational Psychology, 73,* 251–260.

Glasser, W. (1965). *Reality therapy. A new approach to psychiatry.* New York: Harper & Row.

Hazel, J.S., Schumaker, J.B., Sherman, J.A., & Sheldon-Wildgen, J. (1982). *Asset: A social skills program for adolescents.* Champaign, IL: Research Press.

Hoagland, J. (1972, March). Bibliotherapy: Aiding children in personality development. *Elementary English,* pp. 390–394.

Hutton, J.B., & Roberts, T.G. (1986). *Social-Emotional Dimension Scale.* Austin, TX: Pro-Ed.

Kazdin, A.E. (1972). Response cost: The removal of conditioned reinforcers for therapeutic change. *Behavior Therapy, 3,* 533–546.

Kerr, M.M., & Nelson, C.M. (1983). *Strategies for managing behavior problems in the classroom.* Columbus, OH: Merrill.

Kircher, C.J. (1966). *Behavior patterns in children's books.* Washington, DC: Catholic University of America Press.

Kroth, R. (1973). The behavioral Q-sort as a diagnostic tool. *Academic Therapy, 8,* 317–329.

Licht, B.G. (1984). Cognitive-motivational factors that contribute to the achievement of learning-disabled children. *Annual Review of Learning Disabilities, 2,* 119–126.

Lieberman, L.M. (1983). The homework solution. *Journal of Learning Disabilities, 16,* 435.

Lindsley, O.R. (1964). Direct measurement and prothesis of retarded behavior. *Journal of Education, 147,* 62–81.

Lindzey, G., & Borgatta, E.F. (1954). Sociometric measurement. In G. Lindzey (Ed.), *Handbook of social psychology.* Reading, MA: Addison-Wesley.

Lister, J.L. (1969). Personal-emotional-social skills. In R.M. Smith (Ed.), *Teacher diagnosis of educational difficulties.* Columbus, OH: Merrill.

Long, N.J., & Newman, R.G. (1971). Managing surface behavior of children in schools. In N.J. Long, W.C. Morse, & R.G. Newman (Eds.), *Conflict in the classroom: The education of emotionally disturbed children* (2nd ed.). Belmont, CA: Wadsworth.

Meichenbaum, D. (1977). *Cognitive-behavior modification: An integrative approach.* New York: Plenum Press.

Moody, M.T., & Limper, H.K. (1971). *Bibliotherapy: Methods and materials.* Chicago: American Library Association.

Moreno, J.L. (1953). *Who shall survive? Foundations of sociometry, group psychotherapy, and sociodrama* (2nd ed.). New York: Beacon House.

Morse, W.C. (1971). Worksheet on life space interviewing for teachers. In N.J. Long, W.C. Morse, & R.G. Newman (Eds.), *Conflict in the classroom: The education of emotionally disturbed children* (2nd ed.). Belmont, CA: Wadsworth.

Myklebust, H.R. (1981). *The Pupil Rating Scale: Screening for learning disabilities* (Rev. ed.). New York: Grune & Stratton.

Nihira, K., Foster, R., Shellhaas, M., & Leland, H. (1981). *AAMD Adaptive Behavior Scales: School edition.* Washington, DC: American Association on Mental Deficiency.

O'Leary, K.D., & Drabman, R. (1971). Token reinforcement in the classroom: A review. *Psychological Bulletin, 75,* 379–398.

Paine, S.C., Radicchi, J., Rosellini, L.C., Deutchman, L., & Darch, C.B. (1983). *Structuring your classroom for academic success.* Champaign, IL: Research Press.

Pierce, M.M., Stalhbrand, K., & Armstrong, S.B. (1984). *Increasing student productivity through peer tutoring programs.* Austin, TX: Pro-Ed.

Piers, E., & Harris, D. (1969). *The Piers-Harris Children's Self-Concept Scale.* Nashville: Counselor Recordings and Tests.

Polsgrove, L. (1979). Self-control: Methods for child training. *Behavioral Disorders, 4,* 116–130.

Premack, D. (1959). Toward empirical behavior laws: I. Positive reinforcement. *Psychological Review, 66,* 219–233.

Quay, H.C., & Peterson, D.R. (1983). *Behavior Problems Checklist* (Rev. ed.). Coral Gables, FL: University of Miami.

Reid, V.M. (Ed.). (1972). *Reading ladders for human relations* (5th ed.). Washington, DC: American Council on Education.

Remmers, H.H., & Bauernfeind, R.H. (1957). *SRA Junior Inventory, Form S.* Chicago: Science Research Associates.

Remmers, H.H., & Shimberg, B. (1957). *SRA Youth Inventory, Form S.* Chicago: Science Research Associates.

Russell, A.E., & Russell, W.A. (1979). Using bibliotherapy with emotionally disturbed children. *Teaching Exceptional Children, 11,* 168–169.

Schumaker, J.B., & Hazel, J.S. (1984). Social skills assessment and training for the learning disabled: Who's on first and what's on second? Part II. *Journal of Learning Disabilities, 17,* 492–499.

Schwarzrock, S., & Wrenn, C.G. (1984). *Coping with series* (Rev. ed.). Circle Pines, MN: American Guidance Service.

Skinner, B.F. (1953). *Science and human behavior.* New York: Free Press.

Smith, R.M., Neisworth, J.T., & Greer, J.G. (1978). *Evaluating educational environments.* Columbus, OH: Merrill.

Sparrow, S.S., Balla, D.A., & Cicchetti, D.V. (1984). *The Vineland Adaptive Behavior Scales.* Circle Pines, MN: American Guidance Service.

Spivack, G., & Spotts, J. (1966). *Devereux Child Behavior Rating Scale.* Devon, PA: Devereux Foundation.

Spivack, G., Spotts, J., & Haimes, P.E. (1967). *Devereux Adolescent Behavior Rating Scale.* Devon, PA: Devereux Foundation.

Stainback, W.C., Payne, J.S., Stainback, S.B., &

Payne, R.A. (1973). *Establishing a token economy in the classroom.* Columbus, OH: Merrill.

Stephens, T.M. (1977). *Teaching skills to children with learning and behavior disorders.* Columbus, OH: Merrill.

Stephens, T.M., Hartman, A.C., & Lucas, V.H. (1983). *Teaching children basic skills: A curriculum handbook* (2nd ed.). Columbus, OH: Merrill.

Stephenson, W. (1953). *The study of behavior: Q-Technique and its methodology.* Chicago: University of Chicago Press.

Swift, M. (1982). *Devereux Elementary School Behavior Rating Scale* (2nd ed.). Devon, PA: Devereux Foundation.

Swift, M., & Spivack, G. (1972). *Hahnemann High School Behavior Rating Scale manual.* Philadelphia: Departmental Health Sciences, Hahnemann Medical College and Hospital.

Vernon, W.M. (1972). *Motivating children: Behavior modification in the classroom.* New York: Holt, Rinehart, & Winston.

Walker, H.M. (1979). *The acting-out child: Coping with classroom disruption.* Boston: Allyn & Bacon.

Walker, H.M. (1983). *Walker Problem Behavior Identification Checklist.* Los Angeles: Western Psychological Services.

Walker, H.M., McConnell, S., Holmes, D., Todis, B., Walker, J., & Golden, N. (1983). *The Walker social skills curriculum: The ACCEPTS program.* Austin, TX: Pro-Ed.

Walker, H.M., Todis, B., Holmes, D., & Horton, G. (1987). *The Walker social skills curriculum: The ACCESS program.* Austin, TX: Pro-Ed.

Wallace, G., & Kauffman, J.M. (1986). *Teaching students with learning and behavior problems* (3rd ed.). Columbus, OH: Merrill.

Wallace, G., & Larsen, S.C. (1978). *Educational assessment of learning problems: Testing for teaching.* Boston: Allyn & Bacon.

Weller, C., & Strawser, S. (1981). *Weller-Strawser Scales of Adaptive Behavior for the learning disabled.* Novato, CA: Academic Therapy.

Wolf, M.M., Hanley, E.L., King, L.A., Lachowicz, J., & Giles, D.K. (1970). The timer-game: A variable interval contingency for the management of out-of-seat behavior. *Exceptional Children, 37,* 113–117.

PART TWO

Teaching Academic Skills

CHAPTER 6

Assessing
Math Skills

tudents with learning problems often have difficulty mastering math skills and concepts. Arithmetic problems are common at all age levels. During the preschool and primary years, many children cannot sort objects by size, match objects, understand the language of arithmetic, or grasp the concept of rational counting. During the elementary years, they have trouble with computational skills (Otto & Smith, 1980). In the middle and upper grades, students experience difficulty with fractions, decimals, percentages, and measurement. Secondary students may experience problems in these areas, but it is not uncommon for them to make errors like those of younger children—for example, place value problems and difficulty with basic facts.

Learning problems in math have generally received less attention than other academic areas. However, increased interest in arithmetic disabilities in the 1970s resulted in more research activity and the development of numerous tests and materials (Underhill, Uprichard, & Heddens, 1980). The works of Cawley and his associates (Cawley et al., 1976) and Thornton and her associates (Jones, Thornton, & Toohey, 1985; Thornton & Toohey, 1985) represent major efforts to understand and ameliorate the mathematical deficits of students with learning problems.

DEVELOPMENT OF MATH SKILLS

Mathematics content has a logical structure. Students construct simple relationships first and then progress to more complex tasks. As the student progresses in this ordering of math tasks, the learning of skills and content transfers from each step to the next higher step. Several studies (J.L. Brown, 1970; Callahan & Robinson, 1973; Phillips & Kane, 1973) indicate that the best learning sequences come from arranging instruction in learning hierarchies. The hierarchy of math skills in Appendix A provides useful information for assessing and teaching math skills. In using the hierarchy, the teacher should remember that individual students may learn specific skills faster in slightly different orderings or may be able to skip selected subskills.

Since mastery of lower-level math skills is essential to learning higher-order skills, the concept of *readiness* is important in arithmetic instruction. For example, if a youngster has not mastered basic facts in multiplication, he is not ready for division. Many authorities (Copeland, 1979; Reisman, 1982; Underhill et al., 1980) claim that failure to understand basic concepts in beginning math instruction contributes heavily to later learning problems in arithmetic. Unfortunately, students with learning difficulties often are taught math in a rote manner, without ever achieving an understanding of basic concepts.

Readiness for Number Instruction

Piaget (1965) describes several concepts that are basic to understanding numbers: (a) classification, (b) ordering and seriation, (c) one-to-one correspondence, and (d) conservation. Mastering these concepts is necessary for learning higher-order arithmetic skills.

Classification is one of the most basic intellectual activities and must precede work with numbers (Piaget, 1965). It involves a study of relationships, such as likenesses and differences. Activities include categorizing objects according to a specific property. For example, the child may group buttons according to color, then size, then shape, and so on. Most children 5 to 7 years old can judge objects as similar or dissimilar on the basis of properties such as color, shape, size, texture, and function (Copeland, 1979).

Ordering is important for sequencing numbers. Many children do not understand order until they are 6 or 7 years of age (Copeland,

1979). It is important for the child first to understand the *topological* relation of order. When counting objects, the student must order them so that each object is counted only once. In a topological ordering activity, the teacher might display objects in a certain order and ask the child to arrange identical objects in the same order. Ordering activities include (a) sequencing blocks in a certain pattern; (b) lining up for lunch in a specific order; and (c) completing "pattern" games—for example, the child is given a series such as

$$X–O–X–O–X–O–X–\ \_\_$$

and tells what goes in the blank.

Topological ordering involves arranging a set of items without considering a quantity relationship between each successive item. The combination of *seriation and ordering,* however, involves ordering items on the basis of *change* in a property, such as length, size, or color. An example of a seriation task would be arranging items of various lengths in an order from shortest to longest with each successive item being longer than the preceding item. Children 6 to 7 years old usually master ordering and seriation (Copeland, 1979).

One-to-one correspondence is the basis for counting to determine how many, and it is essential for mastering computational skills. It involves understanding that one object in a set is the same number as one object in a different set, whether or not characteristics are similar. If a teacher places small buttons in a glass one at a time and a child places the same number of large buttons one at a time in a glass, the glass containing the large buttons soon displays a higher stack. If the child is asked, "Does each glass have the same number of buttons?" and responds "Yes," the child understands one-to-one correspondence. If the child responds "No, because the buttons are higher in one glass," the child is not applying one-to-one correspondence and instead is judging on the

basis of sensory cues. Most children 5 to 7 years old master the one-to-one correspondence concept. Initial activities consist of matching identical objects, whereas later activities should involve different objects. Sample activities are (a) giving one pencil to each child, (b) matching each head with a hat, and (c) matching a penny to each marble.

Piaget (1965) considers the concept of *conservation* fundamental to later numerical reasoning. Conservation means that the quantity of an object or the number of objects in a set remains constant regardless of spatial arrangement. Copeland (1979) describes two types of conservation: conservation of quantity and conservation of number. Conservation of quantity is illustrated in the familiar Piagetian experiments of pouring identical amounts of water into a tall, thin glass and a low, wide glass and rolling a piece of clay into a ball and a long roll. If the student recognizes that the amount of water or clay remains constant, she probably understands conservation of quantity. Conservation of number involves understanding that the number of objects in a set remains constant whether the objects are close to one another or spread apart. Ask the child to select a spoon for each of seven plates and check her work by putting each spoon on each plate. Then remove the spoons and put them in a stack. Ask her if there is still the same number of spoons and plates. If the child says yes, she probably understands the concept of conservation of number (Copeland, 1979). Most children master conservation between the ages of 5 and 7.

Several authorities consider an understanding of Piaget's concepts as a prerequisite for formal math instruction. Many teachers in preschool through first grade directly teach to help children understand these concepts. Moreover, some authorities recommend that teachers in later grades spot deficits in these concepts and provide remedial instruction.

Readiness for More Advanced Facts and Concepts

Once formal math instruction begins, the student must master operations and basic axioms in order to acquire skills in computation and problem solving. Operations are well known: addition, subtraction, multiplication, and division. Basic axioms are less familiar. Alley and Deshler (1979) list axioms that are especially important for teaching arithmetic skills to students with learning problems: (a) commutative property of addition, (b) commutative property of multiplication, (c) associative property of addition and multiplication, (d) distributive property of multiplication over addition, and (e) inverse operations for addition and multiplication.

Commutative property of addition. No matter what order the same numbers are combined in, the sum remains constant:

$$a + b = b + a$$
$$3 + 4 = 4 + 3$$

Commutative property of multiplication. Regardless of the order of the numbers being multiplied, the product remains constant:

$$a \times b = b \times a$$
$$9 \times 6 = 6 \times 9$$

Associative property of addition and multiplication. Regardless of grouping arrangements, the sum or product is unchanged:

Addition

$$(a + b) + c = a + (b + c)$$
$$(4 + 3) + 2 = 4 + (3 + 2)$$

Multiplication

$$(a \times b) \times c = a \times (b \times c)$$
$$(5 \times 4) \times 3 = 5 \times (4 \times 3)$$

Distributive property of multiplication over addition. This rule relates the two operations:

$$a(b + c) = (a \times b) + (a \times c)$$
$$5(4 + 3) = (5 \times 4) + (5 \times 3)$$

Inverse operations. These axioms relate operations that are opposite in their effects. The following equations demonstrate inverse operations.

Addition and subtraction

$$
\begin{array}{ll}
a + b = c & 5 + 4 = 9 \\
c - a = b & 9 - 5 = 4 \\
c - b = a & 9 - 4 = 5
\end{array}
$$

Multiplication and division

$$
\begin{array}{ll}
a \times b = c & 9 \times 3 = 27 \\
c \div a = b & 27 \div 9 = 3 \\
c \div b = a & 27 \div 3 = 9
\end{array}
$$

Levels of Learning

Understanding the ordering of the basic operations and related axioms that affect computation skills helps the teacher to diagnose math learning problems and plan instruction. Knowledge of the *levels* of understanding specific math concepts also is vital to arithmetic instruction. Underhill et al. (1980) report that there are several basic levels of learning in mathematical learning experiences. Basically, these levels are *concrete, semiconcrete,* and *abstract.*

The concrete level involves the manipulation of objects. This level may be used to help the student relate manipulative and computational processes. At this level, the learner concentrates on both the manipulated objects and the symbolic processes that describe the manipulations (Underhill et al., 1980). For example, in instruction of addition problems involving sums of 8, a concrete activity would be to have the student group eight blocks into all possible combinations of 8 (6 + 2, 5 + 3, and so on). In instruction involving one-to-one correspondence at a concrete level, the learner might be required to put one straw in each milk carton or pass out one book to each child in the room. Some students demonstrate their need for concrete-level activities by counting on their fingers when requested to complete simple addition problems. Concrete experiences are important for learning skills at all levels in the arithmetic hierarchy.

Dunlap and Brennan (1979) stress the use of manipulative aids. However, they note that these should not be used haphazardly. They offer the following guidelines:

1. Prior to abstract experiences, instruction must proceed from concrete (manipulative) experiences to semiconcrete experiences.
2. The main objective of manipulative aids is to help students understand and develop mental images of mathematical processes.
3. The activity must accurately represent the actual process. For example, a direct correlation should exist between the manipulative activities and the paper-pencil activities.
4. More than one manipulative object should be used in teaching a concept.
5. The aid should be used individually by each student.
6. The manipulative experience must involve the moving of objects. The learning occurs from the student's physical actions on the objects, not from the objects themselves.

The Key Math Early Steps Program (Connolly, 1982) teaches beginning mathematics through hands-on activities with specially designed manipulatives: cubes, attribute blocks, card decks, chips, tumblers, numeral cards, and trays. Students gain practice in geometry, numeration, addition/subtraction, measurement, time, fractions, and money.

The semiconcrete level involves working with illustrations of items in performing math tasks. Items may include dots, lines, pictures of objects, or nonsense items. Some authorities divide this level into semiconcrete and semiabstract (Underhill et al., 1980). *Semiconcrete* refers to using pictures of real objects, whereas *semiabstract* involves the use of tallies. In this book, *semiconcrete* refers to both pictures and tallies. A worksheet that requires the learner to match sets of the same number of items is a semiconcrete-level task. Most commercial math programs include worksheets of tasks at this level. Many students with math learning problems need practice at this level to master a concept or fact. Often students demonstrate their reliance on this level by supplying their own graphic representations. For example, the problems

$$6 + 5 = \underline{\hspace{1cm}}$$

and

$$4 \times 2 = \underline{\hspace{1cm}}$$

may be approached in the following manner:

At the semiconcrete level, the emphasis is on developing associations between visual models and symbolic processes.

The abstract level involves the use of numerals. For example, in computation this level involves working only with numerals to solve math problems. Students who have difficulty in math usually need a lot of experience at the concrete and semiconcrete levels before they can use numerals meaningfully.

In a series of studies (Hudson, Peterson, Mercer, & McLeod, 1988; Peterson, 1987) at the University of Florida, the concrete—

semiconcrete—abstract mathematics teaching sequence has produced excellent results with mildly handicapped learners. These studies suggest that the sequence is instructionally efficient and produces excellent retention of targeted skills. Sample concrete, semiconcrete, and abstract learning experiences for each operation are presented in Chapter 7 in the sections on math teaching strategies, activities, and materials.

FORMAL MATH ASSESSMENT

Formal math assessment is accomplished by using published tests. These tests are either norm- or criterion-referenced and include both survey and diagnostic instruments.

Standardized Tests

Standardized math tests are norm-referenced and provide many kinds of information. They are usually classified into two categories: survey or achievement, and diagnostic. Survey tests cover a broad range of math skills and are designed to provide an estimate of the student's general level of achievement. They yield a single score which is compared to standardized norms and converted into a grade- or age-equivalent score. Survey tests are useful in screening students to identify those who need further assessment. Diagnostic tests, in contrast, usually cover a narrower range of content and are designed to assess the student's performance in specific math skill areas. Diagnostic tests aim to determine the student's strengths and weaknesses.

Survey tests. Most achievement tests include sections covering specific academic areas, such as reading, spelling, and math. Each of these specific academic areas is divided into skill areas. For example, a math section may be divided into numerical reasoning, computa-

tion, and word problems. Several of the commonly used survey tests are listed in Table 6.1.

Diagnostic tests. No one diagnostic test assesses all mathematical difficulties. The examiner must decide on the purpose of the assessment and select the test that is most suited to the task. Since quantitative scores are not very useful in developing a systematic instructional program, most diagnostic tests are criterion-referenced. However, five standardized diagnostic math tests are presented in Table 6.2.

The *Key Math Diagnostic Test* features an easy-to-use "easel kit" format and yields a grade-equivalent score for each subtest and for the total test. The manual provides an instructional objective for each of the 209 items on the test. It is individually administered in approximately 30 to 40 minutes. All items are given orally; thus, reading is not a factor affecting the student's performance.

Underhill et al. (1980) review the positive and negative features of the *Key Math*. Among its positive features, they note that the test is well organized and is in a very usable format. Items for each subtest follow an easy—more difficult sequence. Salvia and Ysseldyke (1988) note that the instructional objective that accompanies each item enables the teacher to administer the test in a criterion-referenced format. They state that this procedure is the real value of the test. About the test's negative features, Underhill et al. (1980) report that no test items are at the concrete level. Many place value concepts are not covered. Most items assess at the rote level, and understanding is not evaluated. Also, there are no provisions for error analysis, and items are not equally distributed across grade levels.

The *Key Math—Revised* is a revision of the *Key Math Diagnostic Arithmetic Test* and measures the student's understanding and application of important mathematics concepts and skills. The test is individually administered in

TABLE 6.1
Survey tests of math achievement.

Title: *California Achievement Tests* (1985)

Publisher: California Test Bureau/McGraw-Hill

Grade Levels: K–12

Areas Assessed: Computation and concepts and applications

Comments: This group-administered test has a locator test to identify the level of the test that is more appropriate. There are two forms of the test, and criterion-referenced objectives are available.

Title: *Diagnostic Achievement Battery* (Newcomer & Curtis, 1984)

Publisher: Pro-Ed

Grade Levels: 1–9

Areas Assessed: Mathematics reasoning and mathematics calculation

Comments: The Mathematics Reasoning Subtest consists of 30 items in which a mathematical problem is presented orally and the student must solve the problem without paper or pencil. In the Mathematics Calculation Subtest the subject works directly on a math calculation worksheet of 36 problems that become progressively more difficult.

Title: *Metropolitan Achievement Tests: Survey Battery* (Prescott, Balow, Hogan, & Farr, 1984)

Publisher: Psychological Corporation

Grade Levels: K–12

Areas Assessed: Concepts, problem solving, and computation.

Comments: This group-administered test has been available since 1937. A diagnostic battery that covers specific educational objectives is also available.

Title: *Peabody Individual Achievement Test— Revised* (Dunn & Markwardt, 1988)

Publisher: American Guidance Service

Grade Levels: K–12

Areas Assessed: Matching and recognizing numbers, and solving geometry and trigonometry problems

Comments: The test is individually administered and features an easy-to-use easel kit. Sometimes scores are inflated because the student response always involves selecting the correct answer from among four choices. Reading is not required, and the math subtest takes 10–15 minutes to administer.

Title: *SRA Achievement Series* (Naslund, Thorpe, & Lefever, 1978)

Publisher: Science Research Associates

Grade Levels: K–12

Areas Assessed: Concepts, computation, and problem solving

Comments: The test is group administered and yields grade equivalents, percentiles, stanines, and standard scores.

Title: *Stanford Achievement Test* (Gardner, Rudman, Karlsen, & Merwin, 1982)

Publisher: Psychological Corporation

Grade Levels: 1–9

Areas Assessed: Concepts, computation, and applications

Comments: This group-administered test is both norm-referenced and objective-referenced. A lower level of the test and an upward extension are also available.

TABLE 6.2
Diagnostic tests of math achievement.

Title: Key Math Diagnostic Arithmetic Test (Connolly, Nachtman, & Pritchett, 1976)

Publisher: American Guidance Service

Grade Levels: K–6

Areas Assessed: The *Key Math* consists of 14 subtests divided into three areas—content, operations, and application.

Comments: Underhill et al. (1980) state that the "*Key Math* seems to be a good test for screening purposes, but it does not provide a technique for zeroing in on specific difficulties a student is experiencing. *Key Math* represents a good beginning tool, but the clinician must extend the diagnosis in greater depth as a follow-up" (p. 218).

Title: Key Math—Revised (Connolly, 1988)

Publisher: American Guidance Service

Grade Levels: K–9

Areas Assessed: The *Key Math—Revised* consists of 13 subtests divided into three areas—basic concepts, operations, and applications.

Comments: This revision of the *Key Math Diagnostic Arithmetic Test* contains new items based on a comprehensive scope and sequence. Two parallel forms are available.

Title: Sequential Assessment of Mathematics Inventory (Reisman, 1985)

Publisher: Psychological Corporation

Grade Levels: K–8

Areas Assessed: SAMI includes 300 objectives organized into the eight content strands of mathematics language, ordinality, number/notation, measurement, geometry, computation, word problems, and mathematical applications.

Comments: In addition to classroom survey tests and the individual assessment battery, *SAMI* provides probes for more precise diagnosis of student deficits within each content strand. A concrete materials kit of manipulative materials is available for use with the probes.

Title: Stanford Diagnostic Mathematics Test (Beatty, Madden, Gardner, & Karlsen, 1984)

Publisher: Psychological Corporation

Grade Levels: K–12

Areas Assessed: The *Stanford* is divided into four separate tests, and the appropriate test is selected according to the student's grade level. Each level test is divided into three categories: number system and numeration, computation, and applications.

Comments: Underhill et al. (1980) note that the *Stanford* tests, like most group tests, must be supplemented with additional diagnostic work to determine the specific needs of students with learning problems.

Title: Test of Mathematical Abilities (V.L. Brown & McEntire, 1984)

Publisher: Pro-Ed

Grade Levels: 3–12

Areas Assessed: Information is provided about a student's abilities in two major areas: story problems and computation.

Comments: The test also provides related information regarding attitude toward mathematics, understanding of mathematical vocabulary, and understanding of general information that includes mathematical content.

approximately 35 to 50 minutes and yields standard scores, grade and age equivalents, percentile ranks, and stanines. An optional software program is available that provides quick score conversion and a detailed report of the student's strengths and weaknesses.

The *Sequential Assessment of Mathematics Inventory* assesses math performance of students in kindergarten through eighth grade. The classroom survey tests provide a profile of student performance in math concepts and skills, and the individual assessment battery gives an in-depth evaluation. The test covers 300 objectives organized into eight content strands, and items are sequenced from easy to difficult. In addition to the norm-referenced items in the individual assessment battery, *SAMI* provides follow-up probes to test the student's grasp of the material at various cognitive levels, including the concrete level. Manipulative materials included in the concrete materials kit may be used with the probes for diagnosing concrete representation. *SAMI* offers three types of test activities (paper/pencil, oral interview, and concrete representation) to provide a well-rounded picture of the student's strengths and weaknesses in mathematics skills.

The group-administered *Stanford Diagnostic Mathematics Test* is designed to identify the strengths and weaknesses of the students. Except for the level for grades 1 through 3, the student must read many of the examples. Although some items are at the semiconcrete level, most are at the abstract level. Throughout the test a multiple-choice format is used. The test scores are reported in percentile ranks, stanines, or grade equivalents. The *Stanford* is both criterion- and norm-referenced.

Underhill et al. (1980) review the positive and negative features of the *Stanford*. They note that the test is one of the few group-administered tests aimed at locating strengths

and weaknesses. It is available for all grade levels, and each item is based on a behavioral objective. The manual discusses how the scores can be interpreted to identify students with similar instructional needs. However, no provision is made for error analysis or for determining why a student misses an item. The test may identify the student's difficulty at a general level but fail to isolate the student's specific problem. No provision is made for assessing at the concrete level. Also, the multiple-choice format introduces an element of chance in a student's performance.

The *Test of Mathematical Abilities* is designed for use in grades 3 through 12 to provide standardized information not only about two major skill areas (i.e., story problems and computation) but also to provide related information about attitude, vocabulary, and general cultural application. The test is related to age and to IQ, and standard scores and percentiles are provided. The test scores differentiate diagnostically between groups of students who have problems in mathematics and those who do not.

Criterion-Referenced Tests

Standardized tests compare one individual's score with norms. This comparison generally does not help diagnose the student's arithmetic difficulties. However, criterion-referenced tests, which describe the student's performance in terms of criteria for specific skills, are more suited to assessing the student's specific difficulties. Like standardized tests, criterion-referenced tests are divided into survey and diagnostic tests. The survey tests locate general problem areas, whereas diagnostic tests focus on more specific difficulties.

Survey tests. Criterion-referenced achievement or inventory tests usually cover several academic areas. Each of these areas is further subdivided into skill categories. Selected criterion-referenced survey tests are listed in Table 6.3.

Diagnostic tests. Of all available published tests, criterion-referenced diagnostic tests are the most suited for identifying specific math problems. Several of the most recommended tests are listed in Table 6.4.

The *Adston Mathematics Skill Series* includes four tests. For each of the four tests there is a teacher's guide, an individual analysis chart, and prescription sets. The instruments are criterion-referenced and very comprehensive. For example, the *Working with Whole Numbers* test contains a survey test and respective diagnostic tests in each of the operations (+ , − , × , ÷). The items in the survey test consist of 12 addition items, 8 subtraction items, 16 multiplication items, and 16 division items. The diagnostic tests for each operation include many items. For example, the addition facts test has 100 items, and the addition operations test has 36 items. The *Readiness for Operations* test is designed to help the teacher determine if the child is ready for work in the basic operations. It includes tests in 15 areas (for example, one-to-one correspondence, group identification, number names, write numerals, sequencing). This instrument is pictorial and includes many items at the semiconcrete level. No items are on the concrete level.

Underhill et al. (1980) note that the use of three types of tests (survey, fact test, and operations test) is helpful. The inclusion of a readiness test with items at the semiconcrete level is also useful. The teacher is encouraged to look for error patterns, and corrective teaching sets are provided. However, the survey tests include items only at the abstract level. Further, no provision is made for assessing the areas of place value, money, time, and measurement.

TABLE 6.3
Criterion-referenced survey tests in arithmetic.

Title: Brigance Diagnostic Comprehensive Inventory of Basic Skills (Brigance, 1982); *Brigance Diagnostic Inventory of Essential Skills* (Brigance, 1980)

Publisher: Curriculum Associates

Grade Levels: K–12

Areas Assessed: The *Basic Skills Inventory* is designed for use in grades K–9 and assesses the areas of numbers (readiness skills), number facts, computation of whole numbers, fractions and mixed numbers, decimals, percents, word problems, metrics, and math vocabulary. The *Essential Skills Inventory* is designed for use in grade levels 4–12 and focuses on minimal academic and vocational competencies. The math inventory stresses functional and applied math skills.

Comments: The *Brigance Inventories* provide instructional objectives and include a record-keeping system for monitoring the progress of individual students. Also, placement tests are included which yield an age and grade equivalent. These age and grade levels are not based on norms but were determined by examining the hierarchical content of commercial materials.

Title: Classroom Learning Screening Manual (Koenig & Kunzelmann, 1980)

Publisher: Psychological Corporation

Grade Levels: K–6

Areas Assessed: Items are included in the areas of precomputational number skills, addition facts, subtraction facts, multiplication facts, and division facts through divisor of 9.

Comments: This device uses probes to assess each fact. Students are administered the probes in the selected math facts, and the number of correct and incorrect responses per minute is recorded. Criterion rates are suggested.

TABLE 6.4
Criterion-referenced diagnostic tests in math.

Title: Adston Mathematics Skill Series: Readiness for Operations (Adams & Sauls, 1979); *Adston Mathematics Skill Series: Working with Whole Numbers* (Adams & Ellis, 1979); *Adston Mathematics Skill Series: Common Fractions* (Adams, 1979); *Adston Mathematics Skill Series: Decimal Numbers* (Beeson & Pellegrin, 1979)

Publisher: Adston Educational Enterprises

Grade Levels: Preschool through secondary as appropriate for individual needs

Areas Assessed: The four instruments collectively assess readiness for operations, facts and operations in each area (+ , − , × , ÷), operations with fractions, and decimals.

Comments: Additional materials are available in the areas of operations, problem solving, and prealgebra.

Title: Buswell-John Fundamental Processes in Arithmetic (Buswell & John, 1925)

Publisher: Bobbs-Merrill

Grade Levels: Grade 2 and above as appropriate for individual needs

Areas Assessed: Items are included in whole-number computations in addition, subtraction, multiplication, and division.

Comments: The test does not yield final scores or grade equivalents, but is designed to assess faulty work habits. It does this by providing specific information about the methods a student uses in solving arithmetic problems.

Title: Diagnostic Tests and Self-Helps in Arithmetic (Brueckner, 1955)

Publisher: California Test Bureau/McGraw-Hill

Grade Levels: 3–8

Areas Assessed: Items are included in computation of whole numbers, fractions, decimals, percent, and operations in measurement.

Comments: The tests help the teacher identify general and specific areas of difficulty in arithmetic and may be used in planning remedial work.

The *Buswell-John Fundamental Processes in Arithmetic* test may be administered to a group. Materials include a manual of directions, pupil's worksheet, and teacher's diagnostic charts. The pupil's worksheet includes 46 addition items, 44 subtraction items, 44 multiplication items, and 42 division items. An "error analysis checklist" (see Table 6.5) is included in the teacher's diagnostic charts. The errors for each operation are listed according to their frequency of occurrence. Only errors committed by five or more students are included on the checklist. In using the checklist, the teacher is to check errors that appear five or more times. Although the checklist was developed more than 5 decades ago, it is still useful today.

Underhill et al. (1980) review the Buswell-John test. They note that the test is designed to help the teacher analyze specific mathematical difficulties. Throughout the test, the student reports her thought processes and the teacher records them. This procedure helps the teacher examine both calculating and mental processes. Adequate space is provided on the record sheet to show all work, and suggestions for the remediation of specific errors are provided. Reading is not a factor. However, all evaluation is at the abstract level, and problem-solving techniques and place value understanding are not specifically evaluated. Content is limited to basic operations; skills in money, time, measurement, geometry, fractions, decimals, and percentages are not assessed.

TABLE 6.5
Error analysis checklist in addition, subtraction, multiplication, and division.

Addition

Errors in combinations
Counting
Added carried number last
Forgot to add carried number
Repeated work after partly done
Added carried number irregularly
Wrote number to be carried
Irregular procedure in column
Carried wrong number
Grouped two or more numbers
Splits numbers into parts
Used wrong fundamental operation
Lost place in column
Depended on visualization

Disregarding column position
Errors in reading numbers
Dropped back one or more tens
Derived unknown combination from familiar one
Disregarded one column
Error in writing answer
Skipped one or more decades
Carrying when there was nothing to carry
Used scratch paper
Added in pairs, giving last sum as answer
Added same digit in two columns
Wrote carried number in answer
Added same number twice
Omitted one or more digits

Subtraction

Errors in combinations
Did not allow for having borrowed
Counting
Errors due to zero in minuend
Said example backwards
Subtracted minuend from subtrahend
Failed to borrow; gave zero as answer
Added instead of subtracted
Error in reading
Used same digit in two columns
Derived unknown from known combination
Omitted a column
Used trial-and-error addition

Split numbers
Deducted from minuend when borrowing was
    not necessary
Ignored a digit
Deducted two from minuend after borrowing
Error due to minuend and subtrahend digits
    being same
Used minuend or subtrahend as remainder
Reversed digits in remainder
Confused process with division or multiplication
Skipped one or more decades
Increased minuend digit after borrowing
Based subtraction on multiplication combination

Multiplication

Errors in combinations
Error in adding the carried number
Wrote rows of zeros
Carried a wrong number
Errors in addition
Forgot to carry
Used multiplicand as multiplier
Error in single zero combinations, zero as
    multiplier
Errors due to zero in multiplier
Used wrong process—added

Based unknown combination on another
Errors in reading
Omitted digit in product
Errors in writing product
Errors in carrying into zero
Counted to carry
Omitted digit in multiplier
Errors due to zero in multiplicand
Error in position of partial products
Counted to get multiplication combinations
Illegible figures

TABLE 6.5, *continued*

Error in single zero combinations, zero as multiplicand	Forgot to add partial products
	Split multiplier
Confused products when multiplier had two or more digits	Wrote wrong digit of product
	Multiplied by same digit twice
Repeated part of table	Reversed digits in product
Multiplied by adding	Wrote tables
Did not multiply a digit in multiplicand	

Division

Errors in division combinations	Had right answer, used wrong one
Errors in subtraction	Grouped too many digits in dividend
Errors in multiplication	Error in reading
Used remainder larger than divisor	Used dividend or divisor as quotient
Found quotient by trial multiplication	Found quotient by adding
Neglected to use remainder within problem	Reversed dividend and divisor
Omitted zero resulting from another digit	Used digits of divisor separately
Counted to get quotient	Wrote all remainders at end of problem
Repeated part of multiplication table	Misinterpreted table
Used short division form for long division	Used digit in dividend twice
Wrote remainders within problem	Used second digit of divisor to find quotient
Omitted zero resulting from zero in dividend	Began dividing at units digit of dividend
Omitted final remainder	Split dividend
Used long division form for short division	Counted in subtracting
Said example backwards	Used too large a product
Used remainder without new dividend figure	Used endings to find quotient
Derived unknown combination from known one	

Source: Reprinted from *Diagnostic Studies in Arithmetic* by G. T. Buswell and L. John by permission of The University of Chicago Press. Chicago: University of Chicago Press, 1926.

The *Diagnostic Tests and Self-Helps in Arithmetic* are 4 screening tests, 23 diagnostic tests, and 23 self-helps. The screening tests quickly assess the student's computational skills and locate areas for which a diagnostic test may be needed. The self-helps offer corrective exercises and correlate with the diagnostic tests. In fact, they are located on the reverse side of the corresponding diagnostic test. The tests may be administered to a group or to an individual. Although the tests specify a grade level, they may be used with any student depending on the individual's needs.

In addition to some of the positive features mentioned in the preceding description, other assets of the Brueckner tests include the following: (a) they thoroughly cover selected computation skills and provide a good basis for planning remedial work, (b) the tests are linked with the self-helps aids in assessment and instructional planning, and (c) adequate space is provided for solving test items. Some negative features are as follows: (a) all items are presented in written form on an abstract level, (b) areas such as place value, numeration, money, time, measurement, geometry, and problem solving are omitted, and (c) mathematical understanding is not assessed.

The descriptions of these criterion-referenced tests are not intended to be detailed. They are presented to give the reader some indication of what is included in some of the widely known diagnostic arithmetic tests. This type of information should help the teacher select instruments that will serve specific needs. Other criterion-referenced arithmetic tests that may be useful include the following:

1. The *Kraner Preschool Math Inventory* (Kraner, 1976) is designed for use with children 3 to 6½ years old. It includes 77 items divided into seven categories: counting, cardinal numbers, quantity, sequence, position, direction, and geometry/measurement.
2. The *Enright Diagnostic Inventory of Basic Arithmetic Skills* (Enright, 1983) is designed for use with elementary and junior high school students who have arithmetic difficulties. Three types of tests are included: (a) survey tests to determine computational ability in a specific skill area, (b) basic facts tests in addition, subtraction, multiplication, and division, and (c) skill tests to identify existing error patterns in computation. The inventory is based on a task analysis of basic computation skills and assesses the student's ability in 144 arithmetic computation skills that involve the adding, subtracting, multiplying, and dividing of whole numbers, fractions, and decimals.
3. The *Multilevel Academic Skills Inventory* (Howell, Zucker, & Morehead, 1982) includes criterion-referenced objectives in the math areas of computation and application. It is designed for students in grades 1 through 8 and includes survey tests, placement tests, and specific level tests. Student response booklets are included in four areas: addition/subtraction; multiplication/division; fractions; and decimals, ratios, and percents/applications.
4. The *Regional Resource Center Diagnostic Math Inventories* (Regional Resource Center, 1971) feature the use of rate of correct and incorrect responses from 1-minute samples of behavior. Each subtest consists of a probe sheet that is used for the 1-minute timings. Each probe sheet assesses a specific arithmetic skill. The manual suggests administering each subtest approximately five times over a period of several days. Several samples (usually five) provide more reliable results than one sample. Table 6.6 contains a sample record sheet for Math Inventory III. The record sheet readily shows the student's strengths and weaknesses in the subtest areas.

Traditionally, assessment has focused primarily on the abstract level. However, experts in mathematics education (Denmark, 1976; Engelhardt, 1976; Reisman, 1982; Underhill, 1976) maintain that diagnosis should not be limited to the abstract level. These authorities stress that the goal of diagnosis is to assess the learner's ability to relate to arithmetic computation in a meaningful way. To accomplish this they suggest using tasks at each of the levels. Unfortunately, commercial instruments for diagnosing understanding at the three levels are sparse. Only the *Sequential Assessment of Mathematics Inventory* (Reisman, 1985) includes a concrete materials kit which contains manipulative materials for test activities involving concrete representation. Teachers thus must teach mathematical understanding without the aid of many appropriate instruments. Most available tests, which have test items only at the abstract level, are useful mainly in helping to determine the student's level of achievement and general area of weakness. Once the problem area is identified, the teacher may use informal assessment techniques to determine the levels of instruction necessary for teaching specific concepts and facts. (See Underhill et al., 1980, for a detailed discussion of mathematical diagnostic models and related issues.)

TABLE 6.6
Regional Resource Center Math Inventory III record sheet and proficiency rates.

Name __Kathy__   Teacher __Jones__

Grade __3__   School __Piney Circle__

SUB-TEST NAME	TIME	DAY 1 Date ___ standard X nonstand ___ admin. by: ___		DAY 2 Date ___ standard X nonstand ___ admin. by: ___		DAY 3 Date ___ standard X nonstand ___ admin. by: ___		DAY 4 Date ___ standard X nonstand ___ admin. by: ___		Suggested Rates for Determining Proficiency[a]	
		correct	error	correct	error	correct	error	correct	error	correct	error
Read. Num. 0–10,000	1 min.	97	3	106	1	63	1	84	0	60	0
Write Num total	1 min.	56	0	60	1	39	2	51	0	60	0
sequen.		31	1	34	1	20	4	33	0	60	0
unique		Not Administered									
Order III	1 min.	Not Administered									
Add. Facts	1 min.	29	0	24	1	30	0	32	1	50	0
Sub. Facts	1 min.	18	3	22	1	16	1	19	0	50	0
Equation (Add.)	1 min.	6	11	11	4	7	6	12	5	50	0
Equation (Sub.)	1 min.	10	7	17	6	11	5	8	4	50	0
Add. w/o carry	1 min.	29	1	28	3	20	3	24	1	50	0
Sub. w/o borrow	1 min.	26	2	25	1	16	0	18	0	50	0
Add. w/ carry	1 min.	5	13	5	16	— —	— —	— —	— —	50	0
Sub. w/ borrow	1 min.	2	27	1	30	— —	— —	— —	— —	50	0
Mult.	1 min.	11	0	13	3	7	3	11	3	50	0
Division	1 min.	3	5	1	4	— —	— —	— —	— —	50	0

[a]Based on Haughton's (1972) report of research by Starlin.

Source: Adapted from *Regional Resource Center Diagnostic Inventories.* Eugene, OR: University of Oregon. The material is in the public domain.

INFORMAL MATH ASSESSMENT

Informal assessment involves examining the student's daily work samples or administering teacher-constructed tests. Most teachers find that informal assessment is essential for monitoring the progress of students and for teaching math concepts and skills. It enables teachers to use numerous items to sample specific skills, and it is directly related to the math curriculum. Also, with informal techniques the teacher can determine the student's understanding of math concepts at the concrete, semiconcrete, and abstract levels. Informal assessment thus is the most efficient way of determining the instructional needs of individual students.

Analyzing Error Patterns

The error patterns of each student must be considered individually. Nevertheless, it is helpful to examine the research on types of errors that many students of different grades make. In a study of the computational errors of third graders, Roberts (1968) identified four error categories:

1. *Wrong operation.* For example, the student subtracts when she should add.
2. *Obvious computational error.* The pupil applies the correct operation but makes an error in recalling a basic number fact.
3. *Defective algorithm.* An *algorithm* includes the specific steps used to compute a math problem. It is the problem-solving pattern used to arrive at an answer. An algorithm is defective if it does not deliver the correct answer. For example, if the child adds 24 + 16 by adding each number without regard for *place value*—that is, "2 + 4 + 1 + 6 = 13"—she is using a defective algorithm, because the correct answer is 40. When a defective algorithm is the only error, the pupil is applying the correct operation and recalling the basic facts.
4. *Random response.* In a random response

no relationship is apparent between the problem-solving process and the problem. For example, random responding may consist of guesses that do not even involve estimates.

Roberts (1968) reports that careless numerical errors and poor recall of addition and multiplication facts were found with the same frequency in all levels of ability. Random responses and the wrong operation occurred frequently with students of low ability. Random responses accounted for the most errors in low-ability students; defective algorithm techniques accounted for the most errors of pupils in the other three ability levels. In a study of seventh graders' errors in computation, Lankford (1972) reports that many errors were due to the use of defective algorithms. From her research, Cox (1975) reports that without intervention youngsters persist in making systematic errors for long periods of time.

In a study of multiplication and division errors committed by learning disabled students ($N = 213$), Miller and Milam (1987) found that the majority of the errors were due to a lack of prerequisite skills. Errors in multiplication were primarily due to a lack of knowledge of multiplication facts and inadequate addition skills. Errors in division included many subtraction and multiplication errors. The most frequent error in division was failure to include the remainder in the quotient. Miller and Milam conclude,

> Many of the errors discovered in this study indicated a lack of student readiness for the type of task required. Students were evidently not being allowed to learn and practice the skills necessary for higher order operations. The implications are obvious: students *must* be allowed to learn in a stepwise fashion or they will not learn at all. (p. 121)

The determination of a specific error is important because corrective intervention is influenced by the type of error. For example, the type of error may influence whether the student receives place value instruction or specific algorithm instruction.

Howell and Kaplan (1980) provide the following guidelines for conducting an error analysis:

1. Collect an adequate behavior sample by having the student do several problems of each type in which you are interested.
2. Encourage the student to work, but do nothing to influence the responses the student makes.
3. Record all responses the student makes, including comments.
4. Look for patterns in the responses.
5. Look for exceptions to any apparent pattern.
6. List the patterns you have identified as assumed causes for the student's computational difficulties. (pp. 250–251)

In addition to analyzing the student's work, it is very helpful to ask the student how she solved a problem. The student's response may give immediate insights into the error pattern and its cause.

Specific error patterns. The following common error patterns in addition, subtraction, multiplication, and division illustrate some of the computational problems of students with math learning problems.

1. The sums of the ones and tens are each recorded without regard for place value:

$$\begin{array}{r} 83 \\ +67 \\ \hline 1410 \end{array} \qquad \begin{array}{r} 66 \\ +29 \\ \hline 815 \end{array}$$

2. All digits are added together (defective algorithm and no regard for place value):

$$\begin{array}{r} 67 \\ +31 \\ \hline 17 \end{array} \qquad \begin{array}{r} 58 \\ +12 \\ \hline 16 \end{array}$$

3. When the tens column is added, the single-digit number is added to the numeral in the tens column (the lower addend is added twice):

$$\begin{array}{r} \overset{\prime}{68} \\ +\ 8 \\ \hline 156 \end{array} \qquad \begin{array}{r} \overset{\prime}{73} \\ +\ 9 \\ \hline 172 \end{array}$$

4. Digits are added from left to right. When the sum is greater than 10, the unit is carried to the next column on the right. This pattern reflects no regard for place value:

$$\begin{array}{r} \overset{23}{435} \\ +881 \\ \hline 119 \end{array} \qquad \begin{array}{r} \overset{37}{753} \\ +693 \\ \hline 1113 \end{array}$$

5. The smaller number is subtracted from the larger number without regard for placement of the number. The upper number (minuend) may be subtracted from the lower number (subtrahend), or vice versa:

$$\begin{array}{r} 627 \\ -486 \\ \hline 261 \end{array} \qquad \begin{array}{r} 761 \\ -489 \\ \hline 328 \end{array}$$

6. Regrouping is used when it is not required:

$$\begin{array}{r} \overset{6\prime}{1\cancel{7}5} \\ -\ 54 \\ \hline 1111 \end{array} \qquad \begin{array}{r} \overset{7\prime}{1\cancel{8}5} \\ -\ 22 \\ \hline 1513 \end{array}$$

7. When regrouping is required more than once, the appropriate amount is not subtracted from the column borrowed from in the second regrouping:

$$\begin{array}{r} \overset{5\prime\prime}{\cancel{6}32} \\ -147 \\ \hline 495 \end{array} \qquad \begin{array}{r} \overset{4\prime\prime}{\cancel{5}23} \\ -366 \\ \hline 167 \end{array} \qquad \begin{array}{r} \overset{4\prime}{\cancel{5}63} \\ -382 \\ \hline 181 \end{array}$$

8. The regrouped number is added to the multiplicand in the tens column prior to performing the multiplication operation:

$$\begin{array}{r} \overset{2}{17} \\ \times\ 4 \\ \hline 128 \end{array} \qquad \begin{array}{r} \overset{4}{46} \\ \times\ 8 \\ \hline 648 \end{array}$$

9. The regrouped number is not added:

$$\begin{array}{r} 36 \\ \times\ 9 \\ \hline 274 \end{array} \qquad \begin{array}{r} 43 \\ \times\ 6 \\ \hline 248 \end{array}$$

10. The divisor and dividend are reversed. For example, the student thinks $8 \div 4$ and $4 \div 2$ instead of $40 \div 8$ and $20 \div 4$:

$$8\overline{)40} \qquad 4\overline{)20}$$

11. The zero in the quotient is omitted:

$$\begin{array}{r} 21 \\ 6\overline{)1206} \\ \underline{1200} \\ 6 \\ \underline{6} \end{array}$$

The error checklist in the *Buswell-John Fundamental Processes in Arithmetic* test (see Table 6.5) is an excellent source for analyzing arithmetic errors in all assessment settings. Also, Ashlock (1986) and Reisman (1982) provide a thorough listing of computational error patterns.

Place value problems. Many computational errors stem from an inadequate understanding of place value. Lepore (1979) analyzed the computation errors of 79 mildly handicapped youngsters aged 12 to 14. The type of error they made most frequently involved regrouping, a procedure that requires understanding place value. Place value is introduced in the primary grades; however, pupils of all ages

continue to make mistakes because they cannot comprehend that the same digit expresses different orders of magnitude depending on its *location* in a number. Many of the error patterns presented earlier reflect an inadequate understanding of place value. In the next chapter numerous activities to help students learn place value are presented.

Diagnostic Interview Technique

The diagnostic interview provides the information necessary to determine what math skills to teach the student and how to teach them. In this technique the student expresses her thought processes while solving math problems. This technique often is used in administering diagnostic math tests.

The diagnostic interview enables the teacher to identify specific problems, error patterns, or problem-solving strategies in math. A sample interview illustrates how the procedure can yield important information.

The teacher gave Mary three multiplication problems and said, "Please do these problems and tell me how you figure out the answer." Mary solved the problems in this way:

$$\begin{array}{r} \overset{2}{27} \\ \times\ 4 \\ \hline 168 \end{array} \qquad \begin{array}{r} \overset{4}{36} \\ \times\ 7 \\ \hline 492 \end{array} \qquad \begin{array}{r} \overset{3}{44} \\ \times\ 8 \\ \hline 562 \end{array}$$

For the first problem, Mary explained, "7 times 4 equals 28. So I put my 8 here and carry the 2. 2 plus 2 equals 4 and 4 times 4 equals 16. So I put 16 here." Her explanations for the other two problems followed the same logic.

By listening to Mary and watching her solve the problems, the teacher quickly determined Mary's error pattern: She adds the number associated with the crutch (the number carried to the tens column) *before* multiplying the tens digit. Mary explained that she had been taught to first add the number being carried when regrouping in addition. After identifying Mary's error pattern and its origin, the teacher could then plan instruction for teaching the correct algorithm and developing an understanding of the multiplication process. Without the interview, the teacher incorrectly might have planned instruction in the basic multiplication facts.

The interview session provides an excellent opportunity for the teacher to assess the student's attitude toward math. In addition to observing the student's attitude during the session, the teacher may examine attitude through oral sentence-completion tasks. In this activity, the teacher starts the sentence and the student completes it:

1. Math is very _____ .
2. My best subject is _____ .
3. During math sessions I feel _____ .

How valid the diagnostic findings are depends on the quality of the exchange between teacher and student. The teacher must ensure that rapport exists and that the student feels free to respond honestly. Some general guidelines for conducting an interview include the following:

1. Establish rapport and be alert to the student's attitudes toward math throughout the session. It is often helpful to start with items that are easy for the student to do.
2. Focus only on the student's problem area that is the lowest on the skill sequence. Limit each session to one area of difficulty (for example, two-column addition with regrouping).
3. Allow the student the freedom to solve the problem in her own way.
4. Record the student's thinking processes, and analyze for error patterns and problem-solving techniques.
5. Once an error pattern or faulty problem-solving technique is discovered, introduce

diagnostic activities for assessing the student's level of understanding. These activities should include tasks at the semi-concrete and concrete levels.

For more detailed discussions of diagnostic arithmetic interviews, the reader may consult Lankford (1974) and Underhill et al. (1980).

Teacher-Constructed Tests

Teacher-constructed tests are essential for individualizing math instruction. They enable the teacher to identify problems, determine levels of understanding, and monitor progress. There are numerous types of teacher-constructed tests; the type the teacher selects depends, in part, on the purpose of the assessment.

To identify specific problem areas, the teacher may construct a survey test with items at several levels of difficulty. A four-step process details how to develop and use this type of test:

1. Select a hierarchy that includes the content area to be assessed. This hierarchy may come from a math program series, a curriculum guide, or a textbook. A sample math hierarchy is included in Appendix A.
2. Decide on what span of skills needs to be evaluated. Since a hierarchy includes a wide range of skills, the teacher must select which range of skills needs to be evaluated with an individual student. This is done by examining the student's performance on published tests and by analyzing the arithmetic curriculum per grade level. In deciding on the span, the teacher should begin with items that are easy for the student and proceed to items that are difficult.
3. Construct items for each skill within the range selected. A survey test is designed to assess the student's computation (abstract) performance within a hierarchy; all items thus are at the abstract level. If an untimed

criterion approach is used, it is a good practice to include three items for each skill and set 67% or 100% as a criterion for mastery (Underhill et al., 1980). Most commercial tests do not adequately sample a specific skill. Including three items per skill helps to control for carelessness and provides an adequate test sample. For teachers who prefer to use timed probes, a probe for each skill is constructed, and the criterion is established in terms of correct and incorrect responses per minute. To obtain a valid performance, each probe should be administered at least three times. The highest rate from the three samples is used for determining the criterion. From analyzing the proficiency rates in Table 6.7, it appears that 50 to 60 correct digits per minute with no errors is a useful criterion on most arithmetic skills. E. Haughton (personal communication, January 5, 1983) cautions against setting the aim for the rate correct too low. He notes that levels of performance that are associated with retention, endurance, and application are needed, and these levels are independent of age. He recommends that these respective rate levels be achieved as soon as possible. In Table 6.7 the rates provided by Wood, Burke, Kunzelmann, and Koenig (1978) are based on adults who use math in their occupations. Thus, they may be good indicators of application rates. For more information on application rates across a variety of math skills, the reader is encouraged to review the Wood et al. study.

4. Score the test and interpret the student's performance. The teacher starts with the easiest skill items and applies the "two out of three" (67%) criterion or the criterion of rate correct per minute. At the point where the criterion is not achieved, the teacher analyzes the student's performance (carelessness, faulty algorithm, basic fact deficit,

and so on) to determine what skill to teach the student. Also, the test may be used to monitor the progress of the student. A sample test in division is presented in Table 6.8.

The division test presented in Table 6.8 is based on the math scope and sequence skills list in Appendix A. The skills become progressively more difficult, and three items are presented for each skill. Reisman (1982) notes that it is sometimes less threatening for the student if the items in each skill area are placed on index cards.

In using the test, the teacher scores the student's responses under each skill and determines if the 67% criterion has been obtained. Failure to reach criterion on a skill alerts the teacher to a specific area of difficulty. These areas may become the target of instruction and further assessment. It is common practice to use the type of survey test presented in Table 6.8 for determining what to teach. However, as a teacher becomes more skillful in assessment and teaching, he can construct other diagnostic tests to determine the student's level of understanding. The scope and sequence skills list presented in Appendix A may be used in developing informal tests in other math areas.

Teacher-constructed tests may include a number of formats. Sample skills and related assessment items are presented next.

1. Identifies before or after for numbers to 10.

   Fill in the spaces:

   1 __ 3 __ 5 __ 7 __

   What numbers are missing?

   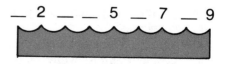

TABLE 6.7
Suggested proficiency rates for math skills.

Write Math Facts

	Digits in Simple Add. and Sub. Equations		Addition Facts 0–9 Gr. 2–3		Sub. Facts (1–5) and Facts Top Numb. 2–9 Gr. 2–3		Add. Facts Sums 10–18 and Sub. Facts Top Numb. 6–9 Gr. 3–4		Two-column Addition with Regrouping Gr. 4–5		Two-column Subtraction with Regrouping Gr. 4–6		Mult. Facts Through ×9 Gr. 5–6		Division Facts Through Divisor of 9 Gr. 6	
	Cor.	Err.	Cor.	Err.	Cor.	Err.	Cor.	Err.	Cor.	Err.	Cor.	Err.	Cor.	Err.	Cor.	Err.
Koenig & Kunzelmann (1980)			60	—	60	—	90	—	60	—	60	—	90	—	60	—
Precision Teaching Project (Montana)			70–90	—	70–90	—	70–90	—	70–90	—	70–90	—	70–90	—	70–90	—
Regional Resource Center (1971) (not grade-specific)	50	0									50	0	50	0	50	0
Smith & Lovitt (1982)			50+	0	45+	0							50+	0	45+	0
Starlin & Starlin (1973)			20–30	0–2	20–30	0–2	40–60	0–2	40–60	0–2	40–60	0–2	40–60	0–2	40–60	0–2
Wood, Burke, Kunzelmann, & Koenig (1978)	125	0			68	0			60	0	56	0	80	0	47	0

TABLE 6.8
Survey test: Division with whole numbers.

Skill

1. Identify symbols for division by circling problems that require division.

$$\begin{array}{c} 4 \\ +4 \end{array} \qquad 6 \times 3 \qquad\qquad 6 \div 2 \qquad\qquad 7 - 4 \qquad\qquad \dfrac{6}{2}$$

$$4\overline{)16} \qquad\qquad 7 \times 4 \qquad\qquad 8 \div 2 \qquad\qquad \dfrac{9}{3} \qquad\qquad \begin{array}{c} 13 \\ \times\,7 \end{array}$$

$$4 \times 1 \qquad\qquad \begin{array}{c} 6 \\ -2 \end{array} \qquad\qquad 8\overline{)64} \qquad\qquad 6 + 2 \qquad\qquad 9 = 3$$

2. Compute basic division facts involving 1.
   $1\overline{)8} \qquad\qquad 1\overline{)7} \qquad\qquad 1\overline{)1}$

3. Compute basic division facts.
   $4\overline{)36} \qquad\qquad 7\overline{)42} \qquad\qquad 8\overline{)56}$

4. Compute division of a nonzero number by itself.
   $7\overline{)7} \qquad\qquad 29\overline{)29} \qquad\qquad 1\overline{)1}$

5. Compute quotient of a one- or two-place dividend and a one-place divisor with a remainder.
   $3\overline{)7} \qquad\qquad 4\overline{)7} \qquad\qquad 2\overline{)9} \qquad\qquad (1D \div 1D)$

   $8\overline{)74} \qquad\qquad 6\overline{)39} \qquad\qquad 3\overline{)17} \qquad\qquad (2D \div 1D)$

6. Compute quotient with expanding dividend.
   $3\overline{)9} \qquad\qquad 9\overline{)90} \qquad\qquad 3\overline{)900}$
   $2\overline{)6} \qquad\qquad 2\overline{)60} \qquad\qquad 2\overline{)600}$
   $4\overline{)8} \qquad\qquad 4\overline{)80} \qquad\qquad 4\overline{)800}$

7. Compute quotient of a three-place dividend and a one-place divisor.
   $8\overline{)638} \qquad\qquad 6\overline{)461} \qquad\qquad 3\overline{)262}$

8. Compute quotient of a many-place dividend with a one-place divisor.
   $7\overline{)47,864} \qquad\qquad 6\overline{)2783} \qquad\qquad 3\overline{)578,348}$

9. Compute quotient of a three-place dividend and a two-place divisor where divisor is multiple of 10.
   $40\overline{)681} \qquad\qquad 30\overline{)570} \qquad\qquad 10\overline{)874}$

TABLE 6.8, *continued*

10. Compute quotient when divisors are 100,
    1000, and so on.

    $100\overline{)685}$ $100\overline{)4360}$ $100\overline{)973}$ (3D−4D ÷ 100)

    $1000\overline{)6487}$ $1000\overline{)99490}$ $1000\overline{)7430}$ (4D−5D ÷ 1000)

11. Compute quotient of a three-place dividend
    and a two-place divisor.

    $27\overline{)685}$ $39\overline{)871}$ $14\overline{)241}$

12. Compute quotient of a many-place dividend
    and a many-place divisor.

    $649\overline{)78,741}$ $3641\overline{)100,877}$ $247\overline{)8973}$

Note. When this test is administered, the directions for items 2–12 should simply state: Solve the following division problems.

Fill in the spaces:

Before		After
—	10	—
—	8	—
—	3	—

2. Identifies the greater or smaller number for
   numbers 0 to 100 and uses > and <.

   Put in order:

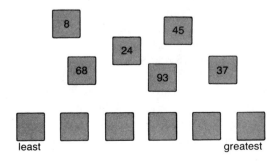

least   greatest

Circle the greater number:

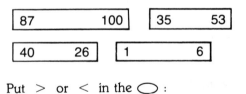

Put > or < in the ◯ :

23 ◯ 32   8 ◯ 19   94 ◯ 76
13 ◯ 42   43 ◯ 29   65 ◯ 59

3. Identifies place value with ones and tens.

   Fill in the spaces:

   36 = ＿＿ tens
        ＿＿ ones

   29 = ＿＿ tens
        ＿＿ ones

   78 = ＿＿ tens
        ＿＿ ones

State the face value and the place value of the underlined digit:

463
face value ____
place value ____

28
face value ____
place value ____

4843
face value ____
place value ____

Complete the following:

7 ones, 3 tens = ____
5 tens, 4 ones = ____
0 tens, 3 ones = ____

4. Computes three two-digit numerals, sum of ones greater than 20.

Add:

$$\begin{array}{r} 26 \\ 18 \\ +47 \end{array} \qquad \begin{array}{r} 57 \\ 38 \\ +49 \end{array} \qquad \begin{array}{r} 29 \\ 47 \\ +36 \end{array}$$

5. Demonstrates mastery of subtraction facts: sums 0 to 9.

Complete:

$$\begin{array}{r} 6 \\ -3 \end{array} \quad \begin{array}{r} 9 \\ -5 \end{array} \quad \begin{array}{r} 8 \\ -0 \end{array} \quad \begin{array}{r} 7 \\ -4 \end{array} \quad \begin{array}{r} 4 \\ -1 \end{array}$$

Subtract:

$8 - 3 =$ ____ $\qquad 5 - 2 =$ ____
$7 - 1 =$ ____ $\qquad 9 - 7 =$ ____

6. Identifies unit fraction inequalities.

Circle the numeral that represents the smaller number of each pair:

$$\frac{1}{2} \quad \frac{1}{3} \qquad \frac{1}{6} \quad \frac{1}{2} \qquad \frac{1}{4} \quad \frac{1}{3}$$

7. Writes fractions in word and numeral forms for ½, ⅓, and ¼.

Write the fractional numerals for each of the shaded areas in words and numeral form:

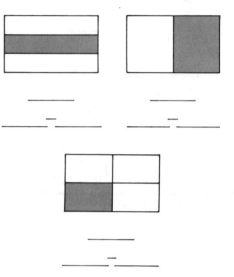

_____   _____
_____ —   _____ —

_____ —
_____

8. Identifies fraction names for 1.

Fill in each ☐:

$$1 = \frac{\square}{8} \qquad 1 = \frac{\square}{77} \qquad 1 = \frac{\square}{689}$$

Teacher-made probes can also be used to identify problem areas. Mixed probes are used to locate areas that need further assessment or instruction. Figure 6.1 presents a mixed probe in addition. There are nine items in each of the following categories: (a) basic addition facts of sums to 9 (first item and then every fourth item), (b) two-digit number plus two-digit number with no regrouping (second item and then every fourth item), (c) two-digit number plus one-digit number with no regrouping (third item and then every fourth item), and (d) basic addition facts of sums to 18 (fourth item and then every fourth item). On this probe, the

4 + 3	22 +41	33 + 6	9 + 7	6 + 2	36 +62	41 + 3	6 + 5	8 + 0
53 +44	78 + 1	5 + 8	7 + 2	43 +36	82 + 5	7 + 4	5 + 3	61 +37
42 + 4	8 + 7	4 + 5	33 +52	31 + 8	9 + 9	6 + 0	24 +53	65 +24
7 + 6	5 + 2	82 +13	37 + 2	6 + 6	4 + 4	31 +18	57 +32	7 + 9

Name _____ Date _____

Correct Digits: _____

Incorrect Digits: _____

Patterns: 0-9 facts _____/9

2D + 2D _____/9

2D + 1D _____/9

0-18 facts _____/9

Comments: _____

_____

_____

FIGURE 6.1
Mixed addition probe with no regrouping.

student may obtain a maximum score of 63 correct digits with no errors. After three timings a high score of 50 or more correct digits per minute with no errors is a reasonable criterion for diagnostic purposes. If the student fails to reach the criterion on a mixed probe, it is very important to analyze the responses and locate the items being missed. This analysis provides the teacher with information for further assess-ment with specific skill probes (such as 0–9 facts). Also, the specific skill probes can be used to monitor the daily progress of the student.

Teacher-constructed analytical tests. As dis-cussed earlier, learning math facts and con-cepts progresses through three levels of under-standing: concrete, semiconcrete, and abstract.

Most published tests consist of abstract-level items; therefore, they do not yield information on the student's understanding at the semiconcrete and concrete levels.

The student's level of understanding determines whether the student needs manipulative, pictorial, or abstract experiences. To obtain the type of information required for effective instructional planning, the teacher must construct analytical tests that focus on both identifying difficulties and determining level of understanding. Items at the concrete level should always involve real objects; items at the semiconcrete level should always use pictures or tallies; and numerals should always be used in items at the abstract level. The examples that follow should help the reader develop analytical arithmetic tests in specific skill areas. Also, the instructional activities presented in Chapter 7 for each of the operations (at all three levels) may provide guidance in developing assessment items. The reader interested in a more detailed discussion of this type of assessment should consult Reisman (1977, 1982) and Underhill et al. (1980).

Skill: Counting 1–5

Concrete level: Count the blocks.

Semiconcrete level: Circle five blocks.

Abstract level: Count to five and circle the number.
1   2   3   4   5   6   7

Skill: Addition Facts (0–9)

Concrete level: Write sum.

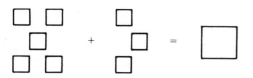

Semiconcrete level: Write sum.

Abstract level: Write sum.

$$\begin{array}{r} 5 \\ +3 \\ \hline \end{array}$$

Skill: Addition Facts (0–18)

Concrete level: Redistribute blocks to show tens and ones, and then write the sum.

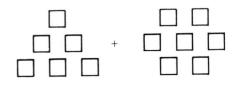

Student work:

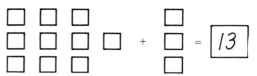

Semiconcrete level: Circle tens and write sum.
Student work:

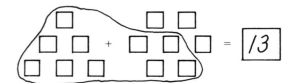

Abstract level: Write sum.

$$\begin{array}{r} 6 \\ +7 \\ \hline \end{array}$$

Skill: Addition Operation Without Regrouping

Concrete level: Let = 1 ten and ☐ = 1 one.
Write sum.

Semiconcrete level: Let ⟨⟩ = 1 ten and ○ = 1 one. Write sum.

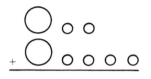

Abstract level: Write sum.

$$\begin{array}{r} 12 \\ +14 \\ \hline \end{array}$$

Skill: Addition with Regrouping Ones and Tens

Concrete level: Write sum and use string to group units.

Student work:

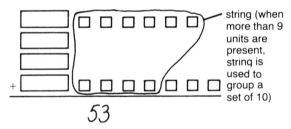

string (when more than 9 units are present, string is used to group a set of 10)

53

Semiconcrete level: Write sum and circle to group units.

Student work:

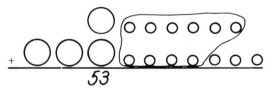

53

Abstract level: Write sum.

$$\begin{array}{r} 16 \\ +37 \\ \hline \end{array}$$

Skill: Addition with Regrouping Ones, Tens, Hundreds

Concrete level: Let ☐ = 1 hundred, ▢ = 1 ten, and ☐ = 1 one. Write sum and use strings to show work. Figure 6.2 is an example of student work with this kind of grouping.

Semiconcrete level: Use the place value chart to show work. Write the sum.

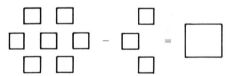

Abstract level: Write sum.

$$\begin{array}{r} 266 \\ +157 \\ \hline \end{array}$$

Skill: Basic Subtraction Facts

Concrete level: Write difference or missing addend.

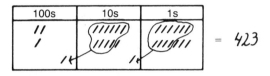

Semiconcrete level: Write difference or missing addend.

Abstract level: Write difference or missing addend.

$$\begin{array}{r} 7 \\ -3 \\ \hline \end{array}$$

Skill: Subtraction Operation with Regrouping

Concrete level: Write difference or missing addend by rearranging blocks and use string to show work, as shown in Figure 6.3.

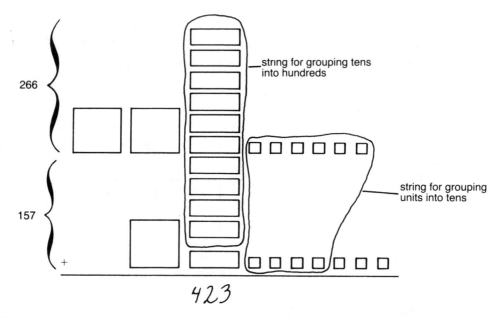

string for grouping tens into hundreds

string for grouping units into tens

266

157

+

423

FIGURE 6.2
Student's grouping of ones, tens, and hundreds.

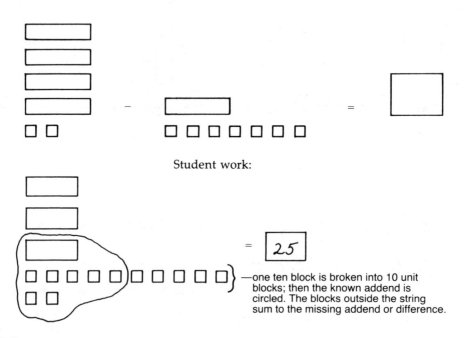

Student work:

= 25

—one ten block is broken into 10 unit blocks; then the known addend is circled. The blocks outside the string sum to the missing addend or difference.

FIGURE 6.3
Regrouping to perform subtraction.

Semiconcrete level: Write difference or missing addend and show work with slashes.

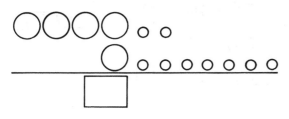

Student work:

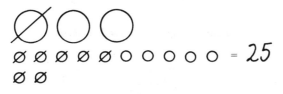

Abstract level: Write difference or missing addend.

42
−17

Skill: Basic Multiplication Facts

Concrete level:
a. Write the product.

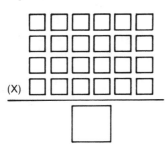

b. Use blocks to show 4 × 6 matrix.

Semiconcrete level: Write the product.

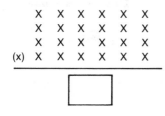

Abstract level: Write product.

4
×6

Skill: Basic Division Facts

Concrete level: Write quotient. Use strings to show work.

Student work:

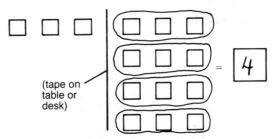

(tape on table or desk)

Semiconcrete level: Write quotient. Circle sets to show work.

Student work:

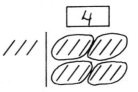

Abstract level: Write quotient.

3)12

Skill: Division with Remainder

Concrete level: Write quotient. Given a large matrix of blocks, figure out how many sets of 4 are in 30, or 30 ÷ 4. Use strings to show work, as shown in Figure 6.4.

Semiconcrete level:
a. Write quotient. Circle sets to show work with tallies.

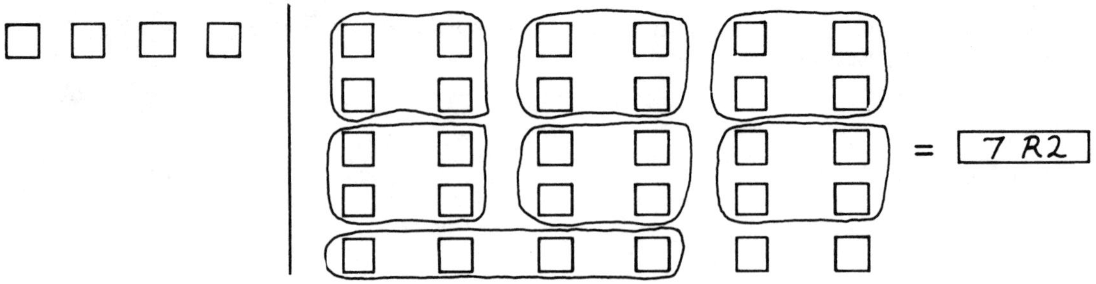

FIGURE 6.4
Student work showing division with blocks.

Student work:

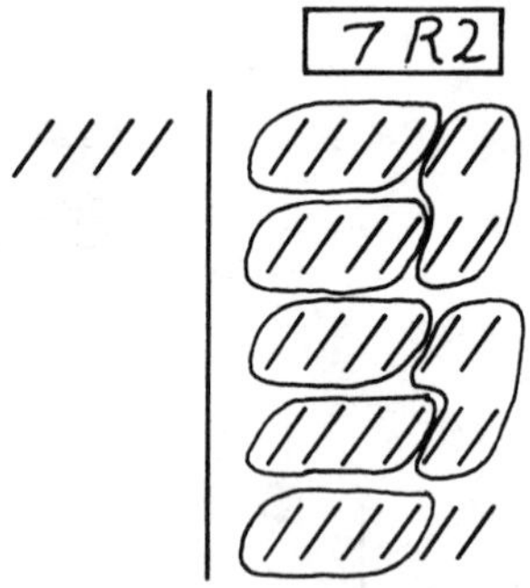

b. Write quotient. Given a large matrix covered with acetate, figure out the number of 4s in 30. Circle sets on matrix to display work.

Student work:

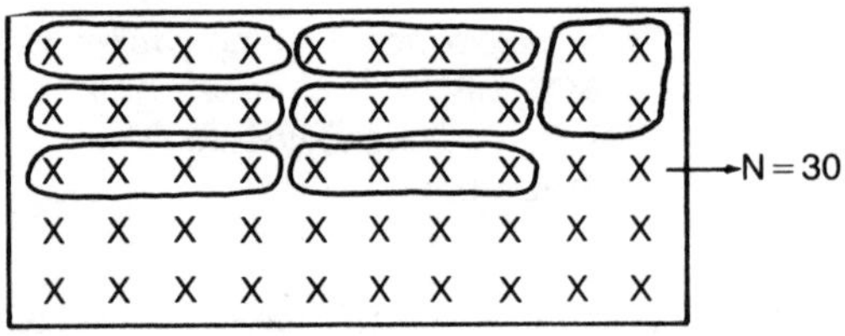

Quotient = 7R2

Abstract level: Write quotient.

$4\overline{)30}$

Skill: Recognize Simple Fractions

Concrete level: Let 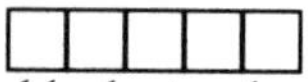 = 1 or 5/5 and  = 1/5. Stack the blocks to show 3/5.

Student work:

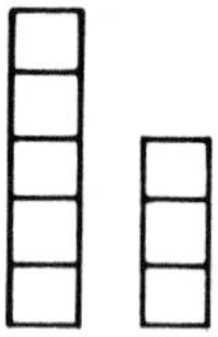

Semiconcrete level: Write a fraction for the shadowed part of the group.

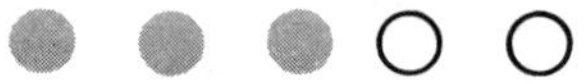

Abstract level: Write the fraction for three-fifths.

Skill: Addition of Fractions with Like Denominators

Concrete level: Let  = 1/3. Write sum of 1/3 + 1/3 and show work with blocks.

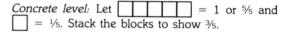

Student work:

Semiconcrete level: Display the sum of ⅓ + ⅓ by shading in the squares.

Abstract level: ⅓ + ⅓ = ____

Skill: Make Change for Amounts up to $1.00

Concrete level: Given real money and items with marked prices, figure out correct change if a $.39 item is purchased with a dollar.

Semiconcrete level: Circle the coins given as change for a dollar when buying a $.39 item.

Abstract level: Answer this problem: How much change would you give when someone buys a $.39 item and gives you a dollar?

Evans, Evans, and Mercer (1986) provide a detailed discussion of math assessment that features guidelines for conducting periodic and continuous assessments in math. Periodic assessment includes an initial testing that generates instructional objectives, and then periodic evaluations include checkups of general progress and in-depth evaluations of students experiencing difficulty. Continuous assessment focuses on monitoring the student's progress and involves frequent assessments—daily, weekly, and/or biweekly. Silbert, Carnine, and Stein (1981) highlight the importance of continuous assessment:

> The importance of careful monitoring cannot be overemphasized. The sooner the teacher

detects a student's skill deficit, the easier it will be to remedy. For each day that a student's confusion goes undetected, the student is, in essence, receiving practice in doing something the wrong way. To ameliorate a confusion, the teacher should plan to spend several days reteaching for every day the student's confusion goes undetected. Thus careful monitoring is a critical component of efficient instruction. (p. 10)

Charts may be developed and used to locate math facts that have not been memorized. The teacher first gives the student a test of selected facts (such as sums: 0–9, 10–18; differences: 0–9, 10–18; products: 0–9). Then the teacher records the student's performance on the chart: ✔ = basic fact memorized; — = basic fact not memorized. Figure 6.5 is a chart for multiplication facts. It shows that the student is experiencing difficulty with facts involving 0. A chart for subtraction facts 0–18 is presented in Figure 6.6. Inspection of Figure 6.6 suggests that the student is having difficulty with two-digit minus one-digit facts, except those involving 9 and those in which the subtrahend equals the difference.

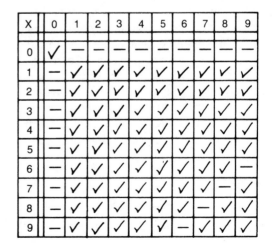

X	0	1	2	3	4	5	6	7	8	9
0	✔	—	—	—	—	—	—	—	—	—
1	—	✔	✔	✔	✔	✔	✔	✔	✔	✔
2	—	✔	✔	✔	✔	✔	✔	✔	✔	✔
3	—	✔	✔	✔	✔	✔	✔	✔	✔	✔
4	—	✔	✔	✔	✔	✔	✔	✔	✔	✔
5	—	✔	✔	✔	✔	✔	✔	✔	✔	✔
6	—	✔	✔	✔	✔	✔	✔	✔	✔	—
7	—	✔	✔	✔	✔	✔	✔	✔	—	✔
8	—	✔	✔	✔	✔	✔	✔	—	✔	✔
9	—	✔	✔	✔	✔	✔	—	✔	✔	✔

FIGURE 6.5
Student's performance on basic multiplication facts.

Minuend

Subtrahend	1	2	3	4	5	6	7	8	9	10	11	12	13	14	15	16	17	18
0	✓	✓	✓	✓	✓	✓	✓	✓	✓	✓								
1	✓	✓	✓	✓	✓	✓	✓	✓	✓	✓								
2		✓	✓	✓	✓	✓	✓	✓	✓	✓	✓							
3			✓	✓	✓	✓	✓	✓	✓	✓	✓	✓						
4				✓	✓	✓	✓	✓	✓	✓	✓	✓	✓					
5					✓	✓	✓	✓	✓	✓	✓	✓	✓	✓				
6						✓	✓	✓	✓	✓	—	✓	—	—	✓			
7							✓	✓	✓	✓	✓	—	—	✓	—	✓		
8								✓	✓	✓	✓	✓	—	—	—	✓	✓	
9									✓	✓	✓	✓	✓	✓	✓	✓	✓	✓

FIGURE 6.6
Student's performance on 0–18 subtraction facts.

Inspection of the sample items readily shows that the student's level of math understanding must be assessed on an individual basis. Developing and administering analytical math tests take time; and some teachers need several years to build an ample file of such tests, which then must be organized and stored in a functional system. Because of the time constraints, some teachers reserve this type of assessment for students who are not progressing with systematic math instruction and who appear to have serious math difficulties. Others include concrete experiences in their teaching and construct tests that include semiconcrete and abstract items. Instruction for students with math learning problems should include experiences at each of the three levels for teaching specific concepts and skills.

REFERENCES

Adams. S. (1979). *Adston Mathematics Skill Series: Common fractions.* Baton Rouge, LA: Adston Educational Enterprises.

Adams, S., & Ellis, L. (1979). *Adston Mathematics Skill Series: Working with whole numbers.* Baton Rouge, LA: Adston Educational Enterprises.

Adams, S., & Sauls, C. (1979). *Adston Mathematics Skill Series: Readiness for operations.* Baton Rouge, LA: Adston Educational Enterprises.

Alley, G., & Deshler, D. (1979). *Teaching the learning disabled adolescent: Strategies and methods.* Denver: Love.

Ashlock, R.B. (1986). *Error patterns in computation: A semi-programmed approach* (4th ed.). Columbus, OH: Merrill.

Beatty, L.S., Madden, R., Gardner, E.F., & Karlsen, B. (1984). *Stanford Diagnostic Mathematics Test* (3rd ed.). San Antonio, TX: Psychological Corporation.

Beeson, B.F., & Pellegrin, L.O. (1979). *Adston Mathematics Skill Series: Decimal numbers.* Baton Rouge, LA: Adston Educational Enterprises.

Brigance, A.H. (1980). *Brigance Diagnostic Inventory of Essential Skills.* North Billerica, MA: Curriculum Associates.

Brigance, A.H. (1982). *Brigance Diagnostic Comprehensive Inventory of Basic Skills.* North Billerica, MA: Curriculum Associates.

Brown, J.L. (1970). Effects of logical and scrambled sequences in mathematical materials on learning with programmed instruction materials. *Journal of Educational Psychology, 61,* 41–45.

Brown, V.L., & McEntire, E. (1984). *Test of Mathematical Abilities.* Austin, TX: Pro-Ed.

Brueckner, L.J. (1955). *Diagnostic tests and self-*

helps in arithmetic. Monterey, CA: California Test Bureau/McGraw-Hill.

Buswell, G.T., & John, L. (1925). *Diagnostic chart for fundamental processes in arithmetic.* New York: Macmillan.

California Achievement Tests. (1985). Monterey, CA: California Test Bureau/McGraw-Hill.

Callahan, L.G., & Robinson, M.L. (1973). Task-analysis procedures in mathematics instruction of achievers and underachievers. *School Science and Mathematics, 73,* 578–584.

Cawley, J.F., Fitzmaurice, A.M., Goodstein, H.A., Lepore, A.V., Sedlak, R., & Althaus, V. (1976). *Project MATH.* Tulsa, OK: Education Development Corporation.

Connolly, A.J. (1982). *Key Math early steps program.* Circle Pines, MN: American Guidance Service.

Connolly, A.J. (1988). *Key Math—Revised: A Diagnostic Inventory of Essential Mathematics.* Circle Pines, MN: American Guidance Service.

Connolly, A.J., Nachtman, W., & Pritchett, E.M. (1976). *Key Math Diagnostic Arithmetic Test.* Circle Pines, MN: American Guidance Service.

Copeland, R.W. (1979). *Math activities for children: A diagnostic and development approach.* Columbus, OH: Merrill.

Cox, L.S. (1975). Diagnosing and remediating systematic errors in addition and subtraction computations. *The Arithmetic Teacher, 22,* 151–157.

Denmark, T. (1976). Reaction paper classroom diagnosis. In J.L. Higgins & J.W. Heddens (Eds.), *Remedial mathematics: Diagnostic and prescriptive approaches.* Columbus, OH: ERIC Center for Science, Mathematics, and Environmental Education.

Dunlap, W.P., & Brennan, A.H. (1979). Developing mental images of mathematical processes. *Learning Disability Quarterly, 2*(2), 89–96.

Dunn, L.M., & Markwardt, F.C., Jr. (1988). *Peabody Individual Achievement Test—Revised.* Circle Pines, MN: American Guidance Service.

Engelhardt, J. (1976). Diagnosis and remediation in school mathematics: Developing continuity among R and D efforts. In J.W. Heddens & F.D. Aquila (Eds.), *Proceedings of the third national conference on remedial mathematics.* Kent, OH: Kent State University Press.

Enright, B.E. (1983). *Enright Diagnostic Inventory of Basic Arithmetic Skills.* North Billerica, MA: Curriculum Associates.

Evans, S.S., Evans, W.H., & Mercer, C.D. (1986). *Assessment for instruction.* Boston: Allyn & Bacon.

Gardner, E.F., Rudman, H.C., Karlsen, B., & Merwin, J.C. (1982). *Stanford Achievement Test* (7th ed.). San Antonio, TX: Psychological Corporation.

Haughton, E. (1972). Aims—Growing and sharing. In J.B. Jordon & L.S. Robbins (Eds.), *Let's try doing something else kind of thing.* Arlington, VA: Council for Exceptional Children.

Howell, K.W., & Kaplan, J.S. (1980). *Diagnosing basic skills: A handbook for deciding what to teach.* Columbus, OH: Merrill.

Howell, K.W., Zucker, S.H., & Morehead, M.K. (1982). *Multilevel Academic Skills Inventory.* San Antonio, TX: Psychological Corporation.

Hudson, P.J., Peterson, S.K., Mercer, C.D., & McLeod, P. (1988). Place value instruction. *Teaching Exceptional Children, 20*(3), 72–73.

Jones, G.A., Thornton, C.A., & Toohey, M.A. (1985). A multi-option program for learning basic addition facts: Case studies and an experimental report. *Journal of Learning Disabilities, 18,* 319–325.

Koenig, C.H., & Kunzelmann, H.P. (1980). *Classroom learning screening manual.* Columbus, OH: Merrill.

Kraner, R.E. (1976). *Kraner Preschool Math Inventory.* Austin, TX: Learning Concepts.

Lankford, F.G., Jr. (1972). *Some computational strategies of seventh grade pupils* (Project No. 2-C-013, Grant No. OEG-3-72-0035). Washington, DC: HEW Office of Education, National Center for Educational Research and Development (Regional Research Program) and Center for Advanced Study, University of Virginia.

Lankford, F.G., Jr. (1974). What can a teacher learn about a pupil's thinking through oral interviews? *The Arithmetic Teacher, 21,* 26–32.

Lepore, A.V. (1979). A comparison of computational errors between educable mentally handicapped and learning disability children. *Focus on Learning Problems in Mathematics, 1,* 12–33.

Miller, J.H., & Milam, C.P. (1987). Multiplication and division errors committed by learning disabled students. *Learning Disabilities Research, 2*(2), 119–122.

Naslund, R.A., Thorpe, L.P., & Lefever, D.W. (1978). *SRA Achievement Series.* Chicago: Science Research Associates.

Newcomer, P.L., & Curtis, C. (1984). *Diagnostic Achievement Battery.* Austin, TX: Pro-Ed.

Otto, W., & Smith, R.J. (1980). *Corrective and remedial teaching* (3rd ed.). Boston: Houghton Mifflin.

Peterson, S.K. (1987). *The concrete to abstract mathematical instructional sequence with learning disabled students.* Unpublished doctoral dissertation, University of Florida, Gainesville.

Phillips, E.R., & Kane, R.B. (1973). Validating learning hierarchies for sequencing mathematical tasks in elementary school mathematics. *Journal for Research in Mathematics Education, 4,* 141–151.

Piaget, J. (1965). *The child's conception of number.* New York: Norton.

Precision Teaching Project. Available from Skyline Center, 3300 Third Street Northeast, Great Falls, MT 59404.

Prescott, G.A., Balow, I.H., Hogan, T.P., & Farr, R.C. (1984). *Metropolitan Achievement Tests* (6th ed.). San Antonio, TX: Psychological Corporation.

Regional Resource Center. (1971). *Diagnostic Math Inventories* (Project No. 472917, Contract No. OEC-0-9-472917-4591 [608]). Eugene, OR: University of Oregon.

Reisman, F.K. (1977). *Diagnostic teaching of elementary school mathematics: Methods and content.* Chicago: Rand McNally.

Reisman, F.K. (1982). *A guide to the diagnostic teaching of arithmetic* (3rd ed.). Columbus, OH: Merrill.

Reisman, F.K. (1985). *Sequential Assessment of Mathematics Inventory.* San Antonio, TX: Psychological Corporation.

Roberts, G.H. (1968). The failure strategies of third grade arithmetic pupils. *The Arithmetic Teacher, 15,* 442–446.

Salvia, J., & Ysseldyke, J.E. (1988). *Assessment in special and remedial education* (4th ed.). Boston: Houghton Mifflin.

Silbert, J., Carnine, D., & Stein, M. (1981). *Direct instruction mathematics.* Columbus, OH: Merrill.

Smith, D.D., & Lovitt, T.C. (1982). *The computational arithmetic program.* Austin, TX: Pro-Ed.

Starlin, C.M., & Starlin, A. (1973). *Guides to decision making in computational math.* Bemidji, MN: Unique Curriculums Unlimited.

Thornton, C.A., & Toohey, M.A. (1985). Basic math facts: Guidelines for teaching and learning. *Learning Disabilities Focus, 1,* 44–57.

Underhill, R.G. (1976). Classroom diagnosis in remedial mathematics: Diagnostic and remedial approaches. In J.L. Higgins & J.W. Heddens (Eds.), *Remedial mathematics: Diagnostic and prescriptive approaches.* Columbus, OH: ERIC Center for Science, Mathematics, and Environmental Education.

Underhill, R.G., Uprichard, A.E., & Heddens, J.W. (1980). *Diagnosing mathematical difficulties.* Columbus, OH: Merrill.

Wood, S., Burke, L., Kunzelmann, H., & Koenig, C. (1978). Functional criteria in basic math skill proficiency. *Journal of Special Educational Technology, 2*(2), 29–36.

CHAPTER 7

Teaching
Math Skills

Math problems may be attributed to a variety of factors—inadequate instruction; immaturity; and problems in memory, perception, reading, language, and abstract thinking. Regardless of the origin of a student's math problems, teachers must provide effective math instruction. This chapter is designed to help the teacher to provide effective instruction to students with math problems. General teaching strategies are discussed, and instructional activities for specific skills, instructional games, self-correcting materials, commercial programs and materials, and computer software programs are presented.

Effective teaching of math skills must start with the belief that it is important for the student to experience success. Ashlock (1986) and Underhill, Uprichard, and Heddens (1980) note that immediate and continuous success for the student is basic to effective math instruction. These authorities suggest guidelines for teaching students with math problems:

1. Involve the student in setting instructional goals in math.
2. Encourage the student to voice his understanding of math concepts.
3. Use a *variety* of instructional techniques and activities.
4. Use practice activities that provide immediate feedback.
5. Provide the student with a means of observing his progress (such as charts, graphs, and checklists).
6. Encourage the student to use instructional aids (number lines, manipulative materials) if they are helpful.
7. Whenever possible, let the student choose from materials designed to improve specific math skills.

Driscoll (1983) reports on the research concerning effective mathematics teaching with secondary students. He found the following factors to be positively correlated with effective mathematics instruction:

1. *Questioning:* Effective teachers ask more process questions (calling for explanations) and more product questions (calling for short answers) than less effective teachers.
2. *Encouragement:* Effective teachers are more encouraging (e.g., providing reinforcement for questions and requests for help) and receptive to student input than less effective teachers.
3. *Modeling:* Effective teachers exhibit more problem-solving behavior and communicate the importance of problem solving better than less effective teachers.
4. *Clarity:* Effective teachers exercise more clarity (i.e., the careful use of vocabulary and systematic explanations) than less effective teachers.
5. *Expectations:* An essential component of effective teaching is a set of firm and appropriate expectations. A study of British secondary schools, which measured effectiveness by student achievement, attendance, behavior, and delinquency records, indicated that high academic expectations are a major factor that differentiates effective schools from ineffective ones.

BASIC TERMS AND PROCESSES

Before beginning arithmetic instruction, the teacher needs to know some of the basic terms used in math. Table 7.1 presents some major terms.

The teacher also should know basic information about the organization of math content. Five areas are essential to learning addition, subtraction, multiplication, and division: (a) understanding, (b) basic facts, (c) place value, (d) structures (laws), and (e) regrouping

TABLE 7.1
Math terms in basic computations.

Operation	Terms
Addition	8 ←addend +4 ←addend 12 ←sum
Subtraction (take away)	9 ←minuend −4 ←subtrahend 5 ←difference
Subtraction (add on)	9 ←sum −4 ←known addend 5 ←missing addend
Multiplication	8 ←multiplicand × 5 ←multiplier 40 ←product
Division	8 ←quotient 6)48 ←dividend ↑ divisor

Note: Although the phrase *addend plus addend equals sum* is used, technically 8 + 4 is a *sum* and 8 × 5 is a *product*.

(Underhill et al., 1980). *Understanding* means comprehending the operation at the concrete, semiconcrete, and abstract levels. *Basic facts* must be memorized; these are the tools of computation. A basic fact is an operation on 2 one-digit whole numbers to obtain a one- or two-digit whole number; for example,

$$6 \times 4 = 24$$

There are 390 basic facts—100 addition, 100 subtraction, 100 multiplication, and 90 division facts. Once understanding and basic facts are mastered, the specific operation can be readily expanded by using *place value*. For example, if the student recognizes that 3×2 is 6, the place value concept can be applied to compute a series of problems such as the following.

3	30	300
× 2	× 2	× 2
6	60	600

3000	30	300
× 2	× 20	× 20
6000	600	6000

Structures are mathematical properties that help the student. If a student memorizes "7×3 is 21" but sees 3×7 as a new problem to memorize, he needs to understand a basic structure—in this case, the commutative property of multiplication—in order to learn multiplication effectively. The last area is *regrouping*, commonly referred to as *carrying* and *borrowing*. It is necessary to understand regrouping to solve more complex problems in each of the four operations.

Another important factor in teaching math is knowledge of algorithms. As noted in Chapter 6, algorithms are the steps used in solving a math problem. Ashlock (1986) discusses the value of trying different algorithms:

> If you are really willing to accept the idea that there are many legitimate ways to subtract, divide, and so on, you may choose to introduce a child having difficulty to an algorithm which is fresh and new to her. By so doing, you may circumvent the mind set of failure which beleaguers the child. . . . If the child learns and remembers the procedure, the needed success experience has been provided. If the child does not, then the procedure can be set aside. (p. 23)

Thornton and Toohey (1985) report strong evidence that modifying the *sequence* and *presentation* of learning tasks can improve basic fact learning among students with learning problems. They offer 10 guidelines that are supported by the literature for planning and implementing basic fact instruction for mildly handicapped students. These guidelines form the basis for MATHFACT, which was developed and successfully used in Queensland, Australia (Thornton & Toohey, 1982-1985). An American miniversion is being used in the United States (Thornton, 1984, 1985; Thornton & Toohey, 1984). Their guidelines include the following:

1. *Consider prerequisite learnings by looking ahead to review or reteach as necessary.* Mathematical concepts and operations are hierarchical. Concepts that are basic to learning a new skill or concept should be taught before introducing the new material. For example, insure that "sums to 9" facts are mastered before introducing subtraction facts.

2. *Provide ongoing diagnosis and assessment.* Attention to the student's rate of progress, types of errors, understanding of concepts, and learning style is basic to successful math facts instruction.

3. *Modify the sequence in which facts are presented for learning.* Traditional fact instruction sequences addition facts by the size of the sum. Thornton and Toohey (1985) maintain that other sequences are more effective for various learners. For example, for immature students or those with serious deficits, they recommend beginning instruction with the 72 easiest addition facts: count-ons ($+1$, $+2$, $+3$) ($n = 45$); zeroes ($n = 19$), doubles ($n = 6$ not previously met), and 10 sums (2 not previously met—$6 + 4$ and $4 + 6$).

4. *Prior to drill, teach students strategies for computing answers to unknown facts.* Many students with learning problems need to be taught specific strategies to help them solve problems independently. For example:

Fact		Strategy
7	6	Start BIG and count on.
$+ 2$	$+ 3$	
6	0	Plus zero stays the same.
$+ 0$	$+ 8$	
8	6	Order of addends does
$+ 6$	$+ 8$	not affect sum.

Overall, the following sequence is suggested: (a) easy addition facts, (b) easy subtraction facts, (c) other addition facts, and (d) other subtraction facts.

5. *Modify the presentation of activities to fit the learning style of each student.* Mildly handicapped students are a very heterogeneous population with a host of different learning styles and preferences. Some procedures for taking advantage of various modality preferences include the following:

For Auditory Learners
a. Precede all actions and demonstrations with spoken instructions. Each step may have two parts: (a) oral instructions only; (b) oral instructions closely followed by a visual stimulus, concrete manipulation, or demonstration.
b. Provide a verbal summary of each step.
c. If necessary, use key words to focus the child's attention (e.g., "listen").
d. Remove extraneous visual stimuli.

For Visual Learners
a. Precede all oral instructions by concrete manipulations or mimed demonstrations. Each step may have two parts: (a) presentation of the visual stimulus only; (b) visual presentation in conjunction with verbalization.
b. Have children describe mimed or demonstrated actions, pictures, or concrete manipulation.
c. Provide a visual summary of each step.
d. Encourage children to make mental images of visual stimuli. Provide opportunity for them to reproduce these images (verbally, pictorially).
e. Use cue cards to focus children's attention.
f. Try a silent lesson.

For Kinesthetic/Tactile Learners
a. Precede all instructions by the physical manipulation of objects by the child. The teacher should guide all manipulations. Each step may have two parts: (a) physical manipulation only, and (b) physical

manipulation in conjunction with oral instructions.

b. Remove visual stimuli if distracting. Have children close their eyes or place objects in their hands behind their backs.

c. Provide a summary (physical manipulation of each step).

d. Use a cueing system to focus the child's attention.

e. Use textured material (pipe cleaners, sandpaper, plasticine, sandtrays, and magnetic boards). (Thornton & Toohey, 1985, pp. 52–53)

6. *Control the pacing.* Knowing when to move faster or slow down is critical to good fact instruction. Continuous monitoring of fact progress provides data that greatly facilitate pacing.

7. *Help students discriminate when to use a strategy and integrate new learnings with old.* Some students learn a strategy and apply it to all situations. For example, a student may learn a count-on strategy and apply it to all addition facts. A student's appropriate use of a strategy should be strengthened by activities that require identifying math facts to which it applies.

8. *Provide verbal prompts.* Repeatedly give students verbal prompts during instruction. This helps some students independently associate the prompts with the specific facts to which they apply.

9. *Help students develop self-monitoring skills.* Many students with learning problems need to acquire skills that focus on *how to learn.* Such techniques as cognitive behavior modification and academic strategy training enable the student to develop self-monitoring skills that are useful across tasks and situations.

10. *Insure provisions for overlearning.* Once facts are mastered, emphasis shifts to activities that help students store them in long-term memory. This usually requires a variety of drill activities and performances on tasks at a high criterion level. Instructional games, self-correcting materials, computer-assisted instruction, peer teaching, and periodic review are a few of the activities appropriate for developing overlearning.

The following sections discuss how to teach place value and each of the operations at the three levels of learning. Alternative algorithms are provided for each operation. In each of the operations, problems are included that involve place value at a complex level.

Place Value

To begin place value instruction at the *concrete level,* gather two plastic cups, a bundle of straws, and a set of blocks. Set the two cups on poster board; label the right one "units" and the left one "tens." Tell the pupil to count the blocks. For each block he counts, place a straw in the units cup. Stop when nine blocks are counted and nine straws are in the units cup. Prior to picking up the 10th straw, explain that one straw in the tens cup represents 10 objects. The pupil then takes the nine straws out of the units cup and places one straw in the tens cup. Next, the pupil continues to count the blocks and place the straws. Counting proceeds in the following manner: 1 ten and 1, 1 ten and 2, . . . 3 tens and 4, 3 tens and 5, and so on. Each time a 10 is reached, empty the units cup and place a straw in the tens cup. Although the pupil is told that 1 ten and 1 is another name for 11, and 3 tens and 5 is another name for 35, during place value instruction encourage him to count using the 3 tens and 5 system. He continues with the blocks and straws until he can do the task readily.

At the *semiconcrete level,* use illustrations instead of the blocks, straws, and cups. A sample task might include the following:

Task: Count the items and place the correct number in each cup.

The completed task would look like this:

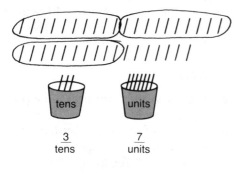

<u>3</u>   <u>7</u>
tens   units

Gradually fade the pictures of the cups and replace them with:

_____   _____
tens   units

The items may change to pictures of real objects.

At the *abstract level,* add numbers gradually in place of items. A sequence of sample tasks might include:

Task 1: Count the items and identify the number of tens and units.

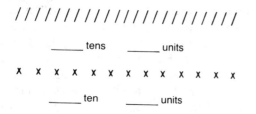

_____ tens   _____ units

X X X X X X X X X X X X X X

_____ ten   _____ units

Task 2: Identify the number of tens and units in each number.

24	_____ tens	_____ units
36	_____ tens	_____ units
87	_____ tens	_____ units

These activities represent only one way of providing place value instruction at the concrete, semiconcrete, and abstract levels. Expand and use different activities across the three levels. These procedures also may be used with different bases. For example, in base 5, counting begins as follows: 3 fives and 2 ones.

Addition

This section features techniques for teaching various addition skills at the three levels. Also, several alternative algorithms are presented.

Sums to 9. Learning sums to 9 underlies later arithmetic functioning. These sums are the initial facts to be mastered. To begin sums to 9 instruction, the teacher can use the following patterns that were developed by Dr. A. Edward Uprichard, of the University of South Florida:

The first instructional goal is to teach the child to recognize and name each pattern without counting the dots. To accomplish this, the teacher begins with a concrete-level task using blocks or other suitable three-dimensional objects. Some activities with blocks include the following: The teacher places the blocks in the

7 pattern and the child copies the pattern. Next, the teacher requests the child to produce the 7 pattern without a model.

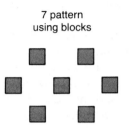

7 pattern
using blocks

Then the teacher asks the child to divide a number pattern into some of its two-group combinations. The 7 pattern may be divided into one or several of its two-group combinations; for example,

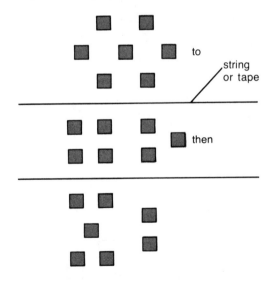

At this point, the teacher stresses that each pattern has a family of two-group combination patterns. For example, the 7 pattern has eight combinations:

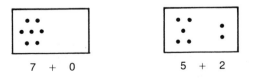

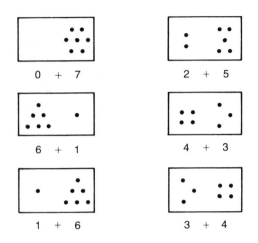

The teacher stresses that each combination is really another name for the number (sum). Thus, *equals* (=) is taught as *another name for* and the word *equals* is not used: "4 + 3 is another name for 7." The child continues to arrange the blocks into the two-group combinations using renaming and the commutative property for addition.

Semiconcrete-level tasks follow the concrete-level activities. At this level, dots or tallies form the patterns. The student works at exercises on cards, worksheets, or the blackboard. The tasks are similar to those used at the concrete level. For example, a worksheet may feature the following exercise:

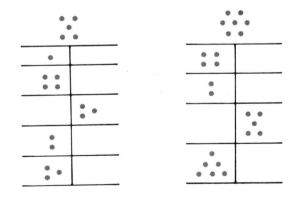

In making the patterns, the pupil must draw 3 + 4 and 4 + 3 to show understanding of commutativity in addition. The pupil should practice with the dots until all two-pattern combinations for each number, including those with zero, are produced or identified readily.

After completing activities at the semiconcrete level, the pupil moves to the abstract level. At this level, he uses numerals. A sample activity would be for the teacher to ask the student to complete the following combinations:

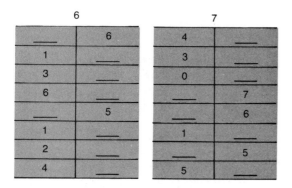

The pupil must learn all the two-addend combinations for each number. In many cases, he must drill extensively. The game of Math War, presented later in this chapter, enables many youngsters to compute or recognize sums to 9 facts very quickly.

Sums to 18. At the concrete level the student begins with two sets of blocks whose sum is greater than 9. For example, the student is presented with a set of 8 blocks and a set of 5 blocks. He identifies the number of blocks in each set and determines the number of blocks that the set of 8 needs to total 10. Then the learner removes two blocks from the set of 5 and rearranges them into two sets, one of 10 blocks and one of 3 blocks.

At this point the student recognizes that another name for 10 blocks and 3 blocks is 13 blocks. This procedure can be used with any 2 one-digit addends whose sum is greater than 10.

At the semiconcrete level, the student is given a paper with a set of 8 dots and a set of 5 dots arranged in the patterns. Next he outlines a set of 10 dots, writes the new numbers for the two sets, and then uses his knowledge of place value to write the total number of dots in both sets.

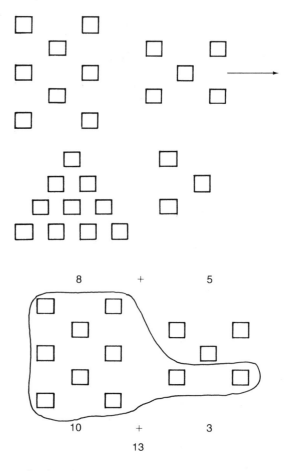

At the abstract level, the learner writes the steps he completes at the concrete and semiconcrete levels:

$8 + 5 = \square$

$8 + (2 + 3) = \square$

$(8 + 2) + (3) = \square$

$10 + 3 = \square$

$13 = \square$

Also,

$8 + 5 = \boxed{10} + 3 = \boxed{13}$

$8 + 5 = \boxed{13}$

In going from the concrete to the semiconcrete level, the teacher simply replaces real objects with pictures of objects or dots or tallies. The step from semiconcrete to abstract involves replacing pictures and tallies with numbers. The following examples are provided to assist the teacher in developing instructional tasks for addition at all three levels.

Concrete level (26 + 17)

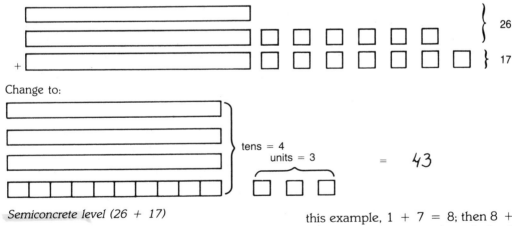

Change to:

tens = 4
units = 3

= 43

Semiconcrete level (26 + 17)

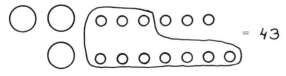

= 43

Abstract level

$$\begin{array}{r} 26 \\ + 17 \\ \hline \end{array}$$

Addition algorithm. Once the student knows addition facts through sums to 18, an adaptation of the *tens method* (Fulkerson, 1963) may be a very useful algorithm. To illustrate:

$$\begin{array}{r} 867 \\ 574 \\ 647 \\ + 786 \\ \hline 2874 \end{array}$$

Beginning at the top right in the example, 7 + 4 equals 11, which can be renamed as 1 ten and 1 one. A horizontal line is drawn through the 4 to represent the ten, and the ones number is written on the extension of the line. Since the line represents the ten the student no longer needs to hold it in mind. The student uses the one (unit digit) that is left over to begin adding until another ten is obtained. In this example, 1 + 7 = 8; then 8 + 6 = 14. Thus, a line is drawn through the 6 to represent the ten, and the 4 ones are written on the line. Since all numbers in the unit column have been added, the 4 is recorded as the unit's digit at the bottom of the column.

The two lines drawn in the units column represent 2 tens; thus, addition in the tens column begins by carrying the 2 tens. These 2 tens are added to the 6 tens, and this continues until there is a sum greater than or equal to 10 tens: 2 tens + 6 tens = 8 tens; 8 tens + 7 tens = 15 tens. A line is drawn across the 7 to represent 10 tens and the remaining 5 tens are written on the line. Then, 5 tens + 4 tens = 9 tens; 9 tens + 8 tens = 17 tens. A line is drawn across the 8, and the 7 is recorded as the tens digit at the bottom. In the tens column each line represents 10 tens or 1 hundred. Thus, the two lines in the tens column are carried to the hundreds column to begin addition there. The 2 hundreds are added to 8 hundreds, and addition proceeds in a similar manner.

Another addition algorithm is referred to as *partial sums*. To illustrate:

$$\begin{array}{r} 47 \\ +\ 28 \\ \hline 15 \\ 60 \\ \hline 75 \end{array}$$

In this algorithm, when the sum of the ones column is greater than or equal to 10, it is written as a two-digit number at the bottom of the ones and tens columns. In the given example, 7 + 8 = 15, so 15 is written at the bottom of the columns. Next, the tens column is added and the sum is written below the ones column sum. In this case, 4 tens + 2 tens = 6 tens or 60. Then the two partial sums are added.

Subtraction

Subtraction facts (1 to 9). Once the addition facts through 9 are learned, the teaching of subtraction facts (1–9) is simple. When the "add on" approach to subtraction is used rather than the "take away" approach, the student is required to find a missing addend instead of a difference. The missing addend approach involves the same logic used in addition; thus a student can use his knowledge

of addition facts in solving subtraction problems. For example, an addition fact can be expressed as an addition *or* a subtraction equation, depending on which unknown the student is seeking to compute.

Addition

$$4 + 3 = \boxed{7}$$

addend + addend = sum

Subtraction

$$7 - 3 = \boxed{4}$$

sum − addend = missing addend

In the missing addend approach to subtraction, the student uses his knowledge of addition facts to answer the subtraction question, "What number goes with 3 to make another name for (equal) 7?" Thus, in solving

$$7 - 3 = \square$$

it becomes

$$3 + \square = 7$$

Subtraction tasks at each of the three levels for the facts through 9 are presented next.

Concrete level (7 − 3)

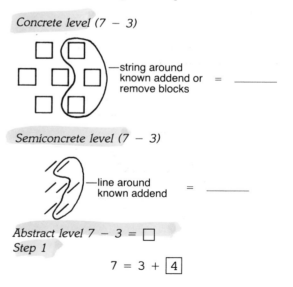

—string around known addend or remove blocks = _____

Semiconcrete level (7 − 3)

—line around known addend = _____

Abstract level 7 − 3 = $\square$
Step 1

$$7 = 3 + \boxed{4}$$

Step 2

$$7 - 3 = \boxed{4}$$

Subtraction facts (10 to 18). When solving subtraction facts involving one-digit addends, the student should be able to regroup a set of ten and ones (sum) to show the known addend as part of the ten and the unknown addend as the total of all remaining blocks, pictures, or tallies (Underhill et al., 1980).

Concrete level (14 − 6)

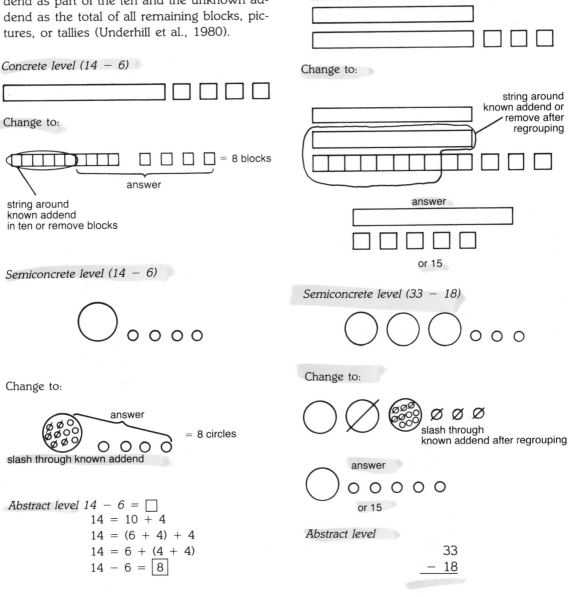

Change to:

= 8 blocks

answer

string around
known addend
in ten or remove blocks

Semiconcrete level (14 − 6)

Change to:

answer

= 8 circles

slash through known addend

Abstract level $14 - 6 = \square$
$$14 = 10 + 4$$
$$14 = (6 + 4) + 4$$
$$14 = 6 + (4 + 4)$$
$$14 - 6 = \boxed{8}$$

Subtraction with regrouping. The following examples are presented to assist the teacher in developing instructional tasks for subtraction at all three levels.

Concrete level (33 − 18)

Change to:

string around
known addend or
remove after
regrouping

answer

or 15

Semiconcrete level (33 − 18)

Change to:

slash through
known addend after regrouping

answer

or 15

Abstract level

$$\begin{array}{r} 33 \\ -\ 18 \\ \hline \end{array}$$

Subtraction algorithm. Hutchings's (1975) *low-stress method of subtraction* is an effective procedure in remedial instruction (Ashlock, 1986). It is based on notation for recording a minuend or sum in several ways. For example, 752 may be recorded as $6^1 52$ or $6^1 4^1 2$ or $74^1 2$. When using this notation, the regrouped sum or minuend is recorded in the middle prior to the recalling of subtraction facts.

For example:

(a)
$$
\begin{array}{r}
8472 \\
-\ 6673 \\
\end{array}
$$

	8	4	7	2
	7	^{13}	^{16}	^{12}
−	6	6	7	3

1 7 9 9

(b)
$$
\begin{array}{r}
65400062 \\
-\ 21450238 \\
\end{array}
$$

6	5	4	0	0	0	6	2
6	4	^{13}	9	9	^{10}	5	^{12}
− 2	1	4	5	0	2	3	8

4 3 9 4 9 8 2 4

In this algorithm, all renaming is completed before subtraction takes place. The student is reminded that renaming is necessary each time the subtrahend (known addend) in each column is greater than the minuend (sum).

Multiplication

Multiplication facts. The 100 multiplication facts ($\times 0$ to $\times 9$) are basic to more complex operations in multiplication.

Concrete level
Task 1: Demonstrate 6×3 using blocks:

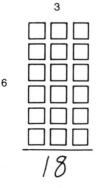

Task 2: Count sets of three blocks to show multiples of 3. For example, show three sets of 3:

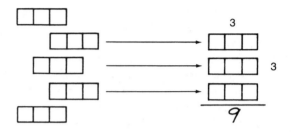

Semiconcrete level
Task 1: Use an array to show 6×3:

$$
\begin{array}{c}
3 \\
6 \quad
\begin{array}{ccc}
x & x & x \\
x & x & x \\
x & x & x \\
x & x & x \\
x & x & x \\
x & x & x \\
\end{array} \\
18
\end{array}
$$

Task 2: On a grid show 6×3 (paper and pencil or chalkboard is good for grid work):

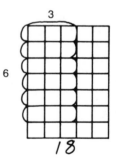

Abstract level

$6 \times 3 = \boxed{18}$ (learned primarily from memory)

The following sequence for teaching multiplication facts is designed to minimize the amount of memorizing required in learning the facts.

1. Teach that 0 times any number is 0.
2. Teach that 1 times any number is that number.
3. Teach that 2 times any number means double that number: 2×3 means $3 + 3$.
4. Teach that 5 times any number involves counting by 5s the number of times indicated by the multiplier. For example, 5×6 means counting "5, 10, 15, 20, 25, 30."
5. Teach the trick in learning the 9s. The trick is to subtract 1 from the multiplier to obtain the tens digit and then add enough to it to make 9 to obtain the ones digit. For example: $9 \times 4 = \underline{36}$—3 is one less than 4 and $3 + 6 = 9$.
6. Now there are only 15 facts left to be memorized:

$$3 \times 3 = 9$$
$$3 \times 4 = 12$$
$$3 \times 6 = 18$$
$$3 \times 7 = 21$$
$$3 \times 8 = 24$$
$$4 \times 4 = 16$$
$$4 \times 6 = 24$$
$$4 \times 7 = 28$$
$$4 \times 8 = 32$$
$$6 \times 6 = 36$$
$$6 \times 7 = 42$$
$$6 \times 8 = 48$$
$$7 \times 7 = 49$$
$$7 \times 8 = 56$$
$$8 \times 8 = 64$$

Some teachers report that these facts are learned faster by grouping the doubles (3×3, 4×4, and so on), thus leaving only 10 facts.

Multiplication algorithm. The *low-stress method of multiplication* (Hutchings, 1976) reduces the amount of remembering required during computation. It is based on notation for recording the products of multiplication facts in a different manner. With *drop notation,* the product of

$$\begin{array}{r} 7 \\ \times\ 8 \\ \hline \end{array}$$

may be written

$$\begin{array}{r} 7 \\ \times\ 8 \\ \hline {}^5 6 \end{array}$$

To illustrate:

Conventional Notation

$$\begin{array}{r} 8 \\ \times\ 7 \\ \hline 56 \end{array} \qquad \begin{array}{r} 6 \\ \times\ 6 \\ \hline 36 \end{array} \qquad \begin{array}{r} 5 \\ \times\ 1 \\ \hline 5 \end{array}$$

Drop Notation

$$\begin{array}{r} 8 \\ \times\ 7 \\ \hline {}^5 6 \end{array} \qquad \begin{array}{r} 6 \\ \times\ 6 \\ \hline {}^3 6 \end{array} \qquad \begin{array}{r} 5 \\ \times\ 1 \\ \hline {}^0 5 \end{array}$$

Using the drop notation, it is possible to compute multiplication problems in the following ways:

(a)
Step 1	*Step 2*	*Step 3*
476	476	476
× 8	× 8	× 8
40	540	3540
8	68	268
		3808

(b)
$$\begin{array}{r} 57764 \\ \times\qquad 7 \\ \hline 344420 \\ 59928 \\ \hline 404348 \end{array}$$

(c) using two multidigit factors:

Step 1	*Step 2*	
476	476	
× 38	× 38	
3540	3540⎱	×8
268	268⎰	
	1210⎱	×3
	218⎰	
	18088	

This low-stress method of multiplication eliminates the regrouping requirement and allows the student to work only with multiplication facts in solving complex multiplication problems.

Another multiplication algorithm is the *partial products* algorithm. This algorithm reduces the regrouping requirement in multiplying multidigit numbers by one-digit numbers. For example:

$$\begin{array}{r} 27 \\ \times\ 6 \\ \hline \end{array}$$
42 (7 × 6) partial product
$\underline{120}$ (20 × 6) partial product
162

$$\begin{array}{r} 362 \\ \times\ \ 4 \\ \hline \end{array}$$
08 (2 × 4)
240 (60 × 4)
$\underline{1200}$ (300 × 4)
1448

Division

Division is considered to be the most difficult of the four operations. For example, long division requires the use of division, multiplication, and subtraction in computing quotients.

Division facts. The 90 division facts are basic to understanding and computing more complex division operations.

Concrete level
Task 1: Determine the number of sets of 4 in 16.

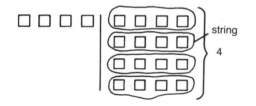
string
4

Task 2: Determine the number of sets of 6 in 42.

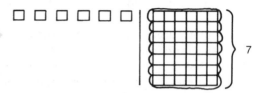
7

The student may also be asked to show how many times 4 can be subtracted from 16 or how many times 6 can be subtracted from 42.

Semiconcrete level
(a) (16 ÷ 4)

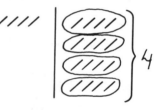
4

(b) (42 ÷ 6)

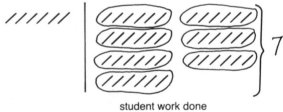
7

student work done
with pencil or on
chalkboard

At this level it may be helpful to use a large grid (on paper or chalkboard) to determine the number of 3s, 4s, 6s, and so on in a number.

Abstract level

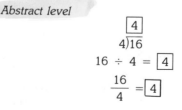

$16 \div 4 = \boxed{4}$

$\dfrac{16}{4} = \boxed{4}$

Sample division problem with regrouping:

Concrete level (20 ÷ 3)

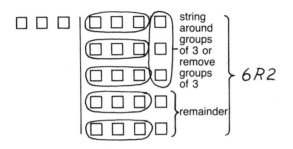

string around groups of 3 or remove groups of 3 } 6 R 2

remainder

Semiconcrete level (20 ÷ 3)

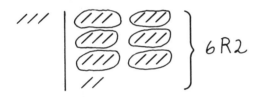

6 R 2

At this level the student may also use a grid (covered with acetate and used with an overhead pen or grease pencil) to solve division problems (for example, determine the number of 4s in 38). In performing the task the student counts until the 38th block is identified. Then 1s are written in the first four blocks, 2s are written in the second four blocks, and so on until no more sets of 4 are left in the first 38 blocks. For example:

1	1	1	1	2	2	2	2	3	3
3	3	4	4	4	4	5	5	5	5
6	6	6	6	7	7	7	7	8	8
8	8	9	9	9	9	X	Ⓧ		

student circles the 38th block

thus,

38 ÷ 4 = 9 R2

Abstract level   repeated subtraction

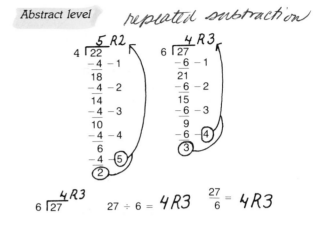

$$6\overline{)27}\,^{4R3} \qquad 27 ÷ 6 = 4R3 \qquad \frac{27}{6} = 4R3$$

Division algorithm. Reisman (1977) notes that the following algorithms are less difficult than the traditional division algorithm. Using the algorithms is made simpler by knowing the shortcut for multiplying by multiples of 10. In algorithm *a*, the student immediately pulls out the largest tens multiple of the divisor; in algorithm *b*, the multiples taken out of the divisor are smaller.

(a) 28)62372

56000	2000
6372	
5600	200
772	
560	20
212	
196	7
16	2227

(b) 28)62372

28000	1000
34372	
28000	1000
6372	
2800	100
3572	
2800	100
772	
280	100
492	
280	10
212	
140	5
72	
56	2
16	2227

Fractions

This section describes procedures for teaching several skills in fractions at the three levels. Also, a low-stress algorithm for adding or subtracting fractions is described.

Recognition of unit fractions:

Concrete level

Let ☐ be 1 and smaller size blocks represent fractional subregions of it.

☐ may be a block or a container which holds fractional blocks. Use the blocks to display ¼, ⅓, ½, and so on.

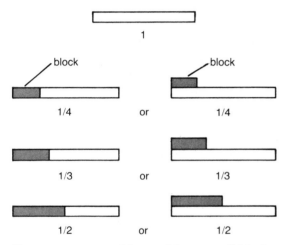

1

block   block

1/4   or   1/4

1/3   or   1/3

1/2   or   1/2

Numerous commercial materials are available for working with fractions at the concrete level (for example, Cuisenaire rods, Unifix cubes).

Semiconcrete level
Write the unit fraction for the designs.

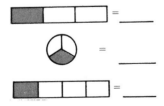

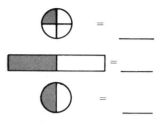

Abstract level
Use numbers to express the unit fractions for one-fourth, one-third, and one-half.

Addition of fractions with same denominators:

Concrete level (⅓ + ⅓)

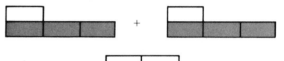

Semiconcrete level (¼ + 2/4)

Abstract level
$$\tfrac{1}{3} + \tfrac{1}{3} = \Box/\Box$$

$$\tfrac{1}{4} + \tfrac{2}{4} = \Box/\Box$$

The following examples are presented to assist the teacher in developing instructional tasks for fractions at all three levels.

Concrete level
Task 1: Use real blocks (3⅔ + 2⅔)
Task 2: Use string (5¼ − 2¾)

Semiconcrete level
Task 1: Use drawings

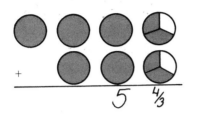

Task 2: Use lines

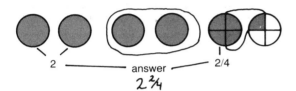

Abstract level

$$3 \ 2/3$$
$$+2 \ 2/3$$
$$5\tfrac{4}{3} = 6\tfrac{1}{3}$$

$5 \ 1/4 =$
$-2 \ 3/4 =$
$$4\tfrac{5}{4}$$
$$2\tfrac{3}{4}$$
$$2\tfrac{2}{4} = 2\tfrac{1}{2}$$

For activities on multiplying and dividing fractions at the various levels, see fraction activities presented later in the chapter.

Fraction algorithm for addition and subtraction. Ruais (1978) describes a low-stress algorithm for teaching the addition and subtraction of fractions. His algorithm is called *ray multiplication* and consists of the following steps:

1. An overhead projection is used to drill the student on the location of geometric shapes and numbers. $\overset{O}{\underset{\triangle}{}} \ \overset{\square}{\underset{\diamond}{}}$ are model items that are used to show the locations of bottom right, bottom left, top right, and top left.

2. The student is instructed to draw three rays (↗): (a) from bottom right to top left, (b) from bottom left to top right, and (c) from bottom left to bottom right. Thus $\overset{O}{\underset{\triangle}{}} \ \overset{\square}{\underset{\diamond}{}}$ would look like

3. On a sheet that has pairs of numerical fractions, the student is directed to draw the three rays and multiply along the rays. The student writes the answers to these multiplication tasks. After the rays are multiplied, the student writes the operation sign between the fractions in a pair. For example:

$$3 \diagdown \nearrow 2$$
$$2 \diagup + \diagdown 6$$

4. In this step the student writes a new fraction for each pair. The new numerator is formed by performing the correct operation on the products of the diagonal ray multiplications. The new denominator for both fractions is the product of the horizontal ray multiplication. For example:

$$\frac{3}{6} + \frac{2}{6}$$

5. Now the student computes the sum or difference of the numerators and writes the result over the denominator. For example:

$$\frac{3}{6} + \frac{2}{6} = \frac{(3 + 2)}{6} = \frac{5}{6}$$

or

$$\frac{3}{6} - \frac{2}{6} = \frac{(3 - 2)}{6} = \frac{1}{6}$$

Ruais (1978) reports that this ray multiplication algorithm leads to reduced stress, reduced teaching time prior to mastery, and increased computation power.

MATH ACTIVITIES

This section provides activities for teaching or practicing math skills. The activities may be used to stimulate interest, individualize instruction, extend practice, and provide variety in teaching methods.

Readiness

In addition to the selected activities in this section, readiness areas and related assessment tasks are provided in Chapter 6.

Classification. Provide the student with a collection of circles, squares, and triangles of various colors. Have the child classify the items according to shape and then according to color. Other objects that are useful in classification activities are buttons, wooden blocks, dominoes, spoons, nails, and golf tees.

Ordering. Provide the child with a set of different-sized objects (wooden blocks, buttons, straws, nails, washers, shapes, Cuisenaire rods, and the like). Have him arrange them in order from the smallest to the largest or vice versa.

One-to-one correspondence. Provide the child with a pegboard design and instruct him to duplicate it. Other helpful activities include putting screws on bolts, passing out papers, playing musical chairs, and adding the same part for several items (such as strings to a kite, sails to a boat, stems to a flower, or straws to a cup).

Counting. Provide the child with Language Master cards with a number of objects to count and a taped message (such as "One, two, three—three cats").

Give the child a picture of several monkeys hanging together or a card with a number on it. Provide the child with a barrel of monkeys and a hook (on the wall or on a stand), and ask him to show the number on the picture or the card by hanging up the same number of toy monkeys.

Have the child circle the number that corresponds to the configuration. This activity may be used to teach the patterns presented earlier for "sums to 9" instruction.

∴∴	4	5	6	8
∴	2	3	4	7
∴∴	7	6	9	8
∷	3	5	6	4

Attach a number line to the top of the student's desk to provide him with a helpful reference:

1	2	3	4	5	6	7	8	9

Place Value

Chip trading games. Use chip trading games to teach place value (Ashlock, 1986). These games stress the idea of exchanging many for one. The values of chips correspond to a numeration place value pattern. For example, white chips represent units, blue chips represent tens, and red chips represent hundreds. The pupil rolls a die and receives the number of units indicated on the die. He makes exchanges for higher valued chips according to the rules of the game (four for one if base 4, ten for one if base 10). The first player to get a chip of a certain high value wins.

Bank game. Use a game board and a bank to help pupils understand place value (Ashlock, 1986). For example:

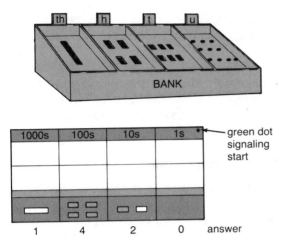

BANK

1000s	100s	10s	1s

green dot signaling start

1   4   2   0   answer

In computing the problem

$$527 \\ +893$$

the pupil places 5 hundreds, 2 tens, and 7 unit blocks in the upper row. Then he places the appropriate blocks for 893 in the second row. Starting with the units (at green dot), the pupil collects 10 units if possible and moves all remaining units below the wide line. He trades to the bank each 10 units collected for the correct number of tens. The tens collected from the bank are placed at the top of the tens column. In this problem (see example), 10 units are traded to the bank for 1 ten, and zero blocks are placed below the wide line in the units column. Next, 10 tens are traded in for a hundreds block, and 2 tens blocks are placed below the wide line in the tens column. He trades in 10 hundreds for a thousands block and then places 4 hundreds blocks below the wide line in the hundreds column. Finally, he moves the thousands block below the wide line in the thousands column. He counts the blocks in each column and writes the answer, 1,420.

Making columns. Draw a line to separate tens and units to help the pupil understand the need to add units to units and tens to tens (Ashlock, 1986):

Labelling columns. Insert the initial letters for units, tens, hundreds, and so on over their respective columns (Bannatyne, 1973):

t th	th	h	t	u
	4	5	4	7
	1	7	5	6
+ | 3 | 3 | 1 | 1 |

Vertical lines may be in colors for additional cuing.

Pegboard. Use a pegboard to aid in learning borrowing and carrying (Wertlieb, 1976). For example:

Use masking tape to divide the pegboard into three rows and three columns, each subdivision having nine holes. An arrow is drawn from right to left on a piece of tape that separates the bottom third. This line serves as an equals sign; answers to problems always are shown by inserting pegs below this line. In addition to helping the student recall the different values for each column, color coding reminds the student to start with green (*go*). The top two rows hold the pegs representing the first two numbers in an addition or subtraction problem. To solve

$$\begin{array}{r} 5 \\ +6 \\ \hline \end{array}$$

the student starts to transfer all the pegs in the units column to the unit section below the arrow. He discovers that not all 11 pegs will fit in the bottom row of the units column. Consequently, he must exchange 10 green pegs for 1 yellow peg (10 units for 1 ten) and carry this yellow peg into the tens column. Borrowing consists of trading 1 yellow for 10 green pegs and putting the green pegs in the top row of the units column.

Dice game. Use a dice game in which three different-colored dice are used (Groves, 1976). The colors correspond to color-coded lines drawn on paper to represent hundreds, tens, and units places. After the student rolls the dice, he writes his number in the appropriate columns and reads it. The student with the highest number wins.

Place value cards. Make cards with numbers on one side and tallies for the number of hundreds, tens, units, and so on in that number on the other side (Wallace & Kauffman, 1986). For example:

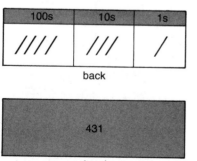

front

Also, strings may be attached to the cards for stringing beads to represent the number in each column.

Tinkertoys. Tinkertoys can be used to teach regrouping (Gallagher, 1979). The round pieces have 10 holes and are helpful in teaching regrouping.

General Computation

This section consists of activities that are easily adapted for any of the four operations. Many of the games and self-correcting materials presented later in this chapter also are useful with all four operations.

Small work samples. Present assignments in small segments. Because of attention problems or lack of interest, some students have difficulty completing an entire sheet of arithmetic problems. Presenting assignments in small segments may help these students complete as many problems as their classmates. Cut a worksheet into small parts (rows), or place problems on cards which the student picks up each time a problem is completed.

Math board (Gallagher, 1979). Glue library pockets on poster board and cover the outside portion of the pocket with transparent, self-

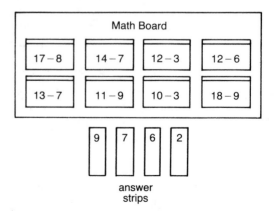

answer strips

adhesive paper. Use water-base felt pens to write problems on the pockets. Corresponding answers are written on cardboard strips. The student is instructed to match the correct answers to the pockets. The problems can be removed with a cloth so new problems can be presented.

Mystery math. Cut tagboard into 5″ × 5″ squares, or draw a square on a ditto. Put a decorative drawing, decal, or picture in the middle. Space off seven or more lines on each side of the decorative square in the middle. Write numbers at random on the left side. If the concept being taught is ÷ 6 and the first number is 42, the first number on the right side should be 7. All other lines on the right side remain blank. The process is repeated with the top and bottom lines. By looking at the top lines on the left and right sides, the student tries to figure out the mathematical function involved. He then fills in the remaining blanks using the same function. Next the process is repeated with the top and bottom lines.

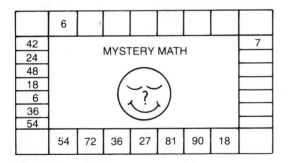

Calculators. Consider allowing the student to use a calculator. In recent years calculators have become inexpensive and commonplace. The National Council of Teachers of Mathematics (1976) provides the teacher with several applications of calculators:

1. Assist in helping the student become a wise consumer.

2. Reinforce learning basic number facts and properties in the four operations.
3. Develop understanding of selected algorithms by using repeated operations.
4. Serve as a check on computations.
5. Promote independence in problem solving.
6. Solve problems that are normally too time-consuming to be computed by hand.

Learning ladders. Provide the student with arithmetic problems in a vertical order on strips of paper or cardboard. Have the student start at the bottom of the "ladder" (strip) and proceed upward as he answers a problem correctly. A marker is placed at the last problem answered correctly. When the student gets three markers (star, tack, pin) on the top problem, progress is recorded and the student is allowed to take the strip home. Learning ladders may also be used to practice number identification, telling time, and coin identification.

4×4	16 -8	$4\overline{)36}$	6 $+7$	$1/2 + 1/2$
6×4	14 -8	$4\overline{)20}$	8 $+7$	$5/6 + 1/6$
9×4	13 -4	$4\overline{)16}$	7 $+4$	$2/3 + 1/3$
5×4	17 -8	$4\overline{)28}$	6 $+5$	$1/5 + 1/5$
7×4	12 -8	$4\overline{)36}$	9 $+7$	$1/4 + 1/4$
8×4		$4\overline{)12}$		

Filmstrip computation. Place number facts on strips cut from transparencies (Lerner & Vaver, 1970). These strips are inserted in a filmstrip projector that exposes the facts for the desired time span. Or make slides and use a slide projector to present the facts. The slide projector can be attached to a timer that regulates the speed of the slide presentation. When using the manual control button, the student can

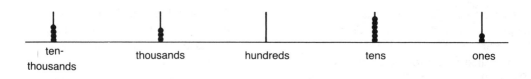

ten-thousands	thousands	hundreds	tens	ones

control the presentation rate by pushing the button.

Addition

Nail abacus. Use a nail abacus for teaching counting, place value (regrouping), and addition. Make the nail abacus by driving five finishing nails at 2″ intervals in a wooden board 2″ by 10″ by ½″. The abacus is used by placing washers or beads on the nails. To display the number 43,062 on the abacus, two washers are placed on the ones nail, six washers are placed on the tens nail, no washers are on the hundreds nail, three washers are on the thousands nail, and four washers are on the ten-thousands nail. (See above.)

The student adds on the abacus by placing washers or beads on the appropriate nails and counting. For example, in solving the problem 43 + 32, the student would first place three washers on the ones nail and four washers on the tens nail. Next, 32 would be shown on the abacus by placing two washers on the ones nail and three washers on the tens nail. Now the student computes the sums of the ones (5) and the tens (7) by counting the washers on the respective nails.

Instruct the student to follow these rules about regrouping when using the abacus:

1. Ten discs on the ones nail are exchanged for one disc on the tens nail.
2. Ten discs on the tens nail are exchanged for one disc on the hundreds nail.
3. No nail can have more than nine discs remaining.

Thus, in solving 18 + 26, several steps are used.

1. Display 18 on the abacus.
2. Leaving the 18, put 26 on the abacus.
3. Check to see if any nails are overloaded (10 or more).
4. Since the ones nail is overloaded with 14 discs on it, make the exchange of 10 ones discs for one more disc on the tens nail.
5. Record the answer in a table. For example:

Tens	Ones	
1	8	
2	6	
3	14	sum
4	4	regrouped sum

Number line. Provide a number line to help the student compute addition facts. Number lines for use in seatwork are easily made by cutting strips from a manila folder. Besides helping the student compute, they provide models for helping him correctly form numerals. In computing 2 + 4 the student is taught to start at 2 and move four spaces to the right to obtain the answer (6). For example, see the number line at the top of page 243. Later, the dot patterns may be eliminated and the numbers can be increased to 18.

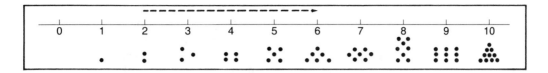

Dot addition. Place reference points on numerals to help students with arithmetic problems (Kramer & Krug, 1973):

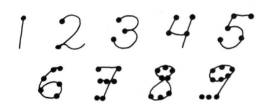

Except for 5, 6, and 8, the dot patterns are identical to the patterns recommended earlier for teaching sums to 9. However, these numbers could be made consistent with the previous patterns:

Kramer and Krug (1973) note that the system offers consistency in perception of the numbers and provides direct association between the number and its value. Actually, the dots provide a semiconcrete-level task for basic addition facts. Also, the dot cues may be faded as the student becomes proficient in learning the facts. For example:

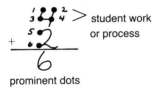

prominent dots

less prominent dots

Computational cues. Provide the learner with cues for helping him remember to regroup or recall the steps in an algorithm. For example, the square reminds the student to carry:

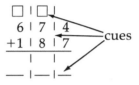

Direction cue. For the student who adds from left to right rather than right to left, place a green dot over the ones column to serve as a reminder to begin computation there.

● —green dot
384
+ 948

Bead addition. Attach a string to cards displaying math facts so the child can put beads on the string when solving the problem. When using the card, the child computes the addition problem by threading the right number of beads onto the shoelace or string. The child can check his answer by looking on the back of the card.

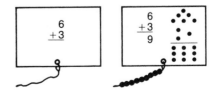

Addition squares. Divide a square into nine smaller squares. Instruct the student to add across and down and to fill in all missing addends or sums. If the computations are accurate, the right column addends and the bottom row addends equal the same sum.

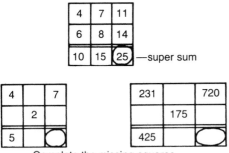

Complete the missing squares

Addition facts family. Present the addition facts (sums 0–18) within a number family framework to help the student learn them (see Figure 7.1). By teaching that any number plus 0 equals the number, and any number plus 1 is counting by 1, there are only 64 facts out of the 100 facts that must be memorized. If the doubles are taught in terms of doubling the addend to compute the sum, only 56 facts remain to be memorized.

Subtraction

Nail abacus. For solving the problem

$$57 - 34 = \square$$

have the student put 57 on the nail abacus: five washers on the tens nail and seven washers on the ones nail. The teacher may use the "take away" or the "find the missing addend" approach. With the take away approach, the student is instructed to take away 34 (3 tens, 4 ones) from the abacus and count the remain-

ing washers to find the difference. With the missing addend approach, the student is instructed to remove the known addend (34) from the sum (57) and count the remaining washers to determine the missing addend. For example:

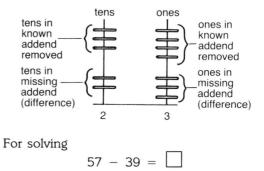

For solving

$$57 - 39 = \square$$

have the student put 57 on the abacus. Since the student cannot take 9 ones from 7 ones, 1 ten is taken off the tens nail and replaced with 10 washers on the ones nail. Now 9 washers are removed from the ones nail, and 3 washers are removed from the tens nail. The number left on the abacus is the answer.

Number line. Provide the student with a number line to help him compute subtraction facts. In solving the problem $14 - 8$, the student is taught to start at 14 and move eight spaces to the *left* to obtain the answer (6). (See below.)

Addition-subtraction pattern. Improve understanding of the relationship between addition and subtraction by having the student compute the sum of two addends and then subtract the two addends from the sum.

$$\begin{array}{r} 47 \\ +23 \\ \hline 70 \end{array} \qquad \begin{array}{r} 70 \\ -23 \\ \hline 47 \end{array} \qquad \begin{array}{r} 70 \\ -47 \\ \hline 23 \end{array}$$

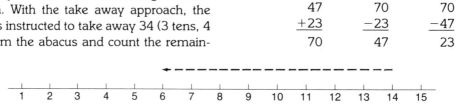

0	1	2	3	4	5	6	7	8	9
0|0*	0|1*	0|2*	0|3*	0|4*	0|5*	0|6*	0|7*	0|8*	0|9*
	1|0*	2|0*	3|0*	4|0*	5|0*	6|0*	7|0*	8|0*	9|0*
		1|1*	1|2*	1|3*	1|4*	1|5*	1|6*	1|7*	1|8*
			2|1*	3|1*	4|1*	5|1*	6|1*	7|1*	8|1*
				2|2*	2|3	2|4	2|5	2|6	2|7
					3|2	4|2	5|2	6|2	7|2
						3|3*	3|4	3|5	3|6
							4|3	5|3	6|3
								4|4*	4|5
									5|4

10	11	12	13	14	15	16	17	18
1|9*	2|9	3|9	4|9	5|9	6|9	7|9	8|9	9|9*
9|1*	9|2	9|3	9|4	9|5	9|6	9|7	9|8	
2|8	3|8	4|8	5|8	6|8	7|8	8|8*		
8|2	8|3	8|4	8|5	8|6	8|7			
3|7	4|7	5|7	6|7	7|7*				
7|3	7|4	7|5	7|6					
4|6	5|6	6|6*						
6|4	6|5							
5|5*								

FIGURE 7.1
Addition facts family.
(Note: Facts marked with an asterisk do not need to be memorized.)

Circle cues. Use circle cues to assist the student to subtract with regrouping.

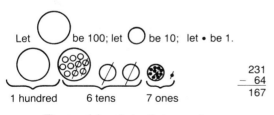

Let ◯ be 100; let ○ be 10; let • be 1.

1 hundred   6 tens   7 ones

$$\begin{array}{r} 231 \\ -\ 64 \\ \hline 167 \end{array}$$

The remaining circles that are not marked through represent the answer.

Multiplication

Array multiplication. Have the student form arrays using tiles, pegboards, or other objects,

and determine the number of rows and columns. Explain that the number of rows and the number of columns represent the factors in a multiplication problem. Then instruct the student to write the multiplication facts represented by various arrays.

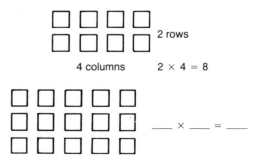

2 rows

4 columns $2 \times 4 = 8$

___ × ___ = ___

Next, give the student multiplication problems and have him form the corresponding arrays.

Dot arrays. Give the student dot arrays and instruct him to write the fact below each array.

```
•  •  •  •        •  •  •  •  •        •  •  •  •  •  •
•  •  •  •        •  •  •  •  •        •  •  •  •  •  •
•  •  •  •        •  •  •  •  •        •  •  •  •  •  •
3 × 4 = 12       _____         •  •  •  •  •  •
                                     _____
```

Napier's rods. Use Napier's rods to strengthen the student's recall of multiplication facts or to check seatwork. They may be constructed from heavy construction paper, tongue depressors, or Popsicle sticks. They consist of 10 strips numbered according to the pattern illustrated below.

The numbers on top of the strips are the multiplicands, and the numbers on the index are the multipliers. The products are in the squares with the diagonal lines. By putting a strip right next to the index, the student can easily determine the product of the respective factors.

For example:

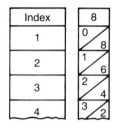

The rods may be used for multiplying more than one digit by a one-digit number. For example, to compute 73 × 4 the rods would be lined up accordingly:

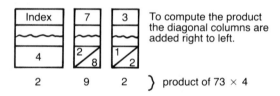

Multiplication chart. Provide the student with a chart for checking his work and doing seatwork. For example:

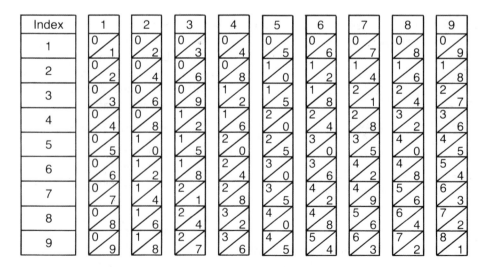

1	2	3	4	5	6	7	8	9
2	4	6	8	10	12	14	16	18
3	6	9	12	15	18	21	24	27
4	8	12	16	20	24	28	32	36
9	18	27	36	45	54	63	72	81

Addition-multiplication pattern. To help the student understand the relationship between addition and multiplication, have him first add the same number several times, then multiply that number by the times it was added. For example:

$$7 + 7 + 7 + 7 + 7 = 35$$
$$7 \times 5 = 35$$

Dot cards. Make 10 sets of cards representing numerals from 1 to 9. Set 1 contains nine cards with *one* dot on each card; Set 2 contains nine cards with *two* dots on each card; Set 3

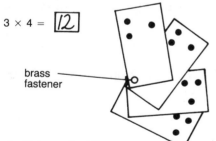

$3 \times 4 =$ ⟨12⟩

brass fastener

The student takes out set three and turns out four cards with three dots. He can count the dots to determine the product or can use the cards to check his work.

contains nine cards with *three* dots on each card; and so on. Instruct the student to use the cards to compute multiplication problems.

Division

Number line. To divide with the number line, have the student count by the set determined by the divisor until the dividend is reached. The quotient is the number of sets used in counting up to the dividend. In computing $18 \div 3$, for example, the student counts by threes since the divisor is 3, and then he counts the loops for the answer. Thus, $18 \div 3 = 6$. (See below.)

Dividing numbers into parts. To help the student understand division, have him divide numbers into equal parts. For example:

12 = ____3s	24 = ____6s
9 = ____3s	36 = ____6s
16 = ____4s	18 = ____6s

Dot division. Use dots to present division problems and have the student write the numerical statement. For example:

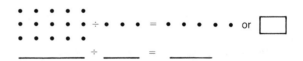

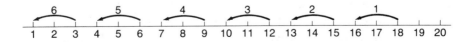

Determining the first digit in the quotient. Provide the student with several long-division problems and ask him to find the first number in the quotient (Wallace & Kauffman, 1986).

Fractions

Number line. Use the fraction number line for illustrating the value of improper fractions. Also, ask the student to indicate if fractions are equal to one whole, greater than one whole, less than one whole, or equal to several wholes.

a stack of cards with graphic representations of a fraction. Have the student match the cards with the correct pocket. For example:

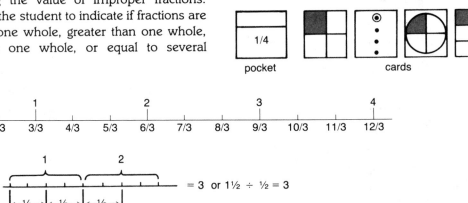

Use the number line to illustrate simple division problems involving fractions. For example, see the illustration above.

Fraction chart. Use fraction charts to show the relationship of a fraction to 1 and to other fractions. Activities with the charts include determining greater-than and less-than values of fractions, finding the lowest common denominator, and determining equivalent fractions.

Use discs (concrete level) or circles (semiconcrete level) to illustrate the division of fractions. For example:

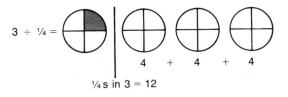

Also, grids are helpful to illustrate division by fractions:

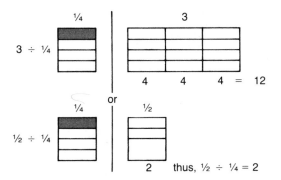

Matching graphic form to numerical symbol. Have the student match fractions in word or graphic form to the numerical symbol for that fraction. To do this, provide the student with library pockets labelled ¼, ⅛, and so forth and

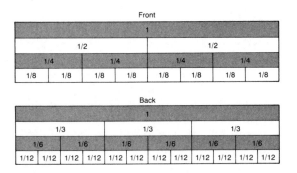

Fraction bars. Make fraction bars out of tongue depressors, Popsicle sticks, or construction paper. On each bar, the multiples of a single-digit number are written. For example:

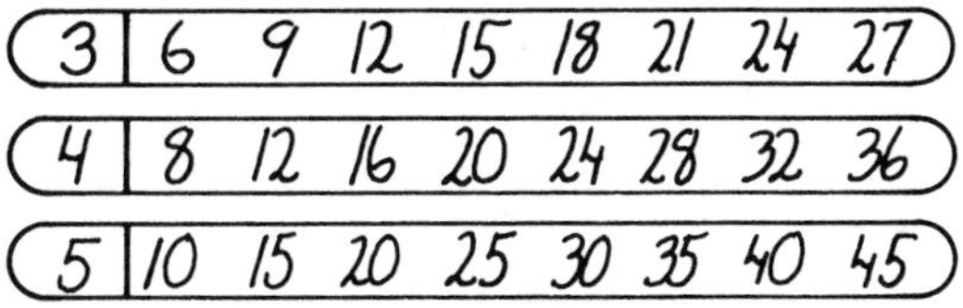
3 6 9 12 15 18 21 24 27
4 8 12 16 20 24 28 32 36
5 10 15 20 25 30 35 40 45

When one bar is placed over another bar, fractions are formed. The two numbers at the extreme left indicate the fraction formed (such as $3/4$); the remaining fractions are a set in which each member of the set is equivalent (such as $3/4$, $6/8$, $9/12$, and so on). The fraction $3/5$ and its equivalents are formed by putting the 3 bar over the 5 bar. For example:

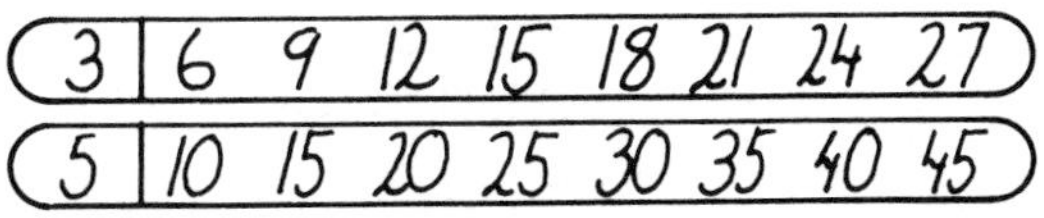
3 6 9 12 15 18 21 24 27
5 10 15 20 25 30 35 40 45

Sample activities include reading the equivalent fractions, forming fractions with other bars, and making new bars.

To compute with fraction bars, instruct the student to use the bars to add two fractions, such as $2/3 + 2/5$. The student is to follow these steps:

1. Form the fraction $2/3$ by placing the 2 bar over the 3 bar.

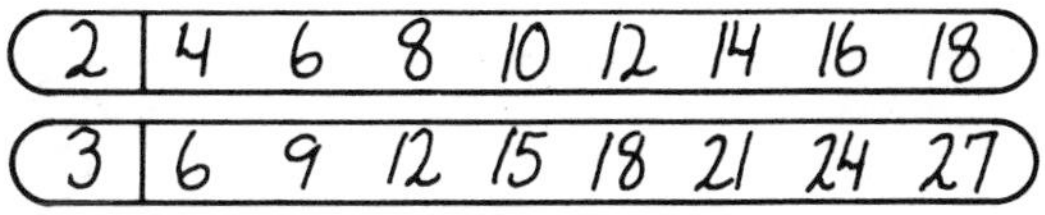
2 4 6 8 10 12 14 16 18
3 6 9 12 15 18 21 24 27

2. Form the fraction $2/5$.

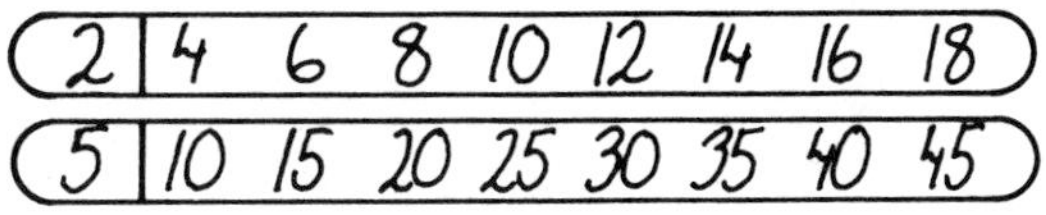
2 4 6 8 10 12 14 16 18
5 10 15 20 25 30 35 40 45

3. Look at the denominators of each fraction and locate the lowest number that is the same on each denominator bar. In this example it is 15.
4. Slide the fraction $2/5$ over until $6/15$ lies directly under $10/15$.

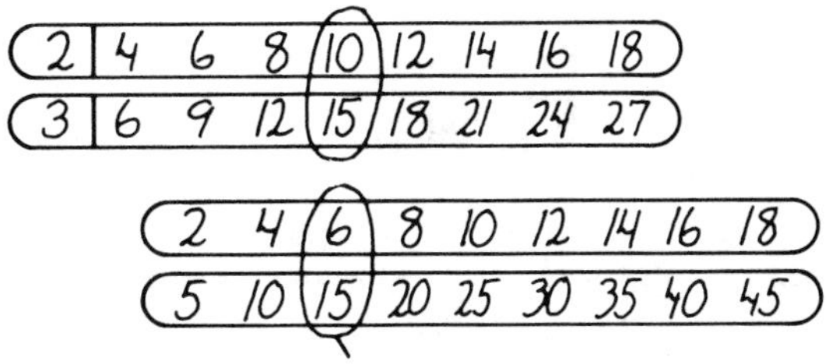
2 4 6 8 10 12 14 16 18
3 6 9 12 15 18 21 24 27
2 4 6 8 10 12 14 16 18
5 10 15 20 25 30 35 40 45

fractions with same denominator

5. To *add*, simply add the numbers on the numerator bars:

$$10 + 6 = 16;$$

thus, the sum is $16/15$.

6. To *subtract*, simply subtract one numerator from the other:

$$10 - 6 = 4;$$

thus, the difference or missing addend is $4/15$.

7. To *divide* $2/3$ by $2/5$, use the common denominator method (D. Howell, Davis, & Underhill, 1974):

$$2/3 \div 2/5 = 10/15 \div 6/15 =$$
$$(10 \div 6) \div (15 \div 15) =$$
$$(10 \div 6) \div 1 = 10 \div 6 = 10/6$$

Multiplying fractions with grids. Have the student draw a grid and represent the two fractions on it that he is multiplying. The student should follow these steps:

1. Make a rectangle and section it equally into the number of squares indicated by the *product* of the denominators. For example, $2/3 \times 1/4 = 12$ squares.

3   4

2. Represent ⅔ on the grid by shading in the correct number of *rows*.

3. Represent ¼ by shading in the correct number of *columns*.

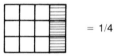

4. The number of squares that overlap represents the numerator of the product of ⅔ × ¼; the total number of squares represents the denominator.

At the concrete level, this activity may use tiles of different sizes.

Time

Number line. Use a circular number line from 1 to 60 to help the student learn to tell time (Reisman, 1982), as shown in Figure 7.2. The number line may be used to help the pupil (a) construct his own clock face, (b) determine the minutes "after the hour," and (c) note the relationship between the hour-hand movement (5 increments per hour) and that of the minute hand (60 increments per hour).

Record schedule. Mark the correct time on clocks for each school bell. Larger clocks may be used to record major events.

FIGURE 7.2
Clock face with number line.

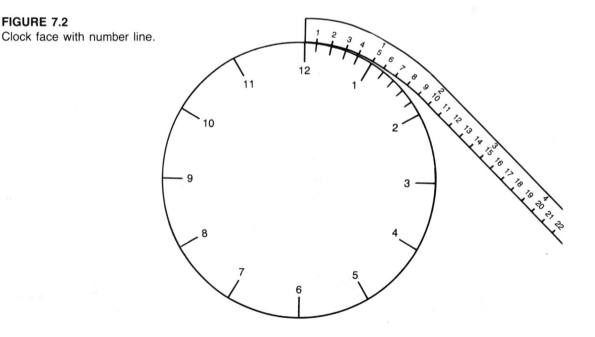

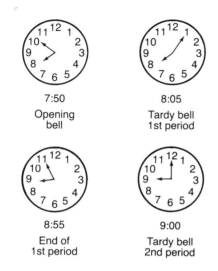

7:50
Opening
bell

8:05
Tardy bell
1st period

8:55
End of
1st period

9:00
Tardy bell
2nd period

Examining schedules. Provide the student with blank clock faces and a variety of schedules (such as those for TV, a movie, or a bus). Have him record schedule times on the clock faces.

Calendar travel. Provide the student with a calendar and a die. The student rolls the die and moves a marker the indicated number of spaces, beginning with the first day. The pupil records the die number and the day of the week on which he lands. The task is over when the student reaches the end of the month.

Calendar quiz. Provide the student with a calendar and a worksheet with numerous ques-

tions. Ask the student to respond to questions like these:

1. How many days are in a week?
2. On what day is the 27th of May?
3. List the dates of all the Wednesdays in January.
4. How many months are in a year?
5. Which month has the fewest days?
6. List the months with 31 days.

Decimals/Money

Cardboard regions. Use cardboard regions for displaying decimals and fractions at the semi-concrete level (Marks, Purdy, & Kinney, 1970). The teacher may shade in various squares and instruct the student to write the equivalent decimal. Graph paper may be glued to the cardboard regions to display specific numbers.

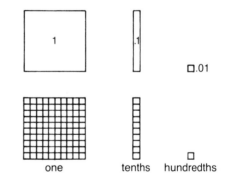

Number line. Use number lines to display decimals and their fractional equivalents. Be-

.0	.1	.2	.3	.4	.5	.6	.7	.8	.9	1.0
$^0/_{10}$	$^1/_{10}$	$^2/_{10}$	$^3/_{10}$	$^4/_{10}$	$^5/_{10}$	$^6/_{10}$	$^7/_{10}$	$^8/_{10}$	$^9/_{10}$	$^{10}/_{10}$

.00	.05	.10	.15	.20	.25	.30	.35	.40	.45	.50
$^0/_{100}$	$^5/_{100}$	$^{10}/_{100}$	$^{15}/_{100}$	$^{20}/_{100}$	$^{25}/_{100}$	$^{30}/_{100}$	$^{35}/_{100}$	$^{40}/_{100}$	$^{45}/_{100}$	$^{50}/_{100}$

0	1.4	2.8	4.2	5.6	7.0	8.4	9.8	11.2
0	$1^4/_{10}$	$2^8/_{10}$	$4^2/_{10}$	$5^6/_{10}$	$7^0/_{10}$	$8^4/_{10}$	$9^8/_{10}$	$11^2/_{10}$

sides using the lines as an aid in computing decimal-fraction problems, the student may be instructed to fill in blank sections of number lines.

Completion of missing parts. Instruct the student to fill in missing parts of various charts and figures as an activity in learning the relationship among fractions, decimals, and percentages. For example:

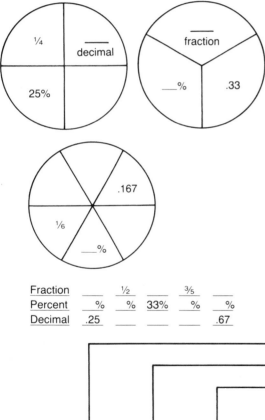

Fraction		½		⅗	
Percent	__%	__%	33%	__%	__%
Decimal	.25				.67

Expanded place value chart. Use an expanded place value chart to demonstrate the relationship among column values, column names, and decimals. An activity consists of leaving parts unlabelled and instructing the student to fill in the missing labels. (See below.)

Money cards. Use money cards to help the student determine correct change. For example, the following $10.00 change card can be used to compute correct change when a $10.00 bill is received:

$10.00 Money Card

$	$	$	$	$	$	$	$	$
(10)	(10)	(10)	(10)	(10)	(10)	(10)	(10)	(10)
(1)	(1)	(1)	(1)	(1)	(1)	(1)	(1)	(1)	(1)

To solve the problem of how much change to give when a $10.00 bill is received and the purchase is for $6.77, the student simply marks out the amount of the purchase on the card. The remaining money is the correct change.

Real money. Use real money as often as possible to teach money values. For example, provide the student with combinations of coins and ask him to total the amounts. Money

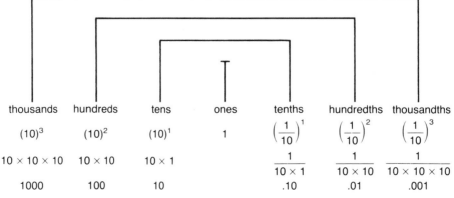

thousands	hundreds	tens	ones	tenths	hundredths	thousandths
$(10)^3$	$(10)^2$	$(10)^1$	1	$\left(\dfrac{1}{10}\right)^1$	$\left(\dfrac{1}{10}\right)^2$	$\left(\dfrac{1}{10}\right)^3$
$10 \times 10 \times 10$	10×10	10×1		$\dfrac{1}{10 \times 1}$	$\dfrac{1}{10 \times 10}$	$\dfrac{1}{10 \times 10 \times 10}$
1000	100	10		.10	.01	.001

stamps from commercial publishers may also be used.

Coupon shopping. On a manila folder, draw a chart. Label the columns *grocery items, price, coupon value,* and *actual cost.* In the coupon column write the value of the coupon or use the real coupon. Ask the student to determine the actual cost of each item. For example:

Grocery Items	Price	Coupon Value	Actual Cost
1. coffee	$3.12	10% off	_____
2. pickles	$1.14	$ .15	_____
3. cereal	$1.39	15% off	_____
4. jelly	$ .79	$ .20	_____

Taking orders. Have the student become a waiter. He can write down orders from a prerecorded cassette tape. Using the menus provided, he can look up the prices of the items ordered, compute the cost of the order, and write the total on the order pad.

Chance shopping. Provide a block with dollar amounts on each side and a laminated shopping card with the following statements:

1. How much do you have to spend?
2. What are you buying?
3. What page is it on in the catalog?
4. How much are you spending?
5. How much do you have left?

The student tosses the block to see how much money he has to spend. Then he looks through a catalog to find items that can be bought for that amount of money. Next, the student answers the questions on the card.

Store comparison. Have the student prepare a list of grocery items and find which supermarket offers the best price. The items and stores can be listed on a chart.

Check the charge. Make worksheets with instructions to check the cashier's slips and see if they are added correctly. For example:

$1.19
.99
.37
1.03
$3.38

$1.38
2.64
.26
.15
$4.43

Measurement

The ruler and Language Master. Draw lines on Language Master cards and record the line's length in inches and centimeters on the tape. Have the student measure the line on a card with the ruler. Number the cards. Have the student put the number on a worksheet and write the length of the line in inches and centimeters next to it. Then the student can insert the card in the Language Master to check his response.

Measure box. Provide the student with a box of objects to measure (such as Popsicle stick, comb, paper clip, straw) and a worksheet with the objects listed on it. Have the student measure the objects and record their length in inches and centimeters on the worksheet. This activity can be repeated for weighing objects.

Measurement and you. Have the student complete the following worksheet:

Your height:
____ feet ____ inches

Your weight:
____ pounds

Your speed:
Number of seconds to run 40 yards: ____ seconds

Your agility:
Number of seconds to deal 52 cards: ____ seconds

Your writing speed:
Number of times you can write your first name in one minute: ____ times

Number of times you can write 6s in one minute: ____ times

Your reading speed:
Number of words read in one minute: ____ words

Circumference of your head: ____ inches

Circumference of your waist: ____ inches

Word Problems

Reality math. Classroom activities may help an adolescent face the realities of adult life (Gallagher, 1979). For example, have the student locate a job in the newspaper and use the salary quoted in the paper to compute net pay. Also, have the student compute living expenses by using newspaper ads, apartment rental ads, car ads, tax guides, catalogs, and brochures with insurance rates.

Word problems. Teach word problems by following the guidelines recommended by Blankenship and Lovitt (1976):

1. Teachers should identify and teach story problems by type, according to various characteristics (for example, extraneous information, verb tense, number and type of nouns).
2. Make up several problems of each type in order to provide practice.

3. A group of instructional techniques should be outlined and used. It may be necessary to vary the techniques according to the needs of each student; however, a systematic plan is essential.

At first, provide the student with very simple, interesting word problems. This helps the student understand that sentences may request specific arithmetic computations. For example:

1. What is the sum of 2 and 3?
2. How much is 3 marbles and 4 marbles?
3. What number represents a triple?
4. How many points is a field goal in football?
5. To get a first down, how many yards must you gain?
6. How many points are 10 baskets in basketball?

Have the student discuss *clue words* in story problems—that is, words indicating mathematical computations. For example:

Operation	Clue Words
Addition	Altogether, sum, and, plus, finds
Subtraction	Left, lost, spent, remain
Multiplication	Rows, groups, altogether
Division	Share, each, cost per month

Have the student write a *number sentence* after reading a story problem (Wallace & Kauffman, 1986). For example:

Mary has 6 comic books. She has read 2 of them. How many books does she have left to read?

$$6 - 2 = \square$$

Table problems. Provide problems that include computing answers from information on a table. An interesting activity that requires computing percentages and decimals from a table is to give the student baseball standings from the newspaper (you can use NFL or NBA standings too, depending on the season) with only the won/lost record beside each team. Have the student do the following:

1. Compute the percentage for each team in the American League East and the National League East.
2. Place the American and National League teams in order based on their won/lost records.
3. Determine how many teams have records over .500.
4. Determine how many percentage points the team in the American League East with the most losses is behind the team with the most wins.

INSTRUCTIONAL GAMES

A variety of games using game boards and sets of stimulus cards can be played to practice various math skills. Game boards are discussed in detail in Chapter 4.

Math War

Materials:

Sets of index cards consisting of family patterns. With sums to 9, each of the numbers from 1 to 9 has a family of two-digit addends. The entire set for sums to 9 includes 54 cards. The family pattern for 7, for example, is $0 + 7$, $7 + 0$, $1 + 6$, $6 + 1$, $2 + 5$, $5 + 2$, $3 + 4$, $4 + 3$.

Directions:

Each player shuffles his 54-card deck. With cards face down, one card at a time is turned over. The player who turns the card showing the number fact with the largest sum wins all the turned cards. The players then turn their next card. If cards of equal sums are turned up at the same time, players with the equivalent cards declare war. They place three

cards face down and turn the fourth card face up. The player whose fourth card has the highest value wins all four cards of the other players (three face down cards, one face up). Whoever has the most cards after 54 cards are played wins. Another way of winning is to play until the other players are down to 5 or 10 remaining cards.

Modifications:

Any set of math facts can be placed on the cards (e.g., multiplication facts, sums to 18). Also, students who play the game during the school day may keep the cards they win and give up the cards they lose. Then for homework each player can complete the missing cards in his deck and remove the extra cards. (Each player always comes to school with one complete deck, with no extra or missing cards.)

Pig Game

Materials:

Dice, scoring pad.

Directions:

Pig Game is usually played by two students with one pair of dice. The object is to be the first player to score 100 points by adding the totals on the dice after each roll. The players take turns rolling the dice; however, a player may roll as many times as he wishes as long as he does not roll a 1 on one or both of the dice. If a 1 is rolled on *one* die, the player gives up the turn and loses all points earned during that turn. If a 1 is rolled on *both* dice, the player gives up the turn, loses all his count, and starts again at zero.

Modification:

Wooden blocks with numerals on all sides except one may be used. A drawing of a pig is placed on the empty side. The pig serves the same function as the 1 on the die.

Make the Numbers Count

Materials:

Dice or a spinner; score sheets.

Directions:

Each player is provided with a score sheet that has five columns—one each for ones, tens, hundreds, thousands, and ten thousands. The left side of the score sheet is numbered from 1 to 10. The die (showing 1–6) or spinner (1–5—may be taken from a commercial game) is rolled or spun 10 times by each player. On each turn the players must enter the number shown on the die or spinner in one of the columns. For a game of 10 turns, only two numbers may be put in each column. After 10 turns the columns are totaled, and the player with the highest number wins.

Spinner Number	10,000s	1000s	100s	10s	1s
1. 3				3	
2. 5	5				
3. 1					1
4. 3		3			
5. 2				2	
6. 2				2	
7. 1					1
8. 4	4				
9. 5		5			
10. 5			5		
Total	9	8	8	4	2

Note: The player in this example would have had a higher score if he had not used the 4 in spin #8 in the 10,000 column. The 5 in either turn 9 or 10 could have been used there.

Rook Math

Materials:

A deck of Rook cards (14 sets of four numbered cards); four dice.

Directions:

The cards are shuffled, and five cards are dealt to each player. The remaining cards are placed on the table, and one card is turned up beside the deck. The player to the left of the dealer throws the four dice. He attempts to match the sum on the dice with a card or cards in his hand. He can lay down a single card or a combination of cards that equals the sum. The player can take the face-up card or draw from the deck. Whether he lays down cards or not, he then discards on the face-up pile. The next player then takes his turn. Play ends when one player is out of cards. The players then total the cards that have been played, and the player with the highest sum wins the game.

Blackjack Math

Materials:

A deck of playing cards.

Directions:

The teacher discusses the value of cards and rules of the game. Aces = 1 or 11; 2–10 are face value; picture cards = 10. The object of the game is to beat the dealer without going over 21. At first, the dealer and each player receive two cards. After that, the players request cards. If a player goes over 21 when taking additional cards, he loses. The winner each time gets to deal.

Golf Math

Materials:

Chalk and chalkboard.

Directions:

The students lay their heads on the desk with their eyes closed. The leader or teacher writes a story problem on the board. At the signal "go," all students look up, read the problem, and begin work. As each student finishes, he raises his hand. The leader gives the first person who finishes 1 point; the second person gets 2 points, and so on. These points represent "strokes" to make the first "hole." Each pupil keeps his score. If a student does not finish the problem within the allotted time, he receives a number of strokes that is more than the highest number given to students who finished the problem. A player then works the problem at the chalkboard. Those who had incorrect answers must add as many strokes to their scores as were given to those who did not finish. Nine holes make up a round, and the player with the lowest total score is the winner.

Math Concentration

Materials:

Ten stimulus cards with arithmetic problems on one side and blank on the other side; 10 cards with the answers to the problems of the stimulus cards on one side and blank on the other side.

Directions:

The cards are placed face down in a 5 × 4 array. Two or more students can play. The first player turns a card over and gives an answer. If he is correct, he turns up a second card. If the second card shows the answer to the first card, the player gets to keep both cards. If an incorrect answer is given to the first card, the player does not turn over a second card. The next player then takes his turn. The winner is the player with the most cards when all cards are taken.

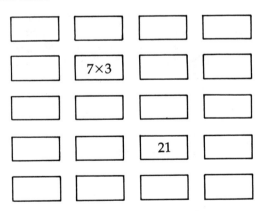

Fraction Game

Materials:

One-inch cubes of wood with gummed stickers on each side marked ½, ¼, ⅙, ¹⁄₁₂, ⅓, and ¹⁄₁₂; 1″ cardboard squares marked as follows: 24 pieces with ¼ label, 31 pieces with ⅙ label, 12 pieces with ½ label, 18 pieces with ⅓ label, and 60 pieces with ¹⁄₁₂ label; six game boards marked into 12 sections.

Directions:

Each player is given a game board. He attempts to collect fractional parts that will cover ¹²⁄₁₂ of his board without overlapping pieces. The first player throws a cube and collects the fractional piece designated by the cube. This piece is placed on the playing board. The next player then takes his turn. Play continues until a player covers ¹²⁄₁₂ of his board. If a player throws the cube and all corresponding pieces have been taken, he receives nothing. Likewise, if the cube indicates a fraction that is larger than needed, the player collects nothing.

Multiplication and Division Facts Rummy

Materials:

Forty to 52 cards containing a family of multiplication/division facts—for example, 9 × 6, 6 × 9, 54 ÷ 6, 54 ÷ 9.

Directions:

Seven cards are dealt to each player. The player on the dealer's left draws a card from the remaining cards. If the card matches two others in his hand in the same family, he lays down the book of cards and gives the answer to each fact. If he gives the wrong answer, the cards must remain in his hand until the next turn. After the player lays down cards or is unable to do so, he discards by placing a card from his hand face up beside the deck so that all the other discards can be seen. The next player may choose from the stack or pick up the previous discard if he can match it with two cards in his hand. If there are two cards in the discard pile that match one in a player's hand, he may pick up both. He does *not* have to take the whole pack, provided he can give the correct answers of the cards between the two he wants. Also, during his turn a player may lay down one or more cards that match another player's books. When one player is out of cards, he says, "Rummy," and wins the game.

Travel Game

Materials:

Large map of the United States; markers or pictures of vehicles; cards with arithmetic problems on them.

Directions:

On a large map of the United States a course across the nation is marked off into 50-mile segments. Each card presents an arithmetic problem and the number of miles it is worth (such as 50, 100, or 200 miles). Each player draws a card and responds to the arithmetic problem. If correct, the player moves the marker the number of miles indicated on the card. If incorrect, the player moves *back* the specified miles. The winner is the first player (or team) to reach the destination.

Modification:

Players can be provided with cards of various levels of difficulty. Each student can select cards from the difficulty level he desires. The more difficult the problem, the more miles it is worth.

Basketball Math

Materials:

A drawing of a basketball court on the chalkboard or on poster board; sets of cards presenting arithmetic problems labelled "lay-ups," "10-foot jump shot," "15-foot jump shot," and "3-point shot."

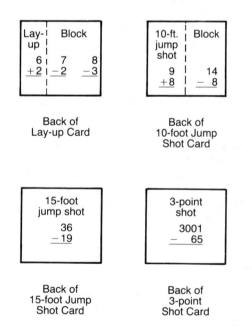

Directions:

The cards are divided into stacks. Each lay-up card has a problem to be answered for 2 points and two problems (slightly more difficult) that may be answered to block the lay-up. If the opposing player can answer either of the "block" problems, the lay-up is blocked. If the shooter answers the lay-up problem correctly and it is not blocked, he receives 2 points. For the next most difficult stack (10-foot jump shot), there is only one block question on the card. The 15-foot jump shot has the next most difficult problem and no block shot questions. The 3-point-shot stack has the most difficult problems and no block shot questions. A time limit (for example, 5 seconds) is set for answering the questions.

Counting Coins

Materials:

Timer; paper and pencil.

Directions:

The object of the game is to use the fewest coins to make a given sum. The leader calls out an amount—say, 65 cents. Each player must write down the coins that make the sum within a given time limit. All players who correctly sum the coins receive 1 point. The player or players who use the fewest coins receive 5 points. The first player to receive 25 points wins the game.

Rate Game

Materials:

A start-to-finish game board; math worksheets and corresponding answer sheets; game markers; dice.

Directions:

Each player is given an individual worksheet at the appropriate instructional level. The first player rolls one die and may elect to move his marker that number of spaces on the game board or to write the answers to problems on his worksheet for 10 seconds and move his marker according to the number of problems answered correctly. The opposing player uses the answer sheet to check the responses. If the player chooses to write answers from the worksheet, he must take these results even if the number is less than the number rolled on the die. The first player to reach the finish space on the board wins the game.

Fraction Blackjack
(Hurwitz, Goddard, & Epstein, 1975)

Materials:

Deck of playing cards.

Directions:

All picture cards are wild and may be given any value from 1 to 10. The cards are separated into two stacks: red cards (diamonds and hearts) and black cards (spades and clubs). The first player draws one card from each stack and forms a fraction using the value of the black card as the numerator and the value of the red card as the denominator. Thus, if he draws a black 8 and a red 2, his fraction is 8/2. The same player continues by drawing two more cards (one black and one red), forming the fraction, and adding the new fraction to the first fraction (8/2). He continues until he makes a sum of 10 or as close to 10 as possible. The sum may be above or below 10, and the winner of each round is the player who gets closest to 10.

Modification:

The game may be played more like traditional blackjack, in which the players take turns receiving their two cards and a player loses if he goes over 10.

Fraction Removal

Materials:

Dice (one green and one white); paper and pencil.

Directions:

Each player writes the following 22 numbers on his paper: 1.00, .50, .33⅓, .25, .20, .26⅔, 2.00, .66⅔, .40, 3.00, 1.50, .75, .60, 4.00, 1.33⅓, 1.20, 5.00, 2.50, 1.66⅔, 1.25, .83⅓, and 6.00. One green die and one white die are used. The green die deter-

mines the numerator, and the white die determines the denominator. Thus, a green 4 and a white 2 is equivalent to 4/2, or 2. The decimal equivalent of this is 2.00. Green 3 and white 5 equals 3/5 or .60. Each player rolls the dice, forms the fraction, computes the decimal form, and crosses it out on his paper. One point is scored for each decimal crossed out. A bonus of 5 points is given for each fraction rolled that is equivalent to 1.00 (2/2, 4/4). The winner is the player who scores 50 points first.

Decimal Shapes
(Bright & Harvey, 1982)

Materials:

A game board with sections containing numbers in decimal form; 10 markers (5 each of two colors); a chip marked *L* on one side and *S* on the other; an answer sheet that has the numbers on the board listed in order from smallest to largest.

Directions:

Both players place their markers on the starting spaces of the board (enclosed with dark lines). The first player flips the chip. If the chip lands on the *L* side, the player must move one of his markers to an adjacent space having a number larger than the number the marker is on. If the chip lands on the *S* side, the player must move one of his markers to an adjacent space having a number smaller than the number the marker is on. If the player can move one of his markers to a space occupied by his oppo-

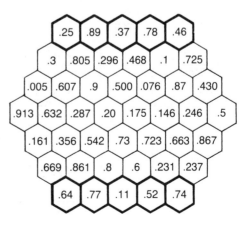

nent, the opponent's marker is moved back to a starting position. Only one marker may be on a space at one time. The player must move one of his markers, no matter what the direction, if he is able to do so. If he cannot move, he loses his turn. The two players take turns, and each move can be checked for correctness by using the answer sheet. The winner is the first player to get all of his markers to the starting spaces on the other side of the board.

SELF-CORRECTING MATERIALS

In addition to the self-correcting materials presented in this section, numerous self-correcting materials for math instruction are described in Chapter 4.

Flip Sider Math Cards

Feedback device:

The correct answer is written on the back of each stimulus card.

Materials:

Stimulus cards with an arithmetic problem on one side and the correct answer on the other side.

Directions:

The student looks at the arithmetic problem on the card and writes the answer on a worksheet. Then he flips the card over to check his response.

Front

Front

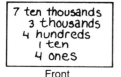

Back

Back

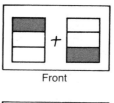

Front

Back

Calculator

Feedback device:

The student computes the problem on the calculator, and the correct answer appears in the read-out area.

Materials:

Low-cost pocket calculator; worksheet of arithmetic problems.

Directions:

The student computes the answer to a problem, writes it on the worksheet, and uses the calculator to check his response.

Clipping Answers

Feedback device:

When the clothespin containing the correct answer is clipped to the problem on the board and the board is turned over, the symbol on the back of the clothespin matches the symbol on the back of the board.

Materials:

Segmented stimulus board showing arithmetic problems on the front and symbols on the back; clothespins with answers on one side and symbols corresponding to those on the stimulus board on the other side.

Directions:

The student matches the answer on the clothespin to a problem by clipping the clothespin to the problem on the board. Then he turns the board over. If the symbol on the back of the clothespin matches the symbol on the back of the board, the answer is correct.

Modifications:

For easy storage, the clothespins may be kept in a plastic bag with a zipper. Also, pizza wheels make good stimulus cards.

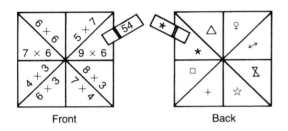

Front　　　　　　　　Back

Arithmetic Squares

Feedback device:

After completing the squares, the student can check his work by turning over the squares. If the squares are correctly placed, a message or picture appears on the back.

Materials:

A set of poster board squares that include arithmetic problems and answers to problems on adjoining squares (a message or picture is written on the back of the large piece of poster board before the squares are cut); a large box with a window in the bottom, made by placing a piece of acetate over an opening.

Directions:

The student fits the squares together so that each fact adjoins its correct answer. He puts the pieces (message or picture side down) inside the box and on top of the acetate. When he has completed the puzzle, he places the cover on the box and flips the

box over. If he is correct, he should be able to read the message or view the picture on the back of the puzzle.

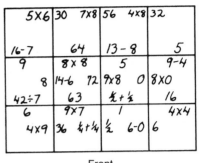

Front

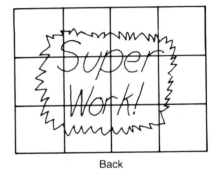

Back

Color Code Folders

Feedback device:

When the worksheet is in the red folder, the problems can be seen but the answers cannot. After completing the problems on a separate sheet of paper, the student removes the worksheet from its folder to check his answers.

Materials:

Red transparent folder (such as a term-paper folder); worksheet with problems written in black felt-tip pen and answers written in yellow.

Directions:

The student inserts the worksheet into the red folder. Then he numbers his seatwork paper and records the answer for each problem. The worksheet is removed from the folder, and the student checks his answers with those written in yellow on the worksheet.

Modification:

Different colors may be used (answers can be written in the same color as the folder).

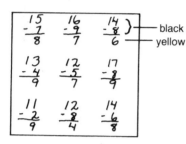

Worksheet

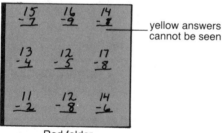

Red folder
with worksheet inside

Fast Facts

Feedback device:

The correct answers are written inside the open folder.

Materials:

Manila folder with arithmetic problems in a column on the *right* side inside the folder and the answers to the problems on the *left* side of the same flap inside the folder. The outside flap of the folder is cut so that only the problems are exposed when the folder is closed.

Directions:

The student computes the problems presented in the closed folder and then opens the folder to check his work.

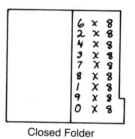

Closed Folder

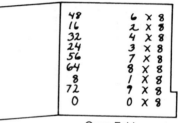

Open Folder

Snoopy Math

Feedback device:

When the student puts his pencil in the hole of the problem he has worked and turns over the cut-out (Snoopy), the correct answer is written next to the hole where his pencil is.

Materials:

Snoopy figure cut out of poster board with (a) holes punched around the cut-out, (b) a number placed near each hole, (c) an operation and a number (such as +8) written in the middle of the cut-out, and (d) answers written on the other side beside the holes; pencil.

Directions:

The student computes problems according to the operation and number presented in the middle of the cut-out. For example, if +8 is presented, the student is to add 8 to each number near each hole. He places his pencil in the hole beside a problem, computes the answer, and turns over Snoopy to check his response by looking at the answer where his pencil is.

Modification:

Each side can be used as the problem or the answer. For example, the problems on the other side of the example +8 become −8.

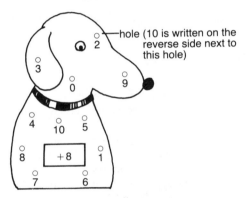

COMMERCIAL PROGRAMS AND MATERIALS

Numerous published materials and programs are available for teaching math concepts and skills. The following selected materials and programs are useful for teaching math skills to students with learning problems.

Computational Arithmetic Program
(Smith & Lovitt, 1982)

Publisher: Pro-Ed

Description:

The *Computational Arithmetic Program* is for students in grades 1 through 6 who need to learn and become proficient in the basic computational skills of whole numbers. It provides 314 sequenced problem worksheets in facts (basic problems for all four computational areas), addition (with and without

carrying), subtraction (with and without borrowing), multiplication (with and without carrying), and division (with and without remainders).

Corrective Mathematics Program
(Engelmann & Carnine, 1982)

Publisher: Science Research Associates

Description:

The *Corrective Mathematics Program* is a remedial series in basic math for students in grades 3 through 12 and adults who have not mastered basic skills. The basic facts are taught in addition, subtraction, multiplication, and division. It includes the concepts of carrying and borrowing as well as story problems. The lessons (65 in each operation area) take between 25 and 45 minutes and include both teacher-directed instruction and independent review activities.

Cuisenaire Rods
(Davidson, 1969)

Publisher: Cuisenaire Company of America

Description:

The Cuisenaire rods are instructional aids for teaching mathematical concepts. They can be used in kindergarten through grade 6; however, they are usually emphasized for kindergarten through grade 3. The Cuisenaire rods are not a complete program and are mainly used to supplement existing mathematical programs. They consist of 291 wood blocks that vary in length and color. Each white cube equals 1, red equals 2, green equals 3, purple equals 4, yellow equals 5, dark green equals 6, black equals 7, brown equals 8, blue equals 9, and orange equals 10 (see Figure 7.3). The rods are used in performing arithmetic operations. For example, to multiply 2×3 or $r \times g$, a cross is made with the rods with the first-named rod on the bottom. It is read as "r cross g." The cross represents the number of red rods ($N = 3$) that would form a floor under the green rod. The three red rods can be placed next to the dark green rod to figure out the product (6).

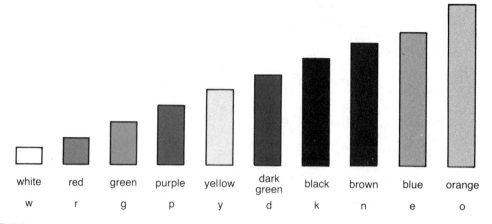

FIGURE 7.3
Cuisenaire rods, with color and letter designations.

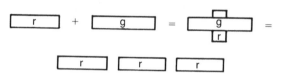

The rods may be used to teach readiness skills as well as all four operations with whole numbers and fractions. Current research suggests that the rods are at least as effective as more traditional mathematical approaches, particularly with certain learners.

DISTAR Arithmetic Kits
(Englemann & Carnine, 1972, 1975, 1976)

Publisher: Science Research Associates

Description:

The *DISTAR Arithmetic Kits* stress direct instruction within a highly systematic, intensive framework. Each kit includes a teacher's guide, teacher's presentation books, take-homes, workbooks for students, and (depending on the level) geometric figures cards, form boards, fact cards, and card stand. DISTAR is primarily designed for use with students in small groups. However, suggestions for teaching large groups are included. The lessons are fast-paced, and the teacher's guide specifies what the teacher should say and do. Simple skills are presented first, followed by more complex skills. Scope and sequence charts are provided. Oral responses are extensively used; however, written work is also required. DISTAR I (Engelmann & Carnine, 1975) focuses on ordinal counting, 35 addition facts, $>$ and $<$ signs, simple story problems, and simple subtraction problems. DISTAR II (Engelmann & Carnine, 1976) covers 60 addition facts, 20 algebra addition facts, 43 subtraction facts, addition with regrouping, multiplication facts, time, money, measurement (metrics and standard), and fractions including all four operations. DISTAR III (Engelmann & Carnine, 1972) extends the basic operations (regrouping, column multiplication, and long division). Also, story problems and problem-solving procedures are stressed. The DISTAR programs have been extensively field tested and evaluated. The results indicate that *DISTAR Arithmetic Kits* are very effective in teaching arithmetic skills to economically disadvantaged children (Abt Associates, 1976; Becker & Engelmann, 1976; Stallings & Kaskowitz, 1974).

Key Math Teach and Practice
(Connolly, 1985)

Publisher: American Guidance Service

Description:

The *Key Math Teach and Practice* program is designed to identify and remediate specific computation difficulties. Math inventories and probes are used to pinpoint a student's strengths and weaknesses. Appropriate activities and worksheets are organized from 32 instructional folders, each of which focuses on specific computational skills. Instructional intervention follows a sequence of foundation steps (practice using concrete and pictorial representations); worksheet activities; and drills, games, and extensions. A teacher's guide, a student progress chart, and a scope and sequence chart are also included.

Montessori Materials
(Montessori, 1964, 1965a, 1965b)

Publisher: Educational Teaching Aids

Description:

Montessori, an Italian physician, organized her developmental materials into three major areas: motor education, sensory education, and language. The arithmetic materials are primarily within the area of sensory training. The materials are designed to stress manipulative experiences and are self-correcting. Some of the basic materials include cylinder blocks, a counting box with spindles, bead frames, number cards and beads, metric number rods, and learning boards with pegs and skittles for addition, subtraction, multiplication, and division. The effectiveness of the Montessori approach is yet to be proven (Goodman, 1974). It appears that the Montessori materials would be helpful as a supplement in providing concrete experiences to children in a systematic arithmetic program. The materials used alone do not offer many experiences at the semiconcrete and abstract levels.

Programmed Math for Adults

Publisher: McGraw-Hill (Sullivan Associates)

Description:

Programmed Math for Adults is a remedial math program consisting of 15 teaching booklets and 8 practice booklets. The program involves very little reading and is self-instructional and self-correcting. It is designed for older students who have inade-

quate math skills. The content ranges from basic addition to trigonometry.

Project MATH
(Cawley et al., 1976)

Publisher: EPC Educational Progress, Educational Development Corporation

Description:

Project MATH was developed at the University of Connecticut by Cawley and his associates. It is designed for children in preschool through grade 6; however, it has been used with secondary students who have learning problems. One of the reasons it was developed was to provide the nonreader with the opportunity to gain skills in math without being hindered by a lack of reading ability (Cawley, 1977). The program stresses multiple options for teaching students with learning problems. The options focus on varying the input and output modes. The program includes a *Mathematics Concept Inventory*, designed to screen and place the learner. There are four kits, and each one covers approximately 1½ grade levels. Each kit contains a *Multiple Option Curriculum* with four ways to demonstrate mastery. The content is organized according to six strands: (a) patterns, (b) sets, (c) geometry, (d) numbers and operations, (e) measurement, and (f) fractions. The program also has units called LABS that stress the social and emotional development of the student. A LABS unit may last from several days to a few weeks. It covers topics such as telephones, calculators, and metrics.

Real-Life Math

Publisher: Hubbard

Description:

This program features role-playing activities in which students establish their own businesses. Students complete files, handle billing forms, and conduct financial transactions with a bank. The program stresses the development of functional math skills in students aged 13 to 18 with learning problems. The materials include a teacher's manual, 15 spirit masters, eight stimulus posters, ten audiocassettes, five student skill books, a mail box, three desk signs, and a kit of expendables for ten students.

Schoolhouse: Mathematics Series

Publisher: Science Research Associates

Description:

This series consists of three kits which can supplement any basal mathematics program for grades 1 through 4. Each kit contains 400 skill cards (two copies each of 200) with plastic overlays. Each card has an answer key on the back for self-checking and immediate reinforcement or correction and thus can be used to provide independent practice or additional drill. The kits offer mathematics skill practice in selected areas including numbers, addition and subtraction, multiplication and division, fractions, word problems, geometry, measurement, and time and money. The *SRA Mathematics Drillpak* is a continuation of the *Schoolhouse Series*. The skill cards offer a review of basic algorithms and focus on skills usually practiced in grades 4 through 6.

Structural Arithmetic
(Stern, 1965)

Publisher: Houghton Mifflin

Description:

Structural Arithmetic is designed for use in grades K through 3. The materials are available in four kits, one for each grade level. Each kit contains a teacher's manual, students' workbooks, and manipulative materials (such as number track, unit blocks, and number guide). Each lesson sets up experiments that guide pupils to make discoveries and generalizations. Stern and Stern (1971) report that the program uses the following approaches:

1. Concrete materials are used to help the child discover number facts.
2. It consists of a carefully arranged sequence of experiments—the student progresses from understanding simple number concepts to mastering computation and problem solving.
3. Illustrations are provided in the workbooks to help the student review any forgotten concepts or facts.

Mastery tests are provided at the end of each workbook and are used throughout the program. Bartel (1986) notes that the program has been used successfully with students who have learning problems.

TELOR Learning System

Publisher: Enrich

Description:

The TELOR is a hand-held, visual cartridge device that uses interchangeable lessons. These plastic cartridges contain 40 frames (questions and answers). Each frame presents a problem and a multiple-choice answer. The student pushes up on a button to respond, and a correct response advances the next frame. The *TELOR Learning Aid* and *Visual Cartridge Lessons* are available in the *Arithmetic Independence Series,* or they may be ordered separately (for example, addition only).

Unifix Materials

Publisher: Educational Teaching Aids

Description:

Unifix materials offer a wide variety of manipulative materials for teaching basic arithmetic concepts and skills. For example, the interlocking Unifix cubes are helpful for teaching basic addition, subtraction, and place value. The materials are available in a kit or separately.

Some additional helpful resources for teachers include the following:

1. *Kids' Stuff—Math* is a book of instructional activities published by Incentive Publications. It covers a wide variety of topics, including numeration, sets, fractions, problem solving, and others.
2. *Number Games to Improve Your Child's Arithmetic* (Hurwitz, Goddard, & Epstein, 1975) is aimed at helping parents design enjoyable arithmetic games for children. It includes over 100 games and is a valuable

resource for teachers who use games to practice and reinforce arithmetic skills.

3. *Plus,* published by Educational Service, includes activities, games, and seatwork ideas in counting, time, facts, money, fractions, and other areas.

COMPUTER SOFTWARE PROGRAMS

Computer software programs in math can be used to provide drill and practice activities in a motivating manner. Some programs present game-playing situations, and others effectively use animation and sound effects to maintain student interest. Also, the computer can provide self-correcting feedback so the student does not practice errors. R.D. Howell, Sidorenko, and Jurica (1987) examined the effects of computer use on the learning of multiplication facts by learning disabled students. They found that it was necessary to combine direct teacher instruction with drill-and-practice and tutorial software for effective results. The following software programs present various math skills and may be useful to the student in developing understanding and mastery of these skills. Appendix C lists the addresses of producers and distributors of educational software programs.

Arcademic Intermediate Math Series

Producer: DLM Teaching Resources

Hardware: Apple II

Description:

The two programs included in this series provide excellent drill-and-practice vehicles for intermediate students. *Decimal Discovery* helps students improve their skills in comparing, adding, subtracting, multiplying, and dividing with decimals. A variety of games and problems are designed around an oil-drilling theme, and players respond by matching, filling in, or scanning the answer. The decimal problems range from tenths to thousandths. *Fast-Track*

Fractions combines the excitement of car racing with fraction drills. Students solve problems that compare, add, subtract, multiply, and divide with fractions. Both programs include an editor system for creating, changing, and printing individualized game content. A listing of the 10 highest-scoring players is displayed to provide a reward system and motivate students to improve their scores.

Arcademic Skill Builders in Math

Producer: DLM Teaching Resources

Hardware: Apple II, IBM PC/PCjr, Commodore 64, Tandy 1000, Atari

Description:

This series is designed to motivate students of all ages to learn fundamental math skills through the fast action and colorful graphics of arcade games. Six individual programs provide practice and drill in the four basic math operations and combinations of operations. *Alien Addition* uses an "alien invasion" theme to provide practice in basic addition facts. *Minus Mission* offers practice in basic subtraction facts as the student uses a robot that fires laser beams to destroy green blobs of dripping slime. Practice in basic multiplication facts is provided in *Meteor Multiplication,* in which the student must disintegrate meteors moving toward a star station. *Demolition Division* gives the student the opportunity to practice basic division facts as tanks move toward cannons that the player can fire. In *Alligator Mix* the student feeds hungry alligators while increasing his skill in both addition and subtraction facts. *Dragon Mix* provides practice in multiplication and division facts as a large dragon protects the city behind it from invading forces. In all the programs the range of numbers can be changed to practice basic facts with the numbers 0–3, 0–6, or 0–9. Also, there are nine speed options, and game time can range from 1 to 5 minutes. Twelve blackline masters and 52 flash cards are included with each program.

Basic Skills in Math

Producer: Love Publishing Company

Hardware: Apple II

Description:

This software pinpoints the student's specific problem area in the basic fundamental math functions (addition, subtraction, multiplication, and division) and provides practice based on individual needs. After assessment, the student is automatically branched to the appropriate part of the program. For practice, the screen shows a numerical and pictorial representation of a problem. Visual and auditory rewards are given for success with each problem. If the student misses a problem twice, the work needed to reach the correct solution is presented visually. After the student progresses to the mastery test and demonstrates the basic skills for that level, he is rewarded with an asteroid math learning game. The program is designed for students in grades 1 through 6, but the format and space theme are compatible with a wide range of ages. Spirit masters accompany each program, and there is a built-in record-keeping system.

Computer Drill and Instruction: Mathematics

Producer: Science Research Associates

Hardware: Apple II, Atari

Description:

Levels A, B, and C of this software series present basic arithmetic skills for the elementary grades, and hundreds of carefully sequenced lessons are included. If the student has difficulty with a problem, he can call for help, and animated tutorials will take him step-by-step through the solution strategy to the correct answer. Level D (available only for Apple computers) is designed for students in junior high through adult age. It includes 208 sequenced lessons covering numbers and numeration, computation with whole numbers, fractions, decimals and percent, measurement, prealgebra, and practical applications.

Mathematics Problem Solving

Producer: Media Materials

Hardware: Apple II, TRS-80

Description:

This series includes 10 programs with instructions and explanations given on an elementary reading level. Correct responses are praised and students are given helpful hints and tutorial assistance for incorrect responses. The following programs are included: *Shoot for Solutions* (five steps to problem solving), *Home Run Logic* (thinking through problems; averages; percents), *Dive into Data* (recognizing essential data in word problems; whole number, fraction, and decimal problem solving), *Answer Matches* (estimating answers by rounding numbers; money problems), *On Your Mark—Go* (word problems; fractions; working with distance), *Score the Goal* (multiplication and division of whole numbers), *Chin Bars and Charts* (interpreting information on charts, tables, and graphs; computations of whole numbers and decimals), *Run a Relay* (using rate tables; reading a table of records), and *Stick to a Plan* (using a five-step plan with word problems; getting data from a bar graph). Supplemental materials for enrichment and reinforcement are included.

Math Sequences

Producer: Milliken

Hardware: Apple II, Atari

Description:

This package consists of 12 diskettes that provide a comprehensive, objective-based mathematics curriculum with structured drill and practice designed for students in grades 1 through 8 or as remediation for older students. Topics covered include number readiness, addition, subtraction, multiplication, division, laws of arithmetic, integers, fractions, decimals, percents, equations, and measurement formulas. The range of problem levels (from 16 to 64) within a sequence makes it possible to place each student at his level of understanding. All the work (e.g., carrying, borrowing, canceling numbers) for each problem is completed on the screen. Graphic or textual reinforcements are given for a correct response. When a problem is missed more than once, the correct solution is displayed, step-by-step, for the student to study. The student is advanced a level after specific achievement criteria are met or moved back a level until mastery is achieved. The management program maintains records for each student and allows the teacher to establish personalized performance levels and make individual and class assignments.

Math Skills—Elementary Level;
Math Skills—Junior High Level

Producer: Encyclopaedia Britannica Educational Corporation

Hardware: Apple II

Description:

These two programs provide practice and drill in mathematical concepts and basic operations and processes. The skills presented at the elementary level include numbers, addition/subtraction, multiplication/division, fractions, and decimals. The skills presented at the junior high level include ratio and proportions, percents, graphics, estimating, and measuring. The programs provide immediate feedback that is supportive when the response is correct and instructional when the response is incorrect. Graphics are used to explain the mathematical concepts and demonstrate them visually. The difficulty of each segment and the content change according to the student's performance.

Micro-Math Programs

Producer: Educational Teaching Aids

Hardware: Apple II, TRS-80

Description:

These computational skills programs are designed to help teach new skills and concepts. The programs complement basal textbooks, and algorithms are presented as they are taught. There are more than 280 levels for grades 1 through 8, and the teacher can choose automatic level adjustment or have the student stay on one level for complete mastery. The programs focus on whole numbers, fractions, decimals, and percents. A record-keeping system is available to record progress or make assignments.

REFERENCES

Abt Associates. (1976). *Education as experimentation: A planned variation model* (Vol. 3). Boston: Abt Associates.

Ashlock, R.B. (1986). *Error patterns in computation: A semi-programmed approach* (4th ed.). Columbus, OH: Merrill.

Bannatyne, A. (1973). Programs, materials and techniques. *Journal of Learning Disabilities, 6,* 204–212.

Bartel, N.R. (1986). Problems in mathematics achievement. In D.D. Hammill & N.R. Bartel, *Teaching children with learning and behavior problems* (4th ed., pp. 179–233). Boston: Allyn & Bacon.

Becker, W.C., & Engelmann, S.E. (1976). *Technical report 1976–1.* Eugene, OR: University of Oregon.

Blankenship, C.S., & Lovitt, T.C. (1976). Story problems: Merely confusing or downright befuddling. *Journal for Research in Mathematics Education, 7,* 290–298.

Bright, G.W., & Harvey, J.G. (1982). Using games to teach fraction concepts and skills. In L. Silvey (Ed.), *Mathematics for the middle grades (5–9): 1982 yearbook.* Reston, VA: National Council of Teachers of Mathematics.

Cawley, J.F. (1977). Curriculum: One perspective for special education. In R.D. Kneedler & S.G. Tarver (Eds.), *Changing perspectives in special education.* (pp. 21–45). Columbus, OH: Merrill.

Cawley, J.F., Fitzmaurice, A.M., Goodstein, H.A., Lepore, A.V., Sedlak, R., & Althaus, V. (1976). *Project MATH.* Tulsa, OK: Educational Development Corporation.

Connolly, A.J. (1985). *Key Math teach and practice.* Circle Pines, MN: American Guidance Service.

Davidson, J. (1969). *Using the Cuisenaire rods.* New Rochelle, NY: Cuisenaire.

Driscoll, M. (1983). *Research within reach: Secondary school mathematics.* St. Louis: Research and Development Interpretation Service.

Engelmann, S., & Carnine, D. (1972). *DISTAR arithmetic level III.* Chicago: Science Research Associates.

Engelmann, S., & Carnine, D. (1975). *DISTAR arith-*

metic level I. Chicago: Science Research Associates.

Engelmann, S., & Carnine, D. (1976). *DISTAR arithmetic level II.* Chicago: Science Research Associates.

Engelmann, S., & Carnine, D. (1982). *Corrective mathematics program.* Chicago: Science Research Associates.

Fulkerson, E. (1963). Adding by tens. *The Arithmetic Teacher, 10,* 139–140.

Gallagher, P.A. (1979). *Teaching students with behavior disorders: Techniques for classroom instruction.* Denver: Love.

Goodman, L. (1974). Montessori education for the handicapped: The methods—the research. In L. Mann & D. Sabatino (Eds.), *The second review of special education.* Philadelphia: JSE Press.

Groves, K. (1976). Teacher idea exchange: Using dice and the blockhead game for skill development. *Teaching Exceptional Children, 8,* 103–104.

Howell, D., Davis, W., & Underhill, L. (1974). *Activities for teaching mathematics to low achievers.* Jackson, MS: University Press of Mississippi.

Howell, R.D., Sidorenko, E., & Jurica, J. (1987). The effects of computer use on the acquisition of multiplication facts by a student with learning disabilities. *Journal of Learning Disabilities, 20,* 336–341.

Hurwitz, A.B., Goddard, A., & Epstein, D.T. (1975). *Number games to improve your child's arithmetic.* New York: Funk & Wagnalls.

Hutchings, B. (1975). Low-stress subtraction. *The Arithmetic Teacher, 22,* 226–232.

Hutchings, B. (1976). *Low-stress algorithms.* Reston, VA: National Council of Teachers of Mathematics.

Kramer, T., & Krug, D.A. (1973). A rationale and procedure for teaching addition. *Education and Training of the Mentally Retarded, 8,* 140–144.

Lerner, J.W., & Vaver, G. (1970). Filmstrips in learning. *Academic Therapy, 5,* 320–324.

Marks, J.L., Purdy, C.R., & Kinney, L.B. (1970). *Teaching elementary school mathematics for understanding.* New York: McGraw-Hill.

Montessori, M. (1964). *The Montessori method.* New York: Schocken Books.

Montessori, M. (1965a). *Dr. Montessori's own handbooks.* New York: Schocken Books.

Montessori, M. (1965b). *The Montessori elementary material.* Cambridge, MA: Robert Bentley.

National Council of Teachers of Mathematics. (1976). Minicalculators in schools. *The Arithmetic Teacher, 23,* 72–74.

Reisman, F.K. (1977). *Diagnostic teaching of elementary school mathematics: Methods and content.* Chicago: Rand McNally.

Reisman, F.K. (1982). *A guide to the diagnostic teaching of arithmetic* (3rd ed.). Columbus, OH: Merrill.

Ruais, R.W. (1978). A low-stress algorithm for fractions. *Mathematics Teacher, 71,* 258–260.

Smith, D.D., & Lovitt, T.C. (1982). *The computational arithmetic program.* Austin, TX: Pro-Ed.

Stallings, J.A., & Kaskowitz, D.H. (1974). *Follow Through classroom observation evaluation.* Menlo Park, CA: Stanford Research Institute.

Stern, C. (1965). *Structural arithmetic.* Boston: Houghton Mifflin.

Stern, C., & Stern, M.B. (1971). *Children discover arithmetic: An introduction to structural arithmetic* (Rev. ed.). New York: Harper & Row.

Thornton, C.A. (1984). *Basic mathematics for the mildly handicapped: First year report* (Grant No. G008301694, Project No. 1029JH30133). Washington, DC: U.S. Department of Education, Office of Special Education and Rehabilitative Services.

Thornton, C.A. (1985). *Basic mathematics for the mildly handicapped: Second year report* (Grant No. G008301694, Project No. 1029JH40016). Washington, DC: U.S. Department of Education, Office of Special Education and Rehabilitative Services.

Thornton, C.A., & Toohey, M.A. (1982–1985). *MATHFACT: An alternative program for children with special needs* (A series of four kits: Basic Addition Facts, Basic Subtraction Facts, Basic Multiplication Facts, Basic Division Facts). Brisbane, Australia: Queensland Division of Special Education.

Thornton, C.A., & Toohey, M.A. (1984). *Matter of facts: Addition; Matter of facts: Subtraction; Matter of facts: Multiplication; Matter of facts: Division.* Oaklawn, IL: Creative Publications.

Thornton, C.A., & Toohey, M.A. (1985). Basic math facts: Guidelines for teaching and learning. *Learning Disabilities Focus, 1,* 44–57.

Underhill, R.G., Uprichard, A.E., & Heddens, J.W. (1980). *Diagnosing mathematical difficulties.* Columbus, OH: Merrill.

Wallace, G., & Kauffman, J.M. (1986). *Teaching students with learning and behavior problems* (3rd ed.). Columbus, OH: Merrill.

Wertlieb, E. (1976). The tool chest: Games little people play. *Teaching Exceptional Children, 9,* 24–25.

CHAPTER 8

Assessing
Language Skills

Oral language is a learned behavior that enables people to transmit their ideas and culture from generation to generation. It is a powerful tool to control the environment. Language also is directly related to achievement and adjustment in school.

Since many mildly handicapped learners have some language problems, educators need to be able to define and describe language. One widely accepted definition of language is that of Bloom and Lahey (1978), who propose that language is "a code whereby ideas about the world are represented through a conventional system of arbitrary signals for communication" (p. 4). Rees (1978) stresses that the purpose of language is communication; this is reflected in messages that express information, needs, and feelings. Hughes (1962) includes communication and a conventional system of vocal symbols in his definition of language.

Both speakers and listeners are involved in oral language—language is heard as well as spoken. A speaker's use of this arbitrary vocal system to communicate ideas and thoughts to a listener is referred to as *expressive language,* or *production.* In this process the listener uses *receptive language,* or *comprehension.* In this chapter the terms *expressive* and *receptive language* will be used instead of production and comprehension.

DIMENSIONS OF LANGUAGE

In addition to defining language, it is important to discuss its components or dimensions. To assess and plan instruction for language problems, educators need to be familiar with these aspects of language. Bloom and Lahey (1978) classify the dimensions of language according to (a) form (phonology, morphology, syntax), (b) content (semantics), and (c) usage (pragmatics).

Form

Phonology. A *phoneme* is a unit of sound that combines with other sounds to form words. A phoneme is the smallest unit of language. It is distinguished from the other language dimensions in that a phoneme alone does not convey meaning. There are approximately 45 phonemes in the English language, classified as either vowels or consonants. Vowels are categorized according to where they are produced in the mouth. The tongue may be moved up, down, forward, or backward in producing vowels. These different tongue positions are used to classify vowels as high, mid, or low and front, central, or back (Dale, 1972). For example, the long /e/ sound is classified as high front because the tongue blade is high in the front of the mouth. The tip of the tongue is down for all vowels. Consonants are classified according to place and manner of production. For example, the phoneme /f/ can be described by place (labial) and manner (voiceless stop).

Jakobson and Halle (1956) propose three principles that influence the order of phoneme acquisition:

1. Children learn to distinguish sounds first that have the fewest features in common, such as oral-nasal (/p/, /m/), labial-dental (/p/, /t/), and stop-fricative (/p/, /f/).
2. Development of front consonants such as /p/ and /m/ precedes the development of back consonants such as /k/ and /g/.
3. Phonemes that occur infrequently among the languages of the world—such as the English short *a* in *bat* (even though it may be frequent in the child's native language)—are the last to be acquired.

Normal acquisition of phonology continues until approximately 7½ years of age (Menyuk, 1971; Templin, 1957).

Problems in phonology frequently show up as articulation disorders. The most common problem is that of the child who is developmentally delayed in consonant acquisition. The child may (a) omit a consonant such as *y* and say "oo" for *you;* (b) substitute one consonant for another, as in "wabbit" for *rabbit;* or (c) distort a consonant. An example of a consonant distortion is the lateral emission of air in the production of /s/. The air escapes over the sides of the tongue, rather than the tip, and results in a noticeably "slushy" quality to the sound.

In addition to problems in expression, problems may also occur in reception, such as discrimination difficulty. For example, the child may hear "Go get the nail" when the command was actually "Go get the mail." The child does not respond correctly, since she cannot tell the difference between /n/ and /m/. Phoneme discrimination errors may occur in comprehension of consonants (/p/ for /b/; /d/ for /t/), consonant blends (/pr/, /fr/, and /kr/ confused with /pl/, /fl/, and /kl/), and vowels (confusion of "front" vowels—produced with the tongue in a forward position—such as in *pit, pet,* and *pat*) (Wiig & Semel, 1976).

Morphology. A *morpheme* is the smallest unit of language that conveys meaning. It can be a root word, such as *dog, run,* or *her. Free* morphemes are root words that convey meaning and stand alone. A morpheme can also be a prefix (such as *un*) or a suffix (such as *ed*). Prefixes and suffixes must be attached to a root word and are referred to as *bound* morphemes. *Derivational* suffixes change word class—for example, the verb *drive* becomes a noun, *driver,* with the addition of the suffix *er. Inflectional* suffixes change the meaning of a word—for example, the addition of the inflectional *s* to the word *boy* changes the meaning to more than one boy.

Children who are delayed in morphological development may not use appropriate inflectional endings in their speech. An elementary school child may not use the third-person *s* on verbs (for example, "He walk") or use *s* on nouns or pronouns to show possession (for example, "Mommy coat") or use *er* on adjectives (for example, "Her dog is small than mine"). Older elementary students and middle school children who are delayed in morphology may lack more advanced morphemes of irregular past tense or irregular plural (such as *drived* for *drove* or *mans* for *men*). Bartel and Bryen (1982) note that such students exhibit much inconsistency regarding morphology usage. For example, they may vacillate in their use of *bringed, branged,* and *brought.*

Some differences in inflectional endings are observed in children who speak black English (Baratz, 1969; Bartel, Grill, & Bryen, 1973). The educator should be aware that some inflectional endings reflect a child's *cultural* difference rather than a developmental delay. Examples of inflectional differences include "John cousin" in black English instead of "John's cousin"; "fifty cent" instead of "fifty cents"; and "she work here" instead of "she works here" (Baratz, 1969).

Syntax. Syntax is a system of rules that determines how words or morphemes are combined to make grammatically correct sentences. Syntax is frequently referred to as *grammar.* Rules of grammar emerge between 18 and 24 months of age, evidenced in children's production of two-word sentences. The child does not change abruptly from single words to grammatical two-word sentences. There is a period of transition in which a distinction can be made between two-word utterances and two words in grammatical form (Bloom, 1976; Braine, 1976; Greenfield & Smith, 1976). Braine (1976) claims that in this transition period the child often is groping for a pattern that is later replaced by a correct grammatical form.

The field of linguistics has been strongly influenced by two features of N. A. Chomsky's (1957) theory of generative transformational grammar. The first feature is that the speaker transforms an underlying sentence structure, such as *girl-throw-ball,* into different "surface" (verbalized) structures: "The girl threw the ball," "The ball was thrown by the girl," "It was the ball that the girl threw." The second aspect is that the speaker generates sentences according to an internalized rule system.

Bloom (1970) started a trend to describe children's early sentences in semantic grammar. She observed that the context in which a child says something must be noted to understand the child's meaning. Schlesinger (1971) also developed a method to describe early sentences based on word relationships. Table 8.1 presents Bloom's and Schlesinger's descriptions of semantic relationships.

TABLE 8.1
Descriptions of semantic relationships.

Bloom (1970)		Schlesinger (1971)	
Semantic Relationships	Example	Semantic Relationships	Example
Subject + predicate	"Car go"	Agent + action	"Daddy go"
Verb + object	"See Daddy"	Action + object	"Throw ball"
Subject + object	"Daddy lunch" (Daddy is eating lunch)	Agent + direct object	"Mommy milk" (Mommy is drinking milk)
Attributive	"Big ball"	Modifier + head	"More milk"
Genitive	"Mary hat" (Mary's hat)		
Recurrence	"More cookie"		
Nonexistence	"No ball" (there is no ball)	Negation + X	"No bed"
Rejection	"No bed" (I do not want to go to bed)		
Denial	"No car" (that is not a car)		
		X + dative	"Throw Mary" (throw it to Mary)
Demonstratives with predicate nominatives	"That cookie"	Introducer + X	"There ball"
Subject + locative	"Coat chair" (the coat is on the chair)	X + locative	"Sit chair" (sit in the chair)
Verb + locative	"Go up"		
Noticing reaction	"Hi Daddy"		

Semantic grammar would describe a young child's sentence of "No go" as denial or negation. Sentences of older children and adolescents are more appropriately described with syntactical analysis. For example, the sentence "I won't go" expresses denial or negation but also has a subject and a predicate.

Wood (1976) outlines six stages in the acquisition of syntax. Stages 1 and 2 can be better described with semantic rules of grammar, whereas the last four stages describe syntactical structure. Stage 3 typically begins when the child is 2 to 3 years old. At this age, the child's sentences contain a subject and a predicate. For example, in Stage 2 she says, "No play," but in Stage 3 she says, "I won't play." Stage 4 begins around 2½ years of age and continues to around 4 years of age. In this stage the child begins to perform operations on sentences. The child learns to add an element to one of her basic sentences through the process of *conjunction*. For example, "Where" can be added to the simple sentence "Daddy go" to form "Where Daddy go?" The child can also *embed*—that is, place words within the basic sentence. For example, the sentence "No glass break" becomes "The glass didn't break." In Stage 4 the word order is changed to ask a question. For example, the question, "Man is here?" is changed to "Is the man here?" During this stage, sentences remain simple in structure (Ingram, 1975). Between 2 and 3 years of age the child does not combine simple sentences but says them next to each other—for example, "John bounced the ball. John hit the lamp." Between 3 and 4 years of age the child combines simple sentences with the conjunction *and*—"John bounced the ball and hit the lamp."

Stage 5 is usually between 3½ and 7 years of age. In this stage the child uses complete sentences that have word classes typical of adult language: nouns, pronouns, adverbs, and adjectives. The child also becomes aware of differences within the same grammatical class. This awareness is evident in the child's use of different determiners and verbs with singular and plural nouns. For example, *this* is inappropriate for use in the sentence, "This chairs are heavy." The proper determiner (singular or plural) and appropriate verb for expressing plurality must be used. This same principle applies to prepositional phrases. For example, the sentence, "We cried to the movie" is not grammatically correct because an inappropriate prepositional phrase is used. In essence, in this stage the child learns the appropriate semantic functions of words and assigns these words to the appropriate grammatic classes.

Wood's Stage 6 begins when the child is around 5 years of age and extends until 10 years of age. The child begins complex sentence structures. She learns to understand and produce sentences that imply (a) a command ("Give me the toy"), (b) a request ("Please pass the salt"), and (c) a promise ("I promise to stop"). Implied commands are the easiest for children to acquire but are often confused with requests. The promise verb is very difficult for children to understand (C. Chomsky, 1969; Kessel, 1970); this type of verb may not be mastered until age 10 (Wood, 1976).

Children who have delay in syntax use sentences that are shorter or lack the syntactical complexity expected for their age. For example, a 6-year-old who uses a mean sentence length of three words may say, "Where Daddy go?" instead of "Where did Daddy go?" Additional deficits in the processing of syntax include problems in comprehending sentences (e.g., questions or sentences that express relationship between direct and indirect objects), negation, mood (e.g., inferences of obligations signified by auxiliary verbs *must, have to,* and *ought*), and passive sentences (Wiig & Semel, 1976, 1984).

Content

Semantics. *Semantics* refers to meanings attached to words and word relationships. For example, the word *cup* has a meaning of a container from which to drink and refers to an object in the child's world. An example of meaning attached to word relationships is the phrase "Daddy's cup." These words add the meaning of possessiveness in relationship to each other: The cup belongs to Daddy.

Clark (1973) and Nelson (1974) express different views concerning the child's development of meaningful words. Clark asserts that children use perceptual cues to acquire word meaning. For example, the word *dog* appears in a child's early vocabulary as the child notes the physical characteristics of a dog (four legs, tail, long ears, fur, and so on). Clark reports that a child relies on perceptual cues when she uses one word to refer to several things. For example, the child may use the word *dog* to refer to all four-legged, furry animals. Nelson, in contrast, proposes that the meanings first expressed by young children are based on dynamic properties of people and objects that are movable, moving, or changeable. For example, *Mommy* is a word that is observed in early vocabularies and refers to a movable, moving, changeable person in the child's world. Words that refer to food, clothing, and toys also appear in early vocabularies because of their dynamic characteristics. Children experience food as they eat it; articles of clothing as they put them on and take them off; and toys as they bounce, roll, and spin them. Nelson also states that children categorize words according to a shared function. Children observe that objects are similar in the way they move and act or in the way they are acted upon; thus, words that refer to food are categorized by the common function of things to eat.

Bloom and Lahey (1978) believe that the child uses *both* functional and perceptual cues in the development of word meaning. They note that the child observes objects that involve movement such as Mommy and bottles (Mommy and bottles come and go). The child also perceives that objects in a class look alike (bottles are cylinder-shaped and have nipples).

The acquisition of meaning extends beyond acquisition of the child's first words. It is a slow, complicated process that continues into adulthood (Wood, 1976). Wood (1976) outlines several stages of semantic acquisition. In Stage 1, a child develops meanings as she acquires her first words. Wood refers to these first words as one-word sentences. The meanings of these sentences are determined by the context in which they were spoken. An 18-month-old child may use the word *doggie* quite frequently, but the contexts in which she says the word may differ and imply different meanings (for example, "There is a doggie," "That is my doggie," "Doggie is barking," "Doggie is chasing a kitty"). As noted earlier, Bloom (1970) is often credited with first suggesting that the context in which something is said determines its meaning.

In about 2 years the child begins to produce two-word utterances with meanings related to concrete actions (such as "Doggie bark" or "My doggie"). In Stage 2, the child conveys more specific information verbally and continues to expand vocabulary and utterance length. However, until around the age of 7, the child defines words merely in terms of visible actions. To a 6-year-old, then, a fish is "a thing that swims in a lake" and a plate is "a thing you can eat dinner on." Also, during this stage, the child typically responds to a prompt word (such as *pretty*) with a word that could follow it in a sentence (such as *flower*). Older children, around 8 years of age, frequently respond with a verbal opposite (such as *ugly*) (Brown & Berko, 1960).

In Stage 3, at 8 years of age, the child's word meanings relate directly to experiences, operations, and processes. If a child's neighbor owns a horse, the child may include this attribute in her word meaning of horse in addition to the attributes of animal, four-legged, and a thing that can be ridden. When asked where horses live, the child may respond, "At the Kahns'." By an adult definition, this answer is not correct. The child's vocabulary is defined by her own experiences, not those of adults. At 12 years of age, the child begins to give dictionary-like definitions for words (Wood, 1976). When asked to define *bear,* she might respond, "a large, warm-blooded animal that hibernates in the winter." At this time the child's word definitions approach the semantic level of adults.

Developmental delay in word meaning (semantics) is observed in children who use or understand a limited number of words. The limited vocabulary may be in specific areas, such as adjectives, adverbs, prepositions, or pronouns. Semantics delay is also evident when children assign a very narrow set of attributes to each word so that each word has limited meaning. In addition, students may have figurative language problems and tend to interpret idioms, metaphors, and proverbs literally (Wiig & Semel, 1984).

Usage

Pragmatics. Bruner (1974/1975) defines *pragmatics* as the "directive function of speech through which speakers affect the behavior of others in trying to carry out their intention" (p. 283). In discussing this definition, McLean and Snyder-McLean (1978) distinguish two broad functions: controlling or influencing the listener's action ("Give me the doll") and influencing attitudes ("I think Jane would make a good class president"). These functions are also referred to as the speaker's intent.

Several studies have examined the development of pragmatic functions between the ages of 18 months and 3 years (Dore, 1975; Gallagher, 1977; Garvey, 1975; Halliday, 1975). Prutting (1979) notes that less is known about the later stages of pragmatic development (from 3 years of age to adulthood). One function that occurs after 3 years of age is the indirect request, or hint (Ervin-Tripp & Mitchell-Kernan, 1977; Leonard, Wilcox, Fulmer, & Davis, 1978). Prutting notes that these indirect requests are frequently used in our culture, as in "My mother always lets me have cookies before lunch." Leonard et al. (1978) studied 4-, 5-, and 6-year-old children's understanding of three types of indirect requests. The three types of indirect requests were (a) affirmative construction ("Can you shut the door?"), (b) responses with a negative element ("Can't you answer the phone?"), and (c) an affirmative construction with a negative intention ("Must you play the piano?"). The 4- and 5-year-old children understood the first two types of requests but not the third type. The 6-year-olds understood the third type of request but made mistakes. Leonard et al. interpret the mistakes to mean that understanding was not complete.

Bloom and Lahey (1978) state that the situation affects the form of the message within the pragmatics of language. J. E. McLean and L. K. Snyder-McLean (personal communication, March 1980) refer to this as *pragmatic presuppositions*. Pragmatic presuppositions are the characteristics of the message that increase the likelihood that the message will be *accepted* as well as understood. In adult speech these presuppositions are apparent in tendencies to be polite and indirect in requests. Children as young as 4 and 5 years of age show these pragmatic presuppositions when they talk politely when making a request. Pragmatic presuppositions develop as the child matures and learns not to interrupt the speaker, talk at the wrong time, or speak too loudly for the situation.

Delay in pragmatics is evident when children do not use functions that are expected for their developmental age. For example, if a student whose developmental age is above 8 years seriously answers "Yes" to the indirect request, "Must you play the piano?"—instead of ceasing to play the piano—she may be developmentally delayed in understanding indirect requests. Other types of pragmatic delay may be expressed by an older child who has difficulty understanding that she should not interrupt a speaker, speak too loudly, or talk at the wrong time. The student also may have difficulty choosing the right linguistic content (e.g., using complexity according to the listener), using questioning strategies, and interacting well verbally in a group (Wiig & Semel, 1984).

LANGUAGE ASSESSMENT

Miller (1978) lists three key questions that should be asked prior to assessing a child for language:

1. What is the reason for assessing the child?
2. What is to be assessed?
3. How will the child be assessed?

The five major reasons for language assessment are as follows:

1. To identify children with potential language problems.
2. To determine a child's language developmental level.
3. To plan educational objectives.
4. To monitor the child's progress.
5. To evaluate the language program.

The last three of these assessment functions are most relevant to daily instructional planning. Among these three functions, the first one performed is *planning objectives*. The assessment information describes the child's language. This description is used in planning objectives that relate directly to the problem. The assessment of a morphological disorder, for example, should be specific: "The child does not use *s* on regular nouns to indicate plurality." The educator then can plan the objective: "The child will use plural *s* on regular nouns with 90% accuracy when naming pictures of plural regular nouns." *Monitoring the child's progress* also is part of daily instructional plans. The educator must determine daily or weekly if the child is reaching short-term instructional objectives. The sample objective of 90% accuracy of plural *s* when naming pictures of plural regular nouns requires an assessment procedure of counting responses. Finally, *program evaluation* is part of daily instructional planning. The educator assesses the child's progress with the materials and techniques used in the program. This information allows the educator to determine if it is necessary to change materials or techniques to achieve the educational objective.

Assessment of a child's language development is an evaluation of the child's receptive and expressive language. The components assessed are semantics, phonology, morphology, syntax, and pragmatics. Language skills in these areas are listed by age in the language scope and sequence skills lists presented by Bartel and Bryen (1982) and Mercer, Mercer, and Bott (1984). The educator can assess all of these components or decide to assess only one or two specific components. An experienced examiner obtains information about the child or observes her before deciding what to assess. The information gathered may include various observations; for example, the child is difficult to understand, the child has difficulty understanding what others say, the child uses short sentences, the child uses few words, or the child cannot start and maintain a discussion topic.

The child who is difficult for others to understand, but who understands what others say and uses many words and long sentences, may have problems in phonology. Thus, assessment should begin in this area. The child who uses only a few words needs to be assessed in semantics, and the student who uses short sentences needs assessment in semantic relationships and syntax.

Language assessment includes the use of formal and informal tests. Whether to use formal or informal measures depends on the reason for assessment. For example, if the examiner wants to determine the child's language development level, formal measures frequently are used. If the examiner wants to determine specific teaching objectives, informal measures are best. Assessment of both language development level and teaching objectives could include both types of tests. School speech/language clinicians are experienced in administering and interpreting formal and informal measures of language. The educator who is unfamiliar with these tests should con-

sider working with the school speech/language clinician in assessing language. For additional information, Wiig and Semel (1984) present a detailed discussion of many language assessment approaches and techniques.

Formal Language Assessment

Common formal language tests are presented in Table 8.2. These tests can be divided into two major types of instruments (Wallace & Larsen, 1978). The first type is a comprehensive measure of all language functioning. This type of test assesses receptive and expressive language in all components. Three comprehensive measures are included in Table 8.2, the *Clinical Evaluation of Language Functions* (Semel & Wiig, 1980), the *Houston Test for Language Development* (Crabtree, 1963), and the *Test of Language Development—2* (Hammill & Newcomer, 1988; Newcomer & Hammill, 1988). Although these tests are described as comprehensive, pragmatics are not assessed in these measures.

TABLE 8.2
Formal language measures.

Test	Dimension Measured	Receptive/ Expressive	Grade/ Age Norms
Screening Tests:			
Clinical Evaluation of Language Functions (Semel & Wiig, 1980)	Phonology, morphology, syntax, semantics	R, E	K–5; 5–12 (grades)

Elementary level uses a "Simon Says" format of 31 items to assess language processing. Language production is assessed using 17 items that include phrase and sentence imitation, phrase completion, serial recall, antonyms, phoneme recall production, abstraction, and formulation of attributes. Advanced level includes 34 items in a card game format to assess language processing (e.g., point to the red queen and the black queen). Language production includes 18 items similar in format to the elementary screening.

(continued)

TABLE 8.2, *continued*

Test	Dimension Measured	Receptive/ Expressive	Grade/ Age Norms
Clinical Evaluation of Language Fundamentals— Revised (Semel, Wiig, & Secord, 1987)	Morphology, syntax, semantics	R, E	K–12 (grades)

The *CELF–R* is a restandardized version of the *CELF* that consists of 11 subtests: *Formulated Sentences, Listening to Paragraphs, Semantic Relationships, Oral Directions, Recalling Sentences, Word Structure, Sentence Structure, Sentence Assembly, Word Associations, Word Classes,* and *Linguistic Concepts.* The test is norm-referenced by age and yields standard scores and percentile ranks.

Test	Dimension Measured	Receptive/ Expressive	Grade/ Age Norms
Merrill Language Screening Test (Mumm, Secord, & Dykstra, 1980)	Syntax, semantics	R, E	K–1 (grades)

This mass screening instrument is used for quick detection of potential language problems in young children. A story is told to the child using colorful pictures, and the child is asked to retell the story and answer questions. Information is obtained on production of complete sentences, utterance length, verb-tense agreements, elaboration, and communication competence. An optional articulation screening inventory is also available. A special scoring procedure is included for nonstandard dialect speakers.

Test	Dimension Measured	Receptive/ Expressive	Grade/ Age Norms
Northwestern Syntax Screening Test (Lee, 1971)	Syntax	R, E	3 yrs., 11 mos.– 7 yrs., 11 mos.

Twenty items assess receptive ability. A sentence is spoken by the examiner, and the child is required to look at four pictures and indicate the one that is most appropriate. Also, 20 items assess the child's expressive ability by having the child repeat sentences spoken by the examiner as the examiner points to various pictures.

Diagnostic Tests:

Test	Dimension Measured	Receptive/ Expressive	Grade/ Age Norms
Clinical Evaluation of Language Functions: Diagnostic Battery (Semel & Wiig, 1980)	Phonology, morphology, syntax, semantics	R, E	K–12 (grades)

This individually administered test contains 13 subtests: six processing subtests, five production subtests, and two supplemental subtests of receptive and expressive phonological factors. The tests are norm-referenced or criterion-referenced.

(continued)

TABLE 8.2, *continued*

Test	Dimension Measured	Receptive/ Expressive	Grade/ Age Norms
Houston Test for Language Development (Crabtree, 1963)	Phonology, morphology, syntax, semantics	R, E	6 mos.–6 yrs.

Part I is for children 6 months to 3 years of age. It is a checklist that is completed by an observer who has ready access to the child. Part II is for children 3 to 6 years of age. The examiner elicits speech from the child with materials from a kit.

Test	Dimension Measured	Receptive/ Expressive	Grade/ Age Norms
Test of Language Development—2: Primary (Newcomer & Hammill, 1988) *Test of Language Development—2: Intermediate* (Hammill & Newcomer, 1988)	Phonology, morphology, syntax, semantics	R, E	4 yrs.–8 yrs., 11 mos. (primary edition); 8 yrs., 6 mos.–12 yrs., 11 mos. (intermediate edition)

The *TOLD—2 Primary* has seven subtests: *Picture Vocabulary* and *Oral Vocabulary* assess the understanding and meaningful use of spoken words; *Grammatic Understanding, Sentence Imitation,* and *Grammatic Completion* assess differing aspects of grammar; *Word Articulation* and *Word Discrimination* measure the abilities to say words correctly and to distinguish between words that sound similar. The *TOLD—2 Intermediate* contains six subtests: *Generals, Malapropisms,* and *Vocabulary* assess the understanding and meaningful use of spoken words; *Sentence Combining, Word Ordering,* and *Grammatic Comprehension* assess differing aspects of grammar.

Test	Dimension Measured	Receptive/ Expressive	Grade/ Age Norms
Auditory Discrimination Test (Wepman, 1973)	Phonology	R	4 yrs.–adult

Forty word pairs are presented to the child for discrimination. Some of the word pairs differ in beginning sounds, some in middle sounds, and others in ending sounds. The child tells the examiner whether the word pairs sound the same or different.

Test	Dimension Measured	Receptive/ Expressive	Grade/ Age Norms
Goldman-Fristoe Test of Articulation (Goldman & Fristoe, 1986)	Phonology	E	2–16+ yrs.

The first subtest, *Sounds in Words,* consists of 35 pictures that elicit the child's articulation of the major speech sounds in the initial, medial, and final positions. The second subtest, *Sounds in Sentences,*

(continued)

TABLE 8.2, *continued*

Test	Dimension Measured	Receptive/ Expressive	Grade/ Age Norms

contains two narrative stories that are read by the examiner and illustrated by action pictures. The child is asked to retell each story using his own words. The third subtest, *Stimulability,* determines if misarticulated phonemes are articulated correctly when the child is given maximum stimulation. The child is asked to watch and listen carefully while the sound is pronounced in a syllable, used in a word, and used in a sentence.

Test	Dimension Measured	Receptive/ Expressive	Grade/ Age Norms
Goldman-Fristoe-Wood-cock Test of Auditory Discrimination (Goldman, Fristoe, & Woodcock, 1970)	Phonology	R	4 yrs.–adult

Student is asked to point to the correct picture from a plate of four pictures upon hearing a stimulus word pronounced on an audiotape.

Test	Dimension Measured	Receptive/ Expressive	Grade/ Age Norms
Photo Articulation Test (Pendergast, Dickey, Selmar, & Soder, 1969)	Phonology	E	3–12 yrs.

Seventy-two color photographs are designed to elicit one consonant, and in some instances one vowel or diphthong as well. The only exception is *hanger,* which tests two consonants. All consonants, vowels, and diphthongs as well as nine blends are tested. A deck of individual test cards is included in the kit.

Test	Dimension Measured	Receptive/ Expressive	Grade/ Age Norms
Grammatic Closure Subtest of *Illinois Test of Psycholinguistic Abilities* (Kirk, McCarthy, & Kirk, 1968)	Morphology	E	2–10 yrs.

Student supplies morphological form to complete a spoken sentence.

Test	Dimension Measured	Receptive/ Expressive	Grade/ Age Norms
Test for Auditory Comprehension of Language—Revised (Carrow-Woolfolk; 1985)	Morphology, syntax	R	3 yrs.–9 yrs., 11 mos.

The test is individually administered and measures auditory comprehension of word classes and relations, grammatical morphemes, and elaborated sentence constructions. No oral response is required of the subject.

(continued)

TABLE 8.2, *continued*

Test	Dimension Measured	Receptive/ Expressive	Grade/ Age Norms
Carrow Elicited Language Inventory (Carrow, 1974)	Syntax	E	3 yrs.–7 yrs., 11 mos.

Teacher reads a sentence to the student and asks him to imitate exactly what he hears. The stimuli range in length from 2 to 10 words with an average length of 6 words. There are 52 oral stimuli including 51 sentences and one phrase.

Test	Dimension Measured	Receptive/ Expressive	Grade/ Age Norms
Developmental Sentence Scoring (Lee & Canter, 1971)	Syntax	E	2 yrs.–6 yrs., 11 mos.

A speech sample from 50 complete sentences is analyzed. Specific directions are given for scoring the sentences.

Test	Dimension Measured	Receptive/ Expressive	Grade/ Age Norms
Multilevel Informal Language Inventory (Goldsworthy, 1982)	Syntax, semantics	R*, E (*if required by the student)	K–6 (grades)

Picture probes are used to assess language at three levels dictated by the skills of the child. At the evoked spontaneous level, the child is asked to tell what is happening in the stimulus picture. If the child does not succeed, indirect imitation procedures are initiated (i.e., examiner tells about one part of the picture and asks the child to tell about another part). If the child is still unsuccessful, the receptive level is administered in which the child is asked to point to what the examiner names. A profile of scores is produced.

Test	Dimension Measured	Receptive/ Expressive	Grade/ Age Norms
Test of Adolescent Language—2 (Hammill, Brown, Larsen, & Wiederholt, 1987)	Syntax, semantics	R, E	6–12 (grades)

The test is used to identify problems in both spoken and written language. Ten areas are included: listening, speaking, reading, writing, spoken language, written language, vocabulary, grammar, receptive language, and expressive language.

Test	Dimension Measured	Receptive/ Expressive	Grade/ Age Norms
The Token Test for Children (DiSimoni, 1978)	Syntax, semantics	R	3 yrs.–12 yrs., 6 mos.

The examiner uses squares and circles of different shapes and sizes, placing these tokens in a standard order in front of the child. Then the examiner presents a series of spoken commands, requiring the child

(*continued*)

TABLE 8.2, *continued*

Test	Dimension Measured	Receptive/ Expressive	Grade/ Age Norms

to manipulate the tokens to perform the operation. The raw scores are converted into standard scores. Suggested cutoff scores denote unsatisfactory performance.

Assessment of Children's Language Comprehension (Foster, Giddan, & Stark, 1973)	Semantics	R	3–7 yrs.

Student points to a picture in response to a linguistic stimulus. On the first subtest the student points to pictures in response to a word spoken by the examiner. The other three subtests involve comprehension of utterances with two, three, or four critical elements.

Boehm Test of Basic Concepts—Revised (Boehm, 1986)	Semantics	R	K–2 (grades)

Fifty pictorial items, in multiple-choice form, are arranged in approximate order of increasing difficulty and divided into two booklets. The test is read by the teacher, and the children mark their answers in the test booklets.

Bracken Basic Concept Scale (Bracken, 1984)	Semantics	R	2 yrs., 6 mos.–8 yrs.

Level 1, the Screening Tests, measures basic concept acquisition to identify students whose concept development is below age-level expectations. Level 2, the Diagnostic Scale, contains more than 250 items which yield information about the ability to understand finely defined concepts in 11 categories (color, shape, size, quantity, counting, letter identification, direction/position, time/sequence, texture, comparisons, and social-emotional responses).

Environmental Language Inventory (MacDonald & Horstmeier, 1978)	Semantics	E	1–30 yrs.

The subject's language is sampled in situations requiring imitative speech, prompted "conversational" speech, and spontaneous speech in play situations.

(continued)

TABLE 8.2, *continued*

Test	Dimension Measured	Receptive/ Expressive	Grade/ Age Norms
Peabody Picture Vocabulary Test—Revised (Dunn & Dunn, 1981)	Semantics	R	2–18 yrs.

Stimulus pictures are presented to the child, who indicates the picture that best represents a stimulus word spoken by the examiner. There are two forms, 175 plates, with four pictures per plate.

Test	Dimension Measured	Receptive/ Expressive	Grade/ Age Norms
Vocabulary Comprehension Scale (Bangs, 1975)	Semantics	R	2–6 yrs.

This individually administered test assesses comprehension of pronouns, prepositions, adverbs, and adjectives. The test has a game format that involves following the examiner's instructions with a toy garage, a tea set, some buttons, and miscellaneous items.

Test	Dimension Measured	Receptive/ Expressive	Grade/ Age Norms
Let's Talk Inventory for Adolescents (Wiig, 1982)	Pragmatics	R*, E (*if required by the student)	9 yrs.–adult

This 40-item inventory is administered with a picture manual. Students are asked to formulate a sentence or series of sentences that the pictured adolescent might say in a particular social situation. Four communication functions are assessed: ritualizing, informing, controlling, and feeling. Drop-back items of a receptive nature are administered to those students who have difficulty with the expressive section.

Test	Dimension Measured	Receptive/ Expressive	Grade/ Age Norms
Let's Talk Inventory for Children (Bray & Wiig, 1987)	Pragmatics	R*, E (*if required by the student)	4–8 yrs.

This inventory contains 34 items that picture a different situation involving peer or adult interactions. The child is asked to formulate a speech act appropriate for the context and the audience. Association items are administered only if the child is unable to respond satisfactorily to the formulation items.

The second type of language test is designed to measure specific components of language. For example, the *Northwestern Syntax Screening Test* (Lee, 1971) assesses receptive and expressive skills in syntax only. Some language tests are more specific and measure only receptive or expressive skills in one component. For example, the *Peabody Picture Vocabulary Test—Revised* (Dunn & Dunn, 1981) assesses receptive semantic skills.

Informal Language Assessment

Informal language assessment measures include charting, probes, checklists, and analysis of speech samples. These devices are used in a number of ways. They can document a delay in a child's language development. Many formal tests use a small number of items to assess a particular skill (Stephens, 1977), and using a small sample may lead to incorrect conclusions about the child's skill level. Informal assessment is often used to affirm or refute the results of formal measures. Also, many formal measures do not give enough specific information to plan educational objectives. Therefore, informal language measures often are used to determine specific instructional objectives. Another common use of informal measures is to monitor a child's daily or weekly progress over a long period of time. Unlike formal measures, which are designed to assess a child over a long period of time, informal measures lend themselves to daily or weekly assessment.

Informal tests of form—phonology. Phonology can be assessed informally by analyzing the child's production of phonemes in single words. The examiner makes a list of all the consonant phonemes and collects pictures to depict words that contain each phoneme. There should be a picture to elicit a word with the consonant in the initial position and a picture to depict the consonant in the final position. For example, a picture of a pot will elicit initial /p/, and a picture of Scotch tape will elicit final /p/. The examiner shows the child each picture and says, "Tell me the name of each picture." It is noted if the child says the word incorrectly, and the results are recorded on a checklist. This type of assessment requires careful, experienced listening for accurate results. Only the *error* sounds are recorded; for example, a /b/ sound is recorded to indicate the child said "bot" for *pot*. Also, comments that describe the error are recorded; for example, a substitution of /b/ for /p/ is recorded as an error in voicing. The examiner lists all the phoneme errors and determines which phonemes should have been mastered at the child's developmental age. These phonemes can become target phonemes for the child's educational objectives.

After the examiner analyzes the phoneme profile and selects a target phoneme, she should collect baseline data on the target phoneme in the child's spontaneous speech. The examiner also needs to monitor change in the child's speech after corrective instruction has begun. Informal assessment is the primary tool used to gather baseline data on the target phoneme and to monitor change in the child's speech.

Diederick (1971) recommends direct observation of a phoneme to obtain baseline data and to monitor the child's progress. The examiner engages the child in spontaneous speech with pictures or toys as stimuli to elicit speech from the child. Older students may respond to prompts such as "Tell me about your weekend." "Adult talking" must be kept to a minimum so that the child is allowed to talk. During a 3-minute sample, the examiner counts the child's correct and incorrect productions of the target phoneme. The target phoneme's frequency can be observed by charting the incorrect and correct responses (see Chapter 2 for a discussion on charting). Accuracy is computed by dividing the number of correct target phonemes the child said by the total number of target phonemes said (correct and incorrect).

One aspect of receptive phonology that is readily assessed by informal measures is auditory discrimination. The examiner may want to verify if the child has difficulty discriminating between two particular sounds that were confused on a formal measure. For example, the child may have confused /p/ with /b/, and the examiner may further assess these sounds with a criterion measure. The measure can consist of a list of *cvc* (consonant-vowel-consonant) words in which only one phoneme is different—*pin-bin* or *cup-cub*, for example. Two words are said in word pairs, and the child is asked whether the words are the same or different. The examiner records the results on a checklist and scores the responses for accuracy. Accuracy levels can be used to indicate whether the child needs help in learning to discriminate these sounds. Accuracy of 90% or above is a good indication that the child can already discriminate these sounds.

Informal tests of form—morphology. Informal measures of morphology can determine mastery level of each morpheme in a hierarchy. Informal assessment of morphology can be based on Berko's (1958) format of sentence closure. The evaluator can use Brown's (1973) rank ordering of morpheme acquisition to make sentences that assess each morpheme. Pictures are presented with the sentences to assess the use of each morpheme. If the objective is to assess use of the present progressive morpheme *ing,* the examiner could show a picture of girls playing and say, "The girls like to play. Here they are _____." The child says the missing word, "playing." Or if the examiner is assessing the use of the morpheme *in,* she might show a picture of a baby sleeping and ask, "Where is the baby? The baby is _____." The child says the missing words, "in bed."

The examiner records the results as correct or incorrect on a checklist. Analysis of the results should help the educator determine which morphemes are mastered and which morphemes need to be taught. Also, assessing the morphemes in a hierarchical order helps the teacher determine which morpheme to teach first.

Another informal assessment of morphology is a measure of accuracy of a specific morpheme in a child's conversational speech. Mastery of a morpheme is indicated by 90% accuracy in a child's conversational speech (Brown, 1973). It would be very time-consuming to obtain a daily or weekly conversational sample with enough occurrences of a specific morpheme to determine accuracy. An informal assessment of a specific morpheme that is less time-consuming is to have the child respond to the prompt, "Tell me about this picture." First the examiner shapes the response by showing the child a picture depicting a boy (or girl) jumping and says, "What is the boy (or girl) doing?" If the child does not describe the action (by saying "jumping" or "jump") the child may need an additional prompt. The examiner can prompt the child: "Say *jumping.*" After the child has given two correct responses (description of action) to two different pictures and the instructions, "What is the boy (or girl) doing?" the instructions can be changed to "Tell me about this picture." The examiner can show a series of 20 pictures, each of which elicits the present progressive *ing* form of a word. As each picture is presented, the examiner says, "Tell me about this picture." She then records the results on a checklist and counts the number the child said correctly and incorrectly. The accuracy percentage is determined by dividing the correct responses by the total number of pictures. If the accuracy is 90% or above, the morpheme is mastered and does not need to be taught. Accuracy below 90% indicates that the morpheme is not mastered and may require teaching. Before teaching, the examiner should note if mastery of this morpheme is expected at the child's developmental age.

An informal measure of receptive morphology is to have the child point to a picture that depicts a morpheme. The examiner says a sentence with a specific morpheme and asks the child to point to the correct picture. For example, to assess the irregular past tense of *eat,* the examiner can show a picture of a girl who has finished eating and a picture of a girl eating. The examiner says, "The girl ate." The child must point to the correct picture of the girl who has finished. Sequence pictures (such as those published by DLM Teaching Resources) can be used with this task. The examiner records the results on a checklist by marking each irregular past tense verb as correct or incorrect. Then she analyzes the results to determine which morphemes the child has mastered receptively. The examiner may recommend that the child master a morpheme receptively before she is taught to use that morpheme expressively.

Informal tests of form—syntax. Expressive syntax can be informally assessed by analyzing the child's spontaneous speech for use of grammatical forms. The examiner can obtain and record a spontaneous sample of the child's speech by the guidelines presented in the next section, "Informal tests of content—semantics." If the sample is used only for grammatical analysis, modify the guidelines so that a tape recorder is used without recording the context of each utterance. After recording, the examiner transcribes the sample and lists each utterance on a checklist, as shown in Table 8.3. Each utterance is then analyzed for the grammatical forms used. A list is compiled

of the grammatical forms that were *not* used. Each form is compared to norms for the child's developmental age. If the particular form is expected for the child's developmental age, a teaching objective should be planned to teach it.

Pflaum (1978) suggests an alternative informal assessment of syntax that involves sentence repetition. The examiner says each sentence, and the child repeats the sentence. To increase the accuracy of the examiner's judgment, the evaluation session can be recorded on tape so that the child's responses can be checked. The examiner records the child's responses on a checklist and analyzes them for critical syntactical features. Omitted syntactical features should be included in the child's educational objectives.

Informal tests of content—semantics. Some tasks that assess semantics are very complex, so informal procedures may be difficult to devise for them (such as in the areas of logical relationships, cause—effect relationships, and verbal problem solving). However, for areas such as verbal opposites, categorization, and classification of words, informal testing is very useful.

For the assessment of verbal opposites, DLM Teaching Resources produces a set of cards that displays pictures of 40 pairs of opposites. When paired correctly, the cards in each set illustrate two opposites—for example, thin and fat. The examiner mixes the cards and asks the child to sort them into sets of opposites. The examiner observes the sets the child combines and records the results on a checklist. Analysis of the incorrect sets aids in determining which opposites to include in teaching objectives for a child.

As an informal assessment of word categorization, Berry (1969) suggests having the child say words in the same category. The examiner

TABLE 8.3
Syntactical analysis of utterances.

Student's Name _Michael Jordan_

Date _3/15/88_

Utterances	present progressive *ing*	is	plural regular *s, es*	possessive *'s*	I, me, mine, my you, yours	irregular past	he, him, his she, her, hers	am, are, was, were	not	can't, don't	and	but	because	reversal of copula (is it)	who, what	where
1. What this is?		X													X	
2. That all of it?																
3. This a wall.																
4. I gonna tell you.					X											
5. Yeah, but her not in today.							X		X			X				
6. Car go up and car go down.																
7. Car go sideways.																

says a word and asks the child to say as many words as possible in the same category. The words can fall into the category because of similar function or physical attribute. The examiner lists the words on a checklist as the child says them. Then the results are analyzed to determine whether the child can say several words in a category or whether the child (a) says a word that is an opposite, (b) says a rhyming word, or (c) tends to repeat the stimulus word.

Bartel and Bryen (1982) recommend using a word association task as a measure of word classification. They note that young children tend to respond to a stimulus word with a word that precedes or follows the stimulus word according to the rules of syntax. This is termed a *syntagmatic* response. For example, if the stimulus word is "apple," the young child may respond with "eat" or "red." Children shift to a response in the same grammatical category around the age of 6 to 8 years. This type

of response is termed *paradigmatic*. For example, if the stimulus word is "apple," the older child may respond with "orange," "banana," or another word from the fruit category. The examiner says the stimulus word, notes which kind of response the child makes, and records the response under that category (syntagmatic or paradigmatic) on a checklist. The checklist shows whether the student is categorized as a younger child with syntagmatic responses or as an older child with paradigmatic responses. The child may have responses in both categories, but with most responses in one category.

Another area of semantics that can be assessed by informal measures is semantic relationships. This can be assessed if the child's language utterances are three or fewer words. If a child uses more words, a syntactical analysis is more appropriate. Semantic relationships can be informally assessed by analyzing the child's spontaneous speech.

McLean and Snyder-McLean (1978) recommend the following guidelines for obtaining a speech sample:

1. Set up a partially structured play situation in which the child interacts with a familiar adult.
2. Use toys that the child is familiar with and that are likely to elicit a variety of responses from the child.
3. Record all the child's speech on a videotape recorder. Continue the sampling until 50–100 intelligible utterances are obtained. If videotape equipment is not available, record the sample on a tape recorder and have an observer record the context of each utterance the child says.
4. Avoid talking excessively or structuring the child's verbal responses by asking questions such as "What is this?" or "What color is the doll's dress?"
5. Transcribe the tape as soon as possible.
6. List each utterance—that is, any meaningful speech segment preceded and followed by a pause (Cohen & Plaskon, 1980). Each word in the utterance must be analyzed for semantic form and listed under the appropriate category. Several two- and three-word utterances are analyzed in Table 8.4. The two-word utterance "that ball" is listed under demonstrative, since "that" plus a noun is used to point out an object or person. The utterance "more milk" is listed under attribute since *more* modifies the noun. "Daddy pipe" is listed under possession, since it refers to Daddy's ownership of the pipe. The utterance "milk cookie" is listed under conjunction, since it refers to milk *and* cookie. The three-word utterance "Mommy drink milk" is placed in the action category (agent—Mommy; action—drink; object—milk).
7. After listing each utterance in the appropriate category, analyze the checklist to determine which semantic relationships the child used or did not use. The forms that the child did not use may be included in teaching objectives of semantic relationships for this child. For example, if the child used three-word utterances but did not use action (verb) + object (noun) + location (noun) forms, this may be an appropriate teaching objective.

After the child's language sample is analyzed for semantic grammar, the mean length of utterance in morphemes is computed. Brown (1973) suggests the following guidelines:

1. Transcribe the language sample.
2. Start the analysis on the second page of the transcription and count the first 100 utterances. Count only fully transcribed utterances, and count utterance repetitions.
3. Count each morpheme in the 100 utterances. Do not count fillers such as "mm" or "oh," but do count "no," "yeah," and "hi." Count as single morphemes compound words, proper names, and idiomatic duplications (such as *night-night, choo-choo, see-saw*). Count as single morphemes all irregular past tenses of verbs (*got, did, went, saw*). Count as single morphemes all diminutives (such as *doggie*). Count as separate morphemes all auxiliaries (*is, have, will, can, must, would*) and catenatives (*gonna, wanna, hafta*). Count as separate morphemes all inflections (such as possessive *s*, plural *s*, third-person singular *s*, regular past *ed*, and progressive *ing*).
4. Compute the mean length of utterance by dividing the total number of morphemes by 100.

The mean length of utterance gives the examiner a quick measure of growth over an extended period of time. Many current studies

TABLE 8.4

Format for semantic analysis of language sample.

Student's Name _Lisa Walker_   Date Collected ___4/3/88___

Total Number of Utterances ___11___

Relationship Components	Demonstrative		Recurrence	Attribute		Possession	Conjunction
	Nomination	Notice		Nonexistence	Descriptive		
Two-word grammatical	That ball	Hi Mommy	More cookie	allgone cookie	Big ball	Daddy pipe	Milk cookie
Three+-word grammatical							
Nongrammatical one-word utterances							

Relationship Components	Action			Location			
	Agent	Action	Object	Agent	Action	Object	Location
Two-word grammatical							
Three+-word grammatical	Mommy	drink	milk	Daddy Mommy	sit put	car doll	here here bed
Nongrammatical one-word utterances							

293

report children's semantic development in terms of this measure rather than chronological age. For example, the agent + action + object semantic form may be reported as occurring in children with a mean length of utterance of three words, rather than in children of any specific chronological age.

Informal tests of usage—pragmatics. Pragmatics can be informally assessed by analyzing a sample of the child's spontaneous speech to determine which pragmatic function was used. The first step is to obtain a videotaped speech sample from the child. (Guidelines for obtaining a speech sample are presented in the semantics section.) If videotape equipment is not available, an observer can record what happened just before and just after each utterance. The second step is to transcribe the tape and list each utterance on a checklist, as shown in Table 8.5. The examiner classifies the pragmatic function of an utterance by analyzing the events before and after the utterance. For example, the child's utterance may be "Throw ball." The examiner notes that before the utterance she was holding the ball and the child's arms were held out to catch the ball. It is also noted that the examiner threw the ball to the child after the utterance. The utterance is classified as a request, and a mark is put in the *Request* column. The examiner examines the checklist for each function the child did or did not use and then lists the functions that the child did not use. For example, it may be noted that the child did not use a protest function, such as "no shoes" to mean "Don't put on my

TABLE 8.5
Checklist of pragmatic functions.

Utterances	Instrumental	Protest	Request	Acquire Information	Metalinguistic	Give Information	Label	Imitate	Answer	Initiate/Terminate Social	Entertain	Other
1. Drink milk	X											
2. No milk		X										
3. Shoes on			X									
4. Car							X					
Question asked: "Where is the ball?" 5. Ball chair									X			
6. Daddy come?			X									

Student's Name _Julie Bates_

Date _2/12/88_

shoes." The educator can select from the pragmatic functions that were not used to determine appropriate teaching objectives.

In older students, informal assessment of pragmatics includes measures of speaking with inappropriate loudness, talking at inappropriate times, interrupting the speaker, and using indirect requests. These behaviors can be assessed by counting and recording them in several situations and on different days. An educator may want to count and record these same behaviors in a speaker of the same age who is not delayed in pragmatics. Select a student who talks to other students and contributes during group activities. Do not choose a student who is quiet or has little to say. Select at least three situations, such as group instructional time, independent work time, lunch time, or playground time. Count the number of times each student interrupts other speakers; talks too loudly; and talks when she should be listening, reading, or working. Record the results on charts (see the section on charting in Chapter 2). Compare the results of the two students. A significant difference in the two students's behaviors points to a teaching objective. An appropriate objective is to decrease interruptions by increasing skills in determining when a speaker is finished talking.

Indirect requests can be informally assessed in students whose developmental age is 8 years and above by asking the student to state the implied direct requests. For example, the examiner says, "Tell me what I want you to do when I say, 'Can you close the door.'" The student says, "You want me to close the door." The examiner then says, "Tell me what I want you to do in each of the following sentences." The examiner reads indirect requests listed on a checklist and puts a check in a column to indicate if the student's response is correct or incorrect. Analyze the results to determine the number of errors made. Determine which form the student is having the most difficulty with—the affirmative "Can you . . . ," the negative "Can't you . . . ," or the affirmative with negative intention "Must you . . . ." These forms of indirect requests can become teaching objectives for the student.

REFERENCES

Bangs, T.E. (1975). *Vocabulary Comprehension Scale.* Allen, TX: DLM Teaching Resources.

Baratz, J.C. (1969). Language and cognitive assessments of Negro children: Assumptions and research needs. *Journal of American Speech and Hearing Association, 11,* 87–91.

Bartel, N.R., & Bryen, D.N. (1982). Problems in language development. In D.D. Hammill & N.R. Bartel, *Teaching children with learning and behavior problems* (3rd ed.). Boston: Allyn & Bacon.

Bartel, N.R., Grill, J.J., & Bryen, D.N. (1973). Language characteristics of black children: Implication for assessment. *Journal of School Psychology, 11,* 351–364.

Berko, J. (1958). The child's learning of English morphology. *Word, 14,* 150–177.

Berry, M. (1969). *Language disorders of children.* New York: Appleton-Century-Crofts.

Bloom, L. (1970). *Language development: Form and function in emerging grammars* (Research Monograph No. 59). Cambridge, MA: MIT Press.

Bloom, L. (1976). *An interactive perspective on language development.* Keynote address, Eighth Annual Forum on Child Language Research, Stanford University. In *Papers and reports on child language development,* Stanford University Department of Linguistics.

Bloom, L., & Lahey, M. (1978). *Language development and language disorders.* New York: Wiley.

Boehm, A.E. (1986). *Boehm Test of Basic Concepts—Revised.* San Antonio, TX: Psychological Corporation.

Bracken, B.A. (1984). *Bracken Basic Concept Scale.* San Antonio, TX: Psychological Corporation.

Braine, M. (1976). Children's first word combinations. *Monographs of the Society for Research in Child Development, 41* (Serial No. 164).

Bray, C.M., & Wiig, E.H. (1987). *Let's Talk Inventory for Children.* San Antonio, TX: Psychological Corporation.

Brown, R. (1973). *A first language: The early stages.* Cambridge, MA: Harvard University Press.

Brown, R., & Berko, J. (1960). Word associations and acquisition of grammar. *Child Development, 31,* 1–14.

Bruner, J.S. (1974/1975). From communication to language: A psychological perspective. *Cognition, 3,* 255–287.

Carrow, E. (1974). *Carrow Elicited Language Inventory.* Allen, TX: DLM Teaching Resources.

Carrow-Woolfolk, E. (1985). *Test for Auditory Comprehension of Language—Revised.* Allen, TX: DLM Teaching Resources.

Chomsky, C. (1969). *The acquisition of syntax in children from 5 to 10.* Cambridge, MA: MIT Press.

Chomsky, N.A. (1957). *Syntactic structures.* The Hague: Mouton.

Clark, E. (1973). What's in a word? On the child's acquisition of semantics in his first language. In T.E. Moore (Ed.), *Cognitive development and the acquisition of language.* New York: Academic Press.

Cohen, S., & Plaskon, S. (1980). *Language arts for the mildly handicapped.* Columbus, OH: Merrill.

Crabtree, M. (1963). *The Houston Test for Language Development.* Houston: Houston Test Company.

Dale, P.S. (1972). *Language development: Structure and function.* Hinsdale, IL: Dryden Press.

Diederick, W.M. (1971). Procedures for counting and charting a target phoneme. *Language Speech and Hearing Services in Schools, 5,* 18–32.

DiSimoni, F. (1978). *The Token Test for Children.* Allen, TX: DLM Teaching Resources.

Dore, J. (1975). Holophrases, speech acts and language universals. *Journal of Child Language, 2,* 21–40.

Dunn, L.M., & Dunn, L.M. (1981). *Peabody Picture Vocabulary Test—Revised.* Circle Pines, MN: American Guidance Service.

Ervin-Tripp, S., & Mitchell-Kernan, C. (Eds.). (1977). *Child discourse.* New York: Academic Press.

Foster, C.R., Giddan, J.J., & Stark, J. (1973). *ACLC: Assessment of Children's Language Comprehension.* Palo Alto, CA: Consulting Psychologists Press.

Gallagher, T.M. (1977). Revision behaviors in the speech of normal children developing language. *Journal of Speech and Hearing Research, 20,* 303–318.

Garvey, C. (1975). Requests and responses in children's speech. *Journal of Child Language, 2,* 41–63.

Goldman, R., & Fristoe, M. (1986). *Goldman-Fristoe Test of Articulation.* Circle Pines, MN: American Guidance Service.

Goldman, R., Fristoe, M., & Woodcock, R.W. (1970). *Goldman-Fristoe-Woodcock Test of Auditory Discrimination.* Circle Pines, MN: American Guidance Service.

Goldsworthy, C.L. (1982). *Multilevel Informal Language Inventory.* San Antonio, TX: Psychological Corporation.

Greenfield, P., & Smith, J. (1976). *The structure of communication in early language development.* New York: Academic Press.

Halliday, M. (1975). Learning how to mean. In E. Lenneberg & E. Lenneberg (Eds.), *Foundations of language development: A multi-disciplinary approach* (Vol. 1). New York: Academic Press.

Hammill, D.D., Brown, V.L., Larsen, S.C., & Wiederholt, J.L. (1987). *Test of Adolescent Language—2.* Austin, TX: Pro-Ed.

Hammill, D.D., & Newcomer, P.L. (1988). *Test of Language Development—2; Intermediate.* Austin, TX: Pro-Ed.

Hughes, J.P. (1962). *The science of language.* New York: Random House.

Ingram, D. (1975). If and when transformations are acquired by children. In D.P. Dato (Ed.), *Georgetown University round table on language and linguistics.* Washington, DC: Georgetown University Press.

Jakobson, R., & Halle, M. (1956). *Fundamentals of language.* The Hague: Mouton.

Kessel, F. (1970). The role of syntax in children's comprehension from age six to twelve. *Monographs of the Society for Research in Child Development, 35*(6), 48–53.

Kirk, S.A., McCarthy, J.J., & Kirk, W.D. (1968). *Illinois Test of Psycholinguistic Abilities* (Rev. ed.). Urbana, IL: University of Illinois Press.

Lee, L. (1971). *The Northwestern Syntax Screening Test*. Evanston, IL: Northwestern University Press.

Lee, L., & Canter, S. (1971). Developmental sentence scoring: A clinical procedure for estimating syntactical development in children's spontaneous speech. *Journal of Speech and Hearing Disorders, 36*, 315–341.

Leonard, L.B., Wilcox, M.J., Fulmer, K.C., & Davis, G.A. (1978). Understanding indirect requests: An investigation of children's comprehension of pragmatic meanings. *Journal of Speech and Hearing Research, 21*, 528–537.

MacDonald, J.D., & Horstmeier, D.S. (1978). *Environmental Language Inventory*. San Antonio, TX: Psychological Corporation.

McLean, J.E., & Snyder-McLean, L.K. (1978). *A transactional approach to early language training*. Columbus, OH: Merrill.

Menyuk, P. (1971). *The acquisition and development of language*. Englewood Cliffs, NJ: Prentice-Hall.

Mercer, C.D., Mercer, A.R., & Bott, D.A. (1984). *Self-correcting learning materials for the classroom*. Columbus, OH: Merrill.

Miller, L. (1978). Pragmatics and early childhood language disorders: Communicative interactions in a half-hour sample. *Journal of Speech and Hearing Disorders, 43*, 419–436.

Mumm, M., Secord, W., & Dykstra, K. (1980). *Merrill Language Screening Test*. San Antonio, TX: Psychological Corporation.

Nelson, K. (1974). Concept, word, and sentence: Inter-relations in acquisition and development. *Psychological Review, 81*, 276–285.

Newcomer, P.L., & Hammill, D.D. (1988). *Test of Language Development—2: Primary*. Austin, TX: Pro-Ed.

Pendergast, K., Dickey, S., Selmar, J., & Soder, A. (1969). *Photo Articulation Test*. Danville, IL: Interstate.

Pflaum, S.W. (1978). *The development of language and reading in young children* (2nd ed.). Columbus, OH: Merrill.

Prutting, C.A. (1979). Process \prä | , ses\n: The action of moving forward progressively from one point to another on the way to completion. *Journal of Speech and Hearing Disorders, 44,* 3–30.

Rees, N.S. (1978). Applications to normal and disordered language development. In R.L. Schiefelbusch (Ed.), *Bases of language intervention*. Baltimore: University Park Press.

Schlesinger, I.M. (1971). Production of utterances and language acquisition. In D.I. Slobin (Ed.), *The ontogenesis of grammar*. New York: Academic Press.

Semel, E.M., & Wiig, E.H., (1980). *Clinical evaluation of language functions*. San Antonio, TX: Psychological Corporation.

Semel, E.M., Wiig, E.H., & Secord, W. (1987). *Clinical Evaluation of Language Fundamentals—Revised*. San Antonio, TX: Psychological Corporation.

Stephens, T.M. (1977). *Teaching skills to children with learning and behavior disorders*. Columbus, OH: Merrill.

Templin, M.C. (1957). *Certain language skills in children: Their development and interrelationships*. Minneapolis: University of Minnesota Press.

Wallace, G., & Larsen, S.C. (1978). *Educational assessment of learning problems: Testing for teaching*. Boston: Allyn & Bacon.

Wepman, J. (1973). *The Auditory Discrimination Test*. Palm Springs, CA: Language Research Associates.

Wiig, E. (1982). *Let's Talk Inventory for Adolescents*. San Antonio, TX: Psychological Corporation.

Wiig, E.H., & Semel, E.M. (1976). *Language disabilities in children and adolescents*. Columbus, OH: Merrill.

Wiig, E.H., & Semel, E. (1984). *Language assessment and intervention for the learning disabled* (2nd ed.). Columbus, OH: Merrill.

Wood, B.S. (1976). *Children and communications: Verbal and non-verbal language development*. Englewood Cliffs, NJ: Prentice-Hall.

CHAPTER 9

Teaching
Language Skills

This chapter presents some of the major points of view in the area of language intervention and offers a variety of activities and materials useful in teaching language skills. The first three sections of the chapter discuss theories of language acquisition, language programs, and general teaching strategies and techniques. The remainder of the chapter presents language activities, instructional games, self-correcting materials, and commercial programs and materials.

THEORIES OF LANGUAGE ACQUISITION

Theories of language acquisition fall within three major camps: (a) behavioristic, (b) nativistic, and (c) interactionistic. The behavioristic position (Skinner, 1957) relies on learning principles to explain language acquisition. Other proponents of the behavioristic position include Braine (1971), Jenkins and Palermo (1964), and Staats (1971). The behaviorist believes that the infant begins with no knowledge of language but possesses the ability to learn it. The child learns through reinforcement of imitation. Reinforcement of babbling (including parent attention and delight) and the shaping of vocal behavior account for the initial stages of learning. Behaviorists emphasize environmental influences and the universal laws of learning, namely operant conditioning principles.

Chomsky (1957, 1965) holds the nativistic position along with Lenneberg (1964, 1967) and McNeil (1966, 1970). Chomsky claims that the child possesses an innate capacity for dealing with linguistic universals. The child generates a theory of grammar to help understand and produce an infinite number of sentences. Lenneberg states that the child is biologically predisposed to learn language as the brain matures. In the nativistic position, humans are believed to be "prewired" for language development, and the environment simply triggers its emergence.

Piaget (1960), the major proponent of the interactionistic position, theorizes that the child acquires language through the interaction of his perceptual-cognitive capacities and experiences. The child's environment and neurological maturation determine learning. Language and thought thus develop *simultaneously* as the child passes through a series of fixed developmental stages requiring more and more complex strategies of cognitive organization. Interactionists consider the capacity for language to be innate; however, unlike the nativist, the interactionist believes the child must internalize linguistic structures from the environment and must become aware of communication's social functions.

On the one hand, the biologists (Lenneberg, 1967) and the linguists (Chomsky, 1965) view the child as a product of his own maturation process. Unless physical or mental complications occur, biologists and linguists believe the child's development is predetermined. This view places heavy emphasis on the child: He is biologically prepared or linguistically preprogrammed to develop language. On the other hand, the behaviorists stress the influence of the environment. The child's role is passive— development depends largely on the individuals in the child's environment who respond to his behavior. The interactionistic position emphasizes the child's active interactions with the environment as the child learns to talk (Bloom, 1975). To date, no single theory has complete support. Many researchers continue to pursue answers about the acquisition and nature of language.

LANGUAGE PROGRAMS

There are numerous language programs available from which the educator can choose. Selection is influenced by two primary factors: the population the program serves and the theoretical model on which it is based. The theoretical model describes normal language acquisition (Schiefelbusch, Ruder, & Bricker, 1976) and includes (a) the content the normal child learns, (b) the sequence in which the child learns, and (c) how the child learns. There is a close relationship between the language program and a theoretical model of language acquisition (McLean & Snyder-McLean, 1978).

Primarily through the work of Wiig and Semel, language intervention has focused on the linguistic model, with its direct concern about language functioning (Hresko & Reid, 1981). The linguists are interested in analyzing the comprehension and performance of language in mildly handicapped students according to the components of language (e.g., phonemes) and their rules.

The linguistic model has served as the basis for the creation of language programs. These programs usually focus on a particular language skill the child should have. Although the content of these programs is similar (morphemes, phonemes), some have their foundations in behavioral theory, some in nativism, and some in interactionism.

Behavioristic Programs

Two programs used with mildly handicapped students based on the behavioral model are DISTAR (Engelmann & Osborn, 1976) and the Monterey Language Program (Gray & Ryan, 1972). Originally developed for culturally disadvantaged children in Project Head Start programs, the DISTAR Language Program is a very structured approach to language intervention. It is designed for students in preschool through third grade and focuses on expressive and receptive language and cognitive development. The program uses a didactic approach,

with repetitive group drills, to teach higher concepts. The teacher models, elicits group and individual responses at a fast pace, and either reinforces the appropriate response or corrects the inappropriate response. Various language skills are taught, such as identity statements (*This* is a ball), pronouns (The dog is *hers*), prepositions (*in* the box), and multiple attributes (The dog is *small* and *black*). The program provides a recommended procedure for teaching each objective, based on imitating the teacher. For example, the recommended procedure for teaching the identity statement is as follows:

1. The teacher presents an object such as a book and says, "This is a book."
2. The teacher asks, "Is this a book?"
3. The teacher answers, "Yes, this is a book."
4. The teacher repeats the question, and this time he encourages the student to answer.
5. The teacher presents the book and asks, "What is this?"
6. The student responds, "This is a book."

DISTAR research has been impressive in both Head Start and Follow Through programs. Stallings (1974) reports that children exposed to the structured model of language learning scored higher on intelligence, math, and reading variables as compared to children exposed to other models. It is important to mention that these children (especially in the Follow Through program) were also enrolled in DISTAR reading and arithmetic programs.

The Monterey Language Program (Gray & Ryan, 1972) is usually used for severe language/learning disabled children. The children are reinforced for imitation of a teacher's response. Imitation and reinforcement can be observed in the following procedure for teaching "is":

1. The teacher says, "The block is red."

2. The student models the sentence closely enough to include "is."
3. The teacher says, "Good."

The skills are taught separately in sequential order. Matheny and Panagos (1978) found that the Monterey phonological and syntactic programs were effective for children with multiple linguistic problems. However, the concept of teaching separate skills was not validated. The phonological intervention produced as much syntactical improvement as the syntactical method, and vice versa.

Nativistic Programs

Programs such as the Interactive Language Development Training Program (Lee, Koenigsknecht, & Mulhern, 1975) and the Semel Auditory Processing Program (Semel, 1976) are representative of the nativistic model. These programs emphasize the teaching of rules for sentence transformations.

The Interactive Language Program (Lee, Koenigsknecht, & Mulhern, 1975) is a syntax development program that is appropriate for use in preschool through primary grades. It may be used with individual children or small groups. Each lesson contains a story to teach specific syntactic and transformational rules. The lesson also provides guidelines for the verbal interactions between the instructor and the child. The teaching procedure is demonstrated in the following story, which is designed to teach the use of *he*, copular *is* + verb + *ing*, and *let's*.

Story: Because Daddy is coming home, he is at the airport. Bobby is going to the airport. Where is he going?

Child's response: "He is going to the airport."

Story: Here is Mommy. She says, "Hurry up. Let's go. It's time to leave. Let's go to the airport." What does Mommy say?

Child's response: "Let's go to the airport."

The Semel Auditory Processing Program (Semel, 1976) is designed to remediate problems in morphological and syntactic rule learning. There are three levels: beginning (developmental—ages 3 to 7 years), intermediate (7 to 11 years), and advanced (11 years and up). The three levels are identical in format but differ in the difficulty of words presented and the structures and activities featured. Sections and activities that focus on linguistic skills emphasize morphological and syntactic rule learning, and task requirements stress segmentation of words into morphemes, analysis and synthesis of structures, sentence completion, and oral closure. Each level contains a teacher's manual, a student's response book, and a set of 96 activity cards. There are also assessment guidelines.

Both of these programs have shown some success in remediation of language problems. A total of 25 language-delayed children (3 to 5 years old) showed improvement on the use of syntax after participation for 8.3 months in the Interactive Language Development Program (Wiig & Semel, 1984). Likewise, exposure to the Semel Auditory Processing Program for 15 weeks resulted in learning disabled children (7 to 11 years old) making some progress on formal measures of language assessment (Semel & Wiig, 1981).

Interactionistic Programs

Programs in the interactionistic model are based on two ideas: (a) meaning is brought to a child's language through interaction with the environment, and (b) the child uses speech to control the environment. The model's treatment approaches emphasize natural language teaching rather than structured exercises and drills. For example, Daddy walking into the room causes the child to say "See Daddy." Moreover, the utterance "Me drink" (which usually produces a drink of water for the child) is demonstrative of the use of speech to control surroundings.

The Preschool Language Intervention Program (Miller, 1978) is an example of the interactionistic model. The activities are child centered around structured play, and the teacher models the intent of the child's message. Miller (1978) provides the following example of how a teacher models the child's intent:

John: (indicates toy horse has drunk water) "He go, 'slurp, slurp.'" (rolls over, putting arms and legs in the air to show what was happening to the horse)

Clinician: He drank some cold water. Then he fell down and he rolled over. It looks like he's dead. (p. 436)

The interactionistic model is also exemplified in Berry's (1980) Global-Ontogenic Teaching Program. This program uses spontaneous talking to emphasize the teaching of phonemes, morphemes, syntax, semantics, and prosody (proper usage of rhythm, intonation, and stress patterns of language) in an interrelated manner. The program includes example teaching units, case examples, and suggestions for ideas and materials. Berry also suggests ways to involve parents and paraprofessionals.

Conclusion

As is evident, there are many programs available. Which to use depends on the needs of the children, the expertise of the teacher, and the program orientation of a particular county or school district. Even though some of the programs have been effective, validation procedures are still highly controversial. In their discussion of these procedures, Panagos and Griffith (1981) conclude that there are no widely accepted methods of validating intervention programs; thus, unfortunately, many "special education teachers/clinicians are implementing untested methods and programs of language intervention" (p. 78).

Before selecting a program, the teacher should determine if the program is designed to serve a specific population. Language enrichment programs cannot serve the needs of children who are severely delayed in language development. Also, the teacher's style may reflect learning principles that cannot be adapted to certain programs. If the teacher chooses to develop an individualized program to teach language objectives, he should select strategies that fit his teaching style as well as the student's special objectives.

GENERAL TEACHING STRATEGIES AND TECHNIQUES

When the teacher designs an individualized program, teaching strategies must be considered. The teaching strategies selected often depend on the particular model acquired. Many special educators who use direct teaching methods for remediation of reading and math problems undoubtedly select this technique for teaching language skills. With these formats, the teacher directs the learning and dictates the content, pace, and sequencing of the lesson. Often the child is allowed little opportunity to engage in spontaneous conversations during this highly structured skills approach.

Conversely, there are special educators who feel that learning should be child centered, with the child dictating the content, pace, and sequencing of the lesson. The teacher controls minimally and emphasizes social interaction so that communication can occur along the lines of normal conversation. Taenzer, Cermak, and Hanlon (1981) provide a detailed discussion of how this approach operates.

Weller (1979) compared the Berieter-Engelmann (DISTAR authors) teacher-directed approach with the child-centered approach of Marion Blank. Weller found that the first method was more effective in teaching descriptor words (adjectives) and functor words (connectives, prepositions, articles) to four subjects (aged 4 to 5 years). More studies need to be conducted before definitive conclusions can be made concerning the most effective technique.

Regardless of whether the technique is primarily teacher or child directed, research findings have some implications for the selection of strategies.

Listening Strategies

The following strategies may be helpful in improving the listening skills of students with learning problems.

1. Teachers should model good listening, especially by giving students full attention and eye contact when they speak (DeHaven, 1983).
2. Both spontaneous speech and written language read orally should be used to teach listening, because different skills are involved (Froese, 1981).
3. Students should be cued into listening through the use of silent pauses or instructions to listen to or look at the teacher. Donoghue (1975) found that poor listeners do not establish a mental set for listening.
4. The use of organization cues such as "These are the important points" or "The first step is . . . " helps the poor listener (Alley & Deshler, 1979; Burns, 1980).
5. Students with learning problems tend to comprehend better when speed of presentation is slower than the normal rate (Blosser, Weidner, & Dinero, 1976; McCroskey & Thompson, 1973).
6. When passive sentences and sentences with a long list of adjectives, negatives, and situationally bound adverbs are used in in-

struction, more processing time should be given to the student.
7. Because of linguistic problems of some students, teachers should use structurally simple and relatively short sentences of not more than 5 to 10 words in their language of instruction (Wiig & Semel, 1984). Also, the number of new and unfamiliar vocabulary words presented in a single lesson should be limited (e.g., five or less).

Production Strategies

The following strategies focus on improving the production or expression skills of students with learning problems.

1. The components (e.g., morphemes) of the formal language system should not be taught separately (Matheny & Panagos, 1978).
2. Language should be taught in various natural settings (e.g., classroom, cafeteria) and not only in isolated groups (Panagos & Griffith, 1981; Spekman & Roth, 1984).
3. Language skills should be taught in connection with other curriculum content (Gerber & Bryen, 1981; Wiig & Semel, 1984). McNutt (1984) suggests that teachers assuming the role of facilitator should teach oral language, reading, writing, discussion of written language, and strategy lessons within a holistic framework.
4. Pragmatic language skills, such as asking questions and taking turns, should be included (Bloom & Lahey, 1978; Bryan, Donahue, & Pearl, 1981; Gerber & Bryen, 1981; Spekman & Roth, 1984).
5. The content of a student's message should be reacted to first, since it is most important in the communication process, and then the syntax error should be corrected (Pflaum, 1978; Spekman & Roth, 1984).
6. Students should not always be asked to speak in complete sentences, since this re-

quest violates ordinary discourse rules. As Spekman and Roth (1984) emphasize, it is perfectly appropriate in normal discourse to answer questions with one or two words or phrases.

7. Generalization of language must be taught, so that the students will learn how to apply rules to novel situations (Vogel, 1983; Weber, 1982).

Imitation and Modeling Strategies

Two teaching strategies that are frequently used in teaching language are imitation and modeling. Some investigators use these terms to refer to the same behavior (Rees, 1975). The child gives a response that is similar to a model's. Courtright and Courtright (1976) distinguish between modeling and imitative behavior that is mimicry. They define imitative mimicry as a one-to-one, literal matching response for each stimulus statement. These investigators maintain that this form is widely used. In contrast to mimicry, modeling involves acquiring an abstract language rule without giving an immediate response to the stimulus (Bandura, 1971). For example, the child observes the teacher modeling a rule several times before the child is required to use the rule. This strategy is apparent in the following method of teaching the use of *s* on singular verbs: The teacher models 20 different singular subject-verb sentences that describe pictures (such as "Dog runs," "Boy walks," "Cat plays," and so on). After this modeling of 20 sentences, the child is requested to describe the pictures.

Leonard (1975) recommends the use of modeling with a problem-solving set. The teacher uses a puppet as a model. Visual stimuli, such as toys or pictures of objects and people, are placed in front of the model (puppet). The teacher tells the child to listen carefully and determine which sentences earn reinforcers for the model. The model produces 10 to 20 utter-

ances that describe the visual stimuli and deliberately gives 25% of the responses incorrectly. The teacher then presents the same visual stimulus to the child and encourages a response that earned a reinforcer for the model. The child and model take turns responding until the child has produced three consecutive appropriate responses that were presented previously by the model. At this point the child is presented with new visual stimuli and is required to produce unmodeled utterances.

The teacher may use imitative mimicry at one point with a child and gradually move to more spontaneous responses. When using this strategy, the teacher needs to structure the event preceding the child's response (that is, the antecedent event). The antecedent event can have varying degrees of cueing. A teacher can use *total* cueing in the antecedent event: "What do you want? Tell me, 'I want apple.'" Or he can use *partial* cueing in the antecedent event: "Is this a ball or an orange?" Partial cueing may also include pointing to or looking at items to help the child make a correct response. *Minimal* cueing can be used when the child is ready to generalize a rule. For example, the teacher can say, "What's happening? What's he doing?"

Muma (1978) discusses modeling techniques that are used for language intervention. Among the modeling techniques suggested by Muma is the expansion model. Parents often use this technique. With this technique, the child's response is commanded by the parent or educator. For example, the child says "Car go," and the parent or educator immediately gives the expanded model, "The car is going."

ACTIVITIES, GAMES, AND MATERIALS

After carefully selecting a program, the teacher may decide to supplement it to meet the specific needs of certain students. Some teachers prefer to plan a complete individualized program rather than use an available commercial program. To supplement or design an individualized program, teachers must plan teaching activities. One advantage of planning activities is that the teacher can select and vary his teaching methods and materials to fit the individual student's needs.

Direct teaching activities are designed to meet specific objectives. They must, however, be supplemented with independent learning and reinforcing activities. Self-correcting materials are a good choice for independent learning of a skill, and instructional games frequently are used to reinforce newly acquired skills. Various teaching activities, games, and self-correcting materials are described in this section. Also included are some commercial programs and materials that can be used in teaching language skills. Activities, games, and self-correcting materials that are appropriate for use with secondary students are presented near the end of each section.

Language Activities

1. *Objective:*
   To teach *is* + verb + *ing (is jumping)*

   For each picture, say a model sentence that includes *is* plus *verb* plus *ing*. The teacher may show a picture of a girl jumping rope and say, "The girl is jumping." The teacher models 10 different sentences with pictures. The child is not encouraged to respond during the modeled sentences. After the modeled sentences, the teacher shows the pictures again and asks the child to tell what is happening in each picture. After successful completion of this task, the teacher shows 10 new action pictures and for each new picture says, "Tell me what's happening." (See Kent, 1974, for a good source of action pictures.)

   Modification:
   The teacher can use modeling to teach semantics, morphology, syntax, and so forth by vary-

ing the stimulus and the modeled response. For example, the morphological form of singular pronouns plus the inflectional verb ending *s*—"She walks"—can be taught by using action pictures with singular subjects and changing the model to "She walks," "He runs," "He jumps," and so on. Courtright and Courtright (1976, 1979) report that generalization of a syntactical rule is significantly higher with this type of modeling than with imitative responses, in which the child repeats the model immediately after the teacher.

2. *Objective:*
   To teach plural morpheme *s* on regular plural nouns

   Use modeling with problem solving to teach language rules (Leonard, 1975). Show a puppet 20 pictures that depict 20 plural nouns. The puppet names each picture and misses 25% of them. The teacher reinforces each correct response with a chip. After the modeling of 20 pictures, the teacher asks the child to name the pictures. After the child correctly responds to these pictures, the teacher presents 20 new pictures and asks the child to name them.

   Modification:
   Modeling with problem solving can also be used to teach semantics, phonology, syntax, and so on. For example, to teach a syntactical rule of *they* + *are* + verb + *ing*, present pictures depicting action with a plural subject (such as children playing) and say to the puppet, "Tell me what's happening in each picture." The puppet responds using the form of *they* + *are* + verb + *ing* for each picture ("They are playing"). The puppet randomly makes 25% of the responses incorrect ("They play"). The teacher reinforces the correct responses with a chip. After the modeling the teacher says, "You give the puppet a chip for each correct sentence." After successful completion of this task, the teacher says to the student, "You tell me what's happening in each picture."

3. *Objective:*
   To teach possessive pronouns *(her, his, their)*

Prepare small cards with mounted pictures of a single girl, a single boy, and several children. Mount pictures of objects on separate cards. Attach the cards to rings and group all the people pictures together on one set of rings and all the object cards on another. Attach the rings and card sets to a folded cardboard stand. The child or teacher flips each card separately to form phrases (*her hat, his ball, their house,* and so forth). Coloring books are good sources of pictures.

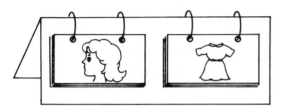

Modification:
Add a third set of color cards. Each card is shaded a different color. The student is required to say phrases, such as "Her dress is red," "His hat is yellow," or "His ball is blue."

4. *Objective:*
To teach classification of associated words

Have the student sort various association pictures. (See Figure 9.1.) Wedemeyer and Cejka (1975) suggest the following procedure:

   a. Mount individual pictures of objects commonly associated with each other on small cards. Select pictures such as ball and bat, cup and saucer, and shoe and sock from reading readiness workbooks.
   b. Make a card holder with strips of tagboard stapled to a large piece of tagboard.
   c. Place a picture in each slot down the left side of the card holder.
   d. Give the student the remaining pictures and have him tell how the two objects are associated.

Modification:
Use matching pictures and pictures that depict opposites. Also, the activity can be made self-correcting by putting matching shapes on the backs of associated pictures. After sorting the pictures, the child can check his work by looking at the backs of the cards to determine if the shapes match.

5. *Objective:*
To develop the use of *him, her,* and *it*

To teach the use of pronouns have the students participate in the following activity suggested by Bartel and Bryen (1982). Arrange the children in a circle, with girls alternating with boys. Each child's task is to roll the ball to another child. Before doing so, however, the child must state if the child who receives is a "him" or a "her." After some children are successful with this task, have them hold pictures of familiar objects (such as car, ball, house) while the other children retain their human identity. Now before a child rolls the ball, he must state if the child receiving is an object and must say "it" before rolling the ball. If the receiver does not have a picture, the child must state "him" or "her" before rolling the ball.

Modification:
Have all students hold pictures of objects. Before each child rolls the ball, ask him to state if the receiver of the ball is a "him" or a "her" and to identify the object that the child is holding. Then the child says the appropriate phrase (such as "her house").

6. *Objective:*
To teach *ed* on regular verbs *(walked, jumped)*

Have the child describe an activity as he is performing it. For example, the child says, "I am jumping" as he is jumping. Upon completion have the child say, "I jumped very high" or "I jumped over the box." This activity can be extended by using small objects that can perform movement; for example, a doll can be made to jump, walk, or hop. Also, this activity can be used to teach irregular verb forms such as *ate, drank,* and *fell.*

7. *Objective:*
To teach the prepositions *in, on, out of, in front of, in back of, beside*

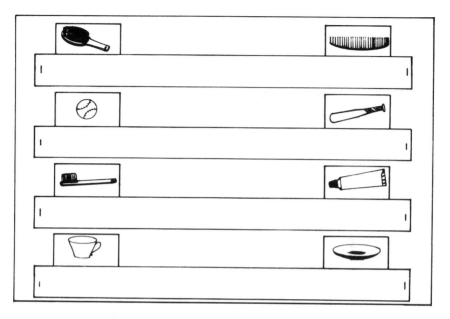

FIGURE 9.1
Associated pictures mounted in card holder.

Use Hula Hoops and physical activity to teach prepositions. Give directions to the students to move in relation to the hoops ("Stand in the Hula Hoops"). At first the teacher announces and performs the activity with the students; then gradually he only announces the activity. Finally, the teacher has the students themselves talk during the activity. For example the students say, "The Hula Hoop is beside me" when they move their hoops by their side.

Modification:
The teacher can stand in some kind of relation to the hoop, such as in the hoop and ask, "Where am I?" The children answer, "You are in the Hula Hoop." Each child then can have a turn standing in relation to his Hula Hoop and asking, "Where am I?"

8. *Objective:*
To teach classification of part/whole relationships

Use a flannelboard activity as suggested by Wedemeyer and Cejka (1975) to teach part/whole relationships. Cut out of flannel the parts of two complete objects such as a truck. Have one truck put together on the flannelboard before beginning. Ask the child to complete the second truck by saying, "Put on the part of the truck that is the wheel," "Put on the part of the truck that is the door," and so on.

Modification:
This activity can also be used to teach functional relationships. For example, ask the child to put on the part of the truck that opens to let people inside, or the part of the truck that turns to change the truck's direction.

9. *Objective:*
To teach classification by function

Collect pictures of objects used for one function. For example, to show a bath, collect pictures of a bathtub, soap, washcloth, and towel. Have the child sort the pictures according to function. For example:

a. *Sandwich:* bread, knife, peanut butter, jelly
b. *Bath:* tub or shower, washcloth, towel, soap

c. *Washing dishes:* dishes, soap, sink, sponge, drainer, towel

d. *Building:* lumber, nails, hammer, sandpaper, paint, screws, tools

Modification:

This task can be made more difficult for older students by making the functional relationships more complex. For example: *Dressing for a party:* washing hair, fixing fingernails, brushing hair, brushing teeth. Moreover, a picture-card deck called Functions (produced by DLM Teaching Resources) can be used to teach classification. It includes 14 five-card sets (e.g., stamp, paper, pen, envelope, mailbox), and the student can use the cards to match objects into sets on the basis of function.

10. *Objective:*

To classify objects that belong to the same class (animals, foods, houses, vehicles)

To teach classification, prepare a large card with four sections (Wedemeyer & Cejka, 1975). In one section put a picture of a house; in the second section put a picture of an animal; in the third, a picture of a vehicle; and in the fourth, a picture of food. Collect and mount pictures of animals, foods, houses, and vehicles. Have the child sort the pictures in the four areas. An area can easily be made with a color or shape so that the child can sort objects or pictures according to the attribute of color or shape.

11. *Objective:*

To teach synonyms

Ask a student to call out a word for which he knows at least one synonym. Then ask the next student to "match" the word by providing a synonym of it. Use a game format in which the student receives one point for each correct synonym he names. If he cannot think of any, he may challenge the first player to state the synonym he had in mind. Any failure in this respect is penalized by one point. A player fails to score a point if he is unable to think of a synonym, and he is penalized one point if he responds with a word that is not a synonym of the word proposed by the preceding player. The object is to squeeze as many synonyms out of the original word as possible. If a player can think of only one or two synonyms, his opponent may add a few points to his score by naming some others. When the possibilities of a given word have been exhausted, a new word is used.

Modification:

This activity can also be used with antonyms. For example, if *big* is the given word, an appropriate response might be *little*. Then the next player must give an antonym of *little* (e.g., *large*) without using the original word, *big*. A point is scored for each correct antonym (or synonym of the original word) given.

12. *Objective:*

To teach classification of weather and seasonal clothes

Have the child make decisions for clothing dolls. Wedemeyer and Cejka (1975) suggest the following procedure to teach classification:

a. Make boy and girl figures from flannel.

b. Cut out flannel articles of clothing for seasonal and weather changes, different times of the day, and different occasions. Use a paper doll book for patterns.

c. Use marking pens to make details—buttons, shoelaces, collars, and so forth.

d. Make articles such as mittens and shoes to correspond to the right and left sides.

e. Place the dolls on a flannelboard and have the students dress the dolls as the teacher directs (for example, "Dress the girl doll for a rainy day").

Modification:

This activity can be modified slightly to teach articles of clothing. The teacher says, "Tell me what I should put on the doll." The child responds, "Shoes." The teacher puts on the shoes. The teacher calls on each child for a clothing word that should be put on or taken off to change the doll.

13. *Objective:*

To teach labels of furniture

Use a playhouse and miniature furniture. Put all the furniture in one group and say, "Tell me what furniture goes in the kitchen. John, you tell me one piece of furniture." The teacher calls on children until all the kitchen items are placed and then starts with another room. Magazine pictures of furniture and rooms can also be used in this activity. The teacher can hold up a picture of a kitchen from a magazine and have pictures of furniture on the table. The teacher says, "Tell me what furniture goes in the kitchen," and the student selects an appropriate picture and names the piece of furniture.

Modification:

Place a piece of furniture in a room where it does not belong—for example, a bed in the kitchen. The teacher asks, "What doesn't belong? Can you tell me why?"

14. *Objective:*

To teach *rough* and *smooth* as modifiers

Collect items that are small and rough (a piece of sandpaper, a piece of window screen, fingernail file, washcloth, a small rough rock, a piece of net, a piece of bark). Also, collect items that are smooth (a marble, a small magnet, a small mirror, a smooth rock). Place the smooth and rough objects in a large bag. Introduce the word *smooth* by letting the children feel a smooth object and talk about how it feels. Introduce the word *rough* by letting them feel a rough object and talk about how it feels. Now let each child reach in the bag and feel one object. Have the child decide if the object feels smooth or rough and then take it out of the bag.

Modification:

Use objects that are hard and soft, or heavy and light.

15. *Objective:*

To increase auditory discrimination between two phonemes

Draw a ladder on a piece of paper. Give the student a marker and tell him to move the marker when he hears two different words. Say some word pairs that consist of the same word and some that are different words. When the child is consistent in moving the marker only for two different words, change the task by having the child listen to words that are different by only one phoneme, such as *pair–fair*. The child moves the marker when he hears two different words. Some suggested pairs differing in only one phoneme are *pair–fair; purr–fur; put–foot; pork–fork;* and *pay–fay.*

Modification:

This activity can be modified according to how the student signals that two sounds are the same or different. The student can raise his hand, tap a pencil, move a space on a game board, or pick up a chip.

16. *Objective:*

To teach negatives

Use the following procedure recommended by Worthley (1978) for teaching negatives. Model a sentence without a negative and then immediately model a sentence containing a negative. For example, the teacher says, "Some for John. None for John." The student imitates the two sentences. When several sentences with negatives have been modeled correctly, the teacher only presents a sentence without a negative. The student responds by saying a sentence with a negative. A recommended sequence of negatives is as follows:

a. no
b. none
c. nothing else
d. no more
e. not enough
f. don't

g. let's not
h. we'll not
i. do not
j. don't do
k. is no more
l. does not
m. is not
n. did not
o. nothing is
p. will not
q. was not

Modification:

This technique can be used to teach morphology. For example, to teach plural *s* on regular nouns, the teacher can present sets of two pictures and two modeled responses, such as "one kite—two kites, one cat—two cats." After the child correctly repeats several modeled sets, the teacher presents a picture of one cat and says, "One cat." Then the teacher presents a picture of two cats, and the child says, "Two cats."

17. *Objective:*

To extend the use of linguistic forms to other environments

The speaker describes an object to the listener such that the listener can select a similar object from several objects placed in front of him (Schiefelbusch et al., 1976). The speaker and listener sit back to back. Place three objects in front of the listener (for example, key, comb, ball) and one similar object (such as the comb) in front of the speaker. The speaker describes the object, and the listener is encouraged to ask questions until he can select the correct object.

Modification:

Use a block-building activity, suggested by Bartel and Bryen (1982). Two children are seated back to back. The speaker and listener each have an identical set of six blocks that vary in shape, color, or size. The speaker builds a construction using all of the blocks and provides enough information to the listener so that he can duplicate the construction.

18. *Objective:*

To use language as an effective communicator

Use the Over-the-Shoulder Game suggested by McCaffrey (1976), in which the speaker is the *encoder* and the listener is the *decoder*. The encoder stands behind the decoder and talks over the decoder's shoulder to tell him what to do next. The encoder must give information so that the decoder understands, and the information must be revised if the decoder does not understand. For example, the encoder may say, "Put the red triangle on top of the blue square." The decoder places the triangle above the square so that it touches the top of the square. The encoder may then say, "You have put the triangle on top of the square like a roof on a house. Instead, lay it on top of the square like a blanket." The encoder must keep revising his instructions until the decoder completely understands the message.

Modification:

Have the encoder draw a simple design and then tell the decoder over his shoulder how to draw the same design. The decoder may stand at the chalkboard while the encoder looks at his own design and the one the decoder is drawing.

19. *Objective:*

To teach the classification of *where, when,* and *what* phrases

Write the word *where* next to the word *place.* Tell the student that *where* refers to place. With the student, list a few phrases that refer to place. Write the word *what* next to the word *thing.* Tell the student to list some phrases that refer to things. Write the word *when* next to the word *time.* Tell the student that *when* usually refers to time. The student needs a broader concept of time than time on a clock. Time can refer to the hour, parts of a day, events of a day (such as breakfast, school, bedtime), day of the week, and so on. Have the student list some time phrases. For practice, give the student a worksheet with the three headings of *Where, What,* and *When* and have him list the following phrases under the appropriate heading:

a. on the playground
b. tomorrow morning
c. beside your bed
d. the blue car
e. last night
f. in your lunchbox
g. on a rainy day
h. her pretty dress
i. my broken cup
j. behind the school
k. a small coat
l. at my house
m. before lunch
n. after school

Modification:
This activity can also be used to classify *who, why,* and *how* phrases. Classification of these phrases can be made self-correcting by putting the phrases on cards in a Poke Box (described in Chapter 4) with the multiple-choice words of *When, Where,* and *What* (or *Who, Why,* and *How*).

20. *Objective:*
To teach vocabulary likenesses

Write the following verbs and objects on the chalkboard:

kicking	swing
pushing	house
sewing	ball
building	dress

Ask the student to tell you how to pair the action words and objects. Then ask the student to tell you how *kicking* the *ball* is like *pushing* a *swing.* (Help the student conclude that when you kick a ball it goes away from you, and when you push a swing it also goes away from you.) Ask the student how *sewing* a *dress* is like *building* a *house.* (Again, help the student conclude that when you build or sew you make a complete item out of parts.) Then give the student a worksheet with incomplete sentences and ask him to select the best word to complete each sentence. For example:

a. *Working* is to job as *playing* is to
_____. (fun, game, children)
b. *Sweeping* is to broom as *hitting* is to
_____. (bat, ball, catch)
c. *Sleeping* is to bed as *sitting* is to
_____. (table, chair, desk)
d. *Smiling* is to happy as *crying* is to
_____. (anger, tears, sad)
e. *Eating* is to food as *drinking* is to
_____. (thirst, water, cup)
f. *Fussing* is to anger as *laughing* is to
_____. (happiness, funny, smile)
g. *Running* is to legs as *throwing* is to
_____. (catching, arms, ball)
h. *Cutting* is to knife as *stirring* is to
_____. (bowl, cook, spoon)
i. *Writing* is to pencil as *painting* is to
_____. (paper, canvas, brush)
j. *Reading* is to book as *listening* is to
_____. (teacher, ear, talk)

Modification:
This vocabulary task of comparison of likenesses can be modified to include items based on part/whole relationships. For example: *Fingers* are to hands as *toes* are to feet.

21. *Objective:*
To teach the use of relative clauses

On the chalkboard give the student several examples of sentences that contain relative clauses. Then give the student a practice sheet with several sets of two sentences. Ask him to combine them into one sentence by using a relative pronoun. For example:

a. The boy broke the window. The boy ran away. (who)   a. The boy who broke the window ran away.
b. Read the book. The book is about dogs. (that)   b. Read the book that is about dogs.

Modification:
Combine sentences with conjunctions such as *and, but, because,* and *so.* For example, the following sentences can be combined with *but.*

a. Bob eats breakfast every day. Bob is always hungry at lunch.

b. The puppy plays outside. The puppy likes to sleep in the house.

a. Bob eats breakfast every day, but he is always hungry at lunch.

b. The puppy plays outside, but he likes to sleep in the house.

22. *Objective:*

To use the conjunctions *and, but, because,* and *so*

Use the cloze procedure with multiple-choice items (Wiig & Semel, 1984). Make a list of sentences that require the use of a conjunction. Leave that space blank and give multiple choices. For example:

a. He goes to school _____ he plays baseball. (and, but, or)

b. I don't want ice cream _____ I would like a dessert. (or, but)

c. You should take a bath _____ you are dirty. (because, but)

d. You must finish your homework _____ you can go out and play. (but, so)

Modification:

The cloze procedure with multiple-choice items can be used to teach semantics, morphology, or other forms of syntax. For example, the following sentence requires an inflectional ending *(ed)* on a regular verb:

The boy _____ to school this morning before breakfast. (walk, walked)

23. *Objective:*

To teach paraphrasing

Use a game format in which the students are divided into two teams. Have the first player on Team A tell the first player on Team B to do something (for example, "Touch your nose"). The Team B player performs the action and then tells the first player on Team A to do the same thing; however, he must give the command using different words (for example, "Put your finger on your nose"). If both players perform correctly, both teams get a point. If the player on Team B is unable to say the same command in different words, only Team A gets

the point. The game continues in this manner, and the team with the most points at the end of the game wins.

Modification:

Present a short paragraph that the students are required to paraphrase. This can be a written or oral task. For example:

Mary woke up early because she had to arrive at school before the bell rang. She needed to go to the library before school so she could return an overdue book.

Paraphrased paragraph:

Mary had to return an overdue book to the library before school began. Therefore, she needed to wake up earlier than usual.

24. *Objective:*

To teach employment vocabulary words to secondary students

Cut out job ads from the newspaper and collect job application forms. Read the ads and application forms to the class and determine what words and phrases they know (such as *experience, minimum wage, waitress, waiter, good working conditions, apply in person, references required*). Define the words they do not understand. With each student, role play a job interview and use the vocabulary on the job applications.

Modification:

Select vocabulary words from credit applications, checkbooks, classified ads, or driver's license applications.

Language Games

His, Her, or Their

Objective:

To teach the use of the possessive pronouns *his, her,* and *their*

Materials:

Game board with start-to-finish format (presented in Chapter 4); one stack of picture cards depicting objects; one stack of picture cards depicting people (should include at least one picture of a boy, one picture of a girl, and one picture of several children); a spinner; markers.

Directions:

1. The stack of object pictures and the stack of people pictures are placed face down on the game board.
2. Each player places a marker at the start position.
3. Each player in turn spins the spinner, notes the number on which it lands, and picks up the number of cards shown on the spinner from each stack.
4. The player turns over the cards and makes as many pronoun and object combinations as possible. For example:

   her hat, his hat, their hat, their ball, her house, his shoe

5. For each combination the player says, he moves his marker ahead one space.
6. After moving his marker, the player puts the used cards face down on the bottom of each stack.
7. The players take turns, and the one who moves to the end of the game board first is the winner.

What Goes Together

Objective:

To teach classification by association

Materials:

Set of 40 playing cards composed of association pictures (for example, a card illustrating a shoe and a card illustrating a sock).

Directions:

1. Six cards are dealt to each player (2–4 players) and the remaining cards are placed face down in the center of the players.
2. Each player combines any association sets in his hand and lays them face up on the table.
3. Then each player in turn takes a card from the deck, discards one from his hand, and places it face up next to the deck.

4. After the first discard, each player can select a card either from the deck or from the discard pile.
5. The first player who displays three association sets wins. (The criteria for winning may be varied to suit the students and the situation.)

The Deck
(Wedemeyer & Cejka, 1975)

Objective:

To teach opposite words

Materials:

Deck of cards composed of pictures depicting opposite words (for example, a card illustrating the word *up* and a card illustrating the word *down*).

Directions:

1. An equal number of cards are dealt to each player until all cards are dealt.
2. Each player combines any sets of opposites in his hand and lays them face up on the table.
3. Then each child draws a card in turn from another player's hand.
4. When a player has a set of opposite pictures in his hand, he lays them on the table.
5. The game continues until one player wins by pairing all the cards in his hand. The number of hands played can vary according to the time available.

Whose Is It?

Objective:

To teach the use of possessive personal pronoun *mine* and *'s*

Materials:

Two matching sets of 12 pictures.

Directions:

1. The dealer lays three pictures from the first set of cards face down in front of each of the four players.

2. He then lays the entire second matching stack of cards face down on the table.
3. The dealer turns the first card in the stack face up and asks, "Whose is it?"
4. The first player guesses who is holding the matching card by saying, "Mine," "John's" "Mary's," and so on. The player must use the possessive 's or possessive pronoun *mine*.
5. Whoever the player guesses must turn over his cards; that is, if the player says, "John's," John must turn over his cards for everyone to see. If the card matches one in John's hand, the player who selected John gets a chip. If it does not, the card is placed face down on the bottom of the deck, and John turns his cards back face down on the table.
6. The dealer turns the next card from the stack face up and asks the next player, "Whose is it?"
7. The player who makes the most correct guesses receives the most chips and wins.

Say the Whole Sentence

Objective:

To teach sentence construction

Materials:

Deck of cards of matching pairs with several of the pairs having only one attribute different from other pairs. (For example, there can be three pairs of Christmas trees—one set with blue lights, one set with red lights, and one with green lights.)

Directions:

1. Six cards are dealt to each player, and the remaining cards are placed face down in a stack on the table.
2. Each player combines any matching sets in his hand and lays them face up on the table.
3. Each player in turn asks for a card from another player by using all the attributes; for example, "Do you have a Christmas tree with green lights?" If the other player has that card, he gives it to the first player. If the other player does not have the requested card, the first player takes a card from the deck.

4. The first player who matches all his cards wins the game.

Phonetic Bingo

Objective:

To teach phoneme identification

Materials:

Cards that have five numbered columns with each column containing five letters; discs.

Directions:

1. Each player receives a bingo card containing letters.
2. The caller calls out a column number and a phoneme, such as 2/p/.
3. If the player has that particular phoneme in the appropriate column, he places a disc over that letter.
4. The winner is the first player to cover five letters in a row. A list of the called-out letters can be kept to check the winning card.

1	2	3	4	5
p	d	g	t	v
g	v	p	v	t
b	t	d	g	p
t	g	b	p	b
d	p	t	d	g

Fishing for Blends

Objective:

To teach /s/ blends

Materials:

Fish-shaped cards displaying /s/ blends: *st, sk, sw, sl.*

Directions:

1. The cards are placed face up in the center of the students.
2. The caller calls out a word containing an /s/ blend, such as *skate*.
3. The players take turns finding the correct blend from the group of fish cards.
4. If the player picks the correct card, he gets to keep the card.
5. When all the cards are gone from the center, the player with the most "fish" wins.

Two-Way Words

Objective:

To improve use of homonyms

Materials:

Set of 20 index cards with a pair of homonyms written on each card; answer key which lists the definition of each homonym.

Directions:

1. Two pairs of partners sit across from each other.
2. The dealer deals five cards to each of the four players.
3. The first player selects one of his cards, makes a statement that includes either of the homonyms on the card, and then repeats the homonym (for example, "She wore a plain dress—plain"). He then challenges his partner to make a statement that includes the other homonym on the card but gives no further clues.
4. When the partner makes a statement (for example, "We were in the plane"), the dealer refers to the answer key to see if the response is correct. If the response is questionable, the dealer can ask for another statement that gives additional information concerning the meaning of the homonym (for example, "We were flying above the clouds in the plane").
5. If his partner's statement is correct, the player can place his card in the middle of the table. If his partner's statement is not correct, the player must keep the card for another turn.
6. The next player challenges his partner in the

same way, and the partner pairs take turns. A player may challenge only his own partner and must use his own cards.
7. The first partner pair to have all their cards in the middle of the table wins the game.

Sentence Game

Objective:

To teach sentence construction

Materials:

A start-to-finish game board (presented in Chapter 4); a deck of cards displaying stimulus pictures; a spinner; markers.

Directions:

1. Each player places a marker at the start position, and the picture cards are placed face down.
2. The first player spins the spinner and moves the designated number of spaces.
3. Then the player selects a card from the deck, and he must use the word or words illustrated in the picture in a sentence.
4. If the sentence is complete and correct, the player remains on the square. If the player cannot use the word or words correctly, he moves back one square at a time and picks up another card until he produces a correct sentence.
5. The first player to reach the finish square wins.

Three Little Words

Objective:

To teach sentence construction using conjunctions

Materials:

A stack of word cards containing two related words and one conjunction on each card; a spinner; chips.

Directions:

1. The first player spins the spinner and selects the designated number of cards from the deck.
2. The player must make a sentence for each card by using the set of words on the card.

3. The player receives a chip for each sentence correctly constructed.
4. The player with the most chips at the end of a set time period wins the game.

Can You Answer with a Question?

Objective:

To teach the use of *who, what,* and *where* questions

Materials:

A game board with categories and points (similar to Jeopardy game); question cards corresponding to the categories and point levels (the words range in difficulty according to their point value, and the answers are written on the back of each card).

Directions:

1. The first player chooses a category and point value from the game board.
2. The player is presented with a word from the category he chose and must define the word with a question. For example, the category may be *clothes,* and the word on the card may be *shoes.* The correct answer on the back of the card is, "What do you wear on your feet?" Object categories require a *what* question. If the player selects from a category of places, the answer must be in the form of a question that uses *where.* For example, if the category is *Community Places* and the word is *library,* the answer is "Where do we get books?" If the student selects from a *who* category, the answer must be in the form of a question that uses *who.* For example, if the category is *Community Helpers* and the words are *police officer,* the answer is "Who catches criminals?" The following are suggested categories for the game board:

What
Clothes (hat, shoes, dress)
Animals (dog, cat, bird)
Sports Equipment (ball, bat, glove)

Where
Community Places (bank, post office, school)
Fun Places (restaurant, zoo, theater)
Travel Depots (train station, airport, bus station)

Who
Community Helpers (firefighter, police officer, mail carrier)
Family Member (mother, father, sister)
School Personnel (principal, teacher, librarian)

Build a Sentence

Objective:

To teach combining independent clauses with conjunctions

Materials:

Thirty flannel-backed cards with independent clauses written on the front of each card; 13 flannel-backed cards with conjunctions written on the front of each card; a flannelboard.

Directions:

1. The flannelboard is placed in the middle of the table, and the cards are dealt to the players.
2. The first player lays down a card containing an independent clause, such as *She was late.*
3. The second player lays down a card containing a conjunction, such as *because.*
4. The third player must lay down a clause to complete the sentence, such as *she missed the bus.*
5. The next player begins a new sentence.
6. A player loses his turn if he does not have an appropriate card to play.
7. The first player who uses all his cards wins the game.

   Suggested clauses:
   She went to bed
   She was tired
   Mary stayed home
   He made a good grade
   John went to the store
   She likes school
   She was hungry
   He studied
   She watched television
   He brought some ice cream
   He washed dishes
   He bought a ticket
   His father fussed

Mother cooked supper
He took a bath
She was dirty

Suggested conjunctions:
because
and
since

Prefix Bingo

Objective:

To teach the prefixes *in*, *re*, *un*, and *non*

Materials:

Bingo cards with various root words that can be combined with the prefixes *in*, *re*, *un*, or *non*; a spinner with four sections that has a prefix in each section; markers with one prefix printed on each marker (see Figure 9.2).

Directions:

1. The first player spins the spinner, notes on which prefix it lands, and picks up a marker with that prefix on it.
2. The player places the prefix marker on a root word it can combine with.
3. The player loses his turn if the spinner lands on a prefix that cannot be combined with a root word on his card.
4. The first player who has his markers in a row (vertically, horizontally, or diagonally) wins the game. To check the winning card, make sure the prefix on each marker can be combined with the root word on which it is placed.

Modification:

This game can be modified by using suffixes, such as *ful, less, ly*.

Deal a Sentence

Objective:

To teach sentence construction

Materials:

Word cards containing words from the following grammatical categories: 9 nouns, 9 pronouns, 15 verbs, 12 adjectives, 3 articles, 3 conjunctions, 3 prepositions, and 1 adverb.

Directions:

1. Each player receives five cards, and the remaining cards are placed face down in the center of the players.
2. Each player organizes his hand to determine if he has a sentence.
3. The first player selects one card from the deck and discards one card face up.
4. The first player to make a sentence wins the hand. The number of hands played can vary according to the time available, and the player with the most points at the end of time period wins. Also, the first player to earn a predetermined number of points could be the winner. Scoring could be: 1 point for a declarative sentence, 2 points for using *not* in a sentence, 3 points for a sentence with a conjunction, and 4 points for a question.

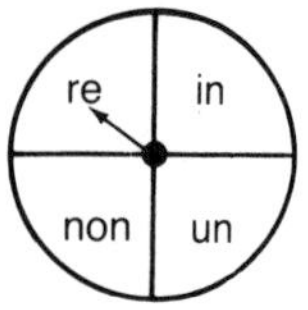

side	build	do	tire	seen
turn	tell	fill	use	sense
sent	claim	call	stick	tend
skid	happy	move	cover	born
to	tie	come	paid	fuel

Spinner: re | in / non | un

FIGURE 9.2
Prefix Bingo game card and spinner.

Suggested words:

Nouns: ball, dress, boy, girl, book, house, doll, bike, dog

Pronouns: I, you, she, he, him, they, them, it, we

Verbs: is, are, was, were, made, can, go, should, may, do, see, ride, walk, run, am

Adjectives: big, round, pretty, small, sad, happy, little, red, fast, slow, fat, funny

Articles: a, an, the

Conjunctions: and, but, or

Prepositions: to, at, with

Adverb: not

Conjunction Square

Objective:

To teach sentence construction using conjunctions

Materials:

A checkerboard with a conjunction written on each square; a stack of cards with a sentence printed on each card; checkers.

Directions:

1. The player makes his checker move (according to the rules of the game of checkers) and takes two sentence cards.
2. The player must combine the two sentences on the cards with the conjunction on which his checker lands. He must make a correct sentence in order to keep his move.
3. If the player is unable to make a sentence, he must move his checker back to its previous position.
4. The players continue taking turns and making sentences until one player wins the checker game.

Self-Correcting Materials

Opposites

Objective:

To teach classification of word opposites

Feedback device:

Windows in the back of the Spinning Wheels show matching symbols to indicate picture or word opposites.

Materials:

Spinning Wheels (described in Chapter 4); a worksheet that has one picture in the left column and two pictures on the right—one of which illustrates the opposite of the picture on the left—corresponding to the pictures on the Spinning Wheels; an acetate overlay (see Figure 9.3).

Directions:

The student places the acetate overlay over the worksheet, selects the picture that is the opposite of the one in the left column, and marks an X on that picture. After completing the worksheet, the student checks his work with the Spinning Wheels. He turns the wheels so the picture opposites he has selected appear in the windows, and then he turns over the wheels to see if there are matching symbols in the back windows.

Modification:

This activity can be used to teach same, different, or associated words by changing the items or pictures on the Spinning Wheels.

Time Slot

Objective:

To increase skills in using verbs relating to time

Feedback device:

Symbols or line drawings on the back of the verb cards match the line drawing on the envelope with the appropriate verb form.

Materials:

Three envelopes for present-, past-, and future-tense verbs with a different line drawing or symbol on each envelope; a set of cards with pictures de-

FIGURE 9.3
Worksheet for Opposites.

picting the time associated with various verb tenses (see Figure 9.4).

Directions:

The student looks at each card to determine which verb tense the picture illustrates. He then places each card in the envelope that denotes his answer. After sorting all the cards, the student takes the cards out of the envelopes and checks to see if the symbol on the back of each card matches the symbol on the front of the envelope in which it was placed.

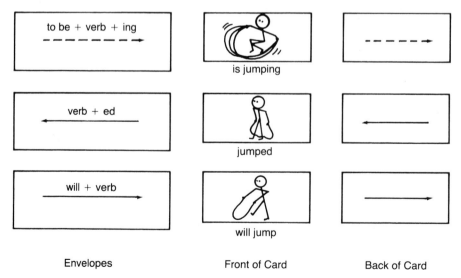

FIGURE 9.4
Envelopes and cards for Time Slot.

Modifications:

Include several syntactical forms such as *are* + verb + *ing* or *has* + verb + *ed.* A different line drawing or symbol should be assigned to each syntactical form. Also, the activity can be further modified by using words instead of pictures and labelling the envelopes with the name of the verb tense.

Flip Siders (presented in Chapter 4)

Objective:

To teach classification by association

Feedback device:

Matching colors or symbols are on the back of pictures that are associated.

Materials:

Flip-sider cards that contain pictures of words which can be categorized by association (such as a sock and a shoe) and have matching colors or symbols on the back of associated pictures.

Directions:

The student looks at each picture and finds the picture associated with it. He combines the cards and turns them over. The pictures that are associated have the same color or symbol on the back.

Modifications:

Flip siders can also be used to teach opposites, verb tenses, and phoneme recognition. Also, the material can be modified for secondary students by combining association pictures that illustrate cause-and-effect relationships. For example, the pictures could show a student studying and a report card with good grades, or an accident and an ambulance.

Make a Question

Objective:

To teach the interrogative reversal

Feedback device:

The pieces of the puzzle strip fit together when the sentence is in question form.

Materials:

A worksheet with declarative sentences; a set of puzzle pieces for each sentence that fit together when the sentence is in the form of a question.

Directions:

The student rewrites each sentence on the worksheet into an interrogative reversal to ask a question. After completing the question, he puts the corresponding puzzle pieces together to check his answer.

(a) The girls are at home.

(b) She is very tall.

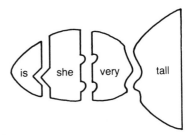

What Came First?

Objective:

To teach sentence order

Feedback device:

The pieces of the puzzle fit together when the critical elements of the sentence are in the correct order.

Materials:

A tape recording of sentences of various lengths, with each sentence containing critical verbal elements—for example, *The boy* (agent) *hit the wall* (action) *with the rock* (object); a worksheet of pictures corresponding to the sentences on the tape recording; picture puzzle pieces for the critical elements in each sentence that fit together only if put in order (see Figure 9.5).

Directions:

The student listens to the tape recording, and when he hears a sentence (such as *The boy hit the wall with the rock*), he numbers the corresponding pictures (boy, wall, rock) on the worksheet according to which came first, second, and third. To check his answer, the student puts together the puzzle pieces for each sentence and looks to see if the pictures are in the same order as he numbered them on his worksheet.

When Did It Happen?

Objective:

To teach the past-tense morpheme *ed*

Feedback device:

A tab pulled from a pocket in the material reveals the correct answer.

Materials:

A tape recording of sentences that contain the morpheme *ed*; a card that contains the sentences and has a smiling face to circle to indicate correct use of *ed* and a frowning face to indicate incorrect use of *ed*; a tab containing the answer key that fits in a pocket in the card; an acetate overlay (see Figure 9.6).

Directions:

The student places the acetate overlay over the card, listens to the sentence on the tape recording, and circles the appropriate face on the answer card to indicate correct or incorrect use of *ed*. A pause on the tape is given after each sentence to allow the student time to circle his answer and pull the tab from the pocket to see if his answer is correct. The numbers next to the faces on the tab correspond to the numbers of the sentences.

Modifications:

The activity can be used to teach *is, ing,* and so on by making a tape with sentences that require *is* or *ing*. The activity can be further modified for older students by using written sentences, each of which the student must judge as grammatically correct or incorrect.

Word Endings with Meanings

Objective:

To teach the suffixes *less* and *ful*

Feedback device:

The correct answer is revealed under a flap.

Materials:

A laminated card that contains incomplete sentences which require a root word and the suffix *less* or *ful*; a laminated card illustrating a tree with roots at the bottom and the same number of branches at the top of the tree: (a) two numbered leaves on each branch are cut so that each leaf will fold

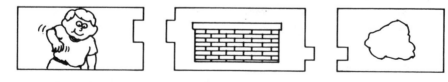

FIGURE 9.5
Puzzle pieces for What Came First?

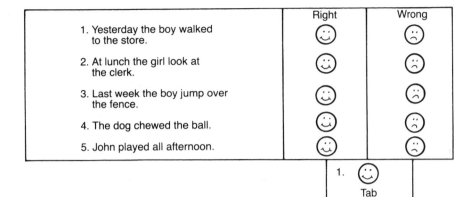

FIGURE 9.6
Card and tab for When Did It Happen?

back to reveal an answer underneath, (b) holes are punched in each corner of the card and a sheet of paper is attached to the back of the card with brass fasteners, (c) under each numbered leaf a suffix is written that matches up with the respective sentence, and (d) root words are written along the tree roots with a grease pencil.

Directions:

The student is given a laminated card that contains incomplete sentences requiring a root word and a suffix. He circles the correct suffix with a grease pencil. After he completes the sentences, he lifts the leaves on the tree card to see the correct answers.

1. The broken car is use(ful/less) until it is fixed.
2. The basket is use(ful/less) to carry groceries.
3. I learned a lot from the meaning(ful/less) speech.
4. The poor directions were meaning(ful/less).
5. The student was very care(ful/less) and wrote a neat letter.
6. The student was care(ful/less) and spilled paint on her dress.
7. She felt help(ful/less) when she couldn't start her car.
8. The neighbor was help(ful/less) when she loaned me her telephone.
9. The flower arrangement was pleasing and taste(ful/less).
10. The food was very bland and taste(ful/less) to me.

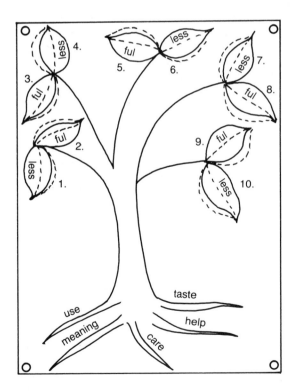

Modification:

Attach a sheet containing different prefixes and suffixes to the back of the tree card and supply a corresponding worksheet.

Make It Say a Sentence

Objective:

To teach sentence order

Feedback device:

An answer key in an envelope attached to the back of the card provides the answers.

Materials:

A card containing scrambled sentences that contain conjunctions; an envelope on the back of the card; an answer key; paper.

Directions:

The student looks at each scrambled sentence on the card and unscrambles the words. He writes the unscrambled sentences on paper, and to check his work he looks at the answer key in the envelope on the back of the card.

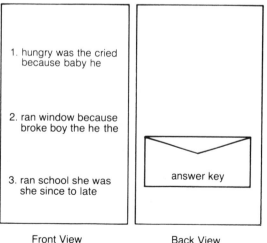

1. hungry was the cried because baby he

2. ran window because broke boy the he the

3. ran school she was she since to late

answer key

Front View   Back View

Modifications:

This self-correcting device can be used with many tasks, such as making grammatical judgment, changing declarative sentences into interrogative sentences, and using conjunctions. The cloze procedure for completing sentences with conjunctions can be adapted to this procedure by putting sentences on a card with an answer key attached. For example:

She went to the store _____ she needed to buy some groceries. (because, and)

She is going to buy milk _____ bread. (since, and)

Does It Mean the Same Thing?

Objective:

To teach similarity of deep structure in two sentences

Feedback device:

An answer key on the back of the card provides the correct answers.

Materials:

A card with sentence pairs, some having the same meaning and others having different meanings; an acetate overlay; an answer key on the back of the card (see Figure 9.7).

Directions:

The student reads each set of sentences and decides if the *deep structure* (meaning) of both sentences is the same or different. He places the acetate overlay over the response section of the card and circles "same" or "different" to indicate his answer. After completing the task, the student turns the card over and places the acetate overlay over the answer key. The circles on the overlay should match the words circled on the answer key.

Modifications:

Acetate overlays and marked answer keys can be used with sentences that use a cloze procedure with multiple choices. For example:

FIGURE 9.7
Card and acetate overlay for Does It Mean the Same Thing?

He heated the water _____ made coffee. (and, because)

This procedure can also be used with grammatical judgment. For example:

Yesterday he walk to school. _____ Correct _____ Incorrect

Descriptors

Objective:

To increase use of effective communication skills

Feedback device:

The correct responses are provided on the back of the stimulus card.

Materials:

Cards with a small object mounted on the front of each card and a list of six descriptive categories pertaining to the object written on the back of each card; six Language Master cards.

Directions:

The student looks at the object on the card and records a different sentence describing the object on each Language Master card. After recording the six sentences, the student turns over the stimulus, listens to each of his recorded sentences, and checks the appropriate descriptive category used on the back of the card.

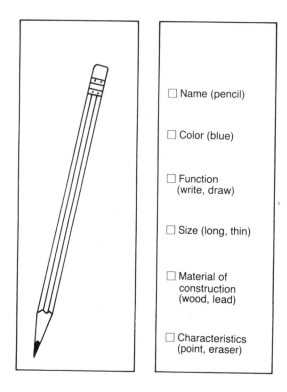

☐ Name (pencil)

☐ Color (blue)

☐ Function
   (write, draw)

☐ Size (long, thin)

☐ Material of
   construction
   (wood, lead)

☐ Characteristics
   (point, eraser)

Modification:

This material can be modified for younger students by giving the child a picture of an object with two attributes (such as a small, red car). The student describes the picture by recording a descriptive sentence on a Language Master card. After recording, he turns the picture card over to the answer key, listens to the recording on the Language Master card, and checks each attribute used. The answers can be coded for nonreaders to check—a color to indicate color category, and a very small object to indicate size category.

Indirect Requests

Objective:

To identify indirect requests

Feedback device:

An answer key is provided on the back of the response card.

Materials:

Various indirect requests and questions taped on a tape recorder; a response card with an answer key provided on the back of the card; an acetate overlay.

Directions:

The student places the acetate overlay over the response card and listens to the taped sentences. He decides if each sentence is a question or an indirect request and records his answer on the overlay. After completing the task, the student turns over the response card and places the acetate overlay over the answer key to check his responses.

Taped sentences:

1. What time is it?
2. Can you shut the door?
3. Won't you stop that?
4. Can't you finish your work?
5. When does the bus arrive?
6. Is the water running?
7. Must you just sit there?
8. Must you slurp your milk?
9. Can't you sit still?
10. Did the dog run away?

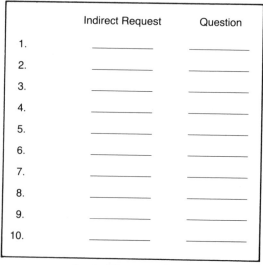

Front of Response Card

	Indirect Request	Question
1.		X
2.	X	
3.	X	
4.	X	
5.		X
6.		X
7.	X	
8.	X	
9.	X	
10.		X

Back of Response Card

Modification:

Change the taped sentences to questions and statements. The student identifies each sentence as a statement or a question.

Commercial Programs and Materials

Numerous commercial language programs are available to help develop language skills of students having difficulty with spoken language. The selection of programs and materials for classroom use should reflect the developmental ages of the students for whom they are selected as well as the purpose of the intervention.

Alike Because

Publisher: DLM Teaching Resources

Description:

This material is composed of two spiral-bound flip books of association pictures. Level 1 is for elementary students, and Level 2 is appropriate for older elementary and junior high students. There are 32 pictures in each book, with 16 pictures on the left side and 16 pictures on the right side. The pictures on the left can be compared with the pictures on the right for likenesses and differences. This comparison of pictures of common objects helps develop association and generalization skills.

All-Purpose Photo Library

Publisher: DLM Teaching Resources

Description:

Set 1 includes 272 lifelike photo cards divided into 12 categories (for example, body parts, household items, tools and hardware, transportation). Set 2 contains 266 photo cards in 16 categories including musical instruments, sports, birds, and insects. In addition to the photo cards, each category contains a question card of general questions and a group card of questions dealing with basic characteristics of the grouped items. The photos and question cards are designed to reinforce and expand language skills through the identification of common objects in photographs and to increase the student's awareness of functions and attributes of various items.

Basic Concept Stories

Publisher: DLM Teaching Resources

Description:

These stories are designed to give students practice in understanding and using basic language concepts. The complete program includes two flip-style books, each of which contains six stories illustrated with full-color photographs. *Spatial Concepts* includes such basics as *in front of/in back of/behind* and *in/into/out of. Comparatives and Opposites* includes such basics as *easy/easier/easiest, bad/worse/worst, rough/smooth,* and *deep/shallow.* Expressive and receptive use of the language concepts is incorporated into the stories, photographs, questions, and activities.

Clinical Language Intervention Program
(Semel & Wiig, 1982)

Publisher: Psychological Corporation

Description:

This program focuses on teaching semantics, syntax, memory, and pragmatics to students in kindergarten through eighth grade. Within each category of language form and content, the materials and tasks are designed to elicit clearly defined intervention targets. The program includes more than 2,000 stimulus pictures, matching verbal stimuli, suggested task formats for intervention, and additional activities for carry-over training. Components include a teacher's guide with suggested training methods and strategies, a picture manual to promote acquisition and use of specific language skills or functions, a language activities manual of maintenance and generalization activities, and student progress checklists for recording progress across time.

Communicative Competence: A Functional-Pragmatic Language Program

Publisher: Communication Skill Builders

Description:

The main focus of this program is the development of structurally adequate, nonegocentric, coherent communication skills. The program includes 644 stimulus cards depicting situations the student must describe accurately. They are categorized by specific semantic-grammatical rules, elaborations of these basic constructions, and categories of objects and people. Four color filmstrips that present several sequential stories are used to reduce egocentric communication styles. In addition, 14 different spinner boards offer various stimuli to develop cognitive-linguistic skills. Also included are a teacher's manual that suggests various teaching strategies and a monograph that presents the theoretical framework for developing communication skills in primary through secondary students.

Concepts for Communication

Publisher: DLM Teaching Resources

Description:

This program aids students in developing receptive, associative, and expressive language skills. In Unit I,

Listening with Understanding, the student works with audiocassette tapes to improve memory, concentration, deduction, and decoding skills. The purpose of Unit II, *Concept Building,* is to increase the student's skill and flexibility in classifying data. Unit III, *Communication,* includes gamelike situations in which students work in pairs or small groups to improve their oral skills of description and inquiry. A teacher's manual, cassette tapes, matrix cards, and activity books are included.

Developmental Syntax Program

Publisher: Learning Concepts

Description:

This 11-part program is designed to remediate syntactical errors in children between the developmental ages of 3 and 10 years. Three basic procedures are used: ear training, production and carry-over, and generalization to a different context. The materials include a file box of 301 3″ × 5″ illustrated cards, 13 story posters, student record sheets, and a manual.

Fokes Sentence Builder

Publisher: DLM Teaching Resources

Description:

This structured oral language program helps students develop skills in verbal expression, comprehension, and sentence construction. The kit contains 201 black-and-white picture cards of drawings of people, animals, and common objects, as well as a guide which explains how to build declarative sentences, questions, and negative sentences in the present, past, and future tenses. Students create grammatically correct sentences by selecting cards from the color-coded boxes, which represent five categories of words: *who, what, is doing, which,* and *where.* Sentence markers, sentence inserts, and a sentence line are included, and 180 additional picture cards are available. Also, the expansion kit provides three additional grammatical categories (*whose, how, when*) that allow students to build more sentences.

*Let's Talk: Developing Prosocial
Communication Skills
(Wiig, 1982)*

Publisher: Psychological Corporation

Description:

This program is designed to develop and strengthen the prosocial communication skills of students who are 9 years old to adult age. A communication card game format and structured training activities are used to help teach effective ways to handle everyday social interaction. Students learn to express positive and negative feelings; present, understand, and respond to information in spoken messages; adapt messages to the needs of others; and approach conversations with expectations of what to say and how to say it. The *Communication Intents* package includes card decks pertaining to asking for favors, making dates, sharing feelings, and dating. Card decks in the *Function Communication* package focus on getting around town, shopping, telephoning, getting a job, and serving people. The card decks are also available separately.

Newby Visualanguage

Publisher: Newby Visualanguage

Description:

This material is suitable for elementary students and is made up of pictures and worksheets for teaching pronouns, verbs, and adjectives. The pictures can be used with nonreaders to elicit parts of speech. There are 13 verb illustrations (present, past, and future tense) on 5″ × 7″ laminated cards. There are also illustrations of 20 adjectives, 20 antonyms, 8 nominative pronouns, 8 possessive pronouns, and 8 objective pronouns. Worksheets are available for verbs, adjectives, and pronouns, and there is a workbook for verbs. The worksheets and workbook require some reading skills.

*Peabody Language Development Kits
(Dunn, Smith, Dunn, Horton, & Smith, 1981)*

Publisher: American Guidance Service

Description:

This multilevel program for developing oral language and cognitive skills in young children consists of four kits—one each for preschoolers, first, second, and third graders. The kits stress overall language development rather than specific psycholinguistic processes. The activities at each level emphasize the skills of *reception* through sight, hearing, and touch; *expression* through vocal and motor behavior; and *conceptualization* through divergent, convergent, and associative thinking. Pictures, records, puppets, manipulative materials, and a teacher's manual are included in the kits. The teacher's manual has descriptions of daily lessons and specifies a teacher script as well as appropriate materials and activities.

*Peel and Put Speech and Language
Development Program*

Publisher: Communication Skill Builders

Description:

The complete program includes 1,000 pictures that stick to any clean, nonporous surface. These pictures are coded according to vocabulary, conceptual categories, and speech sounds and are designed for children whose developmental age is between 3 and 14 years. Also included in the program are four alphabet sheets (upper- and lowercase), two shapes/visual closure sheets, a manual, and 300 blank flash cards. The major objectives of the program are to develop accurate oral communication and articulation, increase concept formation, utilize and develop understanding of word structure, and increase word comprehension skills. The program activity manual includes 89 speech and language activities for the development of the student's thinking, learning, and oral communication processes.

Syntax One; Syntax Two

Publisher: Communication Skill Builders

Description:

Syntax One is designed for children whose syntactical skills are from 1 to 5 years behind other language-related skills. The objective is to develop student awareness of word order and word endings to convey meaning. The kit contains six double-sided syntax wheels that show the syntactical form to be taught. The wheel inserts rotate to expose stimulus pictures in order to elicit a syntactical form or an inflectional word ending. *Syntax Two* also includes 6 two-sided syntax wheels. The student is presented with problem-solving situations in which he must ask questions to get necessary information; thus the form and function of questions are taught.

Teaching Morphology Developmentally

Publisher: Communication Skill Builders

Description:

This developmental program for teaching word formation is designed for students whose language age is between 2½ and 10 years. The 523 color stimulus cards can be used to teach more than 1,000 free morphemes and 700 bound morphemes. Specific morphemes that are focused on include present progressives, plurals, possessives, past tenses, third-person singulars, and derived adjectives (comparative-superlative and irregular forms). Reproducible lists of curriculum items, pre- and posttest forms, and suggestions for developing behavioral objectives are included in the instructional guide.

WH-Questions

Publisher: DLM Teaching Resources

Description:

This program consists of three levels (beginning—preschool to primary; intermediate—middle grades; advanced—junior high), each of which consists of 25 full-color 8″ × 10″ photo cards with 10 questions presented on the back. The components of the program are designed to develop and reinforce the following skills: (a) comprehension words—*who, what, where, which, whose, when, why,* and *how;* (b) appropriate response to questions that require discrimination of the content and details of visual materials as well as interpretation and extrapolation; and (c) verbal reasoning such as interpreting characters' feelings and motives, predicting cause–effect

relationships, sequencing, and making inferences. The materials may also be useful as a springboard for creative writing activities.

REFERENCES

Alley, G., & Deshler, D. (1979). *Teaching the learning disabled adolescent: Strategies and methods.* Denver: Love.

Bandura, A. (1971). Analysis of modeling processes. In A. Bandura (Ed.), *Psychological modeling: Conflicting theories.* New York: Aldine/Atherton.

Bartel, N.R., & Bryen, D.N. (1982). Problems in language development. In D.D. Hammill & N.R. Bartel, *Teaching children with learning and behavior problems* (3rd ed.). Boston: Allyn & Bacon.

Berry, M. (1980). *Teaching linguistically handicapped children.* Englewood Cliffs, NJ: Prentice-Hall.

Bloom, L. (1975). Language development review. In F.D. Horowitz (Ed.), *Review of child development research* (Vol. 4). Chicago: University of Chicago Press.

Bloom, L., & Lahey, M. (1978). *Language development and language disorders.* New York: Wiley.

Blosser, J., Weidner, W., & Dinero, T. (1976). The effect of rate-controlled speech on the auditory receptive scores of children with normal and disordered language disabilities. *Journal of Special Education, 10,* 291–298.

Braine, M. (1971). *On two types of models of the internalization of grammar.* New York: Academic Press.

Bryan, T., Donahue, M., & Pearl, R. (1981). Studies of learning disabled children's pragmatic competence. *Topics in Learning and Learning Disabilities, 1*(2), 29–41.

Burns, P. (1980). *Assessment and correction of language arts difficulties.* Columbus, OH: Merrill.

Chomsky, N.A. (1957). *Syntactic structures.* The Hague: Mouton.

Chomsky, N.A. (1965). *Aspects of the theory of syntax.* Cambridge, MA: MIT Press.

Courtright, J.A., & Courtright, I.C. (1976). Imitative modeling as a theoretical base for instructing language-disordered children. *Journal of Speech and Hearing Research, 19,* 655–663.

Courtright, J.A., & Courtright, I.C. (1979). Imitative modeling as a language intervention strategy: The effects of two mediating variables. *Journal of Speech and Hearing Research, 22,* 389–402.

DeHaven, E. (1983). *Teaching and learning the language arts* (2nd ed.). Boston: Little, Brown.

Donoghue, M. (1975). *The child and the English language arts* (2nd ed.). Dubuque, IA: Brown.

Dunn, L.M., Smith, J.O., Dunn, L.M., Horton, D.B., & Smith, D.D. (1981). *Peabody language development kits* (Rev. ed.). Circle Pines, MN: American Guidance Service.

Engelmann, S., & Osborn, J. (1976). *DISTAR: An instructional system.* Chicago: Science Research Associates.

Froese, V. (1981). Hearing/listening/auding: Auditory processing. In V. Froese & S. Straw (Eds.). *Research in the language arts: Language and schooling.* Baltimore, MD: University Park Press.

Gerber, A., & Bryen, D. (Eds.). (1981). *Language and learning disabilities.* Baltimore: University Park Press.

Gray, B.B., & Ryan, B.P. (1972). *Monterey language program (Programmed conditioning for language).* Palo Alto, CA: Monterey Learning Systems.

Hresko, W., & Reid, D. (1981). From the editors: Language intervention with the learning disabled. *Topics in Learning and Learning Disabilities, 1*(2), viii–ix.

Jenkins, J.J., & Palermo, D.S. (1964). Mediation processes and the acquisition of linguistic structure. In U. Bellugi & R. Brown (Eds.), *The acquisition of language. Monographs of the Society for Research in Child Development, 29*(1, Whole No. 92).

Kent, J. (1974). *Hop, skip and jump book: A first book of action words.* New York: Random House.

Lee, L., Koenigsknecht, R.A., & Mulhern, S.T. (1975). *Interactive language development teaching.* Evanston, IL: Northwestern University Press.

Lenneberg, E. (1964). A biological perspective of language. In E. Lenneberg (Ed.), *New directions in the study of language.* Cambridge, MA: MIT Press.

Lenneberg, E.H. (1967). *Biological foundations of language.* New York: Wiley.

Leonard, L.B. (1975). Modeling as a clinical procedure in language training. *Language, Speech and Hearing Services in Schools, 6,* 72–85.

Matheny, N., & Panagos, J. (1978). Comparing the effects of articulation and syntax programs on syntax and articulation improvement. *Language, Speech and Hearing Services in Schools, 9*(1), 57–61.

McCaffrey, A. (1976). *Talking in the classroom: How can we teach children to use language?* Paper presented at the New York Speech and Hearing Association Convention, New York.

McCroskey, R., & Thompson, N. (1973). Comprehension of rate controlled speech by children with specific learning disabilities. *Journal of Learning Disabilities, 6,* 29–35.

McLean, J.E., & Snyder-McLean, L.K. (1978). *A transactional approach to early language training.* Columbus, OH: Merrill.

McNeil, D. (1966). Developmental psycholinguistics. In F. Smith & G.A. Miller (Eds.), *The genesis of language: A psycholinguistic approach.* (pp. 15–84) Cambridge, MA: MIT Press.

McNeil, D. (1970). The development of language. In P.H. Mussen (Ed.), *Carmichael's manual of child psychology* (Vol. 1, 3rd ed., pp. 1061–1161). New York: Wiley.

McNutt, G. (1984). A holistic approach to language arts instruction in the resource room. *Learning Disability Quarterly, 7,* 315–320.

Miller, L. (1978). Pragmatics and early childhood language disorders: Communicative interactions in a half-hour sample. *Journal of Speech and Hearing Disorders, 43,* 419–436.

Muma, J.R. (1978). *Language handbook: Concepts, assessment, and intervention.* Englewood Cliffs, NJ: Prentice-Hall.

Panagos, J., & Griffith, P. (1981). Okay, what *do* educators know about language intervention? *Topics in Learning and Learning Disabilities, 1*(2), 69–82.

Pflaum, S. (1978). *The development of language and reading in young children.* Columbus, OH: Merrill.

Piaget, J. (1960). *The psychology of intelligence.* Patterson, NJ: Littlefield, Adams.

Rees, N.S. (1975). Imitation and language development: Issues and clinical implications. *Journal of Speech and Hearing Disorders, 40,* 339–350.

Schiefelbusch, R.L., Ruder, K.F., & Bricker, W.A. (1976). Training strategies for language-deficient children: An overview. In N.G. Haring & R.L. Schiefelbusch (Eds.), *Teaching special children.* New York: McGraw-Hill.

Semel, E. (1976). *Semel auditory processing program.* Chicago: Follett.

Semel, E., & Wiig, E. (1981). Semel auditory processing program: Training effects among children with language-learning disabilities. *Journal of Learning Disabilities, 14,* 192–197.

Semel, E., & Wiig, E. (1982). *Clinical language intervention program.* San Antonio, TX: Psychological Corporation.

Skinner, B.F. (1957). *Verbal behavior.* New York: Appleton-Century-Crofts.

Spekman, N., & Roth, F. (1984). Intervention strategies for learning disabled children with oral communication disorders. *Learning Disability Quarterly, 7,* 7–18.

Staats, A. (1971). Linguistic-mentalistic theory versus an explanatory S-R learning theory of language development. In D.I. Slobin (Ed.), *The ontogenesis of grammar.* New York: Academic Press.

Stallings, J. (1974). *What teachers do does make a difference: A study of seven Follow Through educational models* (Paper presented to Early Childhood Conference on Evaluation, Anaheim, CA, ERIC No. ED095186). Menlo Park, CA: Stanford Research Institute.

Taenzer, S., Cermak, C., & Hanlon, C. (1981). Outside the therapy room: A naturalistic approach to language intervention. *Topics in Learning and Learning Disabilities, 1*(2), 41–47.

Vogel, S.A. (1983). A qualitative analysis of morphological ability in learning disabled and achieving children. *Journal of Learning Disabilities, 16,* 416–420.

Weber, R. (1982). A closer look at three measures of English morphology. *Journal of Learning Disabilities, 15,* 86–89.

Wedemeyer, A., & Cejka, J. (1975). *Creative ideas for teaching exceptional children.* Denver: Love.

Weller, C. (1979). The effects of two language training approaches on syntactical skills of language-deviant children. *Journal of Learning Disabilities, 12,* 470–479.

Wiig, E. (1982). *Let's talk: Developing prosocial communication skills.* San Antonio, TX: Psychological Corporation.

Wiig, E.H., & Semel, E.M. (1984). *Language assessment and intervention for the learning disabled* (2nd ed.). Columbus, OH: Merrill.

Worthley, W.J. (1978). *Sourcebook of language learning activities: Instructional strategies and methods.* Boston: Little, Brown.

CHAPTER 10

Assessing
Reading Skills

A bout 10 to 15% of the general school population experience difficulty in reading (Haring & Bateman, 1977; Harris & Sipay, 1980). Several authorities (Brabner, 1969; Carnine & Silbert, 1979; Kaluger & Kolson, 1978) suggest that reading difficulties are the principal cause of failure in school. Reading experiences strongly influence a student's self-image and feeling of competency (Carnine & Silbert, 1979); furthermore, reading failure may lead to misbehavior, anxiety, and a lack of motivation. Athey (1976) concludes that in American culture, learning to read is important for maintaining self-respect and for obtaining the respect of others.

Reading is a very complex task, and numerous definitions exist. In this chapter reading is defined as a visual-auditory task that involves obtaining meaning from symbols (letters and words). Reading includes two basic processes: a *decoding* process and a *comprehension* process. The decoding process involves understanding the phoneme—grapheme relationships and translating printed words into a representation similar to oral language. Thus, decoding skills enable the learner to pronounce words correctly. Comprehension skills enable the learner to understand the meaning of words in isolation and in context.

ORGANIZATION OF READING SKILLS

To assess or teach reading skills effectively, it is helpful to understand the general organization of reading content and related subskills. As implied in the definition, reading content is divided into word recognition skills and comprehension skills. Figure 10.1 illustrates these skills. Reading approaches differ in which reading skills they stress and when to introduce them. For example, a phonics approach emphasizes the early introduction of the sound-symbol system, whereas an approach that fo-

cuses on meaning stresses learning whole words by sight at first and introduces the sound-symbol system later.

There are seven commonly used strategies of word recognition (Ekwall & Shanker, 1985; Guszak, 1978). *Configuration* refers to the outline or general shape of a word. Word length, capital letters, and letter height may provide some visual cues to the unskilled reader. *Context analysis* is "the skill of using the words and meanings surrounding an unknown word or phrase to determine the unknown element"

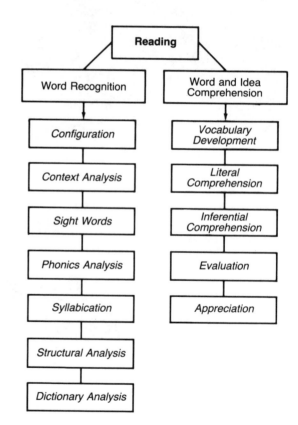

FIGURE 10.1.

An organizational framework of developmental reading skills.

Source: From *Students with Learning Disabilities* (p. 375) 3rd ed., by C.D. Mercer, 1987, Columbus, OH: Merrill. Copyright 1987 by Merrill Publishing Company. Reprinted by permission.

(Guszak, 1978, p. 31). Semantic and syntactic (grammatical) cues help the reader predict word possibilities according to context. Likewise, pictures can provide context cues. *Sight words* are those the reader recognizes without applying phonetic analysis. Sight words include frequently used words, such as those on the Dolch list (Dolch, 1955), as well as words the reader knows instantly from repeated exposure. Many words in English that have irregular spellings are taught as sight words; that is, they are learned as whole words. In reading approaches that focus on meaning, the whole-word method is predominantly used to introduce printed words. *Phonics analysis* refers to decoding words by symbol-sound associations. It involves the learning of phonemes and rules concerning the various sounds. For example, phonics analysis includes learning sounds and rules pertaining to single initial consonants, initial and ending consonant blends, consonant digraphs, silent consonants, short and long vowel sounds, and vowel teams and special letter combinations. *Syllabication* is the process of dividing a word into its component parts. Each syllable contains a vowel sound. Some authorities place syllabication in phonics skills, whereas others include it in structural analysis (Ekwall & Shanker, 1985). In *structural analysis* the reader perceives meaningful units such as root words, prefixes, suffixes, possessives, plurals, word families, and compound words. Comprehension of these structures permits a faster rate of reading than does analyzing individual sounds. *Dictionary analysis* is seldom used for word recognition; however, it does provide the reader with an independent means of pronouncing unknown words. Basically, it involves the use of the pronunciation key symbols included in a glossary or dictionary.

Five major areas are included in reading comprehension (Ekwall & Shanker, 1985; Smith & Barrett, 1974). *Vocabulary develop-* *ment* is essential for the reader to understand the words used by the writer. A background of meaningful experience (exposure to books, people, places) and learning words from context (through a variety of reading material) aid in developing vocabulary. *Literal comprehension* refers to recognition and recall of explicitly stated information. Some of the skills involved in literal reading include the ability to read for the central thought and main ideas, note and remember significant details, note the order or sequence of events, and find answers to specific questions. *Inferential (or interpretative) comprehension* requires the reader to make conjectures or hypotheses based on stated information, her intuition, and her personal experience. Grasping cause–effect relationships, anticipating the remainder of a story, and forming opinions are inferential comprehension skills. *Evaluation* or critical reading deals with judgments based on the reader's experiences, knowledge, or values. Evaluation focuses on qualities of accuracy, acceptability, worth, or probability of occurrence. It includes making judgments of reality or fantasy, fact or opinion, and validity, as well as making value (moral) judgments and analyzing the intent of the author. *Appreciation* deals with the student's emotional and aesthetic sensitivity to the written selection. To function at this level, the student identifies with characters and incidents and is able to verbally express emotional feelings about the word (e.g., excitement, fear, boredom).

In functional reading the student reads to obtain information. Whereas developmental reading (word recognition and comprehension) involves *learning to read,* functional reading involves *reading to learn.* Functional reading is sometimes called *study skills* because it includes locating information (e.g., use of indexes, tables of contents, encyclopedias), comprehending data (technical vocabulary, reading maps and tables), outlining and summarizing, researching, and developing study patterns for specific content areas (Harris & Sipay, 1980).

The scope and sequence skills list for reading presented in Appendix A is organized into word-attack skills and comprehension skills. Authorities disagree about the sequence for teaching reading skills, and research results about the sequence are inconclusive. Thus, a teacher should use a reading scope and sequence skills list in a flexible way and should tailor the sequence for assessing and teaching reading skills according to logic and experience.

DEVELOPMENT OF READING SKILLS

Reading content has a structure in which the student first constructs simple relationships (such as grapheme–phoneme) and then progresses to more complex tasks (such as critical reading). Many authorities (Carrillo, 1976; Harris & Sipay, 1980; Kirk, Kliebhan, & Lerner, 1978) feel that growth in reading skills occurs in several stages. Knowing the stages helps the teacher in selecting assessment tasks, developing instructional goals, and choosing instructional approaches. In addition, when student progress is carefully monitored, the teacher can determine when the student progresses from one level to the next. Harris and Sipay (1980) divide reading development into five stages: (a) development of reading readiness, (b) the initial stage in learning how to read, (c) rapid development of reading skills, (d) wide reading stage, and (e) refinement of reading skills.

Development of Reading Readiness

Readiness refers to the level of development needed for efficient learning. Kirk et al. (1978) report that many factors contribute to reading readiness, including (a) mental maturity, (b) visual abilities, (c) auditory abilities, (d) speech and language development, (e) thinking and attention skills, (f) motor development, (g) social and emotional maturity, and (h) interest and motivation. Kirk et al. state that these factors are interrelated. The readiness period spans a period from birth until formal reading instruction begins. For many children, the period continues through the kindergarten year.

The relationship of mental age to readiness has received much attention. Many educators hold that a minimum mental age of between 6 and 6½ years is essential, but this position—primarily based on studies conducted in large classrooms in the 1930s (Gates, 1937)—is being viewed critically. For example, educators now realize that difficulty of material, pace of instruction, method used, amount of individualized help, and the child's specific abilities affect the minimum mental age required for efficient learning. Harris and Sipay (1980) note that reading can be introduced in an early, relaxed manner to kindergarten children who are ready. They also indicate that the current trend favors a slow, gradual start in beginning reading instruction with readiness skills embedded in the context of reading.

Initial Stage in Learning How to Read

The initial learning usually begins in first grade, but with some children it may begin in kindergarten or earlier, or in the second grade or later. In the initial stage, reading is difficult. Often the student reads slowly, word by word, as she tries to break a detailed, complicated code. In this stage, tools are acquired to make the child an independent and fluent reader.

There is much controversy among researchers concerning this stage. Disagreement centers around the *code-emphasis* approach versus the *meaning-emphasis* approach. The code approach stresses the early introduction of the sound-symbol system and the teaching of phonics. The meaning approach stresses the initial learning of whole words and sentences by sight; phonics instruction comes later in this approach.

Kirk et al. (1978) present a three-phase model for learning to read: (a) reading wholes, (b) learning details, and (c) reading without awareness of details. Reading wholes and learning details occur in this initial stage. The term *reading wholes* refers to providing the child with some initial words and sentences to learn by sight. To learn these words, children rely heavily on memory and configuration clues. *Learning details* involves discriminating between words and acquiring the associations between sound and symbol. In essence, the child learns the code and develops word-attack skills during this phase of learning details.

Stage of Rapid Development of Reading Skills

In the second and third grades, the child refines reading skills acquired earlier. The third phase (Kirk et al., 1978), reading without awareness of details, applies to this stage. The child automatically begins to use the tools acquired previously. She attains fluent reading and is able to read grade-level material in the range of 100 to 140 words per minute with two or fewer errors. The transition from the initial stage to the stage of rapid development is shown by a baby who at first must concentrate intensely when learning to walk and then is able to walk automatically, without thinking about it. Similarly, the child reading at the stage of rapid development does so automatically until she encounters an unknown word. Having mastered most of the sound-symbol relationships, the child tries a variety of word-attack approaches. Once the child reaches this stage, instruction focuses mainly on developing vocabulary, improving comprehension skills, and maintaining interest. However, few

children or adolescents with severe reading disabilities (in word recognition) ever reach this stage of development during their school years. As peers move into this stage of rapid development, upper elementary and adolescent students with reading problems often experience motivation problems and become extremely frustrated.

Stage of Wide Reading

Normally, during the intermediate grades the child realizes the pleasure of reading. It becomes a very meaning-oriented task. Children voluntarily read magazines and books such as those by Judy Bloom. These enthusiastic readers read faster and recognize and comprehend words easily. Their teachers encourage independent recreational reading and help them in their functional reading to expand vocabulary, build further comprehension skills, and review phonics and structural analysis. Students of all ages with reading problems seldom reach this level.

Stage of Refinement of Reading Skills

In the junior and senior high school years, reading increases both in amount and difficulty. The students develop more advanced comprehension skills (critical reading), as well as improve their study skills and reading rate. Continuing into adulthood, this stage principally demands practice in reading skills.

READING PROBLEMS

Once the teacher recognizes the decoding and comprehension processes of the reading task and is aware of the network of reading skills and their general developmental sequence, reading assessment can be undertaken in a meaningful manner. Because reading problems stem from many causes and the reading process is so complex, many reading difficulties can exist (Kaluger & Kolson, 1978; Kirk et al., 1978). Bond, Tinker, and Wasson (1979) provide the following general classification of the more prevalent reading difficulties: (a) faulty word identification and recognition, (b) inappropriate directional habits, (c) deficiencies in basic comprehension abilities, (d) limited special comprehension abilities (such as inability to locate and retain specific facts), (e) deficiencies in basic study skills, (f) deficiencies in ability to adapt to reading needs of content fields, (g) deficiencies in rate of comprehension, and (h) poor oral reading.

In addition to indicating the student's current reading ability, assessment measures can point to specific strengths and weaknesses and aid the teacher in planning instructional objectives. Both commercially prepared instruments and informal measures are useful. To obtain a valid assessment of the student's reading abilities, the teacher should use a variety of assessment procedures—standardized tests, observations, and informal inventories. The information the teacher wants to obtain should help determine the type of assessment device used. For example, a group-administered reading achievement test yields information on the level of reading of the entire class. More specific information about certain skills of one student is better obtained from an individually administered diagnostic reading test or through informal assessment techniques. The remainder of this chapter presents various formal and informal assessment techniques and devices.

FORMAL ASSESSMENT

Many published tests are available that assess reading skills. These commercial tests often have been standardized on large groups of students. Such norm-referenced tests enable the teacher to compare each student's performance with the population upon which the test was standardized. Scores from standardized reading tests are reported in a number of ways (such as reading grade level, reading age score, percentile, stanine score). However, the use of norm-referenced tests requires following strict procedures in administration, scoring, and interpretation. In addition to norm-referenced tests, some published reading measures are criterion-referenced. These tests *describe* performance, rather than compare it, and may be used to determine if the student has mastered specific instructional objectives. In this section, three types of formal assessment devices are presented: (a) standardized achievement and reading survey tests, (b) diagnostic tests, and (c) criterion-referenced tests.

Standardized Achievement and Reading Survey Tests

General achievement tests assess a student's ability in various school subjects. Achievement tests that contain reading subtests often are used to obtain an overall measure of reading achievement. These tests are norm-referenced and thus yield objective results that can be compared to the norms of the standardization sample. Reading survey tests measure reading skills only and are also frequently used to indicate a student's general range of reading abilities. Achievement and reading survey tests basically are screening measures and may help determine which children are experiencing reading difficulties and need further testing. Table 10.1 presents information on selected reading survey tests and achievement tests with reading subtests.

Diagnostic Tests

In contrast to achievement and general reading survey tests, which yield broad information,

TABLE 10.1
Survey and achievement tests with reading subtests.

Test	Publisher	Group or Individual	Grade Level	Reading Areas Assessed
California Achievement Tests: Reading (1985)	California Test Bureau/ McGraw-Hill	G	K–12	Word analysis, vocabulary, comprehension
Gates-MacGinitie Reading Tests (MacGinitie, 1978)	Houghton Mifflin	G	K–12	Vocabulary, comprehension
Iowa Tests of Basic Skills (Hieronymus, Hoover, & Lindquist, 1986)	Riverside	G	K–9	Comprehension, vocabulary, word analysis, work-study skills
Kaufman Test of Educational Achievement (Kaufman & Kaufman, 1985)	American Guidance Service	I	1–12	Decoding, comprehension
Metropolitan Achievement Tests: Survey Battery (Prescott, Balow, Hogan, & Farr, 1984)	Psychological Corporation	G	K–12	Vocabulary, word recognition, reading comprehension
Peabody Individual Achievement Test— Revised (Dunn & Markwardt, 1988)	American Guidance Service	I	K–12	Reading recognition, reading comprehension
SRA Achievement Series (Naslund, Thorpe, & Lefever, 1978)	Science Research Associates	G	1–12	Vocabulary, comprehension
Stanford Achievement Test (Gardner, Rudman, Karlsen, & Merwin, 1982)	Psychological Corporation	G	1–9	Vocabulary, reading comprehension, word reading, word study skills, listening comprehension
Tests of Achievement and Proficiency (Scannell, 1986)	Riverside	G	9–12	Reading comprehension, using sources of information
Wide Range Achievement Test—Revised (Jastak & Wilkinson, 1984)	Jastak Associates	I	Preschool–adult	Letter recognition, word recognition
Woodcock-Johnson Psycho-Educational Battery (Woodcock & Johnson, 1977)	DLM Teaching Resources	I	Preschool–adult	Letter-word identification, word attack, passage comprehension

diagnostic reading tests provide a more precise, comprehensive analysis of specific reading abilities and disabilities. The teacher finds out *how* the student attempts to read. By pinpointing the student's specific strengths and weaknesses in various subskills of reading, diagnostic tests yield detailed information that is useful in planning appropriate individual educational programs. Most diagnostic reading tests are standardized; however, some do not include norm-referenced data. Also, many of these instruments are designed for individual rather than group administration. Diagnostic tests are discussed in two categories: test batteries and tests of specific skills.

Test batteries. Diagnostic reading test batteries are designed to measure many reading subskills. They often include multiple subtests that sample performance in areas such as word analysis, word recognition, comprehension, and various reading-related skills. The following five test batteries are widely used to provide a systematic assessment of reading skills.

1. *Diagnostic Reading Scales* (Spache, 1981). Three word recognition lists and 22 passages of increasing difficulty are used to assess word recognition, word analysis, and comprehension. The student's performance on the word lists, which increase in difficulty, indicates the level at which the reading passages should begin. As the student reads orally from the reading passages, the teacher notes reading errors and then checks comprehension by asking several questions following each passage. Instructional, independent, and potential reading levels are determined. Twelve supplementary phonics and word analysis tests are also included to assess areas such as consonant and vowel sounds, blending, initial consonant substitution, and auditory discrimination. The battery is designed to be individually administered to children in grades 1 through 7 as well as to older students with reading difficulties. Bond et al. (1979) report several advantages of the Spache tests:

   a. Directions are clearly stated and include adequate precautions.
   b. Suggestions to reduce emphasis on rigid standards are useful to the teacher and clinician, and tentative remedial suggestions are offered.
   c. The tests are appropriate for a wide range of students.
   d. The tests may be administered by a classroom teacher.

2. *Durrell Analysis of Reading Difficulty* (Durrell & Catterson, 1980). Designed for individual administration by a trained professional, this test may be used with children from nonreading level to sixth grade. Oral reading passages and accompanying comprehension questions are included, as well as paragraphs for silent reading and listening comprehension. Specific subtests deal with oral reading, silent reading, listening comprehension, and word recognition and word analysis. Additional subtests are included in listening vocabulary, sounds in isolation, spelling, visual memory of words, identifying sounds in words, and prereading phonics abilities. The battery assesses a wide variety of specific skills and may take approximately an hour to administer. In addition to providing a profile of grade-level scores, the test includes a checklist of instructional needs on which the teacher can note particular reading difficulties. Also, the test manual contains helpful information concerning corrective instruction and program planning. Bond et al. (1979) report that this test has several distinct advantages:

   a. The directions are complete and clear.

b. It can be administered in a reasonable time period.

c. The checklist of errors is one of the most complete of its kind.

3. *Gates-McKillop-Horowitz Reading Diagnostic Tests* (Gates, McKillop, & Horowitz, 1981). This comprehensive diagnostic reading battery is a revision of the *Gates-McKillop Reading Diagnostic Tests* (Gates & McKillop, 1962) that assesses a wide range of word analysis skills. It is designed to be individually administered by the classroom teacher to children in grades 1 through 6. The subtest areas include oral reading (with error analysis), flash presentation of words, untimed presentation of words, knowledge of word parts, recognition of visual forms representing sounds, auditory blending, auditory discrimination, and written expression. If given in its entirety, the test is quite lengthy; however, the teacher may choose to administer only certain subtests, depending on the child's age and level of skill development. The Gates-McKillop-Horowitz lacks a subtest assessing reading comprehension, but the battery can be quite useful when used with a child experiencing severe difficulties in word analysis. Bond et al. (1979) note that the Gates-McKillop is one of the most complete diagnostic tests available, and it is helpful with students whose reading difficulties span a wide degree of severity. However, Salvia and Ysseldyke (1988) report that scores obtained on the Gates-McKillop-Horowitz are subject to misinterpretation, and the value of the test is limited to its clinical use.

4. *Stanford Diagnostic Reading Test* (Karlsen & Gardner, 1984). This group test is both norm-referenced and criterion-referenced. It measures specific reading skills in vocabulary (auditory vocabulary, word meaning, word parts); decoding (auditory discrimination, phonetic analysis, structural analysis);

comprehension (word reading, reading comprehension—literal and inferential); and rate (reading rate, fast reading, scanning, and skimming). There are four overlapping levels, identified by color, which may be used with students in grades 1 through 12. Several subtests of the four skill areas are not included at all four levels; for example, word reading is included only in the first level, and rate is assessed in the last two levels. Two forms are available at each level. In addition to yielding percentile ranks, stanines, grade equivalents, and scaled scores, the test results can be used to identify strengths and weaknesses in specific reading skills. Bond et al. (1979) note that this test is effective in diagnosing reading disability cases from grade 3 to college level. The directions are clear, and remedial suggestions are provided.

5. *Woodcock Reading Mastery Tests—Revised* (Woodcock, 1987). This battery of tests yields cluster scores (in readiness, basic skills, and comprehension) and a total reading score, as well as derived scores (age- and grade-based percentile ranks and standard scores, age and grade equivalents) in six subtest areas: *visual-auditory learning*—the student translates sequences of rebuses (unfamiliar visual symbols) into sentences; *letter identification*—the student names 51 various upper- and lowercase manuscript and cursive letters of the alphabet; *word identification*—the student names isolated words sequenced in difficulty; *word attack*—the student identifies nonsense words; *word comprehension*—the student gives antonyms and synonyms, and completes analogy formats that measure knowledge of word meaning; and *passage comprehension*—the student silently reads passages and supplies an appropriate word for each blank space. The test contains two forms (one of which omits visual-

auditory learning and letter identification) and is designed to be individually administered to students in kindergarten through adult age. Norm-referenced scores are yielded, and a microcomputer scoring program can be used to assist the examiner in computing scores and providing score printouts.

Tests of specific skills. Some diagnostic reading tests are designed to measure the student's ability in a specific skill area. Five selected tests of specific reading skills are discussed.

1. *Botel Reading Inventory* (Botel, 1978). Subtests on word recognition and word opposites (in reading or listening) yield independent (free reading), instructional, and frustration reading levels; a phonics mastery test provides an estimate of the child's phonics proficiency. The test may be used with students in grades 1 through junior high school and takes approximately 30 minutes to administer. Only the subtest on word recognition requires individual rather than group administration.

2. *Doren Diagnostic Reading Test of Word Recognition Skills* (Doren, 1973). This group test assesses word recognition skills within the primary and intermediate range. The following skill areas are included: letter recognition, beginning sounds, whole-word recognition, words within words, speech consonants, ending sounds, blending, rhyming, vowels, discriminate guessing, spelling, and sight words. The manual contains remedial activities for each of the skills tested.

3. *Gilmore Oral Reading Test* (Gilmore & Gilmore, 1968). Ten paragraphs of increasing difficulty are used to assess the oral reading performance of students in grades 1 through 8. As the student orally reads each passage, the teacher records reading errors (such as substitutions, mispronunciations,

insertions, hesitations, repetitions, omissions) as well as reading time. Then the student is asked to respond to several comprehension questions. When 10 or more oral reading errors are made on one paragraph, testing is stopped. Grade-level scores and performance ratings (poor–superior) are provided for accuracy and comprehension; rate of reading is scored as slow, average, or fast. The test can be individually administered in approximately 20 minutes.

4. *Gray Oral Reading Test—Revised* (Wiederholt & Bryant, 1986). This individually administered test for students in grades 1 through 12 is comprised of two forms, each of which contains 13 developmentally sequenced passages with five comprehension questions. As the student reads aloud, the teacher notes reading characteristics, errors, and time elapsed in reading each paragraph. Comprehension questions are asked after each paragraph is read. A system for performing a miscue analysis of reader performance yields information in four areas: meaning similarity, function similarity, graphic/phonemic similarity, and self-correction.

5. *Test of Reading Comprehension* (Brown, Hammill, & Wiederholt, 1986). Reading comprehension of students in grades 2 through 12 is assessed by this test, which can be administered to either groups or individuals. Eight subtests are divided into the two major areas of general comprehension core and diagnostic supplements. The general comprehension core subtests include general vocabulary, syntactic similarities, and paragraph reading. The subtests pertaining to diagnostic supplements are mathematics vocabulary, social studies vocabulary, science vocabulary, reading the directions of schoolwork, and sentence sequencing. Thus, the test measures both general reading comprehension and spe-

cific knowledge needed to read in three content areas. Scaled scores, grade equivalents, and reading comprehension quotients are provided.

Criterion-Referenced Tests

Whereas norm-referenced tests compare a child's performance to the scores of others, criterion-referenced tests describe performance according to fixed criteria. In the latter method, the teacher finds out what skills the student has learned, what she is learning now, and what skills still must be taught. Teachers use criterion-referenced reading tests to determine if the student has mastered specific reading instructional objectives, such as recognition of *ed* endings or use of the *ch* consonant digraph. Test items are presented in a hierarchy so that the student is assessed within a sequence of reading skills. If her performance on each skill does not reach the established criterion of success (for example, 95% level of proficiency), the teacher provides instruction specifically for that skill. When the student's performance demonstrates mastery of a skill according to the determined criterion, she progresses to the next skill in the sequence. Thus, criterion-referenced tests focus on the student's ability to master specific skills, and the assessment relates to curricular content and instructional objectives. The student's progress is determined by comparing her current performance with her previous performance. Six criterion-referenced reading assessment measures are discussed.

1. *Brigance Diagnostic Inventory of Basic Skills* (Brigance, 1977). This inventory contains criterion-referenced tests for academic skills from kindergarten through grade 6. It is primarily used to establish educational objectives and monitor progress toward these objectives. Tests related to reading skills are

included in the following areas: *word recognition* (six skill sequences such as basic sight vocabulary, abbreviations, and contractions), *reading* (including comprehension level and oral reading level), *word analysis* (19 skill sequences such as short and long vowel sounds, digraphs and diphthongs, suffixes, and prefixes), and *vocabulary* (five skill sequences such as context clues, antonyms, and homonyms). Student record books show at each testing the point of competence to which the student has progressed. Also, a class record book is provided for the teacher to keep a record of each student's progress. The *Brigance Diagnostic Comprehensive Inventory of Basic Skills* (Brigance, 1982), which is for students in kindergarten through ninth grade, retains the basic components of the *Inventory of Basic Skills* and includes additional skill sequences and a reading comprehension section. In addition, the *Brigance Diagnostic Inventory of Essential Skills* (Brigance, 1980), designed for students in grades 6 through 12, measures minimal competencies in word recognition, oral reading, functional word recognition, word analysis, and reading comprehension.

2. *Classroom Learning Screening Manual* (Koenig & Kunzelmann, 1980). This precision teaching assessment device measures performance according to frequency—a count of behavior during a fixed period of time. Each student's performance is compared to proficiency levels (standards) of performance to determine which students should have further diagnostic work and attention. Probes are included on saying words for one minute.

3. *Fountain Valley Teacher Support System in Reading* (1971). A series of 77 self-scoring, criterion-referenced tests are used to measure specific reading objectives in five areas: phonetic analysis, structural analysis,

vocabulary development, comprehension, and study skills. The tests are color-coded and sequenced according to difficulty. The results of testing indicate the student's strengths and weaknesses in the developmental sequence of reading. Also, continuous pupil profiles enable the teacher to monitor individual progress.

4. *Multilevel Academic Skills Inventory* (Howell, Zucker, & Morehead, 1982). This assessment instrument, designed for students in grades 1 through 8, includes more than 300 criterion-referenced objectives. It includes specific reading skills in decoding, comprehension, and vocabulary. Three levels of assessment are provided: survey tests that sample a wide range of key objectives, placement tests that sample a cluster of closely related skills within a content area, and specific level tests that measure mastery of one specific subskill. In addition, accuracy criteria (number correct) and mastery criteria (accuracy plus speed) are included.

5. *Regional Resource Center Diagnostic Reading Inventory* (1971). This reading test uses rate of correct and incorrect responses from one-minute behavior samples. Each subtest consists of a probe sheet which is used for the one-minute timings to assess a specific reading skill. The following skill areas are assessed in the *Diagnostic Reading Inventory: consonant sounds*—the student orally sounds consonants while pointing to the letter; *vowel sounds*—the student orally sounds long and short vowels while pointing to the letter; *blending I*—the student reads three-letter phonically regular nonsense words; *consonant teams*—the student reads consonant teams in nonsense words; *irregular words*—the student reads irregular words; *blending II*—the student reads nonsense words containing blends

such as digraphs and diphthongs; *"Van's Cave"*—the student orally reads a story from a primer; *classroom reader*—the student orally reads from a classroom reader. The manual recommends that the teacher administer each subtest approximately five times over a period of several days. (Several samples provide more reliable results than a single sample.)

Table 10.2 contains a sample record sheet for the *Diagnostic Reading Inventory*. The record sheet readily displays the student's strengths and weaknesses in the subtest areas. In the example, Greg needs immediate instruction in the areas of simple blending and sight words. Also, the rate of saying vowel and consonant sounds needs to be increased. Thus, through the use of probes, the student's average performance is compared to minimum proficiency levels to indicate mastery of specific reading skills.

6. *Wisconsin Tests of Reading Skill Development* (Kamm, Miles, Van Blaricom, Harris, & Stewart, 1972). A total of 38 short tests at four levels of difficulty are used to assess word-attack skills commonly taught in kindergarten through third grade. The student demonstrates mastery of a specific skill by responding correctly to at least 80% of the items on any given test. Also, comprehension tests are available in five levels of difficulty corresponding to those skills used in kindergarten through sixth grade. The tests assess the comprehension skills of establishing cause-and-effect relationships, using context clues to derive word meanings, drawing conclusions, and judging relevance. The results of testing indicate which skills have not yet been mastered, and the results can be used to plan instruction as well as monitor student progress.

TABLE 10.2
Regional Resource Center Diagnostic Reading Inventory record sheet.

Name __Greg__ Teacher __Jones__

Grade __4__ School __Piney Circle__

weekend

SUBTEST NAME	TIME	DAY 1 Date ___ standard X non-stand ___ admin. by: ___		DAY 2 Date ___ standard X non-stand ___ admin. by: ___		DAY 3 Date ___ standard X non-stand ___ admin. by: ___		DAY 4 Date ___ standard X non-stand ___ admin. by: ___		Suggested Rates for Determining Proficiency[a]	
		correct	error	correct	error	correct	error	correct	error	correct	error
Consonant Sounds	1 min.	18	0	25	0	18	0	35	0	60–80	2 or less
Vowel Sounds	30 sec.	14	0	12	4	11	1	15	3	30–40	2 or less
Blending I	1 min.	6	6	5	2	4	10	9	8	90–100	2 or less
Con. Teams	30 sec.	6	4	7	4	7	4	8	3	45–50	1 or less
Irreg. Words	1 min.	8	3	15	3	21	3	17	9	80–100	0
Blending II	1 min.	2	4	2	2	b				80–100	2 or less
Oral Reading "Van's Cave"	1 min.	9	7	18	4	26	6	28	11	100–120	2 or less
School Book:	1 min.	21	1	18	6	24	7	28	5	100–120	2 or less

Title: __"Tony's Adventure"__ Page __48__ Grade Level __2.1__

Publisher __Science Research Associates__ Basal / (Regular) (circle one)

[a] Based on Haughton's (1972) report of research by Starlin.

[b] Blank boxes show that rate is so low, further testing is not warranted.

Source: Adapted from *Regional Resource Center Diagnostic Inventories.* Eugene, OR: University of Oregon. The material is in the public domain.

INFORMAL ASSESSMENT

Informal assessment involves examining the student's daily work or administering teacher-constructed tests. The teacher can informally assess any measurable reading skill by presenting the student with a task and recording her responses. In addition to evaluating the student's ability in various reading tasks, the teacher can determine specific strengths and weaknesses by analyzing reading errors. Informal procedures usually offer two advantages: they require less time to administer than formal tests, and they can be used with classroom materials during regular instruction periods (Kirk et al., 1978).

Teacher Observations

An experienced teacher can make careful, day-to-day observations to obtain diagnostic information. The teacher has many opportunities to observe and informally assess the student's reading skills. The teacher can obtain information about the student's reading interests and attitudes, as well as her word analysis and comprehension skills, by conducting observation during oral reading activities, seatwork assignments, instructional sessions, testing sessions, and recreational reading periods. Several informal observations over an extended period of time also can confirm or supplement the results of formal assessment tests.

When observing the student's performance on various reading tasks, the teacher should keep the following questions in mind:

1. What is the student's attitude toward reading?
2. What specific reading interest does the student have?
3. Is the student making progress in reading?
4. What strengths and weaknesses in reading does the student exhibit?
5. During oral reading, does the student read word by word or with fluency?
6. What kinds of errors does the student make consistently?
7. What word analysis skills does the student use?
8. Does the student use context clues to recognize words?
9. Does the student have a good sight vocabulary?
10. Does the student appear to pay attention to the meaning of the material as she reads?

Strang (1969) notes that teacher observations should be recorded on a checklist of reading skills and behaviors. Many commercial tests include teacher observation checklists. A reading diagnosis checklist devised by Ekwall (1989) is presented in Table 10.3. This checklist consists of 30 reading abilities or related abilities; the teacher is to check each ability three times. Thus, specific strengths and weaknesses are noted, and progress is charted.

Teacher observation is continuous and permeates all types of informal assessment. This section presents the following informal assessment techniques: (a) graded word recognition lists, (b) Informal Reading Inventory, (c) reading miscue analysis, (d) cloze procedure, and (e) teacher-made tests.

Graded Word Lists

Graded word lists frequently are used to examine the student's word recognition skills. Word lists may be useful in informal diagnosis for three purposes: (a) to indicate the student's sight vocabulary, (b) to estimate the level at which the student can read with fluency and have little difficulty with word attack, and (c) to reveal basic weaknesses in word analysis skills as the student attacks unknown words (Otto & Smith, 1980).

TABLE 10.3
Reading diagnosis checklist.

NAME _____   TEACHER _____

GRADE _____   SCHOOL _____

#	1st Check	2nd Check	3rd Check	Item	Category
1				Word-by-word reading	Oral Reading
2				Incorrect phrasing	
3				Poor pronunciation	
4				Omissions	
5				Repetitions	
6				Inversions or reversals	
7				Insertions	
8				Substitutions	
9				Basic sight words not known	
10				Sight vocabulary not up to grade level	
11				Guesses at words	
12				Consonant sounds not known	
13				Vowel sounds not known	
14				Vowel pairs and/or consonant clusters not known (digraphs, diphthongs, blends)	
15				Lacks desirable structural analysis (Morphology)	
16				Unable to use context clues	
17				Contractions not known	
18				Comprehension inadequate	Oral Silent
19				Vocabulary inadequate	
20				Unaided recall scanty	Study Skills
21				Response poorly organized	
22				Unable to locate information	
23				Inability to skim	
24				Inability to adjust rate to difficulty of material	
25				Low rate of speed	
26				High rate at expense of accuracy	
27				Voicing-lip movement	Other Abilities
28				Lacks knowledge of the alphabet	
29				Written recall limited by spelling ability	
30				Undeveloped dictionary skills	

D—Difficulty recognized
P—Pupil progressing
N—No longer has difficulty

The items listed above represent the most common difficulties encountered by pupils in the reading program. Following each numbered item are spaces for notation of that specific difficulty. This may be done at intervals of several months. One might use a check to indicate difficulty recognized or the following letters to represent an even more accurate appraisal:

The teacher can develop word lists by randomly selecting 20 to 25 words for each level from the glossaries of graded basal readers. To obtain a random sample of 25 words for each level, the teacher would divide the total number of words for each level by 25. For example, 250 total words divided by 25 would mean that every 10th word is included in the random sample for that level. The teacher should check to make sure the words represent various phonics skills (such as consonant and vowel sounds in different positions, consonant blends, digraphs). The words also should include prefixes, suffixes, and compound words. Sample graded word lists for primer through sixth-grade level are presented in Table 10.4. The words for each grade level can be typed on separate cards for the student to read. The teacher should have all the words listed on one sheet of paper. Another method would be to have the student's word list on a sheet of paper and present each word through a window with the use of a tachistoscope made from oaktag or strips cut from manila folders.

Cohen and Plaskon (1980) note that word lists may be presented in two ways. A timed flash exposure (one second) may be given to assess the student's instant recognition or sight-word vocabulary. Second, words the student was unable to recognize at first may be presented in an untimed manner to test the student's ability to apply word-attack skills to unknown words. During the second exposure the teacher may obtain additional information by giving prompts, such as providing an initial sound or covering part of the word.

The teacher can determine a word recognition grade-level score—indicating the student's ability to identify words—by untimed presentation of graded word lists. In general, the level at which the student misses none or only one word is her *independent* reading level. The *instructional* level is indicated when the student

identifies two words incorrectly, and when three or more words are missed, the student has reached her *frustration* reading level. As well as using word lists to determine grade-level placement in word recognition, the teacher should note specific errors in word attack. When the student mispronounces a word, the teacher should write down the mispronunciation in order to analyze the student's method of word attack. Also, the teacher should look for error patterns. For example, the student may recognize only initial consonant sounds and may guess at the remainder of the word, or she may not be able to blend individual sounds into whole words. The student who reads *month* as "mouth" or *long* as "large" may be responding to configuration cues; a response of a completely dissimilar word, such as "after" for *field,* may indicate that the student lacks phonetic word-attack skills. In addition, the teacher should note the student's skill in structural analysis—for example, knowledge of prefixes, roots, and endings.

In addition to graded word lists devised by the teacher, published word lists are available, such as those by Dolch (1955), Durrell (1956), and Fry (1980). The widely used Dolch list includes 220 sight words that make up 50 to 65% of the words the student encounters in elementary school basal readers. The Dolch list was examined by D. D. Johnson (1971) in terms of current word usage. Johnson notes that 82 Dolch words are not among the 220 most frequent words in the Kucera-Francis list, which is an analysis of present-day American English. Table 10.5 presents the 220 most frequent words in the Kucera-Francis list.

Also, the Mann-Suiter Developmental Reading Inventory contains a word recognition section and a paragraph reading section (Mann, Suiter, & McClung, 1979). The Word Recognition Inventory contains 10 word lists (20 words each) of preprimer through eighth-grade level. The Paragraph Reading Inventory

TABLE 10.4
Graded word lists.

Primer	First	Second	Third	Fourth	Fifth	Sixth
not	kind	mile	beginning	worm	abandon	seventeen
funny	rocket	fair	thankful	afford	zigzag	annoy
book	behind	ago	written	player	terrific	dwindle
thank	our	need	reason	scientific	terrify	rival
good	men	fourth	bent	meek	plantation	hesitation
into	met	lazy	patient	rodeo	loaf	navigator
know	wish	field	manage	festival	hike	gorge
your	told	taken	arithmetic	hillside	relative	burglar
come	after	wolf	burst	coward	available	construction
help	ready	part	bush	boom	grief	exploration
man	barn	save	gingerbread	booth	physical	technical
now	next	hide	tremble	freeze	commander	spice
show	cat	high	planet	protest	error	spike
want	hold	bad	struggle	nervous	woodcutter	prevail
did	story	love	museum	sparrow	submarine	memorial
have	turtle	brave	grin	level	ignore	initiation
little	give	reach	ill	underground	disappointed	undergrowth
cake	cry	song	alarm	oxen	wrestle	ladle
home	fight	cup	cool	eighty	vehicle	walnut
soon	please	trunk	engine	shouldn't	international	tributary

Source: From *Analytical Reading Inventory* (pp. 58–60), 4th ed., by M. L. Woods and A. J. Moe, 1989, Columbus, OH: Merrill. Copyright 1989 by Merrill Publishing Company. Reprinted by permission.

TABLE 10.5
Kucera-Francis list of basic sight words.

1. the	45. when	89. many	133. know	177. don't
2. of	46. who	90. before	134. while	178. does
3. and	47. will	91. must	135. last	179. got
4. to	48. more	92. through	136. might	180. united
5. a	49. no	93. back	137. us	181. left
6. in	50. if	94. years	138. great	182. number
7. that	51. out	95. where	139. old	183. course
8. is	52. so	96. much	140. year	184. war
9. was	53. said	97. your	141. off	185. until
10. he	54. what	98. may	142. come	186. always
11. for	55. up	99. well	143. since	187. away
12. it	56. its	100. down	144. against	188. something
13. with	57. about	101. should	145. go	189. fact
14. as	58. into	102. because	146. came	190. through
15. his	59. than	103. each	147. right	191. water
16. on	60. them	104. just	148. used	192. less
17. be	61. can	105. those	149. take	193. public
18. at	62. only	106. people	150. three	194. put
19. by	63. other	107. Mr.	151. states	195. thing
20. I	64. new	108. how	152. himself	196. almost
21. this	65. some	109. too	153. few	197. hand
22. had	66. could	110. little	154. house	198. enough
23. not	67. time	111. state	155. use	199. far
24. are	68. these	112. good	156. during	200. took
25. but	69. two	113. very	157. without	201. head
26. from	70. may	114. make	158. again	202. yet
27. or	71. then	115. would	159. place	203. government
28. have	72. do	116. still	160. American	204. system
29. an	73. first	117. own	161. around	205. better
30. they	74. any	118. see	162. however	206. set
31. which	75. my	119. men	163. home	207. told
32. one	76. now	120. work	164. small	208. nothing
33. you	77. such	121. long	165. found	209. night
34. were	78. like	122. get	166. Mrs.	210. end
35. her	79. our	123. here	167. thought	211. why
36. all	80. over	124. between	168. went	212. called
37. she	81. man	125. both	169. say	213. didn't
38. there	82. me	126. life	170. part	214. eyes
39. would	83. even	127. being	171. once	215. find
40. their	84. most	128. under	172. general	216. going
41. we	85. made	129. never	173. high	217. look
42. him	86. after	130. day	174. upon	218. asked
43. been	87. also	131. same	175. school	219. later
44. has	88. did	132. another	176. every	220. knew

Source: From "The Dolch List Reexamined" by D. D. Johnson, 1971, *The Reading Teacher, 24*, 455–456. Copyright 1971 by the International Reading Association. Reprinted by permission.

consists of 12 passages and accompanying comprehension questions for preprimer through eighth-grade level. Using graded word lists to determine word recognition skills is often the first step in administering an Informal Reading Inventory.

Informal Reading Inventory

The Informal Reading Inventory provides information about the student's general reading level. It uses reading passages of increasing difficulty from various graded levels. The teacher can choose selections from a basal reading series the student is unfamiliar with. In general, the passages should consist of approximately 50 words (at preprimer level) to 200 words (at secondary level). The student begins reading passages aloud at a level where she easily handles word-attack and comprehension tasks. She continues reading passages of increasing difficulty until she can no longer do so. As the student reads aloud, the teacher records her errors. The teacher asks three to five questions about each passage to check comprehension skills. Questions of many kinds should be used: recall of facts (who, what, where), inference (why), and vocabulary (general or specific meanings). Kender and Rubenstein (1977) suggest that the student be allowed to reread or inspect the passage before answering comprehension questions; if the student is not allowed to do so, it is possible that *memory* rather than comprehension is being tested. The percentage of words read correctly for each passage is computed by dividing the number of correctly read words by the number of words in the selection. The percentage of comprehension questions answered correctly is determined by dividing the number of correct answers by the number of questions asked.

Through this method the teacher can estimate the student's reading ability at three lev-els: independent, instructional, and frustration (Johnson & Kress, 1965). At the independent reading level, the student can read the graded passage with high accuracy: She recognizes 98 to 100% of the words and answers the comprehension questions with 90 to 100% accuracy. The reading is fluent and natural, and there is no finger pointing or hesitation. At this level, the teacher can hand out supplementary materials for independent or enjoyment reading. The level at which the student needs some help is the instructional reading level. The student can recognize 95% of the words and comprehends approximately 75% of the material. She reads in a generally relaxed manner, and the material is challenging but not too difficult. The teacher should provide directed reading instruction at this level. At the frustration reading level, the student reads with considerable difficulty. Her word recognition is 90% or less, and her comprehension score is 50% or less. The student shows signs of tension and makes many errors or reversals. Reading material at this level cannot be used for instruction.

According to Carnine and Silbert (1979), one of the major purposes of the Informal Reading Inventory is to help the teacher place the student at her instructional level in a basal series. Lovitt and Hansen (1976) also offer guidelines in placing a student in a basal series: a correct reading rate of 45 to 65 words per minute with eight or fewer errors and 50 to 75% comprehension.

In addition to using the Informal Reading Inventory to record the student's oral reading performance pertaining to word recognition and comprehension, the teacher also notes various types of reading errors. On her copy of the reading material, the teacher should record errors such as omitting words or parts of words, inserting or substituting words, reversing a word or its letters, and repeating words. It is helpful to develop a system for marking oral reading errors. Table 10.6 presents oral reading errors and a corresponding set of appropriate marks.

The Informal Reading Inventory also can be used to assess silent reading. Whereas in oral reading the focus is on word-attack skills, in silent reading the focus is on comprehension. The student silently reads each passage and responds to comprehension questions. The percentage of correct responses indicates the student's independent (90–100%), instructional (75%), or frustration (50%) silent reading level. While the student reads silently, the teacher can note whispering, lip movements, finger pointing, facial grimaces, and fidgeting. Also, the student may have difficulties such as low rate, high rate at the expense of understanding, poorly organized recall, or inaccurate recall. The teacher can compare the student's oral and silent reading performances to determine if there is a great difference.

In addition, the material in the Informal Reading Inventory may be read to the student to determine her listening or hearing capacity level. This is the highest level at which the student can comprehend 75% of the material read to her. This provides an estimate of the student's reading potential or what her level would be if she had no problems with the mechanics of reading.

Several published Informal Reading Inventories are available. The *Classroom Reading Inventory* (Silvaroli, 1982) consists of graded word lists and graded oral paragraphs from preprimer to sixth-grade level. A spelling survey is also included for first- to seventh-grade level. The oral reading test is accompanied by comprehension questions, and results are given in terms of instructional levels. Thus, the teacher assesses the student's word recognition, word analysis, and comprehension skills for instructional purposes. The *Analytical Reading Inventory* (Woods & Moe, 1989) also contains graded word lists and graded passages. There are three equivalent forms, and the seven word lists for each form are graded from primer to sixth-grade level. The 10 passages are from primer to ninth-grade level. The inventory is designed to identify (a) the student's level of word recognition, (b) strengths and weaknesses in word-attack and comprehension skills, (c) levels of reading achievement (independent, instructional, frustration), and (d) the potential for reading growth. Student record summary sheets, error analysis summary sheets, and a class record summary sheet also are included. A sample Informal Reading Inventory for the second-grade level is included in Table 10.7.

Although it is time-consuming to use Informal Reading Inventories because they are individually administered, they are widely used. They help the teacher to plan needed corrective instruction and to provide the student with reading materials suited to her abilities. The Informal Reading Inventory can be administered from time to time to check the student's reading progress.

Reading Miscue Analysis

Reading miscue analysis, based on the work of K. S. Goodman (1969, 1973), is a method of analyzing the student's oral reading strategies. Although comprehension is considered in an Informal Reading Inventory, comprehension is the *major* consideration in reading miscue analysis. Emphasis is placed on the *nature* of the reading errors (miscues) rather than the number of errors made. Miscues can be classified according to the following categories:

1. *Semantic*—the miscue is similar in meaning to the text word. Some miscues indicate that the student comprehends the passage; thus, the simple substitution of a word is not important (e.g., substitution of *dad* for *father*).

TABLE 10.6
Oral reading errors and marking system.

Type of Error	Marking System	Example
Omissions	Circle the word or parts of word omitted.	The boy went in(to) the (burning) building.
Insertions	Use a caret to mark the place of insertion and write the added word or letter/s.	The children sat ^down^ at the table to eat lunch^es^.
Substitutions	Cross out the word and write the substituted word above it.	Now I ~~recognize~~ realize your name.
Reversals	For letter reversals within a word, cross out the word and write the reversal word above it.	The ~~top~~ pot is lost.
	For reversals of words, draw a curved line going over, between, and under the reversed words.	Mary looked often at the clock.
Repetitions	Draw a wavy line under the words which are repeated.	Everyone was cheering for me because I was a baseball hero.
Mispronunciations	Write the mispronounced word (indicating the student's pronunciation) over the correct word.	It was an oc-top-us octopus.
Hesitations	Use a slash to indicate improper hesitation.	The /judge asked the jury /to leave the courtroom.
Aided Words	Underline the word pronounced for the student.	The scared cat began to tremble.
Unobserved punctuation marks	Cross out the punctuation mark the student continued to read through.	The puppy saw the man✗ He barked and barked.
Self-corrected errors	Write **sc** over the error notation.	This ~~month~~ mouth (sc) is November.

Example of a Marked Passage

The three boys were (very) tired from their long /journey✗ Now they had to swim across a river. John plunged into the icy ^cold^ water and started (to swim). He swam slowly but managed to reach the other side of the ~~wide~~ wet river.

TABLE 10.7
Sample informal reading inventory.

Level 2 (118 words)

Student's Name:_____

Date:_____

Motivation Statement: Imagine how you would feel if you were up to bat and this was your team's last chance to win the game! Please read this story.

Passage:

   Whiz! The baseball went right by me, and I struck at the air!

   "Strike one," called the man. I could feel my legs begin to shake!

   Whiz! The ball went by me again, and I began to feel bad. "Strike two," screamed the man.

   I held the bat back because this time I would kill the ball! I would hit it right out of the park! I was so scared that I bit down on my lip. My knees shook and my hands grew wet.

   Swish! The ball came right over the plate. Crack! I hit it a good one! Then I ran like the wind. Everyone was yelling for me because I was now a baseball star!

Comprehension Questions and Possible Answers:

1. What is this story about?
   (*Main idea*—A baseball game, someone who gets two strikes and finally gets a hit, etc.)
2. After the second strike, what did the batter plan to do?
   (*Factual*—Hit the ball right out of the park)
3. Who is the "man" in this story who called the strikes?
   (*Inferential*—The umpire)
4. In this story, what was meant when the batter said, "I would kill the ball"?
   (*Terminology*—Hit it very hard)
5. Why was the last pitch a good one?
   (*Cause and effect*—Because it went right over the plate)
6. What did the batter do after the last pitch?
   (*Cause and effect*—The batter hit it a good one and ran like the wind.)

Error Count:

Omissions	_____	Aided words	_____
Insertions	_____	Repetitions	_____
Substitutions	_____	Reversals	_____

Scoring Guide:

Word Recognition Errors		Comprehension Errors	
Independent	1	Independent	0
Instructional	6	Instructional	1-2
Frustration	12+	Frustration	3+

Source: From *Analytical Reading Inventory* (p. 63), 4th ed., by M. L. Woods and A. J. Moe, 1989, Columbus, OH: Merrill. Copyright 1989 by Merrill Publishing Company. Adapted by permission.

2. *Syntactic*—the miscue is the same part of speech as the text word. Some miscues show that the student fails to comprehend the meaning, but she at least substitutes a word that makes grammatical sense.
3. *Graphic*—the miscue is similar to the sound/symbol relationship for the initial, medial, or final portion of the text word (e.g., *find* for *found*). Some miscues indicate the student's knowledge of phoneme—grapheme relationships.

It must be determined whether each miscue changed or interfered with the meaning of the information conveyed in the sentence or phrase in which it occurred. Basically, the seriousness of miscues depends on whether they form a consistent pattern that alters the meaning of the written passage and thus affects the student's comprehension.

   Some authorities feel the miscue inventory is fine for research but cumbersome for the classroom teacher (Fry, 1977). Some oral mistakes reveal that the student is reading with meaning (K. S. Goodman, 1969, 1973). These errors are not too serious if one believes that the purpose of reading is understanding. Fry suggests that the three types of linguistic errors—semantic, syntactic, and sound–symbol—can be very useful to the classroom teacher in informal observation of any oral reading. For the clinician who wants to pursue a systematic diagnosis of meaning-clue deficiencies, the *Reading Miscue Inventory* by Y. M. Goodman and Burke (1972) is very helpful. Each oral reading miscue is scored according to nine categories: dialect, intonation shift, graphic similarity, sound similarity, grammatical function, correction, grammatical acceptability, semantic acceptability, and meaning change. Also, a short form of the *Reading Miscue Inventory* is available (Burke, 1976).

Cloze Procedure

The cloze procedure can be used as an informal method to measure reading levels and comprehension. The cloze technique can estimate the difficulty the student will have with a specific reading material and thus help determine whether a book is appropriate (Clary, 1976; Karlin, 1973). The teacher presents a reading passage of approximately 250 words to the student. The first sentence is typed completely, but beginning with the second sentence every fifth word is omitted and replaced with a blank. The blanks should be of uniform length. The remainder of the selection is typed as it appears in text. The student reads the passage and fills in the missing words or synonyms. Clary suggests providing the student with an answer key of the omitted words to select from. Karlin suggests deleting only every 10th word. Also, other appropriate words may be omitted instead of every fifth word, in order to avoid the continuous omission of articles or proper names. An example of the cloze procedure for a reading passage is presented in Table 10.8.

A reading passage using the cloze procedure can be administered either individually or in groups. Reading levels are determined by changing the number of correct responses to percentages. Rankin and Culhane (1969) suggest the following scoring of cloze passages: (a) *independent reading level*—61% or more correct responses, (b) *instructional reading level*—41 to 60% correct responses, and (c) *frustration reading level*—40% or fewer correct responses. For additional information the teacher should attempt to analyze why the student makes certain errors. Hafner (1965) suggests that cloze errors may be examined according to linguistic components, cognitive types, and reasoning skills.

Teacher-Made Tests

The teacher can devise an informal test to obtain a quick estimate of a specific skill. Probe sheets can be developed to assess a particular reading objective, such as consonant sounds, vowel sounds, blends, compound words, and so on. A sample probe sheet to assess the student's ability to blend consonant-vowel-consonant sounds is presented in Table 10.9. After the probe is administered for a one-minute period and the correct and incorrect responses are tallied, the student's reading rate can be compared with the suggested proficiency reading rates (see Table 10.10).

Teacher-made tests can be constructed by using items in standardized tests and workbook exercises as guides. A variety of items that measure a specific skill can be used—for example, multiple-choice, true–false, completion, and matching. The teacher should be careful to include enough items to sample the skill adequately. Heilman (1985) provides an excellent informal word recognition skills test (see Table 10.11) which a teacher may adapt or use in informal assessment. It assesses both phonics and structural analysis skills. In addition, short-form word analysis tests can be devised to measure specific skills. Also, items can be developed to assess specific comprehension skills, such as main idea, noting de-

TABLE 10.8
Reading selection illustrating the cloze procedure.

James Cornish lay wounded on the saloon floor! "He's been stabbed in ___1___ chest!" shouted one horrified ___2___. "Someone get him to ___3___ hospital!" another shouted.

It ___4___ a hot and humid ___5___ in Chicago in 1893. ___6___ arrived at the hospital ___7___ a one-inch knife ___8___ in his chest, dangerously ___9___ his heart. Dr. Daniel ___10___ Williams was called in ___11___ operate.

In those days ___12___ blood transfusions and antibiotics ___13___ unknown, chest surgery was ___14___ attempted since it meant ___15___ high risk of death. ___16___ Dr. Williams began to ___17___, he found that the ___18___ wound had cut the ___19___ and the sac around ___20___ heart. Dr. Williams then ___21___ history by becoming ___22___ first surgeon to successfully ___23___ on the human heart. ___24___ Williams did not release ___25___ information for three and ___26___ half years. When he ___27___, the newspaper headline read, "___28___ Up His Heart," and ___29___ news became known to ___30___ entire world. Not only ___31___ Cornish been discharged from ___32___ hospital a well man, ___33___ he lived fifty years ___34___ his surgery. Cornish even ___35___ the surgeon who had ___36___ his life.

Correct Answers:

1. the	13. were	25. this
2. bystander	14. rarely	26. a
3. a	15. a	27. did
4. was	16. As	28. Sewed
5. day	17. operate	29. the
6. Cornish	18. stab	30. the
7. with	19. heart	31. had
8. wound	20. the	32. the
9. near	21. made	33. but
10. Hale	22. the	34. after
11. to	23. operate	35. outlived
12. when	24. Dr.	36. saved

Source: From *Analytical Reading Inventory* (p. 123), 4th ed., by M. L. Woods and A. J. Moe, 1989, Columbus, OH: Merrill. Copyright 1989 by Merrill Publishing Company. Adapted by permission.

TABLE 10.9
Probe sheet for blending consonant-vowel-consonant sounds.

luv	had	mok	hob	cuz
lit	def	cak	met	roc
nom	vig	pit	tik	fam
cum	zot	wet	bag	pod
fif	lid	hat	get	won
pik	soc	jox	vic	sut
sas	far	kah	par	gan
teg	tem	mez	zix	zec
pub	hun	nod	wol	wap
sel	top	nip	ris	dit

Name: _____

Time: _____

Number Correct: _____

Number Incorrect: _____

Comments: _____

tails, and cause-and-effect relationships. Selected items for assessing the short *a* vowel sound are presented in Table 10.12. When the student passes the informal test, the teacher can assume the student has mastered the objective and is ready to progress to another skill. Reading scope and sequence skills lists, such as the one included in Appendix A, are helpful in determining the order of skill assessment and instruction. Finally, teacher-made tests often deal with reading skills the student must use daily. In addition, they provide a measure of student progress over a specific period of time.

TABLE 10.10
Proficiency rates for reading skills.

I. Grade Level Specified

	Say Isolated Sounds (K–3)		Say Words in List (2–4)		(5–6)		(Adult)		Say Words in Text (1–3)		(4–6)		(Adult)	
	Cor.	Err.	Cor.	Err.	Cor.	Err.	Cor.	Err.	Cor.	Err.	Cor.	Err.	Cor.	Err.
Koenig & Kunzelmann (1980)			140	0	120–130	0								
Starlin & Starlin (1973)			100–126 Phonetic words	0	138–148	0	198	0	50–70	2	100–200	2	100–200	2
			90–128 Irregular words	0	134–150	0	198	0	120–132	0	156–180	0	252	0
Wolking (1973) High Achievers	36–52	0–4												
Range:			90–140	0	120–150	0								
Mode:			100–126	0	130+	0								
Median:			115	0	136	0								

II. Grade Level Not Specified

	Say Isolated Sounds		Say Words in List		Say Words in Text	
	Cor.	Err.	Cor.	Err.	Cor.	Err.
Alper, Nowlin, Lemoine, Perine, & Bettencourt (1974)	80	2	60–80	2	100–120	3
Haughton (1972)	100	0				
Henderson, Clise, & Silverton (1971)	100	0				
Precision Teaching Project * (Montana)	60–80	0	80–100 Sight words	0	200+	0
			60–80 Regular words	0		
Regional Resource Center (1971)	60–80	2	80–100	2	100–120	2
	90–100 Blends	2				
Starlin (1971)	40	2	50+	2	100–200	2
SIMS Program (1978)			50	2	100	2
Range:	40–100	0–4	50–100	0–7	100–200	0–2
Mode:	100	0	80	2	100	2
Median:	70	2	80	2	100+	2

*Note. Available from Skyline Center, 3300 3rd Street N.E., Great Falls, Montana 59404.

TABLE 10.11
Informal word recognition skills test.

Subtest A (pronunciation)
(Initial and final consonant sounds; short vowel sounds)

dad	self	but	ten	lift
fuss	yell	hog	sand	muff
lamp	him	jug	get	nap
puff	web	miss	pond	kill
rag	gum	pill	rob	cob
van	top	big	held	fond

Subtest B (pronunciation)
(Initial consonant blends; long and short vowel sounds)

bring	split	blue	smoke	scream
throat	clay	club	string	trip
please	twist	float	trade	glass
sky	prize	grass	flag	snail
crop	drill	blow	scene	sweet
spray	free	sled	spoon	stay

Subtest C (pronunciation)
(Consonant digraphs [*ch, sh, th, wh, qu, ng, ck*]; consonant blends)

quite	thank	check	shrink	crash
church	block	length	queen	shake
shake	quick	shove	choose	think
splash	strong	thing	truck	deck
whale	chose	which	sprung	hung
fresh	wheat	quench	tenth	quack

Subtest D (pronunciation)
(Compound words; inflectional endings; contractions)

keeping	something	it's	bakery	really
pleased	can't	everybody	likes	finding
stops	quickly	lived	someone	helped
I'll	into	calls	he'll	outside
anyone	tallest	you'll	prettiest	loudest
unlock	happily	going	everything	wasn't

(continued)

TABLE 10.11, *continued*

Subtest E (Sight recognition—pronunciation)
Irregular Spellings
Consonant Irregularities

knee	rough	gnaw	is	you	limb
hour	the	who	phone	knew	whole
was	know	cough	enough	whose	knot

Vowel Irregularities

been	have	once	eye	sure	bird
give	any	do	break	chief	cough
they	to	one	love	could	dead
said	some	head	steak	none	their

Subtest F (syllabication)
(In the blank spaces, write the word in separate syllables.)

candy	can dy	detective	_____
moment	_____	situation	_____
locomotive	_____	tiger	_____
formation	_____	education	_____
summer	_____	slippery	_____
tumble	_____	release	_____

Subtest G (prefixes, suffixes, and syllabication)
(Pronounce each word; divide each word into syllables [see example].)

dis/con/tent/ment	prehistorical	disloyalty
recaptured	disgraceful	indebtedness
incapable	imperfection	previewing
unhappily	expandable	readjustment
exporter	independently	impassable
removable	rearrangement	submerged

Subtest II
(Sustained-reading passage)

Fred and Frank planned to go on a trip to the pond. Frank liked to swim, but Fred was not a swimmer. He chose to hunt frogs and trap crabs. With a shout, the boys were off on their hike to the lake. At first, they tried to walk in the shade. Then both took off their shirts to get a suntan.

Source: From *Phonics in Proper Perspective* (pp. 84–86), 5th ed., by A. W. Heilman, 1985, Columbus, OH: Merrill. Copyright 1985 by Bell & Howell Company. Reprinted by permission.

TABLE 10.12
Teacher-made test items for assessing short *a* vowel sound.

I. The student reads the words with short *a* in initial position.

am	ant	at
an	as	act
and	ask	add

Criterion: 7/9

II. The student reads the words with short *a* in medial position.

ham	pant	bat
can	gas	fact
hand	task	mad

Criterion: 7/9

III. The student selects the word of the pair which contains the short *a* sound.

hat—hate	plan—plane
say—sad	past—pay
ran—ray	stay—sand
tale—land	dad—pale

Criterion: 7/8

IV. The student chooses the word with the short *a* sound to complete the sentence.

The boy had a _____ on his head. (cap, cape)

The _____ was blowing. (sail, flag)

His mother was looking at the _____. (mail, map)

There was a _____ in the sidewalk. (crack, nail)

The father did not _____ his son. (blame, spank)

Criterion 4/5

REFERENCES

Alper, T., Nowlin, L., Lemoine, K., Perine, M., & Bettencourt, B. (1974). The rated assessment of academic skills. *Academic Therapy, 9,* 151–164.

Athey, I. (1976). Reading research in the affective domain. In H. Singer & R.B. Ruddell (Eds.), *Theoretical models and processes of reading.* Newark, DE: International Reading Association.

Bond, G.L., Tinker, M.A., & Wasson, B.B. (1979). *Reading difficulties: Their diagnosis and correction* (4th ed.). Englewood Cliffs, NJ: Prentice-Hall.

Botel, M. (1978). *Botel Reading Inventory.* Chicago: Follet.

Brabner, G., Jr. (1969). Reading skills. In R.M. Smith (Ed.), *Teacher diagnosis of educational difficulties* (pp. 69–94). Columbus, OH: Merrill.

Brigance, A.H. (1977). *Brigance Diagnostic Inventory of Basic Skills.* North Billerica, MA: Curriculum Associates.

Brigance, A.H. (1980). *Brigance Diagnostic Inventory of Essential Skills.* North Billerica, MA: Curriculum Associates.

Brigance, A.H. (1982). *Brigance Diagnostic Comprehensive Inventory of Basic Skills.* North Billerica, MA: Curriculum Associates.

Brown, V.L., Hammill, D.D., & Wiederholt, J.L. (1986). *The Test of Reading Comprehension: A method for assessing the understanding of written language* (Rev. ed.). Austin, TX: Pro-Ed.

Burke, C. (1976). *Reading Miscue Inventory—Short form.* Bloomington, IN: Indiana University.

California Achievement Tests. (1985). Monterey, CA: California Test Bureau/McGraw-Hill.

Carnine, D., & Silbert, J. (1979). *Direct instruction reading.* Columbus, OH: Merrill.

Carrillo, L. (1976). *Teaching reading: A handbook.* New York: St. Martin's.

Clary, L.M. (1976). Tips for testing reading informally in the content areas. *Journal of Reading, 20,* 156–157.

Cohen, S., & Plaskon, S. (1980). *Language arts for the mildly handicapped.* Columbus, OH: Merrill.

Dolch, E.W. (1955). *Methods in reading.* Champaign, IL: Garrard Press.

Doren, M. (1973). *Doren Diagnostic Reading Test of Word Recognition Skills* (2nd ed.). Circle Pines, MN: American Guidance Service.

Dunn, L.M., & Markwardt, F.C., Jr. (1988). *Peabody Individual Achievement Test—Revised.* Circle Pines, MN: American Guidance Service.

Durrell, D.D. (1956). *Improving reading instruction* (2nd ed.). New York: Harcourt Brace Jovanovich.

Durrell, D.D., & Catterson, J.H. (1980). *Durrell Analysis of Reading Difficulty* (3rd ed.). San Antonio, TX: Psychological Corporation.

Ekwall, E.E. (1989). *Locating and correcting reading difficulties* (5th ed.). Columbus, OH: Merrill.

Ekwall, E.E., & Shanker, J.L. (1985). *Teaching reading in the elementary school*. Columbus, OH: Merrill.

Fountain Valley Teacher Support System in Reading. (1971). Huntington Beach, CA: Richard L. Zweig Associates.

Fry, E. (1977). *Elementary reading instruction*. New York: McGraw-Hill.

Fry, E.B. (1980). The new instant word list. *The Reading Teacher, 34,* 284–289.

Gardner, E.F., Rudman, H.C., Karlsen, B., & Merwin, J.C. (1982). *Stanford Achievement Test* (7th ed.). San Antonio, TX: Psychological Corporation.

Gates, A.I. (1937). The necessary mental age for beginning reading. *Elementary School Journal, 37,* 497–508.

Gates, A.I., & McKillop, A.S. (1962). *Gates-McKillop Reading Diagnostic Tests*. New York: Teachers College Press.

Gates, A.I., McKillop, A.S., & Horowitz, R. (1981). *Gates-McKillop-Horowitz Reading Diagnostic Tests*. New York: Teachers College Press.

Gilmore, J.V., & Gilmore, E.C. (1968). *Gilmore Oral Reading Test*. San Antonio, TX: Psychological Corporation.

Goodman, K.S. (1969). Analysis of oral reading miscues: Applied psycholinguistics. *Reading Research Quarterly, 5,* 9–30.

Goodman, K.S. (Ed.). (1973). *Miscue analysis: Applications to reading instruction*. Urbana, IL: National Council of Teachers of English.

Goodman, Y.M., & Burke, C.L. (1972). *Reading Miscue Inventory: Manual of procedure for diagnosis and evaluation*. New York: Macmillan.

Guszak, F.J. (1978). *Diagnostic reading instruction in the elementary school* (2nd ed.). New York: Harper & Row.

Hafner, L. (1965). Importance of cloze. In E.T. Thurstone & L.E. Hafner (Eds.), *The philosophical and social bases for reading: 14th yearbook*. Milwaukee: National Reading Conference.

Haring, N.G., & Bateman, B. (1977). *Teaching the learning disabled child*. Englewood Cliffs, NJ: Prentice-Hall.

Harris, A.J., & Sipay, E.R. (1980). *How to increase reading ability: A guide to developmental and remedial methods* (7th ed.). New York: Longman.

Haughton, E. (1972). Aims—Growing and sharing. In J.B. Jordon & L.S. Robbins (Eds.), *Let's try doing something else kind of thing*. Arlington, VA: Council for Exceptional Children.

Heilman, A.W. (1985). *Phonics in proper perspective* (5th ed.). Columbus, OH: Merrill.

Henderson, H.H., Clise, M., & Silverton, B. (1971). *Modification of reading behavior: A phonetic program utilizing rate acceleration*. Ellensburg, WA: H.H. Henderson.

Hieronymus, A.N., Hoover, H.D., & Lindquist, E.F. (1986). *Iowa Tests of Basic Skills*. Chicago: Riverside.

Howell, K.W., Zucker, S.H., & Morehead, M.K. (1982). *Multilevel Academic Skills Inventory*. San Antonio, TX: Psychological Corporation.

Jastak, S.R., & Wilkinson, G.S. (1984). *Wide Range Achievement Test—Revised*. Wilmington, DE: Jastak Associates.

Johnson, D.D. (1971). The Dolch list reexamined. *The Reading Teacher, 24,* 449–457.

Johnson, M.S., & Kress, R.A. (1965). *Informal reading inventories*. Newark, DE: International Reading Association.

Kaluger, G., & Kolson, C.J. (1978). *Reading and learning disabilities* (2nd ed.). Columbus, OH: Merrill.

Kamm, K., Miles, P.J., Van Blaricom, V.L., Harris, M.L., & Stewart, D.M. (1972). *Wisconsin Tests of Reading Skill Development*. Minneapolis: National Computer Systems.

Karlin, R. (1973). Evaluation for diagnostic teaching. In W. MacGinitie (Ed.), *Assessment problems in reading*. Newark, DE: International Reading Association.

Karlsen, B., & Gardner, E.F. (1984). *Stanford Diagnostic Reading Test* (3rd ed.). San Antonio, TX: Antonio, TX: Psychological Corporation.

Kaufman, A.S., & Kaufman, N.L. (1985). *Kaufman Test of Educational Achievement*. Circle Pines, MN: American Guidance Service.

Kender, J.P., & Rubenstein, H. (1977). Recall versus reinspection in IRI comprehension tests. *The Reading Teacher, 30*(7), 776–778.

Kirk, S.A., Kliebhan, J.M., & Lerner, J.W. (1978). *Teaching reading to slow and disabled learners*. Boston: Houghton Mifflin.

Koenig, C.H., & Kunzelmann, H.P. (1980). *Classroom learning screening manual*. San Antonio, TX: Psychological Corporation.

Lovitt, T.C., & Hansen, C.L. (1976). Round one—Placing the child in the right reader. *Journal of Learning Disabilities, 9,* 347–353.

MacGinitie, W.H. (1978). *Gates-MacGinitie Reading Tests.* Boston: Houghton Mifflin.

Mann, P.H., Suiter, P.A., & McClung, R.M. (1979). *Handbook in diagnostic-prescriptive teaching* (Abridged 2nd ed.). Boston: Allyn & Bacon.

Naslund, R.A., Thorpe, L.P., & Lefever, D.W. (1978). *SRA Achievement Series.* Chicago: Science Research Associates.

Otto, W., & Smith, R.J. (1980). *Corrective and remedial teaching* (3rd ed.). Boston: Houghton Mifflin.

Prescott, G.A., Balow, I.H., Hogan, T.P., & Farr, R.C. (1984). *Metropolitan Achievement Tests: Survey battery* (6th ed.). San Antonio, TX: Psychological Corporation.

Rankin, E., & Culhane, J. (1969). Comparable cloze and multiple-choice comprehension test scores. *Journal of Reading, 13,* 193–198.

Regional Resource Center. (1971). *Diagnostic Reading Inventory* (Project No. 472917, Contract No. OEC–0–9–472917–4591 [608]). Eugene, OR: University of Oregon.

Salvia, J., & Ysseldyke, J.E. (1988). *Assessment in special and remedial education* (4th ed.). Boston: Houghton Mifflin.

Scannell, D.P. (1986). *Tests of Achievement and Proficiency.* Chicago: Riverside.

Silvaroli, N.J. (1982). *Classroom Reading Inventory* (4th ed.). Dubuque, IA: Brown.

SIMS Reading and Spelling Program (3rd ed.). (1978). Minneapolis: Minneapolis Public Schools.

Smith, R.F., & Barrett, T.C. (1974). *Teaching reading in the middle grades.* Reading, MA: Addison-Wesley.

Spache, G.D. (1981). *Diagnostic Reading Scales.* Circle Pines, MN: American Guidance Service.

Starlin, C.M. (1971). Evaluating progress toward reading proficiency. In B. Bateman (Ed.), *Learning disorders.* Vol. 4: *Reading.* Seattle: Special Child Publications.

Starlin, C.M., & Starlin, A. (1973). *Guides to decision making in oral reading.* Bemidji, MN: Unique Curriculums Unlimited.

Strang, R. (1969). *Diagnostic teaching of reading* (2nd ed.). New York: McGraw-Hill.

Wiederholt, J.L., & Bryant, B.R. (1986). *Gray Oral Reading Tests—Revised.* Austin, TX: Pro-Ed.

Wolking, W.D. (1973, October). *Rate of growth toward adult proficiency: Differences between high and low achievement children, grades 1–6.* Paper presented at the International Symposium of Learning Disabilities, Miami Beach, FL.

Woodcock, R.W. (1987). *Woodcock Reading Mastery Tests—Revised.* Circle Pines, MN: American Guidance Service.

Woodcock, R.W., & Johnson, M.B. (1977). *Woodcock-Johnson Psycho-Educational Battery.* Allen, TX: DLM Teaching Resources.

Woods, M.L., & Moe, A.J. (1989). *Analytical Reading Inventory* (4th ed.). Columbus, OH: Merrill.

CHAPTER 11

Teaching
Reading Skills

many approaches and materials have been developed to teach reading. Methods of beginning reading instruction may be divided into two major approaches: the code-emphasis approach and the meaning-emphasis approach. The primary difference in the two approaches is the way decoding is taught (Carnine & Silbert, 1979). Beginning reading programs that stress letter-sound regularity are code-emphasis programs, whereas those that stress the use of common words are meaning-emphasis programs.

Code-emphasis programs begin with words consisting of letters and letter combinations that have the same sound in different words. This consistency in the letter-sound relationship enables the reader to read unknown words by blending the sounds together. For example, the word *sit* is sounded out as "sss–ii–tt" and pronounced "sit." The word *ring* is sounded out as "rrr–ii–nng" and pronounced "ring." The letter *i* has the same sound in both words. Moreover, a new word is not introduced unless its component letter-sounds have been learned. For example, the word *bet* is not introduced until the *b*, *e*, and *t* letter-sound relationships have been mastered. Some major code-emphasis programs include: *Basic Reading* (J. B. Lippincott), *Reading Mastery: DISTAR* (Science Research Associates), *Merrill Linguistic Reading Program* (Merrill), *Palo Alto Reading Program* (Harcourt Brace Jovanovich), and *Sullivan Programmed Reading* (Webster/McGraw-Hill). Also, the phonics, linguistic, and programmed programs are classified as code-emphasis programs.

Meaning-emphasis programs begin with words that appear frequently. It is assumed that frequently occurring words are familiar to the reader and thus easier to learn. Students are encouraged to use a variety of decoding techniques, including pictures, context of story, initial letters, and word configuration. Words are not controlled such that a letter has the same sound in different words. For example, the words *at, many,* and *far* may occur, and the *a* represents a different sound in each word. Some of the major meaning-emphasis programs include: *Ginn 720* (Ginn & Company); *Houghton Mifflin Reading Series* (Houghton Mifflin); and *Basics in Reading, The New Open Highways,* and *Reading Unlimited* (Scott, Foresman). Moreover, the language experience and individualized reading approaches are generally classified as meaning-emphasis programs.

Code-emphasis programs are considered to be more effective in teaching students to decode (Bleismer & Yarborough, 1965; Bond & Dykstra, 1967; Chall, 1967; Diederich, 1973; Dykstra, 1968; Gurren & Hughes, 1965). Early systematic instruction in phonics provides the skills necessary for becoming an independent reader earlier than is likely if phonics instruction is delayed and less systematic (Dykstra, 1974).

Those who support the meaning-emphasis approach agree that code-emphasis programs have an advantage in teaching decoding, but they maintain that meaning-emphasis programs have an advantage in teaching comprehension (Carnine & Silbert, 1979). Some educators, however, maintain that the research is inconclusive and that findings are at times conflicting (Carnine & Silbert, 1979). Although the meaning- versus code-emphasis debate continues, Carnine and Silbert strongly recommend the code-emphasis approach, especially for students with learning problems.

A. J. Harris and Sipay (1980) state that teacher skill is more important than reading methodology, and that "efforts should concentrate on determining which program(s) work best with which children when used by certain types of teachers under given conditions and why" (p. 70). Thus, a teacher must know a variety of instructional practices in reading in order to teach students with reading difficulties. Heilman, Blair, and Rupley (1986) make the following statement:

> No single approach to teaching beginning reading is successful with all children. The teacher is a major factor in determining the success of a reading approach by knowing when to modify an approach, combine approaches, or use a different approach to meet students' needs. . . . Thus, the importance of the teacher is highlighted within the implementation of any given approach. It is the teacher who is the *key variable* in whether or not a child is successful in learning to read. (p. 272)

The remainder of this chapter presents numerous reading approaches, programs, activities, and materials aimed at helping the teacher design effective reading instruction for individual students.

DEVELOPMENTAL APPROACHES

Developmental reading approaches emphasize sequential instruction on a daily basis. Most are programmed according to a normative pattern of reading growth. The basic material for instruction is usually a series of books (such as basal readers) that directs what will be taught and when. A well-developed program provides supplementary materials such as workbooks, skillpacks, wall charts, related activities, learning games, and filmstrips. To teach students with reading problems it is often necessary to adapt developmental programs to meet their needs—changing the sequence, providing additional practice activities, and modifying the input-output arrangements of selected tasks. The following developmental approaches are discussed: (a) basal, (b) phonics, (c) linguistics, (d) language experience, and (e) individualized reading.

Basal Reading Approach

Many teachers use a basal reading series as the core of their reading program. Most series include a sequential set of reading texts and supplementary materials such as workbooks, flash cards, placement and achievement tests, and filmstrips. In addition, a comprehensive teacher's manual explains the purpose of the program and provides precise instructional plans and suggestions for skill activities. The teacher's manual is usually highly structured and completely outlines each lesson. For example, in addition to lesson activities, the manual may include skill objectives, new vocabulary words, motivational activities, and questions for checking comprehension on each page of the text.

The readers in a basal series usually begin with preprimers and gradually increase in difficulty, continuing through the eighth grade. Some basals are changing their progression from grade-level readers to levels of readers corresponding to stages in development (Spache & Spache, 1977). The content is based upon common child experiences and well-known interests of children. Materials designed for multiracial and disadvantaged groups sometimes feature story settings and content to appeal to a variety of backgrounds and ethnic groups. Basals may stress either a meaning-emphasis or a code-emphasis approach. A basal series systematically presents reading skills in word recognition, comprehension, and word attack, and it controls the vocabulary from level to level. The reader, accompanying teacher's manual, and the student's workbook provide various activities that aid in (a) learning word-attack skills (including phonics), (b) developing comprehension, and (c) increasing reading rate steadily.

The basal approach has the following advantages:

1. The readers are comprehension oriented and are sequential in content from early readiness to advanced reading levels.
2. The teacher's manual provides suggestions,

activities, and a detailed outline for teaching.

3. Reading skills are developed in a systematic, sequential manner.
4. A basic vocabulary is established and repeated throughout the sequence to provide reinforcement.
5. Assessment, evaluation, and diagnostic materials usually are provided.

A disadvantage of the basal program is that its structured, comprehensive nature may limit the teacher's creativity and may contribute to an inflexible, traditional method of teaching. Also, the basal approach encourages teaching reading in groups rather than concentrating on individual differences and needs. In addition, it may not provide an adequate foundation for reading tasks of the content fields (for example, reading maps, charts, and arithmetic problems; using library skills and organizational skills such as notetaking and outlining).

Most basal readers recommend the *directed reading activity*. This is the procedure for teaching a reading lesson. The steps include the following:

1. Motivate the student to learn the material.
2. Prepare the student for the material by presenting new concepts and vocabulary.
3. Guide the student in reading the story by asking questions that give a purpose or goal for the reading.
4. Develop or strengthen skills relating to the material through drills or workbook activities.
5. Assign work to apply the skills acquired during the lesson.
6. Evaluate the effectiveness of the lesson.

This guided reading approach may be used to increase comprehension skills. Basal readers contain stories with many details and often are divided into small parts. Thus, location exer-

cises can be given in finding the main idea or main characters as well as specific words, phrases, sentences, and paragraphs.

An alternative to the directed reading lesson is the *directed reading-thinking activity* (Stauffer, 1981). In this thought-provoking strategy the student largely determines the purposes for reading and must generate questions about the selection, read the selection, and then validate the answers to the questions through group judgment. The teacher acts as a catalyst and provides thoughtful questions in directing the process (What do you think? Why do you think so? Can you prove your conclusion?).

The basal reading approach is used in the majority of reading programs in the United States. The teacher can easily adjust or supplement the materials to meet the individual needs of students with reading problems.

Phonics Approach

The phonics approach teaches word recognition through learning grapheme–phoneme associations. After learning the sounds of vowels, consonants, and blends, the child learns to sound out words by combining sounds and blending them into words. Thus, the child learns to recognize unfamiliar words by associating speech sounds with letters or groups of letters. Table 11.1 presents the sounds stressed in a phonics program. Spache and Spache (1977) note the increasing stress on phonics: "The move to earlier and stronger phonics programs in the primary grades, now called 'decoding,' has become an almost universal practice in our beginning reading program" (p. ix).

Teachers may use either the *synthetic* method or the *analytic* method to teach phonics (Matthes, 1972). In the synthetic method the child learns that letters represent certain sounds (for example, *b—buh*) and then finds out how to blend, or *synthesize,* the sounds to form words. This method emphasizes isolated

TABLE 11.1
Sounds stressed in a phonics program.

VOWEL SOUNDS

Short Sounds		*Long Sounds*	
a	bat	*a*	rake
e	bed	*e*	jeep
i	pig	*i*	kite
o	lock	*o*	rope
u	duck	*u*	mule

W is sometimes used as a vowel, as in the *ow* and *aw* teams. W is usually a vowel on word endings and a consonant at the beginning of words.

Y is usually a consonant when it appears at the beginning of a word, and a vowel in any other position.

Three consonants usually affect or control the sounds of some, or all, of the vowels when they follow these vowels within a syllable. They are: *r*, *w*, and *l*.

r (all vowels)	*w* (*a,e,* and *o*)	*l* (*a*)
car	law	all
her	few	
dirt	now	
for		
fur		

CONSONANT SOUNDS

b	bear	*k*	king	*s*	six
c	cat	*l*	lake	*t*	turtle
d	dog	*m*	money	*v*	vase
f	face	*n*	nose	*w*	wagon
g	goat	*p*	pear	*x*	xylophone
h	hen	*q*	queen	*y*	yellow
j	jug	*r*	rat	*z*	zebra

The following consonants have two or more sounds:

c	cat	*s*	six
c	ice	*s*	is
g	goat	*x*	xylophone
g	germ	*x*	exist
		x	box

When *g* is followed by *e, i,* or *y,* it usually takes the soft sound of *j,* as in *gentle* and *germ.* If it is not followed by these letters it takes the hard sound illustrated in such words as *got* and *game.*

When *c* is followed by *e, i,* or *y,* it usually takes the soft sound heard in *cent.* If it is not followed by these letters, it usually takes the hard sound heard in *come.*

Qu usually has the sound of *kw;* however, in some words such as *bouquet* it has the sound of *k.*

S sometimes takes a slightly different sound in words such as *sure.*

CONSONANT BLENDS
BEGINNING

bl	blue
br	brown
cl	clown
cr	crown
dr	dress
dw	dwell
fl	flower
fr	from
gl	glue
gr	grape
pl	plate
pr	pretty
sc	score
sk	skill
sl	slow
sm	small
sn	snail
sp	spin
st	story
sw	swan
tr	tree
tw	twelve
wr	wrench
sch	school
scr	screen
shr	shrink
spl	splash
spr	spring
squ	squash
str	string
thr	throw

ENDING

ld	wild
mp	lamp

(continued)

TABLE 11.1, *continued*

nd	*wind*
nt	*went*
rk	*work*
sk	*risk*

CONSONANT AND VOWEL DIGRAPHS

Consonant

ch	chute	*sh*	ship
ch	choral	*th*	three
ch	church	*th*	that
gh	cough	*wh*	which
ph	graph	*wh*	who

Vowel (most common phonemes only)

ai	pain
ay	hay
ea	each
	or
ea	weather
ei	weight
	or
ei	either
ie	piece

(A number of other phonemes are common for *ie*)

oa	oats
oo	book
	or
oo	moon
ou	tough (*ou* may be either a digraph or a diphthong)
ow	low
	or
ow	cow

DIPHTHONGS

au	haul*	*oi*	soil
aw	hawk*	*ou*	trout
ew	few	*ow*	cow
ey	they	*oy*	boy

*Some may hear *au* and *aw* as a digraph.

Source: From *Locating and Correcting Reading Difficulties* (pp. 313–315), 5th ed., by E. E. Ekwall, 1989, Columbus, OH: Merrill. Copyright 1989 by Merrill Publishing Company. Reprinted by permission.

letter sounds before the child progresses to words. The analytic method teaches letter sounds as integral parts of words (for example, *b* as in *baby*). The child must learn new words on the basis of phonics elements similar to familiar or sight words. Phonics methods and materials differ on details, but the main objective is to teach the child to attack new words independently.

Spache and Spache (1977) recommend the sequence outlined in Table 11.2 for teaching phonics. In addition, phonics instruction includes a list of rules introduced at various stages. Spache and Spache's list of rules is presented in Table 11.3.

By emphasizing word recognition, phonics helps the child to associate sounds with printed letters and leads to independence in unlocking new words. However, the phonics approach has the following disadvantages:

1. The emphasis on word pronunciation may be at the expense of comprehension.
2. The student may become confused with words that are exceptions to the phonetic rules.
3. After learning isolated sounds, the student may have difficulty blending the sounds to form complete words.

Kirk, Kliebhan, and Lerner (1978) note that instruction in phonics may be added effectively to the basal reader or language experience approach after the student has acquired a basic sight vocabulary of 50 to 100 words. Phonics is helpful with beginning readers in a developmental program or as a remedial technique for students who have a strong sight vocabulary but are unable to analyze unfamiliar words. A number of phonics programs are commercially available. Phonics programs that are widely used with students who have learning problems include *Phonetic Keys to Reading* (T. Harris, Creekmore, & Greenman, 1967),

TABLE 11.2
Sequence for teaching phonics.

Simple Consonants
    b, p, m, w, h, d, t, n, hard *g* (gate), *k,* hard *c* (cake), *y* (yet), *f* (for)

More Difficult Consonants
    v, l, z (zoo), *s* (sat), *r, c,* (cent), *q* (kw), *x* (ks), *j, g* (engine), *s* (as)

Consonant Blends and Digraphs
    ck, ng, th (the), *zh, sh, th* (thin), *wh, ch*

Simple Consonants with l, r, p, or t, as bl, pl, gr, br, sp, st, tr, thr, str, spl, scr, and others as they appear

Short Vowels
    a (hat), *e* (get), *i* (sit), *o* (top), *u* (cup), *y* (happy)

Long Vowels
    a (cake), *e* (be), *i* (five), *o* (old), *u* (mule), *y* (cry)

Silent Letters
    k (knife), *w* (write), *l* (talk), *t* (catch), *g* (gnat), *c* (black), *h* (hour)

Vowel Digraphs
    ai (pail), *ea* (each), *oa* (boat), *ee* (bee), *ay* (say), *ea* (dead)

Vowel Diphthongs
    au (auto), *aw* (awful), *oo* (moon), *oo* (wood), *ow* (cow), *ou* (out), *oi* (oil), *oy* (boy), *ow* (low)

Vowels with r
    ar (car), *er* (her), *ir* (bird), *or* (corn), *ur* (burn) Same with *l* and *w*.

Phonograms
    ail, ain, all, and, ate, ay, con, eep, ell, en, ent, er, est, ick, ight, ill, in, ing, ock, ter, tion Alternates—*ake, ide, ile, ine, it, ite, le, re, ble*

Source: From *Reading in the Elementary School* (pp. 380–381), 4th ed., by G. D. Spache and E. B. Spache, 1977, Boston: Allyn & Bacon. Copyright 1977 by Allyn & Bacon, Inc. Reprinted by permission.

TABLE 11.3
Phonetic rules.

Consonants

1. When *c* is frequently followed by *e, i,* or *y,* it has the sound of *s,* as in *race, city, fancy.*
2. Otherwise, *c* has the sound of *k,* as in *come, attic.*
3. *G* followed by *e, i,* or *y* sounds soft like *j,* as in *gem.*
4. Otherwise *g* sounds hard, as in *gone.*
5. When *c* and *h* are next to each other, they make only one sound.
6. *Ch* is usually pronounced as it is in *kitchen,* not like *sh* (in *machine*).
7. When a word ends in *ck,* it has the same last sound, as in *look.*
8. When two of the same consonants are side by side, only one is heard, as in *butter.*
9. Sometimes *s* has the sound of *z,* as in *raisin, music.*
10. The letter *x* has the sounds of *ks* or *k* and *s,* as in *box, taxi.*

Vowels

11. When a consonant and *y* are the last letters in a one-syllable word, the *y* has the long *i* sound, as in *cry, by.* In longer words the *y* has the long *e* sound, as in *baby.*
12. The *r* gives the preceding vowel a sound that is neither long nor short, as in *car, far, fur, fir.* The letters *l* and *w* have the same effect.

Vowel Digraphs and Diphthongs

13. The first vowel is usually long and the second silent in *oa, ay, ai,* and *ee,* as in *boat, say, gain, feed.*
14. In *ea* the first letter may be long and the second silent, or it may have the short *e* sound, as in *bread.*
15. *Ou* has two sounds: one is the long sound of *o;* the other is the *ou* sound, as in *own* or *cow.*
16. These double vowels blend into a single sound: *au, aw, oi, oy,* as in *auto, awful, coin, boy.*
17. The combination *ou* has a schwa sound, as in *vigorous,* or a sound as in *out.*
18. The combination *oo* has two sounds, as in *moon* and as in *wood.*

Source: From *Reading in the Elementary School* (pp. 382–383), 4th ed., by G. D. Spache and E. B. Spache, 1977, Boston: Allyn & Bacon. Copyright 1977 by Allyn & Bacon, Inc. Reprinted by permission.

Phonovisual Method (Schoolfield & Timberlake, 1974), *Remedial Reading Drills* (Hegge, Kirk, & Kirk, 1955), *SIMS Reading and Spelling Program* (1978), and *The Writing Road to Reading* (Spalding & Spalding, 1962).

Linguistic Approach

Many linguistic approaches to reading stem from the ideas of various linguists. Linguists, who are mainly concerned with oral communication, have provided important information about the nature and structure of language. Bloomfield and Barnhart (1961) and Fries (1963) provide a linguistic framework for the teaching of reading that emphasizes decoding— changing the printed words into verbal communication.

In many linguistic reading materials, a *whole-word* approach is used. This approach does not use exercises in sounding and blending. Words are taught in word families and only as wholes. In beginning reading, words are introduced that contain a short vowel and consist of a consonant-vowel-consonant pattern. The words are selected on the basis of similar spelling patterns (such as *cab, lab, tab*); the child must learn the relationship between speech sounds and letters (that is, between phonemes and graphemes). The child is not taught letter sounds directly—he learns them through minimal word differences. Words that have irregular spellings are introduced as the child progresses, and he learns them as sight words. After the words are learned in the spelling patterns, they are put together to form sentences.

The following reading selection is from a book in the Merrill Linguistic Reading Program (Wilson & Rudolph, 1986, p. 15):

Mud on a Pup

Gus got a tub for Pam's pup.
"Pam," he said, "you cannot let your pup run
  in the mud.
Get your pup into the tub.
Get him wet and rub suds on him."

Pam gets her pup into the tub.
She wets him and rubs him.
"Is your pup wet yet?" said Gus.
"He is a wet pet," said Pam.

"He lets me get him wet," said Pam.
"He is not a bad pet."

The linguistic approach differs from the phonics approach in that linguistic readers focus on words instead of isolated sounds. It differs from the basal reading approach in that linguistic instruction places emphasis first on breaking the written language code before meaning and comprehension are considered. Thus, many linguistic series contain no pictures or illustrations, which may provide clues and tempt the student to guess rather than decode the printed word.

Cohen and Plaskon (1980) list the following advantages of the linguistic approach:

1. The emphasis on the relationship between phonemes and graphemes helps the student realize that reading is talk written down.
2. Consistent visual patterns are presented as learning progresses from familiar, phonemically regular words to words of semiregular and irregular spellings.
3. The child is taught to spell and read the word as a whole unit.
4. An awareness of sentence structure is developed.
5. Reading is taught by association with the child's natural knowledge of his own language.

Kaluger and Kolson (1978) note also that the frequent repetition of words in this approach may be helpful to students with learning problems. One of the major disadvantages of the linguistic approach is its lack of emphasis on comprehension and reading for meaning in the beginning stages of reading. Other disadvantages include the following:

1. The vocabulary is extremely controlled, and the use of nonsense words and phrases for pattern practice detracts from reading for comprehension.
2. Word-by-word reading is encouraged.
3. The approach strongly emphasizes auditory memory skills.
4. Linguists disagree about the methodology of teaching reading.

The following selected commercial materials use the linguistic approach: *Let's Read* (Clarence L. Barnhart), *Linguistic Readers* (Harper & Row), *Merrill Linguistic Reading Program* (Merrill), *Miami Linguistic Readers* (D. C. Heath), *SRA Basic Reading Skills* (Science Research Associates), and *Structural Reading Series* (L. W. Singer).

Language Experience Approach

The language experience approach (LEA) integrates the development of reading skills with the development of listening, speaking, and writing skills. What the student is thinking and talking about makes up the materials. According to Lee and Allen (1963), LEA deals with the following thinking process: (a) what a child thinks about, he can talk about; (b) what a child says, he can write (or someone can write for him); and (c) what a child writes (or others write for him), he can read.

LEA stresses each child's unique interests. The approach is based not upon a series of reading materials but upon the child's oral and written expression. The child's experiences play a major role in determining his reading material. The child dictates stories to the teacher; these may be taken at first from the child's own drawings and artwork. The teacher writes down the stories, and they become the basis of the child's initial reading experiences. Thus, the child learns to read his own written thoughts. In this approach the language patterns of the reading materials are determined by the child's speech, and the content is determined by his experiences (Hall, 1981). The teacher tries to broaden and enrich the child's base of experiences from which he can think, speak, and read. Eventually, with help, the child can write his own stories. Thus, according to Hall (1981), the approach is based on the concept that "reading has the most meaning to a pupil when the materials being read are expressed in his language and are rooted in his experiences" (p. 2).

At first, the teacher guides the student or group of students in writing an experience chart. The content of the experience chart (story) derives from the students' experiences as they share information through group discussion. Experience charts may comprise several topics: narrative descriptions of experiences, reports of experiments or news events, or fiction stories made up by the students. The teacher writes the ideas in a first draft on the chalkboard. During the writing of the chart, the teacher guides the students' suggestions and revisions and discusses word choice, sentence structure, and the sounds of letters and words. Specific skills—such as capitalization, punctuation, spelling, grammar, and correct sentence structure—can be taught as needed during the editing and revising of the chart. Thus, the teacher provides skill development at the appropriate time instead of following a predetermined sequence of training in reading skills. Since the child creates the content, motivation and interest are usually high.

The language experience approach is mainly a way of teaching beginning reading. However, it may be just as effective in the intermediate grades and often is used with older students for corrective instruction and motivation. Matthes (1972) notes that in the first grade, self-expression and individualized reading can be developed by having the child label paintings and drawings, read and complete sentences (such as "I like to . . ."), and write groups of rhyming words. By the second and third grades, the student might be producing his own experience charts or writing poetry or song lyrics. Picture dictionaries, simple readers, word cards, labels on classroom objects, and lists of interest or topical words should be available to stimulate ideas and extend the student's writing (and reading) vocabulary.

In the language experience approach, each student is encouraged to proceed at his own rate. Progress is evaluated in terms of the student's ability to express ideas in oral and written form and to understand the writings of his peers. Progress or growth in writing mechanics, spelling, vocabulary, sentence structure, and depth of thinking is evident in the student's written work. The stories each student writes can be illustrated and bound in an attractive folder, and students can trade story notebooks.

Allen and Allen's (1970) program, *Language Experiences in Reading,* consists of three levels, each of which is divided into units. The teacher's resource book gives valuable information and suggestions for each lesson; for example, concepts to be developed or reviewed, language skills emphasized, descriptions of ways to work with the pupil books, and suggestions of supplementary books and filmstrips.

One advantage of the language experience approach is that it uses the student's own language as the focus of the reading program. It incorporates speaking, listening, and writing skills into the reading program and makes the student more sensitive to his language, environment, and experiences. Also, the student's interest level tends to be high, and creativity is encouraged in writing original stories. Major disadvantages are that the approach does not provide a structured, systematic method of teaching sequential reading skills, and there is no method of evaluating student progress. Emphasis is placed on the student's own experiences and his speaking vocabulary; however, there may not be enough structure in this approach to develop vocabulary or to generalize from speaking and listening vocabularies to reading and writing vocabularies. When teacher organization is provided as well as provisions for teaching word-attack and comprehension skills, the language experience approach may be used effectively to teach children with learning problems. Also, it may be used to improve comprehension skills of older students who have developed basic decoding skills or to maintain interest and motivation.

Individualized Reading Approach

In an individualized reading program, each child selects his own reading material according to his interests and ability and progresses at his own rate. It is essential to have available a large collection of books at different reading levels, with many subjects represented at each level of difficulty. After each child chooses his reading materials, he paces himself and keeps records of his progress. The teacher teaches word recognition and comprehension skills as each student needs them.

The student and teacher meet once or twice a week, during which time the teacher may ask the student to read aloud and discuss his reading material. The teacher can note reading errors and check the student's sight vocabulary, understanding of word meanings, and comprehension. Also, the teacher may guide the student with regard to his next reading selection, although the choice is left up to the student. From these conferences the teacher keeps a record of the student's capabilities and progress in order to plan activities to develop specific skills. The teacher's role is to diagnose and prescribe; success of the program depends on the teacher's resourcefulness and competence. Individual work may be supplemented with group activities using basal readers and workbooks in order to provide practice on specific reading skills.

Self-pacing and self-selection may be considered advantages of the individualized reading approach. Self-pacing builds self-confidence, and self-selection satisfies personal interests and promotes independent reading. Individualized reading also eliminates "high" and "low" reading groups and avoids competition and comparison. The one-to-one conferences between pupil and teacher may also encourage the teacher to observe and diagnose reading weaknesses. The main disadvantage of the program is that it lacks structure and organization in developing specific reading skills. The teacher must be very competent and skillful in order to conduct beneficial conferences and keep efficient records. Also, a large number of books must be available to meet each student's interests and level of ability. An additional disadvantage is that no provision is made in advance to deal with unknown words, specific word meanings, or difficult concepts; also, since teacher guidance follows the completion of reading, the student may repeat inappropriate responses. The value of the individualized reading approach for students with learning problems is questionable, since it involves self-learning and lacks a systematic check of mastery of developmental skills in the reading process (Kirk et al., 1978).

REMEDIAL PROGRAMS AND APPROACHES

Remedial programs are designed to teach reading to the student who has, or would have, difficulty learning to read in the regular classroom reading program.

Programmed Reading Approach

Programmed reading materials can be presented either in a workbook format or a teaching machine. The materials are designed to be self-teaching and self-correcting. Subject matter is presented in small steps or frames that are in a systematic, logical sequence. The child must make a response to the question in each frame, and then he checks his response by sliding down a marker. Responses may be in the form of answering true–false or multiple-choice questions, completing a sentence, writing a word, or completing a word by filling in letters. When working with a machine, the child responds by pulling a lever or knob, pushing a button, or turning a crank. With all programmed materials the student receives immediate feedback. In workbooks the answers often are in the margin; on teaching machines a light or sound can give feedback, the answer can be uncovered, or the response can appear on the screen. In the *linear* program the student must correct an incorrect response before continuing. In a *branching* program, if an incorrect response is made, the student is referred to another page where his mistake is explained to him before he continues; thus, the student progresses at his own rate and receives positive reinforcement or correction at each step.

Matthes (1972) notes the following advantages of programmed reading instruction:

1. Positive reinforcement or correction is given at each learning step.
2. Each student moves at his own pace.

3. The content is self-instructional and does not need to be explained or reviewed.
4. Completed programs can be used as a record of progress.
5. The teacher is freed from repetitive drilling and can help individual pupils or small groups.

A major disadvantage is that it is difficult to program comprehension skills, and thus little emphasis is placed on their development. Reading short, independent frames does not promote growth in reading long passages or skimming for specific facts.

Repetition and feedback are important when using programmed materials with students with learning problems. The success of the approach depends on providing each student with materials suited to his needs. Two commercially available programmed reading materials are *Programmed Reading* (Buchanan, 1966) and the *Sullivan Reading Program* (Sullivan, 1966).

Reading Mastery: DISTAR Reading and Corrective Reading Programs

The *Reading Mastery: DISTAR* (Direct Instructional System for Teaching Arithmetic and Reading) *Reading Program* (Engelmann & Bruner, 1984), which consists of levels I and II of the SRA Reading Mastery basal reader series, is an intensive, highly structured programmed instructional system designed to remediate below-average reading skills of students through the third grade. The students are grouped according to their current abilities, with no more than five students in a group. They sit in chairs in a quarter-circle around the teacher. Each day, one 30-minute lesson is presented. The manual specifies the sequence of presentation as well as the teacher's statements and hand movements. Each student receives positive reinforcement (praise or

points) for correct responses. As the student masters skills (indicated by his performance on criterion-referenced tests), he changes groups.

The program uses a synthetic phonics approach and emphasizes basic decoding skills, including sound-symbol identification, left-to-right sequence, and the oral blending of sounds to make words. The program includes the following exercises: (a) games to teach sequencing skills and left-to-right orientation, (b) blending tasks to teach children to spell words by sounds ("say it slow") and to blend quickly ("say it fast"), and (c) rhyming tasks to teach the relationships between sounds and words. Take-home sheets are used to practice skills. The program teaches students to concentrate on important sound combinations and word discriminations and to use a variety of word-attack skills. It emphasizes literal and inferential comprehension, including deduction processing and instruction following.

The *DISTAR* program is fast-paced. The student receives immediate feedback, and correction procedures for various student errors are specified. Repetition is built into the program. *DISTAR* has helped children in Head Start programs to learn reading skills (Becker & Engelmann, 1977; Stallings, 1974). However, Kirk et al. (1978) note that the rigidity of the instructional program and its emphasis on auditory skills may be considered disadvantages.

The *Corrective Reading Program* (Engelmann, Becker, Hanner, & Johnson, 1980) is an advanced remedial reading program based on *DISTAR* concepts. It is designed for students in grades 4 through 12 and adults who have not mastered decoding and comprehension skills. The program is divided into two strands, decoding and comprehension; each strand has 340 lessons and three levels of skill development (decoding—word-attack basics, decoding strategies, skill applications; comprehension—thinking basics, comprehension skills, concept applications). Each lesson lasts 35 to

40 minutes and provides teacher-directed work, independent applications, and tests of student performance. The presentation book for the teacher specifies the teacher's role in each lesson. The program gives the student immediate feedback and provides a built-in reinforcement system.

Edmark Reading Program

The *Edmark Reading Program* (Bijou, 1977), published by Edmark Corporation, is designed to teach 150 sight words of varying parts of speech, plus the endings *ing, ed,* and *s,* to students with extremely limited skills. The student needs only to be able to repeat a word the teacher says and point to a response. The 227 lessons are of five formats: (a) prereading lessons that train the student on the match-to-sample format, (b) word recognition lessons of one to two words per lesson, (c) lessons in direction books that teach the child to follow printed directions, (d) lessons in matching pictures to phrases, and (e) lessons in a storybook in which the student orally reads 16 stories. All lessons are broken down into small, sequential steps, and reinforcement is provided. Pretests and review tests are included throughout the program, and procedures are given for charting student progress. A software version of the program is available for Apple computers in which the student selects answers with a joystick. Also, after completing Level I of the *Edmark Reading Program,* the student may move into Level II, which introduces an additional 200 words and reinforces the 150 words previously learned.

Rebus Approach

The rebus approach to readiness and beginning reading instruction involves the use of picture words—rebuses—rather than spelled words. Reading materials use pictures instead of printed words. Since each picture has only one obvious meaning, reading is quite easy; for example, *dog* is simply a picture of a dog.

The *Peabody Rebus Reading Program* (Woodcock, Clark, & Davies, 1979) includes three programmed workbooks and two readers. Each workbook contains 384 frames that present a simple question or reading task. To mark a response, the child uses a moistened pencil eraser. If the response is correct, the area changes color to green. If the response is incorrect, the area becomes red and the child does not move to the next frame until he has made a correct response. Thus, immediate feedback is provided in each frame, and the student proceeds at his own pace. At the readiness level, *Introducing Reading—Book One* introduces a rebus vocabulary of 35 words and several basic reading skills, such as the use of context clues. *Introducing Reading—Book Two* introduces 33 additional rebuses, and structural analysis skills are presented. At completion of the second workbook, the student is using a rebus vocabulary of 68 words in complex reading tasks. A supplementary lessons kit for the readiness level includes 17 comprehension lessons for group instruction that provide a more intensive introduction to the program. Picture cards, word cards, sentence cards, and answer strips also are included.

The *transition* level (from rebuses to spelled words) includes the programmed workbook, *Introducing Reading—Book Three,* which introduces some phonics skills. *Book Three* is used with two rebus readers, *Red and Blue Are on Me* and *Can You See a Little Flea?* In these two readers, spelled words are substituted for rebuses. The first time a word appears in traditional letter form, its rebus appears directly above the word, but reduced to half size. Also, a yellow background is used to indicate every new word. The student can look at the word key at the top of the page if he needs help with the transition word. Upon completion of the transition level the student has a reading vocabulary of approximately 120 spelled words, including the names of numbers and colors and many words commonly used in basal reading programs. A supplementary lessons kit for the transition level includes 35 lessons that provide additional intensive instruction. Thus, the transition level is designed to equip the student with the skills and vocabulary needed to move into the primer level of traditional programs.

REMEDIAL METHODS

Several remedial methods are designed for students with moderate to severe reading problems—for example, nonreaders or students who are more than one year behind in reading achievement. Numerous programs have been developed from some of these remedial methods.

Multisensory Reading Method

The multisensory method is based on the premise that some children learn best when content is presented in several modalities. Frequently, *kinesthetic* (movement) and *tactile* (touch) stimulation are used along with the visual and auditory modalities. The multisensory programs that feature tracing, hearing, writing, and seeing are often referred to as VAKT (visual-auditory-kinesthetic-tactile). To increase tactile and kinesthetic stimulation, sandpaper letters, finger paint, sand trays, raised letters, and sunken letters are used. Some research supports the use of the multisensory method with retarded readers (Gillespie-Silver, 1979). The multisensory method mainly has been used in remedial and special education.

The Fernald (1943) method and the Gillingham method (Gillingham & Stillman, 1968) are reading approaches that highlight VAKT

instruction. The Fernald method stresses whole-word learning. The Gillingham method, based on the work of Orton (1937), features sound blending.

The Fernald method. Vocabulary is selected from stories the student has dictated, and each word is taught as a whole. In the Fernald approach there is no attempt to teach phonics skills. The teacher identifies unknown words, and the student writes the word to develop word recognition. Each word is learned as a whole unit, and it immediately is placed in a context that is meaningful to the child. Success is stressed to help maintain a high level of motivation.

The method consists of four stages. In Stage 1 the student selects a word he would like to learn, and the teacher writes it with a crayon in large letters. The student then traces the word with his fingers, making contact with the paper (tactile-kinesthetic). As he traces it, he says each part of the word aloud (auditory). In addition, the student sees the word (visual) while he is tracing it and hears the word as he says it (auditory). This process is repeated until the student can write the word correctly without looking at the sample. If the student makes an error when tracing or writing, he must start over so that the word is always written as a unit. If the word is correct, it is filed alphabetically in a word bank. The student writes a story using the learned word, and the story is typed so he can read the word in print.

In Stage 2 the student is no longer required to trace each word. Now he learns each new word by looking at the teacher's written copy of the word, saying it to himself, and writing it. He continues to write stories and keep a word file.

In Stage 3 the student learns new words by looking at a printed word and saying it to himself before writing it. Thus, the student learns directly from the printed word; the teacher is not required to write it. At this point the student may begin reading from books. The teacher continually checks to see that the student is retaining learned words.

In the final stage, Stage 4, the student is able to recognize new words because of their similarity to printed words or parts of words already learned. Thus, he can apply his reading skills and expand his reading interests.

The Fernald approach uses language experience and tracing (kinesthetic) techniques. Progress is slow, so to sustain interest the student chooses his own material. Success is stressed to help maintain a high level of motivation. The student is never encouraged to sound out word parts or to copy words he has traced. Each word is learned as a whole unit, and it immediately is placed in a context that is meaningful to the child. Also, the teacher never reads to the student until he has mastered normal reading ability. The four stages must be mastered in sequence. This remedial approach generally is used with students with severe reading problems. However, Otto and Smith (1980) note that the tracing technique alone may be used effectively to help students learn frequently used words with which they are having trouble.

The Gillingham method. The Gillingham method (Gillingham & Stillman, 1968) is a highly structured, phonetically oriented approach based on the theoretical work of Orton (1937). Each letter sound is taught using a multisensory approach. Consonants and vowels having only one sound are presented on drill cards (consonants on white cards and vowels on salmon-colored cards), and letters are introduced by a key word (for example, *fun* for *f*). *Associative* processes are used, beginning with the child associating (linking) the name and sound of a letter with its printed symbol. The method involves the following procedures:

1. A drill card showing one letter is exposed to the student. The teacher says the name of the letter, and the student repeats it. When this has been mastered, the teacher says the sound of the letter, and the student repeats the sound. Then the drill card is exposed and the teacher asks, "What does this letter say?" The student is to give its sound.

2. Without presenting the drill card, the teacher makes the sound represented by the letter and says, "Tell me the name of the letter that has this sound." This is essentially oral spelling.

3. The teacher carefully writes the letter and explains its form, thus instructing the student in cursive handwriting. The student traces the letter over the teacher's lines, copies it, writes it from memory, and writes it with his eyes looking away. Finally, the teacher makes the sound and says, "Write the letter that has this sound."

After the student has mastered the first group of ten letters (*a, b, f, h, i, j, k, m, p, t*), he is taught to blend them into words. The letters are combined to form simple consonant-vowel-consonant words (for example, *bit, map, jab*). Spelling is introduced after blending: When the teacher says a word, the student (a) repeats the word, (b) names the letters, (c) writes the letters as he says them (simultaneous oral spelling), and (d) reads the word he has written. Sentence and story writing is introduced after the child is able to write any three-letter, phonetically pure word. Nonphonetic words are taught through drill. Consonant blends are taught after the student can read, write, and spell the words in the short stories. Also, syllabication, dictionary skills, and additional spelling rules are introduced. Thus, the Gillingham method emphasizes repetition and drill, and spelling and writing skills are taught in conjunction with reading skills.

Instructional materials developed for the Gillingham method include phonetic drill cards, phonetic words, syllable concept cards, and little stories. Lessons and instructions on using the materials to teach various skills are outlined in the manual (Gillingham & Stillman, 1968). The procedure is highly structured, and no other reading or spelling materials may be used. Dechant (1970) and Gates (1947) criticize this method because the teaching procedures are rigid. Also, it lacks meaningful, interesting activities, and the student tends to develop a labored reading style. Kaluger and Kolson (1978) state that an additional weakness is the method's lack of emphasis on comprehension. However, they note that the system does work and may be valuable for use with students experiencing severe reading difficulties. Two adaptations of the Gillingham method include *Recipe for Reading* (Traub & Bloom, 1970) and *Multi-Sensory Approach to Language Arts for Specific Language Disability Children* (Slingerland, 1974). Also, the *Remedial Reading Drills* (Hegge et al., 1955) use a VAKT phonics approach.

Modified Alphabet Method

The alphabetic method in beginning reading instruction often is used with students with learning problems. Two modified alphabetic methods are discussed: initial teaching alphabet and diacritical marking system.

Initial teaching alphabet. The initial teaching alphabet (i.t.a.; Downing, 1965) uses a modified alphabet to insure a consistent correspondence between sound and symbol. Letters in the traditional 26-letter alphabet do not always have just one sound apiece. However, because the i.t.a. presents *one* symbol for each sound, a clear relationship exists between each of the characters and its sound. This pattern helps reduce confusing irregularities in spell-

ing. There are 44 characters, including all the letters of the traditional alphabet except *x* and *q* and 20 other letters that look like traditional letters joined together or are new symbols. These additional letters represent special phonemes, such as *th* sound. In addition, a larger version of the letter indicates uppercase letters instead of capital letters. Some examples of words in the i.t.a. include *larg* (large), *laf* (laugh), *askt* (asked), and *wun* (one). The initial teaching alphabet is used only in the beginning stages of reading. As soon as the child is fluent in the i.t.a., usually by the end of the first grade, he transfers his skills to the traditional alphabet.

The initial teaching alphabet is not a method of instruction. It actually was proposed to simplify beginning reading. The teacher can use the i.t.a. with any method he chooses. For example, it can be combined with the language experience approach or a multisensory method. In listing advantages of the i.t.a., Matthes (1972) notes that it is easier for a child to learn to read when each symbol is represented by one sound. Also, enthusiasm and interest in reading increase as the child finds success. Greater skill in creative self-expression is developed. However, a disadvantage is that the teacher must buy new reading books written in the i.t.a., and the child may be confused when he sees the traditional alphabet in other reading materials. Also, the student may experience difficulty in making the transition from the i.t.a. to the traditional alphabet. Spache and Spache (1973) report that research findings on the i.t.a. are often contradictory and inconclusive, but it shows promise and deserves further study.

Diacritical marking system. In the diacritical marking system (Fry, 1964), phonetic marks are added to the letters in the traditional alphabet. For example, long vowels have a bar over them, silent letters have a slash mark through them, and digraphs have a bar under both letters—for example, fiv¢, wi<u>th</u>, chi¢ks. Short vowels and regular consonants are not changed since these are the most common usages of the letters. In this beginning reading system, nearly every word the child sees (in reading books, on worksheets, and on the chalkboard) is marked according to the diacritical marking system. As the child's reading skill progresses, the use of the marks diminishes.

Neurological Impress Method

The neurological impress method (Heckelman, 1969; Langford, Slade, & Barnett, 1974) was developed to teach reading to children with severe reading disabilities. The method consists of joint oral reading at a rapid pace by the student and the teacher. It is based on the theory that a student can learn by hearing his own voice and someone else's voice jointly reading the same material. The student is seated slightly in front of the teacher, and the teacher's voice is directed into the student's ear at a close range. There is no special preparation of the material prior to the joint reading. The objective is simply to cover as many pages as possible, in the allotted time, without tiring the student. At first, the teacher should read slightly louder and faster than the student; the student should be encouraged to maintain the pace and not worry about mistakes. The teacher slides his finger to the location of the words as they are being read. As the student becomes capable of leading the oral reading, the teacher may lower his voice and read slightly slower, and the student's finger can point to the reading. Thus, the student and teacher alternate between leading and following. No attempt is made to teach any phonics skills or word recognition, and no attention is given to comprehension of the material being read. The basic concern is for the student to attain fluent reading automatically.

Instruction begins at a level slightly below where the student can read successfully. Gradually the student advances until he is reading at the appropriate grade level for his age and measured intelligence. The neurological impress method emphasizes rapid decoding and may be most effective with students 10 years old or older who spend too much time sounding out words and do not read fluently (Faas, 1980). Reading material in phrases rather than isolated words reveals progress, as does learning to pause for punctuation previously ignored. Lorenz and Vockell (1979) conducted a study using the neurological impress method and found that there were no significant gains in word recognition or reading comprehension. Several positive effects, however, were noted: improvement in (a) oral expression, (b) fluency, and (c) the students' confidence in their ability to read.

A variation of the neurological impress method is the method of repeated readings (Samuels, 1979). This method requires the student to reread a short, meaningful passage several times until a satisfactory level of fluency is reached. The procedure is then repeated with a new passage. Kann (1983) notes that this method promotes the development of syntactic competency and provides students with successful reading experiences. Although not complete alone, either the neurological impress method or the method of repeated readings may be used effectively to improve reading fluency (Henk, Helfeldt, & Platt, 1986).

High Interest—Low Vocabulary Method

Older students with reading problems often are frustrated because books geared to their interest level are beyond their reading ability. High interest—low vocabulary books offer a relatively easy vocabulary while maintaining an interest level appropriate for the more mature reader. As indicated in Table 11.4, numerous

TABLE 11.4
High interest–low vocabulary reading materials.

Title	Publisher	Reading Grade Level	Interest Grade Level
Action Series	Scholastic Magazine and Book Services	4–5	7–12
American Adventure Series	Harper & Row	3–6	4–8
Basic Vocabulary Books	Garrard	2	1–6
Breakthrough Series	Allyn & Bacon	2–6	7–12
Checkered Flag Series	Field Educational Publications	2–4	6–12
Childhood of Famous Americans Series	Bobbs-Merrill	4–5	7–9
Cowboy Sam Series	Benefic Press	PP–3	1–6
Dan Frontier Series	Benefic Press	PP–4	1–7
Deep Sea Adventures	Field Educational Publications	2–5	3–11
Everyreader Series	McGraw-Hill	6–8	5–12
Fastback Books	Fearon	4–5	6–12
First Reading Books	Garrard	1	1–4
Folklore of the World Books	Garrard	2	2–8
Interesting Reading Series	Follett	2–3	7–12
Jim Forest Readers	Field Educational Publications	1–3	1–7
Junior Science Books	Garrard	4–5	6–9
Morgan Bay Mysteries	Field Educational Publications	2–4	4–11
Morrow's High Interest/ Easy Reading Books	William Morrow	1–8	4–10
Mystery Adventure Series	Benefic Press	2–6	4–9
Pacemaker Classics	Fearon	2	7–12
Pacemaker True Adventure	Fearon	2	5–12
Pacemaker Story Books	Xerox Education Publications	2	7–12
Pal Paperback Kits	Xerox Education Publications	1–5	5–12
Pleasure Reading Books	Garrard	4	3–7
Racing Wheels Series	Benefic Press	2–4	4–9
Reading For Concepts Series	McGraw-Hill	3–8	5–12
Reading Reinforcement Skilltext Series	Merrill	1–5	1–8
Reading Skill Builders	Reader's Digest Services	1–4	2–5
Sailor Jack Series	Benefic Press	PP–3	1–6
Space Science Fiction Series	Benefic Press	2–6	4–9
Sports Mystery Stories	Benefic Press	2–4	4–9
Super Kits	Warner Educational Services	2–5	4–12
Superstars Series	Steck-Vaughn	4–6	7–12
Teen-Age Tales	D.C. Heath	4–6	6–11
Top Picks	Reader's Digest Services	5–7	5–12
What Is It Series	Benefic Press	1–4	1–8

publishing companies produce these materials covering a wide variety of topics (for example, sports, mysteries, science, adventure).

The teacher can estimate the reading level of any reading material by using the Fry (1977) readability formula, presented in Figure 11.1. A computer software program, *Readability Formulas,* produced by Encyclopaedia Britannica Educational Corporation, allows the user to apply seven different readability formulas (e.g., Fry, SMOG, Spache) to any reading selection simultaneously to determine reading level. The program, which is for Apple II computers, graphically depicts readability results. In addition, the *Foxie Systematic Readability Aides* (Fox, 1979) include a reference book that lists the readability level for more than 7,890 stories in 32 basal series published from 1970 to 1978. The Fry formula was used approximately three times on each story examined. A basal book list is provided listing approximately 400 basal readers in alphabetical order and giving each reader's grade level, year of publication, and publisher. A wall chart summarizes the research on readability levels of stories listed in the reference book; thus, the teacher can compare series at each grade level and among grade levels for each series. For each basal, the chart gives (a) the percentage of stories below, at, and above grade level; (b) the range of stories; and (c) the average readability of the basal.

No one reading approach or program works best for all students with learning problems. The teacher must consider each individual case to determine which skills need corrective instruction and then must select the approach most likely to be effective. In addition, the teacher should encourage independent reading, since reading performance may improve through the frequent use of reading skills. The teacher can stimulate interest in reading by reading parts of stories aloud to students and making displays of various books and reading topics. Book clubs or awards for reading may also motivate some reluctant readers.

READING AND STUDY SKILLS FOR ADOLESCENTS

Most secondary course work requires a relatively large amount of reading, since textbooks and supplementary reading materials are the major sources of information. Roe, Stoodt, and Burns (1983) state that "teachers can promote developmental reading by helping students learn the concepts and vocabulary of [each] content area, and they can enhance their students' reading comprehension by assisting them in interpreting and evaluating the text material" (p. 5). The secondary teacher also should be aware that the older student often needs to develop his rate of reading and study skills, in addition to increasing decoding and comprehension skills.

The adolescent may need to increase his reading speed in order to finish his assignments on time and keep up with other classmates. Roe et al. (1983) note that secondary students should be made aware of poor reading habits that may decrease their reading rate. Such poor habits include forming each word as it is read, sounding out all words (familiar and unfamiliar), going back and rereading previously read material, and pointing at each word with the index finger. Another technique for increasing rate, which is often used in a reading laboratory, is to present words and phrases with a tachistoscope and gradually reduce the presentation time, thus speeding up the student's responses. Also, using timing devices such as stopwatches and egg timers, the teacher can have the student participate in timed readings. Reinforcement should be provided, and progress should be charted continuously. Timed readings should be accompanied by comprehension checks, and teachers

Average number of syllables per 100 words

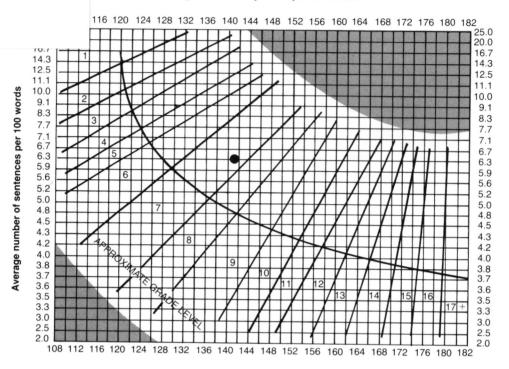

DIRECTIONS: Randomly select 3 one hundred word passages from a book or an article. Plot average number of syllables and average number of sentences per 100 words on graph to determine the grade level of the material. Choose more passages per book if great variability is observed and conclude that the book has uneven readability. Few books will fall in gray area but when they do grade level scores are invalid.

Count proper nouns, numerals and initializations as words. Count a syllable for each symbol. For example, "1945" is 1 word and 4 syllables and "IRA" is 1 word and 3 syllables.

EXAMPLE:

	SYLLABLES	SENTENCES
1st Hundred Words	124	6.6
2nd Hundred Words	141	5.5
3rd Hundred Words	158	6.8
AVERAGE	141	6.3

READABILITY 7th GRADE (see dot plotted on graph)

EXPANDED DIRECTIONS FOR WORKING READABILITY GRAPH

1. Randomly select three (3) sample passages and count out exactly 100 words beginning with the beginning of a sentence. Do count proper nouns, initializations, and numerals.

FIGURE 11.1

Fry's graph for estimating readability—extended.

Reprinted by permission of the author.

2. Count the number of sentences in the hundred words estimating length of the fraction of the last sentence to the nearest 1/10th.
3. Count the total number of syllables in the 100-word passage. If you don't have a hand counter available, an easy way is to simply put a mark above every syllable over one in each word, then when you get to the end of the passage, count the number of marks and add 100. Small calculators can also be used as counters by pushing numeral "1", then push the "+" sign for each word or syllable when counting.
4. Enter graph with average sentence length and average number of syllables; plot dot where the two lines intersect. Area where dot is plotted will give you the approximate grade level.
5. If a great deal of variability is found in syllable count or sentence count, putting more samples into the average is desirable.
6. A word is defined as a group of symbols with a space on either side; thus, "Joe," "IRA," "1945," and "&" are each one word.
7. A syllable is defined as a phonetic syllable. Generally, there are as many syllables as vowel sounds. For example, "stopped" is one syllable and "wanted" is two syllables. When counting syllables for numerals and initializations, count one syllable for each symbol. For example, "1945" is 4 syllables and "IRA" is 3 syllables, and "&" is 1 syllable.

FIGURE 11.1, *continued*

should encourage rate increases only if comprehension does not suffer.

Rupley and Blair (1983) note that successful reading in the content areas requires the ability to adjust one's rate of reading to the type of material being read. Three types of reading are required: skimming, scanning, and studying. *Skimming* refers to covering a selection to get some of the main ideas and a general overview of the material without attending to details. In skimming, the student should (a) read the first paragraph line by line, (b) read boldprint headings as they appear, (c) read the first sentence of every paragraph, (d) examine pictures, charts, and maps, and (e) read the last paragraph. Skimming activities may involve giving the student a short amount of time to skim a content chapter and write down the main ideas or asking him to skim newspaper articles and match them to headlines. *Scanning* refers to reading a selection to find a specific piece of information. When scanning, the student should (a) use headings to locate the pages to scan for the specific information, (b) run his eyes rapidly down the page in a zigzag or winding S pattern, (c) note capital letters if looking for a name, numbers for dates, and

italicized words for vocabulary items, and (d) read only what is needed to verify the purpose. Scanning activities may include having the student scan a history chapter to find the date of a particular event or giving him a telephone directory to locate a specific person's number. In *study-type reading,* the goal is total comprehension, and reading is deliberate and purposeful. Rupley and Blair state that students must have these three types of reading explained to them, practice under teacher supervision, and be given opportunities for independent practice.

As students learn to study various content areas, they should develop effective study skills. The SQ3R method, developed by Robinson (1961), is widely used, especially for social studies and science material. This method may be useful to the student with learning problems in providing a systematic approach to increasing study skills. The method involves the following steps:

1. *Survey:* To get an overview of the reading material, the reader scans the entire assignment. He glances over headings to see the major points that will be developed and

reads introductory statements and summaries. He also should inspect graphic aids such as maps, tables, graphs, and pictures. This survey provides a framework for organizing facts in the selection as the student progresses through the reading.

2. *Question:* To give a purpose for careful reading of the material, the reader devises questions that he expects to find answered in the selection. Questions can derive from rephrasing headings and subheadings.

3. *Read:* The reader reads the material with the intent of finding the answers to questions he posed. Also, notes may be taken during this careful reading.

4. *Recite:* The reader looks away from the reading material and his notes and briefly recites the answers to his questions. This checks on what the reader has learned and helps set the information in memory.

5. *Review:* The reader reviews the material and checks his memory of the content by rereading portions of the selection or notes to verify answers given during the previous step. He may also note major points under each heading. This review activity helps the student retain the material better by reinforcing the learning.

Another strategy to increase students' comprehension is for the content teacher to provide a reading guide or study organizer. A reading guide includes questions and statements on the content of the text material. It should be given to the student prior to reading and completed or filled in by the student as the text is read. A study organizer summarizes the main ideas and important concepts of the material in a factual style or in a schematic form such as a flow chart, diagram, or table.

Setting a purpose for reading through the use of study guides or the SQ3R method may improve the older student's comprehension ability. Students with learning problems may also be taught to use learning strategies designed to increase their reading comprehension (Clark, Deshler, Schumaker, Alley, & Warner, 1984). For example, the visual imagery strategy requires the student to read a passage and to create representative visual images, and the self-questioning strategy teaches the student to form questions about the content of a passage as he reads in order to maintain interest and enhance recall. Developing effective study skills, increasing reading rate, using learning strategies, and adjusting reading rate according to purpose should help the adolescent read more efficiently in numerous content areas at a higher academic level. Additional study methods for secondary students are discussed in Chapter 14.

ACTIVITIES AND MATERIALS

There are many reading activities and commercial and teacher-made materials that aid in the development of reading skills. Supplementary activities and materials are useful in short, concentrated drill or practice; they also may be used to enhance motivation and interest by reinforcing a newly learned skill. Activities, instructional games, self-correcting materials, and computer software programs can be used to individualize instruction according to specific needs and abilities. Additional reading activities for adolescents are presented in Chapter 14.

Word-Attack Activities

1. For practice in initial consonant sounds, glue pictures of simple objects on small cards and make a grid or a pocket chart in which the beginning square or pocket has consonant letters corresponding to initial sounds of the objects. To indicate the initial sound of the word, the student places each picture card next to the appropriate letter. Consonant blends, medial

vowel sounds, and final consonant sounds also may be practiced in the same manner.

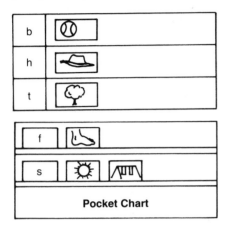

Pocket Chart

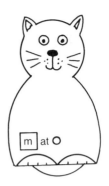

2. Have the child make his own picture dictionary by using a scrapbook indexed with the letters of the alphabet. The child draws pictures or cuts them out of old magazines. When he learns the word shown by the picture, he pastes the picture on the page representing the initial consonant sound. For example, a picture of a dog is pasted on the *D* page. The student-made dictionary invites interest because the child makes it himself and it contains only words that he is using. If desired, completed dictionaries can be exchanged so that each student learns to read other students' dictionaries.

3. Make a rotating circle device to use in practicing initial consonant sounds and word families. Cut an attractive design or object out of poster board and print the desired letters of a word family on it. Cut out a square in front of the

letters. Then cut a small circle out of poster board and print the appropriate initial consonant letters on it. Attach the circle to the back of the larger poster board, positioned so that each letter will be exposed in the square opening as the circle is rotated.

4. Make flash cards: Paste pictures on index cards and print the word or phrase that tells about the picture on both the front and back of the card. Vowel cards can be made by using a picture illustrating a word that uses a specific vowel (for example, *cat*) and writing the word and the marked vowel on the card (căt—ă). Flash cards for blends, digraphs, or diphthongs can be constructed in a similar manner. After the child learns to associate the printed symbol with the picture, he can practice reading the words on the back side of the cards.

5. Make a set of word cards in which the first letter of each word is omitted and a picture illustrates the word. The child is to fill in the missing letter. The cards can be made self-correcting by writing the answer on the back or supplying an answer key that is picture coded. Cards also may be made that omit letters in the medial or final position or that omit blends, digraphs, or diphthongs. The cards can be laminated and written on with a grease pencil so that they can be reusable. (See the cards on page 388.)

6. To develop auditory discrimination of letter sounds, have the student participate in rhyming activities such as matching pictures whose names rhyme. Also, when given one word in a family, the student may be asked to name and list as many other words as he can that belong

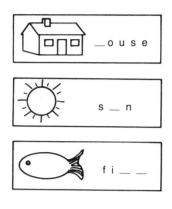

to the same family and to circle like parts of the rhyming words.

7. Have the student make a *sound* dictionary in an indexed scrapbook. On each page, paste pictures of objects or actions that illustrate words beginning with the sound. For example, pictures of a table, tent, and top can be pasted on the *T* page; the page for words with the initial *Ch* sound can have pictures of a church, cheese, and children on it.

8. For general word recognition, attach labels to the door, windows, and objects in the classroom so that the child will begin to associate the printed word with the object. Also, a large picture can be made on poster board with slits next to the objects in the picture. Word cards are made for the objects in the picture, and an envelope containing paper clips is attached to the back of the picture. Instruct the child to match each word card to the appropriate object in the picture by paper clipping it to the slit.

9. To provide practice on basic sight words or sight phrases, make a ladder that will hold word or phrase cards on each rung. The student tries to climb the ladder by saying each word or phrase. When he is able to reach the top by pronouncing each word correctly, he receives a reward (reinforcement) and starts to work on a more difficult set of cards.

10. Construct a word wheel: Two poster board circles, one smaller than the other, are fastened together through their centers so that they rotate freely. A blend can be written on the inner circle with an opening next to it; letters to add to

the blend are printed on the outer circle. The student rotates the inner wheel and reads the words as they appear in the opening. A variation of the word wheel is to print word endings and suffixes on the outer wheel and various root words on the inner wheel. The teacher gives a sentence (for example, "The two boys are _____") and points to the root word on the inner wheel. The student rotates the wheel to find the appropriate ending and reads the word.

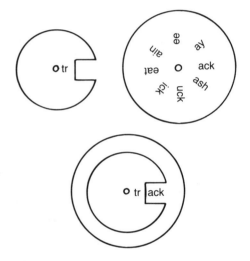

11. Make a tachistoscope by cutting a window in a piece of oaktag and attaching the window card to another card of equal size to form a backing. Words or phrases are written on a strip of paper the width of the window; the student pulls the strip past the window to reveal the written words. This device can be made self-correcting by having two windows, one of which is covered with a flap, and preparing an answer strip with picture clues. The student reads the word in the open window and lifts the flap on the other window to check his response by looking at the picture clue. Also, to develop quick recognition of sight words, a shutter can be attached to the opening so that the teacher can quickly expose or flash each word. If the word is missed, the shutter can be reopened to allow the child more time to analyze the word.

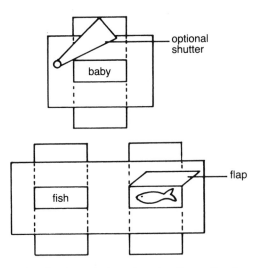

12. To develop knowledge of contractions, give the student sentences to read in which several words are underlined that could be made into contractions. Instruct him to change the words to the appropriate contraction as he reads. For example:

   a. There is nobody she will go with today.
   b. He has not done the work because he can-not see it.
   c. "You are going to the store, are not you?" said Mary.

   Also, the student may be asked to underline all contractions or words that could have been made into contractions in a selected reading passage. An additional activity is to have contraction races. Call out contractions and see who can give the words they stand for, or call out two words and see who can give the contraction. Ekwall (1989) lists contractions and the grade level at which they should be known.

13. To help the student identify compound words, give him two lists of words and have him draw lines to connect two words to make a compound word. Also, the student can be asked to separate compound words into two words. Activities involving compound words encourage focusing on the whole word. Such activities may help the student who has a tendency to read words by looking at the initial sound and guessing at the remainder of the word.

14. If the student has a tendency to read word by word, allow him to read material he is familiar with or material that has a lower-level vocabulary (high interest–low vocabulary stories). Tape record the student's reading of familiar passages and contrast it with other reading to note whether the student reads fluently. The student also may read against a timer to increase his speed and maintain a more appropriate pace.

15. Have the student practice with phrase cards. After he has mastered short, easy phrases, longer and more difficult phrases may be introduced. The phrase cards may be arranged to tell a continuous story. Phrase reading also may be encouraged by giving the student a reading passage in which the words to be read together are underlined—for example, All the children walked quickly to the car.

16. On the chalkboard, write sentences that contain words with prefixes or suffixes. Ask the student to locate the root word, identify the prefix or suffix, and explain how the addition of the prefix or suffix changes the meaning of the root word.

17. If the student tends to omit or repeat words when reading, tape record his reading of a selected passage. Give him a copy of the passage and ask him to follow along with his finger as the tape is played back to him. Have him circle all omitted words or underline words that he repeats. This focuses attention on omitted or repeated words and increases the student's awareness of this tendency as he reads.

18. Emphasize left-to-right orientation to help the student who frequently reverses letters in words (such as was for saw or lap for pal). Present frequently reversed words on flash cards and cover up all but the initial letter. Slowly uncover the remaining letters as the student correctly pronounces the word. Arrows drawn from left to right may also be added under the word. In addition, the student may be asked to trace troublesome words or letters with his fingers and simultaneously sound out the word or letter. After tracing each word or letter, the student should attempt to write it from memory.

19. Encourage the student to use context clues instead of guessing at unknown words or substituting words. Ask the student to complete multiple-choice sentences that provide practice in context reading. For example:

    a. While camping, the boys slept in a
       _____. (lamp, tent, trap)
    b. It was raining, so she brought her
       _____. (umbrella, usher, clock)

    In a reading passage, encourage the student to sound out the first few sounds of a troublesome word and then to read beyond it to see if the following words give any clue concerning its meaning. Context clues as well as beginning sounds may help the student identify a difficult word.

20. Give the student a list of words. Ask him to arrange them in columns according to the number of syllables in each word. Improving skills in syllabication aids the older student in structural analysis and often enhances word recognition.

21. Instruct the student to use the following cognitive strategy for word identification (Ellis & Lenz, 1987):

    D = Dicover the context.
    I = Isolate the prefix.
    S = Separate the suffix.
    S = Say the stem.
    E = Examine the stem using the rules of 2s and 3s:
        If a stem or part of the stem begins with a vowel, divide off the first two letters; if it begins with a consonant, divide off the first three letters.
    C = Check with someone.
    T = Try the dictionary.

Comprehension Activities

1. To help the student remember what he has read, point out key words that reveal the text's organization and show a series of events. The student should be aware of words and phrases such as *to begin with, next, after that,* and *finally.*

2. To emphasize word meaning and develop vocabulary, have the student group various words in categories. For example, words that relate to specific interests may be grouped together, such as baseball words or cooking words. Also, words may be grouped in categories such as "Things That Are Alive," "What Animals Do," or "Things That Eat."

3. Help the student develop a visual image by reviewing the setting of the story before he reads. While reading, he may be asked to describe images from the passage; for example, "Do you think Ruff is a big dog?" Also, after reading, the student may draw pictures to illustrate settings and happenings in the story.

4. Model proper inflection for a particular sentence. Have the student imitate what he has just heard. Reading with expression increases understanding.

5. Write several riddles or short stories that describe a specific word or object. The student must focus on descriptive details in order to answer each riddle. If the riddle is written on a card, the activity can be made self-correcting by writing the answer on the back of each card.

6. Have the student read a story and then make up an appropriate title for it. The teacher could give the student several titles and ask him to select the best one and justify his response.

7. Have the student read a story in which the sentences have been numbered. Ask several detailed questions about the reading selection, and require the student to give the number of the sentence in which he located each answer.

8. After the student has read a selection, ask him to underline the sentences that best state the main idea, or he can tell what the selection is about in his own words. Then have him list important details pertaining to the main idea. The headings "Who," "What," "Where," "When," and "Why" may be written on the paper so that details regarding each heading can be listed in the appropriate column. The student may also draw pictures to illustrate details of the selection or answer questions requiring knowledge of the important details.

9. Cut pictures out of magazines or catalogs and write descriptive statements about them. Have the student match each picture with its description.

10. Cut articles out of the newspaper and cut off the headlines. Have the student read each article and then select the appropriate headline.

11. To help the student attend to specific details of a reading passage, have him read directions on how to do a given activity and then have him perform the activity step by step. Also, ask the student to write directions for playing a game; then another student can read the written directions to see if he could learn to play the game from them.

12. Present the student with a series of paragraphs, each of which contains one word or one sentence that does not fit the meaning of the rest of the paragraph. Have him cross out the irrelevant word or sentence and write a more appropriate one in its place.

13. To enhance vocabulary development and word meaning, make a crossword puzzle in which the clues are word definitions. For young students, a modified puzzle may be made in which the puzzle supplies the first letter for each response.

14. Teach vocabulary with definitions according to the following format (Carnine & Silbert, 1979):

    a. State the definition and ask the student to repeat it.

    b. Teach and test students on positive and negative examples. Positive examples are words of the same class, and negative examples are those of a different class. For example, in teaching the meaning of the word *exit,* a positive example would be a picture of a door leading out of a movie theater, and a negative example would be a picture of a closet door. The teacher presents each example by holding up the picture, pointing to the door, and asking, "Is this an exit? How do you know?"

    c. Review words previously taught.

    Lovitt (1984) suggests several modifications of this approach: (a) let the student select words to be learned, (b) have the student write a story using the words, or (c) have the student use the words in an oral discussion.

15. After the student has read a short story, instruct him to write a telegram telling the main events of the passage. The telegram should be limited to a specific number of words. Blank telegrams can be provided for the student's use. A variation of this activity is to provide a list of topic suggestions and have the student compose a telegram of 10 or fewer words about the chosen topic.

16. To help the student distinguish between the main idea and supporting details of a reading selection, have him diagram the sentences of a paragraph. For example:

Every day the old man and his dog took an early morning walk.
They always walked four blocks.
The dog stayed right next to the man.
Many people spoke to both the man and his dog.

17. To provide practice in distinguishing between cause and effect, have one student describe an event—for example, "the dog barked." The second student must give a reason for the event: "because a cat came into the yard." Then a third student is asked to give a probable effect: "the cat ran home."

18. To help the student increase his speed of reading while focusing on comprehension, have him read a short selection in a limited amount of time. Then present a series of questions based on the selection and have the student answer as many questions as he can. Also, the teacher could present questions prior to reading and then give the student the selection; the student is allowed a short period of time to locate as many answers as possible. An additional method to increase recall of facts involves having the student read a selection orally for a specified amount of time and then write down or recite as many facts as he can remember. The number of correct and incorrect responses can be charted to indicate progress.

19. Read half of a story aloud and ask the student to predict how the story will end. Also, the student can read chapter headings of a book, or

look at pictures from a story, and the teacher can ask him to tell or write what he thinks the story will be about.

20. Present the student with a short story in which the sentences are presented in the wrong order. Ask the student to rewrite the selection, arranging the sentences in logical order so that the story makes sense. Another sequencing activity is to give the student a list of events from a story he has read and ask him to number the events to indicate the order in which they happened. Also, the student could arrange pictures that tell stories or show action in sequence and then write a sentence or paragraph for each picture.

21. To develop comprehension skills involving inference, ask the student several cause–effect questions (for example, "What will happen if . . . ?"). Read part of a story aloud and stop at a crucial point to let the student predict what will happen next. Also, the student may be asked to judge the reading selection as being true or fantasylike.

22. To develop study skills, use the daily newspaper to present comprehension activities. The student can practice locating the main idea and supporting ideas by using the editorial page. Then he can discuss the pros and cons of the viewpoint presented. He also may be asked to study the employment ads to answer various questions concerning available jobs. Grocery store ads give the student an opportunity to read for comparison shopping, and from articles in the sports section he may be required to locate answers concerning (a) to whom it happened, (b) what happened, (c) when it happened, (d) where it happened, and (e) why it happened. Highway maps, available at local service stations, are excellent for practice in the important skill of map reading.

23. Instruct the student to use cognitive strategies for reading comprehension. Chapter 14 includes the following strategies: RIDER (a visual imagery strategy), RAP (a paraphrasing strategy), and FIST (a self-questioning strategy).

Instructional Games

Vowel Spinner

Materials:

A spinner made from a cardboard circle which is divided into five equal segments, with a vowel written in each section; two or more laminated cardboard cards containing three-, four-, or five-letter words with the vowels deleted; grease pencil.

Directions:

The first student spins the spinner, and he must try to use the vowel the spinner stops on to complete a word on his card. The student uses the grease pencil to write the vowel in the selected place, and the word must make sense. If the player cannot use the vowel, he loses that turn. Next, the second student spins and attempts to use his vowel. The players continue to take turns, and the winner is the first student to fill the card by completing every word with an appropriate vowel.

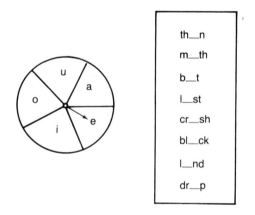

Blend Game

Materials:

A start-to-finish game board; cards with pictures showing words containing initial blends; spinner with numbered segments; markers; answer key that gives the correct initial blend for each picture.

Directions:

The first player draws the top card from the card deck. He identifies the picture (for example, flower) and tells the initial blend (*fl*). Another student can check his response by referring to the answer key. If the player is correct, he spins the spinner and moves his game board marker the number of spaces shown on the spinner. The players take turns; when an incorrect response is made or the player cannot identify the blend, he loses that turn and does not spin the spinner or move his marker. The first player to reach the finish space on the game board wins the game.

Modifications:

Use picture cards that illustrate words containing digraphs, diphthongs, medial vowels, or initial consonants. Also, to boost interest the game board can have various instructions on certain spaces—for example, *Go back one space, Spin again, Lose one turn.*

Word Blender

Materials:

Cards of words containing initial blends, with each card cut in half to show the blend on one half and the remainder of the word on the other half.

Directions:

The deck of blend cards and the deck of word cards are both shuffled and placed face down. The first player turns over the top cards from each deck. If the blend fits the letters on the word card, the player places the cards together and says the word. If he is correct, he keeps the cards. If he is incorrect, or if the blend and letters do not form a word, the cards are placed in their respective discard piles. The players take turns trying to form words. When the decks are finished, the discard piles are shuffled and used. When all the cards have been used (or at the end of a predetermined time period), the players count their cards, and the player with the most matches wins.

Modifications:

The cards may contain words and be cut so that the players have to form words with appropriate prefixes, suffixes, or various endings.

Phonics Rummy

Materials:

Phonics card sets: Each set consists of four cards with the phonics element written at the top, and four words are listed under it containing that phonics element—a different word is underlined on each of the four cards in the set (36 cards are ample for two players; additional card sets can be added for more players).

Directions:

Eight cards are dealt face down to each player, and the remaining cards are placed face down in a stack in the middle of the players. The first player asks another player for a word using a certain phonics element to try to obtain three or four cards in a set. For example: "Mike, give me 'bat' from the *a* group"—the player pronounces the short *a* sound. If the player who was asked has the card, he must give it to the caller. The caller continues to ask for cards from specific players. If the person asked for a card does not have it, the caller takes the top card from the center pile. The players take turns, and when a player has three cards from a certain phonics element set, he lays them down. When the fourth card to a set that has already been laid down is drawn, it may also be put down. The winner is the player who gets rid of all the cards in his hand and in doing so "goes out."

Modifications:

Instead of phonics elements the card sets may contain four synonyms (or four antonyms) for a specific word.

ă	dr .	mad
bat	drink	angry
flat	dress	furious
sat	drop	unhappy
task	drape	insane

Fish

Materials:

A deck of word cards with three cards for each word (the word should be written in the top-right-hand corner and upside down in the lower-left-hand corner of the card; a picture illustrating the word can be placed in the middle).

Directions:

Nine cards are dealt to each player, and the remaining cards are placed face down in the middle of the players. The first player asks another player for a match for a word in his hand. If the asked player has the word card, he must give it to the caller. If he has two cards of that word set, he must give them both to the caller. The caller continues to ask for cards until the person does not have the card asked for and he says, "Go Fish." When told to "Go Fish," the player takes the top card from the pile. If it happens to be the word card he had just asked for, his turn continues. The players take turns, and when a player completes a set (three cards with the same word), he lays it down in front of him. The first player out of cards is the winner.

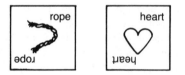

Word Bingo

Materials:

Bingo cards (five squares across and five squares down) with a sight word written in each square; word list of the words included on all the cards; discs to use as markers.

Directions:

Each student is given a bingo card and several discs. The teacher (or caller) reads a word from the word list and checks it off. The players look for the called word on their bingo cards, and if a player has it, he covers it with a disc. The teacher continues to call out words one at a time, and the first player to cover five spaces in any direction calls out "Bingo." After the player calls out "Bingo," he must also pronounce each of the covered words to win.

Modifications:

Bingo cards and word lists can be derived from various categories, such as words with prefixes, words with suffixes, compound words, or words containing blends.

Word War

Materials:

Word cards with several sets of identical words.

Directions:

The cards are shuffled, and all are dealt to the players. All players simultaneously turn over one card at a time from their stacks. When two (or more) identical cards are turned up, the first player to name the word correctly takes the turned-up stacks of cards from the players who were involved in the "war." The winner is the player who gets all the cards or the most cards within a specified period of time.

Dominoes

Materials:

Word cards divided in half by a line, with a different word on each side of the line (the words are repeated several times on different cards).

Directions:

The cards are all dealt out to the players. The first player places a word card in the middle, and the next player must match words in order to play a card. The player must pronounce the word as he matches it. A design is formed by placing the matching card next to the word in any direction. If a player cannot match a word, he loses that turn. The first player to use all his cards is the winner.

Modifications:

Various sets of word cards can be devised, such as words containing blends, digraphs, or diphthongs; compound words; contractions; or words with prefixes or suffixes.

Word Game Board

Materials:

Start-to-finish laminated game board with words or phrases written in the squares—some special squares contain instructions such as *Move back three squares, Take an extra turn,* or *Go back to start;* dice; markers.

Directions:

The first player rolls the dice and moves his marker the number of spaces indicated on the dice. The player must correctly pronounce the word or phrase written on the square he lands on in order to remain there. If the player is unable to pronounce the word or phrase correctly, he moves his marker back to where he was prior to the roll. When the player lands on a special square, he must follow the directions on that square. The players take turns, and the first player to reach the Finish square is the winner.

Modifications:

The board is laminated or covered with clear plastic so that words can be written with a grease pencil and changed as needed.

Word Baseball

Materials:

Vocabulary words written on flash cards; answer key.

Directions:

The teacher divides the class into two teams and marks first base, second base, third base, and home plate on the floor. A member of the first team goes to home plate, and the designated pitcher on the opposing team holds up a word from his set of flash cards. The batter must correctly pronounce the word, define it, and use it in a sentence. If he is correct (as judged by a scorekeeper with an answer key), he advances to first base. Other members of the team bat, and for each "hit" (correct response) the player advances one base. Runs are scored by crossing home plate; an out occurs when a batter misses a word or its definition. Each team gets three outs, and then the opposing team comes to bat. The team with the highest score, after both teams have batted at least three times, is the winner.

Modifications:

The word cards may be labelled *single, double, triple,* or *home run* to indicate the value of the hit.

Also, the word cards may be divided according to words with one, two, three, or four or more syllables. The number of syllables indicates the number of bases a correct response is worth. However, in addition to reading the word, the student must state the number of syllables in that word correctly, or he is out. In addition, the pitcher may be allowed to select his pitches (word cards) depending on who the batter is; however, once a word card has been used, it is out of the game for that team.

Mystery Detective Game

Materials, Directions, Modifications, and Example:

This game, designed to practice reading comprehension of phrases (who, where, why, how, what, when), uses a game-board format and is described in detail in Chapter 4. It features a self-correcting format and can be modified to offer practice in syllabication.

Comprehension Game

Materials:

Start-to-finish game board with each square colored red, blue, or white; several copies of a story; a set of red cards (made from construction paper) containing comprehension questions (who, what, when, why, where, or how questions) about the story's content; a set of blue cards containing vocabulary words from the story; a set of white cards that are synonym cards and give a sentence with one word underlined; markers; spinner.

Directions:

Each player reads a copy of the given story. To begin the game, the first player takes the top card from one of the card sets. If he takes a red card, the player must correctly answer the comprehension question. If the player takes a blue card, he must correctly define the vocabulary word. If he takes a white card, the player must give a synonym for the word underlined on the card. If the player responds to the card correctly, he spins the spinner and moves his marker the number of spaces it shows. On his next turn, he must take the top card from the card set

that is the same color as the space his marker is on. If the player is unable to respond to his card correctly, he does not spin the spinner or move his marker and must try another card of the same color on his next turn. The other players must decide if each task is answered correctly; they may refer to the story to be sure. The first player to reach the Finish square wins the game.

Self-Correcting Materials

Heart Puzzles

Feedback device:

The two pieces of the heart fit together to indicate a correct choice.

Materials:

Sets of heart puzzle pieces: one part of the heart contains a picture, a second part fits together with the picture piece and has the word illustrated by the picture written on it, and two additional heart pieces that do not fit together with the picture piece but contain words with minimal letter differences from the word that identifies the picture.

Directions:

The student looks at the picture and selects the word illustrated by the picture. She fits the two pieces of the heart together to check her choice—only the correct word will fit with the picture.

Modifications:

The puzzle pieces may contain various tasks, such as matching the word with the correct definitions, matching the correct blend with the picture, or matching the correct number of syllables with the card.

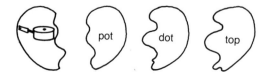

Flip Siders

Feedback device:

A picture clue to identify the word on the front of the card provides feedback.

Materials:

Index cards with a word printed on the front and a picture illustrating that word pasted on the back.

Directions:

The student looks at the word and reads it. Then he flips the card over to check himself by looking at the picture illustrating the word.

Modifications:

For phonics review, have the student look at the pictures and put all the pictures with the same beginning sound in a pile (for example, *cat, cake, can, crack*). Then the student turns over each card to see the printed word and the initial letter. Another variation is to have words written on the front of each card and the number of syllables, or the word divided into syllables, written on the back. The student reads the word, counts the number of syllables, and flips over the card to check his response. Also, for practice in vocabulary development, sets of cards can show a word on one card and its definition on another card. The backs of both cards in the set should have matching objects, numbers, or colors or should go together to complete a picture. When the student pairs a word with its definition, he flips over the cards to see if the reverse sides go together.

Punch-Through Cards

Feedback device:

On the reverse side of the card the hole that indicates the correct answer is circled in a color.

Materials:

Index cards containing pictures, with the word illustrated by each picture written underneath omitting the initial or final consonant or blend, and with three possible answers listed next to three holes—the hole next to the correct answer is circled in a color on the back; pencil (or golf tee).

Directions:

The student looks at the picture and determines what letter or letters are omitted in the word. He punches his pencil through the hole to indicate his response. Then he turns the card over. If his answer is correct, his pencil is in the hole circled in a color.

Modifications:

Vocabulary words with three possible definitions can be presented on the cards, or the student can be required to select the appropriate synonym or antonym for a word. Also, a brief reading selection can be presented with a comprehension question and three possible answers. Commercial sets of Punch-Thru Cards that focus on initial consonants, short vowels, long vowels, final consonants, and consonant blends are produced by Trend Enterprises.

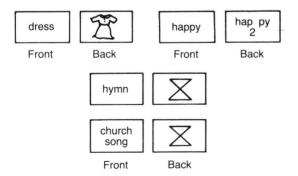

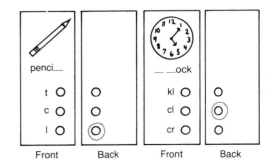

Clothespin Wheel

Feedback device:

The symbol or number on the back of the clothespin matches the symbol or number on the back of the correct section of the wheel.

Materials:

A 10-inch cardboard circle divided into eight sections which have definitions written in them, and a symbol or number on the back of the circle in each section; clothespins with words corresponding to the definitions written on the front and a symbol or number written on the back.

Directions:

The student reads the definition and looks at the words on the clothespins to find the correct answer. He clips the clothespin containing his answer to the section of the wheel with the definition and then turns over the circle. If his response is correct, the symbol or number on the backs of the circle section and the clothespin match.

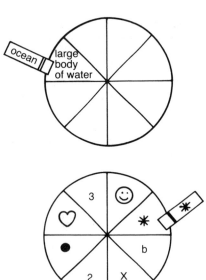

Modifications:

The student can be required to match synonyms, antonyms, or contractions with the appropriate section of the circle. Another variation is to have a word written in each section on the front with a corresponding picture in each section on the back. Then the student reads the word, clips a clothespin to the section, and turns over the circle to check his response by looking at the picture.

Mickey Mouse Contractions

Feedback device:

A flap is raised to reveal the correct response.

Materials:

A laminated cardboard figure of Mickey Mouse's head with holes cut for the eyes and nose; a flexible flap of thick black felt material held in place over the nose opening with two fasteners; a long piece of cardboard with the two words to be made into a contraction written so that they will show in the eye openings, and the correct answer (the contraction form) positioned in the middle column so that it will appear in the nose opening; three strips of cardboard taped on the back of Mickey Mouse's head to hold the large task card of contractions in place and allow it to slide through to present each contraction task; a piece of paper.

Directions:

The student places the large task card through the strips on the back of Mickey Mouse's head so that the first two words to be made into a contraction appear in Mickey's eyes. The student writes down the contraction form of these two words on a piece of paper and then lifts the flap over the nose to reveal the answer and check his response. Then he continues by sliding the card up to present the next two words.

Modification:

This task can also be presented in the Answer Box format, described in detail in Chapter 4.

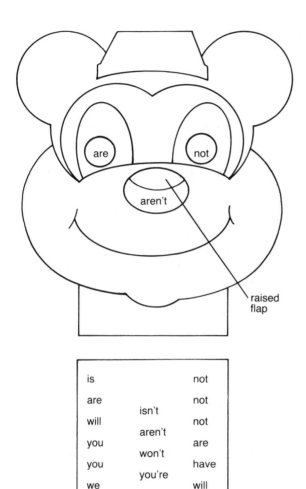

are not

aren't

raised flap

is		not
are		not
	isn't	
will		not
	aren't	
you		are
	won't	
you		have
	you're	
we		will
	you've	
they		will
	we'll	
was		not
	they'll	
he		is
	wasn't	
	he's	

Poke Box

Feedback device:

A stylus is inserted in the hole in the Poke Box to indicate the student's response. If the answer is cor-

rect, the task card can be removed from the box because the area below the correct answer is cut out and offers no resistance to the stylus.

Materials, Directions, Modifications, and Example:

The Poke Box is described in detail in Chapter 4 and may be used to present various reading tasks, including synonyms, antonyms, vocabulary definitions, or comprehension questions for a selected reading passage.

Synonym Lotto

Feedback device:

The correct answer is written on the back of each word card.

Materials:

A large cardboard square, six squares across and six squares down, with a word written in each of the 36 squares; word cards containing synonyms for the words included on the large board and the correct responses written on the back (see Figure 11.3).

Directions:

The student selects a word card and matches it with its synonym on the large board. After he makes his choice, he turns the word card over to see if he is correct. He continues until the entire board is covered.

Modifications:

Require the student to match antonyms with words, words with pictures, contractions with contracted words, or words with definitions.

Tape Recorder Reading

Feedback device:

The correct answers are provided on the tape.

Materials:

A tape recording of 25 words numbered on the tape and separated by a pause between each word, and

LITTLE	ENDED	SMILED	CENT	WOMAN	TRAIL
GLAD	PRESENT	CRY	REPLY	PRETTY	SCARED
MAD	LARGE	BAG	CORRECT	DISTANT	FAST
NEARLY	GRANDMA	CHIEF	STONE	SPEAK	BEACH
HARD	BEGAN	FLAT	TRIP	SHOUT	ODD
WOODS	HURRY	WEARY	NEAR	HUNGRY	AUTO

Cards containing the following words with the appropriate synonym from the large square written on the back:

small	finished	grinned	penny	lady	path
happy	gift	weep	answer	beautiful	afraid
angry	big	pouch	right	faraway	quick
almost	Grandmother	leader	rock	talk	shore
difficult	started	level	journey	tell	strange
forest	rush	tired	close	starved	car

FIGURE 11.3
Game board and cards for Synonym Lotto.

at the end of the tape a list of the correct responses; paper numbered from 1 to 25.

Directions:

The student listens to the tape recording and writes the sound he hears at the beginning (or end) of each word. At the end of the 25 words he continues to listen to the tape to hear the correct answers and check his responses.

Modifications:

The student may be instructed to write down vowel sounds, blends (in initial or final positions), or digraphs. Another variation of using the tape recorder is to present a short reading passage on the tape. After the student listens to the selection, he is instructed to turn off the recorder and write down the main ideas. Then he can turn the recorder back on to check his work by listening to the reader's summary of the main ideas on tape. Also, by recording a reading selection on tape, the student can be presented with various comprehension questions, and the answers can be provided on tape. Another device that can be used to provide oral feedback is the Language Master. The student can read the word printed on the Language Master card and then run the card through the machine to hear the word read for him.

Comic Strips

Feedback device:

The numbers to indicate correct sequence are written on the back of each section.

Materials:

Laminated newspaper comic strips mounted on cardboard and cut into frames, with each frame numbered on the back to indicate its proper position in the sequence.

Directions:

The student is given the mixed-up frames of a comic strip. He reads each frame and then unscrambles them and arranges them in order. This develops

and improves the student's ability to recognize and follow a sequence of happenings and his ability to anticipate the outcome of a situation. After arranging the frames in order, the student turns over the frames to see if they are numbered in order, thus indicating the correct sequence.

Packaged Comprehension

Feedback device:

The correct answers are provided on an answer key included in an envelope attached to the back of the folder.

Materials:

Manila folder with a label or wrapper (such as a food can label or a candy bar wrapper) attached to the front and comprehension questions concerning the label or wrapper written inside the folder (*What company makes the product? What does the product weigh?*); an answer key in an envelope attached to the back of the folder.

Directions:

The student reads the label or wrapper on the front of the folder and then opens the folder up to read the comprehension questions. He answers each question on a sheet of paper without rereading the label or wrapper and then checks his responses with the answers included in the answer key.

Modification:

A brief reading selection or short story can be attached to the front of the folder instead of a label or wrapper. Comprehension questions concerning the reading passage are included inside the folder.

Commercial Programs and Materials

A large number of commercial reading programs and materials are available for use with students who have learning problems. These materials may supplement one of the basic reading approaches to develop or improve specific skills, such as word attack or comprehension. This section presents 15 well-known commercial reading materials.

Dolch Reading Materials

Publisher: DLM Teaching Resources

Description:

Popper Words, Sets 1 and 2, consist of the 220 Dolch basic sight words. These words comprise 65 to 75% of primary reading materials and 50 to 75% of elementary reading materials. These commonly used words must be recognized instantly by sight so that the child can read with interest and confidence. The *Group Word Teaching Game* contains nine sets of six word cards and is played like bingo to help children in the second grade and above learn to recognize the 220 basic sight words. The *Picture Word Cards* present the Dolch 95 most common nouns, with each word written beside its picture. The *Sight Phrase Cards* consist of 140 two- and three-word phrases derived from the basic sight words and the 95 most common nouns. The cards are appropriate for use with children reading at the second-grade level. The student can use the phrase cards alone to improve phrase recognition, or several students can play a game to build sentences from phrases. *First Reading Books* include 12 paperback readers that contain the easier half of the 220 basic sight words as well as the 95 most common nouns. The eight *Basic Vocabulary Books* are written almost entirely with the Dolch basic sight words and most common nouns.

Essential Sight Words Program
(Sundbye, Dyck, & Wyatt, 1980)

Publisher: DLM Teaching Resources

Description:

This teacher-directed program is divided into two levels, each of which focuses on the identification of 100 frequently used words. A structured approach is used that combines sight-word drill and the actual reading of sight words in context. The program focuses on the interests of students in grades 1 to 4 and is appropriate for low-achieving readers and students with reading disabilities.

Learning Strategies Curriculum

Publisher: University of Kansas

Description:

This curriculum is designed to improve a student's ability to cope with specific curriculum demands and to perform tasks independently. The learning strategies in the acquisition instructional strand enable students to gain information from written material. The *Word Identification Strategy* (Lenz, Schumaker, Deshler, & Beals, 1984) is aimed at quick decoding of multisyllabic words. The strategy teaches students a problem-solving procedure for quickly attacking and decoding unknown words in reading materials. The *Paraphrasing Strategy* (Schumaker, Denton, & Deshler, 1984) is designed to improve comprehension by focusing attention on the important information of a passage. It directs students to read a limited section of material, ask themselves the main idea and the details of the section, and put that information in their own words. Additional acquisition learning strategies are being developed. The *Visual Imagery Strategy* improves reading comprehension by having the student form mental pictures of the events described in a passage. In the *Self-Questioning Strategy* students form questions about key pieces of information in a passage and then read to find answers to these questions. The *Interpreting Visual Aids Strategy* increases the ability to obtain information from visuals such as pictures, diagrams, charts, tables, and maps. Finally, *Multipass* is a strategy for attacking textbook chapters that involves making three passes over the chapter to survey it, obtain key information from it, and study the key information. The *SOS Strategy* is an alternative version of Multipass that includes a visually marked and an audiotaped version of the text.

Phonetic Keys to Reading
(T. Harris, Creekmore, & Greenman, 1967)

Publisher: Economy Company

Description:

This supplementary phonics material places emphasis on sounding in beginning reading. The child initially is taught 40 phonics skills (keys), including long and short vowel sounds, all consonant sounds, and a number of blends and consonant digraphs. The keys are learned as the child first learns the sounds, and the specific phonetic principles must be memorized and applied when attacking a new word.

Phonovisual Method
(Schoolfield & Timberlake, 1974)

Publisher: Phonovisual Products

Description:

In this phonetic system the sounds of 26 initial and final consonants plus 18 vowel sounds are introduced orally through the use of pictorial wall charts. The child is taught to associate each letter sound with a visual image—for example, a monkey for /m/, a cat for short vowel sound /a/. Game materials and books are included, and the 15- to 30-minute lessons are presented in a game format. This sound–symbol approach provides adequate phonetic instruction and practice in auditory and visual discrimination and may supplement a basal reading program and other approaches.

Programmed Reading
(Buchanan, 1966)

Publisher: McGraw-Hill

Description:

Programmed workbooks and textbooks are used to teach reading skills from readiness to seventh-grade level. A linguistic approach is used to strengthen decoding skills and word recognition. The material follows a single pattern, regardless of the response of the student. In workbook exercises the student must circle the correct word or write a letter or letters. The student is allowed to proceed at his own pace and receives immediate feedback; however, the materials rely heavily on visual discrimination, and much emphasis is placed on word parts or individual letters. Placement tests and criterion-referenced achievement tests are included.

Reading for Understanding

Publisher: Science Research Associates

Description:

These individualized multilevel comprehension-building kits help develop critical thinking, inferential logic, and ability to draw sound conclusions. The exercises, which focus on inferential comprehension, are of the idea-completion type, in which the student reads a selection and then chooses a logically appropriate ending from four suggested conclusions. Level 1 is designed for students in grades 1 through 3, Level 2 is for students in grades 3 through 7, and Level 3 is for grades 7 through 12.

Reading Skill Builders

Publisher: Reader's Digest Services

Description:

This series of books, from first- to sixth-grade reading level, uses a magazine format with short reading selections. The interesting stories and articles are well illustrated and are accompanied by comprehension, vocabulary, and discussion questions. *Advanced Reading Skill Builders* are designed for students in grades 7 through 9, and emphasis is on critical thinking skills, study skills, and literary skills as well as comprehension. Four readers are provided for each grade (1–9), and there are four taped lessons on two cassettes correlated to each reader. The material appeals to all ages and can be used for directed or supplementary reading to develop comprehension skills.

Remedial Reading Drills
(Hegge, Kirk, & Kirk, 1955)

Publisher: George Wahr

Description:

The drills are designed to teach phonetic reading and word-attack skills to students who are reading below the fourth-grade level and need remedial assistance. The 55 remedial reading drills are divided into four parts. Part I introduces the most frequent sounds, including sounds of short vowels and consonants. Part II consists of combinations of sounds previously learned in isolation. Part III includes more advanced and less frequently used sounds presented in whole words. Part IV provides 37 supplementary exercises which cover exceptions to sounds previously taught. The drills emphasize learning the sounds of letters and blending letters together, and they should be used only with children who are trainable in sound blending and do not have extreme visual or auditory deficiencies.

SIMS Reading and Spelling Program (1978)

Publisher: Minneapolis Public Schools

Description:

This program consists of a criterion-referenced teaching and testing sequence of reading and spelling objectives. Measures are provided for monitoring student progress through the objectives. Each of the 53 *SIMS* categories represents a specific word structure generalization (for example, consonant-vowel-consonant plus endings, digraphs, blends, diphthongs, prefixes, and suffixes). The teacher monitors student progress by testing ability to decode and encode words in each category. This precision teaching program uses probes and one-minute timings to determine fluency as well as accuracy. Data are provided on the average amount of time to achieve 50 words per minute correct with three or fewer errors on the *SIMS* category word lists.

Specific Skill Builders

Publisher: Barnell Loft

Description:

The exercise booklets are designed to provide practice in reading comprehension skills for students reading between the first- and sixth-grade levels (books A–F) and students reading on levels 7 through 12 (books G–L). At each level there is a booklet for each of the following skills: (a) using the context, (b) getting the main idea, (c) drawing conclusions, (d) following directions, (e) working with sounds, (f) locating the answer, (g) getting the facts,

(h) detecting the sequence, and (i) identifying inferences. The booklets can be used to provide follow-up work, supplementary activities, or self-directed work.

SRA Reading Laboratories

Publisher: Science Research Associates

Description:

This developmental reading program has kits available for students in first grade through high school. Comprehension, vocabulary, and word-attack skills are covered, as well as aspects of reading such as study skills and reading rate improvement. The materials are color-coded and may be used as a supplement to provide individualized reading instruction.

Sullivan Reading Program (Sullivan, 1966)

Publisher: Behavioral Research Laboratories

Description:

This programmed series is available in five ability levels. Each level includes four programmed textbooks and related readers. The readers provide practice in using the vocabulary the student has learned in the corresponding programmed text. Pictures are used to enhance motivation and provide clues to meaning. Placement tests are included, and the student proceeds at his own pace. He responds to tasks within the textbook and receives immediate feedback by self-checking each response. At the completion of each programmed textbook, the student takes a progress test.

TR Reading Comprehension Series

Publisher: DLM Teaching Resources

Description:

This series features a structured framework for teaching comprehension skills to remedial students in grades 2 to 7 who are reading one to three grades below level. The program consists of eight work-texts (readability level—low first grade to high fourth grade) that can be used in conjunction with phonics/decoding programs and with graded readers. Each worktext contains 42 lessons that focus on the following areas of skill development: context and references, form, topic, main ideas, details, sequence, spatial relationships, comparison, cause and effect, author's purpose and technique, and study skills.

The Writing Road to Reading
(Spalding & Spalding, 1962)

Publisher: William Morrow

Description:

This structured phonics system is designed for group use. In this method, 70 phonograms representing 45 basic sounds are presented. Only phonetic sounds are used, and the letters are not referred to by name. Much drill is provided in which the teacher pronounces the phonogram and the students say its sound and then write its letter symbol in lowercase manuscript form. After phonograms have been mastered, words are taught and are presented in groups that correspond to phonetic rules. Forms of words that do not follow phonetic rules are taught as sight words. As the students master the rules, they are introduced to a primer.

Computer Software Programs

Microcomputer programs can be effectively used to develop basic skills in reading by providing varied drill and extra practice. Word identification skills as well as comprehension skills can be reinforced. Numerous software programs are available to reinforce sight words, expand vocabularies, provide drill in phonics, analyze words according to structural analysis, and test comprehension. Also, the teacher can use a microcomputer to develop language experience lessons, store individual reading vocabulary tests, and produce cloze tests. In addition, a microcomputer scoring program is available to help compute scores for the *Woodcock Reading Mastery Tests.* The following programs provide examples of available software that focus on reading skills. Appendix C lists addresses of producers and distributors of educational computer software.

Cloze-Plus

Producer: Milliken

Hardware: Apple II

Description:

This program develops reading comprehension skills and vocabulary through the use of structured cloze and context analysis activities. A factual reading selection with one word omitted is presented along with five possible word choices. The student reads the paragraph and types the letter of the best word choice. If desired, he may request context clues in which pertinent information is underlined. After two wrong responses, the correct answer is displayed along with explanatory information. After a correct response, a positive reinforcement appears. Upon completion of a selection or session, the student receives a summary of his performance. The cloze exercises focus on meaning completion, vocabulary in context, or syntax completion. The following skills are reinforced: interpretation and association, same or opposite meaning, identifying definition, making comparisons and contrasts, identifying time and order, using signal words and phrases, identifying pronoun antecedents, and noting similarities and differences. Six levels are available with vocabulary controlled from third-grade to eighth-grade level. The programs may also be used for remediation with older students.

Comprehension Power

Producer: Milliken

Hardware: Apple II

Description:

This program is designed to build comprehension skills of students reading at grade levels 4 through 12. In addition to the nine individual levels, there are three programs for junior and senior high school students who are reading at extremely low levels. The programs consist of three activities: preparation (new vocabulary words used in context), preview (key sentences from the reading selection), and comprehension reading. Stories are presented on a wide range of high-interest topics including adventure, sports, contemporary issues, and career awareness. The reading selection is presented either one line at a time at a preassigned rate (from 50 to 650 words per minute) or page by page with the student advancing the page manually. After each segment, the student answers comprehension questions. Responses are followed by immediate feedback and positive reinforcement. The student may reread the segment, if needed, and may also adjust the reading rate. At the end of the session, the student receives an overall summary of performance. The programs provide practice and measurement of 25 commonly accepted reading comprehension skills in five main areas: literal understanding (e.g., recalling information and details, identifying speaker), analysis (e.g., recognizing cause and effect, identifying analogies), appreciation (e.g., recognizing emotional reactions, identifying mood and tone), interpretation (e.g., making inferences, predicting outcomes), and evaluation (e.g., detecting author's purpose, judging validity). Thus, this software provides the opportunity to practice major comprehension skills and increase reading speed at the same time.

Construct-a-Word I and II

Producer: DLM Teaching Resources

Hardware: Apple II

Description:

These two software programs help the student read words more quickly and accurately by upgrading his knowledge of consonants, consonant clusters, and phonograms. The words and sounds presented in the programs are the same as those introduced in basal reading series. The student creates words by selecting appropriate word beginnings and endings. The programs require the addition of a speech peripheral such as a plug-in board called the Supertalker (available from DLM Teaching Resources). This allows the student to hear a digitized voice pronounce the words with which he is working. The programs provide extensive practice in identifying the important units that make up words and help the student add words to his repertoire as well as increase his speed in making those words.

Diascriptive Reading I and II

Distributor: Educational Activities

Hardware: Apple II, TRS–80, Commodore 64, PET, Atari

Description:

Diascriptive Reading I includes diagnostic tests in five skill areas (main ideas, details, vocabulary, sequence, and inference) and 20 developmental reading lessons for grade levels 1.5 to 5.5. *Diascriptive Reading II* includes an additional test on fact/opinion (total of six tests) and 36 reading lessons for grade levels 3 to 8. Each self-directing lesson contains a short, informative selection which the student must carefully read to respond to questions that follow. The student receives immediate reward or instruction using advanced graphics animation for reinforcement. An automatic management system is included that remediates or advances the student through each skill area and records the student's progress on the disk.

Hint and Hunt I and II

Producer: DLM Teaching Resources

Hardware: Apple II

Description:

These two programs focus on vowels and vowel groups to teach basic decoding skills. The words and sounds contained in the programs are correlated to those introduced in basal reading series. The instructional phase, *Hint,* features realistic voice stimulus and animated graphics. The practice phase, *Hunt,* is designed in a fast-action game format. There are four speed options as well as an untimed option. The programs require the addition of Supertalker, a plug-in board available from the producer, to allow the student to hear the selected words pronounced. Repetitive drill helps the student develop automatic decoding and word recognition with little conscious effort.

Micro-Read

Producer: American Educational Computer

Hardware: Apple II

Description:

This program includes eight levels covering reading skills in grades 1 through 8. The complete program includes the Supertalker circuit board, microphone, and speaker, which allow the student to hear instructions and the modeling of sounds and words in natural speech. In addition, there are story cards for levels 3 through 8. The program provides practice in word analysis and vocabulary skills (e.g., digraphs, silent letters, root words, prefixes and suffixes), comprehension skills (e.g., cause and effect, pronoun referents, imagery, sequence), and study skills (e.g., summarizing, skimming, taking notes).

Syllasearch I, II, III, and IV

Producer: DLM Teaching Resources

Hardware: Apple II

Description:

These four programs provide students with intensive practice in seeing and hearing multisyllable words. Each level has three phases: (a) meet the words (pronunciation of each word in a given level), (b) yank the syllables (analyzing whole words to find particular syllables), and (c) collect the words (synthesizing syllables to form words). A speech output system (available from DLM Teaching Resources) is used to provide actual human speech for instruction, feedback, and correction. The programs deal with two-, three-, and four-syllable words that contain many of the most common syllables in the English language and have an interest level appealing to remedial and special education students in grades 3 through 9.

Word Man; Word Radar

Producer: DLM Teaching Resources

Hardware: Apple II, IBM PC/PCjr, Commodore 64, Tandy 1000, Atari

Description:

These two programs are included in the series *Arcademic Skill Builders in Language Arts* published by DLM Teaching Resources. *Word Man* uses a game format that consists of a tricky maze of rectangular tracks with groups of letters placed along the rows. As a consonant moves past the letter combinations, the student must decide when a word is formed. Thus, the student practices basic phonetic patterns by forming words with the consonant-vowel-consonant or consonant–vowel–consonant–silent *e* patterns. Only words with one syllable and three to four letters are used. *Word Radar* provides practice in matching basic sight words by having the student role play a control tower operator who scans words that increase in length. In both programs, the speed and length of the game can be altered, as well as content and difficulty level.

REFERENCES

Allen, R.V., & Allen, C. (1970). *An introduction to a language-experience program: Level I.* Chicago: Encyclopaedia Britannica Press.

Becker, W.C., & Engelmann, S. (1977). *The Oregon direct instruction model: Comparative results in Project Follow Through: A summary of nine years of work.* Eugene, OR: University of Oregon Follow Through Project.

Bijou, S.W. (1977). *Edmark Reading Program.* Bellevue, WA: Edmark.

Bleismer, E.P., & Yarborough, B.H. (1965, June). A comparison of ten different beginning reading programs in first grade. *Phi Delta Kappan,* 500–504.

Bloomfield, L., & Barnhart, C.L. (1961). *Let's read—A linguistic approach.* Detroit: Wayne State University Press.

Bond, G.L., & Dykstra, R. (1967). The cooperative research program in first-grade reading instruction. *Reading Research Quarterly, 2,* 5–142.

Buchanan, C.D. (1966). *Programmed reading.* New York: McGraw-Hill.

Carnine, D., & Silbert, J. (1979). *Direct instruction reading.* Columbus, OH: Merrill.

Chall, J. (1967). *Learning to read: The great debate.* New York: McGraw-Hill.

Clark, F.L., Deshler, D.D., Schumaker, J.B., Alley, G.R., & Warner, M.M. (1984). Visual imagery and self-questioning: Strategies to improve comprehension of written material. *Journal of Learning Disabilities, 17,* 145–149.

Cohen, S., & Plaskon, S. (1980). *Language arts for the mildly handicapped.* Columbus, OH: Merrill.

Dechant, E.V. (1970). *Improving the teaching of reading* (2nd ed.). Englewood Cliffs, NJ: Prentice-Hall.

Diederich, P.I., II. (1973). *Research 1960–70 on methods and materials in reading.* Princeton, NJ: Educational Testing Service.

Downing, J. (1965). *The initial teaching alphabet reading experiment.* Chicago: Scott, Foresman.

Dykstra, R. (1968). Summary of the second-grade phase of the cooperative research program in primary reading instruction. *Reading Research Quarterly, 4,* 49–70.

Dykstra, R. (1974). Phonics and beginning reading instruction. In C.C. Walcutt, J. Lamport, & G. McCracken (Eds.), *Teaching reading: A phonic/linguistic approach to developmental reading.* New York: Macmillan.

Ekwall, E.E. (1989). *Locating and correcting reading difficulties* (5th ed.). Columbus, OH: Merrill.

Ellis, E.S., & Lenz, B.K. (1987). A component analysis of effective learning strategies for LD students. *Learning Disabilities Focus, 2*(2), 94–107.

Engelmann, S., Becker, W., Hanner, S., & Johnson, G. (1980). *Corrective Reading Program.* Chicago: Science Research Associates.

Engelmann, S., & Bruner, E. (1984). *Reading Mastery: DISTAR Reading.* Chicago: Science Research Associates.

Faas, L.A. (1980). *Children with learning problems: A handbook for teachers.* Boston: Houghton Mifflin.

Fernald, G. (1943). *Remedial techniques in basic school subjects.* New York: McGraw-Hill.

Fox, A.C. (1979). *The Foxie systematic readability aides.* Coeur d'Alene, ID: Fox Reading Research.

Fries, C.C. (1963). *Linguistics and reading.* New York: Holt, Rinehart & Winston.

Fry, E. (1964). A diacritical marking system to aid beginning reading instruction. *Elementary English, 41,* 526–529.

Fry, E. (1977). Fry's readability graph: Clarifications, validity, and extension to level 17. *Journal of Reading, 21,* 242–252.

Gates, A.I. (1947). *The improvement of reading* (3rd ed.). New York: Macmillan.

Gillespie-Silver, P. (1979). *Teaching reading to children with special needs: An ecological approach.* Columbus, OH: Merrill.

Gillingham, A., & Stillman, B. (1968). *Remedial teaching for children with specific disability in reading, spelling, and penmanship.* Cambridge, MA: Educator's Publishing Service.

Gurren, L., & Hughes, A. (1965). Intensive phonics vs. gradual phonics in beginning reading: A review. *Journal of Educational Research, 58,* 339–346.

Hall, M. (1981). *Teaching reading as a language experience* (3rd ed.). Columbus, OH: Merrill.

Harris, A.J., & Sipay, E.R. (1980). *How to increase reading ability: A guide to developmental and remedial methods* (7th ed.). New York: Longman.

Harris, T., Creekmore, M., & Greenman, M. (1967). *Phonetic keys to reading.* Oklahoma City: Economy Company.

Heckelman, R.G. (1969). The neurological impress method of remedial reading instruction. *Academic Therapy, 4,* 277–282.

Hegge, T.G., Kirk, S.A., & Kirk, W.D. (1955). *Remedial reading drills.* Ann Arbor, MI: George Wahr.

Heilman, A.W., Blair, T.R., & Rupley, W.H. (1986). *Principles and practices of teaching reading* (6th ed.). Columbus, OH: Merrill.

Henk, W.A., Helfeldt, J.P., & Platt, J.M. (1986). Developing reading fluency in learning disabled students. *Teaching Exceptional Children, 18,* 202–206.

Kaluger, G., & Kolson, C.J. (1978). *Reading and learning disabilities* (2nd ed.). Columbus, OH: Merrill.

Kann, R. (1983). The method of repeated readings: Expanding the neurological impress method for use with disabled readers. *Journal of Learning Disabilities, 16,* 90–92.

Kirk, S.A., Kliebhan, J.M., & Lerner, J.W. (1978).

Teaching reading to slow and disabled learners. Boston: Houghton Mifflin.

Langford, K., Slade, K., & Barnett, A. (1974). An explanation of impress techniques in remedial reading. *Academic Therapy, 9,* 309–319.

Lee, D.M., & Allen, R.V. (1963). *Learning to read through experience* (2nd ed.). New York: Appleton-Century-Crofts.

Lenz, B.K., Schumaker, J.B., Deshler, D.D., & Beals, V.L. (1984). *Learning strategies curriculum: The word identification strategy.* Lawrence: University of Kansas.

Lorenz, L., & Vockell, E. (1979). Using the neurological impress method with learning disabled readers. *Journal of Learning Disabilities, 12,* 420–422.

Lovitt, T.C. (1984). *Tactics for teaching.* Columbus, OH: Merrill.

Matthes, C. (1972). *How children are taught to read.* Lincoln, NE: Professional Educators Publications.

Orton, S.T. (1937). *Reading, writing, and speech problems in children.* New York: Norton.

Otto, W., & Smith, R.J. (1980). *Corrective and remedial teaching* (3rd ed.). Boston: Houghton Mifflin.

Robinson, F.P. (1961). *Effective study.* New York: Harper & Row.

Roe, B.D., Stoodt, B.D., & Burns, P.C. (1983). *Secondary school reading instruction: The content areas* (2nd ed.). Boston: Houghton Mifflin.

Rupley, W.H., & Blair, T.R. (1983). *Reading diagnosis and remediation: Classroom and clinic* (2nd ed.). Boston: Houghton Mifflin.

Samuels, S.J. (1979). The method of repeated readings. *The Reading Teacher, 32,* 403–408.

Schoolfield, L.D., & Timberlake, J.B. (1974). *The phonovisual method* (Rev. ed.). Rockville, MD: Phonovisual Products.

Schumaker, J.B., Denton, P.H., & Deshler, D.D. (1984). *Learning strategies curriculum: The paraphrasing strategy.* Lawrence: University of Kansas.

SIMS Reading and Spelling Program (3rd ed.). (1978). Minneapolis: Minneapolis Public Schools.

Slingerland, B.H. (1974). *A multi-sensory approach to language arts for specific language disability children.* Cambridge, MA: Educator's Publishing Service.

Spache, G.D., & Spache, E.B. (1973). *Reading in the elementary school* (3rd ed.). Boston: Allyn & Bacon.

Spache, G.D., & Spache, E.B. (1977). *Reading in the elementary school* (4th ed.). Boston: Allyn & Bacon.

Spalding, R.B., & Spalding, W.T. (1962). *The writing road to reading.* New York: Morrow.

Stallings, J.A. (1974). *Follow Through classroom observation evaluation 1972–1973* (Executive Summary SRI Project URU–7370). Menlo Park, CA: Stanford Research Institute.

Stauffer, R.G. (1981). Strategies for reading instruction. In M.P. Douglas (Ed.), *Reading: What is basic? 45th yearbook, Claremont Reading Conference.* Claremont, CA: Center for Developmental Studies.

Sullivan, M.W. (1966). *Sullivan Reading Program.* Palo Alto, CA: Behavioral Research Laboratories.

Sundbye, N.W., Dyck, N.J., & Wyatt, F.R. (1980). *Essential Sight Word Program.* Allen, TX: DLM Teaching Resources.

Traub, N., & Bloom, F. (1970). *Recipe for reading.* Cambridge, MA: Educator's Publishing Service.

Wilson, R.G., & Rudolph, M.K. (1986). *Catch On— Merrill Linguistic Reading Program* (4th ed.). Columbus, OH: Merrill.

Woodcock, R.W., Clark, C.R., & Davies, C.O. (1979). *Peabody Rebus Reading Program.* Circle Pines, MN: American Guidance Service.

CHAPTER 12

Assessing and
Teaching Spelling Skills

Spelling is the forming of words through the traditional arrangement of letters. Generally, spelling instruction is introduced at the beginning of the second grade or at the end of the first grade. The ability to spell is essential because it allows one to read correctly what is written. In addition, incorrect spelling often results in an unfavorable impression, and the poor speller may be considered uneducated or careless.

The English language presents inconsistent relationships between phonemes (speech sounds) and graphemes (written symbols). There are 26 letters in the alphabet; however, more than 40 phonemes are used in English speech. Thus, differences exist between the spelling of various words and the way the words are pronounced. Many children with learning problems have difficulty mastering the regular spelling system. Inconsistent spelling patterns make learning to spell even more complex for some mildly handicapped learners.

Children who have trouble recognizing words in reading usually have poor spelling skills as well (Carpenter & Miller, 1982; Lerner, 1985). However, children may be skilled in the ability to read words but may be unable to reproduce words in spelling. Thus, it appears that spelling a word may be a more difficult task than reading a word. Reading is a *decoding* process in which the reader receives clues (such as context) for word recognition. Spelling is an *encoding* process in which the learner must respond without the benefit of a complete visual stimulus; thus there are fewer clues. Spelling requires concentration on each letter of every word, but in reading it is not necessary to know the exact spelling of words or to attend to every letter in most words. Ekwall (1989) notes that the same types of errors may be present in both reading and spelling. For example, a phonetic speller may mispronounce phonetically irregular words when reading. In addition, a student who lacks phonetic word-attack skills in reading may not be able to spell because of her poor phonetic skills.

To spell, the child must be able to (a) read the word, (b) possess knowledge and skill in certain relationships of phonics and structural analysis, (c) apply phonics generalizations, (d) visualize the word, and (e) use the motor capability to write the word (Lerner, 1985). Spelling problems may stem from problems in visual memory, auditory memory, auditory and visual discrimination, and motor skills.

ASSESSMENT OF SPELLING DIFFICULTIES

A variety of techniques assess the child's spelling performance. Also, specific patterns of spelling errors may be pinpointed. Spelling assessment may be divided into three broad categories: (a) standardized tests, (b) criterion-referenced tests, and (c) informal assessment techniques. In choosing spelling assessment techniques, the tester should (a) know what the test measures and its limitations, (b) supplement the test where possible with other measures, and (c) use informal evaluation techniques to gain specific information for planning a remedial program.

Standardized Tests

Standardized spelling tests provide a wide range of information. Achievement tests that contain spelling subtests are designed to provide an estimate of the child's general spelling ability. They yield a single score that is compared to the standardized norms and converted to a grade-equivalent score. Thus, achievement tests provide a general survey measure, and they may be useful for identifying children who need corrective instruction and further diagnosis. In contrast, diagnostic tests provide detailed information about a child's performance in various spelling skill areas. These tests are aimed at determining the child's strengths and weaknesses. The achievement and diagnostic spelling tests presented next are widely used and represent the types of tests available.

Achievement tests. On achievement tests, spelling is assessed by two procedures: recall and recognition. On tests using recall, the student must write words presented orally and used in sentences. On tests using recognition, the student is required to select the correctly spelled word from several choices. Tests with recall items are considered to be more difficult, but also more valid, than tests with recognition items (Otto, McMenemy, & Smith, 1973).

The *Iowa Tests of Basic Skills* (Hieronymus, Hoover, & Lindquist, 1986) are designed for grade levels 1 through 9 and are group administered. The *Tests of Achievement and Proficiency* (Scannell, 1986) assess spelling of students in grades 9 through 12. In both tests, spelling is assessed as an area within the language subtest. As the teacher reads a word, the child must choose the correctly spelled word from four words. Grade-equivalent norms and grade percentile norms are given. Percentile grade norms are provided for testing done in the beginning, middle, or end of the school year.

The *Peabody Individual Achievement Test—Revised* (Dunn & Markwardt, 1988) is individually administered and can be used with students in kindergarten through 12th grade. On the first 14 items in the spelling subtest, the child must distinguish a printed letter of the alphabet from pictured objects and associate letter symbols with speech sounds. On items 15 through 84, the student must choose from four words the correct spelling of the word read aloud by the examiner. Age equivalents, grade equivalents, percentile ranks, and standard scores are obtained.

The *SRA Achievement Series* (Naslund, Thorpe, & Lefever, 1978) is group administered and includes spelling assessment for grade levels 2 through 12. At the second-grade level, the student must identify which of four alternative spellings of a word is correct. At the third-grade level, words are given in context so that context cues may be used to help spell them. In the remaining levels, words are given in phrases only. The test yields grade equivalents, percentiles, and stanine scores.

The *Stanford Achievement Test* (Gardner, Rudman, Karlsen, & Merwin, 1982) assesses spelling of children in grades 1.5 through 9. The *Test of Academic Skills* (Gardner, Callis, Merwin, & Rudman, 1983), an extension of the *SAT,* assesses spelling of students in grades 8 through 13. The student must detect misspellings of words that contain various types of errors. The test is group administered and yields stanines, grade-equivalent scores, percentiles, age scores, and standard scores.

The *Wide Range Achievement Test—Revised* (Jastak & Wilkinson, 1984) is an individually administered test for students aged 5 to adult. The spelling subtest assesses a child's skill in copying marks on paper, writing his name, and writing single words from dictation. Grade equivalents, percentiles within grades, and standard scores are obtained.

Diagnostic tests. The *Diagnostic Spelling Potential Test* (Arena, 1981) measures traditional spelling, word recognition, visual recognition, and auditory-visual recognition. The four subtests of 90 items assess ages 7 through adult and take 25 to 40 minutes. Raw scores from each subtest can be converted to standard scores, percentiles, and grade ratings.

The *Gates-Russell Spelling Diagnostic Test* (Gates & Russell, 1937) provides a variety of diagnostic information concerning spelling problems. The subtests measure nine areas related to spelling ability: (a) spelling words orally; (b) word pronunciation; (c) giving letters for letter sounds; (d) spelling one syllable; (e) spelling two syllables; (f) word reversals; (g) spelling attack; (h) auditory discrimination; and (i) effectiveness of visual, auditory, kinesthetic, or combined methods of study. A grade-level score is obtained for performance in each area.

The *Test of Written Spelling—2* (Larsen & Hammill, 1986) can be administered individually or to small groups of children in grades 1 through 12 in approximately 20 minutes. This dictated-word test consists of words chosen from 10 basal spelling series and assesses the student's ability to spell words whose spellings are (a) readily predictable in sound-letter patterns, (b) less predictable (spelling demons), and (c) both types of words considered together. The test yields a spelling quotient and percentile ranks. Thus, it provides the teacher with an index of overall spelling skill and indicates the types of words that are difficult for the student.

Criterion-Referenced Tests

Standardized norm-referenced tests (achievement and diagnostic) *compare* a child's performance to the scores of those in the norm population. Criterion-referenced tests *describe* performance in terms of fixed criteria. Teachers can use criterion-referenced spelling tests to determine if the child has mastered specific spelling instructional objectives (for example, *wh* spelling, contractions, vocational words, and so on). The teacher finds out what skills the child has learned and what skills still must be taught. Also, an objective measure of progress is provided as the child moves from task to task and her current performance is compared with her previous performance.

The *Brigance Diagnostic Comprehensive Inventory of Basic Skills* (Brigance, 1982) contains a section that assesses spelling skills of children whose achievement is in the kindergarten through ninth-grade levels. The skill area is arranged in a developmental and sequential hierarchy. Tests include spelling dictation grade placement, initial consonants, initial clusters, suffixes, and prefixes. Also, the reference skills section contains a test on the important skill of dictionary use. The instructional objectives related to each test are clearly defined. In addition to revealing the child's level of achievement, the results can help the teacher to develop an individualized instructional program in spelling.

Kottmeyer's (1970) *Diagnostic Spelling Test* is a criterion-referenced test that measures specific phonics and structural spelling elements (for example, doubled final consonants, nonphonetic spellings, long and short *oo*). The examiner says a word and a sentence using the word, and the child is required to write the word. One test is for children in the second and third grades; another test is for children in the fourth grade and above. The 32-item tests are designed so that each item measures a particular spelling element. A grade score is computed from the total number of correct spellings. Specific information on skills not yet mastered is obtained through an analysis of the child's errors.

Spellmaster (Greenbaum, 1987) is a series of nonstandardized, criterion-referenced tests that includes eight diagnostic tests for measuring the spelling of phonetically regular words, eight irregular-words tests, eight homophone (homonym) tests, and entry-level tests. The tests pinpoint the precise strategies students use and the errors they make when spelling words.

Criterion-referenced tests mainly aid in specific instructional planning, rather than determining grade-level scores or percentile ranks. In the *Brigance Diagnostic Comprehensive Inventory of Basic Skills,* some tests were *texts-referenced:* the most commonly used texts were examined to determine a grade level at which a specific skill first is introduced. Thus, a grade-level score is obtained. In the future, criterion-referenced tests may also be norm-referenced. They then would be useful for both establishing instructional objectives and placement in terms of grade level.

Informal Assessment Techniques

According to Wallace and Larsen (1978), "the informal assessment should clearly outline the relevant skills a student has or has not mastered, pinpoint patterns of errors, provide direction for systematic remedial instruction, and permit a nonsubjective measure of gain as the pupil moves from task to task" (p. 380). The spelling scope and sequence skills list presented in Appendix A may be used to devise informal assessment measures and to determine appropriate instructional objectives as the child progresses in spelling.

Teacher observation. The teacher can obtain diagnostic information through structured observation and evaluation of the child's attitudes, written work, and oral responses. Negative attitudes toward spelling and willingness to use a dictionary may be noted, as well as the child's work habits and her ability to handle frustration. Analysis of written work can provide information about handwriting problems that are causing errors (such as letter forms or spacing), specific types of errors, range of the child's vocabulary, and knowledge of important spelling rules (Brueckner & Bond, 1966). In addition, the teacher should observe the child's oral responses and should note problems in pronunciation, articulation, and dialect. Oral spelling responses can also indicate phonics ability and method of spelling words orally—for example, as units, by letter, by digraphs, or by syllables.

Dictated tests. The dictated spelling test is a commonly used procedure for assessing various skills in spelling and determining spelling grade level. Words can be selected from any graded word list; the student's performance indicates at what grade level she experiences difficulty. Stephens, Hartman, and Lucas (1982) present sample assessment tasks that use dictated word lists of increasing difficulty. The instructional level is determined when the student achieves 70 to 90% accuracy. Dictated word lists can also assess skills in areas such as phoneme–grapheme association (such as *like, bike,* and *hike*), spelling generalizations (such as *stories, cries, tries*), homonyms (*pain, pane; pear, pair*), and functional words (*menu, restaurant, cashier*). The dictated test presented in Table 12.1 assesses selected spelling objectives for students in the grades 2 and 3. Through error analysis the teacher can readily determine areas of weakness.

The child's proficiency in spelling words frequently used and words that are often misspelled also may be determined. Horn (1926), after studying 10,000 words, reported that 10 words accounted for 25% of all words used. In order of most frequent to least frequent these words include: *I, the, and, to, a, you, of, in, we, for.* He also noted that 100 words accounted for 65% of the words written by adults. In addition, Kuska, Webster, and Elford (1964) present a list of commonly misspelled words that are linguistically irregular and do not follow spelling rules—for example, *ache, fasten, nickel, scratch, double.*

Informal spelling inventory. The informal spelling inventory (ISI) may be used to determine the child's approximate grade level in spelling achievement. An ISI can be constructed by selecting a sample of words from spelling books in a basal spelling series (Mann, Suiter, & McClung, 1979). Approximately 15 words should be chosen from the first-grade

TABLE 12.1
A dictated spelling test and objectives.

Spelling Words	Spelling Objectives	Spelling Words Used in Sentences
1. man 2. pit 3. dug 4. web 5. dot	short vowels and selected consonants	The *man* is big. The *pit* in the fruit was hard. We *dug* a hole. She saw the spider's *web*. Don't forget to *dot* the i.
6. mask 7. drum	words beginning and/or ending with consonant blends	On Halloween the child wore a *mask*. He beat the *drum* in the parade.
8. line 9. cake	consonant-vowel-consonant-silent *e*	Get in *line* for lunch. We had a birthday *cake*.
10. coat 11. rain	two vowels together	Put on your winter *coat*. Take an umbrella in the *rain*.
12. ice 13. large	variant consonant sounds for *c* and *g*	*Ice* is frozen water. This is a *large* room.
14. mouth 15. town 16. boy	words containing vowel diphthongs	Open your *mouth* to brush your teeth. We went to *town* to shop. The *boy* and girl went to school.
17. bikes 18. glasses	plurals	The children got new *bikes* for their birthdays. Get some *glasses* for the drinks.
19. happy 20. monkey	short *i* sounds of *y*	John is very *happy* now. We saw a *monkey* at the zoo.
21. war 22. dirt	words with *r*-controlled vowels	Bombs were used in the *war*. The pigs were in the *dirt*.
23. foot 24. moon	two sounds of *oo*	Put the shoe on your *foot*. Three men walked on the *moon*.

TABLE 12.1, *continued*

Spelling Words	Spelling Objectives	Spelling Words Used in Sentences
25. light 26. knife	words with silent letters	Turn on the *light* so we can see. Get a fork and *knife*.
27. pill	final consonant doubled	The doctor gave me a *pill*.
28. bat 29. batter	consonant-vowel-consonant pattern in which final consonant is doubled before adding ending.	The baseball player got a new *bat*. The *batter* hit a home run.
30. didn't 31. isn't	contractions	They *didn't* want to come. It *isn't* raining today.
32. take 33. taking	final *e* is dropped before adding suffix	Please *take* off your coat. He is *taking* me to the show.
34. any 35. could	nonphonetic spellings	I did not have *any* lunch. Maybe you *could* go on a trip.
36. ate 37. eight 36. blue 39. blew	homonyms	Mary *ate* breakfast at home. There are *eight* children in the family. The sky is *blue*. The wind *blew* away the hat.
40. baseball	compound words	They played *baseball* outside.

book and 20 words from each book for grades 2 through 8. *Random* selection is obtained by dividing the total number of words at each level by 20. For example, 300 words at each level divided by 20 equals 15; therefore, every 15th word should be included in the ISI. For children in grades 4 and below, testing should begin with the first-level words. For students in grades 5 and above, assessment should start with words at the third level. The test is administered in a dictated-word format: The teacher says the word, uses it in a sentence, and repeats the word. Testing ends when the child responds incorrectly to six consecutive words. The child's achievement level is the highest level at which he responds correctly to 90 to

100% of the items, and the instructional level is the highest level at which the child scores 75 to 89% correct. Various errors made on the ISI may be analyzed to provide additional diagnostic information.

Spelling error analysis. Cartwright (1969) suggests the use of a spelling error analysis chart to provide a profile of spelling strengths and weaknesses. Each time the child makes a specific error, it is recorded on the chart. Edgington (1967) suggests some specific types of errors that should be noted: addition of extra letters; omission of needed letters; reversals of whole words, consonant order, or syllables; errors resulting from a child's misinterpretation or dialect; phonetic spelling of nonphonetic words. Spelling errors can be analyzed in written composition as well as on dictated tests. Burns (1980) notes that the majority of errors in spelling occur in vowels in midsyllables of words; 67% of the errors result from substitution or omission of letters, and 20% are in addition, insertion, or transposition of letters. Through a careful analysis of spelling errors, the teacher can focus on consistent patterns of errors and plan appropriate instruction.

Cloze procedure. The cloze procedure is a visual means of testing spelling. The child may be required to complete a sentence by writing the correct response in the blank—for example, "The opposite of down is _____" (*up*). In addition, the child may complete a word or supply missing letters: "The clouds are in the s_____" (*sky*), or "Please give me a glass of w__t__r" (*water*). Cartwright (1969) notes that the cloze procedure is especially useful in evaluating the child's knowledge of spelling generalizations. In this case, the child is required to fill in blanks that all pertain to a general spelling rule, such as doubling the final consonant before adding *ing.* A multiple-

choice format may also be used; for example, "Mary needed _____ to pay for her lunch" (*munny, mony, money, monie*). The cloze procedure, which is visual, may be used effectively along with the auditory dictated spelling test.

Probes. Spelling skills may be assessed through the use of probe sheets. The child works on the probe sheet for one minute and the teacher records the rate of correct and incorrect responses and notes any error patterns. The task on the probe sheet may be administered several times to give the teacher a reliable index of how well the student can perform. Starlin and Starlin (1973) suggest a proficiency rate for children in kindergarten through grade 2 of 30 to 50 correct letters per minute with two or fewer errors at the independent level and 15 to 29 correct letters with three to seven errors at the instructional level. For third grade through adult, the independent level is 50 to 70 correct letters per minute with two or fewer errors, and the instructional level is 25 to 49 correct letters with three to seven errors. Koenig and Kunzelmann (1980) provide the following proficiency rates according to grade levels:

1. Grade 2: 60–90 correct letters per minute.
2. Grade 3: 90–100 correct letters per minute.
3. Grade 4: 100–120 correct letters per minute.
4. Grade 5: 110–130 correct letters per minute.
5. Grade 6: 120–140 correct letters per minute.

In addition, the teacher may collect data from children who are achieving satisfactorily and use their rates for comparison when assessing a child with spelling difficulties. A sample probe sheet for spelling contractions is presented in Table 12.2. Probe sheets may also be devised in which a picture of an object appears and the child is required to spell the word.

Modality testing. Sensory modality preference testing, described by Westerman (1971), assesses the child's performance through various combinations of input and output channels. The five input/output channels are as follows:

1. *Auditory-vocal:* The teacher spells the word aloud, and then the child orally spells the word.

TABLE 12.2
Probe sheet for spelling contractions.

Task: See words—Write contractions

do not	_____
I will	_____
can not	_____
have not	_____
we are	_____
I am	_____
could not	_____
is not	_____
it is	_____
you are	_____
she is	_____
are not	_____
would not	_____
I have	_____
did not	_____
they would	_____
has not	_____
was not	_____
they are	_____
he will	_____

Name: _____
Time: 1 minute
Number of correct letters written: _____
Number of incorrect letters written: _____

2. *Auditory-motor:* The teacher spells the word aloud, and the child writes the word on paper.
3. *Visual-vocal:* The teacher shows the word on a flash card, and the child orally spells the word.
4. *Visual-motor:* The teacher shows the word on a flash card, and the child writes the word on paper.
5. *Multisensory combination channel:* The teacher shows the word on a flash card and spells it aloud, and the child orally spells the word and writes it on paper.

In modality testing, 40 unknown words are divided into five sets of eight words each. Two words are taught in each of the five modalities for four consecutive days, and the child is tested on a written dictation spelling test at the end of each day. On the fifth day the child is tested on all 40 words. The number of correct responses in each modality indicates whether the child shows a pattern of preference among modalities. This kind of assessment information is useful in planning individualized instruction. For example, children with an auditory-motor preference may learn new spelling words by using a tape recorder and writing each word after hearing it. Similarly, visual learners should be provided with many opportunities to see the word.

TEACHING STRATEGIES

Stephens (1977) notes that there are nine spelling competencies that enable the child to be an effective speller. These nine skills and corresponding subareas are presented in Table 12.3. Various teaching methods and strategies may be used to help the child with spelling difficulties. The following selected techniques provide alternatives for teaching spelling skills.

TABLE 12.3
Spelling competencies.

Competency Area	Subareas
Auditory discrimination	Ability to discriminate consonant sounds and vowel sounds and use correct word pronunciation
Consonants	Knowledge of consonants in initial, final, and medial positions in words and knowledge of consonant blends
Phonograms	Ability to identify phonograms in initial, medial, and final positions in words and ability to identify word phonograms
Plurals	Ability to form plurals by adding *s*, adding *es*, changing *f* to *v*, making medial changes, and knowledge of exceptions
Syllabication	Ability to divide words into syllables
Structural elements	Knowledge of root words, prefixes and suffixes
Ending changes	Ability to change ending of words which end in final *e*, final *y*, and final consonants
Vowel digraphs and diphthongs	Ability to spell words in which a vowel digraph forms one sound (*ai, ea, ay, ei, ie*) or a diphthong forms a blend (*oi, ou, ow*)
Silent *e*	Knowledge of single-syllable words that end in silent *e*

Rule-Based Instruction

Spelling instruction can be based on teaching rules and generalizations. After learning a general spelling rule, the child is able to use it in spelling unfamiliar words. Spelling rules can apply to instruction using both linguistics and phonics.

The linguistic approach to teaching spelling is based on the idea that there is regularity in phoneme–grapheme correspondence. Thus, linguists stress the systematic nature of spelling patterns. Spelling rules, generalizations, and patterns are taught which apply to whole words. Words are selected for spelling instruction according to their particular linguistic pattern—for example, *cool, fool, pool; hitting, running, batting.*

In spelling instruction related to phonics, rules are taught concerning phoneme–grapheme relationships within parts of words. The child learns to associate a sound with a particular letter or combination of letters. Thus, phonetic rules can help the child determine how sounds should be spelled. Through phonics instruction the child can learn to spell words according to syllables. The child breaks up the word into recognizable sound elements, pronounces each syllable, and writes the letter or letters that represent each sound.

In rule-based instruction (in both linguistics and phonics), only those spelling rules and generalizations that apply to a large number of words and have few exceptions should be taught. The general rule should be applicable more than 75% of the time. Spelling rules may be taught by guiding the student to discover rules and generalizations on her own. After analyzing several words that share a common linguistic property, the student may be asked to apply the generalization when spelling unfamiliar words. After the student can generalize, exceptions to the rules can be discussed. The child should be taught that generalizations are not steadfast and that some words do not conform to spelling rules.

Multisensory Approach

Spelling involves skills in the visual, auditory, and motor sensory modalities. The child must be able to exhibit visual and auditory recognition and discrimination of the letters of the alphabet and must have motor control to write the word. Hodges (1966) notes the following:

> A child who has learned to spell a word by the use of the senses of hearing, sight, and touch is in a good position to recall the spelling of that word when he needs it in his writing because any or all the sensory modes can elicit his memory of it. (p. 39)

Fernald's (1943) multisensory approach involves four sensory modalities: visual, auditory, kinesthetic, and tactile (VAKT). In this approach, Fernald focuses on the following areas as being important in learning spelling: (a) clear perception of word form, (b) development of a distinct visual image of the word, and (c) habit formation through repetition of writing until the motor pattern is automatic.

The following steps are included in learning to spell a new word:

1. The teacher writes and says a word while the student watches and listens.
2. The student traces the word while simultaneously saying the word. Then the student copies or writes the word while saying it. Emphasis is placed on careful pronunciation, with each syllable of the word dragged out slowly as it is traced or written.
3. Next, the word is written from memory. If it is incorrect, the second step is repeated. If the word is correct, it is put in a file box. Later the words in the file box are used in stories.
4. At later stages the tracing method for learning is not always needed. The student may learn the word by observing the teacher write and say it and then by writing and saying it herself. As the student progresses, she may learn the word by looking at it in print and writing it and, finally, merely by looking at it.

Since the student hears, sees, and traces the word in the Fernald approach, four sensory modalities (auditory, visual, kinesthetic, tactile) are involved.

The Gillingham method (Gillingham & Stillman, 1968) uses an alphabetic system and emphasizes repetition and drill. Letter–sound correspondences are taught using a multisensory approach—visual, auditory, and kinesthetic. Words introduced initially include only those with consistent sound–symbol correspondences. The student is given experience reading and spelling one-syllable words as well as detached regularly spelled syllables. Words of more than one syllable are learned syllable by syllable (e.g., *Sep tem ber*). Words whose spelling is not entirely consistent are carefully sequenced according to structural characteristics, and words following a pattern are grouped. The technique used in studying spelling words is called simultaneous oral spelling. When the teacher says a spelling word, the student repeats the word, names the letters, writes the letters as she says them, and reads the word she has written. Letter names rather than sounds are used in this practice so the technique can be applied to nonphonetic words. Sentence and story writing is introduced after the child is able to write any three-letter, phonetically pure word. Nonphonetic words are taught through drill. Thus, the Gillingham method differs from the Fernald (1943) approach in two major respects: (a) words to be taught are carefully selected and sequenced rather than being of the student's own choosing or as she needs them for her own writing, and (b) instruction focuses on individual letters and sounds rather than on whole words.

Another multisensory approach that features repetition and often is used with slow learners is the cover-and-write method. The child is taught to spell words through the following steps:

1. The child looks at the word and says it.
2. She writes the word twice while looking at it.
3. The child covers the word and writes it again.
4. She checks her spelling by looking at it.

The steps are repeated with the child writing the word as many as three times while looking at it, covering the word, writing it, and checking her spelling.

Study-Test Techniques

The test-study-test approach to teaching spelling frequently is used. The child is given a pretest at the beginning of each unit of study. The words the child misspells on the pretest become her study list. After instruction, a posttest is given to determine the student's degree of mastery. A progress chart is kept, and words missed on the posttest are added to the list of words for the following unit of study.

The study-test plan is similar to the test-study-test approach, except that it does not include a pretest. The child's study list consists of all of the words in the unit of study. The student is tested after completing various spelling activities. Petty (1966) and Stephens et al. (1982) note that the test-study-test method obtains better spelling results than the study-test approach.

Some studies indicate that added reinforcement procedures can encourage students to study harder to obtain higher test scores. For example, Lovitt, Guppy, and Blattner (1969) noted a substantial increase in the number of perfect spelling papers when students were given the test four days a week (Tuesday through Friday) and, after receiving 100% on that week's word list, were excused from spelling for the rest of the week and given free time. Also, Sidman (1979) used group and individual reinforcement contingencies with middle school students. Accuracy increased when free time was provided as a reward for improved test scores. (The increase was greater during group contingency conditions.)

Fixed and Flow Word Lists

Spelling words frequently are presented and taught in fixed word lists. Generally, a new list of words is assigned each week. The words may be either somewhat unfamiliar or completely unknown to the student. Usually a test on each list is given on Friday. This method seldom results in spelling mastery for all students, since misspelled words on the test usually are ignored or left for the child to practice on her own. Another procedure using fixed word lists is to have the child practice the words at her own rate until she is able to spell them all correctly on a certain number of tests.

On a flow list of spelling words, each word is dropped from the list when mastered (for example, spelled correctly on two consecutive days); then a new (unpracticed) word is added. Thus, the list is individualized, and the child does not spend time practicing known words. McGuigan (1975) developed a teaching procedure, the Add-a-Word Program, which uses flow word lists. McGuigan found that students (aged 7 to 13 and adults) learned words more quickly with add-a-word lists than fixed lists and also showed similar or superior retention of learned words.

Burns and Broman (1983) recommend presentation of only 5 or 10 words per week to poor spellers (20 words per week may be presented to adequate spellers). In a study of students with learning problems, Bryant, Drabin, and Gettinger (1981) found that a higher failure rate and greater variance in performance may occur when the number of words presented each day exceeds 3. They suggest that 7 to 8 new spelling words per week may be an appropriate number for such students.

Imitation Methods

Stowitschek and Jobes (1977) present a method of spelling instruction that involves imitation. It is designed for children who have failed repeatedly to learn to spell through traditional procedures. The teacher provides an oral and written model of the spelling word, and the child is required to imitate the model by spelling the word aloud and writing it. The child receives immediate feedback and praise for correct responses. Incorrect responses are followed by retraining. The procedure is repeated until the child can spell and write the word without models or prompts. A spelling probe is administered after each training ses-

sion to determine which words have been mastered and to check retention of learned words.

Kauffman, Hallahan, Haas, Brame, and Boren (1978) tested the effectiveness of showing the child a correct model of a spelling word as opposed to providing first a written imitation of the child's spelling error and then showing the correct model. Kauffman et al. found that the method of including imitation of the child's errors was more effective, especially for nonphonetic words. Kauffman et al. suggest that imitation may be particularly useful in teaching words that do not follow regular phonetic rules—words for which the child must use visual memory.

Additional Considerations

Different types of correctional procedures should be used with various kinds of spelling errors. Visual image should be emphasized with a child who omits silent letters or misspells phonologically irregular words; incorrect spelling of homonyms indicates a need to stress word meanings. Also, words the child misspells in written compositions may be included in the child's spelling program. This is motivating, since words the child uses are being taught, and the need to learn to spell those words is apparent.

Spelling also may be taught and reinforced throughout the total language arts curriculum. One way to improve spelling is through word study in reading (Templeton, 1986). In oral reading the child gives close attention to the sounds of the entire word. In addition, reading gives the student the meanings of words, increasing interest in them. The student learns the correct usage of a word in sentences and can determine whether or not the word is written correctly. Thus, learning to spell may accompany learning to read; a program that stresses both skills may be effective and motivating. As discussed in Chapter 11, the language experience approach (Lee & Allen, 1963) incorporates reading and spelling. The *SIMS* program (1978), a precision teaching program, teaches the student to spell words as she learns to read them. Shinn (1982) stresses that no student should be forced to learn to spell words that she cannot read and understand. Otherwise, she is really memorizing a nonmeaningful series of letters that she will not retain. Thus, spelling lists should be produced from the student's reading vocabulary. Shinn provides a linguistic spelling program that is designed to assist in the diagnosis and intervention of spelling difficulties as well as in the evaluation of instruction through specific charting procedures.

Training in dictionary usage also should be included in the spelling program. Dictionaries help the child become more independent in locating spellings and provide such information as syllabication, meaning, pronunciation, synonyms, and homonyms. Picture dictionaries can be used in the primary grades. Beginning in the fourth grade, special practice in using the dictionary often is included in the curriculum, and the use of dictionaries may be encouraged during writing tasks.

In teaching spelling skills at the secondary level, the teacher should help the adolescent understand the social and practical significance of correct spelling. For example, employers place value on accurate spelling on job applications. The student's own interests and the various subject areas can provide new words to study. Also, vocational words can be emphasized. At the secondary level it might be best to teach spelling in conjunction with other activities, rather than to use class time solely for spelling instruction (Marsh, Gearheart, & Gearheart, 1978). Practice in reading and other learning activities may help the adolescent learn to spell. Finally, strategies to compensate for poor spelling should be taught to students whose spelling problems may affect their grades in content areas. For example, the teacher can provide such students with a spelling checker which contains frequently used words and words they often misspell.

ACTIVITIES AND MATERIALS

Many activities and materials may be used to supplement a spelling program. Games and activities stimulate interest, provide practice, and add variety in teaching techniques. In addition, spelling instruction may be individualized by developing games and activities for particular individuals or small groups. The following activities, instructional games, self-correcting materials, commercial materials, and computer software programs promote the development of spelling skills.

Activities

1. Ask the student to complete words in sentences by filling in omitted letters. Lists of words from stories in basal readers or spelling textbooks may be used to develop reusable worksheets or dittos. For example:

   The bo__ and __irl were bak____ a cak__.

2. Give the child various words and their configurations. Ask her to match each word with its configuration. Worksheets of specific words (for

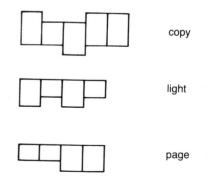

example, reading selections, weekly spelling lists) can be made and reused for this seatwork activity.

3. Use a hidden-word format to provide practice in letter sequence of spelling words. Give the student a list of spelling words and a puzzle. Ask her to locate the hidden spelling words and to draw a circle around them.

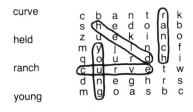

curve

held

ranch

young

4. Have each child keep a file box of spelling words that have caused her some difficulty. The words should be arranged in alphabetical order, and the cards may also contain definitions or pictures. Encourage each child to study her cards and to practice writing the words from memory. New words may be included and others deleted as the child progresses.

5. In compiling the weekly spelling word list, ask class members to volunteer words, such as those they have misspelled in writing or have encountered in independent reading. The teacher may want to include on the spelling list those words the children will use frequently in their writing. Give a pretest on the words on Monday and a second test on Friday. Keep a scoreboard graph for the entire class, scaled to 10. Have each child try to move "up 10" each week on the graph by spelling more words correctly on Friday than were spelled correctly on the pretest. Thus, the child is competing against her own previous score. The advanced student who gets a perfect score and the less able student who improves by 10 words both receive the "up 10" mark on the graph.

6. Describe a current spelling word phonetically. For example, the word *move* may be described as "a one-syllable word beginning with a consonant and ending with a vowel." Call on a child to find the word in her spelling list, and

then give her a turn to describe a word and to call on another classmate.

7. Use the Language Master to provide visual, auditory, and kinesthetic experiences for the student. Blank cards can be reused by laminating the top portion so that the words may be erased and changed. Also, pictures or letters written in yarn may be added to the blank cards. Once the card has been placed through the recorder, the student can trace the word.

8. Have each student work with *anagram* activities: The student is given a word and must rearrange all the letters to make a new word. For example, *smile* is an anagram for *miles,* and *sister* is an anagram for *resist.* For students having particular difficulty, *Scrabble* letter tiles may be used, or the student can copy the word, cut it apart, and rearrange the letters. Also, have each student work anagram puzzles, in which one letter is changed each time until the top word is changed into the bottom word. Definitions or clues may be provided. For example:

POND	small lake
_____	young horse (pony)
_____	nickname for Anthony (Tony)
_____	dial _____ (tone)
BONE	dog's treat

9. Have a spelling bee in which the students stand in a line, and each time a student spells a word correctly she "jumps" two persons toward the end of the line. When a student jumps enough people to reach the end, she goes to her seat. Thus, those students who need practice remain, and those who know the words have time for independent work.

10. Begin an add-a-letter activity with a one- to two-letter word (for example, *to*). Call on a student to make a different word by adding one letter (for example, *top*). The letters may be rearranged, but one letter must be added each turn (for example, *spot*). When no one can continue the process, start a new word. This can become a seatwork activity, in which each child works independently on a worksheet to add letters and make new words.

11. Provide the student with a jar containing approximately 40 wooden cubes with letters on them (similar to alphabet blocks or *Spill and Spell* cubes). Have the student spill the letters from the jar and see how many words she can make in five minutes with the given letters. Link letters (letters that fit together to form words) also may be used for this activity.

12. Give the student spelling word cards (two cards for each word) and have her play a concentration game. The cards are mixed up and placed face down in rows. The student turns over two cards at a time and tries to remember their location so that she can make spelling matches. When the student turns up two cards that match (that is, the same spelling word), the cards are removed. Two students may play together, taking turns to see who can make the most matches.

13. Have each student write a story or theme using the spelling list words. The theme may be on any subject and as long or as short as the student wishes to make it; however, *every one* of the spelling words must be included in what is written. Encourage the student to pay attention to spelling and using the words correctly.

14. Encourage the student to develop memory devices to help her remember the spelling of difficult words or words that are not spelled as they sound. For example:

Station*ery* is writing pap*er*.
The princi*pal* is your *pal*.

15. Present crossword puzzles that contain spelling words in order to give practice in writing the words and learning their meanings. Also, the student may be asked to make up a crossword puzzle that includes new and review spelling words and everyday words.

16. For dictionary practice, give the student a list of words (for example, *overcoat, tongue-tied, well-known*). Ask her to locate them in the dictionary and write *yes* or *no* to indicate whether each word is hyphenated. Also, give the student sentences containing some unfamiliar words and ask her to supply synonyms for four words in each sentence. For example:

Across
1. small cat
3. not wild
6. what you hear with
7. a small clue
8. a father's boy
10. not old

Down
1. room you cook in
2. short periods of sleep
4. more than one man
5. puts in mouth and chews
9. opposite of yes

The clandestine meeting was interrupted by incorrigible bandits who came incognito.

17. Have a student describe a spelling word from the current week's list by giving rhyming, meaning, or descriptive clues. The other class members are given one minute to guess the word. The first person to say the correct word goes to the chalkboard and writes it. If she spells it correctly, she gets to describe a word.

18. To motivate a student, allow her to practice spelling words on the typewriter. She can say the letters as she types them, thus combining sight, sound, and touch.

19. Select a student to pick a word from the dictionary and write on the chalkboard the exact pronunciation for the word as found in the dictionary. It should be written letter for letter with all diacritical marks and accents. Class members are then asked to pronounce and spell the word the correct way.

Instructional Games

Find-a-Word

Materials:

Two words containing the same number of letters written on the chalkboard.

Directions:

The teacher divides the class into two teams. The first child from each team goes to the chalkboard and writes any word that can be made from the letters in the given word. She gives the chalk to the next child on her team and goes to the end of the line. Each child must write a new word or correct a misspelled one. The game continues until the teacher calls time. The team with the most correctly spelled words at the end of the time limit is the winner. For example:

The given words are:	*place*	*dream*
The children may write:	pace	read
	cap	mad
	leap	dear
	pal	me

Detective

Materials:

Spelling words with various letters omitted written on the chalkboard.

Directions:

The teacher gives the definition of each word and calls on a student to fill in the missing letters. The student goes to the board and writes in the missing letters. One point is given for each correct word or letter. The student with the most points at the end of the game is the winner. For example:

n_____ghb_____r person who lives next door
stor_____s short reading selections
ni_____t opposite of day

Jaws

Materials:

Twenty-one index cards with one consonant printed on each card; 21 index cards with pictures corresponding to the sound of each consonant; one index card with "Jaws" (a shark) drawn on it.

Directions:

The cards are dealt to three or more players. The players check for pairs and place them on the table.

(A pair consists of one consonant card and a picture card that has the same beginning consonant sound.) The first player picks a card from the player sitting on her left. If it matches a card in her hand, she places the pair on the table. The game continues until all the cards have been matched and one student is left holding "Jaws."

Modification:

The players may be asked to write the names of the pictures in the pairs. The player who spells the most pairs correctly wins the game.

Spell It–Keep It Card Game

Materials:

Cards with spelling words printed on them placed on the chalkboard ledge with backs to the class.

Directions:

The teacher divides the class into two teams. A student from the first team selects a card and reads the word. A student from the other team spells the word. If the word is spelled correctly, the student who spelled it gets to keep the card. If the word is spelled incorrectly, a child from the first team has a chance to spell it and get the card. Then a student from the second team selects a card, and the process is repeated until all cards are gone from the ledge. The winner is the team having the most cards at the end of the game.

Telegraph Spelling

Materials:

Two sets of 2″ × 6″ cards with letters used in the spelling words printed on them.

Directions:

The class is divided into two teams, and each child receives a card. The teacher pronounces a spelling word. The members of each team arrange themselves in the proper order at the front of the room. The team that correctly spells the word the quickest wins a point. After a specified time limit, the team with the most points wins the game.

Modification:

For older students, each member of the team may be assigned one or two letters of the alphabet. When the teacher gives the spelling word, the members of the team begin verbally to "transmit" (call out) the spelling of the word. There can be no more than 5 seconds between calling out letters, and other team members are not allowed to help. One point is earned for each correct response.

Spelling Bingo

Materials:

Cards divided into 24 squares (four squares across and six squares down), with a different spelling word printed in each space and words in different order on each card; numerous discs or markers.

Directions:

Each child receives a card and several discs. As the teacher calls out and spells a word, each student covers the given word on her card with a disc. The first student to complete a column going across, down, or diagonally calls "Bingo" and wins the game.

Modifications:

1. The students can make their own cards by dividing their paper into 24 squares. The spelling words are written on the chalkboard, and each student writes the words in any squares on her paper. One child is selected to stand with her back to the board, and the teacher calls out words for her to spell. For each word she spells correctly, the other students place a disc on the corresponding square on their card. The game

continues until someone calls "Bingo." The teacher keeps a list of the words and checks the winning card.

2. For young children, the bingo cards may consist of rows of selected consonants, short vowels, and long vowels. When the teacher calls a word, the child puts discs on the appropriate letters on her card.

A game-board format may be used to present spelling instructional tasks. Game boards may be made on poster board to depict various themes, such as a race track, rocket path, mountain path, safari, or any other start-to-finish sequence. Also, stacks of index cards containing spelling words may be color-coded or numbered according to difficulty level. Students may play with two different stacks of cards according to their ability levels. The players roll dice to determine the number of spaces they can move on the game board if they spell the word on the spelling card correctly. The following instructional game uses a game-board format.

Golf Game Board

Materials:

Large game board on tagboard or laminated poster board; different-colored golf tees for markers; cards with spelling words printed on them, with stars on the cards of the most difficult words (see Figure 12.1).

Directions:

Two players each choose a golf tee and place it on the "tee off" square. The first player takes the top card and reads the word to the other player, who tries to spell the word. If she spells the word correctly, she moves ahead one space. If the word is spelled incorrectly, she moves back one space. When a player correctly spells a word that has a star on the card, she moves her marker ahead two spaces. The first player to reach the golf hole wins the game.

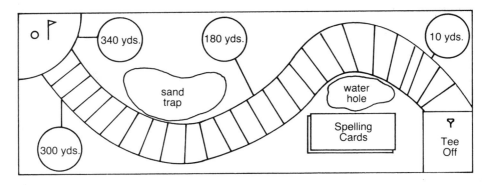

FIGURE 12.1
Golf game board.

Modifications:

1. The spelling cards may consist of some words spelled correctly and some words spelled incorrectly. The player draws a card and must decide whether or not the word is correctly spelled. If it is misspelled, the player must spell it correctly. Each player moves one space for a correct answer. A third student can use a key to check responses.

2. For older students, the words on the spelling cards may be assigned a number of yards (in multiples of 10) according to the difficulty level of the word. Each space on the board is worth 10 yards. When the player spells a word correctly, she moves the number of yards indicated on the card. If she misspells the word, she does not advance.

Tic-Tac-Toe

Materials:

A tic-tac-toe game square made of tagboard or laminated poster board; five tagboard Xs and five Os; cards with spelling words written on them.

Directions:

One student chooses to mark with Xs and the other student uses Os. The first student takes the top spelling card and reads it to her opponent, who attempts to spell it. If the student spells the word correctly, she places her marker in a square on the board. The game continues until one player has three of her markers in a horizontal, vertical, or diagonal row.

Modification:

The class can be divided into two teams, and each student can pin a paper marked X or O on herself to indicate her team. Nine chairs are placed in three rows similar to a tic-tac-toe board. A member of one team selects a card and reads the spelling word, and a member of the other team must spell it. If the student spells the word correctly, she sits in the chair of her choice. The game continues until one team gets three members sitting in a row.

Connect the Dots

Materials:

Twenty-five dots (rows of five across and five down) drawn on the chalkboard; cards with spelling words printed on them.

Directions:

The students are divided into two teams, Team 1 and Team 2. A member of the first team draws the top spelling card and reads the word to a member of the opposite team, who tries to spell it (either in writing or aloud). If the student spells the word correctly, she draws a line connecting two dots, and her team gets another turn to try to spell a word. If a word is spelled incorrectly, the other team gets a turn. When a square is closed in by four lines, the number of the team is written in the square. The team that obtains the most squares is the winner.

Modification:

Two players may play the game with a game board of dots made of tagboard covered with acetate so that marks made with a grease pencil can be erased. When a player makes a square, she can write her initial in it.

Checkers

Materials:

A checker game board made of tagboard; 24 tagboard checkers (12 of one color and 12 of another), each of which has a spelling word printed on the bottom.

Directions:

Two players place their checkers on the board, and they take turns moving their checkers. If one player can "jump" her opponent's checker, the opponent looks on the bottom of the checker to be jumped and reads the word aloud. If the jumping player correctly spells the word, she is allowed to jump and pick up the opponent's checker. If she misspells the word, she is not allowed to make the move. The game continues until one player has obtained all her opponent's checkers through jumping.

Modifications:

1. Additional checkers may be made so different spelling words are used each time the game is played.
2. Regular checkers may be used when spelling word cards are provided. When a player wants to make a jump, she must correctly spell the word on the top card to her opponent.

TV Talent

Material:

Three decorated shoe boxes; spelling words of varying difficulty printed on index cards.

Directions:

The game is presented as a television show with one student acting as master of ceremonies (MC). The words are placed in the three boxes, and two players are chosen from the "audience." The first player picks a card from one of the boxes and hands it to the MC without looking at it. The MC pronounces the word, and the player writes the word on the chalkboard. If the player spells the word correctly, she gets 5 points. The players take turns until one player earns 50 points.

Modification:

The spelling words may be divided into three levels of difficulty. The easiest words are placed in the box marked 1 point; the next level, in the box marked 3 points; and the most difficult words, in the box marked 5 points. The student chooses a card from a box according to how many points she wants to try for on that turn.

Bowling

Materials:

Two sets of 10 numbered bowling pins; file-card box divided into 10 sections, with spelling words filed according to the number of points each word is worth (1–10).

Directions:

The bowling pins are set up or pinned to a backboard in the arrangement of a bowling game. The first player calls the number of a pin, and her opponent reads the first word from that section in the file box. If the player spells the word correctly, the pin is removed and she gets the number of points that pin is worth. The second player takes a turn using her set of pins. The winner is the player who earns the most points after trying to knock down all her pins.

Modification:

Two pairs of players may play. The first player of the pair tries to get a strike (worth 55 points) by spelling all the words. If she misses a word, her partner may try to get a spare (worth 45 points) by spelling the word her partner missed and the words for any remaining pins. If the second member of the pair misses a word, she and her partner receive points according to the numbered pins they knocked down. The first pair of players to score a specified number of points wins the game.

Dictionary Store Hunt

Materials:

One dictionary per player; a stack of cards with nouns written on them that are unlikely to be familiar to the players (for example, *cockatiel, metronome, colander*).

Directions:

Each player picks at random five word cards. At the same starting time, each player begins to look up the words in her dictionary, reads the definition to herself, and writes down the kind of store she would shop in for that item. The winner is the first person to complete the hunt. Other players may check her responses by looking up the words as she names the stores.

Baseball Spelling Game

Materials:

Baseball diamond with three bases and home plate drawn on the chalkboard; cards with spelling words written on them.

Directions:

The class is divided into two teams, and the top speller in each group may act as pitcher. The pitcher draws a card and reads the word to the first batter of the other team. If the first batter spells the word correctly, she is given a single and stands in front of first base on the chalkboard. If the second batter correctly spells the word she is given, she goes to first base and the player on first base moves to sec-

ond base. If a player misspells her word, she is "out"; there are three outs for each team in each inning. Prior to hearing her word, any batter may declare "home run," and if she spells the word correctly, she clears the bases and the home run(s) is added to the score. However, if she misspells the word it automatically counts as the third out for the team, regardless of the actual number of outs for the team. The team with the most runs at the end of a set number of innings is the winner.

Modifications:

1. The word cards may be labelled "single," "double," "triple," and "home run" according to the difficulty level of the spelling word. After the batter spells the word correctly, the pitcher tells her what her "hit" was worth according to the card. The batter moves to the appropriate base, and batters already on base advance.
2. A baseball diamond may be arranged in the room, using chairs for the bases, and the "runners" can sit in the appropriate chair when they get "hits."

Football Spelling Game

Materials:

A football field including yard lines drawn ⊂E chalkboard; index cards with spelling words w on them.

Directions:

The class is divided into two teams, and the ba⎯ placed (drawn) on the 50-yard line by the "refere⎯ The referee reads a word to a member of the fi⎯ team. If she spells the word correctly, the ball⎯ moved 10 yards toward the opponent's goal line.⎯ the word is misspelled, the offensive team loses 10 yards. Each team gets four words in one turn; then the other team takes a turn. A team is given 6 points each time it crosses the opponent's goal line. The winner is the team with the most points at the end of a specified time period.

Modifications:

1. The football field may be made on tagboard, and two players can play using small tagboard foot-

balls for their markers. One player draws a card and reads the word to her opponent. If the opponent spells the word correctly, she advances her marker 5 yards closer to her goal; and if she misspells the word, she moves her marker back 5 yards. The players take turns (one word a turn), and the first one to reach the goal line scores a touchdown and wins the game.

2. The word cards may include the number of yards each spelling word is worth (1–10 yards), and the ball is moved accordingly.

3. In addition to spelling word cards, there may be "gain" cards and "loss" cards. When the student correctly spells the word on the spelling card, she picks a gain card; and when she misspells a word, she draws a loss card. The gain cards denote the number of yards gained—for example, "completed pass, 30 yards," "20-yard run." The loss cards denote the number of yards lost— "quarterback sack, lose 10 yards," "tackled, 5-yard loss." The player moves her football accordingly.

4. Rather than drawing, erasing, and redrawing the ball throughout the game, a chalkboard eraser can be used as the ball. It is easy to move and see if set vertically on the chalkboard tray.

Nym Game

Materials:

Two sets of three decorated coffee cans—one labelled "antonyms," one labelled "homonyms," and one labelled "synonyms"; cards with pairs of words written on them which are antonyms, homonyms, or synonyms (all appropriate and acceptable antonyms, homonyms, or synonyms are given for each initial word in the word pair).

Directions:

The first player draws the top card and reads and spells the first word on the card to her opponent. The opponent must (a) spell the word that completes the word pair, (b) use the words in sentences, and (c) identify the word pair as antonyms, homonyms, or synonyms. If correct, the opponent places the word card in the appropriate can of her set. If incorrect, the first player gets to put the card in the

appropriate can of her set. The players take turns, and when all the cards are gone, they count their score. For each card in the homonym can, the player gets 3 points; for each antonym card she gets 2 points; and for each synonym card she gets 1 point. The player with the highest total score wins the game.

Spelling Dart Game

Materials:

Target divided into sections for 15, 10, 5, and 1 points, drawn on heavy poster board; suction darts; a file box divided into sections labelled 15, 10, 5, and 1 containing spelling word cards of four levels of difficulty (the most difficult words are in the 15-point section).

Directions:

The target is mounted on the wall, and the first player throws a dart at it from approximately 10 feet away. The players decide which section of the target the dart landed in. Another player takes a card from the section of the file box corresponding to the target section. For example, if the dart landed in the 5-point section, the card would be drawn from the 5-point section in the file box. The spelling word is pronounced, and the player who threw the dart must correctly spell the word to receive that number of points. The players take turns until one player scores 50 points and wins the game.

Charades

Materials:

Spelling words printed on index cards.

Directions:

The class is divided into two teams. A member of the first team selects a card, reads the word to herself, and then acts out the word without saying anything. There is a 2-minute time limit, after which the student picks another team member to take her place. The first team to guess the word gets 1 point. If the person who guesses the word can also spell it correctly, her team gets 2 points. The person who guessed the word then draws a card and acts out her word. The team with the most points at the end of a specified time period wins the game.

Bottle Top Scrabble

Materials:

One hundred fifty bottle tops with letters of the alphabet written inside them with a marking pen and point values written on the outside (letters most often used should appear most; point values may be the same as those in *Scrabble*).

Directions:

Each student selects 10 tops without looking. The first player spells a word using as many of her letters as possible and adds the point values of the letters used. Then she picks more tops so that she again has 10 tops. The players take turns spelling words that connect with previously spelled words, as in a *Scrabble* game. After all possible bottle tops have been used, the player with the highest score is the winner.

Modification:

For older students, there can be a minimum number of letters for each word (for example, four or more). Also, the number of tops may be increased.

Self-Correcting Materials

Spelling Word Puzzles

Feedback device:

The pieces of the puzzle fit together to indicate a correct choice.

Materials:

Spelling words printed on heavy cardboard and then cut into two or more puzzle pieces.

Directions:

The child looks at the puzzle pieces and fits together the pieces that correctly spell a word.

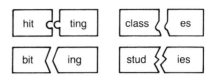

Flip-Sider Spelling Cards

Feedback device:

Picture completion or the matching of objects, numbers, or colors provides feedback.

Materials:

Sets of index cards with a spelling word on one card and the definition or a picture representing the word on another card; the reverse sides of the two cards that go together have the same object, number, or color, or the two cards complete a picture.

Directions:

The student looks at the spelling word on a card and selects the card with the definition of that word or a picture representing it. Then the student flips over the two cards. If she has chosen the correct definition or picture, the backs of the two cards will have the same object, number, or color, or they will complete a picture. (See the cards on page 434.)

Modification:

The front of the card can have a sentence in which the spelling word is omitted. The sentence may be a definition of the missing word, or there may be a picture illustrating the word in the blank. The spelling word that goes in the blank is written on the back of the card. The student reads the sentence, writes down the missing word, and then flips over the card to check her response.

Spelling Spinner

Feedback device:

A flap is located on the poster board. When the flap is raised, the answer is revealed.

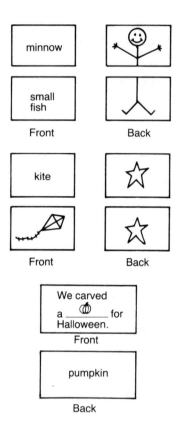

Modification:

Discs of spelling words selected from reading selections or spelling lists may be numbered and stored so that the teacher can select a disc appropriate for an individual child.

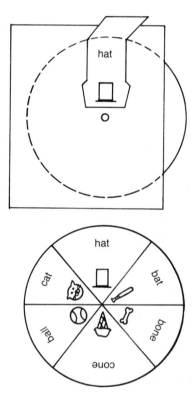

Materials:

A round disc of poster board divided into several sections, each of which has a word written at the top and a picture or definition written in the lower portion of the section; a square piece of poster board which has the round disc attached to the back with a brass fastener, with a small window cut out at the top to reveal the top portion of the disc and a larger window below it to reveal the lower portion of the disc; a flexible flap (such as vinyl wallpaper) placed over the top window.

Directions:

The student turns the spinner to reveal a picture or definition in the window. She writes the spelling word for the picture or definition and then lifts the flap to check her answer.

Tape Recorder Spelling

Feedback device:

Following the spelling activity presented on the tape, the correct answers are given on the tape.

Materials:

A tape recorder and a tape cassette that contains a spelling activity—for example, a dictated spelling test or directions instructing the student to draw a house and label objects (such as "Add a chimney to your house and write the word *chimney*").

Directions:

The student follows the instructions given to her on the tape recorder and writes the specified words. Following the activity she continues to listen to the tape to hear the correct responses and thus checks her answers.

Answer Box (presented in Chapter 4)

Feedback device:

A flap is placed over the window; when lifted, the window reveals the answer.

Materials:

An Answer Box and a set of index cards that present a spelling exercise.

Directions:

The student writes an answer to the presented spelling problem and then lifts the flap to see the answer.

Modification:

Change the two "eyes" to one long opening. Then activities such as definitions or sentences with missing words can be presented.

Contraction cards to use in the Answer Box:

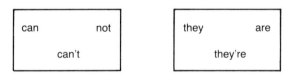

Definition cards to use in the modified Answer Box:

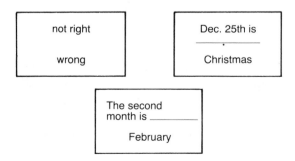

Fill in the Letters

Feedback device:

When the correct letters are filled in, the message at the bottom of the page is completed. Deciphering the code thus provides feedback.

Materials:

Worksheets on which the student must either cross out or add a letter so that the word is spelled correctly; blanks at the bottom of the page which give a message when the crossed out or added letters are written in them.

Directions:

The student completes the worksheet by crossing out or adding letters as indicated. Then each letter is written in the appropriate blank at the bottom of the page. If the correct letters are chosen, the student reads a message.

Color Spelling Sheet

1. rsed	5. whirte
2. bl e	6. yeljlow
3. orpange	7. br wn
4. belack	8. greben

1 2 3 4 5   6 7 8

☐☐☐☐☐▦☐☐☐ (super job)

Spelling Crossword Puzzles

Feedback device:

Only a correct response will fit in the squares and complete additional words.

Materials:

A crossword puzzle in which spelling words are used (for example, the crossword puzzle presented on p. 426).

Directions:

The student completes the crossword puzzle and receives feedback as she fills in the squares.

Scrambled Letters

Feedback device:

The backs of the letters are numbered in the correct sequence of the spelling word.

Materials:

Envelopes with pictures illustrating a word or definitions written on the front; square cards placed inside the envelopes, with each card giving a letter needed to spell the word; numbers written on the backs of the cards to represent the correct letter sequence of the word.

Directions:

The student reads the definition or looks at the picture on the envelope, takes the letters out of the envelope, and places them face up. She unscrambles the letters and arranges them to spell the word. Then she turns the letters over. The number order on the back of the cards indicates if the word is spelled correctly.

Poke Box (presented in Chapter 4)

Feedback device:

The student places a stylus in the hole to indicate her response. If the correct answer is selected, the card can be easily pulled out of the Poke Box.

Materials:

A Poke Box and a set of index cards that present a spelling exercise—for example, a word and three abbreviations, or a definition or picture and three words.

Directions:

The student selects an answer to the presented spelling problem by inserting the stylus in the hole below the answer. She then pulls the card, which can be removed if her answer is correct.

Abbreviation and picture cards to use in a Poke Box:

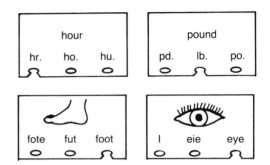

Color Magic

Feedback device:

The student receives feedback by opening the folder to see the answers written in colored pencil.

Materials:

A plastic colored folder (such as the type typically used to hold term papers), inside of which is a spelling worksheet; answers written on the worksheet in the same color as the plastic folder (that is, if the plastic folder is red, the answers are written with a red colored pencil so they will not show through the folder).

Directions:

The student follows the instructions on the worksheet, which she reads through the colored plastic folder. She writes her answers on a sheet of paper and, when finished with the activity, she opens the folder to check her responses.

Commercial Materials

Basic developmental programs and corrective materials for spelling instruction are available, as are games and materials stressing dictionary skills. Appendix B lists the addresses of the publishers and producers of the materials presented.

Common Words

Publisher: Merrill

Description:

This developmental spelling and vocabulary program for students in grades 9 through 12 reviews commonly misspelled words from elementary grades and then emphasizes the correct spelling and usage of high-utility high school and adult vocabulary. The program consists of two consumable workbooks containing units that emphasize word meanings, word analysis, word building, and dictionary usage.

Corrective Spelling through Morphographs

Publisher: Science Research Associates

Description:

This is an intensive 1-year program for students in grade 4 through adult age. The program includes 140 twenty-minute lessons that cover more than 12,000 words, including problem words. The student is taught basic units of meaning in written language (morphographs) that are always spelled according to specific rules. Thus, the student learns analytic techniques and generalizations that can be applied to words not in the program.

Flash-X

Producer: Arista

Description:

This manually operated tachistoscope gives a flash exposure to words printed on discs. The device is simple to operate and exposes a word at a set rate of 1/25 of a second. In addition to discs that contain words at various difficulty levels, there are blank discs for printing words selected by the teacher.

Gateways to Correct Spelling

Publisher: Steck-Vaughn

Description:

This high school worktext for students in grades 7 through 12 provides instruction in basic spelling, dictionary habits, and vocabulary. Vocabulary sections include 720 commonly misspelled basic spelling words as well as practical words that are frequently used in business, literature, and general correspondence.

Speed Spelling; Advanced Speed Spelling

Publisher: C. C. Publications

Description:

Speed Spelling is an individualized, phonetically based spelling program designed for children in grades 1 through 6. *Advanced Speed Spelling* is designed to increase written spelling skills at the 7th- through 12th-grade levels. *Speed Spelling* focuses on the regularities of written spelling, while *Advanced Speed Spelling* teaches the irregularities. Both programs include lessons in word reading, word writing, and sentence writing. A record of student performance is included so that the student can chart her own progress.

Spelling Mastery

Publisher: Science Research Associates

Description:

This five-level basal spelling series is designed to teach a high level of mastery of spelling words to students in grades 2 through 6. Levels A and B stress phonemic spelling (by sounds) and whole-word spelling (by words), and Levels C through E include more multisyllable words and also emphasize morphological spelling (by base words, prefixes, etc.).

Spelling Workbook Series

Publisher: Educators Publishing Service

Description:

The four workbooks in this series present a corrective program for elementary and secondary students experiencing difficulty with spelling. The first two workbooks emphasize the phonetic elements of words in context; the third workbook is designed for students who have poor visual recall of letters and words. The secondary level workbook emphasizes spelling rules and generalizations.

Target: Spelling

Publisher: Steck-Vaughn

Description:

This series of six consumable books is designed to teach spelling to students with learning problems in grades 1 through 7. A systematic, highly ordered format is used in which 1,260 words are presented sequentially and with constant reinforcement throughout the six books. Students are asked to learn only six new words per week, and learning experiences to ensure mastery include activities such as word shapes, word search, visual discrimination, recognition in context, matching words with pictures, sound blending, rhyming, and supplying missing letters.

Teaching Resources Spelling Series

Publisher: DLM Teaching Resources

Description:

This linguistically based program emphasizes mastery of crucial spelling rules, phonetic patterns, and sight words most frequently misspelled. The series consists of student workbooks on three reading levels (grades 2, 3, and 4), with the interest level ranging from third to seventh grade. The workbooks each contain 30 weekly lessons accompanied by review lessons and reinforcement activities.

Dictionary Materials

(a) Learning How to Use the Dictionary

Publisher: Macmillan

Description:

This programmed approach emphasizes basic skills used in locating words in the dictionary and skills needed for defining, spelling, and using words appropriately.

(b) The Perfect Speller

Publisher: Grosset and Dunlap

Description:

This is a reference book of commonly misspelled words and may be used by elementary or secondary students. Thousands of words are listed in alphabetical order, with correct spellings always printed in red. A student looks up a word any way she thinks it is spelled and is given the correct spelling. For example, if the student makes a phonetic error in her spelling, the word as she spells it is listed in black type in the left-hand column and the correct spelling is in red in the right-hand column.

(c) Spellex Word Finder

Publisher: Curriculum Associates

Description:

This student reference book helps students quickly verify the correct spelling of over 15,000 root words and their derivatives. Each base word is presented with its other common forms (for example, *empty— empties, emptied, emptying, emptiness*).

Spelling Calculators

(a) Spelling B

Producer: Texas Instruments

Description:

This calculator, designed for children at least 6 years old, is accompanied by a book of numbered pictures. A number is displayed on the calculator, the child locates the picture with that number in the book, and she punches in the correct spelling for that item. If the child spells the word correctly, the calculator gives another number and the student continues. If the child misspells the word, the calculator displays the word *wrong* and the child tries the word again. If the word is spelled incorrectly a second time, the calculator displays the word spelled correctly and then a new number is given. Thus, this electronic learning aid uses word-picture associations and the corrected-test method to help students learn more than 260 useful words.

(b) Speak & Spell

Producer: Texas Instruments

Description:

This calculator is more complex than *Spelling B* and is geared for children who are 7 years and older. The calculator "speaks" a word, and the student punches in what she thinks is the correct spelling. If the spelling is correct, the calculator responds "That is correct" and proceeds with a new word. If the word is misspelled, the calculator indicates so and the student tries the word again. After a second misspelling, the calculator verbalizes the correct spelling and then dictates a new word. Also after giving a word, the calculator allows time for the student to say the word before spelling it. A booklet accompanies the calculator and contains instructions for spelling games that can be played with others or with the calculator only. In addition, DLM Teaching Resources offers nine supplemental modules and activity books (for example, Noun Endings, Vowel Ventures, Homonym Heroes) which introduce more than 200 spelling words.

Spelling Games

(a) Hangman

Producer: Milton Bradley

Description:

Hangman is a word-guessing game designed for two players from age 8 to adult. It consists of two L-shaped trays, a total of 112 letter tiles (56 in each color) and lists of 5-, 6-, 7-, and 8-letter words. Each player chooses a word to play, spells the word with her letter tiles, and places the letters in the slots at the top of her tray so that, when turned, the opponent will read the letters left to right. The object of the game is to be the first player to guess the opponent's concealed word. The players take turns guessing letters, and a player's turn continues until she calls an incorrect letter. For each incorrect letter guess, the opponent turns the dial in her tray which shows a diagram of stages of "hanging the man" in the window of the tray. After 11 turns of the dial, the player is "hanged" and thereby loses the game.

Also, a player who guesses an incorrect word or misspells a word automatically loses the game. The winner is the first player to correctly spell out or guess her opponent's word before being "hanged."

(b) Scrabble

Producer: Selchow and Righter

Description:

Scrabble is a crossword game designed for two to four players. Letter tiles with various score values are used to form interlocking words in crossword fashion on the *Scrabble* playing board. Since less frequently used letters (such as *q, z,* and *x*) are worth more points, the student is encouraged to spell more difficult words. The players compete for high score by using the letters in combinations and locations that take the best advantage of the values of the tiles and the premium squares (such as *double word score*) on the board. Students can learn new words from plays made by their opponents. Also, any misspelled words may be challenged by other players, and a dictionary may be used to check correct spellings.

(c) Spill and Spell

Producer: Parker Brothers

Description:

Spill and Spell is a word game for any number of players. Fifteen wooden cubes with letters printed on each side are placed in a cup and spilled. Each player must make words using the letters shown on the top surface of her spilled cubes. After making the first word, the player continues to try to use the remaining letters in crossword puzzle fashion. The score is determined by squaring the number of letters in each word; therefore, it is to the player's advantage to use as many letters as possible in each word. Also, the number of cubes not used are squared and subtracted from the player's score. *Spill and Spell* can be played by a single student to see how high a score she can get in a single throw. Also, players may take turns rearranging the letters of a single throw to see who can get the highest score. Young children can play to see who can come closest to using all the letters in spelling simple words. In addition, an hourglass timer is included so that players can race against time for the highest score.

Computer Software Programs

Microcomputer software can be effectively used to give students additional learning opportunities to improve or enrich their spelling skills. Some programs provide practice activities and tutorials through a systematic approach, whereas others feature a game format. The following computer programs are described to give examples of types of software that are available to reinforce spelling skills. Addresses of the producers and distributors of educational computer software are listed in Appendix C.

Dieting Dinosaur Series

Distributor: Charles Clark Company

Hardware: TRS-80

Description:

This series of games uses the format of *Hangman* to promote spelling skills. The games can be used by one or two players, or the class can be divided into teams to compete for total points. The program features a dinosaur who is on a strict diet and can only eat letters that fit into the word to be guessed. Students feed letters to the creature and thus expand their vocabulary and sharpen spelling skills. Words and hints in the program were derived from a variety of texts and are separated into grade levels (grades 3–4, grades 5–6, grade 7, and grade 8). If desired, teachers can replace the word bank with their own chosen words and hints.

Pop 'R Spell; Pop 'R Spell Challenge

Producer: Milliken—EduFun

Hardware: Apple II, IBM PC, Atari

Description:

Pop 'R Spell is designed for students in grades 3 through 8 and uses a game format in which one to four students may play. In the game three letters pop out, and the student must guess which one belongs in the secret word. If the correct letter is chosen, the player's turn continues; otherwise, another player gets a turn. The sooner the secret word is spelled, the more bonus points are earned. The first player to score 100 points wins. *Pop 'R Spell Challenge* is for students in the fifth grade and above and focuses on advanced spelling and vocabulary development. The secret words become more challenging as new, difficult words are presented. Students can challenge each other or have round-robin tournaments.

Spelling Rules

Distributor: Charles Clark Company

Hardware: Apple II

Description:

This software contains instruction with illustrative examples, exercises for practice opportunities, and a mastery quiz. The program explains rules related to *ie* or *ei*, final *e*, adding *k*, final consonant, *-sede*, *-ceed*, *-cede*, and final *y*. It is designed for students in the fifth grade and above.

The Spelling System

Producer: Milliken

Hardware: Apple II

Description:

This program is designed to teach the major principles and patterns that occur in the spelling of English words. In addition, many spelling irregularities are covered. The program gives special attention to sound spellings and teaches more than 1,400 words. Teachers can also add new words. Each lesson is composed of three separate exercises. First the student receives a brief introduction to the concept or fact being presented. Then she works through three practice activities (unscrambling words, deciphering words by determining if a before-letter or after-letter code is used, and locating misspelled words). Finally, the student tests her mastery of the lesson words. In the testing format, a sentence is presented with a word missing, and the student may request a sound spelling clue if desired. Only one chance is given for a correct answer. Four diskettes are available (vowel spellings, consonant spellings, special vowel spellings, and word building) as well as a reproducible activity book for supplementary exercises. The program provides instruction for students in grades 4 through 8, as well as review for older students.

Spelling Wiz

Producer: DLM Teaching Resources

Hardware: Apple II, IBM PC/PCjr, Commodore 64, Tandy 1000, Atari

Description:

This software program is included in DLM Teaching Resources' *Arcademic Skill Builders in Language Arts* and assists students in spelling words commonly misspelled in grade levels 1 through 6. The game features a colorful wizard who uses his magic wand to zap missing letters into words. The following game control options can be preset according to an individual student's needs: speed at which game is played (nine different speeds), difficulty level of content, length of game (1–5 minutes), and sound effects on or off. Additional activities for review and reinforcement are provided on 24 blackline masters.

Spelltronics

Distributor: Educational Activities

Hardware: Apple II, TRS-80, Commodore 64 with emulator, Atari

Description:

This program uses the letter cloze technique to reinforce correct spelling and build visual memory. The entire program teaches 240 words, and it allows the teacher to add additional words. Each word is presented three separate times with different letters deleted. The student adds the missing letters and must type the word into a sentence. If the student is unable to provide the correct spelling after two opportunities, the correct answer is displayed and the student tries again. Correct answers are rewarded in all drills. Words are grouped according to linguistic, phonic, or spelling concepts. Six programs are included: vowel patterns, long vowel patterns, consonant patterns, word endings, useful words, and unexpected spellings. Each pattern has four units containing 10 programmed words and a review unit. The student advances from simple to more complex patterns. The program is useful for all students who have difficulty spelling.

REFERENCES

Arena, J. (1981). *Diagnostic Spelling Potential Test.* Novato, CA: Academic Therapy.

Brigance, A.H. (1982). *Brigance Diagnostic Comprehensive Inventory of Basic Skills.* North Billerica, MA: Curriculum Associates.

Brueckner, L.J., & Bond, G.L. (1966). *The diagnosis and treatment of learning difficulties.* New York: Appleton-Century-Crofts.

Bryant, N.D., Drabin, I.R., & Gettinger, M. (1981). Effects of varying unit size on spelling achievement in learning disabled children. *Journal of Learning Disabilities, 14,* 200–203.

Burns, P.C. (1980). *Assessment and correction of language arts difficulties.* Columbus, OH: Merrill.

Burns, P.C., & Broman, B.L. (1983). *The language arts in childhood education (5th ed.).* Chicago: Rand McNally.

Carpenter, D., & Miller, L.J. (1982). Spelling ability of reading disabled LD students and able readers. *Learning Disability Quarterly, 5*(1), 65–70.

Cartwright, G.P. (1969). Written expression and spelling. In R.M. Smith (Ed.), *Teacher diagnosis of educational difficulties* (pp. 95–117). Columbus, OH: Merrill.

Dunn, L.M., & Markwardt, F.C., Jr. (1988). *Peabody Individual Achievement Test—Revised.* Circle Pines, MN: American Guidance Service.

Edgington, R. (1967). But he spelled them right this morning. *Academic Therapy Quarterly, 3,* 58–59.

Ekwall, E.E. (1989). *Locating and correcting reading difficulties* (5th ed.). Columbus, OH: Merrill.

Fernald, G. (1943). *Remedial techniques in basic school subjects.* New York: McGraw-Hill.

Gardner, E.F., Callis, R., Merwin, J.C., & Rudman, H.C. (1983). *Test of Academic Skills* (2nd ed.). San Antonio, TX: Psychological Corporation.

Gardner, E.F., Rudman, H.C., Karlsen, B., & Merwin, J.C. (1982). *Stanford Achievement Test* (7th ed.). San Antonio, TX: Psychological Corporation.

Gates, A., & Russell, D. (1937). *Gates-Russell Spelling Diagnostic Test.* New York: Teachers College, Columbia University.

Gillingham, A., & Stillman, B. (1968). *Remedial teaching for children with specific disability in reading, spelling, and penmanship.* Cambridge, MA: Educators Publishing Service.

Greenbaum, C.R. (1987). *Spellmaster: The Spellmaster Assessment and Teaching System.* Austin, TX: Pro-Ed.

Hieronymus, A.N., Hoover, H.D. & Lindquist, E.F. (1986). *Iowa Tests of Basic Skills.* Chicago: Riverside.

Hodges, R.E. (1966). The psychological bases of spelling. In T.D. Horn (Ed.), *Research on handwriting and spelling.* Champaign, IL: National Council of Teachers of English.

Horn, E.A. (1926). *A basic writing vocabulary.* University of Iowa Monographs in Education, First Series No. 4. Iowa City, IA: University of Iowa.

Jastak, S.R., & Wilkinson, G.S. (1984). *Wide Range Achievement Test—Revised.* Wilmington, DE: Jastak Associates.

Kauffman, J.M., Hallahan, D.P., Haas, K., Brame, T., & Boren, R. (1978). Imitating children's errors to improve their spelling performance. *Journal of Learning Disabilities, 11,* 217–222.

Koenig, C.H., & Kunzelmann, H.P. (1980). *Classroom learning screening manual.* San Antonio, TX: Psychological Corporation.

Kottmeyer, W. (1970). *Teacher's guide for remedial reading.* New York: McGraw-Hill.

Kuska, A., Webster, E.J.D., & Elford, G. (1964). *Spelling in language arts 6.* Don Mills, Ontario, Canada: Nelson.

Larsen, S.C., & Hammill, D.D. (1986). *Test of Written Spelling—2.* Austin, TX: Pro-Ed.

Lee, D.M., & Allen, R.V. (1963). *Learning to read through experience* (2nd ed.). New York: Appleton-Century-Crofts.

Lerner, J.W. (1985). *Learning disabilities: Theories, diagnosis, and teaching strategies* (4th ed.). Boston: Houghton Mifflin.

Lovitt, T.C., Guppy, T.E., & Blattner, J.E. (1969). The use of free-time contingency with fourth graders to increase spelling accuracy. *Behavior Research and Therapy, 7,* 151–156.

Mann, P.H., Suiter, P.A., & McClung, R.M. (1979). *Handbook in diagnostic-prescriptive teaching* (2nd ed.). Boston: Allyn & Bacon.

Marsh, G.E., II, Gearheart, C.K., & Gearheart, B.R. (1978). *The learning disabled adolescent: Program alternatives in the secondary school.* St. Louis: Mosby.

McGuigan, C.A. (1975). *The effects of a flowing words list vs. fixed word lists and the implementation of procedures in the add-a-word spelling program.* (Working Paper No. 52). Seattle: University of Washington, Experimental Education Unit.

Naslund, R.A., Thorpe, L.P., & Lefever, D.W. (1978). *SRA Achievement Series.* Chicago: Science Research Associates.

Otto, W., McMenemy, R.A., & Smith, R.J. (1973). *Corrective and remedial teaching* (2nd ed.). Boston: Houghton Mifflin.

Petty, W.T. (1966). Handwriting and spelling: Their current status in the language arts curriculum. In T.D. Horn (Ed.), *Research on handwriting and spelling.* Champaign, IL: National Council of Teachers of English.

Scannel, D.P. (1986). *Tests of Achievement and Proficiency.* Chicago: Riverside.

Shinn, T.K. (1982). Linguistic and functional spelling strategies. In D.A. Sabatino & L. Mann (Eds.), *A handbook of diagnostic and prescriptive teaching* (pp. 263–295). Rockville, MD: Aspen Systems.

Sidman, M.T. (1979). The effects of group free time and contingency and individual free time contingency on spelling performance. *The Directive Teacher, 1,* 4–5.

SIMS Reading and Spelling Program (3rd ed.). (1978). Minneapolis: Minneapolis Public Schools.

Starlin, C.M., & Starlin, A. (1973). *Guides to decision making in spelling.* Bemidji, MN: Unique Curriculums Unlimited.

Stephens, T.M. (1977). *Teaching skills to children with learning and behavior disorders.* Columbus, OH: Merrill.

Stephens, T.M., Hartman, A.C., & Lucas, V.H. (1982). *Teaching children basic skills: A curriculum handbook* (2nd ed.). Columbus, OH: Merrill.

Stowitschek, C.E., & Jobes, N.K. (1977). Getting the bugs out of spelling—or an alternative to the spelling bee. *Teaching Exceptional Children, 9,* 74–76.

Templeton, S. (1986). Synthesis of research on the learning and teaching of spelling. *Educational Leadership, 43*(6), 73–78.

Wallace, G., & Larsen, S.C. (1978). *Educational assessment of learning problems: Testing for teaching.* Boston: Allyn & Bacon.

Westerman, G.S. (1971). *Spelling & writing.* San Rafael, CA: Dimensions.

CHAPTER 13

Assessing and Teaching Handwriting and Written Expression Skills

Writing is a tool for communication, and it is both a skill and a means of self-expression. The complex process of writing integrates visual, motor, and conceptual abilities and is a major means through which students demonstrate their knowledge of advanced academic subjects. Moreover, Hammill and McNutt (1981) report that writing skills are among the best correlates of reading. Such skills include competence in writing, spelling, punctuation, capitalization, studying, making sound—letter correspondences, knowing the alphabet, and distinguishing one letter from another. Hammill and McNutt conclude that "a strong relationship exists between reading, which is theroretically a receptive form of written language, and almost all other aspects of written language" (p. 35).

Classroom instruction in handwriting usually begins in kindergarten or first grade. Readiness activities such as tracing, coloring, and copying are emphasized at first. Until approximately the third grade, instruction is given on the formation of letters, numbers, and words. After the third grade, more emphasis is placed on writing as a form of meaningful self-expression, and instruction focuses on using grammar correctly and developing the quality of ideas expressed. In this chapter the teaching of writing skills is divided into the two major areas of handwriting and written expression.

HANDWRITING

The major objective of instruction in handwriting is *legibility*. In order to communicate thoughts in writing, the student first must be taught to write legibly and easily. Thus, instruction focuses on holding the writing instrument, forming manuscript and cursive letters correctly, and maintaining proper spacing and proportion when writing. Many students with learning problems have difficulty with handwriting. Numerous factors contribute to handwriting difficulties: motor problems, emotional problems, faulty visual perception of letters and words, poor visual memory, poor instruction, and/or lack of motivation.

Fine motor problems can also interfere with handwriting, and thus with schoolwork. For example, a student may know how to spell a word, but he may be unable to write with enough legibility and speed to keep up with the teacher; thus, his spelling evaluation may be poor. The same situation may exist in copying material from the chalkboard and working on seatwork activities. Unfortunately, many parents and teachers view the student as academically slow when, in fact, the real problem is handwriting.

Children show a variety of handwriting problems: (a) slowness, (b) incorrect directionality of letters and numbers, (c) too much or too little slant, (d) spacing difficulty, (e) messiness, (f) inability to stay on a horizontal line, (g) illegible letters, (h) too much or too little pencil pressure, and (i) mirror writing. Newland (1932) examined the cursive handwriting of 2,381 people. Approximately 50% of the illegibilities involved the letters *a, e, r,* and *t.* Most commonly, people (a) failed to close letters, (b) closed top loops in letters like *e,* (c) looped strokes that should be nonlooped (such as writing *i* like *e*), (d) used straight-up strokes rather than rounded strokes (such as writing *n* for *u*), and (e) exhibited problems with end strokes. In a study of illegibilities in cursive handwriting of sixth graders, Horton (1970) reported that 12% of all errors were incorrect formations of the letter *r.* Thus, the majority of handwriting errors involve the incorrect writing of a few letters. Common number malformations include writing 5 like 3 (**5**), 6 like 0 (**6**), 7 like 9 (**9**), and 9 like 4 (**4**).

Wiederholt, Hammill, and Brown (1983) suggest that teachers in the primary grades should devote at least 10 to 15 minutes each day to teaching handwriting. Teachers should demonstrate the correct way to form letters and should supervise students' handwriting efforts carefully. Also, the teacher should help the student develop a positive attitude toward handwriting by encouraging progress and stressing the importance of the skill. In the upper elementary grades and in secondary classrooms, greater emphasis is placed on identifying and remediating individual handwriting deficits revealed in the student's daily written work. Hofmeister (1981) lists six instructional errors to *avoid*: (a) unsupervised handwriting practice while skills are being formed, (b) lack of *immediate* feedback to correct errors, (c) lack of emphasis on student analysis of errors, (d) failure to provide close-range models of correct letter formation, (e) repeated drill of both correct and incorrect letter production, and (f) misplaced emphasis on activities of limited value. A scope and sequence chart of handwriting skills by grade level is presented in Appendix A.

Assessment of Handwriting Skills

In assessing the young student (8 or 9 years old and younger), the teacher should remember that occasional reversals, omissions, and poor spacing are normal. However, a writing problem exists if such errors continue over a long period of time and if the student does not improve his ability to perform simple handwriting tasks. Unlike other academic skill areas, there are few standardized devices for measuring handwriting, and informal procedures are widely used. It is difficult to set minimum standards since activities differ in emphasis placed on speed, legibility, and character of handwriting.

Published assessment devices. To assess a student's overall readiness for handwriting instruction, the writing section of the *Basic School Skills Inventory—Diagnostic* (Hammill & Leigh, 1983) may be used. The scale assesses a child's handwriting ability in various tasks: writing from left to right, grasping a pencil, writing his first name, maintaining proper writing position, writing letters upon request, copying words, copying from chalkboard to paper, staying on the line, and writing his last name. The instrument is norm-referenced for ages 4 years to 6 years, 11 months to identify children who are low in handwriting readiness as compared to other children their age. The scale also can be used as a criterion-referenced test to determine what skills need to be taught.

The *Zaner-Bloser Evaluation Scales* (1979) are based on a national sampling of students' handwriting and are frequently used for assessing manuscript and cursive handwriting. There are scales for grades 1 and 2 written in manuscript style and scales for grades 2 through 8 written in cursive style. Five specimens of handwriting—excellent, good, average, fair, and poor—are provided for each grade level. Each scale contains a sentence or paragraph which the teacher writes on the chalkboard. The students practice writing the model and then copy the sentences in their best handwriting onto a sheet of paper. The teacher compares each paper with the five specimen sentences for the child's grade level and judges the following five elements: letter formation, vertical strokes in manuscript and slant in cursive, spacing, alignment and proportion, and line quality. Each student's writing is rated according to the number of satisfactory elements. Through this method a student's handwriting can be compared to that of students in the same grade level; however, a thorough analysis of errors is needed prior to planning instructional programs.

For assessing cursive handwriting, the *Test of Written Language* (Hammill & Larsen, 1983) contains a norm-referenced test of handwriting for students in grades 3 through 8. The student's handwriting ability is estimated by rating (from 0–10) his sample of spontaneous writing according to various graded writing samples included in the manual. The most important consideration in this subtest is legibility of the writing.

Various legibility scales have traditionally been used to provide a subjective evaluation of general handwriting competence. However, the objectivity of the scales has been questioned, and they do not highlight specific errors and illegible forms in writing. Thus, handwriting scales may best be used to aid the teacher in rating a writing specimen for screening purposes. To obtain information for instructional purposes, various informal assessment techniques may be helpful.

Informal assessment. The teacher can obtain diagnostic information informally through a close visual examination of the student's handwriting. Writing samples may be used to determine problem areas in legibility. Mann, Suiter, and McClung (1979) suggest obtaining three samples: the student's usual, best, and fastest handwriting. The usual writing sample shows the student's work under normal, nonfatiguing conditions. For the best sample, the student is asked to take his time and write the sentence with his best effort. Then the student is timed for 3 minutes to see how many times he can write a given sentence. Sometimes a student can write legibly but only when specifically asked to do so. Also, some students write well but at an extremely slow rate. By comparing the three writing samples, the teacher can determine the student's ability with regard to speed and legibility.

While observing the student during handwriting activities, the teacher should note possible problem areas by answering the following questions:

1. Does the student grip the pencil correctly and in a comfortable and flexible manner?
2. Is the student's paper in the proper position on his writing surface?
3. Does the student sit correctly when writing, or does he hold his head too close or too far away from the paper?
4. Does the student consistently use the same hand for writing?
5. Does the student appear extremely frustrated, nervous, or emotional when writing?
6. Does the student have a negative attitude toward handwriting and appear bored and disruptive?

Additional instructional information can be obtained by analyzing the student's writing samples for error patterns in the following various aspects of handwriting:

1. *Letter formation:* Letter formation involves the strokes that make up each letter. To check letter formation for legibility, a piece of cardboard may be used with a hole cut in the center that is slightly larger than a single letter. By exposing one letter at a time, the hole helps the teacher to see which letters are illegible or poorly formed.

2. *Letter size, proportion, and alignment:* The size and proportion of letters are indicated by their height relationship to one another; *alignment* refers to the evenness of letters along the baseline, with letters of the same size being the same height. These legibility elements can be measured by using a ruler to draw lines that touch the base and tops of as many letters as possible.

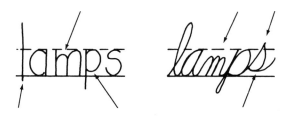

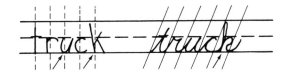

3. *Spacing:* There should be consistent spacing between letters within words, as well as between words and between sentences.

4. *Line quality:* There should be consistent thickness and steadiness in the lines used to form letters. The teacher should mark lines that waver or are too thick or too fine. Incorrect hand or body position or cramped fingers could result in inconsistent line quality.

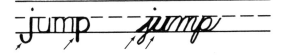

5. *Slant:* The slant of letters should be uniform. In general, manuscript letters are perpendicular to the baseline and have a straight up-and-down appearance. In cursive writing the paper is slanted, and strokes are pulled toward the body. Straight lines or lines with a uniform slant may be drawn through the letters to indicate which letters are off slant.

6. *Rate:* Speed of handwriting can be determined on a writing sample by asking the student to write as well and as rapidly as he can. The rate of handwriting—*letters per minute* (lpm)—is figured by dividing the total number of letters written by the number of writing minutes allowed. Handwriting proficiency rates include the following:

a. Zaner-Bloser scales:
   grade 1—25 lpm
   grade 2—30 lpm
   grade 3—38 lpm
   grade 4—45 lpm
   grade 5—60 lpm
   grade 6—67 lpm
   grade 7—74 lpm

b. Precision Teaching Project (Montana):
   think—write alphabet (emphasizing speed): 80–100 lpm
   see—write letters (emphasizing accuracy): 75 lpm correct (count of three for each letter—slant, form, ending)
   see—write random numerals random: 100–120 digits per minute
   see—write connected cursive letters: 125 lpm (count of three per letter)

c. Koenig and Kunzelmann (1980):
   see—write letters: 70 lpm
   see—write random numerals random: 70 digits per minute

Table 13.1 displays a diagnostic chart for manuscript and cursive writing that highlights errors, likely causes, and remediation procedures.

TABLE 13.1

Diagnostic chart for manuscript and cursive writing.

Factor	Problem	Possible Cause	Remediation
		Manuscript Writing	
Shape	Letters slanted	Paper slanted	Place paper straight and pull straight line strokes toward center of body.
	Varies from standard	Improper mental image of letter	Have pupil write problem letters on chalkboard.
Size	Too large	Poor understanding of writing lines	Reteach size concept by pointing out purpose of each line on writing paper.
		Exaggerated arm movement	Reduce arm movement, especially on circle and part-circle letters.
		Improper mental image of letter	Have pupil write problem letters on chalkboard.
	Too small	Poor understanding of writing lines	Reteach size concept by pointing out purpose of each line on writing paper.
		Overemphasis on finger movement	Stress arm movement; check hand-pencil and arm-desk positions to be sure arm movement is possible.
		Improper mental image of letter	Have pupil write problem letters on chalkboard.
	Not uniform	Adjusting writing hand after each letter	Stress arm movement; move paper with nonwriting hand so writing hand can remain in proper writing position.
		Overemphasis on finger movement	Stress arm movement; check arm-desk and pencil-hand positions.
Space	Crowded letters in words	Poor understanding of space concepts	Reteach uniform spacing between letters (finger or pencil width).
	Too much space between letters	Improper lowercase letter size and shape	Review concepts of size and shape; provide appropriate corrections under size and shape.
Alignment	Letters not sitting on baseline	Improper letter formation	Evaluate work for letter shape; stress bringing straight line strokes all the way down to baseline.
		Poor understanding of baseline concept	Review purpose of baseline on writing paper.
		Improper hand-pencil and paper-desk positions	Check positions to make sure pupil is able to reach baseline with ease.

(continued)

Factor	Problem	Possible Cause	Remediation
	Letters not of consistent height	Poor understanding of size concept	Review concept of letter size in relationship to lines provided on writing paper.
Line quality	Too heavy or too light	Improper writing pressure	Review hand-pencil position; place wadded paper tissue in palm of writing hand to relax writing grip; demonstrate desired line quality.

Cursive Writing

Factor	Problem	Possible Cause	Remediation
Shape	Letters too oval in size	Overemphasis of arm movement and poor image of letter size and shape	Check arm-desk position; review letter size and shape.
	Letters too narrow in shape	Finger writing	Check positions to allow for arm movement.
		Overemphasis of straight line stroke	Make sure straight line stroke does not come all the way down to baseline in letters like *l, b,* and *t.*
		Poor mental image of letter shape	Use transparent overlay for pupil's personal evaluation of shape.
			In all problems of letter shape review letters in terms of the basic strokes.
Size	Letters too large	Exaggerated arm movement	Check arm-desk position for over-movement of forearm.
		Poor mental image of letter size	Review base and top line concepts in relation to 1/4 space, 1/2 space, and 3/4 space; use transparent overlay for pupil's personal evaluation of letter size.
	Letters too small or letters not uniform	Finger movement	Check arm-desk and pencil-hand positions; stress arm movement.
		Poor mental image of letter size	Review concept of letter size (1/4 space, 1/2 space, and 3/4 space) in relation to base and top lines; use transparent overlay for pupil's personal evaluation of letter size.
Space	Letters in words crowded or spacing between letters uneven	Finger movement	Check arm-desk, pencil-hand positions; stress arm movement.

(continued)

Factor	Problem	Possible Cause	Remediation
		Poor understanding of joining strokes	Review how letters are joined; show ending stroke of one letter to be beginning stroke of following letter; practice writing letters in groups of five.
	Too much space provided between letters in words	Exaggerated arm movement	Check arm-desk position for over-movement of forearm.
		Poor understanding of joining strokes	Review joining strokes; practice writing groups of letters by rhythmic count.
	Uneven space between words	Poor understanding of between-word spacing	Review concept of spacing between words; show beginning stroke in second word starting under ending stroke of preceding word.
Alignment	Poor letter alignment along baseline	Incorrect writing position; finger movement; exaggerated arm movement	Check all writing positions; stress even, rhythmic writing movement.
		Poor understanding of baseline concept	Use repetitive exercise with emphasis on relationship of baseline to written word.
		Incorrect use of joining strokes	Review joining strokes.
	Uneven alignment of letters in words relative to size	Poor understanding of size concept	Show size relationships between lower- and uppercase, and $1/4$ space, $1/2$ space, and $3/4$ space lowercase letters; use repetitive exercise with emphasis on uniform height of smaller letters.
Speed and Ease	Writing becomes illegible under stress and speed (grades 4, 5, and 6)	Degree of handwriting skill is insufficient to meet speed requirements	Improve writing positions; develop more arm movement and less finger movement.
	Writing becomes illegible when writing activity is too long	Handwriting positions have not been perfected to allow handwriting ease	Improve all writing positions, especially hand-pencil position; stress arm movement.
Slant	Back slant	Left-handedness	Correct hand-pencil and paper-desk positions.
	Vertical	Poor positioning	Correct hand-pencil and paper-desk positions.

(continued)

Factor	Problem	Possible Cause	Remediation
	Too far right	Overemphasis of finger movement	Make sure pupil pulls slant strokes toward center of body if right-handed and to left elbow if left-handed.
			Use slant line instruction sheets as aid to teaching slant.
			Use transparent overlay for pupil's personal evaluation.
			Review all lowercase letters that derive their shape from the slant line.
			Write lowercase alphabet on chalkboard; retrace all slant strokes in colored chalk.

Probes may be used to assess a specific handwriting skill and determine instructional targets. On the Precision Teaching Project (Montana) handwriting probe sheets, the student is timed for one minute. Tasks include repeatedly writing the same letter, writing manuscript capitals, writing cursive letters, writing two cursive letters joined together, and writing words in small cursive letters. Daily performance on the probe sheets is charted to monitor progress. The *Sequential Precision Assessment Resource Kit (SPARK II)* (Trifiletti, Rainey, & Trifiletti, 1979) also contains sequenced handwriting probe sheets. Probes are included on tracing manuscript letters, copying manuscript letters, tracing capital cursive letters, tracing small cursive letters, copying capital cursive letters, and copying small cursive letters. Koenig and Kunzelmann (1980) provide probe sheets for writing uppercase letters, writing lowercase letters, writing one's first name, writing the first letter of one's first name, and writing words for one minute. A probe sheet on writing uppercase manuscript letters is presented in Figure 13.1

In assessing handwriting difficulties, the teacher also can encourage the student to use self-evaluation. Diagnostic charts and evaluation scales may be made available to the student so that he can identify his own handwriting inaccuracies. When the student monitors his own writing, he can quickly and easily change his writing performance. Also, positive attitudes may be increased as the student assumes some responsibility for learning and improving his handwriting. A commercial material that may be useful in self-evaluation is *Peek-Thru* (Zaner-Bloser). This is a plastic overlay which the student places on top of his writing and "peeks thru" to check correct letter formation and alignment. A manuscript set is provided for grades 1 through 3, and a cursive set is available for transition, grade 3, and grade 4. For grades 5 and above there are two similar plastic overlay rulers, one in manuscript and one in cursive.

Teaching Handwriting Skills

After assessment, the teacher can establish instructional objectives based upon errors pinpointed and the student's overall development of handwriting skills. Skills should be taught through activities that are meaningful and motivating to the student. Repetitious drills and mass practice without supervision should be avoided, and the student should receive im-

Name: _____ Date: _____

Time: _____

Rate (letters per minute): _____ Correct

_____ Error

Comments: _____

_____

FIGURE 13.1
Probe sheet for writing uppercase manuscript letters.

mediate feedback. Models should be provided of both good and poor work so that the student eventually can make comparisons to determine necessary changes. The development of handwriting skills and teaching strategies is presented next in the areas of readiness skills, manuscript writing, transitional writing, and cursive writing.

Readiness skills. Writing requires muscular control, eye-hand coordination, and visual discrimination. The teacher needs to help develop skills in these areas before the student is ready to begin handwriting. Muscular coordination may be developed in the young child through manipulative experiences—for example, cutting with scissors, finger painting, tracing, and coloring. Activities in eye-hand coordination include drawing circles and copying geometric forms. Also, developing visual discrimination of sizes, shapes, and details aids the child's visual awareness of letters and how they are formed. Chalkboard activities provide practice and give the student the opportunity to use muscle movement of the shoulders, arms, hands, and fingers. Prior to beginning handwriting instruction, the child should be able to do the following:

1. Perform hand movements such as up–down, left–right, and forward–back.
2. Trace geometric shapes and dotted lines.
3. Connect dots on paper.
4. Draw a horizontal line from left to right.
5. Draw a vertical line from top to bottom and bottom to top.
6. Draw a backward circle, a curved line, and a forward circle.
7. Draw slanted lines vertically.
8. Copy simple designs and shapes.
9. Name letters and discern likenesses and differences in letter forms.

Determining the student's hand preference is also very important. The teacher should determine which hand the student uses most often in natural situations, such as eating or throwing a ball. Also, the teacher can ask the child to use one hand to take a pencil out of a box, cover one eye, or make a mark on the chalkboard. The child who indicates a strong preference for using his left hand should be allowed to use his left hand when writing. If the student uses both hands well, he should be encouraged to make a choice and consistently use one hand for writing, or the teacher may encourage him to become a right-handed writer.

The proper position of paper and pencil also must be taught before extensive handwriting instruction. During writing, the child should be in a comfortable chair, with feet flat on the floor. The desk or table should be at a height that allows the child to place his forearms on the writing surface without discomfort. The nonwriting hand holds the writing paper at the top. To prevent elbow bumping, left-handers should be seated in a left-hand desk chair or along the outside at a work table. The pencil should be held lightly in the triangle formed by the thumb and the first two fingers, and the hand should rest lightly on its outer edge. The pencil is held approximately an inch above its point by right-handers, and the pencil top points in the direction of the right shoulder. For left-handers, the pencil is held about $1\frac{1}{4}$ inches from its writing point, and the pencil end points toward the left shoulder. Commercial pencil grips (triangular shaped) or masking tape may be placed on the pencil to make it easier to hold. For manuscript writing the paper should be placed straight on the desk directly in front of the eyes. For some left-handers it may be helpful to slant the paper so that the lower right corner of the paper points to the left of the center of the body. For cursive writing the paper is tilted. The right-handed child places the paper so that the lower left corner points toward the center of the body and the writing stroke is pulled toward the center of the body. For the left-handed child the paper is slanted north-northeast; the lower right corner points to the center of the body and the writing stroke is pulled toward the left elbow. Some left-handers begin "hook-

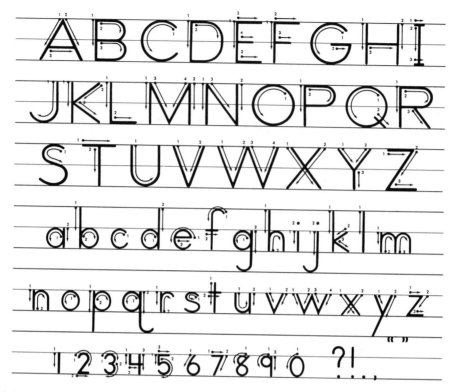

FIGURE 13.2

Formation of uppercase and lowercase manuscript letters and numbers.

Source: Used with permission from *Creative Growth with Handwriting* (p. 96) by W.B. Barbe, V.H. Lucas, C.S. Hackney, and C. McAllister, Columbus, OH: Zaner-Bloser, Inc. Copyright 1975, 1979.

ing" their hand and wrist while writing, in order to see what they have written and to avoid smudging their writing. This should be avoided and can be controlled by helping the student find the right slant for his paper.

Manuscript writing. Manuscript writing usually is taught in kindergarten and first grade and is based entirely upon the basic shapes of circles and straight lines. The strokes for both uppercase and lowercase manuscript letters are presented in Figure 13.2 with arrows and numbers to indicate the direction and sequence of strokes.

The teacher often demonstrates letter forms on the chalkboard. He should be careful to stand to one side and not to block the student's vision so that the student can observe the handwriting *process* as well as the finished product. When the child is writing on the chalkboard, he should write at eye level and stand at arm's length directly in front of the writing.

A *multisensory approach* often is used in teaching letter forms. The child sees, hears, and traces the letter model. The following steps may be used:

1. The teacher shows the student the letter (or word) to be written.

2. The teacher says aloud the letter name and stroke directions; for example, "First we go up; then we go down."
3. The student traces the model with his finger and may report his movements aloud as he traces.
4. The student traces the letter model with his pencil.
5. The student copies the letter on paper while looking at the model.

A *fading model* also may be used in teaching handwriting. The letter model is presented at first in heavy, dark lines, and the student traces over the model with his finger and the nonwriting end of his pencil. Gradually, portions of the model are faded out, and the student traces the model with his pencil. Eventually the model is not given for tracing purposes, and the student writes the letter independent of the model. For example:

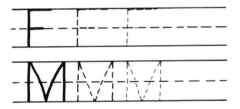

As soon as possible, activities should be provided in which words are used and the writing says something. Copying meaningless letters may result in boredom and negative attitudes toward writing. Also, in copying exercises, the letter or word model should be presented at first on the kind of paper the student uses.

Letters that consist entirely of vertical and horizontal strokes (such as *E, F, H, I, L, T, i, l, t*) are learned more easily than letters in which straight and curved lines are combined (such as *b, f, h, p*). Letters with easier strokes may

be taught first. The teacher should give more attention to the formation of difficult letter forms.

In a study of first graders' errors in the formation of manuscript letters, Lewis and Lewis (1965) made the following observations:

1. Incorrect size was the most common type of error, and it was more frequent with descender letters (*p, q, y, g, j*).
2. The most frequently reversed letters were *N, d, q,* and *y*.
3. Incorrect relationship of parts occurred most frequently in the letters *k, R, M,* and *m*.
4. Partial omission occurred most frequently in the letters *m, U,* and *I*.
5. Additions often occurred in the letters *q, C, k, m,* and *y*.
6. The most frequently misshaped letter forms were *j, G,* and *J*.

Numerous letters are often reversed, such as *b, d, p, q, s, y,* and *N*. In teaching these letters, the teacher should emphasize the correct beginning point and direction of letters. In addition to difficulties in forming letters, some children have problems in spacing manuscript letters and poor alignment. In general, the widest space is left between straight-line letters, and the least amount of space is between circle letters. Spacing between words equals approximately the size of one finger or a lowercase *o*, and twice as much space is left between sentences. Poor alignment should be pointed out to the student; however, if the student has extreme difficulty staying on the lines of writing paper, the teacher may choose to provide Right-Line Paper (Modern Education Corporation) until the student develops this skill. Right-Line Paper (both wide- and narrow-rule) has a raised line superimposed on the printed line so that the writer can *feel* as well as see the base line.

Transitional writing. The transition from manuscript to cursive writing usually occurs during the second or third grade, after the student has demonstrated a mastery of manuscript letter forms. However, some controversy exists concerning whether to begin with manuscript or cursive writing. Those who favor manuscript writing (Anderson, 1966; Barbe, Milone, & Wasylyk, 1983; Herrick, 1960) claim that it requires less complex movements and reduces reading problems because most printed pages are in manuscript. In addition, manuscript writing tends to be more legible and has received acceptance in business and commercial contexts. Advocates of cursive writing (Strauss & Lehtinen, 1947) believe that cursive writing results in fewer reversals because of its rhythmic flow. Also, transference problems are avoided if writing begins with cursive. However, some educators (Hildreth, 1963; Templin, 1960; Western, 1977) question the need for teaching cursive writing at all and feel that manuscript writing meets the adult needs of speed and legibility. After reviewing research data concerning manuscript versus cursive writing, Graham and Miller (1980) indicate that most evidence supports manuscript instruction; however, the advantages of manuscript writing have yet to be conclusively demonstrated. Since good arguments are presented on all sides for manuscript or cursive writing, the teacher should assess each individual situation. It may be best to teach each child the form of writing used by his peers in the classroom. Also, many young children want to learn cursive writing because older peers and adults use it. Regardless of the type of writing instruction, the child should be allowed to choose his mode of writing for tests and expressive writing activities.

Mann, Suiter, and McClung (1979) suggest the following method for transitional writing:

1. The word is printed in manuscript.
2. The letters are connected with a dotted line in colored pencil.
3. The student traces over the manuscript letter and the connecting dotted line to form the cursive writing.

The teacher may begin teaching transitional writing with the easier letters and add more difficult letters one at a time. Certain letters must be taught specifically, such as *b, e, f, k, r, s,* and *z.* Also, when the letter *n* is in the middle or end of a word, enough space must be allowed in front of it for the additional hump needed in the cursive formation of the letter.

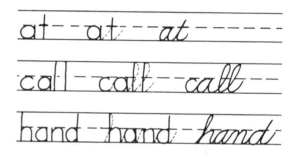

Hagin (1983) recommends a simplified handwriting method based on the vertical downstroke rather than the diagonal slant necessary to cursive writing. Manuscript letters are used as a bridge to a simplified writing style with connections between letters made by the natural movement to the next vertical downstroke. Thus, the simplicity of manuscript writing is combined with the speed of cursive writing. In this approach letter forms are taught through four simple motifs (waves, pearls, wheels, arrows) that serve as foundations for lowercase letters. After practice at the chalkboard, lessons at the desk include (a) tracing letters on an acetate sheet placed over the printed model, (b) trying to write the letter on the acetate without a model, (c) matching the written letter with the model to determine if more practice is needed, and (d) providing a permanent record of the letters worked on in that lesson that can later be compared in self-evaluation. This approach may be helpful to students who have difficulty learning conventional cursive writing patterns.

Cursive writing. Instruction in cursive writing usually begins in the second or third grade, depending upon the skill development of the individual student. In cursive writing the strokes are connected, and fine motor coordination is required to perform many of the precise movements in letter formation. Figure 13.3 presents the letter formation of uppercase and lowercase cursive letters, with arrows and

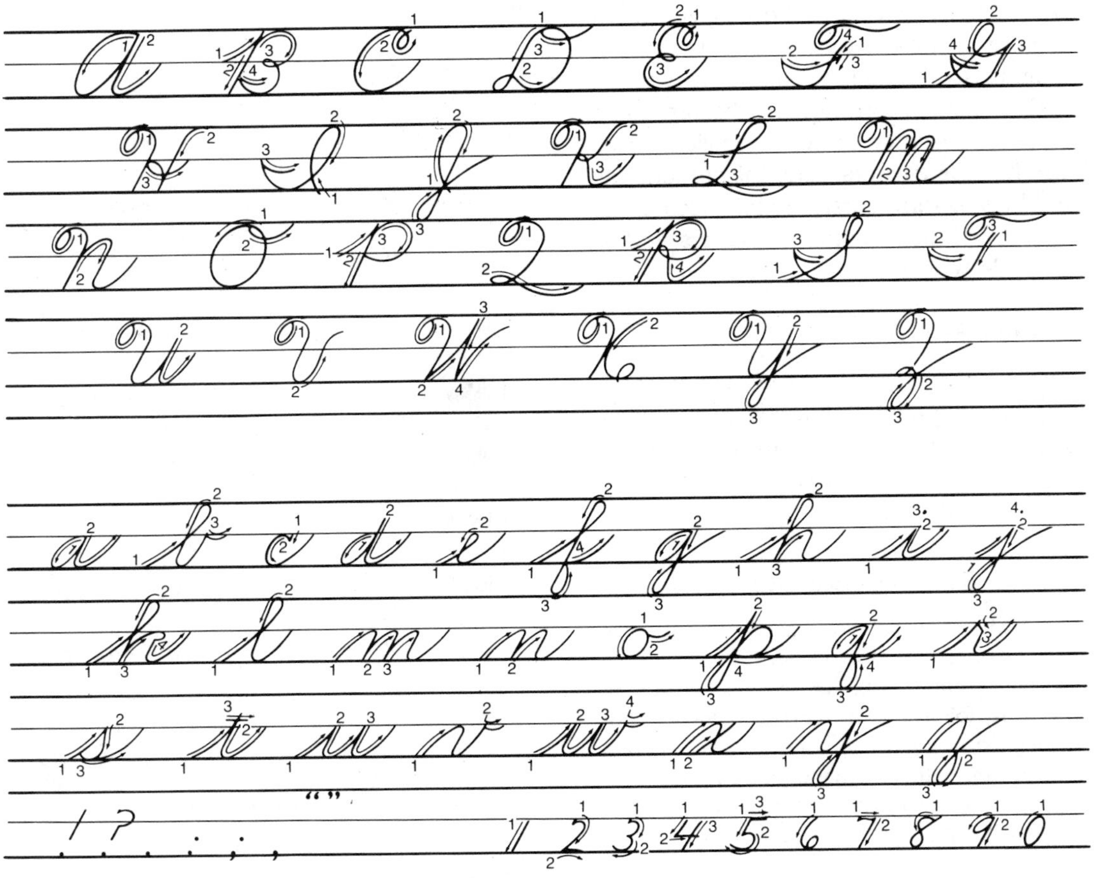

FIGURE 13.3

Formation of uppercase and lowercase cursive letters and numbers.

Source: Used with permission from *Creative Growth with Handwriting* (p. 96) by W.B. Barbe, V.H. Lucas, C.S. Hackney, and C. McAllister, Columbus, OH: Zaner-Bloser, Inc. Copyright 1975, 1979.

numbers indicating the direction and sequence of the strokes.

Many techniques used to teach manuscript writing, such as the multisensory approach and fading model, also may be used in cursive writing instruction. The proper slant in cursive writing is achieved by slanting the paper and pulling strokes to the body, as described earlier in the discussion of readiness skills. Newland (1932) notes that four specific letters—*a, e, r, t*—contribute to a large number of errors in cursive writing. The teacher should give special attention to the proper formation of these four letters and also should focus upon the types of errors that result in common illegibilities. Table 13.2 illustrates numerous common illegibilities in forming cursive letters. After the student has learned how to form cursive letters accurately, he should be taught to connect letters and to write simple words.

Handwriting Activities

Numerous activities and materials enhance the development of handwriting skills. Activities, games, and learning centers are presented in three areas: readiness skills, manuscript writing, and cursive writing.

Readiness Activities

1. Use body exercises to practice movements such as up and down, left and right, and forward and backward. For example, give the child the following instructions: "Raise your writing hand *up* in the air"; "Make a long straight line with your hand going from *top* to *bottom*"; "Make a *circle* with your hand in front of your body"; "Make a long line from *left* to *right*."
2. Have the child use scissors to cut out shapes or large letter forms. Coloring activities may also help the child develop muscle control and learn how to use a writing instrument and stay in lines. The child may be asked to color shapes or objects before cutting them out.

TABLE 13.2
Common illegibilities in handwriting.

a like u	*(cursive)*	m like n	*(cursive)*
a like o	*(cursive)*	n like u	*(cursive)*
a like ce	*(cursive)*	o like a	*(cursive)*
b like li	*(cursive)*	o like v	*(cursive)*
be like bl	*(cursive)*	p like js	*(cursive)*
b like k	*(cursive)*	r like n	*(cursive)*
c like e	*(cursive)*	r like v	*(cursive)*
c like a	*(cursive)*	r like i	*(cursive)*
d like cl	*(cursive)*	t like i	*(cursive)*
e like i	*(cursive)*	t like l	*(cursive)*
g like y	*(cursive)*	u like ee	*(cursive)*
g like q	*(cursive)*	u like ei	*(cursive)*
i like e	*(cursive)*	w like n	*(cursive)*
h like li	*(cursive)*	w like ue	*(cursive)*
h like k	*(cursive)*	w like eu	*(cursive)*
k like ls	*(cursive)*	x like v	*(cursive)*
m like w	*(cursive)*	y like ij	*(cursive)*

3. In seatwork activities, have the child practice drawing circles: balls, balloons, funny faces, coins, apples.
4. To help the child develop fine motor skills and strengthen hand and finger muscles, have him

participate in finger painting and clay modeling activities. Squeezing and molding clay is good exercise. Also, the child may be required to manipulate small objects such as nuts and bolts, cubes, buttons, and bottle caps.

5. Have the child connect dots in dot-to-dot activities to form geometric shapes or pictures. To help the child draw straight lines by himself, place dots in a straight line and gradually increase the distance between them. Also, circles and squares may be completed in dot-to-dot fashion. The figures eventually may include actual letters.

6. Use chalkboard activities for exercises in copying, dot-to-dot, and completing incomplete figures. The large, free movements made at the chalkboard help develop muscles of the shoulders, arms, hands, and fingers. Academic skills also may be practiced through the use of a chalkboard. A child's lack of handwriting development should not be allowed to impede his completion of academic tasks.

7. Have the child practice writing movements in a tray filled with a layer of sand, salt, or cornmeal. The child may use a stick or a pointed finger to practice forming shapes, letters, and numbers.

8. Provide tracing activities by making dark-line figures (shapes, letters, numbers, objects) on white paper and covering the paper with a sheet of onionskin on which the child can trace. Also, the child can trace on sheets of acetate or plastic with a felt-tip pen or a grease pencil. Clipboards may be used to hold tracing paper in its place, or the paper can be taped to the child's desk.

9. Make stencils and templates of shapes, numbers, and letters from plastic, styrofoam, or cardboard. Fasten the stencil to the child's paper with paper clips so that he can write or trace the forms. When the stencil or template is removed the child can view the figure he has made.

10. To help develop visual discrimination, provide the child with pictures that contain hidden uppercase and lowercase manuscript letters. Ask the child to locate the hidden letters. A variation of this activity is to have the child produce a picture from a letter—for example, draw an

umbrella from the letter *f.* Also, the child may be asked to think of things that different letters look like.

Manuscript Writing Activities

1. Provide the child with an individual copy of the alphabet and numbers 0–9 to use at his desk. Zaner-Bloser produces self-adhesive alphabet strips (both manuscript or cursive) that have arrows showing correct stroke directions and sequence. Encourage the child to refer to the model during writing exercises.

2. Have the child form manuscript letters and numbers by drawing between the double lines of outlined letters.

3. Use paper with squares to help the child maintain correct letter size and proportion.

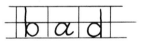

4. Have the child form manuscript letters and numbers by completing slash-to-slash and dot-to-dot activities.

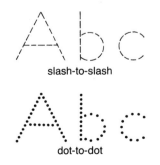

slash-to-slash

dot-to-dot

5. On pieces of oaktag, print uppercase letters and their corresponding lowercase letters and cut the pair to form puzzle pieces. Have the child match the uppercase and lowercase manuscript pairs. This activity is self-correcting, since the puzzle pieces will fit together only if the letters correspond to each other. A variation of this activity would be to match manuscript letters to corresponding cursive letters.

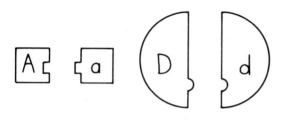

6. Use arrows to provide the child with direction clues in forming specific letters. Also, *rol 'n write*

(Educational Performance Associates) is a commercial material that may be used to illustrate letter formation. The set consists of rectangular plastic boards containing grooves that mark the letters of the alphabet. When a ball is placed at the starting point, it automatically traces the strokes used in forming the letter.

7. Use colored dots to indicate the starting and stopping positions for each letter stroke. Also, letters may be color-coded to indicate their position with respect to the line on which the student is writing. Letters that stay on the line are written in green (grass letters), letters that extend above the line are written in blue (sky let-

ters), and letters that extend below the line are written in brown (root letters). Eventually the color cueing is faded out.

8. For the child who reverses letters such as *b* and *d*, have him form an association to help him remember the direction of the letters. For example, the student can learn to associate lowercase *b* with uppercase *B* or identify the stem of *b* with the left hand. Another method is to have the child raise his left arm in front of him and grasp his left elbow with his right hand. When he looks down he will see the letter *b*. For all reversal problems, encourage the child to refer to an alphabet taped to his desk before writing the letter.

9. Have the child announce his strokes as he writes certain letters. For example:

   m—"short line down; back up, around, and down; back up, around, and down"

   h—"tall line down, back up halfway, around, and down"

   i—"short line down, dot"

10. On balsa wood, print manuscript letters and numbers and use a razor-sharp knife to groove out the wood deep enough for a pencil to follow. Have the child practice forming letters by tracing the letters and numbers with a pencil in the grooves.

11. For the student who has difficulty with letter size and staying on the baseline, make a cardboard frame with a rectangular piece cut out. The child writes within the window area and thus has a barrier that stops his downward movement. Frames may be made for words with one-line, two-line, and three-line letters.

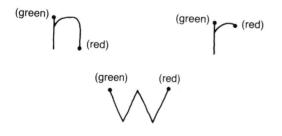

Masking tape also may be used on paper to represent baselines and margins.

12. For the student who has difficulty with spacing between letters within a single word and between words themselves, make an underlay sheet. Trace over the lines on a piece of notebook paper with a felt-tip pen; then draw vertical lines on the paper one letter distance apart. This makes squares the appropriate size for letters. The student places his notebook paper on top of this underlay sheet. He can see the felt-tip pen lines and use them as cues for proper spacing. One letter is written in each square, and one square is skipped between words. An additional method for the student who has difficulty remembering to space between words involves giving him a two-leaded pencil that has red on one end and blue on the other end. Have the student alternate colors each time he writes a new word (first a blue word, then red, then blue, etc.). Changing the color serves as a cue to stop and space properly. Also, if the student runs words together, have him place the index finger of his nonwriting hand at the end of each word to allow space for the next word.

13. Use the Practice Pad as a handwriting center to offer motivation and handwriting exercise. The student can practice any of the handwriting skills provided by the model.

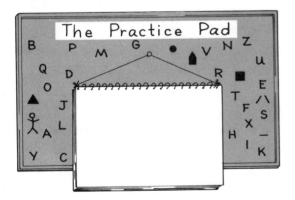

Cursive Writing Activities

1. To help the student see the similarity of manuscript and cursive letters, make a chart that has manuscript and corresponding cursive letters written next to each other.

2. Make dot-to-dot cursive letters and have the student form the letter by connecting the dots. The dots gradually can be faded out so that the student is required to complete the letter.

3. Have the student trace a cursive letter several times. Gradually reduce the cues to only the first stroke and have him finish forming the letter.

4. Arrows and color-coded dots may be used to show direction of the stroke and beginning and ending points.

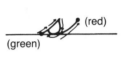

(green)   (red)

5. Encourage the student to practice forming cursive letters until his letters look like the model and show his best effort; then he may stop and proceed to another writing activity. With this method, the student practices only those letters that present difficulty.

6. Have the student practice letters with similar movement patterns at the same time. Also, the student can say the strokes of the letters as he writes.

7. After the student has learned the correct letter formation of cursive writing, his practice should involve writing that has meaning. For example, on the chalkboard write an informative letter to parents and have the student copy it while giving special attention to good handwriting.

8. Have the student copy a series of 10 stories and draw a picture to accompany each story. When he has completed all the stories and pictures in the series, put them together in a booklet to be displayed or taken home.

Commercial Programs and Materials

Many commercial programs and materials are available to develop or improve handwriting skills. The following selected programs and materials may be helpful to students having difficulty with handwriting.

Alphabet 68

Publisher: Numark Educational Systems

Description:

This 68-page booklet presents simplified letters in a stroke-by-stroke sequence, and then traditional letter forms are introduced. This approach is designed for students in grades 3 through 12. It may be used with young students as an introduction to cursive writing or with older students as a refresher course or remedial program.

Better Handwriting for You
(Noble, 1966)

Publisher: Noble and Noble

Description:

This program is a series of eight workbooks and teacher editions. Books 1 and 2 deal with manuscript writing; Books 3 through 8 present cursive writing. Between Books 2 and 3 there is a transitional book that begins with manuscript writing and then introduces cursive writing. Numbers and arrows help teach the sequence and direction of strokes used to write various letters. The student is provided with models of uppercase and lowercase letters and numbers and is required to copy them in the workbooks. The last two books provide devices that allow the student to evaluate the quality of his own handwriting. Throughout the program the teacher is provided with instructions on managing left-handed students and determining correct positions for paper and pencil.

D'Nealian Handwriting Program
(Thurber & Jordan, 1981)

Publisher: Scott, Foresman

Description:

This program is designed to simplify handwriting for the readiness student through eighth grade. The forms of most lowercase manuscript letters are the basic forms of the corresponding cursive letters. Each manuscript letter is made with a continuous stroke, except the dotted letters *i* and *j* and the crossed letters *f, t,* and *x.* The transition to cursive writing is simplified, since the addition of simple joining strokes is all that is needed for every letter except five (*f, r, s, v, z*). The program includes student workbooks and teacher's editions for each grade level, and alphabet cards and self-sticking alphabet tapes are available.

Handwriting with Write and See
(Skinner & Krakower, 1968)

Publisher: Lyons and Carnahan

Description:

This series includes programmed books for grades 1 through 6 and two books for the transition from manuscript to cursive writing, which can be used either at the second- or third-grade level. A step-by-step instructional sequence is followed. The unique feature of this program is the special paper and pen. The paper in the workbooks is specially treated so that when the student forms a letter correctly the mark appears in one color, but when an incorrect mark is made a different color appears. Thus, the student receives immediate feedback on each response. Writing activities and exercises are suggested, such as filling out bank deposit slips or library cards.

Imaginary Line Handwriting Series

Publisher: Steck-Vaughn

Description:

This program is designed to help students in kindergarten through eighth grade develop a legible, individualized style of handwriting. "Imaginary" lines—light blue guide lines—help develop a kinesthetic understanding for the formation of letters by aiding such factors as where to begin, where to stop, height, and width. The program contains a series of nine workbooks, and lessons take 10 to 15 minutes per day. Imaginary-line practice paper and alphabet-card writing guides are also available.

*Improve Your Handwriting
for Job Success*

Publisher: Macmillan (Peterson Handwriting System)

Description:

This 64-page booklet is designed for use with secondary students. The proper position in writing and the correct grip of the pencil or pen are stressed. In addition, the color red indicates new writing strokes as well as the sequence of strokes used in producing each letter form. Activities in applying writing skills are provided, such as filling out employment forms and a social security application.

Learning-to-Write Kit

Publisher: Educational Teaching Aids

Description:

This kit provides writing exercises that progress in difficulty from finger tracing alphabet letters to forming alphabet letters and numerals with a pencil. Also included are a teacher's guide, a kinesthetic tracing alphabet, tactile sandpaper letters, 12 directional letter guide cards, 24 pencil control tracing charts, six acetate overlays, letter tracing stencils, spirit masters of manuscript letters and numerals, 25 pencil grips, and six writing exercise books.

The Talking Pen

Producer: Wayne Engineering

Description:

The Talking Pen is an electronic pen with a small beam of infrared light in its tip. This infrared sensor picks up reflected light and triggers a buzzer. The battery-operated pen will respond to any pattern of light and dark. When the tip of the pen is on a dark area, the pen is silent. If the pen is moved to a light area, it "squawks." This sound can only be silenced by placing the tip of the pen back on a dark area. Thus, by providing a dark pattern on a light background, the pen will "talk" only when the pattern is traced incorrectly. Because the pen provides immediate auditory feedback, it is self-correcting and can be used without direct supervision. To develop handwriting skills, complete uppercase and lowercase alphabet and number patterns (manuscript or cursive) are available. The teacher can also use workbook patterns or make various patterns on any surface with any marker. In addition, the pen can be used with optional standard headphones so that only the student knows when he has made a mistake.

Trace-a-Bet

Publisher: Zaner-Bloser

Description:

This material includes a series of four plastic laminated manuscript or cursive cards. The 11″ × 12″ cards are reusable, and the student uses a grease pencil to trace model letter forms. After tracing the letters, the student can practice free-hand writing in the space under the model. The cards are suitable for every grade level and may be used for individualized handwriting practice.

A Writing Manual for Teaching the Left-Handed
(Plunkett, 1954)

Publisher: Educators Publishing Service

Description:

This cursive writing program is designed for the left-handed student. A teacher's manual and a student exercise pad are included. The program provides sequential writing exercises that emphasize correct position, regularity of slant and alignment, and rhythmic spacing.

*Zaner-Bloser Handwriting: Basic Skills and
Application*
(Barbe, Lucas, Hackney, Braun, & Wasylyk, 1984)

Publisher: Zaner-Bloser

Description:

This program contains a series of workbooks for kindergarten through eighth grade. Manuscript is introduced in kindergarten, developed through grade 2, and maintained through all the grades. Primary cursive is introduced in grade 2 or 3 and developed in grades 3 and 4, and adult cursive is focused on in grades 5 through 8. Letters are introduced systematically: K through 4, by similarity of stroke; grade 5, by size and proportion; grades 6 and up, by rhythmic motion. The elements of legibility are emphasized, and there is immediate application of skills in a practical context. In addition to a teacher's edition for each grade level, there is a supportive materials pack containing materials such as an alphabet wall chart, an evaluation scale, and a peek-through overlay.

WRITTEN EXPRESSION

Written expression, one of the highest forms of communication, reflects a person's level of comprehension, concept development, and abstraction. It differs from handwriting in that handwriting is primarily a visual-motor task that does not require complex cognitive abilities. Whereas handwriting includes such tasks as copying, tracing, and writing from dictation, written expression demonstrates how an individual organizes his ideas to convey a message.

The skill of written expression usually is not acquired until an individual has had extensive experience with reading, spelling, and verbal expression. Problems in written expression may not be diagnosed until the upper elementary school years. In these years the student is required to use the various language components in written composition, and emphasis is placed upon refining writing skills. Written expression is the most complex of the language arts skills and is based on listening, talking, handwriting, reading, and spelling. Thus, it generally is not stressed in instructional programs for mildly handicapped learners. Teachers tend instead to focus on the skills prerequisite to written expression. However, as the student acquires those prerequisite skills, instruction in written expression is warranted.

Assessment of Written Expression

Assessment of written expression yields information about a student's skill level and aids in instructional planning. The teacher can assess various components of written expression to determine deficiencies. A scope and sequence chart for written expression is provided in Appendix A according to the areas of capitalization and punctuation, written composition, and creative expression. It provides a skill hierarchy by grade level for assessing skills that need to be taught. Assessment techniques are presented in two broad categories: published tests (achievement and diagnostic) and informal techniques specifically related to instructional planning.

Published assessment devices. Many standardized tests are designed to provide only a rough estimate of the student's ability in written expression. In standardized achievement tests, skills usually are presented in isolation, and no attempt is made to analyze a composition actually written by the student. Some commonly used standardized achievement tests that include written expression sections are the following:

1. *California Achievement Tests* (1985): Assess mechanics (punctuation and capitalization), word usage, and understanding of sentence structure and paragraph organization for grade levels 1–12.
2. *Iowa Tests of Basic Skills* (Hieronymus, Hoover, & Lindquist, 1986): Assess word usage and mechanics for grade levels 1–9.
3. *Stanford Achievement Test* (Gardner, Rudman, Karlsen, & Merwin, 1982): Assesses mechanics and grammatical structure for grade levels 1–9.
4. *Tests of Achievement and Proficiency* (Scannell, 1986): Assess word usage, capitalization, punctuation, and skill in organiz-

ing and expressing ideas for grade levels 9–12.

Diagnostic tests of written expression provide additional basic information useful in planning instruction. The *Picture Story Language Test* (Myklebust, 1965) measures written language in children aged 7 through 17. The student is asked to write a story based upon a presented picture. The composition is then evaluated along three dimensions: (a) productivity, (b) syntax, and (c) meaning. *Productivity* is the total number of words, sentences, and words per sentence; *syntax* (correctness) refers to word usage, word endings, and punctuation. Meaning of content is judged along a continuum of abstract–concrete. Scores in these three areas may be converted into age equivalents, percentiles, and stanines. Although the reliability and validity of the test have been questioned, it may be useful as an informal observational technique (Wallace & Larsen, 1978).

The writing test of the *Sequential Tests of Educational Progress* (1972) consists of four levels (grade 4 through junior college) and contains objective items in the following categories: (a) *organization*—ordering of ideas, events, facts; (b) *conventions*—syntax, word choice, punctuation, spelling; (c) *critical thinking*—detection of unstated assumptions, cause-and-effect relationships, anticipation of readers' needs; (d) *effectiveness*—adequacy of emphasis and development, exactness of expression, economy, simplicity, variety; and (e) *appropriateness*—choice of tone and vocabulary appropriate to purpose and readership. On most items the student is required to identify errors in written passages and select revisions that correct the errors. The subject matter is presented in the form of essays, directions, reports, letters, or meeting minutes. Items were taken from actual writing specimens of students in school. Normative information is provided, and specific error patterns also can be analyzed.

The *Test of Adolescent Language—2* (Hammill, Brown, Larsen, & Wiederholt, 1987) includes two writing subtests and is designed for use with students in grades 6 through 12. The writing/vocabulary subtest requires the student to read a series of words and write a sentence using them correctly. The writing/grammar subtest requires the student to complete a sentence-combining task. The raw scores can be converted into scaled scores, and the writing subtests combine to form a writing composite score.

The *Test of Written Language—2* (Hammill & Larsen, 1988) can be used to identify students in grades 2 through 12 who have problems in written expression and to note specific deficits for corrective instruction. The student is required to look at pictures and write a complete story based on the pictures. Subtests with spontaneous formats include (a) *thematic maturity*—the number of content elements included in the student's story, (b) *contextual vocabulary*—the number of nonduplicated long words used in the story, (c) *syntactic maturity*—the number of words in the story that are used in grammatically and syntactically correct sentences, (d) *contextual spelling*—the number of words in the story that are spelled correctly, and (e) *contextual style*—the number of different capitalization and punctuation rules that are used by the student in composing an essay. Subtests with contrived formats include (a) *vocabulary*—the student writes sentences that show knowledge of stimulus words, (b) *style and spelling*—the student writes dictated sentences that are checked for spelling, capitalization, and punctuation, (c) *logical sentences*—the student corrects sentences that contain common illogicalities, and (d) *sentence combining*—the student combines ideas expressed in simple sentences to write compound or complex sentences. Two equivalent forms are available, and percentiles and standard scores are provided.

Informal assessment. The first step in informal assessment of written expression is to obtain representative writing samples from the student. These samples are analyzed in order to determine specific problems. Fluency, vocabulary, structure, and content are four major components that may be analyzed.

Cartwright (1969) defines *fluency* as quantity of verbal output. Fluency is related to age and includes sentence length and complexity (McCarthy, 1954; Meckel, 1963). The average sentence length in a composition is determined by counting the number of words and the number of sentences in the composition and dividing the number of words by the number of sentences. Cartwright (1968) found that the average sentence length of an 8-year-old child is eight words and that this length increases one word per year through age 13. He suggests that any deviation of more than two words indicates a problem.

The variety of sentence types a student uses also can reflect fluency problems. Cartwright (1969) identifies four types of sentences that can be used to measure competency: incomplete, simple, compound, and complex. The percentage of usage of the four sentence types in a writing sample can be computed to provide comparisons and a record of the student's progress. Cartwright suggests that the number of compound and complex sentences increases with age and the use of incomplete and simple sentences decreases with age.

Vocabulary refers to the variety of words used in the written task. The student's vocabulary should increase with age and experience (Cartwright, 1969). The Type Token Ratio (TTR) (Johnson, 1944) is a measure of vocabulary that is the ratio of different words used (types) to the total number of words used (tokens). For example, the sentence *The two boys went fishing in Noonan's Lake early yesterday morning* has a high TTR (1.0)—11 total words are used, and all 11 words are different. In contrast, the sentence *The little girl saw the little boy in the little house* has a fairly low TTR (.63)—11 total words are used, but only 7 of these words are different. A low TTR could indicate inadequate vocabulary for the written expression task. This technique also can be used for measuring long compositions. However, the number of different vocabulary words decreases as the total number of words in the composition increases (Carroll, 1938). When comparing several compositions produced by the same student or by different students, the same type of sample should be taken. For example, the first 50 words should be used from each composition instead of selecting the first 50 words from some compositions and the last 50 words from others.

Vocabulary variety can also be assessed by using the index of diversification (Carroll, 1938; Miller, 1951). This refers to the average number of words between each occurrence of the most frequently used word in the writing sample. Cartwright (1969) suggests dividing the total number of words in the sample by the number of *the*s or by the number of times the word used most often appears. The higher the value of the index, the more diverse the vocabulary.

Finally, vocabulary can be assessed by measuring the number of unusual words. For this assessment, a sample of the student's written expression should be compared with a list of words frequently used by other children—for example, the Dolch (1955, 1960) word list. The number of words the student uses that do not appear on the list indicates the extent of his vocabulary.

Structure, Cartwright's third component of written expression, includes the mechanical aspects of writing, such as punctuation, capitalization, and rules of grammar. The Grammatical-Correctness Ratio (GCR) (Stuckless & Marks, 1966) may be used to assess structure. The GCR quickly analyzes the total number of grammatical errors produced by the student. To obtain the GCR, a sample of the student's written expression (for example, 50 words from a composition) is scored by counting the number of grammatical errors. The error count is then subtracted from 50, and this difference is divided by 50. To obtain a percentage score, this last number is multiplied by 100. Because the final result can be displayed as a percentage, GCRs can be calculated for any number of words and still yield a score that can be compared with the student's previous scores. A GCR score also can be calculated for one specific type of grammatical error or for errors in punctuation or capitalization.

Structure can also be assessed by tabulating types of errors in the writing sample. The frequency of specific errors can be recorded to pinpoint individual weaknesses. An error analysis chart (presented in Table 13.3) provides a profile of errors in writing structure.

In addition to spontaneous writing samples, teacher-made test items also may be used to analyze specific elements of writing structure. Written compositions may not include enough opportunities for various errors to occur. For example, the student may write only sentences that contain grammatic forms or punctuation he knows how to use. Thus, to assess punctuation, the teacher may devise a number of short sentences in which punctuation rules are used. The sentences may be dictated for the student to write correctly or may be presented unpunctuated for the student to correct. For example:

1. School starts at 8 30
2. Twenty two boys are in the class
3. Dr Goodman lives in Richmond Virginia
4. His birthday is January 31 1943
5. Our dog Duchess had nine puppies

Content, the fourth component of written expression, can be divided into accuracy, ideas, and organization (Cartwright, 1969). The nature of the written assignment determines how the different factors should be weighed. For example, accuracy carries more weight when the written exercise is a presentation of historical facts. Cartwright suggests rating each factor on a scale from 0 to 10. A 10 in ideas would indicate that the ideas were pertinent to the topic and represented a high degree of originality; 0 would indicate lack of originality or understanding of the task. Wallace and Larsen (1978) note that content is an abstract component of written expression, and the teacher should formulate minimal competencies or objectives according to each individual student's intelligence, experiences, and motivation to communicate.

By examining a student's writing sample, such as an autobiography, the teacher can determine which skills need to be introduced or remediated as well as which have been acquired. Poteet (1980) developed the *Checklist of Written Expression Skills,* containing these areas: penmanship, spelling, grammar (capitalization, punctuation, syntax), and ideation (type of writing, substance, productivity, comprehensibility, reality, and style). Likewise, Weiner (1980a) devised the *Diagnostic Evaluation of Writing Skills (DEWS),* consisting of these areas: graphic (visual features), orthographic (spelling), phonologic (sound components), syntactic (grammatical), semantic (meaning), and self-monitoring. Weiner (1980b) verified the efficacy of the *DEWS* in identifying students requiring special remedial instruction.

A profile of the assessment of written expression components is presented in Table 13.4. The profile may be used with an individual student or an entire class to record strengths and weaknesses and student progress. Although some interpretation is required,

TABLE 13.3
Writing structure error analysis chart.

Sample
Elicitation
Procedure: _____

Date: _____

Students' Names	Verbs		Pro-nouns		Words					Sen-tences		Capitals			Punctuation						Total
	Agreement	Tense	Personal	Possessive	Additions	Substitutions	Modifiers	Negatives	Plurals	Incomplete	Run-on	Beginning sentences	Proper nouns	Inappropriate use	Period	Comma	Question mark	Apostrophe	Colon	Other	

TABLE 13.4

Profile of written expression assessment.

Students' Names	Fluency		Vocabulary			Structure		Accuracy Rating	Content Ideas Rating	Organization Rating
	Average Sentence Length	Sentence Type Variety	Type Token Ratio	Index of Diversification	Number of Unusual Words	Grammatical Correctness Ratio	Types of Errors			

the use of a profile helps to standardize observations and thus yields a more reliable and valid informal assessment.

Teaching Written Expression

Hammill (1986) states three goals of individualized instruction in written composition:

> The first goal is to teach students at least the minimum competencies that they will need to succeed in the school curriculum. The second goal is to instruct them in those forms of writing in which ability will be required for success outside the school (letter writing, completion of forms, note-taking, etc.). The third goal is to teach them to express their creativity in writing poetry, fantasies, and stories. (p. 105)

The student must organize his thoughts logically and follow the proper mechanics of writing (including punctuation and capitalization) in order to communicate clearly and accurately. One of the most effective means of teaching writing skills to mildly handicapped learners is through spontaneous written expression (Cohen & Plaskon, 1980). Each student's writing samples may be used as a base from which to introduce instruction in various writing skills. In other words, the objective of the writing program may be for the student to express his ideas and thoughts with ease. The written work he produces then is used as the basis for skill development.

Written expression can involve either functional or creative writing. *Functional* writing refers to conveying information in a structured form, such as social and business letters, invitations, reports, or minutes of a meeting. *Creative* writing is the personal expression of thoughts and experiences in a unique manner, as in poetry, story writing, and personal narratives. The writing program for mildly handicapped learners should include a range of writing experiences in both functional and creative writing.

The first step in writing instruction is to promote a positive attitude to motivate the student to write. The student must feel comfortable expressing himself. The teacher can promote discussion by encouraging students to share their ideas. Writing should be integrated into the entire curriculum, and the teacher should help the student understand that the purpose of writing is to communicate. Writing instruction thus begins with establishing a positive environment and then proceeds to skill development.

The language experience approach is often adapted in teaching written expression. Writing activities may start with the student dictating a story to the teacher, who writes it down and reads it back to him. As the student becomes familiar with the components of writing, he gradually assumes more responsibility for writing his own thoughts and ideas and composes one or two related sentences on his own. Later the student writes entire paragraphs and stories and receives instruction on organizing ideas and using proper writing mechanics.

Language experience stories may be written by one student or composed by the entire class. *Experience* is an important factor: The teacher should provide experiences (discussions, field trips, films) that stimulate ideas to write about. At first, students may be most comfortable writing about personal material, such as family, trips, or holidays. Students also enjoy writing stories about pictures or intriguing titles; unfinished stories or "story starters" can provide writing topics. Wordless picture books in which the pictures are presented in sequence can provide stimuli for writing activities. Commercial materials also are sources of writing assignments—for example, *Creative Story Starters* (published by DLM Teaching Resources), *Slithery Snakes and Other Aids to Children's Writing* (Petty & Bowen, 1967), *Story Starters—Primary and Intermediate* (Moore & Woodruff, 1980), and *Writing Aids*

Through the Grades (Carlson, 1970). Also, *Wishes, Lies, and Dreams* (Koch, 1970) is a helpful resource in teaching children to write poetry. Since the student produces the story himself in the language experience approach, the material is meaningful to him, and he is motivated to study it. This may be especially important for adolescents, since the stories they compose are on their level of maturity. A student's involvement or interest in a given topic influences his ability to write about it.

While the student continues to be encouraged to express his ideas well in writing, instruction on the more mechanical aspects of writing begins. In teaching punctuation and capitalization skills, the teacher can call attention to places in the student's written work that require punctuation or capitalization. The teacher can show the proper use of the skill and point out how its use enhances meaning. Thus, writing mechanics are explained as needed, and the student is made aware of their importance.

The teacher should avoid excessive correction of the mechanical aspects of writing. Too much correction may discourage the student from trying to express his ideas. He may feel that *how* he writes is more important than *what* he writes and may begin to limit his vocabulary use, write only simple sentences, and avoid expressing complex and creative thoughts. Good writing models should be provided for the student, and reinforcement should be combined with constructive criticism. The teacher should always say something positive about the student's work prior to offering correction, and encouragement and praise should be given for whatever amount the student has written. In general, more attention should be given to developing the written expression of ideas than to correcting mechanical errors. Of course, students who learn to use the right punctuation, correct grammar, and good organization are likely to become better writers. Hansen (1978) states, "Instruction should provide a balance between appreciation and enthusiasm for a student's ideas and a dedication to improving the presentation and organization of those concepts" (p. 122).

In improving a student's writing, the teacher should give considerable attention to sentence and paragraph development (Otto & Smith, 1980). The student should be helped to recognize the different syntactical patterns in which ideas can be expressed. Having the student read interesting material at his independent reading level will expose him to good sentences in the writing of others and may help him develop a sense of English sentence constructions. Also, through reading orally what he has written or tape-recording his stories, the student is likely to notice his own faulty sentence constructions. Learning to write unified, coherent paragraphs may be facilitated by activities in which the student categorizes or classifies ideas or organizes ideas in a logical sequence. Suggesting the use of transitional words (e.g., *finally, in addition to*) may help the student put his compositions together.

A sentence-writing strategy designed by Schumaker and Sheldon (1985) can be used to teach the basic principles of sentence construction and expression. The student learns a set of steps and formulas that enables him to recognize and write different kinds of sentences. The acronym PENS helps the student remember the steps to sentence writing:

1. P—*Pick* a formula.
2. E—*Explore* words to fit the formula.
3. N—*Note* the words.
4. S—*Subject and verb* identification comes next.

As basic writing skills are acquired, the student should learn to proofread and edit his work. In proofreading, the student reads his written work to identify and correct errors. To edit his own work, the student may be guided to look for elements in his writing such as capitalization, sentence sense, punctuation, misspelled words, margins, and paragraph indention. At first it may be helpful for the student to proofread his work several times with a different purpose in mind each time. Individual conferences with the teacher in a supportive atmosphere may also result in constructive editing. As the student reads his work aloud, he may spot errors such as omitted words, improper punctuation, or poor organization.

To give the student specific questions designed to cue him to detect four kinds of common errors, the teacher may introduce COPS questions to be used as an error-monitoring strategy (Schumaker, Nolan, & Deshler, 1985). The student is instructed to ask the following questions and look for these errors:

1. C—Have I *capitalized* the first word and proper names?
2. O—How is the *overall* appearance? Have I made any handwriting, margin, messy, or spacing errors?
3. P—Have I used end *punctuation*, commas, and semicolons correctly?
4. S—Do the words look like they are *spelled* right, can I sound them out, or should I use a dictionary?

Periodically the teacher can review COPS and encourage each student to use it daily so that it will become a habit. The teacher may require all papers to be "COPSed" before being accepted.

Since the goal of writing is to communicate ideas, students should be encouraged to share their written work. Notebooks or books of stories the students want to share may be exchanged for reading material. Also, students can be given the opportunity (on a voluntary basis) to read their selections in front of other students. Through sharing stories, students

receive feedback and become more motivated to improve the quality of their work. Also, the students are provided with models to help them improve their writing.

At the junior and senior high school levels, greater written expression demands are placed on students. Not only are students required to take notes during class lectures and express themselves on written tests, but they also frequently must write themes and reports. Teaching theme writing through the use of the acronym TOWER provides a structured approach.

1. T—*Think*.
2. O—*Order* ideas.
3. W—*Write*.
4. E—*Edit*.
5. R—*Rewrite*.

Prior to writing, the student can be encouraged to fill in a form with the topic at the top and ideas organized according to subtopics or paragraphs. After writing a rough draft, the student can ask COPS questions to edit his work and monitor errors. Activities concerning the development of written expression skills related to test taking and notetaking at the secondary level are presented in Chapter 14.

Written Expression Activities

Writing skills improve through practice. Instructional activities should be chosen for each student according to his particular skill deficits. In this section numerous activities are presented for developing skills in fluency, vocabulary, structure, and content. Additional activities and strategies for developing written expression skills in adolescents are presented in Chapter 14.

Activities in Fluency Development

1. Give the student several words and ask him to arrange them to form a sentence. For example:

her quietly cat the food ate
friends yesterday Jane's left

Also, give the student several words and have him write a sentence that contains all the words.

2. Have the student complete partial sentences. Gradually decrease the number of words presented. For example:

Yesterday morning the dog barked at . . .
Yesterday morning the dog . . .
Yesterday morning . . .

3. Give the student a written paragraph that contains both incomplete and complete sentences. Ask him to underline the subject and verb in each statement and determine which sentences are incomplete.

4. Have the student practice connecting two simple sentences to make compound or complex sentences. Give a list of various words for the student to choose from when writing the compound or complex sentences (such as *but, because, or, and, after, before*).

5. Give the student various noun and verb phrases and have him expand each sentence by adding descriptive words. For example:

man ate	The man in the blue shirt ate his dinner slowly.
dog barked	The big, black dog barked at the man with the stick.

Also, the student can combine related sentences into one sentence. For example:

The policeman is young.	The young policeman stopped the car.
The policeman stopped the car.	
Yesterday the boys played a football game.	Yesterday the boys played a football game that lasted two hours.
The game lasted two hours.	

Activities in Vocabulary Development

1. Provide the student with a variety of experiences (structured field trips, reading stories and poems) and include follow-up discussions of what was seen and heard. In addition, viewing films, listening to guest speakers, making a picture dictionary, and reading books, magazines, and newspapers may increase a person's vocabulary. Whenever the student uses a new vocabulary word appropriately, he should be praised.

2. Discuss special interests with each student (for example, baseball, music, cooking) and make lists of words pertaining to the interests. New words and their definitions may be written on index cards and filed in a word box so that they can be referred to for use in written compositions.

3. Give the class a list of vocabulary words to learn. Write each word on a slip of paper, fold the paper slips, and place them in a decorated coffee can. The first student draws out a word and must begin a story by using his word in a sentence. Each student takes a turn drawing a word and then adds to the story by using his word. After all vocabulary words have been used, the teacher can develop an ending to the story.

4. Have the student discover new words by looking and listening for them outside the classroom—on signs, on television, in reading material. One day each week the students can share newly found words and definitions with their classmates.

5. Give the student a written paragraph in which various words or phrases are underlined. Have him substitute appropriate words or expressions in each underlined area.

6. Divide the class into two teams and play a game involving synonyms and antonyms. Present a word and ask each team member (alternating teams) to give a synonym. One point is awarded to each team for a correct response; five points are taken away from the first team no longer able to give a synonym. The same word or a new word may then be presented with the team members giving antonyms.

7. Present the student with a reading passage and ask him to locate words or phrases according to specific questions. For example: "Tell me the word in the second paragraph that describes Jim's car"; "Find the phrase in the last paragraph that tells you that Mary was mad at herself."

8. Develop a crossword puzzle that includes words

related to a single subject. Have the student complete the puzzle and then write a paragraph using all the puzzle words.

Activities in Structure Development

1. To help develop proper use of punctuation, cut large punctuation marks from black construction paper and pin them to students. After reviewing rules of punctuation usage, write an unpunctuated story on the chalkboard or present it on the overhead projector. As the story is read aloud, the student wearing the appropriate punctuation mark should call out its name when it is needed in the story.

2. To make the student aware of the use of capital letters, have him make a list of all words that are capitalized in a specific reading passage and give the reasons for their capitalization. Lists of words that begin with capital letters can be made according to various classifications, such as cities, people's names, states, and months.

3. Give the student a written paragraph that does not contain any capitalized words. Have him correct the words that should be capitalized and give reasons for capitalizing them. Also, a reading selection could be dictated for the student to add capitals where necessary while he writes it.

4. Provide the student with written sentences that contain no capitals or punctuation and ask him to write each sentence correctly. Also, the teacher can give the student a paragraph without punctuation and capitalization for him to rewrite correctly. Tell the student the type and number of punctuation marks and capitals that must be added. To make the activity self-correcting, provide an answer key.

5. Give the student a list of verbs or singular nouns and ask him to write the past-tense form of each verb or plural of each noun. For example:

do	*did*	child	*children*
ride	*rode*	boy	*boys*
eat	*ate*	deer	*deer*
sing	*sang*	hero	*heroes*
walk	*walked*	story	*stories*

In addition, the student may be asked to use each past-tense verb or plural noun in a sen-

tence. Sentences may be given with the verb omitted, and the student is required to choose the correct verb form from multiple-choice answers. For example:

I (*ride, rode, ridden*) the bus to school this morning.
Last Saturday we (*go, went, gone*) on a picnic.
When he (*fell, fall, fallen*), he hurt his leg.

6. To work on grammatical skills, give the student a paragraph with blanks he must complete. The blanks can require the use of different grammatical elements (for example, plurals, verb tenses, possessive pronouns, adverbs). A list of words for the student to choose from can be provided at the top of the worksheet.

7. To practice editing skills, have students exchange papers and "COPS" each other's work. After the teacher goes over the material, each student can make a corrected copy of his work. The teacher can also give the student a paragraph and ask him to correct it according to the COPS questions.

Activities in Content Development

1. Read the beginning of an exciting story to the class and ask each student to write an ending for the story. The students may share their work to see how others finished the story. Also, after watching a film or reading or listening to a story, the students may write a summary or abstract.

2. To provide ideas for writing stories, cut three windows in a large piece of poster board. Make three circles, each of which is divided into eight sections. Write eight *Who* words on the first circle, eight *When* words on the second circle, and eight *Where* words on the third circle. Attach the circles to the back of the poster board so that the writing shows through the windows (see Figure 13.4). To find a story starter, the student spins all three wheels. Also, to give the student story ideas, the poster board can contain two windows. Two circles can be made with one containing names of circus acts (or any subject) and the other containing phrases of things they might do (see Figure 13.5). The circles are at-

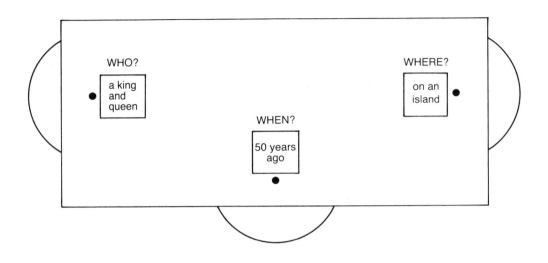

FIGURE 13.4
Who-when-where story board.

tached to the poster board, and the student spins the wheels to find the subject for his composition.

3. Encourage letter writing by establishing a post office in the classroom. Make mailboxes for each student out of cardboard or milk cartons. Have the students write letters, invitations, birthday cards, poems, and so forth and send them through the class postal system. Also, the teacher can use the mailboxes to return papers, give feedback, or send notes to go home.

4. On a large piece of poster board draw four circles, each divided into six sections. On each circle write characters, descriptors, settings, or actions. In the middle of each circle attach an arrow. Have the student spin all four arrows

and then write a paragraph that includes the four designated elements in the story (see Figure 13.6).

5. Give the student a written paragraph in which the sentences are out of sequence. Have him rewrite the paragraph by arranging the sentences in a meaningful order. Also, the student may be given a topic sentence and a closing sentence and be asked to write three detail sentences to form a paragraph.

6. To provide practice in organization skills, give the student a set of cards, each containing a different but related idea. Have the student first arrange the cards in a logical sequence to form an outline and then write a composition from his outline.

FIGURE 13.5
Circus story board.

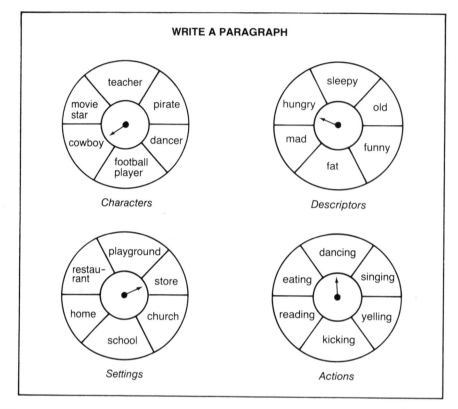

FIGURE 13.6
Write-a-paragraph story board.

7. Reproduce on ditto sheets several cartoons without captions or comic strips without the words spoken by the characters. Have the student write appropriate captions or fill in the conversations. Also, the student may be given frames from a comic strip which he must arrange in proper sequence before writing a comic strip story. These may be shared with the class, and the funniest or best ones may be included in a book.

8. Prepare a worksheet on poems. The student must arrange the lines in the proper order or fill in blanks with appropriate words. Then give the student an opportunity to select from various titles and compose a poem of his own. To help the student get started, suggest a first line.

9. Read a tall tale to the class and ask the students to identify parts of the story that are "tall" (exaggerated). Discuss the importance of accurate or truthful statements in compositions that are not tall tales. Have each student write his own tall tale, which may be shared with the class.

10. Have the student keep a daily diary in a spiral notebook. At the end of class each day, have him write a diary entry in which he expresses himself by summarizing his experiences, feelings, and activities of the day.

11. Make up letters like those that appear in a newspaper advice column such as *Dear Abby*. Have each student give advice by writing responses to the letters. The responses can be

shared with classmates or compared with actual newspaper replies.

12. Encourage the students to develop a monthly class newspaper to which each student can contribute some form of writing. The newspaper might contain current events articles, interviews, short stories, poems, jokes, cartoons, comic strips, advertisements, sports articles, and want ads. Groups of students can take turns serving as editors, printers or typists, proofreaders, and distributors.

Commercial Programs and Materials

Various published materials and programs are available for developing written expression skills. This section presents selected commercial written expression materials and programs that may be helpful to students with learning problems.

Grammar and Composition

Publisher: Merrill

Description:

This supplementary workbook series provides practice and reinforcement in the fundamentals of basic grammar and helps students develop writing skills. The lessons are student directed and focus on grammar, composition, usage, mechanics, and words. The three workbooks are designed for students in grades 7 through 9, as well as for remedial use in high school.

Learning Strategies Curriculum

Publisher: University of Kansas

Description:

The goal of the learning strategies curriculum is to enable students to learn skills and content and to perform tasks independently. The instructional strand of the curriculum that deals with expression and demonstration of competence includes strategies that enable students to express themselves effectively in writing. The *Sentence Writing Strategy* (Schumaker & Sheldon, 1985) is designed to teach

students how to recognize and generate four types of sentences—simple, compound, complex, and compound-complex. The *Error Monitoring Strategy* (Schumaker, Nolan, & Deshler, 1985) is used by students to detect and correct errors in their written products. Students are taught to locate errors in paragraph organization, sentence structure, capitalization, overall editing and appearance, punctuation, and spelling by asking themselves a series of questions. Additional learning strategies pertaining to writing are being developed. The *Paragraph Writing Strategy* teaches students how to write well-organized paragraphs, and the *Theme Writing Strategy* is designed to enable students to compose themes or essays of at least five paragraphs in length.

Lessons for Better Writing

Publisher: Curriculum Associates

Description:

This writing improvement program for students in grades 6 through 12 includes a concise text with writing and editing exercises that provide intensive practice in clear, effective writing. Three independent spirit-master books are also provided. *Better Sentences* features lessons containing sentences that all incorporate the same writing weakness, and students are asked to rewrite each sentence, making the necessary edit. *Better Writing* focuses on effective pupil writing directed toward different audiences. *Better Words* contains exercises that provide practice in understanding pairs of often-confused, related words with subtle distinctions in meaning.

Moving Up in Grammar

Publisher: DLM Teaching Resources

Description:

This program is designed to help students in the elementary and intermediate grades improve their grammar skills. Six independent kits of varnish-coated cards, blackline masters, answer cards, and award certificates provide well-organized practice in various areas. *Sentences* consists of 16 units covering such skill areas as simple and complete subjects and predicates, types of sentences, and compound subjects and verbs. *Nouns and Verbs* contains eight units on nouns (e.g., proper nouns, singular and plural possessive nouns) and eight units on verbs (e.g., linking verbs, the verb *be*, irregular past tense verbs). *Capitalization and Punctuation* covers such skill areas as titles of respect and rank; names of relatives; and periods, question marks, exclamation points, quotation marks, and commas. *Word Usage* consists of 16 units covering words such as *accept* and *except*, *can* and *may*, *lay* and *lie*, and *sit* and *set*. *Adjectives and Adverbs* covers eight adjective skill areas and eight adverb skill areas (e.g., comparatives, superlatives, irregular comparisons). *Pronouns* presents 16 units in areas such as noun substitutes, pronoun/verb agreement, relative pronouns, and demonstrative pronouns.

Paragraphing Kit

Publisher: Curriculum Associates

Description:

This kit contains 120 reusable activity cards that offer exercises aimed at teaching basic paragraph writing to students in grades 5 through 9. Each section contains an explanation and sample activity, and answers and explanations are provided on the back of each activity card; thus, the exercises are self-directing and self-correcting. Students are given opportunities for writing simple paragraphs and are provided with definitions for skills being taught, examples, and correct formats for paragraph writing.

Phelps Sentence Guide Program
(Phelps-Terasaki & Phelps, 1980)

Publisher: Academic Therapy

Description:

This written expression program for language remediation is divided into nine hierarchical stages, beginning with the simple sentence and progressing to paragraphs and stories. Initially, the teacher shows a picture to the student and elicits sentences to describe the picture. The sentence guide contains category headings (for example, Who? What? When? Where? How?) that provide the student with a visual system of structuring sentences. The interactive teacher-child dialogue helps the student expand sentences by using additional sentence categories. The student is required to read entire sentences in response to questioning. For example, through these procedures, an initial sentence, "He's kicking it," may become, "The tall boy is kicking the ball in the park." Phelps-Gunn and Phelps-Terasaki (1982) note that the program may be tailored to meet the individual needs of students with learning problems.

SIMS Written Language Program

Publisher: Minneapolis Public Schools

Description:

This program provides systematic practice in written communication skills through the use of probes (informal timed assessments). It is designed to develop writing skills ranging from copying simple words to writing meaningful paragraphs. The student works on vocabulary, sentence structure, the mechanics of capitalization and punctuation, and the writing of meaningful paragraphs.

Think and Write

Publisher: DLM Teaching Resources

Description:

This writing skills program for students in the elementary grades consists of five kits, each of which includes a minimum of 124 teaching and activity cards. Kit 1 is teacher directed with concepts presented on activity cards and taught by the teacher through examples. Kits 2 through 5 are student directed with concepts and skills introduced on teaching cards and practice and application provided on activity cards. Students work on various skills such as word usage (including the major parts of speech), punctuation, sentence building, writing paragraphs, editing, and organizing compositions.

Computer Software Programs

The use of the computer as a word processor can facilitate the teaching of writing. Word processing allows the student to correct, edit, revise, and manipulate text. The ease of changing words in a word processor prior to printing can motivate the older student to proofread for spelling and mechanical errors as well as make improvements in other aspects of composition writing. *Bank Street Writer* (published by Broderbund Software and available from Opportunities for Learning) is a popular word-processing program that is designed to meet the writing needs of students in grades 4 to 12. In addition, numerous software programs are available that focus on specific written expression skills. The following selected microcomputer programs provide examples of software that may be used to facilitate instruction of students having difficulty with written expression skills. The addresses of producers and distributors of educational software are listed in Appendix C.

Grammar Problems for Practice

Producer: Milliken

Hardware: Apple II

Description:

This software package is divided into three separate modules that provide extensive drill and practice in troublesome grammar and usage areas related to homonyms, verbs, and pronouns. After entering a program, the student takes a pretest on the lesson. If mastery is achieved, he will advance to the next lesson. If mastery is not reached, the student must review and then work practice exercises pertaining to the failed portions of the pretest. During practice, the student is intermittently congratulated with positive reinforcements. If necessary, the student can branch to "help" screens which provide review of the homonym, verb, or pronoun form, as well as definitions and context sentences. The student may review his progress at any time, and a performance summary is given at the completion of the practice exercises. A posttest is given at the end of each lesson. If mastery is not achieved, the student is returned to the practice exercises. The programs focus on skills generally introduced in the third through sixth grades; however, they are

well suited for remediation in the seventh through ninth grades.

M–ss–ng L–nks

Producer: Sunburst Communications

Hardware: Apple, Atari, Commodore 64, IBM PC, TRS–80

Description:

This software includes language puzzles designed to improve reading, writing, spelling, and grammar skills as well as develop an appreciation of syntax, vocabulary, and the mechanics of writing. A passage appears with certain letters missing. The pattern of missing letters varies, thus providing more than 500 different puzzles. The student fills in the blanks by making educated guesses based on knowledge of word structure and spelling, grammar, meaning in context, and sense of literary style. Four diskettes are generally available; they are appropriate for students in the third grade through adult age. *Young People's Literature* offers passages from nine classics of children's literature. *MicroEncyclopedia*, especially appropriate for students in grades 4 through 8, gives factual information on various topics. *Classics, Old and New* includes 81 passages from such authors as Hemingway and Dickens. *English Editor* (not available for Commodore 64) enables the teacher to enter passages of his own choice, thus tailoring the game to the individual student's interests and needs. In addition, for the IBM PC, *Foreign Language Editors* allows the teacher to enter passages of his choice in French, Spanish, or German.

Sentence Combining I and II

Producer: Milliken

Hardware: Apple II

Description:

These programs use creative graphics to teach the writing of more fluent sentences. Through graphics and minimal keyboard input, the student builds sentences by combining elements of shorter sentences displayed on the screen. Each lesson uses the same tutorial procedure to teach and drill the student on one or two topics. First the student receives a brief introduction to the concept being presented. Next, the student is guided through interactive example exercises which are personalized by using the student's name. Finally, the student works practice exercises until mastery or failure is achieved. The exercises follow different formats, which usually involve moving a graphics-created box over parts of sentences to indicate how they are to be combined into new sentences. Other formats include multiple-choice selection or stopping a moving comma to indicate the correct placement of commas in a sentence. Each correct exercise is rewarded with a star, and when the student demonstrates mastery, he is congratulated and moved to the next lesson. *Sentence Combining I,* appropriate for students in grades 4 through 6 and as review for older students, includes lessons on the following topics: compounding with *and* (subjects and predicates); inserting adjectives and adverbs; inserting prepositional phrases; subject and object pronouns with *and;* coordinating conjunctions; singular, plural, and irregular possessives; relative pronouns (*who, that,* and *which*); subject/verb agreement; and using *because, before,* and *after. Sentence Combining II* is appropriate for students in grades 6 through 9 and as review for older students. It includes lessons on movability of adverb and prepositional phrases, complements of linking verbs, restrictive relative clauses, nonrestrictive relative clauses, appositives, gerund phrases (-*ing* phrases as subjects), using semicolons, present and past participles, and making infinitive phrases.

Verb Viper; Word Invasion; Word Master

Producer: DLM Teaching Resources

Hardware: Apple II, IBM PC/PCjr, Commodore 64, Tandy 1000, Atari

Description:

These three programs are included in DLM Teaching Resources' *Arcademic Skill Builders in Language Arts.* In *Verb Viper,* a friendly elastic-necked creature helps the student master subject agreement with regular and irregular verbs in present tense, past tense, and past participle form. *Word Invasion* provides practice in identifying words representing six parts of speech (nouns, pronouns, verbs, adjectives, adverbs, and prepositions) by letting the student control the magic ring of a friendly alien octopus. *Word Master* gives the student practice in identifying pairs of antonyms, synonyms, or homonyms at three difficulty levels, while racing against time and advancing electronic rays. In all three programs, speed, length of the game, content levels, and sound effects can be preset according to the student's needs. A teacher's manual and 24 blackline masters of activities are included for each program.

The Writing Adventure

Producer: DLM Teaching Resources

Hardware: Apple II, Commodore 64

Description:

This software program provides instructional support while allowing students to develop their own stories. In each adventure the student directs the main character through intriguing scenes and takes notes on computer note cards for later reference. The student must make choices and think logically in developing stories and must end the stories by writing the main character out of a trap. When writing his story, the student can call his notes up on the computer screen or can print them. A proofing aid highlights potential errors and displays grammar rules and examples that relate to them. The stories can then be printed and shared with other students. The program package is designed for students age 9 and older and consists of two disks: *Story Starter—* presents the adventure scenes, brief scene descriptions, note cards, and prompting questions, and *Story Writer—*has word-processing capabilities for notetaking, editing, and printing stories.

Writing Competency Program

Distributor: Educational Activities

Hardware: Apple II, TRS-80, PET, Commodore 64 with emulator

Description:

This program is designed to instruct junior and senior high school students in three basic and essential areas of writing skills. The following areas are included: (a) business letters (request and complaint)—format and basic parts, content, punctuation, audience, tone, and capitalization; (b) organizing a report—types of organization, outlining skills, unity and coherence, and details; and (c) persuasion—arguments and facts, topic sentences, supporting details, and audience. The program actively involves students in real-life situations and provides tutorial instruction, motivating graphic rewards, and a management system that allows the teacher to monitor student achievement.

Written Expression Series

Producer: Media Materials

Hardware: Apple II, TRS-80

Description:

This series includes seven programs designed to develop various written expression skills: (a) *Nuts and Bolts*—using verbs, nouns and pronouns, adjectives and adverbs, and singular and plural forms; (b) *Gears and Cogs*—using prepositions, capital letters, words that are similar, and forms to show possession; (c) *Link It All Together*—writing sentences with subjects, action verbs, and adverbs; sentences with linking verbs; and sentences with objects; (d) *Sentence Helpers*—adding helping verbs, words with negative meanings, modifiers to sentences, and verbal modifiers; (e) *Compound? Complex?*—writing compound sentences, complex sentences with adverb clauses, complex sentences with adjective clauses, and direct and indirect quotations; (f) *The Sentence Road Map*—using beginning and end punctuation, using commas in sentences, avoiding major sentence errors, and avoiding fragments; and (g) *Final Assembly*—composing narrative paragraphs, descriptive and enumerative paragraphs, explanatory paragraphs; and using topic and supporting sentences. The programs are designed for students in grades 4 through 12. Sup-

plemental materials for enrichment and reinforcement as well as an instructor's guide are included.

REFERENCES

Anderson, D. (1966). Handwriting research: Movement and quality. In T.D. Horn (Ed.), *Research on handwriting and spelling*. Champaign, IL: National Council of Teachers of English.

Barbe, W.B., Lucas, V.H., Hackney, C.S., Braun, L., & Wasylyk, T.M. (1984). *Zaner-Bloser handwriting: Basic skills and application*. Columbus, OH: Zaner-Bloser.

Barbe, W., Milone, M., & Wasylyk, T. (1983). Manuscript is the "write" start. *Academic Therapy, 18*, 397–406.

California Achievement Tests. (1985). Monterey, CA: California Test Bureau/McGraw-Hill.

Carlson, R.K. (1970). *Writing aids through the grades*. New York: Teachers College Press, Columbia University.

Carroll, J.B. (1938). Diversity of vocabulary and the harmonic series law of word-frequency distribution. *The Psychological Record, 2.*

Cartwright, G.P. (1968). Written language abilities of normal and educable mentally retarded children. *American Journal of Mental Deficiency, 72*, 499–508.

Cartwright, G.P. (1969). Written expression and spelling. In R.M. Smith (Ed.), *Teacher diagnosis of educational difficulties* (pp. 95–117). Columbus, OH: Merrill.

Cohen, S., & Plaskon, S. (1980). *Language arts for the mildly handicapped*. Columbus, OH: Merrill.

Dolch, E.W. (1955). *Methods in reading*. Champaign, IL: Garrard.

Dolch, E.W. (1960). *Better spelling*. Champaign, IL: Garrard.

Gardner, E.F., Rudman, H.C., Karlsen, B., & Merwin, J.C. (1982). *Stanford Achievement Test* (7th ed.). San Antonio, TX: Psychological Corporation.

Graham, S., & Miller, L. (1980). Handwriting research and practice: A unified approach. *Focus on Exceptional Children, 13*(2), 1–16.

Hagin, R.A. (1983). Write right—or left: A practical approach to handwriting. *Journal of Learning Disabilities, 16,* 266–271.

Hammill, D.D. (1986). Problems in written composition. In D.D. Hammill & N.R. Bartel, *Teaching students with learning and behavior problems* (4th ed., pp. 91–121). Boston: Allyn & Bacon.

Hammill, D.D., Brown, V.L., Larsen, S.C., & Wiederholt, J.L. (1987). *Test of Adolescent Language—2.* Austin, TX: Pro-Ed.

Hammill, D.D., & Larsen, S.C. (1983). *Test of Written Language.* Austin, TX: Pro-Ed.

Hammill, D.D., & Larsen, S.C. (1988). *Test of Written Language—2.* Austin, TX: Pro-Ed.

Hammill, D.D., & Leigh, J.E. (1983). *Basic School Skills Inventory—Diagnostic.* Austin, TX: Pro-Ed.

Hammill, D.D., & McNutt, G. (1981). *Correlates of reading: The consensus of thirty years of correlational research* (Pro-Ed Monograph No. 1). Austin, TX: Pro-Ed.

Hansen, C.L. (1978). Writing skills. In N.G. Haring, T.C. Lovitt, M.D. Eaton, & C.L. Hansen, *The fourth R: Research in the classroom* (pp. 93–126). Columbus, OH: Merrill.

Herrick, V.E. (1960). Handwriting and children's writing. *Elementary English, 37,* 248–258.

Hieronymus, A.N., Hoover, H.D., & Lindquist, E.F. (1986). *Iowa Tests of Basic Skills.* Chicago: Riverside.

Hildreth, G. (1963). Simplified handwriting for today. *Journal of Educational Research, 56,* 330–333.

Hofmeister, A.M. (1981). *Handwriting resource book: Manuscript/cursive.* Allen, TX: DLM Teaching Resources.

Horton, L.W. (1970). Illegibilities in the cursive handwriting of sixth graders. *Elementary School Journal, 70,* 446–450.

Johnson, W. (1944). Studies in language behavior. I. A program of research. *Psychological Monographs, 56*(2).

Koch, K. (1970). *Wishes, lies, and dreams: Teaching children to write poetry.* New York: Vintage Books/Chelsea House.

Koenig, C.H., & Kunzelmann, H.P. (1980). *Classroom learning screening manual.* San Antonio, TX: Psychological Corporation.

Lewis, E.R., & Lewis, H.P. (1965). An analysis of errors in the formation of manuscript letters by first grade children. *American Educational Research Journal, 2,* 25–35.

Mann, P.H., Suiter, P.A., & McClung, R.M. (1979). *Handbook in diagnostic-prescriptive teaching* (Abridged 2nd ed.). Boston: Allyn & Bacon.

McCarthy, D. (1954). Language development in children. In L. Carmichael (Ed.), *Manual of child psychology.* New York: Wiley.

Meckel, H.C. (1963). Research on teaching composition and literature. In N. Gage (Ed.), *Handbook of research on teaching.* Chicago: Rand McNally.

Miller, G.A. (1951). *Language and communication.* New York: McGraw-Hill.

Moore, G.N., & Woodruff, G.W. (1980). *Story starters—Primary and intermediate.* North Billerica, MA: Curriculum Associates.

Myklebust, H.R. (1965). *Development and disorders of written language: Picture Story Language Test* (Vol. 1). New York: Grune & Stratton.

Newland, T.E. (1932). An analytical study of the development of illegibilities in handwriting from the lower grades to adulthood. *Journal of Educational Research, 26,* 249–258.

Noble, J.K. (1966). *Better handwriting for you.* New York: Noble & Noble.

Otto, W., & Smith, R.J. (1980). *Corrective and remedial teaching* (3rd ed.). Boston: Houghton Mifflin.

Petty, W.T., & Bowen, M.E. (1967). *Slithery snakes and other aids to children's writing.* New York: Appleton-Century-Crofts.

Phelps-Gunn, T., & Phelps-Terasaki, D. (1982). *Written language instruction: Theory and remediation.* Rockville, MD: Aspen Systems.

Phelps-Terasaki, D., & Phelps, T. (1980). *Teaching written expression: The Phelps sentence guide program.* Novato, CA: Academic Therapy.

Plunkett, M. (1954). *A writing manual for teaching the left-handed.* Cambridge, MA: Educators Publishing Service.

Poteet, J.A. (1980). Informal assessment of written expression. *Learning Disability Quarterly, 3*(4), 88–98.

Scannell, D.P. (1986). *Tests of Achievement and Proficiency.* Chicago: Riverside.

Schumaker, J.B., Nolan, S.M., & Deshler, D.D. (1985). *Learning strategies curriculum: The error monitoring strategy.* Lawrence: University of Kansas.

Schumaker, J.B., & Sheldon, J. (1985). *Learning strategies curriculum: The sentence writing strategy.* Lawrence: University of Kansas.

Sequential Tests of Educational Progress: Writing. (1972). Princeton, NJ: Educational Testing Service.

Skinner, B.F., & Krakower, S.A. (1968). *Handwriting with write and see.* Chicago: Lyons & Carnahan.

Strauss, A., & Lehtinen, L. (1947). *Psychopathology and education of the brain-injured child.* New York: Grune & Stratton.

Stuckless, E.R., & Marks, C.H. (1966). *Assessment of the written language of deaf students* (USOE Cooperative Research Project 2544). Pittsburgh: University of Pittsburgh.

Templin, E. (1960). Research and comment: Handwriting, the neglected R. *Elementary English, 37,* 386–389.

Thurber, D.N., & Jordan, D.R. (1981). *D'Nealian handwriting.* Glenview, IL: Scott, Foresman.

Trifiletti, J.J., Rainey, N.S., & Trifiletti, D.T. (1979). *Sequential precision assessment resource kit (SPARK II).* Jacksonville, FL: Precision People.

Wallace, G., & Larsen, S.C. (1978). *Educational assessment of learning problems: Testing for teaching.* Boston: Allyn & Bacon.

Weiner, E.S. (1980a). Diagnostic evaluation of writing skills. *Journal of Learning Disabilities, 13,* 48–53.

Weiner, E.S. (1980b). The Diagnostic Evaluation of Writing Skills (DEWS): Application of DEWS criteria to writing samples. *Learning Disability Quarterly, 3*(2), 54–59.

Western, R.D. (1977). Case against cursive script. *Elementary School Journal, 78,* 1–3.

Wiederholt, J.L., Hammill, D.D., & Brown, V.L. (1983). *The resource teacher: A guide to effective practices* (2nd ed.). Austin, TX: Pro-Ed.

Zaner-Bloser Evaluation Scales. (1979). Columbus, OH: Zaner-Bloser.

CHAPTER 14

Teaching at the
Secondary Level

Teaching students with learning problems at the secondary level is a great challenge. For years, special and remedial education focused primarily on programming for younger children, under the assumption that early intervention prevents later learning problems (Mercer, 1987). Although early intervention has helped numerous children with special needs, many adolescents continue to enter high school with debilitating learning or behavioral problems. Initial efforts in programming for these adolescents have primarily involved applying approaches developed with younger children (for example, academic remediation in word-attack skills). However, educators have quickly realized that differential programming is needed for adolescents. Adolescents are not simply elementary children grown up, and they exhibit unique characteristics that demand a variety of services. Basically, effective special and remedial education programs must consider that in addition to their learning difficulties, adolescents are in a complex transition from childhood to adulthood that typically has dramatic effects on social, emotional, sexual, physical, and academic development. Moreover, adolescents are placed in a new setting—the high school—which places a multitude of demands on them.

Fortunately, recent efforts, especially in the area of learning disabilities, have focused on developing programs for secondary students with learning problems. For example, a research institute was established at the University of Kansas in 1978 to examine the demands of the secondary setting and the educational needs of learning disabled adolescents. Successful demonstration programs have been developed in many states, and the federal government has funded several projects (Riegel & Mathey, 1980) for developing services for adolescents with learning problems. Although few programs have been empirically validated, the recent surge of programs and literature has certainly increased our knowledge about secondary programming for students with learning problems. Although these recent efforts are primarily in the field of learning disabilities, most of the findings are applicable to mildly handicapped students (for example, mildly mentally retarded and emotionally handicapped). This position is feasible because of the heterogeneous nature of learning disabilities.

Deshler and his associates at the University of Kansas Institute for Research in Learning Disabilities contributed some very helpful information in planning secondary programs for adolescents with learning problems. They examined the demands placed on students in secondary mainstreamed classrooms. Schumaker and Deshler (1984) summarize this literature, discussing their findings in three demand areas: work habit demands, knowledge acquisition demands, and knowledge expression demands. *Work habit demands* include the students' ability to work independently with minimum feedback or help from the teacher. Students must be able to complete homework and other assignments as well as follow classroom rules. *Knowledge acquisition demands* are numerous. Students must be able to listen to presentations and take accurate notes. They must gain information from materials written at a secondary level through reading or using strategies for coping with such high-level material. Also, students must be able to acquire information through studying. Finally, *knowledge expression demands* are vital to success at the secondary level. Students must be able to demonstrate knowledge on classroom tests (short-answer and objective-type questions), and they are required to take minimum competency tests. Students must be able to spell and express themselves in writing, including descriptive and narrative prose. In addition, they need to participate in classroom discussions.

When the mildly handicapped adolescent, with her complex needs, enters the secondary setting, with its extensive demands, the need for a diversity of services becomes apparent. For example, Marsh and Price (1980) identify six types of program services at the secondary level; Deshler, Schumaker, Lenz, and Ellis (1984) discuss four; and Riegel and Mathey (1980) present seven. An analysis of the various programs indicates that at least five types of program services are required to accommodate the various needs of secondary students with learning problems. As presented in Figure 14.1, these include academic remediation, learning strategies, regular course work with supportive instruction, functional living skills, and career-related instruction. These services are provided in a variety of instructional arrangements (for example, resource room, regular class, self-contained class, etc.) by a diverse faculty (special educators, regular class teachers, counselors, vocational educators, etc.).

The heterogeneous nature of the adolescent with learning problems underscores the need to offer a variety of services. Some students need one type of service (for example, academic remediation) in the early stages of their high school program and another service (for example, career-related instruction or functional living skills) in the latter part of their program. Still others may require only one service (for example, learning strategies) during their high school program, while others need a combination of yet different services (for example, academic remediation and regular course work with supportive instruction). To date, it appears that no one approach is appropriate for all adolescents with learning problems. Deshler, Schumaker, Lenz, and Ellis (1984) report that the real challenge is not in determining which approach is right or wrong but in ascertaining under what conditions and with whom a given service is most effective.

Determining who provides the various services depends on many variables (for example, number of teachers, specific expertise, resources, etc.) in diverse secondary settings. Certainly, coordination and cooperation between special and regular educators are essen-

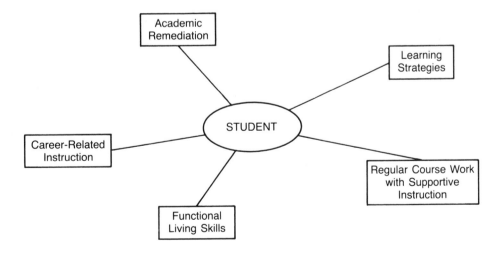

FIGURE 14.1
Program services at the secondary level.

tial for effective programming. Typically, special educators are primarily responsible for academic remediation, learning strategies, and functional living skills. Although some special education teachers offer all of these services, they are usually divided among a team of special education teachers. The resource room teacher is widely used, with the special educator providing direct instruction with students and consultation with regular teachers. In regular course work with supportive instruction, regular class teachers are primarily responsible, and the special educator serves as a consultant who suggests parallel curriculum materials, compensatory techniques, and material adaptations. Career-related instruction is typically provided by regular educators (for example, vocational-business teachers) in conjunction with special education services, especially functional living skills. Finally, the entire program of services must be supported by the school administration and facilitated by responsive guidance and counseling services.

In all instructional settings the teacher of adolescents with learning problems must follow effective teaching practices. Many of these practices are covered in Chapter 1; however, Zigmond, Sansone, Miller, Donahoe, and Kohnke (1986) highlight several teaching practices that are especially useful with adolescents. They recommend the following:

1. Maximize the time students have to learn new skills. Minimize the amount of time used in transitions, getting materials, and dealing with disruptions. Plan activities in which the students overtly participate. Maintain a positive yet businesslike classroom atmosphere to help curb absenteeism.
2. Structure the daily classroom activities in a way that promotes much teacher-directed instruction yet maintains individualized education. During discussions, plan active question-and-answer activities. Monitor seatwork activities and provide feedback.
3. Maximize the amount of time the teacher spends talking about academic content. Provide information through lecturing, giving illustrations, and offering explanations. Use questioning that requires short, factual answers. Provide feedback and be careful to make sure praise is contingent and specific. Do not overuse praise or criticize students for poor performance.
4. Provide lessons that have clarity, appropriate sequencing, and explicit structure. Eliminate or minimize irrelevant information and vagueness from presentations and class discussions. Provide advance organizers, and make certain students are following each lesson.

One service delivery model is not appropriate for all secondary settings. Administrators and teachers must organize the program to match their respective situations; however, the quality and type of services should be maintained in all administrative arrangements. In addition to a discussion on motivation, this chapter provides instructional information (activities, techniques, materials, and resources) in the five program areas (academic remediation, learning strategies, regular course work with supportive instruction, functional living skills, and career-related instruction). Moreover, other sections of the book that relate to secondary services are referred to where applicable.

MOTIVATION

Many secondary students with learning problems have serious motivational problems about schoolwork (Adelman & Taylor, 1983; Deshler, Schumaker, & Lenz, 1984); thus, the incorporation of techniques to enhance motivation is essential to foster effective instruction. The frustration of a school history highlighted by limited academic success and the numerous activities (such as driving a car, getting a job, being with friends) available to the adolescent combine to create substantial motivation problems for some students. Much literature exists that emphasizes the relationship of motivation to problems in learning and performance. Adelman and Taylor (1983) express it simply:

> If a student is motivated to learn something, (s)he often can do much more than anyone would have predicted was possible. Conversely, if a student is not particularly interested in learning something, resultant learning may not even be close to capability. (p. 384)

In essence, there are times when motivation, not academic development, becomes the focus of an intervention program.

A variety of motivation techniques are available to help high school low achievers. Deshler, Schumaker, and Lenz (1984) divide these approaches into two broad categories: those using extrinsic controls and those focusing on developing intrinsic motivation. From their review of motivation studies, Deshler, Schumaker, and Lenz report that several extrinsic control techniques have been successfully used to improve the academic skills of learning disabled adolescents. Zigmond et al. (1986) provide a list of extrinsic reinforcers that appear to be effective with adolescents. The reinforcers include the following:

1. Time for listening to tapes or records
2. Tokens for progress on academics
3. Charting or self-recording of academic accomplishments
4. Allowances at home tied to grades
5. Time to play games or enjoy a recreational activity
6. Opportunity to participate in scheduling academic activities

7. Tangible reinforcers such as restaurant coupons, magazines, and movie tickets
8. Exemption from some homework or assignment
9. Extra time for a break or lunch

Some of the most useful techniques include token economies, contingency contracting, and verbal feedback (see Chapter 5 for descriptions of these techniques). Also, techniques aimed at facilitating intrinsic motivation are receiving support. Schumaker, Deshler, Alley, and Warner (1983) report that the focus of the motivation component at the University of Kansas Institute is to produce independent and active learners. To accomplish this purpose, the intervention is aimed at training self-control skills, including one or more of the following: goal setting, self-recording of progress, self-evaluation, and self-reinforcement. Seabaugh and Schumaker (1981) taught all four of these self-control subskills to learning disabled adolescents with positive results. (That is, the number of lessons completed by the students increased from an average of one-half lesson completed per day to four lessons completed per day.) Deshler, Schumaker, and Lenz (1984) report that self-control training holds much promise for helping low achievers complete their assignments. They note that the training procedures are easily implemented and are not dependent on expensive extrinsic reinforcers.

From their review of the motivation literature, Adelman and Taylor (1983) list tactics for enhancing intrinsic motivation, including the following:

1. Enhance the student's perception that learning is worthwhile, in part by providing the student with some choices relative to curriculum content and procedures. Also, discussions concerning the relevance (real-

life applications) of various content is helpful.

2. Through discussion, obtain a commitment to those options the student values and indicates a desire to pursue. Contractual agreements are helpful.

3. Hold informal and formal conferences with the student to enhance his role in making choices and negotiating agreements.

4. Provide feedback that conveys student progress. The student must not perceive the feedback as an effort to entice and control. To this end self-correcting materials are useful.

One of the recurring themes that permeates the literature on managing and motivating adolescent low achievers is *involve the student.* For example, in their discussion of secondary classroom management for adolescents with behavior disorders, Kerr and Nelson (1983) state, "We strongly recommend that you encourage pupils to participate in all aspects of the curriculum. Specifically, they should be involved in selecting and ordering their own academic and social goals, in making decisions about the classroom structure, and in setting consequences and contingencies" (p. 100). Additional information on classroom management and techniques for enhancing student motivation is presented in Chapter 5.

ACADEMIC REMEDIATION

Most educators agree that the curriculum for elementary-aged students with learning problems should focus on teaching basic academic skills. Basically, this approach stresses that improved academic skills help the student benefit from course work in all content areas. In a survey of secondary programs for the learning disabled adolescent, Deshler, Lowrey, and Alley (1979) report that 49% of the pro-

grams stressed instruction in the basic academic skills. From a survey of 741 high school learning disabilities teachers, Schmid, Algozzine, Wells, and Stoller (1980) found that teachers considered the ability to remediate academic skills as the most important teaching skill. Moreover, they reported that of time spent teaching, the remediation of basic skills was the area in which the teachers spent the most time.

This emphasis on academic remediation is easily understood when the characteristics of secondary students with learning problems are examined. Schmid et al. (1980) found that the majority of learning disabled students placed in secondary programs demonstrated reading and math grade levels in the fourth- to sixth-grade range. Furthermore, a significant number of other learning disabled students were functioning below third-grade level in reading and math. When the learning disabled students below third-grade level are joined by adolescents with learning problems that result from mental retardation, economic deprivation, and emotional problems, the number of students with severe academic problems is substantial. Warner, Schumaker, Alley, and Deshler (1980) report that many learning disabled students reach a plateau at fourth- or fifth-grade academic achievement during the tenth grade and fail to gain thereafter. When the academic deficiencies are considered in light of expectancies placed on many students with learning problems to meet minimal competencies and earn a high school diploma, the need for intense academic remediation is great.

Although the need for academic remediation is apparent, some educators (Deshler, Schumaker, Lenz, & Ellis, 1984) express concern about its application at the high school level. They note that many materials used in this approach were developed with elementary children and may not be appropriate for adolescents. Moreover, many adolescents have difficulty understanding the relevance of academic remediation content. Also, Deshler, Schumaker, Lenz, and Ellis (1984) question the effectiveness of this approach to help the student cope with the complex demands of the high school curriculum. Finally, they report that time may be too limited or it may be too late to make a meaningful impact on academic skills at the high school level.

In spite of concerns with academic remediation for adolescents with learning problems, many educators promote it. It seems especially appropriate for 9th and 10th graders who are achieving below fourth-grade level in one of the basic skill areas. Also, it appears that academic remediation should be provided in conjunction with other services (for example, career-related instruction, functional living skills).

Programming Considerations

A variety of projects have evolved that provide academic remediation to secondary students with learning problems. The Pittsburgh Child Service Demonstration Center developed a model that is widely used in Pittsburgh high schools (Buchwach, 1980). Students attend a resource room (called a learning lab) for not more than two periods daily. The students are removed only from English or math to receive basic skill intervention. A diagnostic systematic approach to skill development is provided, and generalization of newly learned skills is fostered by having students eventually use materials from mainstream classes in the learning lab. A second special education resource teacher functions as a liaison between the students and their mainstream teachers. In addition, once a week this teacher works with the learning lab teacher to provide a school survival skills curriculum (that is, strands pertaining to behavior control, teacher-pleasing behavior, and study skills). Thus, this model demonstrates the use of both academic remediation services and learning strategies intervention.

The Synergistic Model Program for learning disabled adolescents was developed under the direction of Dr. Charles Meisgeier at the University of Houston. In this program a high-intensity learning center is used to provide academic remediation in a very positive environment. The student attends the high-intensity learning center 3 hours a day for 12 weeks. The student receives 2 hours of reading remediation and 1 hour of social-behavioral curriculum each day. Dembrowsky (1980) reports excellent results from the 12-week program. For example, initial data indicate the mean growth in reading was 1.2 years in comprehension and 1.5 years in reading accuracy. Encouraging results were also reported in social-emotional areas. Once the student completes the 12-week program, she returns to mainstream classes. To help maintain academic growth, an essential skills program is provided through part-time special education services. Initial data indicate that academic growth is not only maintained but continues to develop.

Because high school students face numerous curriculum demands and have a limited amount of time to ameliorate deficits, educators are seeking ways to increase the intensity of instruction (for example, learning labs, high-intensity learning centers). This may be done effectively through better use of instructional time (that is, increasing the amount of time students spend on remedial activities). Also, summer school programs may be considered to provide an opportunity for high-intensity instruction without delaying graduation. In addition, to increase student motivation and involvement in the instructional program, it may be helpful to involve adolescents in all major programming decisions.

Much of this book emphasizes individualizing instruction in basic academic skills. Each of the academic areas that are most appropriate for secondary instruction (math, reading, spelling, and written expression) follows a presentation sequence that includes assessment procedures, teaching activities, self-correcting materials, instructional games, commercial materials, and computer software programs. The appropriate age or grade level is given for each assessment instrument, commercial material, and software program. For activities, self-correcting materials, and instructional games, the content generally is arranged starting with material that is most appropriate for young children and going on to material that is most appropriate for secondary students. Thus, instructional activities, self-correcting materials, and games that are designed for teaching basic academics in secondary programs are featured at the end of each respective section.

LEARNING STRATEGIES

As students progress through the grades, it is generally recognized that the demands for successful performance increase. Some educators feel that the complexity of the secondary demands contributes as much to the adolescent's failure as learning deficits. In an effort to understand the demands placed on students in high school content classes, researchers at the University of Kansas Institute analyzed these classes to ascertain the skills needed to succeed. In a series of studies they pinpointed a variety of demands. In an observational study of high school classes, Moran (1980) reports much use of the lecture method coupled with heavy demands in listening and writing. Knowlton and Schlick (in preparation) note that secondary teachers expect performance in the following areas: independent work habits,

skills to cope with subject content, study skills, and communication skills. Link (1980) surveyed secondary teachers to ascertain their feelings regarding the reasons learning disabled adolescents have difficulty with high school curriculum. The teachers reported problems in the areas of following written and oral directions, skimming reading material, locating information in textbooks, taking notes from discussions, and recalling information for tests.

In addition to academic deficits, many adolescents with learning problems exhibit deficits in the spontaneous use of study skills and learning strategies (Alley, Deshler, & Warner, 1979; Carlson & Alley, 1981; Mercer & Snell, 1977; Schumaker, Sheldon-Wildgen, & Sherman, 1980). Moreover, other researchers (Butterfield & Belmont, 1977) report that many adolescents with learning problems have immature executive function (that is, the ability to formulate and apply a strategy to a novel task).

To help students with learning problems cope with the complex demands of secondary curriculum, Alley and Deshler (1979) recommend a learning strategies approach. Deshler and his colleagues define *learning strategies* as techniques, principles, or rules that enable a student to learn, solve problems, and complete tasks independently. This approach is not designed to teach specific course content (such as geography) but to help students develop and use skills necessary to acquire, store, and express content. Basically, it focuses on teaching students "how to learn" and how to demonstrate command of their knowledge in performing academic tasks. For example, a reading strategy might be used by a student with fifth-grade reading skills to obtain relevant information from a textbook chapter written at the tenth-grade level. Deshler and his colleagues at the University of Kansas Institute developed a learning strategies curriculum. Components have been specified, developed, and validated in classrooms. Early field-testing and evaluation data support good student progress and a high degree of consumer satisfaction (Schumaker, Deshler, Alley, & Warner, 1983). In addition, Cronin and Currie (1984) provide a comprehensive resource guide on learning strategies and study skills that may be helpful to the secondary teacher in developing a learning strategies curriculum.

This section presents instructional procedures and activities in the following areas: learning strategies teaching sequence, preparatory study skills, information-gathering and organization skills, sequential study methods, study-rehearsal skills, and knowledge expression and application skills. Within this organization, the University of Kansas Institute strategies are incorporated along with content from other projects and researchers. Selected commercial materials and computer software programs for teaching learning strategies are also presented.

Learning Strategies Teaching Sequence

The teaching methods used with students exhibiting learning problems are crucial to the success of the instruction. The staff at the University of Kansas Institute developed and validated a teaching sequence that is based on sound learning principles. These acquisition steps focus on providing the student with the knowledge, motivation, and practice required to apply a skill or strategy to materials and situations comparable to regular secondary classroom demands (Schumaker et al., 1983). The steps (with examples) are as follows:

Step 1. The student is assessed in terms of her current learning habits on a specific task. She is provided with feedback regarding her strengths and weaknesses. The need for acquiring a new skill is discussed until the student makes a commitment to learning a new

skill to remedy her weaknesses. This step is very important for older students. If they readily see the discrepancy that exists between their approach to a task and a new strategy, they often become actively involved in learning.

Example: Test to determine the student's current paragraph-writing skills. (Task—teaching a paragraph organization strategy.) The student is instructed to write three types of paragraphs (sequential, enumerative, and compare/contrast) with at least five sentences in each one. The teacher scores the paragraphs and discusses the results with the student. Specific feedback is given regarding strengths and weaknesses. It is mutually established that the student exhibits some deficits in writing paragraphs.

Step 2. The new skill is broken down into its component parts and described to the student. Reasons for learning the skill are reviewed, and its applications are delineated.

Example: Describe the paragraph-writing strategy for one paragraph style. Describe the steps involved in the paragraph writing strategy for the first paragraph style (for example, sequential). The steps include the specific behaviors in which the student engages when writing a paragraph. As each step is explained, a rationale for the behavior is discussed in terms of how it helps the student express ideas in writing more clearly.

Step 3. The new skill is modeled for the student from start to completion, and each step is specified aloud. The student is encouraged to ask questions to ensure understanding.

Example: Model the strategy. In this step, the teacher initially presents a paragraph. The role of each sentence is discussed. The teacher models (that is, describes each step of) the paragraph-writing strategy on the chalkboard by writing a different paragraph. Next the teacher and student write a paragraph together. Before each sentence is written, the type of sentence needed is discussed.

Step 4. The student learns to instruct herself on the steps involved in the skill. Verbal rehearsal is practiced until the student describes each step fluently.

Example: Verbally rehearse the strategy. The student verbally rehearses the steps involved to a 100% correct criterion without prompts. This instructional step focuses on familiarizing the student with the steps of the strategy so she can instruct herself in the future.

Step 5. The student practices the new skill to a specified criterion in controlled materials. For reading, the controlled material is at the student's ability level, whereas in listening the material may involve a 3-minute tape of a lecture presented very slowly. Corrective feedback and reinforcement are provided after each practice trial.

Example: Practice writing controlled topic paragraphs. The student practices applying the strategy to successive controlled paragraph topics. As the student develops proficiency in writing paragraphs, she is encouraged to go from overt self-instruction to covert self-instruction.

Step 6. The student practices the skill to criterion in materials that approximate the difficulty level of materials in the regular classroom. For example, the student may apply a study-skill strategy to reading material at grade level or apply a listening–notetaking strategy to a 20-minute tape of a regular classroom lecture. Reinforcement and corrective feedback are given after each trial.

Example: Practice writing paragraphs using regular class content. The student practices applying the strategy to topics from her mainstream classes.

Step 7. The student is assessed to show how much she has progressed from the initial test. Moreover, if daily measures of progress (for example, charting) are used to provide feedback in steps 5 and 6, the student is able to see her progress over a period of time.

Example: Provide feedback. The teacher uses assessment procedures similar to those used in step 1 (for example, pre/posttest). The student's original paragraphs are compared to her final paragraphs with the teacher pointing out improvements. When the student reaches criterion on writing one paragraph style (for example, sequential), steps 2 through 7 are repeated to teach a different paragraph style (for example, enumerative and compare/contrast).

Step 8. Once acquisition training is accomplished, the student engages in three types of generalization activities. *Awareness* activities focus on helping the student realize how the strategy can be used in her daily life. *Activation* activities involve the student using the strategy in her regular classes. Products from the regular classes are periodically evaluated. *Maintenance* activities focus on the student setting goals for use of the strategy. The teacher periodically tests the student to determine if the student is using the strategy.

In addition to the teaching sequence, some helpful guidelines in teaching the learning strategies include the following:

1. Always use the first three steps in teaching the strategies. Steps 4 through 7 may be varied as a function of the student's needs and time available.
2. Always give a pre- and posttest.
3. Reinforce previously learned strategies and periodically check to see if the student is using them.
4. Before teaching a strategy, cover prerequisite skills if necessary.
5. Maintain contact with mainstream teachers to obtain feedback for planning.
6. Remember that the strategies are for assisting students with mainstream content.

7. Require all students to have an organized notebook.
8. Require products as proof. Keep a before-and-after file.
9. Have the student experience the strategy with different people.
10. Teach how strategies are applicable in a variety of situations.

The learning strategies curriculum organized by Deshler, Schumaker, and their colleagues features strategies to help in the areas of acquisition, storage, and expression/demonstration (see Table 14.1). Additional information can be obtained by contacting Dr. Frances L. Clark, Coordinator of Training, Institute for Research in Learning Disabilities, 206 Carruth-O'Leary Hall, University of Kansas, Lawrence, KS 66045-2342 (913/864-4780).

Preparatory Study Skills

Preparatory study skills involve skills and factors that are relevant precursors to efficient learning. The attitude and motivation of the student are critical to student effort and consequent learning. The adolescent with learning problems needs to understand the relevance of assigned tasks and exhibit an attitude that facilitates effort. Chapter 5 and the previous discussion on motivation in this chapter present strategies and activities aimed at improving motivation and social skills.

Time management. Considering the many demands placed on high school students to complete tasks at specific times and participate in a host of competing activities (such as being with peers, joining clubs, watching television, listening to music, driving a car, etc.), it is apparent that time management is critical to surviving in the secondary setting. The adolescent with learning problems usually needs instruction in time management. Activities for teaching time management include making schedules, making time estimates, and establishing priorities.

1. Give the student a 5-day schedule of after-school time and ask her to record how she spends these time blocks. Next, have the student allocate time blocks for specific activities (see Table 14.2, p. 500) and follow the schedule as much as possible. Initially it may help the student to plan a day and then gradually build to a week.
2. Provide or have the student make a calendar to assist her in scheduling her daily or weekly activities. Notations can be made on the calendar to remind the student of project due dates or test dates (Dexter, 1982). Also, the student may keep a notebook with all academic assignments and due dates.
3. Remind the student that some flexibility should be allowed in the daily schedule. Occasionally unexpected events will take precedence over the planned activity. Introduce new events in the daily schedule and explain how adjustments can be made. (For example, if friends invite the student to go out for a pizza during study time, she can replace TV time with study time.) Finally, the student should show the teacher her schedule with adjustments written out when applicable.
4. Either provide assignments or have the student list at least four of her school assignments and estimate how long it will take to do each task. Then have her record the amount of time it actually takes to complete the assignments. These times may be written on the student's schedule. On tasks or subject areas in which the student's estimates are consistently inaccurate (off by more than 20%), have her practice in these areas until the estimates become realistic.
5. Have the student list school assignments and prioritize them. For example, the student may rank the activities in the order she would complete them (that is, place a 1 beside the first activity, a 2 beside the next activity, and so on). For example:

   ___ Work on social studies project due in 2 weeks.

   ___ Write a lab report in science due in 2 days.

TABLE 14.1
Learning strategies curriculum.

Acquisition Strand

Word Identification Strategy: This strategy teaches students a problem-solving procedure for quickly attacking and decoding unknown words in reading materials, allowing them to move on quickly for the purpose of comprehending the passage.

Paraphrasing Strategy: This strategy directs students to read a limited section of material, ask themselves the main idea and the details of the section, and put that information in their own words. The strategy is designed to improve comprehension by focusing attention on the important information of a passage and by stimulating active involvement with the passage.

Self-Questioning Strategy: This strategy aids reading comprehension by having students actively ask questions about key pieces of information in a passage and then read to find the answers for these questions.

Visual Imagery Strategy: This strategy is designed to improve students' acquisition, storage, and recall of prose material. Students improve reading comprehension by reading short passages and visualizing the scene that is described, incorporating actors, action, and details.

Interpreting Visuals Strategy: This strategy is designed to aid students in the use and interpretation of visuals such as maps, graphs, pictures, and tables to increase their ability to extract needed information from written materials.

Multipass Strategy: This strategy involves making three passes through a passage for the purpose of focusing attention on key details and main ideas. Students survey a chapter or passage to get an overview, size up sections of the chapter by systematically scanning to locate relevant information that they note, and sort out important information in the chapter by locating answers to specific questions.

Storage Strand

First-Letter Mnemonic Strategy: This strategy is designed to aid students in memorizing lists of information by teaching them to design mnemonics or memorization aids, and to find and make lists of crucial information.

Paired Associates Strategy: This strategy is designed to aid students in memorizing pairs or small groups of information by using visual imagery, matching pertinent information with familiar objects, coding important dates, and using a first-syllable technique.

Listening and Notetaking Strategy: This strategy is designed to teach students to develop skills that will enhance their ability to learn from listening experiences. These skills include identifying the speaker's verbal cues or mannerisms which signal that important information is about to be given, noting key words, and organizing notes into an outline for future reference or study.

Expression and Demonstration of Competence Strand

Sentence-Writing Strategy: This strategy is designed to teach students how to recognize and generate four types of sentences: simple, compound, complex, and compound-complex.

TABLE 14.1, *continued*

Paragraph-Writing Strategy: This strategy is designed to teach students how to write well-organized, complete paragraphs by outlining ideas, selecting a point of view and tense for the paragraph, sequencing ideas, and checking their work.

Error-Monitoring Strategy: This strategy is designed to teach students a process for detecting and correcting errors in their writing and for producing a neater written product. Students are taught to locate errors in paragraph organization, sentence structure, capitalization, overall editing and appearance, punctuation, and spelling by asking themselves a series of questions. Students correct their errors and rewrite the passage before submitting it to their teacher.

Theme-Writing Strategy: This strategy teaches students to write a five-paragraph theme. They learn how to generate ideas for themes and how to organize these ideas into a logical sequence. Then the students learn how to write the paragraphs, monitor errors, and rewrite the theme.

Assignment-Completion Strategy: This strategy teaches students to monitor their assignments from the time an assignment is given until it is complete and turned in to the teacher. Students write down assignments; analyze the assignments; schedule various subtasks; complete the subtasks, and ultimately, the entire task; and submit the completed assignment.

Test-Taking Strategy: This strategy is designed to be used by students during a test. Students are taught to allocate time and read instructions and questions carefully. A question is either answered or abandoned for later consideration. The obviously wrong answers are eliminated from the abandoned questions, and a reasonable guess is made. The last step is to survey the entire test for unanswered questions.

____ Complete a math worksheet due tomorrow.

____ Practice baseball for the game in 3 days.

____ Read 20 pages in a book in preparation for an oral report due in 4 days.

____ Call the local television meteorologist and invite her to speak to the science class next week about pollution factors.

Discuss the need to consider consequences and time factors in prioritizing lists of things to do. Review the rankings and point out the correct and incorrect rankings in terms of consequences, breaking large tasks into smaller amounts (for example, subdividing reading material into a number of pages per day), and time factors. Also, have the student practice using "value" steps in prioritizing activities and tasks by grouping her list into three areas: activities with high value, activities with medium value, and activities with low value.

6. To complete academic tasks efficiently, encourage the student to work in an environment conducive to studying. Ideally, the study area should be a relatively quiet, unstimulating environment. If noise (television, classmates) becomes too distracting, the student may consider using earplugs. Some comfortable earplugs are designed to screen out noise (Dexter, 1982).

Information-Gathering and Organization Skills

To survive in the secondary setting, the student must acquire and organize information from written and spoken input. High school teachers use the lecture/notetaking format extensively (Moran, 1980). Also, students are required to obtain and organize information from textbooks. This section presents teaching activities

TABLE 14.2
A student's after-school schedule.

	Monday	Tuesday	Wednesday	Thursday	Friday
3:00–4:00	with friend eat snack	with friend eat snack	with friend eat snack	with friend eat snack	with friend eat snack
4:00–5:00	play ball	play ball	play ball	study	play ball
5:00–6:00	play ball	play ball	play ball	study	play ball
6:00–7:00	eat dinner	eat dinner	eat dinner	eat dinner	eat dinner
7:00–8:00	study	study	study	go to game	go to movie
8:00–9:00	study	watch TV	study	go to game	go to movie
9:00–10:00	watch TV	watch TV	play tapes	watch TV	watch TV

and strategies aimed at developing information-gathering and organization skills. The skills are organized into the following areas: listening and notetaking, textbook usage, reading-study skills, reading-notetaking skills, and using visual aids.

Activities for listening and notetaking. Notetaking is defined as an individualized process for recording and organizing information into a usable format and is dependent on *active* student participation (Devine, 1981; Pauk, 1978). Saski, Swicegood, and Carter (1983) report that researchers agree that notetaking is advantageous to the student, yet no one approach is considered superior. To date, notetaking strategies have included (a) an outline format which stresses the identification of a main idea and supporting subordinate ideas and (b) a columnar format which serves as a guide for organizing and classifying information. Moreover, Devine (1981) reports that any notetaking strategy is better than none at all. The importance and complexity of the notetaking process suggest the need for guidelines and activities to facilitate its development.

1. To assist with listening/notetaking, teach the student to use the following strategies (Towle, 1982):

a. Physically prepare for listening and notetaking by sitting alertly (for example, leaning forward) in a comfortable desk with the essential materials (for example, notebook, two or more pencils or pens, textbook). Remove all extraneous materials from the desk.

b. Review vocabulary (for example, from text or handouts) related to lecture topic prior to the lecture. It helps some students to have a list of difficult vocabulary words on their desks during the lecture/notetaking session.

c. Listen for organizational cues or signal words (for example, statements referring to time spans or sequences—*first, second, phase, period, era, next, finally,* etc.). H. A. Robinson (1978) provides a list of signal words to help the student. It includes words indicating a sequence or additional ideas (for example, *first, second, also, furthermore, again, plus, next, after that*); caution words which point to concluding ideas (for example, *consequently, thus, therefore, in conclusion, to summarize, finally, as a result*); turn words which indicate a change in ideas (for example, *in contrast, opposed to, however, to the contrary, on the other hand, in spite of, although, yet, despite*); stop words which signal special significance (for example, *significantly, absolutely, whenever, without doubt, without question*); and application words which indicate concrete application of a thought (for example, *because, for example, specifically, for instance*).

d. Listen for content importance by noticing such cues as change in voice, tone, pitch, pauses, and volume.

e. Ask for elaboration on specific points or content when confusion exists.

f. Request examples to illustrate specific concepts.

g. Paraphrase certain points to check understanding.

h. Ask for visual references (for example, pages in the text).

Initially these notetaking strategies may be taught by lecturing to the student and having her practice a couple of the strategies. Gradually, more strategies can be practiced until all are being used appropriately.

2. Use the following guided listening/notetaking activities to provide the student with opportunities to practice a variety of skills.

a. The teacher plays a 5- to 8-minute tape recording of a lecture on content appropriate to the student's needs. The teacher and student sit beside each other and simultaneously take notes.

b. At the end of the tape the teacher provides corrective feedback by sharing her notes with the student and explaining listening and notetaking strategies. The teacher may elect to replay the tape and point out key factors (for example, content organization, voice cues) in listening/notetaking.

c. The student listens to the tape again and takes a new set of notes. At the end of the tape she compares her notes with the teacher's model notes and makes corrections. The student practices this procedure to criterion with several different tapes.

d. Short tapes are made of selected regular classroom teacher's lectures. The student practices listening and notetaking on these tapes with corrective feedback until criterion is obtained.

e. As the student progresses, the lecture tapes—feedback sequence is expanded to include more teachers in a variety of subject areas.

f. Eventually the student only takes notes from live lectures and uses a set of model notes (for example, from the teacher or a classmate) to correct or complete her notes.

This activity may be used with an individual or group to assess and remediate listening and notetaking skills. Notes from proficient peers may be used as models. In addition, teacher aides can be trained to tape lectures and provide model notes.

3. To improve legibility, have student pairs read each other's notes and circle illegible words. Have each student rewrite the circled words.

4. Present directed listening activities according to the following three stages developed by Cunningham and Cunningham (1976):

1. The Readiness Stage
   a. Establish motivation for the lesson.
   b. Introduce any new or difficult concepts.
   c. Introduce any new or difficult words.
   d. Set purposes for listening.

2. The Listening-Reciting Stage
   a. Students listen to satisfy the purposes for listening set during readiness.
   b. The teacher asks several literal and inferential questions that relate to the purposes set during readiness.
   c. The students volunteer interpretive and evaluative comments about the lesson. Some class discussion may ensue.
   d. If there are errors or gaps in the students' understanding of the lesson, the teacher directs the students to relisten to certain parts of the lesson.

3. The Follow-Up Stage
   a. The teacher provides opportunities for and encourages students to engage in activities that build on and develop concepts acquired during the lesson. These may include writing, reading, small group discussions, art activities . . . (pp. 27–28)

5. To improve listening comprehension and retention, use the following sequence of activities which is adapted from Manzo's (1975) guided listening procedure:

a. The teacher asks the student to try to remember everything she is about to hear.

b. The teacher lectures or plays a recorded selection. If the teacher lectures, she records it.

c. The teacher reminds the student about the instructions that were given. She then writes everything on the board without making any corrections or asking specific questions.

d. The teacher reads everything listed on the board and asks the student to note incorrect information and think about missing information.

e. The student listens to the tape again, corrects inaccurate information, and obtains missing information.

f. The information on the chalkboard is amended and expanded.

g. The teacher asks which ideas on the board are the main and important ideas and which ones should be remembered for a long time. She highlights these items.

h. Now that the student has mastered the literal content of the selection, the teacher asks inferential questions that appear vital for understanding.

i. The teacher erases the board and tests memory with items (for example, oral multiple choice, true–false) that are not too dependent on reading or writing skills.

j. The teacher tests long-term memory with a similar test several weeks later.

6. Teach the student to recognize the main idea and the contributing points from which it arrives. In this way she gains control of what to write by determining how much detail is needed in terms of expected outcome (that is, main idea). Looking for the main and contributing ideas helps make the student a more active listener by encouraging thinking, comprehension, and questions (Alley & Deshler, 1979). Also, teach the student to look for the order and organization of the lecture. Stress that notes are a skeletal representation of the material (Alley & Deshler, 1979).

7. Teach the student to use abbreviations to reduce the writing demands of the task (for example, w/ for with, U.S. for United States).

8. Encourage the use of columnar notetaking formats. Saski, Swicegood, and Carter (1983) report that feedback from secondary learning disabilities teachers is very positive regarding the use of such formats. One of their notetaking formats contains a topic sentence at the top of the page, and the columns (5″, 2″, and 1″ wide) are designed for recording three types of information. The first column is for Basic Ideas (that is, material such as facts, figures, dates, people, and places) that will be needed for future tests. The second column, Background Information, includes pertinent related information plus ideas, facts, and topics that interest the student. This column may begin with key words or concepts from the preceding lecture. The third column, Questions, includes space for marking unclear information that needs clarification or elaboration.

Activities for textbook usage. The textbook is a primary source of information for secondary students. Practice in the correct use of textbooks is very beneficial to students with learning problems. It assists them in completing assignments and reviewing pertinent information. This section features a variety of activities to help students improve their skills in textbook usage.

1. To assist in developing instructional objectives and measuring competence in textbook usage, administer a pre/posttest. A test format may include the following questions:

   a. What part of the book explains how the book is organized?

   b. The authors are listed in what part of the book?

   c. On what page(s) would you look for information on _____?

   d. What part of the book gives meanings of words?

   e. How many chapters are in the book?

   f. What part of the book provides page references for any given topic?

   g. Define _____.

   h. On what page would you find a chapter titled _____?

   i. In what part of the book would you find information on a topic in the form of visual aids?

   j. Who publishes the book?

   k. On what pages does chapter ___ begin and end?

l. On what page would you find out about
    _____ ?

m. What is the meaning of the term _____ ?

n. What information is included in the appendix
    of this book?

2. Instruct the student to locate specific parts of a
    textbook. Allow 15 seconds for each part (for
    example, the index). The following format is use-
    ful.

    Name of textbook _____

    On what page will you find the following:

    a. Table of contents   _____

    b. Index   _____

    c. Glossary   _____

    d. Appendix   _____

3. Instruct the student to use the table of contents to
    determine page numbers where specific chap-
    ters begin and end.

4. Instruct the student to use the table of contents to
    name the chapter in which a given topic is lo-
    cated. The following format is helpful:

    Directions: Place the chapter listed on the right
    under the correct section heading listed on the
    left.

    Section I,   Weather   Reptiles
    A.   Precipitation
    B.   Nutrition—proteins
                            and vitamins
    Section II, Animals   Amphibians
    A.   High-pressure system
    B.   Medications
    Section III, Health
    A.
    B.

5. Discuss the purpose of a glossary, and have the
    student look up several words in a textbook glos-
    sary.

6. From a content reading assignment, instruct the
    student to identify key words and find their
    meanings in the glossary.

7. Explain what an index is, how it is developed,
    and how it can be used. Provide the student with
    a page from an index, and instruct her to locate a
    list of terms and write down corresponding page
    numbers.

8. Give the student a question, and have her iden-
    tify the key words and look them up in the index.
    Have the student write the page number(s) per-
    taining to the question topic. A suggested format
    is as follows:

    Underline key words. Locate them in the index
    and write the page number on which you would
    find the answer.

    a. What was the population of San Francisco in
        1980?   _____

    b. What causes a tidal wave?   _____

9. Instruct the student to use the following cognitive
    strategies to help learning (Ellis & Lenz, 1987):

    a. CAN-DO: A strategy for learning content in-
        formation

        C = Create a list of items to be learned.

        A = Ask yourself if the list is complete.

        N = Note the main ideas and details using a
            tree diagram.

        D = Describe each component and how it
            relates to others.

        O = Overlearn main parts, then supporting
            details.

    b. RIDER: A visual imagery strategy for reading
        comprehension

        R = Read (Read the sentence.)

        I = Image (Make an image or picture in
            your mind.)

        D = Describe (Describe how the new image
            is different from the last sentence.)

        E = Evaluate (As you make the image,
            check to make sure it contains every-
            thing necessary.)

        R = Repeat (As you read the next sentence,
            repeat the steps to RIDE.)

    c. RAP: A paraphrasing strategy for reading
        comprehension

        R = Read a paragraph.

        A = Ask yourself what were the main idea
            and two details.

        P = Put the main idea and details in your
            own words.

    d. FIST: A self-questioning strategy for reading
        comprehension

        F = First sentence in the paragraph is read.

        I = Indicate a question based on informa-
            tion in the first sentence.

        S = Search for the answer to the question.

T = Tie the answer to the question with a paraphrase.

Activities for reading-study skills. The demand for gaining information from reading material is extensive at the high school level. Students with learning problems are faced with obtaining content from a variety of reading materials. Several reading styles and rates are needed for these students to acquire essential information. Thus, students with learning problems must be taught strategies to help them acquire information quickly from a variety of printed materials.

Skimming is a reading strategy that assists students in dealing with the reading and study demands of secondary classes. It is a systematic and efficient way of determining the main ideas of a book or other printed material. In this strategy, key sentences, phrases, and words are isolated and read rapidly. The steps in skimming are as follows:

1. Read the title and headings (dark print) as they appear.
2. Read the introduction (that is, a few paragraphs at the beginning of a chapter or article).
3. Read the first sentence of each subsequent paragraph. In textbooks the first sentence usually contains the main idea of the paragraph.
4. Read the captions of pictures and study any illustrations in the chapter.
5. Read the conclusion or summary of the chapter.

The following activities involving skimming are helpful in developing this reading-study skill:

1. Have the student skim the major headings of a classroom text and formulate several questions for each heading. As a group activity the teacher may require each student to generate one question for each heading.
2. Discuss the terms *chronological, sequential,* or *causal* and provide examples of each.
   a. Chronological—topics or events in the order of their happening. Most history books are organized chronologically.
   b. Sequential—a step-by-step procedure. This frequently occurs in a science lab experiment or in instructions for assembling a project.
   c. Causal—an "if–then" presentation pattern. Some texts use a causal pattern to explain a phenomenon (for example, conditions that lead to weather happenings such as rain, lightning, hurricanes).
3. Give the student a content reading selection and a list of comprehension questions covering several main themes. Instruct her to skim the selection and answer the questions.
4. Use the following skimming activity as a pre/posttest or as practice. Provide the student with a four- to five-page passage and a list of 20 comprehension questions covering main ideas and key words. Instruct her to use skimming techniques to read the passage quickly and gain the most important information. At the end of five minutes, have the student answer the comprehension questions. Set the criterion for mastery at 90% correct on the comprehension questions.

Scanning is another reading and study strategy which helps students with learning problems deal with the demands of acquiring information from printed material. It involves the quick reading of key sentences, phrases, and words to locate specific information. This information could be an important term, definition, or answer to a question. Scanning is a great help in reading and studying because it enables the reader to find specific items rapidly. The steps in scanning are as follows:

1. Remember the specific question to be answered.

2. Estimate in what form the answer will appear (that is, word, name, number, graphic, or date).
3. Use the expected form of the answer as clues for locating it.
4. Look for clues by moving the eyes quickly over the page. When a section that appears to contain the answer is found, read it more carefully.
5. Find the answer, record it, and stop reading.

The following activities involve scanning:

1. Give the student a list of alphabetized items. Call out an item on the list and instruct the student to circle the item within 15 seconds. Once the student becomes proficient, the activity can be repeated with an unalphabetized list.
2. Give the student an unalphabetized list and related questions. Read a question and instruct the student to write the number of the question next to the appropriate word. Initially the time limit for each question is 30 seconds. As the student progresses, the time limit can be shortened to 10 seconds. A sample format is as follows:

___equator	___green	___sophomore
___mammals	___mare	___ewe
___sentence	___blue	___six
___red	___hog	___bull

1. What is the name for warm-blooded animals with fur or hair?
2. What do you call a female sheep?
3. What color is grass?
4. What do you call a group of words that expresses a complete thought?
5. The American flag is red, white, and _____.
6. In 10th grade you are called a _____.
7. How many class periods are in a day?
8. What do you call a female horse?
9. What do you call male cattle?
10. What color is an apple?
11. What do you call a male pig?
12. What is the imaginary line that runs around the earth?

This activity can be adapted to independent seatwork by having the student complete the task (match questions to words) within a specified time (for example, 2 to 6 minutes).

3. Give the student some questions from a chapter(s) she is studying in one of her classes. Indicate the page number where the answer to each question is found. Have the student answer each question using the following instructions and format:

Directions: Answer each question in 60 seconds or less. Each question has four steps: (a) find the page listed, (b) read the question, (c) scan the page to find the answer, and (d) write your answer.

1. (page 118) How long did Nat Turner's rebellion last? _____
2. (page 72) What states were included in the Northwest Territory? _____
3. (page 164) Why did Dred Scott think he should be a free man? _____
4. (page 210) What does the term "Jim Crow" mean? _____

4. Give the student some questions from a chapter she is studying in a content area. Vary the questions so that some key words are found in the index (for example, names, places, events) and others are found in the chapter (for example, section headings, italicized words, boldface print). Instruct the student to (a) identify key words for locating information in text, (b) locate the appropriate page number, (c) read the question, (d) scan the page to locate key words, and (e) answer the question.
5. Use the following activity as a pre/posttest or as a practice activity. Select 10 pages from different textbooks, and write 10 questions on 3″ × 5″ cards (one question per card). Have two questions each to cover (a) information contained in the heading, (b) information contained in topic sentences, (c) information contained in charts, graphs, or maps, (d) information contained in the index, and (e) information contained in key words or terms. Give the student one question along with the page number where the question is answered in the text. Have the student read

the question (begin timing), locate the answer, and write the answer (stop timing). Record the time. Continue in this manner until all questions are answered. Criterion is obtained when the student answers all questions correctly in a 10-minute time period (one question per minute).

Activities for reading-notetaking skills. Taking notes on material read for classes facilitates memory and often makes it unnecessary to reread the material at a later time. When a student takes notes on reading material, she is forced to think about the material and thus enhance recall of the content at a later date (Roe, Stoodt, & Burns, 1983). Moreover, the act of writing ideas helps the student remember content. Notetaking from reading material usually follows either an outline or a paraphrasing format. This section presents activities designed to develop or improve reading-notetaking skills.

1. Teach students how to use an outline format. The first step in making an outline is determining the main ideas. The next step involves locating the supportive ideas for each of the main ideas. The sequence continues by locating specific details that go with respective supportive ideas. A blank outline format is helpful in demonstrating the proper form.

Title

I. Main concept
   A. Information supporting I
   B. Information supporting I
      1. Specific information supporting B
      2. Specific information supporting B
         a. Specific information supporting 2
         b. Specific information supporting 2
   C. Information supporting I
II. Main concept
   A. Information supporting II
   B. Information supporting II
   C. Information supporting II
      1. Specific information supporting C
      2. Specific information supporting C

2. To demonstrate outlining, show the student how the headings in her textbook chapter indicate different levels of subordination. For example, in many textbooks the center headings would be Roman numerals in an outline, side headings would be capital letters in an outline, and italic or paragraph headings would be Arabic numerals in an outline.

3. Provide partially completed outlines and instruct the student to complete them (Roe, Stoodt, & Burns, 1983).

Title (Given by teacher)

I. (Given by teacher)
   A. (Given by teacher)
      1. (Completed by student)
      2. (Completed by student)
   B. (Given by teacher)
      1. (Given by teacher)
      2. (Completed by student)
II. (Completed by student)
   A. (Given by teacher)
   B. (Completed by student)

This technique may gradually increase in difficulty until the teacher provides only the structural arrangement. For example:

Title

I.
   A.
      1.
      2.
   B.
      1.
      2.
II.
   A.
   B.

The relevancy of this task is enhanced if the teacher uses textbooks from the student's regular content classes.

4. To facilitate notetaking from printed material, teach the student to use a columnar format (Saski, Swicegood, & Carter, 1983). For example, in the following format, the 2″ column on the left side is used to record main ideas, the 6″ col-

umn is used to record supporting details of the main ideas, and the 2" space at the bottom is used to summarize ideas, raise questions, and pinpoint areas of concern.

2"	6"	
major ideas, concepts, topics	supportive information, details, ideas	
summary information and questions		2"

5. Give the student several paragraphs and several summaries. Instruct her to select the best summary of the paragraphs. Point out the importance of locating the main idea (usually the topic sentence of a paragraph) and essential supporting details.

6. Give the student passages from a textbook she is using and instruct her to write a summary by following these steps: (a) locate the main idea, (b) locate essential supportive details, and (c) write information as concisely as possible, leaving out illustrative material and statements that merely elaborate on main ideas.

Activities for using visual aids. Secondary textbooks are replete with visual aids, and adolescents with learning problems need to be taught how to use and understand them. This section presents activities and techniques for developing skills in the use of various types of visual aids.

1. Explain that a map represents a geographic area. Review the following map-reading steps (Roe, Stoodt, & Burns, 1983): locate and comprehend the title of the map; determine map directions; interpret the map legend; apply the map's scale; discuss common map terms (for example, latitude, longitude, equator, gulf, bay, continent); and make inferences from map material (for example, climate, population, industry).

2. Provide the student with index cards with a map legend on one side and its use or definition on the other side. Instruct the student to define or describe the legend's use and turn the card over to check her answer.

3. Present the student with road maps, and instruct her to estimate miles between locations and write directions from one place to another.

4. Provide the student with a table, and explain that it includes information arranged in vertical columns and horizontal rows. Review the following table-reading steps: locate and comprehend the title of the table; determine information located in columns; determine information located in rows; and locate specific information through pinpointing intersections.

5. Instruct the student to make a table of respective cities and their average monthly temperatures or of her class periods and corresponding 6-week grades.

6. Use sample graphs to explain the four basic types of graphs: picture, circle, bar, and line graphs. Roe, Stoodt, and Burns (1983) recommend that teachers help students interpret graphs by reviewing the following steps:

a. The purpose of the graph (Usually indicated by the title, the purpose becomes more evident when the accompanying narrative is studied.)

b. The scale of measure on bar and line graphs

c. The legend of picture graphs

d. The items being compared

e. The location of specific pieces of information within a graph (For example, finding the intersection of the point of interest on the vertical axis with the point of interest on the horizontal axis.)

f. The trends indicated by a graph (For example, does an amount increase or decrease over a period of time?)

g. The application of graphic information to actual life situations (A graph showing the temperatures for each month in Sydney, Australia, could be used for planning what clothes to take for a particular time of the year.) (p. 134)

7. Instruct the student to make a line graph using her reading rate (words per minute) in textbooks for various subjects.

8. Instruct the student to make a bar graph of the heights of the starting lineups for two basketball teams. A basketball program may be used to provide the data. This activity can be adapted to various sports and selected information (for example, football—weights; baseball—batting averages).

9. Have the student make a circle graph of how she spends time (for example, in school, sleeping, playing, eating, and miscellaneous).

10. Instruct the student to make a picture graph from the following information: Dallas scored 70 touchdowns; Washington scored 76; Miami scored 47; Pittsburgh, 64; San Francisco, 37; New York, 54; Denver, 62. Let the symbol ⊕ = 10 touchdowns.

11. Use a model to demonstrate how diagrams are used to picture events, processes, structures, relationships, or sequences described in a textbook. Highlight the use of arrows, labelling, and various degrees of shading in diagrams.

12. Instruct the student to make a diagram of a basketball play and orally present it to the teacher or class.

13. For practice or for a pre/posttest format in assessing visual aids, provide the student with a map, table, graph, or diagram, and ask questions pertaining to purpose, legend, columns, and specific information from the visual aid.

14. Instruct the student to use the following cognitive strategy for reading visual aids (Ellis & Lenz, 1987):

R = Read the written material until you are referred to a visual aid or until the material is not making sense.

V = View the visual aid using CLUE.

    C = Clarify the stated facts in the written material.

    L = Locate the main ideas (global) and details (specific parts).

    U = Uncover the signal words (look for captions or words in the visual aid).

    E = Examine the logic (Does what you "read" from the picture make sense in light of what you read in the material?).

A = Ask yourself about the relationship between the visual aid and the written material using FUR.

    F = Ask how the visual aid and the written material "Fit" together.

    U = Ask how the visual aid can help you "Understand" the written material.

    R = Ask how the visual aid can help you "Remember" the written material.

S = Summarize the most important information.

Sequential Study Methods

Several methods have been developed to help students obtain and organize information from textbooks. F. P. Robinson (1946) developed the SQ3R method, which remains one of the most widely known study methods. The steps in SQ3R (survey, question, read, recite, and review) are discussed in Chapter 11. It is apparent that study methods hold much promise for teaching secondary students with learning problems, but systematic applications are needed to determine the effectiveness of various methods with specific populations (Schumaker, Deshler, Alley, Warner, & Denton, 1982). This section presents study methods for students with learning problems.

Multipass. Multipass is an adaptation of SQ3R designed to teach learning disabled adolescents effective study skills. The Multipass steps include the following:

1. *Survey Pass* is designed to obtain the main ideas and organization of the chapter. In this step the student is instructed to do the following:

a. Read the chapter title.

b. Read the introductory paragraph.

c. Review the chapter's relationship to adjacent chapters by examining the table of contents.

d. Read primary subtitles of the chapter and determine the chapter organization.

e. Note illustrations and read their captions.

f. Read the chapter summary.

g. Paraphrase the information gained in the preceding steps.

2. *Size-Up Pass* is designed for the student to gain specific information and facts from the chapter without reading it from beginning to end. In this step the student's instructions are as follows:

a. Read each question at the end of the chapter, and determine what information is important to learn. If the student can answer a question, a checkmark is placed next to the question.

b. Go through the entire chapter following these guidelines: look for textual cues (for example, italicized words, boldface print, subtitles); make the cue into a question (for example, if the cue italicized word is *mitosis,* the student asks "What is mitosis?"); skim through surrounding text to locate the answer to the question; and orally paraphrase the answer without looking at the book.

c. Paraphrase all the ideas and facts obtained from applying these four steps to all contextual cues in the chapter.

3. *Sort-Out Pass* is designed to get the student to test herself on the material in the chapter. In this step the student reads and answers each question at the end of the chapter. If the student can immediately answer a question, a checkmark is placed next to the question. If the student is unable to answer the question, she should follow these steps:

a. Think about the section that most likely contains the answer.

b. Skim through that section for the answer, and checkmark the question if the answer is found.

c. If the answer is not in that section, continue to think and skim until the answer is located and the question is checkmarked.

S.O.S. The S.O.S. strategy is an alternative version of Multipass for students with reading abilities four or more years below their grade level. It includes the same three passes over the textbook as specified in Multipass but, in addition, uses a visually marked version and an audiotaped version of the chapter. Schumaker et al. (1983) recommend that a paraprofessional modify the chapter (that is, mark and tape the chapter). The marking system consists of highlighting important facts, main ideas, key words, and the like. After the chapter is marked, it is read (not verbatim but according to markings) into a cassette tape recorder. Thus, the tape stresses important content and reduces information that can be presented in a few sentences. Each chapter tape is limited to no more than 90 minutes. The students are taught to survey, obtain details, and test themselves (that is, Multipass steps). During the use of the S.O.S. strategy, students complete an organizer outline. Schumaker et al. (1983) report that this process makes the student an active learner while she is listening to the tape.

PANORAMA. The PANORAMA study technique includes eight steps divided into three stages (Edwards, 1973), as follows:

Preparatory Stage:

1. Purpose. The learner determines why the material is being read.

2. Adapting rate to material. The teacher decides at what rate the material should be read. This involves maintaining flexibility of rate within sections as a function of the type of content being covered. For example, on an initial reading, if the main idea is being presented, the rate is slow, whereas elaboration and expansion content may be read more rapidly.
3. Need to pose questions. The student uses headings or cue words to develop questions.

Intermediate Stage:

4. Overview. The student surveys the major parts of the chapter to determine the organization of the material.
5. Read and relate. The student reads the material in terms of a specified purpose. Specific answers to questions are sought.
6. Annotate. Written annotations (paraphrases, outlines) of main ideas, key words, and concepts are made.

Concluding Stage:

7. Memorize. The student uses outlines and summaries to learn the important content. Acronyms and associations are used to facilitate recall of main points.
8. Assess. The student assesses her efforts in relation to the purpose of the reading (for example, answers questions).

Study-Rehearsal Skills

Secondary students are expected to retain much of the information they obtain through lectures and readings. The retention of material is greatly facilitated by study-rehearsal strategies. Towle (1982) states, "Rehearsal involves practicing or using information under cued conditions" (p. 92). She notes that students need a strategy for rehearsing organized content (notes, outlines, summaries, discussions, or demonstrations).

Activities. A number of activities for rehearsal of material are suggested below:

1. Have the student rehearse from various content formats (Towle, 1982). For example:
   a. Rehearsing notes: Rework notes, make up test questions, construct lists of important points, write summaries, review with classmates.
   b. Rehearsing outlines: Verbalize the content by giving a lecture from the outline, construct graphic aids (diagrams, charts, graphs) from the outline.
   c. Rehearsing discussion: Write a summary, use supplementary materials, give examples to support important points.
   d. Rehearsing demonstrations: Role play, practice segments of behavior chains, practice with peers and critique each other.
2. Encourage the student to use verbal rehearsal in reviewing content. This basic step in the learning-strategies teaching sequence can be used in the initial learning of material and in reviewing it. Verbal rehearsal basically involves self-instructional training, which has received much support in facilitating learning (Flavell, 1976; Meichenbaum, 1975). (The cognitive behavior modification section in Chapter 5 presents the steps in verbal rehearsal.)
3. Instruct the student to use questioning strategies when reviewing content. Alley and Hori (1981) increased the reading comprehension of learning disabled adolescents through a questioning treatment based on Manzo's (1969) ReQuest Procedure. The treatment consisted of the following steps:
   a. Appropriate reading material is selected, and the teacher and student read two or three paragraphs following these steps: Both read the first sentence silently; the student asks as many questions as she can pertaining to the sentence, and the teacher answers them; the teacher asks the student questions pertaining

to the sentence, and the student answers them.

b. After several paragraphs are read using the above steps, the student is instructed to write a question or make a prediction about the outcome of the story. The student then reads and answers her question or checks her prediction.

4. To help the student rehearse information for later recall, use the following activities and suggestions (Roe, Stoodt, & Burns, 1983):

a. Have the student review material with a specific purpose (for example, to answer a question).

b. Encourage the student to obtain an understanding of the organization of the material through outlining. This helps the student categorize information to be learned under main headings.

c. Instruct the student to visualize what the text or notes are trying to present.

d. Encourage the student to make notes during rehearsal. In addition to facilitating retention, writing keeps the learner actively involved.

e. Have the student summarize main and supporting information in her own words. Rewording the content helps improve understanding.

f. Encourage the student to discuss the material with a classmate.

g. Instruct the student to review notes or the text as soon as possible after initial contact with the material. Immediate review can strengthen understanding, accuracy, and associations involving the material.

h. Instruct the student to rehearse to a criterion level (for example, answer review questions at 100% accuracy without referring to notes or the book).

5. Instruct the student to use the following cognitive strategies (Ellis & Lenz, 1987):

a. EASY: A strategy for studying content
   E = Elicit *wh* questions to identify important information *(who, what, when, where, why).*
   A = Ask yourself which information is least troublesome.

S = Study easy parts first, hardest parts last.
Y = Yes—do use self-reinforcement.

b. LISTS: A strategy for learning content
   L = Look for clues.
   I = Investigate the items.
   S = Select a mnemonic device using FIRST.
      F = Form a word.
      I = Insert letters.
      R = Rearrange letters.
      S = Shape a sentence.
      T = Try combinations.
   T = Transfer information to a card.
   S = Self-test.

Knowledge Expression and Application Skills

To succeed in high school, students must be able to demonstrate knowledge on classroom tests, minimum competency tests, and written assignments. Moreover, the application of knowledge in real-life settings becomes important to successful independent living during and after high school.

Activities for developing test-taking skills.

The following activities are suggested for helping students develop their test-taking skills:

1. Instruct the student to determine what general information is relevant in preparing for a test. The following list may be used as a guide or reminder:

   Subject content _____

   Date of test _____

   Chapters covered _____

   Notes covered _____

   Type of questions _____

   Number of questions _____

   Timed or untimed test _____

   Information emphasized in class _____

   Also, to facilitate test preparation, give the student a test that has been used previously.

2. Identify vocabulary terms that are frequently used in test directions. Instruct the student to define the terms and perform the specified behavior. For example:

a. Compare means . . .
Contrast means . . .
Compare and contrast milk and water.

b. Criticize means . . .
Criticize some aspect of your school schedule.

c. Illustrate means . . .
Illustrate the difference between a triangle and a circle.

d. Evaluate means . . .
Evaluate the importance of reading.

Other words that may be covered include *discuss, list, justify, outline, diagram, trace, match, define,* and *elaborate.*

3. Present the SCORER system (Carman & Adams, 1972) as a strategy for helping students take tests. Each letter represents an important rule in test taking.

S = *Schedule* your time. The student reviews the entire test and plans time according to the number of items, point value per item, and easy and difficult items.

C = Look for *clue* words. The student searches for clue words on each item. For example, on true–false items words such as *always* and *never* usually indicate the statement is incorrect. Words such as *usually* and *sometimes* frequently indicate the statement is correct.

O = *Omit* difficult questions. Postponing hard questions until later in the testing session can greatly improve a student's score. Specifically, Carman and Adams (1972) suggest that the student use the following procedure:

(a) Move rapidly through the test.

(b) When you find an easy question or one you are certain of, answer it.

(c) Omit the difficult ones on the first pass.

(d) When you skip a question, make a mark in the margin (– or $\sqrt{}$). (Do not use a red pencil or pen. Your marks could get confused with grader's marks.)

(e) Keep moving. Never erase. Don't dawdle. Jot brief notes in the margin for later use if you need to.

(f) When you have finished the easy ones, return to those with marks (– or $\sqrt{}$), and try again.

(g) Mark again those answers you are still not sure of. Change the – to + or $\sqrt{}$ to $\sqrt{}\sqrt{}$.

(h) In your review (that's the last R in SCORER), you will go over all the questions time permits, first the $\sqrt{}\sqrt{}$, then the $\sqrt{}$, then the unmarked. (p. 217)

R = *Read* carefully. A careful reading of test directions and each item can significantly improve test performance. Careless reading can lead to confusion on essay items and careless errors on objective items.

E = *Estimate* your answers. On test items requiring calculations or problem solving the student should roughly estimate the answer. This helps correct careless errors. Moreover, if guessing is not penalized, it is important to answer all questions. After eliminating alternatives that are obviously incorrect, the student should take a best guess.

R = *Review* your work. The student should be encouraged to use every minute available. After she has answered all items, have her review the test. Carman and Adams (1972) suggest the student use the following checklist:

(a) Return to the double-checked ($\sqrt{}\sqrt{}$) difficult questions. Reread them. Look for clue words. Look for new hints. Then go to the $\sqrt{}$ questions, and finally to the unmarked ones if there is still time.

(b) Don't be too eager to change answers. Change only if you have a good reason for changing.

(c) Be certain you have considered all questions.

(d) PRINT your name on the test. If there are separate sheets, print your name on each sheet. (p. 222)

4. Present the following activities and guidelines to help the student with answering true–false test items:
   a. Note the following rule to remember with true–false items: A statement must be completely true to be true. If any part of the statement is false, the whole statement is false.
   b. Instruct the student to be careful about tricky words. Some of these words include *some, many, most, everyone, no one, never,* and *always.* Demonstrate how these words cue true and false statements.
   c. Instruct the student to notice that directions to true–false items may vary. Sample directions include the following:
      (1) Next to each statement, print *T* for true or *F* for false.
      (2) Write the word *true* or the word *false* on the line next to each statement.
      (3) If a statement is true, do nothing to it. If a statement is false, cross out the part that makes it false. Rewrite the part you crossed out to make a true statement.
   d. Instruct the student to look for reworded statements in which positive or negative words have been used to change the answer.
5. Present the following activities and guidelines to help the student with answering multiple-choice test items:
   a. Explain to the student that in most multiple-choice questions several alternatives are usually easy to eliminate because they are obviously incorrect. Frequently two alternatives seem correct, but instructions require the selection of the *best* answer.
   b. Provide the student with sample multiple-choice items that illustrate different ways of thinking. For example, use items that include such key words as *except, not,* and *all of the above.*
   c. Encourage the student to use the following guidelines with multiple-choice items:
      (1) Know how many answers to select.
      (2) Be aware of the kind of answer you are seeking (for example, for a negative question).

   (3) Remember the question.
   (4) Eliminate the obvious wrong answers.
   (5) Choose the answer that fits best.
   (6) Be careful in recording the answer.
6. Present the following activities and guidelines to help the student with answering essay questions:
   a. Instruct the student to read the directions and questions carefully and underline key words. In directions, the student should underline such parts as *answer two of the following questions.* In questions, key words include *discuss, compare, list,* etc.
   b. Instruct the student to outline or organize the answer before attempting to write it (Alley & Deshler, 1979). If time becomes a serious factor, the question can be finished in outline form.
   c. Teach the student to use the SCORER system with essay questions.
7. Instruct the student to use the following techniques when taking all tests:
   a. Review the entire test.
   b. Know the time allotted for taking the test.
   c. Know the value of specific questions.
   d. Follow the directions very carefully.
   e. Notice key words in instructions and questions.
   f. Reread directions and questions.
   g. Go through the test and answer questions you are sure of first.
   h. Place a checkmark beside questions you need to return to later.
   i. Return to questions that have been checked.
   j. Mark an *X* at the bottom of each completed page.
   k. Review all questions.
8. Use a test that the student has taken previously to review ways in which her performance can be improved.
9. Provide the student with a machine-scorable sheet and a set of multiple-choice questions. Instruct her to answer each test question by filling in the appropriate space. Many students with learning problems have difficulty with standardized and minimum competency tests. Practice in using different types of answer formats helps students develop skills with these formats.

Activities and strategies for developing written expression skills. To survive in the secondary curriculum, students with learning problems must be able to express their knowledge in writing. Projects, papers, and essay tests require a degree of writing skills. Several methods (for example, COPS and TOWER) and activities for teaching written expression are presented in Chapter 13. This section features some of the work from the University of Kansas Institute that pertains to teaching written expression strategies.

Moran, Schumaker, and Vetter (1981) conducted a study in which learning disabled adolescents were able to write organized paragraphs after receiving paragraph organization training. The students learned to write three paragraph styles (enumerative, sequential, and compare/contrast) by following these three steps: (a) write a topic sentence; (b) write a minimum of three detail sentences; (c) write an ending or clincher sentence.

Schumaker et al. (1981) conducted a study in which learning disabled adolescents were taught an error-monitoring strategy. This strategy is designed to enable a student to locate and correct errors in written material. Their results indicate that the training improved learning disabled students' ability to detect and correct errors in written work. Moreover, the error rate in the students' self-generated products was very low (almost zero) after training. In addition to following the teaching sequence described at the beginning of the learning strategies section, Schumaker et al. (1981) used these steps to teach the error-monitoring strategy:

1. Provide the student with teacher-generated one-page passages, with some at the student's ability level and some at her grade level. Capitalization errors, appearance errors, and spelling errors are included in each passage.

2. Teach the student to detect and correct errors in the teacher-generated passages by following these procedures:
   a. Read each sentence separately.
   b. Ask the COPS questions (explained in Chapter 13).
   c. When an error is detected, circle it and put the correct form above the error.
   d. Ask for help if unsure of an item.
3. Teach the student to monitor her own work by following these steps:
   a. Use every other line as you write the rough draft.
   b. As you read a sentence, ask the COPS questions.
   c. When an error is located, write the correct form above it.
   d. Ask for help if unsure about a correct form.
   e. Copy the paragraph neatly before giving it to the teacher.
   f. Reread the paragraph as a final check.

Ellis and Lenz (1987) present two cognitive strategies for developing written expression skills:

1. DEFENDS: A writing strategy for defending a position
   D = Decide on your exact position.
   E = Examine the reasons for your position.
   F = Form a list of points that explain each reason.
   E = Expose your position in the first sentence.
   N = Note each reason and supporting points.
   D = Drive home the position in the last sentence.
   S = SEARCH for errors and correct.
     S = See if it makes sense.
     E = Eject incomplete sentences.
     A = Ask if it is convincing.
     R = Reveal COPS errors and correct.
       C = Capitalization
       O = Overall appearance
       P = Punctuation
       S = Spelling
     C = Copy over neatly.
     H = Have a last look.

2. WRITER: A monitoring for written-errors strategy

W = Write on every other line.

R = Read the paper for meaning.

I = Interrogate yourself using COPS questions.

    C = Have I capitalized the first word and all proper nouns?

    O = How is the overall appearance?

    P = Have I used end punctuation, commas, and semicolons correctly?

    S = Do the words look like they are spelled right, can I sound them out, or should I use the dictionary?

T = Take the paper to someone to proofread again.

E = Execute a final copy.

R = Reread your paper a final time.

Commercial Materials for Teaching Learning Strategies

The following selected commercial materials may be helpful in teaching various learning strategies to secondary students.

Learning How to Learn: Teaching Strategies

Publisher: DLM Teaching Resources

Description:

This program presents learning techniques for use in academic, social, and vocational settings. It is designed for students with learning problems from junior high level to adult age. The program consists of five resource manuals which focus on skills in studying, reading, writing, listening, and teaching. For example, in the writing skills manual, instructional activities are provided in areas such as highlighting main ideas, taking lecture notes, and using appropriate format. An implementation guide and 20 blackline masters are also included.

Listening and Notetaking Skills

Publisher: Educational Activities

Description:

This material consists of 10 cassette tapes and activity books which teach students how to prepare for listening to a lecture, how to grasp the main and supporting ideas, and how to write a simple summary. In addition, students learn abbreviations and speedwriting and are taught to use the indented outline form and edit their own notes. Each lesson gives relevant methods of listening or notetaking, as well as practice using the methods taught through actual lectures presented on the cassette tapes.

Study Skills Series

Publisher: Media Materials

Description:

This series consists of five filmstrips and accompanying activity workbooks written at the fourth- to fifth-grade reading level. *How to Follow Directions* shows how to read and follow oral and written directions. *Learning to Outline* presents the correct format of an outline and teaches how to locate information needed for an outline. *Reading Tables* focuses on being able to read and interpret one-column and multicolumn tables, and *Reading Graphs* teaches how to read and interpret picture graphs, circle graphs, line graphs, and bar graphs. Finally, *Taking Tests* is designed to help students develop a strategy for taking objective and essay tests.

Test Taking Techniques

Publisher: Educational Activities

Description:

This program consists of four cassette tapes and 10 activity books that teach ways to approach actual test situations and help establish positive mental attitudes toward test taking. Students are taught how to prepare for tests by using lecture and textbook notes to study, and emphasis is placed on the skill of predicting possible test questions. Specific hints are given on how to deal with objective as well as essay questions. In addition, practice sessions using sample material stress techniques such as making margin notes and underlining important points to make reviewing material more efficient.

Computer Software Programs for Teaching Learning Strategies

The following software programs focus on teaching effective study skills to secondary students, as well as helping them learn how to read in the content areas.

Essential Study Skills Series

Producer: Media Materials

Hardware: Apple II, TRS–80

Description:

This series includes five programs designed to develop essential study skills: (a) *Test Taking Success*—preparing for a test and recognizing answers; (b) *Learning to Read and Understand Tables*—using a chart, retrieving data, and making inferences and conclusions; (c) *Discover What Graphs Can Tell You*—identifying line, bar, circle, and picture graphs, extracting data, and making inferences and conclusions; (d) *Following Directions*—using clue words, picturing the directions, and noticing the order; (e) *Using Outlining Skills*—finding topic sentences, main ideas, and details, and making an outline; and (f) *Key References Skills*—alphabetizing, using parts of a book, and using reference materials. Supplemental materials in workbook format and an instructor's guide are included.

How to Read in the Content Areas

Distributor: Educational Activities

Hardware: Apple II, TRS–80, PET, Commodore 64 with emulator, Atari

Description:

These programs are designed to help students learn how to read effectively in the content areas of science, social studies, literature, and mathematics. The following concepts are featured: (a) spotlighting (vocabulary building); (b) surveying to determine the information given in a particular reading; (c) detecting main ideas and inferences; (d) recalling important facts, ideas, and details; and (e) utilizing skills by applying them to content areas. The programs are self-correcting and include immediate reteaching and reinforcement of skills not mastered.

REGULAR COURSE WORK WITH SUPPORTIVE INSTRUCTION

Most secondary students with learning problems spend the majority of their school day in mainstream classes. Mainstream class teachers use numerous instructional alternatives designed to ameliorate the problems of these students. These alternatives often are referred to as accommodation techniques, compensatory techniques, or instructional adaptations. Laurie, Buchwach, Silverman, and Zigmond (1978) recommend that special and regular educators follow a problem-solving sequence in developing instructional alternatives for students with learning problems. Steps in a problem-solving sequence include the following:

1. Determine the requirements for "making it" in the regular class.
2. Specify the course requirements that the student is not satisfying.
3. Identify factors hindering the student's performance.
4. Brainstorm possible classroom modifications.
5. Select a plan of action.
6. Implement the plan.
7. Evaluate the plan.

Determining the types of modifications needed is critical in providing program alternatives. The discussion in Chapter 2 on factors that influence how a student learns offers many areas for consideration. In addition, the alternatives listed by Laurie et al. (1978), shown in Table 14.3, provide possibilities for modifications.

This section presents instructional alternatives in the following areas: (a) presenting information, (b) adapting materials, (c) administering tests, and (d) applying administrative programming. Finally, specific activities and programs in science and social studies are presented.

Alternatives for Presenting Information

1. Use *advance organizers* to enhance the student's comprehension of content area material (Lenz, 1982). The following components should be included in an advance organizer:
   a. Provide background information.
   b. Motivate students to learn.
   c. Point out the advance organizer to the students.
   d. Identify topics and tasks.

TABLE 14.3
Instructional alternatives for a mainstream teacher.

Classroom Organization	Classroom Management	Methods of Presentation	Methods of Practice	Methods of Testing
Vary Grouping Arrangements •large group instruction •small group instruction •individual instruction •peer tutoring •independent self-instructional activities •learning centers **Vary Methods of Instruction** •teacher directed •student directed	**Vary Grading System** •homework •tests •class discussion •special projects **Vary Reinforcement System** •praise •notes sent home •grades •free time •special activity •tangibles •progress charts **Vary Rules** •differentiated for some students •explicit/implicit	**Vary Content** •amount to be learned •time to learn new information •conceptual level **Vary General Structure** •advanced organizers •previewing questions •cues, mnemonic devices •provide immediate feedback •involve students actively **Vary Type** •verbal — lecture, discussion •written – texts, worksheets •demonstration •audio-visuals •tape recorders •filmstrips •movies •opaque projectors •transparencies	**Vary General Structure** •amount to be practiced •time for practice •group/individual •teacher-directed/ independent •items ranging from easy to difficult **Vary Level of Response** •copying •recognition •recall with cues •recall without cues **Vary Type of Materials** •worksheets •texts •audio-visual equipment	**Vary Type** •verbal •written •demonstration **Vary General Structure** •group/individual •amount to be tested •time for completion **Vary Level of Response** •recognition •recall with cues •recall

Source: From "Teaching Secondary Learning Disabled Students in the Mainstream" by T.E. Laurie, L. Buchwach, R. Silverman, and N. Zigmond, 1978, *Learning Disability Quarterly*, 1(4), p. 68. Copyright 1978 by the Division for Children with Learning Disabilities. Reprinted by permission.

e. Provide a structured framework for the class period.

f. Clarify required activity.

g. Introduce vocabulary.

h. State concepts to be learned.

i. Clarify concepts to be learned.

j. State expected outcome.

2. Provide a list of simple questions prior to a lecture or reading assignment to serve as an effective advance organizer (Marsh, Price, & Smith, 1983).

3. Provide written backup to oral directions and lectures (for example, use outline on handout or overhead).

4. Use the following activities for presenting information to the student who has difficulty with auditory input (Towle, 1982):

a. Provide pre-presentation questions.

b. Develop vocabulary prior to presentation.

c. Pace presentation and give frequent examples.

d. Cluster main points.

e. Summarize.

f. Provide opportunities for student questions and discussion.

g. Repeat important points.

h. Relate content to other topics.

5. For the student who has difficulty following oral presentations, provide tapes of the lectures or allow her to record the class presentation and discussions. In addition, good notetakers can use carbon paper to make copies of their notes for problem learners, or photocopies of notes can be given to problem learners.

6. Instruct the student with learning problems to sit in front of the class. This encourages her to attend to teacher-directed activities and reduces distractions.

7. Match a problem learner with a peer helper who can assist her by (a) explaining directions and assignments, (b) reviewing essential information from a lecture, (c) sharing and correcting notes, and (d) working on joint assignments or projects.

8. Use the following suggestions to help the student maintain attention and learn:

a. Combine visual and auditory presentations.

b. Establish eye contact with students during oral directions and lectures.

c. Write assignments, directions, and lecture objectives on the chalkboard.

d. Pause after questions to provide thinking time.

e. Pause after each segment while giving directions and presenting content.

f. Give examples and demonstrations.

g. Briefly review information from previous lectures, and summarize information at the end of each lecture.

h. Provide the student with time after the lecture for reviewing and improving her notes.

i. Talk distinctly and at a reasonable rate.

j. Give cues concerning what is important, and refer students to textbook pages for more clarification or information.

9. Use a pause procedure during lectures to improve the recall of adolescents with learning problems (Hughes, Hendrickson, & Hudson, 1986). Pause several times during a lecture (for example, every 6 to 8 minutes) in order for students to discuss the content covered.

Alternatives for Adapting Materials

The difficulty level of texts and materials used in mainstreamed classes presents a problem to secondary students with learning difficulties, because the reading level is usually several grades above that of the student. To assist the student in learning, it is often necessary to modify or adapt the ways in which content is presented. The goal of these modifications is to change the format and mode of presentation while maintaining the basic content. Alternatives for adapting materials are presented in the following areas: (a) developing parallel curriculum, (b) simplifying texts, and (c) taping texts.

Developing parallel curriculum. Wiseman (1980) popularized the Parallel Alternative Curriculum (PAC) by means of a demonstration project. He notes that it is a compensatory model primarily developed by regular educators with special education support. Although the total PAC program has numerous components (for example, parent involvement, remediation), the heart of the program features the development of curriculum materials that present essential content in ways that help the problem learner organize, practice, and master important information.

School districts provide regular and special educators with release time or summer employment to write curriculum guides for various courses. These guides are designed for use with all low achievers. Thus, a low achiever receives the standard text and a curriculum guide or booklet. For example, Project PASS (Packets Assuring Student Success) is a mainstreamed secondary program for students experiencing difficulties in U.S. history and American government. The materials consist of 98 instructional packets in U.S. history and 55 packets in American government. A module contains vocabulary, glossary, pre/posttest, subject content, activities, and projects, and the material is written at the third- to fifth-grade reading level. (Information is available from Project PASS, Livonia Public School District, 15125 Farmington Road, Livonia, MI 48154.)

Likewise, in Tallahassee, Florida, a series of Parallel Alternative Curriculum (PAC) booklets and Parallel Alternative Strategies for Students (PASS) booklets have been developed in Project IMPRESS. To date, these materials exist for 11th- and 12th-grade American history, 8th- and 9th-grade social studies, 7th- and 8th-grade science, English I BASIC, comparative economic systems, and health and human biology. Most instructional units in a packet contain target vocabulary, vocabulary exercises, content exercises, unit test, and answer key. Project IMPRESS is a Title IV–B program funded by the Florida State Department of Education. It includes eight components (for example, learning strategies, remediation, PAC) and has had excellent success through-out Florida. The PAC and PASS booklets are credited with much of the program's positive impact. (Additional information on Project IMPRESS is available from Kent Hamilton, Project Manager; Debra Stokes-Coachman, Project Secretary; Project IMPRESS, Fairview Middle School, 3415 Zillah Road, Tallahassee, FL 32310.)

Simplifying texts. The simplification of textbooks assists low achievers to master essential information efficiently. The following activities and procedures can be used for simplifying texts:

1. Provide the student with a highlighted text. Highlighting the main ideas, words, and concepts with a marker pen or underlining helps the student focus on relevant material. Also, the deletion of irrelevant or nonessential words with a dark pen serves to identify important content.
2. Provide the student with a cut-and-paste revision. The main ideas or specific content can be cut from the text and pasted on separate sheets of paper. This procedure has several advantages: (a) material can be arranged sequentially, (b) additional headings can be inserted to aid organization, (c) distracting and nonessential material can be removed, (d) segments of content can be presented in small units, (e) material can be used without rewriting it, and (f) the revision can be photocopied for use with several students.
3. Transform words into graphic aids by creating charts, graphs, drawings, or models. Also, real materials are helpful in presenting content.
4. Use advance organizers to prepare the student for the reading material. These include outlines, diagrammatic overviews, study guides, questions, and directed previewing (for example, attention to selected headings or illustrations).
5. Reduce the complexity and length of work units to the extent that the low achiever receives periodic and consistent closure.
6. Provide self-correcting learning materials. Self-checking answer keys at frequent intervals are helpful checkpoints to guide the student through the material.

7. When simplifying texts, concentrate on content, sentence structure, and vocabulary (Beech, 1983). In simplifying content, it is helpful to (a) present generalizations first and follow with supporting details, (b) sequence events in chronological order, and (c) cluster related material.

8. For the student with limited reading skills, consider using rewritten texts. Some school districts employ paraprofessionals to give teachers extra time, or they offer summer employment for rewriting of texts. In situations where rewriting is feasible, the following guidelines are helpful:

   a. Keep sentences short; a five- to eight-word total is best.
   b. Use basic words of few syllables. Coleman (1979) recommends using the 850 words included in Ogden's (1970) *Basic English Dictionary.*
   c. Use present tense and avoid passive voice.
   d. Use simple sentences and try to begin each sentence with a subject. Avoid appositives and parenthetical expressions. Simple sentences with the verb following the subject are easier to read than compound and complex sentences or sentences in inverted order.
   e. Avoid figurative or symbolic language (for example, change "thundering herd" to, "The herd galloped so hard the hoofs sounded like thunder when they hit the ground").
   f. Use picture clues as much as possible.
   g. Be certain that every pronoun has an unmistakable antecedent.
   h. Use new words sparingly. Repeating key words rather than using synonyms results in simpler content.
   i. Eliminate unnecessary words.

Taping texts. An alternative to reading a textbook is to listen to it on tape. Taped texts can be provided to the student in two ways. One is to qualify the student for the special recordings provided for the blind and learning disabled. (Applications are available from Recordings for the Blind, 214 East 58th Street, New York, NY 10022.) In addition to their existing tapes, this service provides book taping of requested books at no charge. Another way to provide

tapes is for teachers, students, or parents to prepare them. The following is a list of guidelines for taping:

1. Tape in a quiet place where there are rugs, draperies, and upholstered furniture to absorb extraneous noises.
2. Place the microphone on the table approximately six inches from the recorder's mouth. Turn the volume control approximately halfway, and read a portion of the material. Listen to the tape, and adjust the volume and microphone location until desirable recording is obtained.
3. Eliminate clicks by turning the volume on low before turning the recorder on. At the end of the recording let the tape run for a few moments and then gradually turn the volume down and off.
4. Avoid recording during the first 5 seconds and take a break every 15 seconds. Use alternating voices to reduce boredom.
5. Monitor the tape before giving it to the student.
6. At the beginning of the tape, identify the title of the text, author, and chapters or portions to be read.
7. Include the following directions in the initial text information: "Please stop the tape any time you wish to answer questions, write notes for yourself, or look at a section of the book more carefully. You will hear this sound (ring bell) at the end of each page to help you follow along in your textbook. Please turn to page ____ for the beginning of chapter ____."
8. Include selected study questions at the beginning of the tape. This alerts the student to important content.

Alternatives for Administering Tests

Students with learning problems often have difficulty displaying their knowledge or skills on tests. Modifications in test formats often help them perform better. This section presents suggestions for improving test performances.

1. Give frequent, timed minitests so that testing is not such an isolated anxiety-provoking situation. Give practice tests and have students test each other and review answers.

2. Use alternative response forms when existing formats appear to be a barrier to student expression (Towle, 1982). Variations between and within response formats (for example, essay, multiple choice, short answer) are possible.

   a. Multiple-choice alternatives include using yes or no questions, reducing the number of choices, providing more information from which to make a choice, and using matching items.

   b. Short-answer alternatives include providing a list of facts and information to use in the answer, allowing the student to list information or choose from several prepared short answers, using the cloze technique in prepared paragraphs, and scrambling information to be arranged.

   c. Essay alternatives include providing a partial outline for the student to complete, allowing the student to tape answers, noting important points to be included in the response, and using take-home tests.

3. Back up the written test with a tape of the test items. Tapes allow the student to hear instructions and items as well as read them. Also, tapes are convenient for test makeups.

4. Leave ample white space between test questions, and underline key words in the directions and test items.

5. Provide test-study guides which feature a variety of answer formats (for example, essay, multiple choice, fill in the blank).

6. Provide additional time for the student who writes slowly, or use test items that require minimal writing. Oral tests may also be given and answers recorded on tape.

Administrative Suggestions for Helping Low Achievers

Administrative support is critical to the development and maintenance of a viable program for low achievers. Principals need support from central office staff, and teachers and counselors definitely need the support of the building principal. The following supportive activities and procedures are helpful for facili-

tating quality programs for low-achieving students by administrative actions:

1. Identify regular class teachers who are the most sensitive to the needs of students with learning problems. Schedule the student with these "sensitive" teachers, and support the teachers through such activities as (a) providing favorable scheduling—for example, an extra planning period, (b) assigning teacher aide(s) to their classes, (c) releasing time to develop curriculum, (d) placing volunteers in their classes, (e) providing in-service training tailored to their needs, (f) offering summer employment to develop curriculum, (g) providing opportunities to attend conferences and workshops, (h) offering support for university course work, (i) providing salary supplements, (j) recognizing the value of the program to the entire faculty, and (k) providing a budget that allows the purchase of some useful materials.

2. Support the development of a homework hotline.

3. Help establish a parent involvement and training program.

4. Work with guidance counselors to schedule the students so that a balanced workload is maintained. (For example, maintain a balance between demanding courses or teachers and less demanding courses or teachers.)

5. Encourage the development of parallel alternative curriculum for the content classes.

6. Support the development of equitable diploma options for mainstreamed students.

Science and Social Studies

Many students with learning problems who enroll in science and social studies classes need help to learn the content of these courses. Science and social studies both follow an inquiry approach and focus on values development. Also, in both kinds of courses much of the content is taught by lecture, discussion, and projects. Assessment considerations and activities as well as commercial materials and computer software programs are presented for each subject area.

Assessment. Various standardized achievement tests include science and social studies subtests that measure general knowledge and skills in these areas. For example, subtests in science and social studies are included in the *SRA Achievement Series* (Naslund, Thorpe, & Lefever, 1978) for students in grades 4 through 12, and in the *Tests of Achievement and Proficiency* (Scannell, 1986) for students in grades 9 through 12. Also, the *Woodcock-Johnson Psycho-Educational Battery* (Woodcock & Johnson, 1977) contains subtests that measure science and social studies knowledge of students from preschool to adult age.

To design a student's individual program, the teacher may construct her own assessment tools. The teacher first must identify the major concepts and skills to be covered during the year. Once this is done, each major topic must be divided into subtopics, with the important skills and concepts specified. Curriculum guides and textbooks are very helpful in identifying these skills and concepts. After the teacher has specified the content, she needs to develop a survey test and administer it to the student. The purpose of this testing is to discover the student's general readiness and instructional needs with regard to the content that will be covered. Testing also provides information on which prerequisite skills may be lacking—for example, map reading, measurement, vocabulary, concept formation, problem solving, and graph reading. The test may include oral responses, short essay responses, reading with comprehension questions, objective test questions, and timed and untimed tasks.

Reading is a primary medium for learning science and social studies. Thus, it is useful to develop and administer Informal Reading Inventories (IRIs) on science and social studies content. For example, an IRI can clue the teacher in on the student's ability to read the text independently. (The procedure for constructing an IRI is discussed in Chapter 10.) Also, the teacher should be aware of the reading level of the text used. Johnson and Vardian (1973) examined the readability level of social studies texts and found that texts at the intermediate level had a 10-year range. Their findings suggest that many social studies texts have readability levels above grade expectations. Similar findings may also apply to science texts.

For some students the teacher will not change the content but will alter techniques to cover it. For other students—particularly those who lack prerequisite skills—the teacher needs to be flexible in regard to the content. Schulz and Turnbull (1983) note: "It is virtually impossible to meet the unique needs of every student in the class during every class period, but teachers have to work on foundation skills with students who are achieving substantially below grade level" (p. 296). For these students, Schulz and Turnbull advise the teacher to consider the following questions about science and social studies content:

1. Will it help the student be more independent in daily living situations?
2. What is the loss if the student does not know the information?
3. Will the student obtain this information from other sources?

The final assessment concentrates on determining *how* the student learns best. For example, Breuning and Regan (1978) found that secondary special education students retained as much as 80% of the regular content in biology when allowed to participate in a preferred activity after satisfactory academic performance. Factors that influence how a student learns are discussed in detail in Chapter 2.

Science Teaching Strategies and Activities

1. To help the student with a short attention span during science instruction, vary instructional approaches and add active learning periods around periods of lecture and discussion. Change-of-pace activities include working at a science learning center, playing a game, conducting an experiment, and watching a filmstrip. In addition, during lecture and discussion periods it may be helpful to seat the student near the teacher and ask questions frequently to encourage attention and involvement. An outline of the lecture material may be written on the chalkboard for the student to follow.

2. Since science concepts include many technical terms, introduce new vocabulary words before having the student read the words in context. The student may be required to keep a file box of science words. Have her look up the definition of each new word and write the word, its definition, and an appropriate sentence or picture on an index card.

3. As supplementary reading, provide science books written on a lower reading level. Books should be chosen carefully; they should have high-interest content and should not be recognizable as lower-grade books.

4. To help the student increase her science vocabulary, follow these three steps (Russell & Karp, 1951):
   a. Make sure the student can pronounce the word correctly.
   b. Have the student practice writing the word correctly.
   c. Give meaning to the word (for example, conduct an experiment relating to the word).

5. Tape textbook information on a cassette recorder to allow the student to review material. To insure attention, the taped lessons should be brief (approximately 10 minutes). In a taped introduction the student may be given a brief description or overview of the material, and specific points to listen for may be noted. If the tape corresponds to textbook content, the student may be asked to refer to pictures in the text. The tape also may include study questions at the end to check the student's comprehension of the material. To self-check her responses, the student may respond and then turn the tape back on to listen for the correct answers. In addition, short books or selections of books for extra reading can be taped and placed in a special area of the room. The student can follow along in the book as she listens to the tape.

6. To help the student complete science reading assignments, pair a peer tutor with a student who has difficulty identifying words. The two students can read orally, and the tutor can help her partner identify difficult words. After reading the selection, the two students can discuss the material to check each other on comprehension. Also, a peer tutor can underline important concepts in the text or write summaries of selected material.

7. To improve understanding among students with reading problems, use various media to present science concepts—pictures, charts, films, and filmstrips. The use of visual and audiovisual materials often increases motivation and interest.

8. Adapt science projects so that student participation is based on each student's strengths (Mann, Suiter, & McClung, 1979). For example, in a group activity, one student can read the material, another student can conduct the experiment, a third student can take notes or give an oral presentation, and all members of the group can contribute to (and be responsible for) the final written report.

9. Provide a list of materials and step-by-step instructions to build simple machines (such as wheel and axle, pulley, wedge) and conduct simple experiments (for example, connecting pieces of copper wire to the positive and negative ends of a battery, making static electricity by rubbing a balloon with a piece of wool). Learning by doing is highly motivating and effectively attaches meaning to science concepts.

Science Commercial Materials

Elementary Science Study Program

Publisher: McGraw-Hill

Description:

This program consists of 56 units that introduce a variety of science concepts. An inquiry approach is used that removes emphasis from book learning and allows students to learn from their own experiments. The reading level of the materials is approximately first to eighth grade with an interest level of 7 to 16 years. The form, complexity, and function of the materials depend on the unit. In general, they include manipulative materials, worksheets, booklets, film loops, and charts. Of the 56 units, 30 are specifically for use with students with learning problems. These units include topics such as butterflies, growing seeds, ice cubes, match and measure, batteries and bulbs, rocks and charts, sand, and sink or float. Teachers may select units suited to the individual student's interests and abilities. A special education teacher's guide provides detailed guidelines for adapting the program to the needs of special students.

I.D.E.A.L. Science Curriculum

Publisher: Opportunities for Learning

Description:

This individualized, self-directing program emphasizes the human body and health science. The reading level is approximately fifth grade, with content suitable for junior and senior high age. In addition to reading, writing, lab, and follow-up activities, each booklet contains objectives, directions, and review tests. Each student should complete the first three books (*Introduction, Methods,* and *Cells to Systems*) and then choose from the remaining seven books (*Skeletal System, Muscular System, Digestive System, Excretory System, Respiratory System, Circulatory System, Nervous System*) according to interests. The teacher's manual contains instructions as well as more than 150 reproducible worksheets, tests, and answer keys.

Inquire

Publisher: Educational Service

Description:

Inquire includes 208 pages of science activities and projects for the intermediate-level student. The scientific method is used to investigate science areas ranging from simple machines to electricity and magnetism. *Inquire Volume I* contains 40 duplicating masters in such subjects as constellations, electrical circuits, electromagnets, and measuring calories.

Me and My Environment

Publisher: Hubbard

Description:

This environmental science program is designed for mildly mentally handicapped students aged 13 through 16. The program moves the student in sequence through an exploration of five aspects of the environment and his relationship to it. The five content areas included are (a) exploring my environment, (b) me as an environment, (c) transfer and cycling of materials in my environment, (d) water and air in my environment, and (e) energy relationships in my environment.

Me in the Future

Publisher: Biological Sciences Curriculum Study

Description:

This science program focuses on career education for special students from age 14 to adulthood. The introductory program consists of activities on career awareness and includes three games, a filmstrip and audiotape, a student handbook, and a teacher's guide. The program includes four main components divided into clusters containing activities:

1. *Science and Metrics* introduces the student to the metric system and measuring skills.
2. *Science and Vocations* contains seven clusters that provide information relating to vocations (agribusiness, natural resources, construction, manufacturing, personal services, public services, transportation).

3. *Science and Leisure Activities* contains three clusters relating to leisure-time activities (sports, nature, crafts).

4. *Science and Daily Living Skills* contains seven clusters related to daily living skills (homes and furnishings, self-mobility, raising children, clothing management, food management, communication, personal hygiene).

All clusters are at third-grade readability and high school to adult interest level. Audiotapes are provided for all printed material, and enrichment activities are included for the more able student. Each component contains a teacher's guide. The program may be purchased as a whole or in individual components or clusters.

Me Now

Publisher: Hubbard

Description:

This science and health program is designed for special students aged 10 to 13 years. It focuses on building self-image by developing a basic understanding of how the body works. The program is activity centered; there is very little written material for students to read. Four content areas are included: (a) digestion and circulation; (b) respiration and body wastes; (c) movement, support, and sensory perception; and (d) growth and development. A comprehensive curriculum guide is provided for each of the four content areas. Also included are 140 slides, posters and pictures relating to identification of food and food sources, seven film loops, a supplies kit of nonconsumable items (for example, stethoscope, test tubes, magnifying glass), and worksheets. In addition, a three-foot-tall, functioning torso model is available which shows five body systems—digestive, circulatory, urinary, breathing, and nervous. A teacher's guide with teaching strategies and step-by-step procedures accompanies the torso. Standard laboratory supplies and evaluation materials are also available in separate kits.

Science Computer Software Programs

The Physical Science Series

Distributor: Micro Center

Hardware: Apple II

Description:

These 14 tutorial programs present common topics in junior high school science (for example, motor, light, electricity, atoms, energy, and sound). There are 30 to 40 questions in each subject area, and the program automatically branches to give extra information on concepts the student finds difficult. The teacher can change the questions the student is asked, and the student's scores are recorded for teacher records.

Your Body Series

Distributor: Opportunities for Learning

Hardware: Apple II, TRS–80, PET, Commodore 64

Description:

This two-part series covers all of the major body systems and is designed for the junior high school student. The programs in set 1 include *The Human Organism, Your Blood, Your Digestive System,* and *Your Circulatory System.* Set 2 features *Your Muscular System, Your Skeletal System, Your Brain and Nervous System,* and *Your Endocrine System.* The programs present body parts and their functions in an interactive learning-game format, such as a simulated road race through the circulatory system in which the student can only proceed by correctly answering questions. If needed, the student can ask for "extra help" information.

Social Studies Teaching Strategies and Activities

1. Several suggestions listed in the science section for maintaining interest and motivation also apply to teaching social studies. In addition, use the language experience approach to reading in

social studies. After presenting information through lecture, filmstrips, or textbook reading, have each student summarize the main points of the material in her own words. The student can use magazine pictures or drawings to illustrate the written work. Peer tutors may help with vocabulary or spelling in the written compositions.

2. Point out to the student that reading history requires different kinds of reading (Russell & Karp, 1951). For example, to find a date or fact or to see a series of related events, the student may skim or read the passage quickly. However, to organize the material by main ideas and subtopics, the student may first read it quickly to get an idea of the entire selection and then read it more slowly on the second reading. The student can make notes as she reads or when she finishes reading, and the notes should be organized into main topics and subtopics. If the student is reading to note a number of causes of a particular event, she may skim several pages until she comes close to the discussion of the event. Then she should read more carefully to discover the facts.

3. Help the student learn the historical reason for major dates, including holidays, by collecting several different calendars that note holidays. Note the variety of types of holidays, and have the student use reference materials to learn historical information about the following types of dates: education milestones, famous persons, historical events, religious observances, and recreational holidays. Provide the student with an individual calendar, and require her to mark major dates and give information about them. Also, the student may locate dates of events pictured on stamps and paste the stamps on the appropriate day on her calendar.

4. Have the students play "Twenty Questions" using the category of historical figures. One player (or team) decides upon a name, writes it down, and keeps it out of sight. The opposing players can ask up to 20 questions to determine the name. Questions must be answered only with "yes" and "no." Players should be cautioned not to waste questions with wild guesses. Questions should narrow down the time period, sex, field of involvement, and so on until some-

one correctly guesses the name within the 20 questions. If no one is able to guess the person, that player (or team) gets another turn. Twenty Questions also may be played with geography questions. A map is hung in front of the students, and places on the map are the object of the game. Questions may be asked concerning latitude, longitude, surrounding geographical locations, and so on. Another variation of the question game is to have a volunteer choose a famous person or place and tell the class the first letter of the person's last name or the place. Each student asks questions to determine the name until she gets a "no" answer. Then the next player begins questioning. The person asking questions can make a guess at any time; however, if she is wrong, the next questioner begins. The student who correctly guesses the name gets to choose a person or place and continue the game.

5. Prepare a display of several maps of one geographical area, with each map depicting a different aspect of that area—for example, climate, natural resources, population distribution, yearly rainfall, agricultural products. Make a list of questions that require reading each map. Also, the student may be provided with several copies of outline maps of a continent. Ask her to refer to a world atlas, encyclopedia, and other reference books to make five different types of maps for that continent.

6. Explore the concept of patriotism by developing an understanding and respect for the democratic process in America. Have small-group discussions about rights that are free of government control—such as freedom in selecting occupation and freedom of worship—and areas of governmental regulation, such as taxes on property and building codes. In discussing freedom of speech, provide newspaper editorials and have students underline parts that might have been deleted in a country that censors public information. Also, each small group of students can research the history of the American flag and share the information. Voting rights and responsibilities of American citizens can be explored through holding a mock election and discussing the duties of elected officials.

Social Studies Commercial Materials

Insights about America

Publisher: Opportunities for Learning

Description:

These history materials are presented in a cartoon format with follow-up questions. The reading level is approximately fourth grade, but the content is a high-interest level and appeals to older students. American history is presented according to three eras: the American Revolution, the War Between the States, and Frontiers West. A total of 48 booklets are provided, with 16 booklets in each era. Various topics are covered such as Robert E. Lee, the Pony Express, the Oregon Trail, and Daily Life of the Colonists. The follow-up questions are designed to stimulate open-ended discussion and further activities. A teacher's guide is provided.

A Sound History of the World
A Sound History of America

Publisher: DLM Teaching Resources

Description:

These two audiocassette-plus-print programs are designed to help students achieve success in history. Both programs include important historical events normally covered in the traditional curriculum. *A Sound History of the World* covers prehistoric to contemporary time, and *A Sound History of America* spans the time of discovery and exploration into the 1980s. The audiotapes present factual information complemented by period music, dramatizations, and sound effects. The lessons are 10 to 15 minutes in length, and the accompanying scripts can be used as a read-along activity.

Target American History

Publisher: Mafex Associates

Description:

This history workbook is written in a simplified manner and outlines the major historical periods of the United States. Activities include fill-in-the-blanks, coloring projects, historical plays, map completion, crossword puzzles, true-or-false questions, and definitions. Also, each workbook features a time line for displaying American history in pictures. As the student finishes studying a particular segment of American history, she cuts out a symbol that represents the period and pastes it on the time line. Content ranges from the discovery of America to the present, covering topics such as the first explorers, the wild West, the Civil War, famous Americans, and the Vietnam War. A teacher's guide is included as well as ditto supplements.

World History and You

Publisher: Steck-Vaughn

Description:

This consumable two-book survey of world history was written for older students who have reading difficulties. The reading level is approximately fourth-grade level, and emphasis is placed on reading comprehension, vocabulary, and other language skills as well as presenting world history. Book 1 presents areas such as ancient civilizations, growth of major religions, and exploration and colonization of the New World. Book 2 begins with the Industrial Revolution, explores the growth of democracy, and continues through contemporary world history. Exercises and chapter reviews reinforce facts presented in the text.

Social Studies Computer Software Programs

Regions of the United States

Distributor: Educational Activities

Hardware: Apple II, TRS–80, Commodore 64

Description:

This gamelike program, designed for students in grades 5 through 12, focuses on the geography of the United States. In Part 1, "The Fifty States," the student reviews the states, region by region, and then takes a quiz in which she must identify the states and spell their names correctly. In Part 2, "The Regions," the computer gives clues about a particular region, and the student must figure out the region by using as few clues as possible. In addition, the game teaches the major cities, landforms, products, and climates of the different regions of the United States.

The World Traveler: Geography Drills

Producer: Sunburst Communications

Hardware: Atari

Description:

These four programs provide a global perspective of the student's knowledge of geography. *States* helps the student recognize the distinct shape and location of each state in the United States. In *Capitals,* the student matches states with their capitals. *Continents* requires the student to match countries with continents, and *Countries* focuses on matching countries with their capitals.

FUNCTIONAL LIVING SKILLS

A functional or essential living skills program is typically designed for secondary students whose academic skills are very low (that is, below fourth-grade level). Functional living skills are essential for successful living in modern society. For some students with learning problems, functional living skills must be taught directly and systematically. If they are not taught directly, the students may never acquire them or may learn them through trial-and-error experiences that are both costly and time-consuming. Kokaska and Brolin (1985) list nine important areas in planning a functional living curriculum. These areas and their subareas are presented in Table 14.4. Many of these skills can be taught within the traditional curriculum. For example, area 1 may be included in arithmetic; areas 3 and 5 in science; areas 4, 7, and 9 in social studies; areas 2 and 6 in home economics and shop; and area 8 in music, art, and physical education.

Bender and Valletutti (1982) present a functional curriculum based on six roles of the

TABLE 14.4
Functional living curriculum areas.

Areas
1. *Managing family finances*   Identify money and make correct change   Make wise expenditures   Obtain and use bank and credit facilities   Keep basic financial records   Calculate and pay taxes
2. *Selecting, managing, and maintaining a home*   Select adequate housing   Maintain a home   Use basic appliances and tools   Maintain home exterior
3. *Caring for personal needs*   Dress appropriately   Exhibit proper grooming and hygiene   Demonstrate knowledge of physical fitness, nutrition, and weight control   Demonstrate knowledge of illness prevention and treatment
4. *Raising children—family living*   Prepare for adjustment to marriage   Prepare for raising children (physical care)   Prepare for raising children (psychological care)   Practice family safety in the home
5. *Buying and preparing food*   Demonstrate appropriate eating skills   Plan balanced meals   Purchase food   Prepare meals   Clean food preparation areas   Store food
6. *Buying and caring for clothes*   Wash clothing   Iron and store clothing   Perform simple mending   Purchase clothing
7. *Engaging in civic activities*   Generally understand local laws and government   Generally understand the federal government   Understand citizenship rights and responsibilities

(continued)

TABLE 14.4, *continued*

Understand registration and voting proce-
dures
Understand Selective Service procedures
Understand civil rights and responsibilities
when questioned by the law
8. *Using recreation and leisure*
Participate in group activities
Know activities and available community re-
sources
Understand recreational values
Use recreational facilities in the community
Plan and choose activities wisely
9. *Getting around the community (mobility)*
Demonstrate knowledge of traffic rules and
safety practices
Demonstrate knowledge and use various
means of transportation
Drive a car

Source: From *Career Education for Handicapped Individuals*
(pp. 46–47), 2nd ed., by C. J. Kokaska and D. E. Brolin, 1985,
Columbus, OH: Merrill. Copyright 1985 by Bell & Howell Company. Reprinted by permission.

individual. Reading, writing, and math skills
essential to each role are taught. The roles
include (a) resident in home, (b) learner in traditional and nontraditional school settings, (c)
participant in community, (d) consumer
of goods and services, (e) employee, and (f)
participant in leisure activities. Bender and
Valletutti urge teachers of functional curriculum
to examine the functional reality of intervention activities. They report, "To do so requires
a simple technique, namely the performance
of the learning task in its actual context from
the viewpoint of the learner and his role in that
content" (p. 1).

To establish and monitor educational or
prevocational objectives, the *Brigance Diagnostic Inventory of Essential Skills* (Brigance,
1980) may be used. This instrument includes
measures of functional academics at the secondary level and thus assesses minimal academic and vocational competencies. The in-

ventory includes rating scales to measure
applied skills that cannot be assessed objec-
tively, such as health practices and attitude,
responsibility and self-discipline, job interview
preparation, auto safety, speaking skills, and
listening skills. Other practical assessments
include sections on food and clothing, money
and finance, travel and transportation, and oral
communication and telephone skills.

Activities

1. To help the student learn to manage family finances, have her keep a record of expenses for a
certain period of time. The budget should include
areas such as food, clothing, transportation, savings, medical expenses, recreation, and so forth.
She also may itemize her family's purchases during a period of time. To encourage the student to
spend money wisely, provide her with a shopping list of products available at different stores,
and require her to compare prices or to select
items based on a fixed amount of money.

2. Take a field trip to a bank and a savings and loan
facility or arrange classroom demonstrations by
representatives from these establishments. A
classroom bank and individual accounts can be
set up to acquaint the student with checks, deposits, withdrawals, passbooks, and so on. Extensive practice in writing checks, filling out deposit slips, and balancing a checkbook should be
provided. To learn about other banking services,
the student may also be required to fill out forms
for obtaining a loan or opening a charge account.

3. Have small-group discussions in which the students examine various kinds of taxes (such as
sales, gas, property, income). Have them identify
items that are taxed and determine the amount,
how the tax is collected, and how it is used. The
procedure for filing income tax forms can be presented by requiring the student to fill out a 1040
short form. Cut instructions from a tax guide according to numbered sections (for example, 1—
name and address; 2—social security number;
and so on). Fasten each instruction and the corresponding section of the 1040A form to a card.
Provide one sample form filled out as well as

blank 1040A forms that are laminated for reuse. Instruct each student to fill out a 1040A form number by number, referring if necessary to the completed form and the individual instruction cards.

4. Discuss various types of housing available in the community. Have the students explore the advantages and disadvantages of each according to factors such as cost, space, utilities, and location. In discussing renting a home or apartment, include such factors as deposits, leases, and tenant rights and responsibilities. Cut out newspaper ads that list rentals and tape them to the inside of a manila folder. On index cards write questions related to the rental ads and place the cards in a pocket pasted to the folder. The student picks a card, looks for the answer in the classified ads mounted on the inside of the folder, and writes her response. An answer key can be provided by numbering the questions and assigning letters to the ads.

5. Have the students role play potential problems in marriage and child raising and discuss solutions. Encourage the students to refer to their own life experiences when suggesting appropriate practices in raising children. Also, have the students identify community agencies and sources that provide assistance in family planning and marriage problems.

6. Identify emergency situations that can occur in the home (such as fire or storm damage) or with a family member (such as accident or injury). Have the students look up emergency phone numbers and make a booklet containing information on how to get help for emergencies. First-aid procedures for injury situations should be demonstrated in the classroom and listed in the student's booklet. Also, safety procedures for hazardous situations can be discussed.

7. Have each student determine recreational activities in which she can participate, and list resources and facilities available in the community. If music is an area of interest, the teacher can tape five different types of music and have the student select her favorite. Then the student can explore places where that type of music is available or composers she enjoys. To develop an interest in art as a leisure activity, the teacher can present prints of various types of art. The student can determine places or events in which she can enjoy art during recreational time. Also, the student can participate in clubs or hobbies to explore using leisure time effectively.

8. To help the student learn traffic signals, arrange pictures of traffic signs on bingo cards with five pictures in each of the five rows and a "free" space in the middle. Make call cards by writing the names of the signs on paper squares. Each student receives a bingo card, and the caller draws and reads call cards. When a traffic sign is called which appears on a player's bingo card, she covers the sign with a marker (disk). The first player to cover all the signs in a row calls "Bingo" and must then give the meaning of each sign covered in that row.

9. Use a start-to-finish game board to stimulate interest in driver education and understanding of driving procedures. Write various directions on the game-board squares, including some squares instructing the player to pick an Accident card or a Good Driver card (see Figure 14.2). Make green Go cards with a question written on the front and the correct answer written on the back. The back of each Go card also tells the number of spaces to move ahead if the answer is correct and the number of spaces to move back if the player's response is incorrect. The Go cards are placed face up. The player takes the top card, responds to the question, turns the card over to check her answer, and moves her marker the number of spaces indicated. Sample Go card questions include the following:

a. What colors are railroad signs?
b. What does *mph* mean?
c. What papers must you have when you drive?
d. What color is the bottom bulb in a traffic light?
e. Which car has the right of way when they both arrive at the intersection at the same time?

If the player lands on an Accident space or a Good Driver space, she takes a card and follows the directions on the card. Accident cards should be red and may include the following:

a. You made a U-turn in the middle of the block. Move back 1 space.
b. You were driving at night with one headlight. Move back 2 spaces.

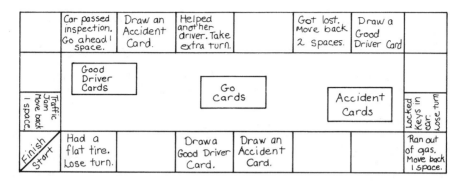

FIGURE 14.2
Driver education game board.

c. You made a turn without signaling. Move back 2 spaces.

d. You parked in front of a fire hydrant. Move back 1 space.

Good Driver cards should be blue and may include the following:

a. You slowed down to 25 mph in an unmarked speed zone. Move ahead 2 spaces.

b. You pulled to the far right of the road and stopped when you heard a siren. Move ahead 2 spaces.

c. You checked your parking meter before you went shopping. Move ahead 1 space.

d. You reduced your speed in a construction zone. Move ahead 1 space.

The players take turns, and the first one to reach the Finish square wins.

Commercial Materials

How to Write for Everyday Living

Publisher: Educational Activities

Description:

This writing competency program focuses on real-life writing tasks and specific applications of writing skills. The student receives instruction and practice in various skills as she works with samples of actual forms. Lessons are included in areas such as filling out an application, writing business letters, taking telephone messages, and writing a résumé. The program includes five cassettes and 10 activity books, and a diagnostic pretest and evaluative posttest are provided.

MATH . . . for Everyday Living

Publisher: Educational Activities

Description:

This program, presented through cassette tapes and activity books, teaches and develops the necessary basic math skills involved in real-life activities. The lessons introduce and reinforce computational skills needed to cope with everyday situations such as shopping, traveling, banking, getting the best-paying job, paying bills, and using credit. A computer software version of this program is available for use with the Apple II, TRS–80, PET, and Commodore 64.

SAIL: Skills to Achieve Independent Living

Publisher: Melton Peninsula

Description:

The SAIL Program fosters independent community living through developing skills in personal management, home management, community access, and applied academics. The personal management area stresses interpersonal relations and focuses on skills related to communication, health and hygiene, sexuality, and personal and social adjustment. Selection and preparation of foods, proper maintenance of clothing, home safety, and minor repairs in the home are featured in the home management area. The area on community access focuses on skills necessary to reach and use community resources (for example, transportation, emergency services, prevocational and leisure-time activities). Academic skills in reading and writing, arithmetic, time management, and money management are featured in the applied academics area. Task objectives, mastery criteria, and strategies are provided on 433 color-coded task cards. The student's progress through the program is monitored on a progress profile, which indicates the skills targeted and the dates they were mastered. A teacher's manual, a skills inventory booklet, and skills inventory checklist sheets are included in addition to 46 sign and symbol cards, 105 number cards, and 12 color storytelling posters.

Survival Math Series

Publisher: Mafex Associates

Description:

This series includes six sets of workbooks that allow students to apply basic math skills to practical, everyday situations. For example, the student is required to work multiplication and addition problems to buy grocery items and to figure weekly pay according to given pay rates. Income tax and social security deductions are explained. In addition, activities are provided in filling out credit cards, making change, and maintaining a checking account.

Survival Words Program

Publisher: DLM Teaching Resources

Description:

This program teaches automatic identification of 90 words and phrases considered most essential for survival. It is designed for use by students with reading problems and has an interest level directed at adolescents. The program includes nine storybooks as well as worksheets containing six types of exercises for each word or phrase.

Computer Software Programs

Daily Living Skills

Producer: Encyclopaedia Britannica Educational Corporation

Hardware: Apple II

Description:

These programs provide interactive instruction and practice in survival reading. *Prescription Medicine* and *Product Labels* deal with labels and appropriate consumer information. *Classified Ads* and *Telephone Directories* focus on common reference sources that require searching through categorized information. *Banking* and *Credit* introduce the fundamental aspects of bank accounts and basic credit concepts. *Job Applications* presents the basic concepts pertaining to applying for a job, and *Paychecks* focuses on the general nature of pay periods, gross and net pay, earnings, and deductions. Graphics are used to present concepts, and questions are included on each program.

Lifeskill Mathematics Series I

Producer: Media Materials

Hardware: Apple II, TRS-80

Description:

This series consists of the following six math programs which are written at the second- to fourth-grade reading level: (a) *On the Road with Basic Math Skills*—computing distance, average speed, miles per gallon; (b) *Car Owner's Manual for Better Math Skills*—buying a new car, financing a car; (c) *The Math in Your Insurance Policies*—auto, house, life, medical, and social security insurance; (d) *Essential Math Skills for Computing Taxes*—sales taxes, property taxes, income taxes, and deductions from payroll; (e) *Math and Your Personal Finances*—housing, clothing, credit; and (f) *Math Around the House*—wall and floor area, buying paint, changing square feet to square yards. Supplemental workbooks are included.

Lifeskill Reading I

Producer: Media Materials

Hardware: Apple II, TRS–80

Description:

This series includes the following eight programs: (a) *Stop, Look, and Learn Highway Warning Signs,* (b) *Set Your Course Using Highway Signs,* (c) *Shop and Save! Food Purchasing Skills,* (d) *Money Matters: Banking and Consumer Transactions,* (e) *Consumer Talk: Everyday Reading Skills* (income and taxes, insurance, real estate, taking care of your health), (f) *Bon Voyage! Basic Travel Skills,* (g) *What's the Scoop? Exploring the Newspaper,* and (h) *You Decide: The Influence of Media* (billboards, ads, propaganda). The reading level of the series is second to fourth grade, and supplemental activities are provided in workbook format.

Survival Math: Simulations

Producer: Sunburst Communications

Hardware: Apple II, TRS–80, Commodore 64, Atari

Description:

These four simulations require students to use math skills as a basis for making sound judgments. *Smart Shopper Marathon* requires students to use unit prices and percent discounts to figure out best buys. In *Hot Dog Stand,* students must purchase food and set prices as they operate a hot-dog stand to raise money. In *Travel Agent Contest,* students are asked to plan a 7-day trip and allocate money for expenses without exceeding a spending limit. *Foreman's Assistant* requires students to help plan a playroom and buy materials for building it while staying within a time frame and budget. Thus, the programs provide practice in calculating or estimating answers and help teach students to use mathematics as an analytical tool.

CAREER-RELATED INSTRUCTION

The emphasis on career education began in the early 1970s and evolved from dissatisfac-

tion with the educational system's ability to prepare students adequately for the future. Students with learning problems are often the ones who most need attractive options in career training. Cegelka (1985) makes the following statement:

> By emphasizing the relationship of subject matter to various careers and occupations and by developing needed work skills, career education has sought to make education more relevant to the economic and employment realities of the day. . . . In short, it has sought to increase the life satisfaction of workers, restore the work ethic, and increase national productivity. (p. 575)

Most states and local school districts now include career education in some form as part of their overall educational philosophies (Wimmer, 1982). In addition, career education is receiving increased federal and state funding.

Career education involves a comprehensive educational program, focusing on careers, that begins in early childhood and continues throughout adulthood. At the elementary level, the major objective is to introduce the student to various occupations. The primary objective at the secondary level is to shape the student's awareness of occupations into preparation for a career. Figure 14.3 presents the stages of career development.

Career education enables an individual to explore the occupational world, to identify with it, and to make job decisions that increase self-fulfillment (Marland, 1972). The U.S. Office of Education (1971) delineated 15 occupational clusters appropriate for career education content. Moreover, this content places value on all kinds of work, regardless of its current social status.

Career education has a broad emphasis and includes vocational training. Vocational training specifically focuses on developing vocational skills essential to entering the world of work. Historically, it has been difficult to obtain voca-

FIGURE 14.3
Career development stages.

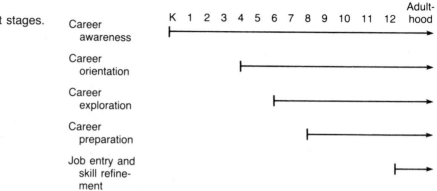

tional training for mildly handicapped students (Marsh & Price, 1980; Smith, 1981). A variety of options and services are needed for providing low achievers with the programs they need. Mori (1980) lists four possible methods of providing students with learning problems with specialized skills in a career area. These include area vocational-technical school, special vocational school, work-study off campus, and work-study on campus. Postschool alternatives include entry-level jobs, trade school, community college, college, and referral to the Bureau of Vocational Rehabilitation or other appropriate community or government agencies (Mori, 1980).

A variety of measures and procedures can be used to assess students in terms of appropriate decisions on career direction. Information can be informally obtained through student–teacher interaction and a consultative process. In addition, a number of standardized tests are available to assess vocational interest or aptitude. The following instruments may be used to help secondary students choose appropriate careers based on their particular abilities and interests: *Harrington-O'Shea Career Decision-Making System* (Harrington & O'Shea, 1982), *Occupational Aptitude Survey and Interest Schedule* (Parker, 1983), *Reading-Free Vocational Interest Inventory* (Becker,

1987), and *Strong-Campbell Interest Inventory* (Strong, Hansen, & Campbell, 1985). In addition to standardized testing procedures, the work-sample method provides a means of prevocational evaluation. The work sample is a simulated task or occupational activity that is representative of tasks and activities in various employment settings. As the individual attempts different work samples, personality characteristics and skill aptitudes can be observed to indicate vocational potential.

Activities

1. Invite students who have recently graduated to return to the school to discuss their jobs or problems in leaving high school for college, work, or military service. Selected students may be responsible for inviting alumni and for developing appropriate questions. The discussions should include positive aspects about their careers and how they handle problems they encounter on the job. If possible, interested members of the class should have the opportunity to observe the graduates actually working.

2. Plan field trips to visit businesses and industries and request personnel to speak with the students. A person from the business may be invited to speak to the class before or after the visit to answer questions or distribute information. During the trip, students should have enough time to observe persons performing various jobs

and to record pertinent information about the job (such as job requirements, working conditions, good and bad features of the job). Students can share their observations in class discussions after the visit.

3. Divide the class into small groups and have them obtain information on one particular job per week. During group discussion the students can determine job responsibilities, identify personal and social values met through the work, and compile a list of words used on the job.

4. Have each student write a want ad for what she considers to be the perfect job. The ad should include information such as hours, salary, qualifications, responsibilities, and so on. Then have the students check the want-ad section of the newspaper to locate ads for jobs in their interest area and compare these ads with their ideal ad. If appropriate, students can contact personnel directors of various business establishments to find out the number of people recently hired, their salaries, and their qualifications. Also, visits may be arranged or volunteer or observation work can be set up with the business the student is most interested in.

5. Cut out several newspaper ads for jobs available. Have each student choose a job from the given ads and state why she would want that particular job and what preparation and qualifications she must have. Then have the student complete an application form for that job. The completed application can be reviewed for improvement.

6. Role play interviews for various jobs. Discuss punctuality, appropriate dress, and questions to ask during the interview and acceptable responses. Role playing can build a student's self-confidence in an actual interview situation.

Commercial Materials

Career Card File

Publisher: DLM Teaching Resources

Description:

This teacher-resource file contains 200 color-coded 5″ × 8″ cards which focus on nine different careers. Introductory career awareness activities, a career objectives key, and bibliography cards encourage career research. The card file offers practical ideas for developing academic skills in reading, spelling, geography, and mathematics while investigating the careers of cosmetology, postal services, food services, law enforcement, telephone company services, auto mechanics, plumbing, carpentry, and truck driving. In addition, award certificates and two blank game spinners are included.

Careers in Focus

Publisher: McGraw-Hill

Description:

This program consists of materials with an interest level of 10 to 16 years and a reading level of sixth to seventh grade. One student manual deals with personal values and self-identity in exploring careers. The remaining 13 manuals present information about various industries and jobs. A sound filmstrip accompanies each manual to introduce the student to the particular occupational field. For each manual, there are three interview audiocassettes focusing on insights and feelings of actual job holders. Worksheet booklets also are included.

Exploring Careers

Publisher: Opportunities for Learning

Description:

This material is for grades 5 to 12 and includes a 52-page spirit master book of student instructions and one or more worksheets for each activity. The student is guided in obtaining information to make successful career decisions through 16 career-related activities. The activities focus on (a) specific careers, (b) the relationship between careers and life-styles, and (c) one's individual talents and preferences. A teacher's manual is also provided that lists teaching objectives, materials, and methods as well as discussion guides and related subjects for each activity.

Expo 10: Exploring Career Interests

Publisher: Science Research Associates

Description:

This career exploration program is designed for grades 5 through adult. It includes 58 games (for example, board games, card games, and variations of traditional games) that provide occupational information in the following interest areas: scientific, computational, musical, artistic, persuasive, literary, mechanical, outdoor, social service, and clerical. Basic occupational facts including description of duties, education and training, required talents or abilities, and places of employment are explored in each of the 10 interest areas.

Get Set for Work!

Publisher: Mafex Associates

Description:

This material includes a teacher's handbook, a student activity book, and competency test records. The teacher's handbook includes 46 step-by-step daily lessons to guide the student in preparing for and getting a job. The following units are covered: (a) identifying and preparing for a job, (b) basic job facts, (c) personal factors affecting work, (d) steps that lead to a job, (e) application forms and related forms, and (f) summer employment. The student activity book includes tasks such as answering help-wanted-ad questions, working crossword puzzles, unscrambling sentences, and finding key words in job-related sentences. The competency test record evaluates the student's comprehension of the material and includes pre- and posttests and terminal objective records for each unit.

Me and Jobs

Publisher: Opportunities for Learning

Description:

This program is designed to enable the student to discover and like herself and then to look at jobs in terms of her own unique abilities and needs. Self-awareness, job awareness, and job acquisition are featured in a set of five filmstrips: *What Do I Have That a Job Needs?*, *The Job Environment and Me*, *Want Ads*, *Application Forms*, and *Job Interview Skills*. These films may be used independently or

along with a 96-page workbook divided into four sections: (a) *Me*—explores personal interests, assets, and opinions; (b) *Jobs*—focuses on various kinds of jobs and how to explore them; (c) *Me and Jobs*—fits personal abilities and interests into different jobs; and (d) *Applications and Interviews*—focuses on how to find and apply for a job. A teacher's manual is included in the program.

Secondary Career Series

Publisher: Media Materials

Description:

This series includes three reproducible cassette activity books. In *Career Awareness*, students discover the reasons why people work, what people do at work, and how and why people choose careers. *Career Exploration* focuses on the skills, interests, educational requirements, and work environments of nine occupational clusters. The lessons in *Career Planning* cover interests, personality traits, skills, and life objectives and how they relate to specific careers, education, on-the-job training, and the process of finding a job. With each cassette activity book, 38 blackline master activity pages and eight self-directing cassette lessons are provided.

Computer Software Programs

Computerized Career Assessment and Planning Program

Distributor: Educational Activities

Hardware: Apple II, TRS–80

Description:

These four programs are designed to help students in grades 9 through 12 (a) determine their career interests, preferences, and abilities, (b) select and explore career clusters, (c) delineate and select relevant occupations, and (d) develop a plan to enter or prepare to enter the occupation of their choice. *Career Assessment* involves students in assessing their career interests and abilities and provides a printout of relevant career clusters. *Selecting Alternatives* allows students to determine what occupational characteristics are important to them and provides a list of occupations related to their characteristics and capabilities. In *Career Exploration,* students can look up specific clusters and occupations to determine what capabilities and interests are required by each. *Career Planning* helps students develop plans to find a job, select a college, or select a vocational school. Each program takes approximately 40 minutes to complete and allows students to gain occupational knowledge while learning career decision-making skills.

REFERENCES

Adelman, H.S., & Taylor, L. (1983). Enhancing motivation for overcoming learning and behavior problems. *Journal of Learning Disabilities, 16,* 384–392.

Alley, G., & Deshler, D. (1979). *Teaching the learning disabled adolescent: Strategies and methods.* Denver: Love.

Alley, G.R., Deshler, D.D., & Warner, M.M. (1979). Identification of learning disabled adolescents: A Bayesian approach. *Learning Disability Quarterly, 2*(2), 76–83.

Alley, G.R., & Hori, A.K.O. (1981). *Effects of teaching a questioning strategy on reading comprehension of learning disabled adolescents* (Research Report No. 52). Lawrence, KS: University of Kansas Institute for Research in Learning Disabilities.

Becker, R.L. (1987). *Reading-Free Vocational Interest Inventory.* Monterey, CA: Publishers Test Service, California Test Bureau/McGraw-Hill.

Beech, M.C. (1983). Simplifying text for mainstreamed students. *Journal of Learning Disabilities, 16,* 400–402.

Bender, M., & Valletutti, P.J. (1982). *Teaching functional academics: A curriculum guide for adolescents and adults with learning problems.* Baltimore: University Park Press.

Breuning, S., & Regan, J. (1978). Teaching regular class materials to special education students. *Exceptional Children, 3,* 180–187.

Brigance, A.H. (1980). *Brigance Diagnostic Inventory of Essential Skills.* North Billerica, MA: Curriculum Associates.

Buchwach, L. (1980). Child service demonstration center for secondary students with learning disabilities. In R.H. Riegel & J.P. Mathey (Eds.), *Mainstreaming at the secondary level: Seven models that work.* Plymouth, MI: Wayne County Intermediate School District.

Butterfield, E.C., & Belmont, J.C. (1977). Assessing and improving the executive cognitive functions of mentally retarded people. In I. Bailer & M. Sternlicht (Eds.), *Psychological issues in mental retardation.* New York: Psychological Dimensions.

Carlson, S.A., & Alley, G.R. (1981). *Performance and competence of learning disabled and high achieving high school students on essential cognitive skills* (Research Report No. 53). Lawrence, KS: University of Kansas Institute for Research in Learning Disabilities.

Carman, R.A., & Adams, W.R. (1972). *Study skills: A student's guide for survival.* New York: Wiley.

Cegelka, P.T. (1985). Career and vocational education. In W.H. Burdine & A.E. Blackhurst (Eds.). *An introduction to special education* (2nd ed., pp. 573–612). Boston: Little, Brown.

Coleman, L.J. (1979, April). *Translating curriculum materials at the secondary level for mainstreaming students.* Paper presented at the Council for Exceptional Children Convention, Dallas.

Cronin, M.E., & Currie, P.S. (1984). Study skills: A resource guide for practitioners. *Remedial and Special Education, 5*(2), 61–69.

Cunningham, P.M., & Cunningham, J.W. (1976, December). Improving listening in content area subjects. *NASSP Bulletin,* pp. 26–31.

Dembrowsky, C. (1980). Synergistic education: A comprehensive plan for learning disabled adolescents. In R.H. Riegel & J.P. Mathey (Eds.), *Mainstreaming at the secondary level: Seven models that work.* Plymouth, MI: Wayne County Intermediate School District.

Deshler, D.D., Lowrey, N., & Alley, G.R. (1979). Programming alternatives for learning disabled adolescents: A nationwide survey. *Academic Therapy, 14*(4), 389–397.

Deshler, D.D., Schumaker, J.B., & Lenz, B.K. (1984). Academic and cognitive interventions for LD adolescents: Part I. *Journal of Learning Disabilities, 17,* 108–117.

Deshler, D.D., Schumaker, J.B., Lenz, B.K., & Ellis, E. (1984). Academic and cognitive interventions for LD adolescents: Part II. *Journal of Learning Disabilities, 17,* 170–179.

Devine, T. (1981). *Teaching study skills.* Boston: Allyn & Bacon.

Dexter, B.L. (1982). Helping learning disabled students prepare for college. *Journal of Learning Disabilities, 15,* 344–346.

Edwards, P. (1973). Panorama: A study technique. *Journal of Reading, 17,* 132–135.

Ellis, E.S., & Lenz, B.K. (1987). A component analysis of effective learning strategies for LD students. *Learning Disabilities Focus, 2*(2), 94–107.

Flavell, J. (1976). Metacognitive aspects of problem solving. In R. Resnick (Ed.), *The nature of intelligence.* Hillsdale, NJ: Erlbaum.

Harrington, T.F., & O'Shea, A.J. (1982). *The Harrington-O'Shea Career Decision-Making System.* Circle Pines, MN: American Guidance Service.

Hughes, C.A., Hendrickson, J.M., & Hudson, P.J. (1986). The pause procedure: Improving factual recall from lectures by low and high achieving middle school students. *International Journal of Instructional Media, 13*(3), 217–226.

Johnson, R., & Vardian, E.R. (1973). Reading, readability, and the social studies. *The Reading Teacher, 26,* 483–488.

Kerr, M.M., & Nelson, C.M. (1983). *Strategies for managing behavior problems in the classroom.* Columbus, OH: Merrill.

Knowlton, H.E., & Schlick, L. (in preparation). *Secondary regular classroom teachers' expectations of LD students* (Research Report). Lawrence, KS: University of Kansas Institute for Research in Learning Disabilities.

Kokaska, C.J., & Brolin, D.E. (1985). *Career education for handicapped individuals* (2nd ed.). Columbus, OH: Merrill.

Laurie, T.E., Buchwach, L., Silverman, R., & Zigmond, N. (1978). Teaching secondary learning disabled students in the mainstream. *Learning Disability Quarterly, 1*(4), 62–72.

Lenz, B.K. (1982). *The effect of advance organizers on the learning and retention of learning disabled adolescents within the context of a cooperative planning model.* Unpublished dissertation, University of Kansas, Lawrence.

Link, D.P. (1980). *Essential learning skills and the low achieving student at the secondary level: A rating of the importance of 24 academic abilities.* Unpublished master's thesis, University of Kansas, Lawrence.

Mann, P.H., Suiter, P.A., & McClung, R.M. (1979). *Handbook in diagnostic-prescriptive teaching* (Abridged 2nd ed.). Boston: Allyn & Bacon.

Manzo, A.V. (1969). The ReQuest procedure. *Journal of Reading, 13,* 123–126.

Manzo, A.V. (1975). Guided reading procedure. *Journal of Reading, 7,* 287–291.

Marland, S.P., Jr. (1972). Career education: Every student headed for a goal. *American Vocational Journal, 47*(3), 34–36, 62.

Marsh, G.E., II, & Price, B.J. (1980). *Methods for teaching the mildly handicapped adolescent.* Saint Louis: Mosby.

Marsh, G.E., II, Price, B.J., & Smith, T.E.C. (1983). *Teaching mildly handicapped children: Methods and materials.* Columbus, OH: Merrill.

Meichenbaum, D. (1975). Self-instructional methods. In F. Kanter & A. Goldstein (Eds.), *Helping people change.* New York: Pergamon Press.

Mercer, C.D. (1987). *Students with learning disabilities* (3rd ed.). Columbus, OH: Merrill.

Mercer, C.D., & Snell, M.E. (1977). *Learning theory research in mental retardation: Implications for teaching.* Columbus, OH: Merrill.

Moran, M.R. (1980). *An investigation of the demands on oral language skills of learning disabled students in secondary classrooms* (Research Report No. 1). Lawrence, KS: University of Kansas Institute for Research in Learning Disabilities.

Moran, M.R., Schumaker, J.B., & Vetter, A.F. (1981). *Teaching a paragraph organization strategy to learning disabled adolescents* (Research Report No. 54). Lawrence, KS: University of Kansas Institute for Research in Learning Disabilities.

Mori, A.A. (1980). Career education for the learning disabled—Where are we now? *Learning Disability Quarterly, 3*(1), 91–101.

Naslund, R.A., Thorpe, L.P., & Lefever, D.W. (1978). *SRA Achievement Series*. Chicago: Science Research Associates.

Ogden, C.K. (1970). *The general basic English dictionary*. London: Evans Brothers.

Parker, R.M. (1983). *Occupational Aptitude Survey and Interest Schedule*. Austin, TX: Pro-Ed.

Pauk, W. (1978). A notetaking format: Magical but not automatic. *Reading World, 17,* 96–97.

Riegel, R.H., & Mathey, J.P. (Eds.). (1980). *Mainstreaming at the secondary level: Seven models that work*. Plymouth, MI: Wayne County Intermediate School District.

Robinson, F.P. (1946). *Effective study*. New York: Harper and Brothers.

Robinson, H.A. (1978). *Teaching reading and study strategies: The content areas* (2nd ed.). Boston: Allyn & Bacon.

Roe, B.D., Stoodt, B.D., & Burns, P.C. (1983). *Secondary school reading instruction: The content areas* (2nd ed.). Boston: Houghton Mifflin.

Russell, D.H., & Karp, E.E. (1951). *Reading aids through the grades: Three hundred developmental reading activities*. New York: Teachers College Press, Columbia University.

Saski, J., Swicegood, P., & Carter, J. (1983). Notetaking formats for learning disabled adolescents. *Learning Disability Quarterly, 6*(3), 265–272.

Scannell, D.P. (1986). *Tests of Achievement and Proficiency*. Chicago: Riverside.

Schmid, R., Algozzine, B., Wells, D., & Stoller, L. (1980). *Final report: The national secondary school survey*. Unpublished manuscript, University of Florida, Gainesville.

Schulz, J.B., & Turnbull, A.P. (1983). *Mainstreaming handicapped students: A guide for classroom teachers* (2nd ed.). Boston: Allyn & Bacon.

Schumaker, J.B., & Deshler, D.D. (1984, March). Setting demand variables: A major factor in program planning for the LD adolescent. *Topics in Language Disorders,* 22–40.

Schumaker, J.B., Deshler, D.D., Alley, G.R., & Warner, M.M. (1983). Toward the development of an intervention model for learning disabled adolescents: The University of Kansas Institute. *Exceptional Education Quarterly, 4,* 45–74.

Schumaker, J.B., Deshler, D.D., Alley, G.R., Warner, M.M., & Denton, P.H. (1982). Multipass: A learning strategy for improving reading comprehension. *Learning Disability Quarterly, 5*(3), 295–304.

Schumaker, J.B., Deshler, D.D., Nolan, S., Clark, F.L., Alley, G.R., & Warner, M.M. (1981). *Error monitoring: A learning strategy for improving academic performance of LD adolescents* (Research Report No. 32). Lawrence, KS: University of Kansas Institute for Research in Learning Disabilities.

Schumaker, J.B., Sheldon-Wildgen, J., & Sherman, J.A. (1980). *An observational study of the academic and social behaviors of learning disabled adolescents in the regular classroom* (Research Report No. 22). Lawrence, KS: University of Kansas Institute for Research in Learning Disabilities.

Seabaugh, G.O., & Schumaker, J.B. (1981). *The effects of self-regulation training on the academic productivity of LD and NLD adolescents* (Research Report No. 37). Lawrence, KS: University of Kansas Institute for Research in Learning Disabilities.

Smith, D.D. (1981). *Teaching the learning disabled*. Englewood Cliffs, NJ: Prentice-Hall.

Strong, E.K., Jr., Hansen, J.C., & Campbell, D.P. (1985). *Strong-Campbell Interest Inventory*. Monterey, CA: Publishers Test Service, California Test Bureau/McGraw-Hill.

Towle, M. (1982). Learning how to be a student when you have a learning disability. *Journal of Learning Disabilities, 15,* 90–93.

U.S. Office of Education. (1971). *USOE career clusters*. Washington, DC: U.S. Government Printing Office.

Warner, M.M., Schumaker, J.B., Alley, G.R., & Deshler, D.D. (1980). Learning disabled adolescents in public schools: Are they different from other low achievers? *Exceptional Education Quarterly, 1*(2), 27–36.

Wimmer, D. (1982). Career education. In E.L. Meyen (Ed.), *Exceptional children in today's schools: An alternative resource book*. Denver: Love.

Wiseman, D.E. (1980). The parallel alternative curriculum for secondary classrooms. In R.H. Riegel & J.P. Mathey (Eds.), *Mainstreaming at the secondary level: Seven models that work.* Plymouth, MI: Wayne County Intermediate School District.

Woodcock, R.W., & Johnson, M.B. (1977). *Woodcock-Johnson Psycho-Educational Battery.* Allen, TX: DLM Teaching Resources.

Zigmond, N., Sansone, J., Miller, S.E., Donahoe, K.A., & Kohnke, R. (1986). Teaching learning disabled students at the secondary school level: What research says to teachers. *Learning Disabilities Focus, 1*(2), 108–115.

APPENDIX A

Scope and Sequence Skills Lists

Math Scope and Sequence Skills List[1]

ADDITION HIERARCHY

Recognizes inequalities of numbers less than 10.
Understands seriation of numbers less than 10.
Recognizes the words *addend* and *sum*.
Understands the "+" sign.
Computes sums less than 10 (memorize).
Understands place value of ones and tens.
Computes sums 10–18, both addends less than 10 (memorize).
Computes 2D + 1D without regrouping.
Computes 2D + 2D without regrouping.
Understands place value concerning regrouping tens and ones.
Computes 2D + 1D with regrouping.
Computes 2D + 2D with regrouping.
Computes 2D + 2D + 2D with sums of ones greater than 20.
Understands place value of hundreds, tens, and ones.
Computes 3D + 3D without regrouping.
Understands place value concerning regrouping hundreds and tens.
Computes 3D + 3D with regrouping.
Estimates sums.

[1]Key:
1D	= one-digit number	< = less than
2D	= two-digit number	> = more than
3D	= three-digit number	≤ = less than or equal to

SUBTRACTION HIERARCHY

Finds missing addends (e.g., 4 + ___ = 9).
Understands the "−" sign.
Uses set separation as model for subtraction.
Expresses a related addition statement in subtraction form (e.g., addend + *addend* = sum ↔ sum − *addend* = addend).
Relates the words *minuend*, *subtrahend*, and *difference* to *sum, given addend,* and *missing addend.*
Memorizes basic subtraction facts 0–9.
Understands place value of ones and tens.
Memorizes basic subtraction facts 0–18.
Names the difference between a two-place whole number (2D) and a one-place whole number (1D) (not a basic fact and no regrouping).
Names the difference between 2D and 2D with no regrouping.
Names the difference between 3D and 2D with no regrouping.
Names the difference between 3D and 3D with no regrouping.
Names the difference between two many-digit whole numbers with no regrouping.
Names the difference between 2D and 1D (not a basic fact) with regrouping.
Names the difference between 2D and 2D with regrouping from tens to ones.
Names the difference between 3D and 2D with regrouping from tens to ones.
Names the difference between 3D and 2D with double regrouping.
Names the difference between 3D and 3D with single regrouping.
Names the difference between 3D and 3D with double regrouping.
Names the difference between two many-place whole numbers with several regroupings.
Names the difference when a zero appears in a single place in the minuend.
Names the difference when zeros appear in the tens and ones place of the minuend.
Estimates differences.

MULTIPLICATION HIERARCHY

Recognizes sets as a model for multiplication (number of sets and number of objects in each set).
Recognizes and uses arrays as a model for multiplication; for example,

$$
\begin{array}{ccc}
2 & & \\
\times & \times & \\
\times & \times & 3 \\
\times & \times & \\
\end{array}
$$

Understands the words *factor* and *product.*
Understands the "×" sign.
Understands the commutative property of multiplication; for example, $a \times (b + c) = (a \times b) + (a \times c)$ [$a \leq 5, b \leq 5$].
Memorizes basic multiplication facts for $a \times b$ ($a \leq 5, b \leq 5$).
Memorizes basic multiplication facts for $a \times b$ ($5 < a < 10, b < 10$).
Names the product if one factor is 10, 100, etc.
Expands the basic multiplication facts (e.g., 4×3 to 4×30).
Computes 2D × 1D without regrouping.

Understands place value of tens, ones, regrouping.
Computes $a \times (b + c) = (a \times b) + (a \times c)$ [$a < 10$, $a \times (b + c) < 100$ with regrouping] (e.g., $6 \times (10 + 3) =$ ___ $+$ ___ $=$ ___).
Computes 2D $\times$ 1D with regrouping, product < 100.
Understands place value of hundreds, tens, ones.
Computes 2D $\times$ 1D with regrouping, product < 100.
Computes 2D $\times$ 2D with regrouping.
Computes 3D $\times$ 1D with regrouping.
Computes 3D $\times$ 2D with regrouping.

DIVISION HIERARCHY

Finds missing factor (e.g., $6 \times$ ___ $= 36$).
Uses symbols that indicate division ($2\overline{)6}$, $6 \div 2$, $6/2$).
Expresses a related multiplication sentence as a division sentence (product $\div$ factor $=$ factor).
Computes division facts with 1 as divisor (e.g., $1\overline{)6}$).
Computes basic division facts ($a \div b$ where $a \leq 81$, $b \leq 9$).
Computes division of a nonzero number by itself (e.g., $12\overline{)12}$).
Computes 1D $\div$ 1D with a remainder.
Estimates 2D $\div$ 1D and computes 2D $\div$ 1D with a remainder.
Computes quotients with expanding dividend (e.g., $3\overline{)9}$, $3\overline{)90}$, $3\overline{)900}$).
Estimates 3D $\div$ 1D and computes 3D $\div$ 1D (e.g., $6\overline{)747}$).
Computes quotient of many-place dividend with a one-place divisor (e.g., $4\overline{)78,743}$).
Estimates 3D $\div$ 2D and computes 3D $\div$ 2D where divisor is multiple of 10 (e.g., $20\overline{)684}$).
Computes quotient with divisors of 100, 1,000, etc. (e.g., $1,000\overline{)6,897}$).
Estimates 3D $\div$ 2D and computes 3D $\div$ 2D (e.g., $17\overline{)489}$).
Computes quotient of many-place dividend and many-place divisor (e.g., $3,897\overline{)487,876}$).

FRACTION HIERARCHY

Readiness Areas

Separates regions into subregions that are equivalent.
Expresses 1 in many different ways.
Uses the terms *fraction, fraction bar, numerator,* and *denominator.*
Models, on the number line, equivalent fractions.
Generates sets of equivalent fractions.
Renames fractions in simplest form.
Rewrites improper fractions as mixed numerals.
Rewrites mixed numerals as improper fractions.
Develops concept of least common denominator using the concept of least common multiple.
Compares fractional numbers.
Develops concept of least common denominator using the concept of greatest common factor.

Addition

Computes sums less than 1, same denominator.
Computes sums of mixed numerals, no regrouping, same denominator.
Computes sums between 1 and 2, same denominator, regrouping.
Computes sums of mixed numeral and nonunit fraction, regrouping, same denominator (e.g., $3\frac{2}{5} + \frac{4}{5}$).
Computes sums of mixed numerals with regrouping, same denominator (e.g., $8\frac{3}{5} + 2\frac{4}{5}$).
Computes sums less than 1, different denominators.
Computes sums of mixed numerals, no regrouping, different denominators.
Computes sums of mixed numerals, regrouping, different denominators.
Computes sums of three nonunit fractions, different denominators.
Solves word problems requiring addition of fractions.

Subtraction

Computes differences between two fractions with like denominators without regrouping, then with regrouping.
Computes differences between two fractions with unlike but related denominators without regrouping, then with regrouping.
Computes differences between two fractions with unlike and unrelated denominators without regrouping, then with regrouping.
Solves word problems requiring subtraction of fractions.

Multiplication

Computes product of whole number × unit fraction, product < 1 (e.g., $3 \times \frac{1}{4} = $ ___).
Computes product of whole number × nonunit fraction, product < 1 (e.g., $2 \times \frac{2}{5} = $ ___).
Gives fraction names for one (e.g., $1 = \frac{?}{7}$).
Solves regrouping problem by writing fraction as mixed numeral, $1 < a < 2$ (e.g., $\frac{7}{5} = $ ___).
Computes product of whole number × nonunit fraction, $1 < $ product < 2 (e.g., $3 \times \frac{3}{5} = $ ___).
Computes product of unit fraction × unit fraction (e.g., $\frac{1}{3} \times \frac{1}{4} = $ ___).
Computes product of nonunit fraction × nonunit fraction (e.g., $\frac{2}{3} \times \frac{4}{5} = $ ___).
Computes $a \times (b + c) = (a \times b) + (a \times c)$, a and b are whole numbers, c is a unit fraction, no regrouping (e.g., $3 \times (2 + \frac{1}{4}) = $ ___ $+ $ ___).
Computes $a \times (b + c) = (a \times b) + (a \times c)$, a and b are whole numbers, c is a nonunit fraction, regrouping (e.g., $4 \times 3\frac{2}{5} = 4 \times (3 + \frac{2}{5}) = $ ___ $+ $ ___ $= $ ___).
Computes product of nonunit fraction × mixed numeral using improper fractions—e.g., $\frac{5}{6} \times 2\frac{1}{3}$ (change to improper fractions).
Computes product of mixed numeral × mixed numeral using improper fractions—e.g., $3\frac{3}{4} \times 1\frac{7}{8}$ (use improper fractions).

Division

Computes quotient of $1 \div$ unit fraction (e.g., $1 \div \frac{1}{5}$).
Computes quotient of whole number ÷ nonunit fraction, $1 < $ whole number < 10—e.g., $2 \div \frac{3}{5}$ (use repeated subtraction and remainder as fractional part).

Computes ¼ ÷ ⅙ where $a < b$ (common denominator approach) (e.g., ½ ÷ ⅓).
Computes ⅚ ÷ ¾ (common denominator approach) (e.g., ⅗ ÷ ¾).
Computes quotient of two mixed numerals (common denominator approach) (e.g.,
2⅕ ÷ 1⅔).

DECIMAL HIERARCHY

Readiness Areas

Generates decimal place value by rewriting fractions with denominators of powers of 10.
Recognizes decimal place value to millionths place.
Reads and writes rational numbers expressed as decimals.
Rewrites fractions as decimals.
Models rational numbers expressed as decimals using the number line.
Generates equivalent decimals by appending zeroes.

Addition

Names the sum of two rational numbers expressed as decimals having the same place value.
Names the sum of two rational numbers expressed as decimals having different place values.
Names the sum of more than two rational numbers expressed as decimals having different
place values.
Solves word problems requiring addition of rational numbers expressed as decimals.

Subtraction

Names the difference between two rational numbers expressed as decimals having the same
place value (without regrouping and with regrouping).
Names the difference between two rational numbers expressed as decimals having different
place values (without regrouping and with regrouping).
Solves word problems requiring subtraction of rational numbers expressed as decimals.

Multiplication

Names the product of two rational numbers expressed as decimals when it is necessary to
append zeroes to the left of a nonzero digit as decimal holders.
Names the product of more than two rational numbers expressed as decimals.
Solves word problems requiring multiplication of rational numbers expressed as decimals.

Division

Names the quotient of rational numbers expressed as decimals when the divisor is a whole
number.
Names the quotient of any two rational numbers expressed as decimals by using the division
algorithm.
Solves word problems requiring division of rational numbers expressed as decimals.

Percents

Interprets the symbol for percent (%) as a fraction and as a decimal.
Rewrites percents as decimals and fractions for percents less than 100% and then for percents
   equal to or greater than 100%.
Rewrites fractions or decimals as percents.
Solves word problems requiring percents.

MONEY HIERARCHY

Identifies coins.
Recognizes relative value of coins.
Makes change for amounts up to $1.00.
Recognizes and uses money notation.
Recognizes currency and makes change for currency.
Solves examples and word problems involving money.

TIME HIERARCHY

Relates the face of the clock with the number line through 12 for hours.
Relates the face of the clock with the number line through 60 for minutes.
Tells time by the hour.
Tells time by the minute.
Understands the difference between A.M. and P.M.
Solves examples and word problems involving time.

MEASUREMENT HIERARCHY

Linear

Uses a straightedge of arbitrary length to measure an object.
Makes a ruler of at least 12″ with 1″ markings.
Uses an inch-marked ruler to measure items.
Recognizes that 12″ measure the same length as 1 foot.
Identifies measurements of objects that are less than, greater than, or equal to 1 foot.
Introduces the symbols for inches and feet.
Makes a ruler with ½″ and ¼″ markings to measure objects.
Uses a ruler with ½″ and ¼″ markings to measure objects.
Estimates heights and lengths in feet and inches.
Recognizes and relates inch, foot, yard, and mile.
Solves examples involving denominate numbers related to linear measurement.
Solves word problems applying the concepts of linear measurement.
Recognizes metric units and relates them to one another.

Liquid and Dry

Recognizes relationships between and relative values of cup, pint, quart, half-gallon, and gallon.

Recognizes metric units and relates them to one another.

Solves examples involving denominate numbers related to liquid or dry measurements.

Solves word problems involving liquid measurement.

Weight

Compares relative weights of objects using a balance.

Recognizes relationships between and relative values of ounce, pound, and ton.

Weighs objects to nearest pound and ounce.

Uses the abbreviations *oz, lb,* and *T* in recording weights.

Recognizes metric units and relates them to one another.

Solves examples involving denominate numbers related to weight measurement.

Solves word problems involving weight measurements.

Note: Portions of this skills list were adapted from *Diagnosing Mathematical Difficulties* (pp. 262–267, 278–290) by R.G. Underhill, A.E. Uprichard, and J.W. Heddens, 1980, Columbus, OH: Merrill. Adapted by permission.

Reading Scope and Sequence Skills List

GRADE 1

Word Attack

Relates spoken sounds to written symbols.

Recognizes all initial and final consonant sounds (single sounds and blends up to first vowel in word).

Identifies likenesses and differences in sounds and structure of words.

Names the letter of the alphabet for single sounds she hears.

Recognizes short vowels in one-syllable words and substitutes different vowels to form new words (*bad:* substitute *e* = *bed*).

Substitutes initial consonant to form new words.

Substitutes final consonant to form new words.

Recognizes long vowels in words ending in silent *e.*

Identifies rhyming words; decodes words with same phonogram/phonemic pattern (*at, cat, bat*).

Recognizes endings: *s, es, ed, ing.*

Identifies compound words (*football*).

Uses context clues to read words within her experience.

Comprehension

Relates printed words to objects or actions.

Follows printed directions (*Find the boy's house*).

Reads to find information.

Draws conclusions from given facts (*What do you think happened then?*).

Recalls main ideas of what has been read aloud.

Recalls details in story.

Arranges increasing numbers of events in sequence.

Uses pictures and context clues for meaning.

Makes comments and asks questions that indicate involvement with characters and story line.

Predicts events in a story.

Relates causes and effects.

Describes characters' feelings.

Discusses feelings evoked by stories.

Tells whether story is factual or fanciful (true-to-life or make-believe).

GRADE 2

Word Attack

Produces the consonant blends in isolation: *bl, br, cl, cr, dr, dw, fr, fl, gl, gr, mp, nd, pl, pr, qu, sc, sl, st, str, sw, scr, sm, sn, sp, spl, squ, sk, spr, tr, tw, thr, -nt, -nk, -st.*

Decodes words with consonant blends.

Substitutes initial consonant blends to form other words.
Identifies forms and sounds of consonant digraphs in initial position: *sh, ch, ph, th, wh.*
Identifies forms and sounds of consonant digraphs in final position: *sh, ch, gh, ng, ph, th, sh.*
Decodes four- and five-letter words that have regular short-vowel sounds.
Decodes words in which the vowels are long.
Decodes words with final consonant blends.
Decodes words ending in vowel-consonant plus silent *e (make, smoke, bone).*
Decodes consonant variants *(s—has, see; g—garden, large; c—music, ice).*
Decodes long *e* and *i* sound of *y.*
Decodes vowel diphthongs: *oi, oy, ou, ow, ew.*
Decodes words in which vowel is controlled by *r (far, fur, bar, more).*
Forms compound word with two known words *(baseball).*
Identifies root/base words in inflected forms of known words *(helpful, help; darkness, dark;*
  unhappy, happy; recall, call).
Decodes words in which final silent *e* is dropped before adding ending *(smoke, smoking).*
Identifies sounds and forms of consonant digraphs in medial position *(wishing).*
Decodes vowel digraphs/vowel teams: *oa, ai, ay, ee, ea, ie, ei.*
Identifies sounds of *a* followed by *l, w,* or *u.*
Decodes suffixes *(less, ful, ness, er, est, ly).*
Decodes prefixes *(un, re, dis, pre, pro, ex, en).*
Identifies multiple sounds of long *a, (ei, weigh; ai, straight; ay, day; ey, they).*
Decodes words with vowel digraph/vowel team irregularities *(bread, heart).*
Recognizes and knows meaning of contractions with one-letter omission.
Identifies plural endings, irregular plurals, and *'s* possessive.

Comprehension

Skims for information.
Reads to answer questions *who, when, where, how,* and *what.*
Makes judgments from given facts.
Draws conclusions, answering such questions as, "What do you think happened next?"
Begins to use contextual clues to determine meaning of a new word.
Interprets simple figurative expressions.
Interprets feelings of characters in stories.
Recognizes the stereotyping of people in stories.

GRADE 3

Word Attack

Uses phonetic clues to recognize words.
Identifies the beginning, middle, and end sounds of each word given orally.
Recognizes silent vowels in words.
Uses consonant digraphs as an aid to word attack.
Identifies diphthongs *(ou, ow, oi, oy)* and pronounces words containing diphthongs.
Knows when to double the final consonant before adding *ing.*
Uses vowel digraphs correctly.

Reads unfamiliar words that contain *r*-controlled vowels.
Reads root words and recognizes prefixes and suffixes *(er, est, ing, ed, es, ly, un, re, less)*.
Decodes silent *k* in *kn (know)*.
Decodes silent *gh (through)*.
Decodes words ending in *ed (ed, crooked; t, looked)*.
Decodes *dg (edge)*.
Divides two-syllable words.
Recognizes contractions.
Recognizes the use of the apostrophe to show ownership.
Hyphenates words using syllable rules.
Recognizes the meanings of words used in different contexts.
Selects the meaning that fits best according to the context in which the word is used.

Comprehension

Finds main idea.
Selects facts to support main idea.
Draws logical conclusions.
Reads for a definite purpose: to enjoy, to obtain answers, and to obtain a general idea of
    content.
Recognizes shifts of meaning caused by using words in different context.
Answers specific questions about material read.
Follows written directions.
Interprets descriptive words and phrases.
Selects an appropriate title after reading an untitled selection.
Composes his own questions about material read.
Makes inferences about material read.
Recognizes structure of plot (summarizes sequence of events).
Recognizes that characters change as a story develops.
Identifies relationships among characters in a story.
Compares similar elements in different stories.

GRADE 4

Word Attack

Uses phonetic clues to accent unfamiliar words correctly.
Uses dictionary as an aid to attacking and pronouncing new words.
Identifies and defines prefixes and suffixes.
Reads synonyms, antonyms, and homonyms correctly at her reading level.
Recognizes and uses words that signal relationships *(and, or, except, still, but, furthermore,
    especially, in this way, such as, on the other hand)*.

Comprehension

Summarizes main ideas and selects facts to support main ideas.
Identifies the subtopics of a selection.

Finds factual and inferential information in answer to questions.
Compares or contrasts selections.
Compares information from different sources.
Interprets literal and figurative language.
Selects the meaning of a specific word when the meaning is implied but not stated.
Predicts possible endings based on previous events in an unfinished selection.
Recognizes theme of story.
Describes times, place, characters, and sequence of action in a story.

GRADE 5

Word Attack

Applies phonetic principles and structural analysis skills in combination with context clues to read unfamiliar words.
Uses context clues to derive meaning from unfamiliar words.
Uses phonetic clues to accent unfamiliar words correctly.

Comprehension

Investigates facts.
Identifies and recalls story facts and significant details.
Infers a character's appearance, moods, feelings, traits, and motives.
Recognizes large thought division within an expository work including parts, chapters, sections, acts, and scenes.
Distinguishes between good and poor summaries.
Identifies the point of view in a selection.
Analyzes a story in terms of who acted, what action was taken, and what resulted from the action.
Cites examples of one good and one bad quality of a character treated in a biography.
Recognizes structure of plot and identifies conflict or problems.
Identifies influence of setting on characters and events.

GRADE 6

Word Attack

Uses a repertoire of word-attack skills.
Uses root words, prefixes, and suffixes to derive the meaning of words.

Comprehension

Compares reading selections as to suitability for a given purpose (dramatization, reading to others, inclusion in a bibliography).
Recognizes elements of characterization (presentation of the characters, completeness of characters, function of the characters, and relationships with other characters).

Recognizes transitional paragraphs that connect chapters, sections, and episodes.

Proves a point with factual information from the reading selections.

Interprets colloquial and figurative expressions.

Describes the rising action, climax, and falling action in a story.

Summarizes the main conflict in a story, giving the underlying causes of the conflict and the events that contributed to the conflict.

Identifies the mood of a selection and the words or phrases that establish the mood.

Identifies the basic elements of a news story *(who, what, where, when, why,* and *how).*

Analyzes and describes the point of view in an editorial.

Spelling Scope and Sequence Skills List

Many spelling skills are repeated at each grade level. However, the difficulty level of the words that the spelling skill applies to increases with grade level. An asterisk (*) denotes the initial introduction of a specific skill.

GRADE 1

*Spells two- and three-letter words.
*Spells own first and last name correctly.

GRADE 2

Spells Consonant Sounds Correctly:

*regular consonants (bed, hat, sun, yes)
*sh, ch, ng, wh, and th (fish, much, sing, which, this, with)
*x spelling of ks (box, fox)
*c spelling of k (cold)
*c and k (cat, kept)
*ck (duck, black)
*s spelling of s and z (sun, as)
*consonant blends (flag)
*silent consonants (doll, hill, who, know, would)

Spells Vowel Sounds Correctly:

*short vowel in initial or medial position (am, did)
*long vowel spelled by a single vowel (go, be)
*two vowels together (meat, rain)
*vowel–consonant–silent e (home, ride)
*ow spelling of long o (snow, grow)
*ay spelling of long a (day, play)
*final y spelling of long e (baby, very)
*final y spelling of long i (my, why)
*oo spelling of u̇ and ü (good, soon)
*ow and ou spellings of the ou sound in owl and mouse (down, house)
*oy spelling of the oi sound (boy, toy)
*vowel sounds before r
*   the er spelling of r at the end (over, teacher)
*   er, ir, or, and ur spellings of er (her, bird, work, hurt)
*   the or and ar spelling of ôr (for)
*   the ar spelling of är (car)
*unexpected single-vowel spellings (from, off, cold)
*unexpected vowel–consonant–silent e (give, done)

*unexpected spellings with two vowels together *(been, said)*
*other unexpected vowel spellings *(they, are)*

Uses Morphemes to Make Structural Changes:

*s plural *(cats, cows)*
*s or *es* for third-person singular *(live, lives)*
*s to show possession *(yours, ours)*
*d or *ed* ending for past tense *(played)*
ing ending *(blowing)*
*er noun agent ending *(singer, player)*
*er and *est* endings *(old, older, oldest)*

Uses Devices to Aid Spelling Recall:

*syllabication *(yel low, go ing)*
*recognizing compounds *(today)*
*recognizing rhyming words *(pet, get)*

Spells Selected Words Correctly:

*simple homonyms *(to, two, too)*

GRADE 3

Spells Consonant Sounds Correctly:

regular consonants *(must, trip, ask, zoo)*
sh, ch, ng, wh, and *th (shoe, child, sang, while, those, thank)*
*nk *(drunk, drank)*
*x *(next)*
c spelling of *k (cup)*
c and *k (ask, cake)*
ck (chicken, clock)
s spelling of *s* and *z (gas, has)*
*gh spelling of *f (laugh)*
consonant blends *(twin)*
silent consonants *(bell, grass, walk, catch, wrote, night)*

Spells Vowel Sounds Correctly:

short vowel in initial or medial position *(bad, send, stop)*
long vowel
* single vowel in open syllables *(paper, table)*
   two vowels together *(soap, cream, train)*
   vowel–consonant–silent *e (game, side, snake)*
   ow spelling of long *o (window)*
   ay spelling of long *a (always, yesterday)*

final y spelling of long e *(city, study, sorry)*
final y spelling of long i *(cry, try)*
oo spelling of u̇ and ü *(cook, shoot)*
ow and ou spellings of the ou sound in owl and mouse *(flower, ground)*
vowel sounds before r
* the er spelling of r at the end *(ever, another)*
* the or spelling of r at the end *(color)*
  er, ir, or, and ur spellings of er *(person, third, word, turning)*
  the or and ar spelling of ôr *(horse, warm)*
  the ar spelling of är *(star, party)*
unexpected single vowels *(kind, full, cost)*
unexpected vowel–consonant–silent e *(whose, sure)*
unexpected spellings with two vowels together *(bread, great, friend)*
other unexpected vowel spellings *(aunt, says, could)*
*le spelling of the el sound *(people, table)*

Uses Morphemes to Make Structural Changes:

*s or es plural *(cups, buses, dishes)*
*changing y to i before es *(cry, cries)*
 s or es for third-person singular *(jumps, races, misses)*
 d or ed ending for past tense *(asked, laughed)*
 ing ending *(reading, thinking)*
*ing ending with doubled consonant *(clapping, beginning)*
*ing ending with dropped silent e *(skating, moving)*
 er noun agent ending *(painter, builder)*
 er and est endings *(high, higher, highest)*

Uses Devices to Aid Spelling Recall:

syllabication *(bas ket, ta ble)*
recognizing compounds *(airplane, something)*
recognizing rhyming words *(hand, land)*

Spells Selected Words Correctly:

homonyms *(its, it's; eight, ate)*

Uses Dictionary Skills:

*alphabetizing—sequencing of words in alphabetical order

GRADE 4

Spells Consonant Phonemes Correctly:

sh, ch, and ng *(ship, rich, hang)*
*voiced and unvoiced th *(bath, those)*

*ch spelling of k *(schoolhouse)*
*wh spelling of hw *(wheel)*
*g spelling of g or j *(frog, bridge)*
*c spelling of k or s *(cage, circus)*
*ck spelling of k *(luck)*
*x spelling of ks *(fix)*
*qu spelling of kw *(queen)*
*nk spelling of ngk *(monkey)*
*ph spelling of f *(elephant)*
consonant blends *(brain)*
silent consonants *(answer)*

Spells Vowel Phonemes Correctly:

short medial vowel *(cap)*
long sound spelled with vowel–consonant–silent e *(bone)*
long sound spelled with two vowels *(tie)*
long sound spelled in open syllables *(hotel)*
vowels before r *(fur, born)*
ou and ow spellings of ou *(count, cowboy)*
*ow spelling of the ö sound *(unknown)*
oo spelling of the ů and ü sounds *(hook, stood)*
*oi and oy spellings of oi *(noise, enjoy)*
*o, al, au, and aw spellings of ô *(north, tall)*
*əl and l *(castle, jungle)*
*y spelling of ē *(busy)*

Uses Morphemes to Make Structural Changes:

d and ed ending *(recalled, untied)*
s and es ending *(socks, chimneys, churches)*
*irregular plurals *(feet)*
doubling a final consonant before ing *(stepping)*
dropping final silent e before ing *(trading)*
er and est endings *(paler, palest)*
*ly ending *(finally)*
changing of y to i before es *(bodies)*
ing ending *(interesting)*
*number suffixes *(fifteen, fifty)*
*suffixes to change part of speech *(kindness, playful, friendly)*
*prefixes to change meaning *(unlock, exchange, replace, promote)*

Uses Devices to Aid Spelling Recall:

syllable divisions *(bot tom, ho tel, cab in)*
*unexpected spellings *(minute)*
compounds *(upstairs, watermelon)*

Spells Selected Words:

homonyms *(whole, hole; hymn, him)*
*contractions *(aren't)*
*months *(February)*

Uses Dictionary Skills:

*using guide words—recognition of words grouped by alphabetical similarities

GRADE 5

Spells Consonant Phonemes Correctly:

sh, *ch*, and *ng (shade, chest, among)*
voiced and unvoiced *th (sixth, either)*
ch spelling of *k (echo)*
wh spelling of *hw (whistle)*
g spelling of *g* or *j (gate, damage)*
c spelling of *k* or *s (cook, princess)*
ck spelling of *k (attack)*
x spelling of *ks (expect)*
qu spelling of *kw (quarter)*
nk spelling of *ngk (trunk)*
silent consonants *(ghost)*

Spells Vowel Phonemes Correctly:

short medial vowels *(bunch)*
vowel–consonant–silent *e (prize)*
various spellings before *r (term, artist)*
ou and *ow* spellings of *ou (outfit, shower)*
ow spelling of *ō (crow)*
oo spelling of the *u̇* and *ü* sounds *(loose, choosing)*
oi and *oy* spellings of *oi (join, voice)*
o, al, au, and *aw* spellings of *ô (crawl, chalk)*
*spellings of *el* and *l (model, central)*
y spelling of *ē (worry, crazy)*

Uses Morphemes to Make Structural Changes:

d or *ed* ending *(excited, earned)*
s or *es* ending *(beads, beaches)*
doubling final consonant before *ing (chopping, snapping)*
dropping final silent *e* before *ing (ruling, shaking)*
number suffixes *(thirteen, sixty)*

Spells Selected Words:

contractions *(they're)*

Uses Dictionary Skills:

*locating words in a dictionary—ability to find words of uncertain spelling in a dictionary

GRADE 6

Spells Consonant Phonemes Correctly:

sh, *ch*, and *ng* consonants *(shelf, chain, gang)*
voiced and unvoiced *th (thread, leather)*
ch spelling of *k (orchestra)*
wh spelling of *hw (whale)*
g spelling of *g* or *j (cigar, pledge)*
c spelling of *k* or *s (cabbage, voice)*
ck spelling of *k (ticket)*
x spelling of *ks (expedition)*
qu spelling of *kw (acquaint)*
nk spelling of *ngk (plank)*
**ph* spelling of *f (alphabet)*

Spells Vowel Phonemes Correctly:

long sound with two vowels *(coach)*
long sound in open syllables *(soda)*
various spellings before *r (stairs, skirt)*
ou and *ow* spellings of *ou (growl, surround)*
ow spelling of *ō (narrow)*
oo spelling of *ú* and *ü (bloom, shook)*
oi and *oy* spellings of *oi (spoil, voyage)*
o, al, au, and *aw* spelling of *ô (author, naughty)*
əl and *l* sounds *(carnival, barrel)*

Uses Morphemes to Make Structural Changes:

changing *y* to *i* before *es (pantries, colonies)*
*forming plurals of nouns that end in *o (pianos, potatoes)*
ing ending *(stretching)*
er and *est* endings *(tinier, tiniest)*
ly ending *(dreadfully, especially)*
suffixes and prefixes *(harmless, attractive, dishonest, incorrect)*
d or *ed* ending *(continued, contracted)*
s or *es* ending *(insects, sandwiches)*
irregular plurals *(calves, geese)*

Uses Dictionary Skills:

*locating appropriate word meaning—awareness and selection of multiple word meanings and
   appropriate word usage

GRADES 7 AND ABOVE

Spells Selected Words:

*hyphenated words *(tongue-tied)*
 silent letters—*b, h, m, g, p (pneumonia)*
*letter combinations: *-ient, -ian, -ium, -iasm, -iable, -ure (transient, enthusiasm)*
*word endings: *-ance, -ence, -ense, -ogy, -cede, -ceed (biology, ignorance)*

Uses Dictionary Skills:

*understanding pronunciation marks—ability to interpret diacritical markings

Handwriting Scope and Sequence Skills List

Many handwriting skills are emphasized at more than one grade level. An asterisk (*) denotes a skill that has not been emphasized at a previous grade level.

KINDERGARTEN

*Begins to establish a preference for either left- or right-handedness.
*Voluntarily draws, paints, and scribbles.
*Develops small-muscle control through the use of materials such as finger painting, clay, weaving, and puzzles.
*Uses tools of writing in making letters, writing names, or attempting to write words.
*Understands and applies writing readiness vocabulary given orally, such as left/right, top/bottom, beginning/end, large/small, circle, space, around, across, curve, top line, dotted line, and bottom line.
*Begins to establish correct writing position of body, arms, hand, paper, and pencil.
*Draws familiar objects using the basic strokes of manuscript writing.
*Recognizes and legibly writes own name in manuscript letters using capital and lowercase letters appropriately.
*Uses writing paper that is standard for manuscript writing.

GRADE 1

Establishes a preference for either left- or right-handedness.
Understands and applies writing readiness vocabulary given orally, such as left/right, top/bottom, beginning/end, large/small, circle, space, around, across, curve, top line, dotted line, and bottom line.
Draws familiar objects using the basic strokes of manuscript writing.
*Begins manuscript writing using both lowercase and capital letters introduced to correlate with the child's reading program.
*Writes at his desk with correct posture, pencil grip, and paper position; works from left to right; and forms letters in the correct direction.
Uses writing paper that is standard for manuscript writing.
*Copies words neatly from near position.
*Writes with firm strokes and demonstrates good spacing between letters, words, and sentences.
*Writes manuscript letters independently and with firm strokes.
*Writes clear, legible manuscript letters at a rate appropriate for ability.
*Arranges work neatly and pleasingly on a page (i.e., uses margins and paragraph indentions and makes clean erasures).

GRADE 2

Establishes a preference for either left- or right-handedness.
Uses correct writing position of body, arm, hand, paper, and pencil.

Writes with firm strokes and demonstrates good spacing between letters, words, and sentences.
Writes clear, legible manuscript letters at a rate appropriate for ability.
Arranges work neatly and pleasingly on a page (i.e., uses margins and paragraph indentions and makes clean erasures).
*Evaluates writing using a plastic overlay and identifies strengths and weaknesses.
*Writes all letters of the alphabet in manuscript from memory.
*Recognizes the differences in using manuscript and cursive writing.
*Reads simple sentences written in cursive writing on the chalkboard.
*Demonstrates physical coordination to proceed to simple cursive writing.

GRADE 3

Uses correct writing position of body, arm, hand, paper, and pencil.
Uses writing paper that is standard for manuscript writing.
Evaluates writing using a plastic overlay and identifies strengths and weaknesses.
Writes with firm strokes and demonstrates good spacing between letters, words, and sentences.
Arranges work neatly and pleasingly on a page (i.e., uses margins and paragraph indentions and makes clean erasures).
*Demonstrates ability to decode cursive writing by reading paragraphs of cursive writing both from the chalkboard and from paper.
*Identifies cursive lowercase and capital letters by matching cursive letters to manuscript letters.
*Begins cursive writing with lowercase letters and progresses to capital letters as needed.
*Uses writing paper that is standard for cursive writing.
*Writes all letters of the cursive alphabet using proper techniques in making each letter.
*Recognizes the proper joining of letters to form words.
*Writes from memory all letters of the alphabet in cursive form.

GRADE 4

Uses correct writing position of body, arm, hand, paper, and pencil.
Evaluates writing using a plastic overlay and identifies strengths and weaknesses.
Writes with firm strokes and demonstrates good spacing between letters, words, and sentences.
Arranges work neatly and pleasingly on a page (i.e., uses margins and paragraph indentions and makes clean erasures).
Uses writing paper that is standard for cursive writing.
*Slants and joins the letters in a word and controls spacing between letters.
*Uses cursive writing for day-to-day use.
*Begins to write with a pen *if* pencil writing is smooth, fluent, and neat.
*Maintains and uses manuscript writing for special needs, such as preparing charts, maps, and labels.
*Writes clear, legible cursive letters at a rate appropriate for ability.

GRADE 5

Uses correct writing position of body, arm, hand, paper, and pencil.

Evaluates writing using a plastic overlay and identifies strengths and weaknesses.

Writes with firm strokes and demonstrates good spacing between letters, words, and sentences.

Arranges work neatly and pleasingly on a page (i.e., uses margins and paragraph indentions and makes clean erasures).

Uses cursive writing for day-to-day use.

Begins to write with a pen *if* pencil writing is smooth, fluent, and neat.

Writes clear, legible cursive letters at a rate appropriate for ability.

Maintains and uses manuscript writing for special needs, such as preparing charts, maps, and labels.

*Reduces size of writing to "adult" proportions of letters (i.e., one-quarter space for minimum letters, one-half space for intermediate letters, and three-quarters space for tall lowercase and capital letters).

*Takes pride in presenting neat work.

GRADE 6

Uses correct writing position of body, arm, hand, paper, and pencil.

Evaluates writing using a plastic overlay and identifies strengths and weaknesses.

Writes with firm strokes and demonstrates good spacing between letters, words, and sentences.

Arranges work neatly and pleasingly on a page (i.e., uses margins and paragraph indentions and makes clean erasures).

Uses cursive writing for day-to-day use.

Begins to write with a pen *if* pencil writing is smooth, fluent, and neat.

Maintains and uses manuscript writing for special needs, such as preparing charts, maps, and labels.

Reduces size of writing to "adult" proportions of letters (i.e., one-quarter space for minimum letters, one-half space for intermediate letters, and three-quarters space for tall lowercase and capital letters).

Writes clear, legible cursive letters at a rate appropriate for ability.

*Customarily presents neat work.

*Evaluates his own progress in the basic handwriting skills pertaining to size, slant, shape, spacing, and alignment.

Written Expression Scope and Sequence Skills List

KINDERGARTEN

Dictates experience stories.
Creates pictures for stories she dictates.

GRADE 1

Capitalization and Punctuation

Copies sentences correctly.
Capitalizes first word of a sentence.
Capitalizes first letter of a proper name.
Uses period at the end of a sentence.
Uses question mark after a written question.
Uses period after numbers in a list.

Written Composition

Arranges scrambled words in correct sentence order.
Writes answers to simple questions.
Dictates thoughts to scribe and does copy work.
Suggests titles for dictated stories.
Forms sentences in dictating and in writing.
Writes own name and address without using a model.
Writes from both personal experience and imagination.
Writes given sentences from dictation.
Writes phrases that describe location.

Creative Expression

Dictates and begins to write captions and comments about pictures.
Writes group poems.
Writes riddles, songs, or poems.
Creates make-believe stories.
Shows increasing selectivity in choice of words to convey meanings effectively.

GRADE 2

Capitalization and Punctuation

Capitalizes titles of compositions.
Capitalizes proper names used in written compositions.

Uses comma after salutation and after closing of a friendly letter.
Uses comma between day of the month and the year.
Uses comma between names of city and state.

Written Composition

Recognizes kinds of sentences—statement and question.
Writes a paragraph of three to five sentences in accordance with specified criteria: relate to topic, capitalize first word of each sentence, use correct end punctuation, indent first line.
Supplies titles for sentence groups.
Writes given sentences from dictation.
Copies sentences correctly.

Creative Expression

Responds to sensory stimuli with descriptive words.
Uses a variety of descriptive words or phrases.
Writes imaginative stories in which ideas and feelings are expressed.
Draws pictures to express a theme, to inform, or to persuade.

GRADE 3

Capitalization and Punctuation

Capitalizes correctly the names of months, days, holidays; first word in a line of verse; titles of books, stories, poems; salutation and closing of letters and notes; and names of special places.
Begins to apply correct punctuation for abbreviations, initials, contractions, items in a list, quotations, questions, and exclamations.
Uses proper indention for paragraphs.

Written Composition

Gives written explanations using careful selection, relevant details, and sequential order.
Begins to proofread for accuracy and to do occasional revising.
Writes simple thank-you notes using correct form.
Builds ideas into paragraphs.
Uses a variety of sentences.
Combines short, choppy sentences into longer ones.
Avoids run-on sentences.
Keeps to one idea.
Correctly sequences ideas in sentences.
Finds and deletes sentences that do not belong in a paragraph.

Creative Expression

Writes imaginative stories—imagines how others feel or how he might feel in another situation.
Uses a variety of words to express action, mood, sound, and feeling.

Writes original poetry.
Writes interesting dialogue.

GRADE 4

Capitalization and Punctuation

Uses capital letters correctly in the following areas: proper nouns, first word of poetry line,
principal words in titles, common and proper nouns, seasons as common nouns.
Uses commas correctly in the following areas: after introductory adverbial clause, to set off
interjections, to separate items in a series, to separate coordinate clauses, to set off words
in direct address, after salutation.
Uses periods correctly after declarative sentences.
Uses apostrophes correctly to show possession.

Written Composition

Makes simple outline with main ideas.
Proofreads for accuracy in writing.
Uses correct form and mechanics in writing invitations and business letters.
Compiles a list of books read, including the title and author of the books and their subjects.
Writes a paragraph defining a term, using an example.

Creative Expression

Writes descriptions of people, places, events.
Writes narrative paragraphs in which events are presented chronologically.
Writes a story including characters, setting, and plot.
Distinguishes between imaginative and factual description.
Writes a brief story in response to a picture.

GRADE 5

Capitalization and Punctuation

Uses capitals correctly in the following areas: first word of poetry line, first word of direct
quotation, seasons as common nouns, ordinary position titles (not capitalized).
Uses commas correctly in the following areas: after introductory phrases, to set off nonrestric-
tive clauses, in addresses, in dates, to separate subordinate clause from main clause, to set
off appositives, to set off parenthetical elements, to separate quotations from rest of sentence.
Uses periods correctly.
Uses colons after introductory lines.
Uses apostrophes correctly in contractions and to show possession, and not in possessive
pronouns.
Uses quotation marks correctly in direct quotations.
Uses hyphens in compound numbers.
Uses semicolons correctly with coordinate clauses.

Written Composition

Uses a variety of sentences—declarative, interrogative, exclamatory, and imperative.
Uses compound subjects and compound predicates.
Writes paragraph from outline.
Begins to organize writing by sticking to one subject and striving for a continuous thought flow.
Produces a factual report from notes and an outline.
Outlines main ideas (I, II, III) and subordinate ideas (A, B, C).
Edits writing for errors in spelling, capitalization, punctuation, and usage.
Writes a paragraph that contains a topic sentence based upon a fact and supports that fact with at least three additional facts.

Creative Expression

Records and expands sensory images, observations, memories, opinions, and individual impressions.
Writes patterned and free verse.
Develops a story plot including at least two characters, a challenge or a struggle, and a climax which results from events that prepare the reader.
Writes short scripts based on stories read by the group.

GRADE 6

Capitalization and Punctuation

Capitalizes names of outline divisions.
Writes correctly punctuated dialogue.
Correctly punctuates dictated paragraphs.
Uses underlining and quotation marks correctly for titles.
Edits own writing for correct spelling, punctuation, capitalization, and usage.

Written Composition

Develops concise statements by avoiding wordiness.
Uses complex sentences.
Checks paragraph for accurate statements.
Uses transition words to connect ideas.
Shows improvement in complete composition—introduction, development, and conclusion.
Writes from point of view that is consistent with the intention.
Plans carefully before beginning to write and revises periodically.
Edits all writing to be read by another person and revises it in accordance with accepted mechanics of writing.
Writes a well-constructed paragraph (topic sentence, supporting details, and conclusion).
Writes a newspaper story from given facts.
Narrows topics for reports.
Writes a paragraph of comparison and contrast.
Uses correct form for business letters.

Creative Expression

Uses figurative language—similes, metaphors.

Writes descriptions and narratives.

Writes a variety of prose and verse based on personal experience.

Writes a variety of short fiction—tall tales, fables, mysteries, adventure stories.

Describes a character by including details (the way the character looks, behaves, dresses, or speaks).

Writes original scripts to be produced by groups in the class.

APPENDIX B

Publishers and Producers

Academic Therapy Publications
20 Commercial Boulevard
Novato, CA 94947

Adapt Press
808 West Avenue North
Sioux Falls, SD 57104

Addison-Wesley Publishing Company
2725 Sand Hill Road
Menlo Park, CA 94025

Adston Educational Enterprises
945 East River Oaks Drive
Baton Rouge, LA 70815

Allied Education Council
P.O. Box 78
Galien, MI 49113

Allyn and Bacon
7 Wells Avenue
Newton, MA 02159

American Book Company
450 West 33rd Street
New York, NY 10001

American Guidance Service
Publishers' Building
Circle Pines, MN 55014

Appleton-Century-Crofts
440 Park Avenue South
New York, NY 10016

Argus Communications
P.O. Box 4000
One DLM Park
Allen, TX 75002

Arista Corporation
2 Park Avenue
New York, NY 10016

Aspen Systems Corporation
1600 Research Boulevard
Rockville, MD 20850

Barnell Loft
958 Church Street
Baldwin, NY 11510

Clarence L. Barnhart
Box 250
Bronxville, NY 10708

Behavioral Research Laboratories
P.O. Box 577
Palo Alto, CA 94302

Benefic Press
10300 West Roosevelt Road
Westchester, IL 60153

Biological Sciences Curriculum Study
P.O. Box 930
Boulder, CO 80306

Bobbs-Merrill Company
4300 West 62nd Street
Indianapolis, IN 46206

Bowmar/Noble Publishers
4563 Colorado Boulevard
Los Angeles, CA 90039

Wm. C. Brown Publishers
2460 Kerper Boulevard
P.O. Box 539
Dubuque, IA 52001

California Test Bureau/McGraw-Hill
Del Monte Research Park
Monterey, CA 93940

C. C. Publications
P.O. Box 23699
Tigard, OR 97223

Communication Skill Builders
3130 North Dodge Boulevard
P.O. Box 42050-H
Tucson, AZ 85733

Continental Press
520 East Bainbridge Street
Elizabethtown, PA 17022

Council for Exceptional Children
1920 Association Drive
Reston, VA 22091

Cuisenaire Company of America
12 Church Street
New Rochelle, NY 10805

Curriculum Associates
5 Esquire Road
North Billerica, MA 01862

DLM Teaching Resources
P.O. Box 4000
One DLM Park
Allen, TX 75002

Devereux Foundation Press
Devon, PA 19333

Dormac
P.O. Box 752
Beaverton, OR 97075

EBSCO Curriculum Materials
Box 11542
Birmingham, AL 35202

Economy Company
P.O. Box 25308
1901 North Walnut Street
Oklahoma City, OK 73125

Edmark Corporation
P.O. Box 3903
Bellevue, WA 98009

Educational Activities
P.O. Box 392
Freeport, NY 11520

Educational Performance Associates
600 Broad Avenue
Ridgefield, NJ 07657

Educational Progress Corporation
P.O. Box 45663
Tulsa, OK 74145

Educational Service
P.O. Box 219
Stevensville, MI 49127

Educational Teaching Aids
A. Daigger & Company
159 West Kinzie Street
Chicago, IL 60610

Educational Testing Service
Princeton, NJ 08540

Educators Publishing Service
75 Moulton Street
Cambridge, MA 02138

Enrich
Mafex Associates
90 Cherry Street
Johnstown, PA 15907

Exceptional Education
P.O. Box 15308
Seattle, WA 98115

Fearon Publishers
6 Davis Drive
Belmont, CA 94002

Field Educational Publications
2400 Hanover Street
Palo Alto, CA 94302

Fisher-Price Toys
East Aurora, NY 14052

Follett Publishing Company
1010 West Washington Boulevard
Chicago, IL 60607

Fox Reading Research Company
P.O. Box 1059
Coeur d'Alene, ID 83814

Garrard Publishing Company
1607 North Market Street
Champaign, IL 61820

General Learning Corporation
250 James Street
Morristown, NJ 07960

Ginn and Company
191 Spring Street
Lexington, MA 02173

Grosset and Dunlap
51 Madison Avenue
New York, NY 10010

Grune and Stratton
111 Fifth Avenue
New York, NY 10003

Gryphon Press
220 Montgomery Street
Highland Park, NJ 18904

Guidance Associates
1526 Gilpin Avenue
Wilmington, DE 19806

H and H Enterprises
946 Tennessee
Lawrence, KS 66044

Harcourt Brace Jovanovich
Orlando, FL 32887

Harper and Row Publishers
10 East 53rd Street
New York, NY 10022

Haworth Press
28 East 22nd Street
New York, NY 10010

D. C. Heath and Company
125 Spring Street
Lexington, MA 02173

Holt, Rinehart and Winston
383 Madison Avenue
New York, NY 10017

Houghton Mifflin
One Beacon Street
Boston, MA 02107

Hubbard
P.O. Box 104
Northbrook, IL 60062

Human Development Training Institute
1081 East Main Street
El Cajon, CA 92021

Human Sciences Press
72 Fifth Avenue
New York, NY 10011

Ideal School Supply Company
11000 South Lavergne Avenue
Oak Lawn, IL 60453

Incentive Publications
P.O. Box 12522
Nashville, TN 37212

Initial Teaching Alphabet Publications
6 East 43rd Street
New York, NY 10017

International Reading Association
800 Barksdale Road
Newark, DE 19711

Janus Books
2501 Industrial Parkway, West
Hayward, CA 94545

Jastak Associates
1526 Gilpin Avenue
Wilmington, DE 19806

Learning Concepts
2501 North Lamar Boulevard
Austin, TX 78705

Learning Skills
17951-G Sky Park Circle
Irvine, CA 92707

J. B. Lippincott Company
Educational Publishing Division
East Washington Square
Philadelphia, PA 19105

Little, Brown and Company
34 Beacon Street
Boston, MA 02106

Longman
95 Church Street
White Plains, NY 10601

Love Publishing Company
1777 South Bellaire Street
Denver, CO 80222

Lyons and Carnahan
407 East 25th Street
Chicago, IL 60616

Macmillan Publishing Company
866 Third Avenue
New York, NY 10022

Mafex Associates
90 Cherry Street
Box 519
Johnstown, PA 15907

McGraw-Hill Book Company
1221 Avenue of the Americas
New York, NY 10020

Media Materials
Department 840251
2936 Remington Avenue
Baltimore, MD 21211

Melton Book Company
111 Leslie Street
Dallas, TX 75207

Melton Peninsula
1949 Stemmons Freeway, Suite 690
Dallas, TX 75207

Merrill Publishing Company
1300 Alum Creek Drive
Columbus, OH 43216

Milton Bradley Company
74 Park Street
Springfield, MA 01101

Minneapolis Public Schools
807 N.E. Broadway
Minneapolis, MN 55413

Modern Curriculum Press
13900 Prospect Road
Cleveland, OH 44136

Modern Education Corporation
P.O. Box 721
Tulsa, OK 74101

William C. Morrow
105 Madison Avenue
New York, NY 10016

C. V. Mosby Company
11830 Westline Industrial Drive
Saint Louis, MO 63141

New Readers Press
1320 Jamesville Avenue
Box 131
Syracuse, NY 13210

Newby Visualanguage
Box 121-E
Eagleville, PA 19408

Noble and Noble Publishers
1 Dag Hammarskjold Plaza
New York, NY 10017

Numark Publications
104–20 Queens Boulevard
Forest Hills, NY 11375

Open Court Publishing Company
1039 Eighth Street
Box 599
LaSalle, IL 61301

Opportunities for Learning
20417 Nordhoff Street
Chatsworth, CA 91311

Parker Brothers
P.O. Box 900
Salem, MA 01970

Phonovisual Products
12216 Parklawn Drive
Rockville, MD 20852

Prentice-Hall
Educational Books Division
Englewood Cliffs, NJ 07632

Pro-Ed
5341 Industrial Oaks Boulevard
Austin, TX 78735

Psychological Corporation
555 Academic Court
P.O. Box 9954
San Antonio, TX 78204

Rand McNally and Company
P.O. Box 7600
Chicago, IL 60680

Random House/Singer School Division
201 East 50th Street
New York, NY 10022

Reader's Digest Services
Educational Division
Pleasantville, NJ 10570

Reading Joy
P.O. Box 404
Naperville, IL 60540

Research Press
Box 31773
Champaign, IL 61821

Riverside Publishing Company
8420 Bryn Mawr Avenue
Chicago, IL 60631

Scholastic Magazine and Book Services
50 West 44th Street
New York, NY 10036

Science Research Associates
155 North Wacker Drive
Chicago, IL 60606

Scott, Foresman and Company
1900 East Lake Avenue
Glenview, IL 60025

Selchow and Righter
505 East Union Street
Bay Shore, NY 11706

Select-Ed
117 North Chester
Olathe, KS 66061

L. W. Singer
A Division of Random House
201 East 50th Street
New York, NY 10022

Slosson Educational Publications
140 Pine Street
East Aurora, NY 14052

Society for Visual Education
1345 Diversey Parkway
Chicago, IL 60614

Special Child Publications
4635 Union Bay Place, N.E.
Seattle, WA 98105

Special Learning Corporation
42 Boston Post Road
Guilford, CT 06437

Special Press
P.O. Box 2524
Columbus, OH 43216

Steck-Vaughn Company
807 Brazos
P.O. Box 2028
Austin, TX 78768

Stoelting Company
1350 South Kostner Avenue
Chicago, IL 60623

Syracuse University Press
1011 East Water Street
Syracuse, NY 13210

Teachers College Press
Teachers College, Columbia University
1234 Amsterdam Avenue
New York, NY 10027

Texas Instruments
2305 University Avenue
Lubbock, TX 79415

Charles C Thomas Publisher
301–27 East Lawrence Avenue
Springfield, IL 62717

Trend Enterprises
P.O. Box 43073
Saint Paul, MN 55164

Troll Associates
320 Route 17
Mahwah, NJ 07430

University of Illinois Press
Box 5081, Station A
Champaign, IL 61820

University Park Press
233 East Redwood Street
Baltimore, MD 21202

VORT Corporation
P.O. Box 11552H
Palo Alto, CA 94306

George Wahr Publishing Company
316 State Street
Ann Arbor, MI 41808

Walker Educational Book Corporation
720 Fifth Avenue
New York, NY 10019

Warner Educational Services
75 Rockefeller Plaza
New York, NY 10019

Wayne Engineering
1825 Willow Road
Northfield, IL 60093

Webster
A Division of McGraw-Hill Book Company
1221 Avenue of the Americas
New York, NY 10020

John Wiley and Sons
605 Third Avenue
New York, NY 10016

B. L. Winch and Associates
45 Hitching Post Drive
Building 29
Rolling Hills Estates, CA 90274

Xerox Education Publications
245 Long Hill Road
Middletown, CT 06457

Zaner-Bloser Company
2500 West Fifth Avenue
P.O. Box 16764
Columbus, OH 43215

Richard L. Zweig Associates
20800 Beach Boulevard
Huntington Beach, CA 92648

APPENDIX C

Producers and Distributors of Educational Computer Software

Academic Software
c/o Software City
22 East Quackenbush Avenue
Dumont, NJ 07628

American Educational Computer
525 University Avenue
Palo Alto, CA 94301

American Micro Media
P.O. Box 306
Red Hook, NY 12571

Avant-Garde Creations
P.O. Box 30160
Eugene, OR 97403

BMI Educational Services
Hay Press Road
Dayton, NJ 08810

Borg-Warner Educational System
600 West University Drive
Arlington, IL 60004

Cambridge Development Laboratory
P.O. Box 605
Newton Lower Falls, MA 02162

Charles Clark Company
168 Express Drive South
Brentwood, NY 11717

Classroom Consorta Media
28 Bay Street
Staten Island, NY 10301

COMPU-TATIONS
P.O. Box 502
Troy, MI 48099

Computer Courseware Services
300 York Avenue
Saint Paul, MN 55101

Computer-Ed
1 Everett Road
Carmel, NY 10512

Cross Educational Software
1802 North Trenton
Box 1536
Ruston, LA 71270

DLM Teaching Resources
P.O. Box 4000
One DLM Park
Allen, TX 75002

Dilithium Software
P.O. Box 606
Beaverton, OR 97075

Dorsett Educational Systems
Box 1226
Norman, OK 73070

Educational Activities
P.O. Box 392
Freeport, NY 11520

Educational Computing Systems
106 Fairbanks
Oak Ridge, TN 37830

Educational Micro Systems
P.O. Box 471
Chester, NJ 07930

Educational Software Consultants
P.O. Box 30846
Orlando, FL 32862

Educational Systems Software
23720 El Toro Road, Suite C
P.O. Box E
El Toro, CA 92630

Educational Teaching Aids
159 West Kinzie Street
Chicago, IL 60610

Edu-Ware Services
28035 Dorothy Drive
Agoura, CA 91301

Encyclopaedia Britannica Educational Corporation
425 North Michigan Avenue
Chicago, IL 60611

Follett Library Book Company
4506 Northwest Highway
Crystal Lake, IL 60014

Gamco Industries
Box 1911
Big Spring, TX 79720

J. L. Hammett Company
Box 545
Braintree, MA 02184

Harcourt Brace Jovanovich
Orlando, FL 32887

Hartley Courseware
Box 431
Dimondale, MI 48821

Houghton Mifflin
One Beacon Street
Boston, MA 02107

Huntington Computing
P.O. Box 1297
Corcoran, CA 93212

K–12 Micromedia
172 Broadway
Woodcliff Lake, NJ 07675

Krell Software
1320 Stony Brook Road, Suite 219
Stony Brook, NY 11790

The Learning Company
4370 Alpine Road
Portola Valley, CA 94025

Learning Systems
P.O. Box 9046
Fort Collins, CO 80525

Little Bee Educational Programs
P.O. Box 262
Massilon, OH 44648

Love Publishing Company
1777 South Bellaire Street
Denver, CO 80222

Magic Lantern Computers
406 South Park Street
Madison, WI 53715

MARCK
280 Linden Avenue
Branford, CT 06405

McGraw-Hill School Division
1221 Avenue of the Americas
New York, NY 10020

Media Materials
2936 Remington Avenue
Baltimore, MD 21211

Mercer Systems
87 Scooter Lane
Hicksville, NY 11801

Merry Bee Communications
815 Crest Drive
Omaha, NE 68046

The Micro Center
P.O. Box 6
Pleasantville, NY 10570

Microcomputer Workshops
103 Puritan Drive
Port Chester, NY 10573

MICROGRAMS
P.O. Box 2146
Loves Park, IL 61130

Midwest Visual Equipment Company
6500 North Hamlin
Chicago, IL 60645

Milliken Publishing Company
1100 Research Boulevard
Saint Louis, MO 63132

Milton Bradley Educational Division
443 Shaker Road
East Longmeadow, MA 01028

Opportunities for Learning
20417 Nordhoff Street
Department 9
Chatsworth, CA 91311

Orange Cherry Media
7 Delano Drive
Bedford Hills, NY 10507

Queue
5 Chapel Hill Drive
Fairfield, CT 06432

Quicksoft
537 Willamette
Eugene, OR 97401

Random House School Division
201 East 50th Street
New York, NY 10022

Reader's Digest Services
Educational Division
Pleasantville, NY 10570

Right On Programs
Division of Computeam
P.O. Box 977
Huntington, NY 11743

Science Research Associates
155 North Wacker Drive
Chicago, IL 60606

Scott, Foresman and Company
1900 East Lake Avenue
Glenview, IL 60025

Society for Visual Education
1345 Diversey Parkway
Department CC–1
Chicago, IL 60614

Southwest EdPsych Services
P.O. Box 1870
Phoenix, AZ 85001

Sunburst Communications
39 Washington Avenue
Box 40
Pleasantville, NY 10570

Texas Instruments
P.O. Box 10508
Mail Station 5849
Lubbock, TX 79408

AUTHOR INDEX

SUBJECT INDEX

ABOUT THE AUTHORS

Cecil D. Mercer is a professor of education at the University of Florida. He received his Ed.D. in special education from the University of Virginia in 1974. Cecil has written numerous articles and books on educating exceptional children. One of his major works is *Students with Learning Disabilities.* Cecil remains involved in the educational programs of exceptional children through his participation in the learning disabilities clinic at Shands Teaching Hospital in Gainesville, Florida. He also is Codirector of the University of Florida Multidisciplinary Diagnostic and Training Program. In addition, he works with children in nonschool settings by coaching Little League baseball.

Ann R. Mercer is an educational diagnostician and participates in the learning disabilities clinic at Shands Teaching Hospital in Gainesville, Florida. She is a former special education teacher of emotionally handicapped students and children with learning problems at both the elementary and secondary levels. Ann is coauthor of *Self-Correcting Learning Materials for the Classroom* in addition to several articles and book chapters in the field of special education. Her three sons keep her active in school and sports activities.